Les monnaies de fouille du monde grec (VIe-Ier s. a.C.)

Frédérique Duyrat
est directrice du département des Monnaies, médailles et antiques de la Bibliothèque nationale de France, codirectrice de la *Revue numismatique*, UMR 8167 - Orient et Méditerranée - Mondes sémitiques.

Catherine Grandjean
est professeur d'histoire ancienne à l'université François-Rabelais, Tours EA 6298 CeTHiS et codirectrice de la *Revue numismatique*

Illustration de couverture :
Droit au type de Héra d'une monnaie de bronze d'Argos trouvée en 1970 lors des fouilles du secteur delta par l'EfA à Argos (Inventaire 1523)

Ausonius Éditions
— Scripta Antiqua 93 —
École française d'Athènes
— Hors collection —

Les monnaies de fouille du monde grec (VIe-Ier s. a.C.) Apports, approches et méthodes

textes réunis par
Frédérique DUYRAT *& Catherine* GRANDJEAN

Ouvrage publié avec le concours du CeTHiS - EA 6298 (Université François Rabelais, Tours), dans le cadre de la convention cadre EfA/CeTHiS et de l'UMR 8167 du CNRS - Orient et Méditerranée. Mondes sémitiques

— Bordeaux 2016 —

Notice catalographique :
Duyrat, F. et C. Grandjean, éd. (2016) : *Les monnaies de fouille du monde grec* (*VI*^{e}-*I*^{er} *s. a.C.*). *Apports, approches et méthodes*, Ausonius Scripta Antiqua 93, Bordeaux.

Mots-clés :
numismatique, archéologie, archéométrie, histoire ancienne grecque, monnaies de fouille, économie, Levant, Syrie, Argos, Thasos, trésors, Macédoine, Délos, cartographie, SIG, Israel, Égypte, fouilles sous-marines, épaves, Asie mineure, Pergame, Seleucides

AUSONIUS
Maison de l'Archéologie
F - 33607 Pessac cedex
http://ausoniuseditions.u-bordeaux-montaigne.fr

Directeur des Publications : Olivier Devillers
Secrétaire des Publications : Nathalie Tran
Graphisme de Couverture : Stéphanie Vincent Pérez

ÉCOLE FRANÇAISE D'ATHÈNES
6, rue Didotou
10680 Athènes (Grèce)
www.efa.gr

Directeur : Alexandre Farnoux
Responsable des publications : Géraldine Hue

ISSN : 1298-1990
ISBN Ausonius Éditions : 978-2-35613-170-6
ISBN École française d'Athènes : 978-2-86958-283-5

Achevé d'imprimer sur les presses
de l'imprimerie SEPEC - 15435161001
ZA des Bruyères
01960 Peronnas

31 octobre 2016

FSC
www.fsc.org
MIXTE
Papier issu
de sources
responsables
FSC® C121954

Auteurs

Nikos Akamatis	International Hellenic University School of Humanities Academic Associate
Donald T. Ariel	Coin Department, Israel Antiquities Authority
Kevin Butcher	Université de Warwick
François de Callataÿ	Bibliothèque Royale de Belgique, EPHE IVe section
Véronique Chankowski	Université Lyon 2, HiSoMA UMR 5189
Katerina Chryssanthaki-Nagle	Université de Paris X-Nanterre
John Davies	Université de Liverpool
Frédérique Duyrat	BnF, Département des Monnaies, médailles et antiques – UMR 8167
Lionel Fadin	École française d'Athènes
Thomas Faucher	Centre Ernest Babelon (Orléans) – UMR 5060 IRAMAT
Christos A. Gatzolis	Musée archéologique de Thessalonique
Catherine Grandjean	CeTHiS, Université François-Rabelais (Tours)
Panagiotis P. Iossif	École belge d'Athènes, Université de Liège
Sophia Kremydi	KERA, National Hellenic Research Foundation
John H. Kroll	Université du Texas (Austin), Université d'Oxford
Marie-Christine Marcellesi	Université Paris-Sorbonne – UMR 8167
Andrew Meadows	Université d'Oxford
Olivier Picard	Institut de France
Selene E. Psoma	Université d'Athènes
Panagiotis Tselekas	Université Aristote (Thessalonique)

Sommaire

1. Monnaies de fouille et histoire

2. Traiter les données

3. Faciès

4. Masses monétaires et contextes

Avant-propos

Ce volume coédité par l'École française d'Athènes et par Ausonius Éditions est issu d'un colloque international que nous avons organisé à Athènes, dans les locaux de l'École française d'Athènes, où il s'est tenu les 29 et 30 novembre 2014. E. Apostolou, V. Stéphanaki, A. Moustaka, B. Demetriadi, G. Kakavas, M. Amandry, A. Rizakis et un public nombreux l'ont honoré de leur présence.

Nous remercions vivement Alexandre Farnoux, directeur de l'EfA, qui a bien voulu cofinancer et accueillir dans les locaux de l'École ce colloque associant principalement des spécialistes de la Grèce, de l'Asie Mineure, du Proche-Orient et de l'Égypte Ptolémaïque. Nous adressons aussi l'expression de notre gratitude à Julien Fournier, directeur des études anciennes et médiévales à l'EfA, qui a encouragé et accompagné ce projet, et à Géraldine Hue, chargée des publications de l'EfA, qui a relu le manuscrit et dont les remarques nous ont été précieuses, comme celles des deux experts de l'EfA. Notre reconnaissance va aussi à nos équipes de recherche, l'EA CeTHiS de l'Université François-Rabelais de Tours et l'UMR Orient et Méditerranée dans sa composante Mondes sémitiques, qui ont contribué au financement du colloque et de sa publication. Enfin, nous remercions chaleureusement Olivier Devillers, directeur d'Ausonius Éditions, qui a œuvré pour une coédition de ce volume avec l'EfA, et l'a menée à bien, avec le soutien amical et l'expertise de Nathalie Tran et de Stéphanie Vincent, dont l'efficacité et le professionnalisme se sont une nouvelle fois vérifiés.

Frédérique Duyrat et Catherine Grandjean

Introduction

Catherine Grandjean

L'idée d'un colloque sur les monnaies de fouille grecques est née des expériences respectives des deux éditrices de ce volume avec des monnaies de fouilles et des trésors. Les monnaies grecques des fouilles de l'EfA à Thasos, jadis, et plus récemment celles de l'EfA à Argos ou encore celles trouvées lors du *survey* mené en Béotie par les universités de Cambridge et de Leyde m'ont fait découvrir les difficultés et les enjeux propres à ce type d'études : problèmes de nettoyage et de conservation, identification des pièces délicate, dès lors que les sols, l'usure ou le feu ont fait leur œuvre de destruction. Il y a aussi le problème de la fiabilité de l'échantillon – pour l'essentiel jeté ou perdu par les Anciens –, que les archéologues nous transmettent : reconstituer la circulation monétaire à partir de ces monnaies pose donc toute une série de problèmes de méthodes. Il en va de même de l'utilisation archéologique des monnaies de fouilles comme élément de datation, puisque les monnaies étaient susceptibles de circuler longtemps après leur émission, avec parfois des phases de décri et de remise en circulation. Une autre question, à l'heure des banques de données et des SIG, est celle de l'utilisation de ce matériel. L'enrichissement des corpus monétaires en est une, traditionnelle et toujours d'actualité. L'accent est mis de plus en plus actuellement sur la capacité d'approcher, via ce matériel, la monétarisation tant d'un point de vue social, via la petite monnaie, la seule accessible à toutes les couches des sociétés antiques[1], que d'un point de vue spatial, avec l'étude des monnaies trouvées dans l'*astu*, la *chôra* voire dans les périphéries urbaines, dont l'étude se développe, ou encore dans différents types de sites (habitat, sanctuaire, nécropole, zone artisanale, forteresse, etc.)[2].

Nous avons monté ce projet de colloque alors que Frédérique préparait la publication de son habilitation à diriger les recherches pour laquelle elle a travaillé en utilisant des monnaies de fouilles comme une donnée statistique, à partir des publications. La variété des modes de publication et la difficulté à les exploiter en séries invitaient à réfléchir aussi au mode de publication susceptible d'être le plus utile, non seulement aux numismates, mais à la communauté plus large des spécialistes de l'Antiquité.

Nos approches étaient complémentaires et invitaient à examiner les manières d'appréhender les monnaies de fouilles. Près de vingt ans après la conférence sur les monnaies de fouille tenue à Athènes en l'honneur de la regrettée Mando Oikonomides, il était temps de faire un nouveau point sur les méthodes d'approche des monnaies de fouilles du monde

1 Butcher 2003.

2 Grandjean 2015.

grec[3]. Pour ce second colloque international sur les monnaies de fouille tenu à Athènes, nous avons décidé d'élargir les réflexions au monde grec au sens le plus large d'un point de vue spatial et d'y associer des spécialistes de la Grèce, de l'Égypte et de l'Orient grecs.

Les monnaies de fouille grecques constituent un sujet peu attractif à première vue pour un colloque, et, le constat de Tony Hackens les concernant, lors de la conférence de Nancy *Numismatique antique, Problèmes et méthodes*, en 1971, n'a pas pris une ride : l'analyse des trésors est mieux accréditée auprès des numismates et des historiens[4]. Mais les découvertes au gré des fouilles et des prospections archéologiques renouvellent chaque année le matériel. Les grandes collections bougent peu et offrent une image bien différente des monnayages, plus proche des représentations de l'Antiquité au fil du temps dans le monde occidental que des réalités antiques, à l'exception de ce que l'on observe au Musée numismatique d'Athènes dont les collections comprennent une grande quantité de monnaies de fouille. Faute de spécialistes disposant de temps pour les étudier, un grand nombre de monnaies de fouille restent à publier et leur volume est sans doute sous-évalué[5]. Il faut espérer que les publications se multiplient, car ces monnaies enrichissent les corpus monétaires, permettent de préciser la datation de certaines séries, et leur apport, tant sur les techniques de frappe que sur les usages monétaires, est irremplaçable.

Les numismates ont pris conscience depuis longtemps des spécificités, du potentiel, mais aussi des difficultés d'exploitation de ce matériel. Dans sa célèbre adresse à la Royal Numismatic Society en 1965 consacrée à l'interprétation des trouvailles monétaires, Philip Grierson proposait une typologie double du matériel en fonction des circonstances de découverte (en contexte ou hors contexte) et de la nature des trouvailles (monnaies groupées ou isolées, celles qu'il appelait les "step-children" de la numismatique). Et surtout, il insistait sur l'impossibilité à reconstituer la circulation à partir du témoignage des monnaies de fouille, posant le problème essentiel de la représentativité de l'échantillon dont nous disposons :

> The coins available for study are only a sample of those that have been found. The coins that have been found are only a sample of those which were lost. These in turn were only a sample of those that had originally been in circulation. Those that had been in circulation in the area for which information is available would be only a sample of the total number of coins issued[6].

De l'autre côté de la Manche et quelques années plus tard, lors de la conférence de Nancy, Tony Hackens évoquait aussi la nécessité, pour une interprétation correcte des monnaies de fouille, de connaître la manière dont les contextes archéologiques s'étaient formés : il soulignait qu'en cas de destruction soudaine et violente, l'image de la circulation monétaire était bien différente de ce que l'on observe en cas d'abandon sans précipitation : ainsi en

3 Sheedy & Papageorgiadou-Banis, éd. 1997.

4 Hackens 1975.

5 F. de Callataÿ évalue leur nombre à 100 000 dans le même volume (voir infra p. 239-262) en se fondant sur les publications, ce qui, rapporté aux millions de monnaies présentes dans des collections, paraît faible, voire négligeable. Reste que peu de monnaies de fouille ont été publiées, faute de spécialistes et parce que le ratio heures de travail/publication, pour les monnaies de fouille, est particulièrement bas, ce qui décourage les vocations.

6 Grierson 1965, p. I-XVI.

est-il à Délos à l'ilot des Comédiens où une majorité de petits bronzes domine la statistique, les monnaies en argent étant quasi absentes. Dans l'ilot voisin, détruit par la violence, on a retrouvé des monnaies d'argent en plus d'un endroit, car la même sélection n'avait pu s'opérer[7].

En Grèce, la conférence organisée à Athènes en l'honneur de la regrettée Mando Oikonomides en 1995 par Kenneth Sheedy et Charikleia Papageorgiadou-Banis[8] a été une étape importante dans la réflexion sur les relations entre numismatique et archéologie. Plusieurs communications sur les monnaies de fouille de Susan Rotroff, Olivier Picard, Yannis Touratsoglou et Alan Walker, n'ont rien perdu de leur actualité. Susan Rotroff y démontrait toute l'expertise pionnière des Américains en la matière, évoquant les problèmes de corrosion liés à la nature des sols et aux nettoyages chimiques. Elle indiquait les opérations à effectuer (tant pour le nettoyage que pour la conservation), insistait sur la nécessité dans les inventaires de faire une double numérotation, celle des trouvailles archéologiques et, en regard, celle de l'inventaire numismatique. Plus généralement, elle invitait les archéologues et les numismates à travailler vraiment ensemble. Dans le même volume, Olivier Picard insistait sur la nécessité d'éviter la confusion entre date de frappe et date d'enfouissement des monnaies, nombre de monnaies circulant longtemps. Il indiquait en outre que les monnaies de fouille reflètent les pratiques sociales structurant la vie d'une communauté et non l'activité économique et ses variations[9].

Travailler sur des monnaies de fouille est un travail d'équipe où le numismate doit s'accorder avec les archéologues, dont il dépend pour la fiabilité des trouvailles et les données sur les contextes. Albert France-Lanord attirait ainsi déjà l'attention, lors de la conférence de Nancy, sur le fait que les petites monnaies échappaient souvent aux fouilleurs[10]. Et, comme l'écrivait Susan Rotroff en 1995 :

> Some numismatists are archaeologists and some archaeologists are numismatists. Usually, however, the two species are quite distinct, and they regard coins in very differing lights [...] The archaeologist sees a tool, and he or she makes a simple demand but an insistant one. What is the date?[11]

Depuis l'important colloque tenu à Athènes, les choses ont un peu changé. La relation duelle entre archéologue et numismate reste essentielle, mais tend peu à peu à s'élargir à d'autres spécialistes, dont les céramologues, à mesure que se précise la connaissance de la céramique commune et des timbres amphoriques. Les archéologues s'appuient sur les céramologues et le dialogue entre ces derniers et les numismates se développe aussi, car il est le plus souvent fructueux. Plusieurs publications, notamment celle des monnaies d'Alexandrie ou celle des monnaies de Monte Iato, veillent à établir une table de concordance entre unité stratigraphique et catalogue monétaire, ce qui facilite le dialogue avec les archéologues et autorise des rapprochements fructueux entre plusieurs matériels ; ces publications visent

7 Hackens 1975.
8 Sheedy & Papageorgiadou-Banis, éd. 1997.
9 Picard 1997.
10 France-Lanord 1975.
11 Rotroff 1997.

en outre à être utiles à des non spécialistes de la monnaie de fouille, intéressés par l'histoire économique et financière notamment[12].

Les bases de données simplifient désormais beaucoup le travail, notamment pour les gros volumes qu'elles permettent d'appréhender et de manipuler aisément. Les bases constituées par Thomas Faucher (sur les monnaies ptolémaïques trouvées en Égypte) et par Panagiotis Iossif (sur les monnaies séleucides) sont prometteuses, tant pour l'étude de la circulation que pour celle des faciès et des usages de la monnaie. Et la mise en ligne de plusieurs collections publiques et de trésors de monnaies grecques facilite déjà le travail des numismates de terrain, qui peuvent travailler sans s'encombrer de volumineux volumes de référence, dès lors qu'ils ont une connexion internet sur site.

Depuis quelques décennies, des numismates de terrain et des mathématiciens ont mis au point, surtout en Grande-Bretagne, mais aussi en Belgique, en France et ailleurs, des outils spécifiques de quantification et de cartographie destinés à mettre en valeur des normes applicables aux monnaies de fouille. On citera notamment les travaux de Richard Reece, Jean-Marc Doyen et Stéphane Martin. Ils mettent en regard les études de monnaies de fouille de très nombreux sites, à l'échelle parfois d'un pays entier, distinguent des phases chronologiques de dix à vingt ans dans les arrivées de matériel ou considèrent les faciès de tel ou tel type de site (militaire, sanctuaire, habitat, urbain, village). Il est évidemment possible pour les spécialistes du monde grec d'adopter ce type d'approche, là où nous disposons de bons contextes et d'une masse de monnaies bien datées issues des mêmes ateliers. Mais cela nous est-il possible en dehors du monde des monarchies hellénistiques[13] ? Dans le monde des colonies grecques au contact de populations barbares, où circulait souvent un type dominant de monnaie grecque, à l'ouest de la Sicile ou dans le Pont-Euxin par exemple, cette méthode est vraisemblablement susceptible de donner aussi des résultats fructueux. Il n'est pas évident en revanche, comme le notait déjà Olivier Picard en 1995, qu'elle puisse s'appliquer au monde des cités de Vieille Grèce, parce que leurs monnaies sont rarement datées avec précision et que la part des émissions locales est importante.

En revanche, ce que Jean Marc Doyen appelle l'analyse chronostratigraphique fine au sein d'un même site est envisageable dès lors que les fouilles sont bien conduites. Elle permet notamment de distinguer les monnaies résiduelles encore en circulation de celles qui sont mises au rebut et inactives : cela n'est pas sans conséquence pour expliquer la présence si fréquente des monnaies classiques et hellénistiques dans des contextes très tardifs, comme l'a montré Kevin Butcher pour Beyrouth[14]. L'étude des facies monétaires au sein d'une cité fouillée nous est souvent accessible et gagnerait à distinguer différents types de sites, les nécropoles bien sûr, mais aussi les sanctuaires, les postes militaires, les zones d'habitat et d'artisanat. Cela apporterait des informations sur les pratiques monétaires.

Les possibilités de développement sont donc très étendues. La masse d'informations que peuvent livrer les monnaies de fouilles est cependant en partie limitée par l'absence de standardisation des publications qui rend toute entreprise de comparaison des sites

12 Picard 2012 ; Frey-Kupper 2013.

13 Reece 2003 (= *id.* 1996).

14 Doyen 2011 ; Butcher 2003.

ardue. La rareté des images disponibles rend donc quasiment impossible la mise à jour les catalogues de monnaies de fouilles lorsque, la bibliographie ayant évolué, ils sont devenus partiellement obsolètes.

Ce rapide tour d'horizon des différentes approches et des problèmes méthodologiques nous ramène à ce volume. Nous avons eu le souci d'y proposer un panorama des monnaies de fouilles du monde grec aussi complet que possible, mais il y a évidemment des lacunes, dont la plus importante concerne le monde colonial occidental ; plusieurs contributions reflètent les découvertes de Grèce, d'Égypte et de l'Orient grecs. La question des faciès des sites archéologiques a été traitée à partir d'études de cas, dont la majorité donne à connaître des matériels et sites inédits. Reste que l'ambition principale de cet ouvrage est de marquer une étape dans la réflexion méthodologique sur l'apport des monnaies de fouilles. La réflexion sur l'exploitation historique des monnaies de fouille est au cœur de ce volume, avec les modes de traitement des données qu'elles fournissent, depuis leur classement et leur conservation jusqu'aux moyens actuels de gérer ces données et de les mettre en relation avec les autres informations livrées par le site d'où elles sont extraites (cartographie, SIG).

I - MONNAIES DE FOUILLES ET HISTOIRE

An Economic Historian's Agenda

John K. Davies

Two discourses

I begin with a comparison. Some years ago I gave an inaugural address at a colloquium in Bruxelles-Brussel which was devoted to the theme of "Pottery markets"[1]. I did so as an amateur self-appointed spokesman on behalf of the economic historians of classical antiquity, and emphasised that we were generalists who approached "as amateurs" the information which specialists – papyrologists, epigraphists, ceramicists, numismatists, archaeologists of every kind, etc. – were offering us in their publications: information which we then attempted to digest and use as best we could. In that specific context I offered a list of the sorts of information which we wanted and needed from ceramic finds and publications, but then went on to report with regret that all too often we found information about pottery to be intractable and indigestible. Distribution maps (when they existed) were partial and misleading in the absence of reliable information about find-spots; the agendas of art history impeded the activity of quantification; dates of production became depressingly vague once one moved from Attic or Corinthian wares to less well-studied or less attractive fabrics, and especially once one moved beyond the death of Alexander; plain wares tended to be ignored (at least until recently); and so on. The sub-title of that address, "Mixed messages and unharmonised agendas", was therefore bleak but à propos.

Fortunately, in this – again inaugural – address[2] I take a rather more sanguine view of the information which our numismatic colleagues provide for the historian. Art history is far less influential[3]; quantification is firmly on the agenda, even if it has provoked ferocious debate[4]; the bulk of the material is more manageable, at least as regards AR and AV issues; dates are mostly precise enough to be useful; issues of composition, purity, and the origins of the bullion used for this or that series have long been addressed; and in any case, since figures for the numbers of obverse dies in an issue already tell us something, one can advance some

1 Davies 2013a.

2 For the invitation to deliver it I thank Catherine Grandjean and the staff of the EfA most warmly. I thank Zosia Archibald, Colin Adams, Jack Kroll, Stephen Todd, and Koenraad Verboven for subsequent comments and improvements. I also thank Yale U.P. for granting permission for the reproduction of fig. 1.

3 Apart perhaps from the well-known issues of Surakousai. The artistically notable bronzes singled out by Kroll 1993, 168 are of a much later (Imperial) date.

4 For which an overview is provided by the papers assembled in de Callataÿ 2006 and 2014.

way economically in using numismatic information without needing to know much about distribution and findspots.

Yet, that much said, all is not well. Though there are shining exemplars, I know from my own experience that it is very difficult for a historian of antiquity to turn her/himself into a numismatist – and the transition is probably equally difficult in the other direction. That is not just a matter of different sources, different skills, or different bibliographies, important though they all are: it is more a matter of using different units of discourse. For numismatists, If I may comment as an outside observer, the fundamental unit of discourse is the object – held in the hand, weighed, described, drawn, photographed, maybe analysed, and then catalogued, with all detectable die-links, within a series within an issue within a currency.

I fully acknowledge the magnetic appeal of the object. As a post-graduate In Oxford, a century ago now, I was privileged to sit week after week tête-à-tête with C. Kraay in the old Ashmolean coin room, handling Corinthian and related pegasi and hearing much of what became his 1969 book[5]. The experience was both formative and hugely constructive, precisely because it was at once both intellectual and tactile: you hold a thing, and it is real, and it has a history. And yet a set of hoard-descriptions in the *Inventory*, or even a catalogue of civic issues, induces a sense of remoteness and impersonality, even with such lucid examples as that of J. Barron for Samos or those of the Elayis for the 4th c. Phoenician cities[6]. That is a handicap, since for an economic historian the fundamental unit of discourse is not the coin, or even the issue, let alone the currency. Instead, it is two-fold: first, and immediately, it is the transaction, along with the human needs and desires which it satisfies. Secondly, both immediately and remotely, it is the commodity – what is being moved or transferred or exchanged or provided, in what quantities, within what trajectories of manufacture, movement, use, and loss or decay, within what institutional and political structures, and within what physical and human contexts. Neither "unit of discourse" is simple, for the "transaction" may be illegal, or conducted by violence or fraud, and the "commodity" may be an intangible good or service that leaves no physical trace.

We therefore have two separate – and perhaps conflicting – discourses. Yet they can converge, and that possibility is both the key to this colloquium and the very core of it, for they come together above all in the case of the single find. In such a case the naive question "How did it get there?" is nourished both by current archaeological preoccupations with "The secret life of things" and the biography of the single object, and also by the knowledge that the man or woman or child who lost this coin had passed by its findspot and was the last in an untraceable chain of people who had handled it and used it, in exchange for whatever purpose, service, or commodity it was being used for. Its "biography" therefore takes us into the heart of exchange patterns and commodity procurement and movement, while the imaginable biography of the human actors opens up the whole world of human movement.

5 Kraay 1969.
6 Barron 1966; Elayi & Elayi 1993 and 2014.

Three warning flags

All the same, I have to raise three warning flags. They all have to do with the relationship between coins as found in surveys and excavations and the actual pattern of economic activity in the community or region concerned, and they all suggest that that relationship was much more complex and more indirect than one would like to be able to assume.

In order to explain my first warning, and with apologies for what to a professional readership will appear banal and elementary, I need briefly to sketch the wider historical context within which Greek coinage emerged. If we think in terms of a very simple generative sequence, the motor, as always, has been the human being, whose needs and desires prompt actions of outreach of every conceivable kind. They range from Eve's literal outreach for the apple of knowledge in the garden of Eden, through the traditional (and not just human) male pursuit of a mate, to today's sophisticated and costly underwater prospections for hitherto inaccessible mineral resources. Such actions in turn generate the emergence of intermediaries, who act as agents in the search for, and acquisition of, commodities that are in demand, and convey them back to the area where active demand is located –unless of course, as so often, the commodity in demand is land or work itself, in which case the commodity-seeker has to move (or be moved) to the commodity via violent or capillary processes of migration. In turn, again, such actions on the part of customers and agents generate institutions and systems of management. They range from language itself, through the technologies of transportation and warfare, to the emergence and eventual consolidation of the state and its institutions, coinage of course being one.

It may seem absurd and pretentious to offer this grotesquely over-simplified model of the evolution of human societies, couched in terms of the demand and supply of commodities and covering thousands of years in a single paragraph. It may well be pretentious, but it is not absurd, for it is only by transforming the discourse in a generative hyper-long-term way that the evidence which this colloquium presents can be placed within an appropriate framework. That is because, as hardly needs to be stated, the activity of procuring commodities from distant locations had already had a past history of many millennia in our macroregion of AfroMedAsia by the time that the use of coinage became firmly established in the Aegean in the 6th c. BC[7]. Such procurement, well outside any plausible range of the exercise of power, had long since required the adoption of systems of exchange. We have no idea what those early systems were (we may learn more when proto-Elamite or the early Balkan scripts are deciphered)[8], but clearly they worked well and endured for centuries into the Early Iron Age and beyond[9]. This is not the place to review the trajectory of the adoption of coinage within or outwith the Aegean, still less to enter detailed debate over chronologies, but simply to note plain facts: that, for example, the Aramaic-speaking communities of the Mediterranean – for all that they were the market leaders in exchange and procurement activity – took a century and more to adopt the new intrusion, and that other communities of the Mediterranean

7 Fuller exegesis of this topic in Davies 2016. It is sufficient to think not merely of tin, or amber, or lapis lazuli, but also of the procurement of obsidian from as early as the tenth millennium BC.

8 Kuhrt 1995, I, 25-26, with references.

9 Exhaustive survey for first millennium BC Babylonia in Jursa & Hackl 2010.

littoral and hinterland took even longer to embrace processes of silverisation[10]. Especially in light of the growing evidence for the use of bagged hacksilber[11], we should not therefore expect all acts of exchange wholly to supersede existing custom and to use minted coin. Nor should we expect it until the silver supply came closer to being adequate for the weight and intensity of transactions – a moment of equilibrium which there is no means of identifying and may well be imaginary in any case.

That argument therefore sets up my first warning flag:

(a) That coin finds cannot be trusted to reflect the full range of economic transactions that took place in a given region during a given period.

A second warning flag is closely linked to the first. We are all aware that the convenience and portability of coinage as adopted and developed in Classical Antiquity allowed it to supplement the use of precious metals by weight, just as the latter had replaced other measures of value such as the ox or vessels of bronze[12]. In the Greek context, with which this colloquium is principally concerned, a large part of that convenience derived from the use of the precious metals AR and AV, since their relative and absolute availability in an Aegean-Eastern Mediterranean context was such as to render their use practicable[13]. Such coins were not just stores of value and measures of value, for the metals of which they were composed were also commodities in their own right. That is also true of bronze, though it took time for that metal to be as central to Greek coining as it had been from the start in Latium, and though Greece shows a far poorer array of surviving bronze tools and domestic accoutrements than the museums of Etruria display. The universal logic of supply and demand will therefore have applied to all four raw metals (Ag, Au, Cu, Sn) as commodities (as also, of course, to iron and lead) in ways and to extents that varied by period, by region, by the uses of each metal, and by technological change[14]. On top of that variability we have to place a derivative "demand" for coined AR and AE that had comparably variable components (for hoarding, for military and civic payments, for exchange, etc), and a corresponding "supply" that was totally fragmented, fluctuating, and unco-ordinated, at least until the 350s[15]. It is therefore essential to assume that "supply" and "demand" were virtually independent variables, and correspondingly to display a second warning flag:

10 Spek 2011.

11 Thompson 2003 and 2011.

12 For the ox, Poll. 9.61 cites the phrase ἀποτίνειν εἰκοσάβοιον from Drakon's laws (= Solon, F 10 Ruschenbusch) (I thank Stephen Todd for retrieving this reference); for bronze vessels, Guarducci 1946.

13 At the same time, Jursa's analysis of the ways in which silver was used in the Babylonian economy of the EIA (Jursa & Hackl 2010, 469-753) is a salutary warning against over-simplification.

14 Treister 1996, 248-260.

15 The degree to which the reprise of the Athenian silver mines in the 350s was a planned initiative, of which Xenophon's *Poroi* was part, is arguable, and there may well have been a drive to maximuse output at various earlier junctures, but there is no positive evidence that they were planned or co-ordinated by a *polis* authority. In contrast, there is no debate about Philip II's drive to maximise the returns from the Pangaion mines (Diod. 16.8.6-7, with Le Rider 1996).

(b) That one cannot posit any direct or close relationship between metal supply, level of economic activity, and coin production[16].

The anomalous relationships detected for Thasos by Picard[17] therefore find some broader theoretical contextualisation.

My third warning flag has to do with the much wider issue of contexts of exchange, and of the way in which coin finds serve as a proxy for them. Here we have to think of at least four kinds of exchange, two pertaining to the fiscal economy and two pertaining to the real economy. One fiscal exchange is that generated by the services rendered *by* a polity to its inhabitants and paid for by taxation. We may well regard the services rendered as being largely notional, but the coins that comprised the payments will have been real enough as they passed through the hands of tax-farmers, officials, *oikonomoi*, and bankers, and we may all have our own views about the chances that all those coins reached their proper destination in a civic or royal treasury. A second kind of exchange on the fiscal level is that generated by services rendered – whether voluntarily or compulsorily – *to* a polity or a ruler, or to an institution such as a sanctuary: I think here primarily of pay for direct military and naval activity, but also of contract work on military or civil or cultic construction projects. If such services generate remuneration other than subsistence, it has to be both acceptable and easily portable: considerations which, as I have argued recently[18], help to explain the adoption of coinage proper and apply with especial force to what V. Gabrielsen has called the largest single market in Greek antiquity, that for mercenary service.

These first two types have no one single or preferred location of exchange. Like the fiscal economy itself, they are diffused, though not randomly: *bouleuteria* and *agorai* are likely to have figured prominently, but also dockyards and sanctuaries. Matters are otherwise, not surprisingly, if we consider exchanges within the real economy, especially those which involve the acquisition of actual objects. Here too one must make a distinction, this time between long-distance and short-distance exchange. By "long-distance exchange", which is my third type, I mean that which I have already referred to, namely the procurement of raw materials or finished products (including potential or actual slaves) from areas of production which lie well outside any political or patronal or military "reach" that the consuming parties or regions might have been able to deploy: the consuming parties therefore have to engage in some form of exchange. In a recent paper E. Fentress has called this type "elite communication", and I have published a paper which illustrates it in detail by using the movement of aromatics from South Arabia as a case-study[19]. One may reasonably expect that the specie involved in exchanges of this type will have tended to be high-value: silver certainly, tetradrachms or the equivalent probably.

That will contrast strongly with my fourth and final type, namely that generated by short-distance procurement, especially of perishables such as fish or vegetables or bread or of services such as cooking or prostitution. It is this type above all which has to be envisaged

16 The point is explored in much greater detail by Bresson 2005.

17 Picard 1997.

18 Davies 2013b.

19 Fentress 2013; Davies 2016.

in order to account for the emergence of real physical markets in central places that could meet the needs of out-and-back movement in a single day from a hinterland within a radius of not more than (say) 20 km. This is not the occasion to rehearse the process of evolution which turned Homeric *agorai* as assembly-places, dancing-floors, running-pistes, and cultic theatres into periodic temporary open markets, still less to re-open the debate about the date and extent of that evolution, but simply to note the consequences. Just as text after text of Athenian Comedy Old and New, not to mention Theophrastos' *Kharakteres*, casually note the low-value silver or (later) bronze fractions that such trade required, so too, and strikingly, paper after paper in this colloquium has reported and emphasised the predominance of bronze, reinforcing yet again thereby the overwhelming figures reported by Kroll and de Callataÿ[20].

It will be clear that my four types of exchange are not clearly separated "Ideal Types" à la Max Weber: on the contrary, they overlap, as when a tax on retail sales links the real and the fiscal economy – and even that sort of tax need not only involve low value bronze, for purchases from the silversmiths' street will have required the transfer of staters or tetradrachms in significant quantity. All four types, moreover, could have been transactions that were carried out not via the physical transfer of specie on the spot but by means of some credit-debit facility, whether bilaterally, or indirectly through a broker, money-lender, or banker, or collectively through a group such as a *koinòn eranistôn*. Though the extensive Athenian evidence for such transactions over-influences the picture, they were clearly widespread. The reader will therefore understand the reason for my third warning flag:

(c) The range of transactions that may be reflected by coin finds is too wide and too intricate to lend itself to simple interpretations[21].

Seven minor case studies

I turn now to review the relationship between coin finds and the contextual information that we have from other sources – literary, epigraphical, archaeological – about the economic and political profile of the polity or region concerned. Here, it will be helpful to begin by offering a check-list of the information about the publication of coin finds that it would be valuable to have. Specifically:

- On the coins as objects: What coins were found? What were their weights and denominations? What were their approximate dates of minting? How long had they

20 From the Athenian agora, "[...] all but one-tenth of 1 per cent of the identifiable coins are bronze" (Kroll 1993, 1). Detailed conspectus of AR:AE ratios from a wide range of sites in de Callataÿ 2006, 178-183.

21 By the same token, it will be even more futile to invoke the Fisher equation for the Greek world than it is for the Roman world. Brief exegesis in Howgego 2009, 287-289; in extenso in Cairncross 1960, 457-465.

been in circulation at the date of loss? What was the split between AV, AR and AE? What proportion were imitations or *falsi*[22]?

- What were their issuing authorities? What was the split between indigenous and other? Which other issuing authorities are attested, and in what numbers?
- What was the distribution of find-spots, *e.g.* among categories such as agora, port, fortress/akropolis, sanctuary, cemetery, urban area, or countryside, and of precise find-spots within each site?
- What was the intensity of deposition within each site, in terms of its physical extent and chronological span of use?
- How do coin finds in excavations compare with the profile of hoards from the same region and period?

Various examples reveal a very varied level of information, and indeed a situation wherein interpretation sometimes has to move from coinage to context, at other times from context to coinage[23]. I offer a rapid survey of (mostly) small-scale or briefly-reported examples before focussing at greater length on two excavated sites where the difference between older catalogue publication and more recent studies reveals the emergence of radically different and – for the economic historian, at least – far more informative approaches.

Within this series, my first is a case where the coins tell us precious little. In the relevant volume of the publication of the American excavations at the sanctuary of the Kabeiroi on Samothrake, under "Minor objects" precisely five coins are listed: all of bronze, all locally minted, and all Hellenistic[24]. Given the town's prosperity and power in the 6th c., given the popularity of the sanctuary as a place of pilgrimage by the 6th c., and given its key position in the post-Alexander world as a place of competitive monarchical display, to find a mere five coins reported, none from outside, is astonishing. It is all the more so if compared with the coin finds from a much less notable[25] sanctuary, that of Poseidon and Amphitrite on Tenos, where the editors of *Ténos I* report some 35 specimens of Imperial date, five being of Tenos or Andros, and some 80 pre-Imperial specimens[26]. All but one[27] of the latter are AE, 58 being of Tenos itself, while the remainder are mostly Aegean and (if datable) Hellenistic[28]. Without

22 At least in some contexts, a high proportion, on the evidence from the Athenian Agora (Kroll 1993, 4) and from various Hellenistic Italian sites (Stannard 2005, citing his own earlier work). Stannard also raises the possibility of "company-issued" imitations, which prompts the speculation that such unofficial issues were a response to a shortage of liquidity, especially but not only for AE in active retail contexts. This is not the place to enter the debate about the role of Nikophon's law (RO 25) in that response: brief comments by Kroll 2011, 18-19, with earlier bibliography.

23 Thus, literary information allows Kroll to link the find-spot of a "forger's hoard" in the Athenian Agora spatially with a particular group of vendors (Kroll 1993, 9 n. 33). Other examples are cited by Rotroff 1997.

24 Lehmann *et al.* 1969, 241-243.

25 For which a single sentence of Str. 10.5.11, C487, is the most substantial literary notice. Discussion in Étienne & Braun 1986, 7-9.

26 *Ibid.*, 259-266. Tableau I in: Étienne 1990, 203, restates the data but adds 19 further specimens of HL date from the Belgian excavations (17 AE, 2 Rhodian AR). They do not alter the earlier picture.

27 N° 83, a Rhodian plinthophoros drachma.

28 From the Aegean: Andros (3), Athens (8), Delos (2), Keos (2), Khios (1), Knidos (1), and Rhodes (1). From elsewhere: Egypt (1), Makedon (1), Sikuon (1), and Seleukid Syria (1).

more material from comparable sites, one cannot be confident that the profile reported at Tenos should be seen as "normal" and that at Samothrake "abnormal", but the discrepancy remains, each extremity prompting further trains of thought. Thus, various explanations of the dearth of coinage at Samothrake are possible[29], while the preponderance of locally minted material at Tenos raises a spectre, that of the so-called "festival issues", which is the subject of much current debate[30].

A third instance, that of the coin finds from the Antigonid palace at Demetrias, does tell us something. Those reported in 1976 from the 1970 and 1971 campaigns amount to 17 specimens, all AE (table 1). That six are Makedonian royal issues, seven are from adjacent Greek states, and three from the Akhaian League, is just what one would expect, and they provide a clear pointer both to the early 3rd c. as the date of the construction of the palace[31] and to the identities of those who frequented it. Indeed they give us more information yet, for the two overstruck royal issues take us firmly beyond 168, all the more as they are two of the six specimens found in the burnt destruction layer. We could date that layer even more precisely if we knew whether the number 106 borne by the exotic from Seleukid Marathos on the Phoenician coast was an ordinal in the Seleukid era or in the era of neighbouring Arad[32]. While therefore the coins from this site provide a minor but vivid illustration of how they can shape the historical understanding of the site, the economic lead which they give us hardly extends beyond a broad hint of local procurement for, and local employment at, a high-status site.

Table. 1. Demetrias: The Antigonid palace.

(Specimen nos from Milojcic & Theocharis 1976, 73 and 140-141.
Asterisked specimens were found in the burnt destruction layer)
Makedonian royal issues: 52; 227; 228; 229; *234; *237
Thessaly: Larisa 50; 51; 52; Gomphoi 226.
Magnesian League: 53; 235; (&*234 & *237 overstruck)
Euboia: 230
Akhaian League: *231; *232; *233
Marathos: *236

29 Candidates include: (a) especially for an excavation conducted in the early post-war period, a lower level of expertise in sifting fill and spotting tiny bronze coins within it than would now be achieved: (b) intensive activity by *clandestini*: (c) adverse soil conditions, as in the Athenian Agora (Rotroff 1997, 9): and (d) the existence of a law proscribing all (or most, or specific) metals from being brought into the sanctuary. (For this last possibility one may compare the laws that prohibited the use of aromatics in some sanctuaries (Plu., *De Virt. Mor.*, 397a, etc.). In any case hoards add a few more data. *IGCH* 696 (Kiourpet on Samothrake GR, 1930), dated *c.* 470, reports *c.* 100 AR, with 1 st. and "the remainder triob. and smaller fr." evidently all local: *IGCH* 858 (Samothrake GR, before 1968), dated before *c.* 275, reports 3+ local AE [*NB*: the mint index reads 856 in error]: *IGCH* 1774 (Babylon 1900), dated *c.* 155-150, reports 1 tetradr. of Samothrake among 100 AR.

30 Raised afresh, with especial reference to the ΑΡΚΑΔΙΚΟΝ issues, by Nielsen 2002, 145-152, but see now Psoma 2008 and Nollé 2014, 285-323.

31 Fuller discussion in Davies 2005, 117-135.

32 The choice is between 206 (S.E., 312/11 a.C.) and 154 (Arad era, 258 a.C.): see Beyer *et al.* in : Milojcic & Theocharis 1976, 88-90.

A fourth case is potentially much more helpful, though it takes us outside the implicit chronological limits of this colloquium. Some 15 pages of Safrai's fundamental study of the economy of Roman Palestine[33] report coin finds from the various communities of the Land of Israel and well beyond in the Roman-Byzantine period, with much quantitative information and a lavish provision of informative bar-graphs. He emphasises the same distinction between local and international exchange as I do, but is concerned above all with links with[34] and within the land of Israel rather than with the general profile presented by the finds. Moreover, he does not distinguish between hoards and stray finds or between metals, and regrettably ignores fiscal transactions, assuming that all such finds reflect commercial ties. Hence, partly because of space constraint but mainly because so little had been published by 1994, his information is not fine-grained enough, and is therefore tantalising rather than satisfying.

A fifth example raises different issues. In a chapter summarising his team's work at Euesperides just outside Benghazi, Andrew Wilson reports[35] that of the 365 coins found and catalogued, one comes from each of Athens, Kroton, and Aigina, two are unidentified, five are Carthaginian, and all the rest – 355 – are of Kurene. He notes that this overwhelming preponderance of local issues, together with the absence of issues from Egypt, parallels other evidence for seeing Kurenaike as a separate currency area even within the (itself closed) Ptolemaic empire: "foreign coin must have been exchanged and remelted to produce local coinage". Plainly, that was the case: we have here to do with information reflecting numismatic practice that has been drastically influenced by public policy. We cannot therefore judge whether Ptolemaic Egypt was in fact the dominant partner economically as well as fiscally, nor whether the ten non-local specimens accurately reflected other exchange relationships.

A sixth example raises a different issue again. In 2006 F. de Callataÿ briefly explored the application to Greek sites of both the "Ravetz index" and a "surface index", the former attempting to assess how many coins had been found on a specific site per year of occupation, the latter attempting to assess how many coins had been found per m^2 [36]. Plainly, both indices would potentially provide the economic historian with invaluable proxy data about the intensity of coin use at the site. Though, as he noted, the problems of creating a meaningful Ravetz index in Greek contexts are probably insurmountable, the figures which he calculates for the "surface index" of three sites lie sufficiently within a single order of magnitude[37] for them to provide a provisional basis of comparison. By courtesy of Z. Archibald, I can now report that a fourth site, that of Pistiros in Thrace, has revealed 1 610 coins on a site of *c.* 0,5 ha, *i.e.* a ratio of 1 coin per 6,21 m^2. That that figure too lies within the same range is encouraging, though the wide differences in both the periods of occupation of the four sites and their functions enjoin extreme caution.

33 Safrai 1994, 399-414.

34 A subject which he reports "has not been studied at all" (*ibid.*, 402).

35 Wilson 2013, 125.

36 de Callataÿ 2006, 187-192, with references at p. 187 n. 5.

37 1 coin for *c.* 3,8 m^2 (Delos, Îlot de la maison des Comédiens); 1 coin for *c.* 8,4 m^2 (Paphos, House of Dionusos); 1 coin for *c.* 4,8 m^2 (Athens, Agora).

Lastly in this section, I adduce one more from the very valuable suite of papers on the Hellenistic West published in Prag & Quinn 2013. A. Wallace-Hadrill summarises Clive Stannard's 2005 study of the coin finds from Regio I *insula* 9 at Pompeii, and reports:

> [...] a strikingly consistent <distribution pattern>: a good number of local Campanian mintages, especially Naples itself; a certain number of South Italian, Sicilian and Punic issues; a substantial presence from Massalia; a massive presence[38] of the extraordinarily small bronze pieces of Ebusus (Ibiza), with the type of the Punic god Bes; and a tiny handful from the eastern Mediterranean. That is to say, not surprisingly, that Pompeii looks West more than East, and links to the Greek cities of Neapolis and Massalia, and the once-Punic Panormus, more strongly than to central Greece, let alone Asia[39].

He then goes on to allude briefly to P. Guzzo's idea that "Ebusus might have played a role analogous to Delos for trade with the western Mediterranean" (39). Again what we are given is tantalising, but this time on a much more solid basis.

Corinth and Olynthos

So much as a sketch or summary of some small-scale illustrations, which indicate the various levels of information that the historian might hope to extract. In this final section I report on the publications of finds from two major sites in more detail, doing so partly because the numbers of finds are far higher, and partly because recent work moves beyond cataloguing to offer real economic interpretations.

I travel first to Corinth[40], where the 1933 catalogue offers a profile of information for the pre-146 city (table 2). If we leave aside the city's own coins for a moment[41], and take rather more interest in those of the other Greek states than K. Edwards was inclined to do in 1933[42], the heavy preponderance of Corinth's immediate neighbours is exactly what we should expect, while the 33 Makedonian royals, ten being of Antigonos Gonatas[43], are wholly comprehensible in the light of the Makedonian hold on Akrokorinthos for most of Antigonos' reign. So too are the 16 Egyptian coins, all of Ptolemaios III (247-222)[44], again probably far more reflecting a trickle-down from politico-military subsidy via a garrison than a simple reflection of market exchange. The only surprise, as Edwards rightly noted, is the paucity of coins minted in the West. Given all that we know about Corinthian activity in that region over at least five centuries, to have a mere four specimens reported is simply bizarre, but no persuasive explanation offers itself.

38 No less than 42,3% of the 130 identifiable coins found (Stannard 2005, 120-121).

39 Wallace-Hadrill 2013.

40 Edwards 1933, 2-4 and 10.

41 *Ibid.*, 13-16.

42 "The total number of coins from Greek states other than Corinth is not large, and their evidence presents little of general interest" (*ibid.*, 10).

43 *Ibid.*, 41-42.

44 *Ibid.*, 73. The connexion, on the basis of Plu., *Arat.*, 41.5 and *Cleom.*, 19.8, due to Mme Varoucha-Christodouloupoulou, is reported by Price 1967, 363.

Table. 2. Coin finds (nearly all AE) from pre-146 Corinthos

(from Edwards 1933, 13-74)
Corinth itself: 10 AR, 286 AE.
NE Peloponnese: Sikyon 104; Argos 14; Akhaia (cities & League) 11; Megara 5; others 4. Total 138.
Rest of Peloponnese: West Pel. 7; Sparta 6; Central Pel. 2. Total 15.
Central Greece: Euboia 12; Athens 11; others 12. Total 36.
Aegean & beyond: Egypt 16; Central islands 3; WAM & offshore islands 4. Total 23.
Northern Greece: Makedonia 33; others 8. Total 41.
Magna Graecia etc: Carthage 1; Rome (pre-146) 1; Bruttium 1; Surakousai 1. Total 4

So much for the limited information which this catalogue presents: limited in part also because the exact find-spots or even sectors in which the coins were found are not recorded therein[45]. One may now contrast that presentation with the approach adopted by Martin Price in his paper in *Hesperia* 1967. He re-catalogues the coins from a particular area, the South Stoa (so the find-spots were recorded after all) and then groups them by find-spot or find-area (table 3), in such a way as not merely to construct "a brief geographical analysis of the deposits" (table 4) but also to ask "Is it possible from the comparison of these deposits to tell how far the coins found were used as currency?" To which his reply is that:

> The number of coins is not great, and therefore we must be hesitant in making general conclusions. There are, however, three types of deposit. Some are from fills or packing to floors, suggesting the use of rubbish or unwanted material. In these circumstances the coins were probably lost haphazardly, and their *intentional* inclusion, except perhaps for a few possibly useless coins, seems unlikely. The destruction fill of the wells, secondly, is certainly débris from a destroyed building, inclcuding shops, and the coins are likely to represent currency *in circulation* at the time of the disaster, a few bronze coins abandoned in the last moments of chaos. Thirdly, the habitation fill from the wells is an accumulative deposit, many of the coins, such as those of silver, accidently lost, but including some [...] which may have been thrown away intentionally[46].

Not only do we get that tentative model of the processes which generated the pattern of finds, but we are also offered a study of the relative numbers of Corinthian and Sikuonian coins through the Hellenistic period which suggests that Corinth "had ceased to issue autonomous coins by *c.* 200 BC, and for the next fifty years, in spite of her supposed freedom, relied considerably on the coins of neighboring Sicyon[47]". One could hardly have a more signal example of how the numismatics, the archaeology, and the history are indissoluble.

Table 3. Corinth – find-areas.

(from Price 1967, 348-361)
PD: Pottery deposit from Shop I of the South Stoa
TCD: Terracotta deposit from Shop III of the South Stoa (?Sanctuary? 363n17)
S: Deposit from Shop XXXII of the South Stoa
Wells A: Habitational fill from 23 wells of South Stoa
Wells D: Destruction deposit of 146 BCE in those wells

45 All that is reported is that "The few Greek coins occur in the same sections as the earlier Roman ones" (Edwards 1933, 2).

46 Price 1967, 363.

47 *Ibid.*, 369.

Table 4. Corinth - Distribution by area.

(from Price 1967, 363)

	PD	*?PD*	*TCD*	*?TCD*	*S*	*Wells A*	*Wells D*
Corinth	23	28	36	22	35	58	61
Mak. Kings	1	4	3	2	1	18	6
N.Greece	4	4	-	1	4	14	14
Sikuon	14	3	3	1	3	13	55
Peloponnesos	2	3	3	1	3	11	11
Egypt	1	-	1	-	3	18	10
Other	-	-	-	1	1	5	6
Illegible	8	9	1	3	11	12	25
Total	53	51	47	31	59	149	188

Except that one can, for the evidence from Olynthos, my final and prime exhibit, provides an even more signal example. The basic material will be familiar. Those of the coins found in 1928 and in 1931 were given preliminary but detailed publication by D. Robinson in *Olynthos*, Parts III and VI respectively, and those of the entire corpus of finds from Olynthos and Mekuberna by D. Robinson and P. Clement in Part IX in 1938: a sequence commendable alike for its rapidity and for its depth of detail. As with Corinth, excavators and interpreters had the great advantage of a firm *terminus post quem non* for the bulk of the finds from the site – 146 for Corinth, 348 for Olynthos. However, there was one major difference, for at Olynthos the category "monnaies de fouille" also included a number of hoards, by no means all of which were to be given 348 as the date of deposition. The 1938 volume identified and numbered them, along with some others found by *clandestini*, reported the find-spots, listed the contents in detail, and offered likely dates of deposition: using *Inventory* numbers I have set the details out in Table 5. Not only that, but the authors used the new evidence not just for the history of the sites[48] but also for a detailed 200-page analysis of the coinage and history of the Khalkidian League[49]. Insofar as an outsider can judge, the publication was numismatically exemplary: one might think there was little more to be said.

Table 5. Pre-348 Hoards at Olynthos.

(Ordinal numbers from Robinson & Clement 1938, 161-196)

1. *IGCH* 356 (Olynthos 1, 1928), c.479: 11 AR (Sermule 2, Terone 3): *Olynthos* III 8-12 and IX 165-6.
2. *IGCH* 359 (Olynthos 5, 1931), c.421: 19 AR (Akanthos 12; Chalkidian League 3; Perdikkas II 3; Athens 1): *Olynthos* VI 13-14 & IX 173-176.
3. *IGCH* 366 (Olynthos 7, 1934), 379: 9 AR (Chalkidian League 7; Terone 1; Perdikkas II 1); *Olynthos* IX 177-179.
4. *IGCH* 367 (Olynthos 6, 1934), 379: 9 AR (Chalkidian League 9): *Olynthos* IX 176-177.
5. *IGCH* 372 (Olynthos 4, 1931), c.348: 34 AR (Akanthos 1; Chalkidian League 33): *Olynthos* VI 12-13 & IX

48 Robinson & Clement 1938, 363-374.

49 To the relevant materials should now be added *CH* VIII 108 and 113.

171-173.

6. ***IGCH* 373 (Olynthos 9, 1931), 348: c. 46 AR (Akanthos 2 or 3; Amphipolis 1; Chalkidian League c.43). *Olynthos* IX 183-185. Not from the excavations.
7. ***IGCH* 374 (Olynthos 10, 1934), 348: c.84 AR (Akanthos 3; Amphipolis 2; Chalkidian League c 79). *Olynthos* IX 186-190. Not from the excavations.
8. *IGCH* 375 (Olynthos 8, 1934), 348: 75 AR (Akanthos 4; Chalkidian League 53; Olynthos 2; Skione 2; Terone 3; Perdikkas II 11). *Olynthos* IX 179-183.
9. *IGCH* 376 (Olynthos 2, 1928), c.348: 35 AR (Chalkidian League 28; Perdikkas II 7). *Olynthos* III 12-13 & IX 167-168.
10. *IGCH* 377 (Olynthos 3, 1931), c.348: 63 AR (Aineia 1; Chalkidian League 50; Olynthos 1; Perdikkas II 10; Skione 1). *Olynthos* VI 11-12 & IX 168-171.

----

11. *IGCH* 378 (Olynthos 2AE, 1934), 348?: 34 AE (Akanthos 2; Chalkidian League 25; Poteidaia 5; Skione 2). *Olynthos* IX 193-194.
12. *IGCH* 379 (Olynthos not numbered, 1938), c.348?: 35 AE (Olynthos 34; Lamia 1). *AJA* 1939, 62.
13. *IGCH* 380 (Olynthos 3AE, 1934), 348?: 12 AE (Chalkidian League 4; Bottike 1; Amuntas III 4; Perdikkas III 3). *Olynthos* IX 195-196.
14. *IGCH* 383 (Olynthos 1AE, 1931), 359-336: 10 AE (Amuntas III 5; Philip II 2; Lamia 1; Larisa 2). *Olynthos* IX 191-193.

Not so, for two more recent publications have added new dimensions. The first was Tsekelas' paper of 1996, which listed *inter alia* the 30 "hoards" of various dates found in graves at Olynthos[50], mostly comprising a few low-value coins in each grave and interpreted by him either as offerings to the deceased or as "coins for Charon". Given that such coins were palpably "monnaies de fouille" found in controlled excavations, their existence, as coins plainly taken from current use at the time of burial, further weakens the intellectual membrane which separates hoards from casual finds.

The second publication, Cahill's book of 2002, goes much further, indeed leaps forward into that new world wherein numismatics, archaeology, topography, and history are again indissoluble. His section on "Trade and exchange"[51] focuses above all on the distribution of coins within the excavated area, at a level of detail made possible by the cataloguing style of Robinson and Clement. He deals separately with street finds, with house finds, and with hoards, also depicting separately the distribution of AR and of AE: hardly surprisingly, the latter (fig. 1) is the more immediately informative. For hoards, he interprets their distribution as a reflection both of "the association between monetary wealth and trade and industry <in the case of those households> rather than with traditional pursuits" and follows E. Cohen in seeing them as evidence of participation in the "hidden economy", in *aphanès ousía*. For house finds, he detects a direct correlation between numbers of coins per house and closeness to the Agora, with all that that may mean for the activities carried on in those houses. For street finds, he interprets them as the detritus of street trading. These conclusions are supplemented by observations on the balance between AR and AE and between domestic and imported currency. Along with the non-numismatic finds, they allow Cahill to paint a

50 Tsekelas 1996b, n° 1-30, whence *CH* IX 27-29, 34-57, 62-63 and 74.

51 Cahill 2002, 265-276.

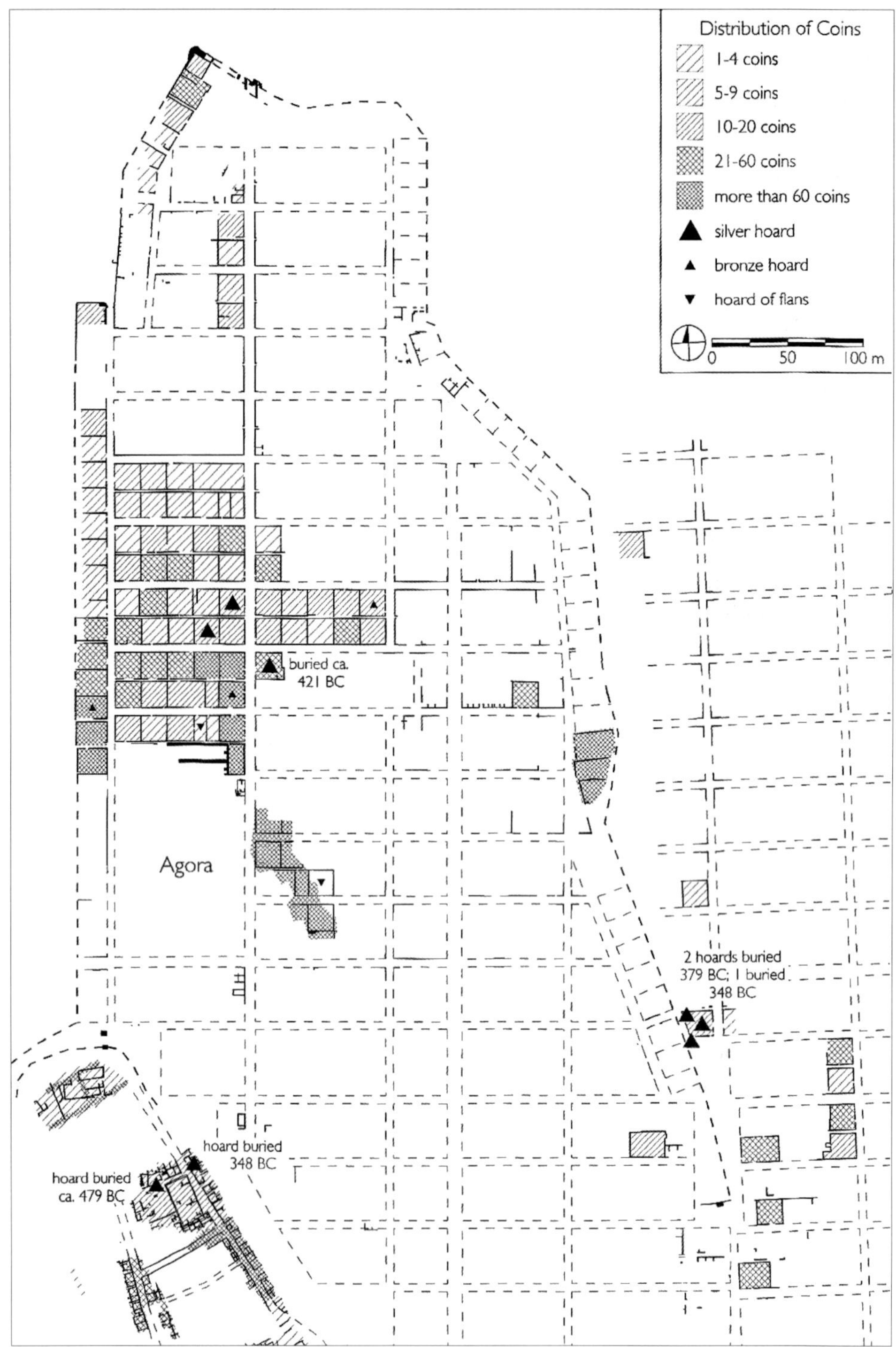

Fig. 1. Distribution of bronze coins and of hoards, North Hill, Olynthos (from N. Cahill, Household and city organisation, 267, fig. 60, reproduced by permission of Yale U.P.).

real portrait of the economic activity of the excavated section of the town: one awaits with lively interest what will emerge from the renewed excavations[52].

The reader will therefore readily understand the basis for a fourth warning flag:

(d) Traditional catalogues are a necessary but a wholly insufficient basis for inferences about economic activity of any kind. The precise find-spots of *monnaies de fouille* are essential – indeed primordial – clues to the final uses that were made of the coins concerned, especially if the location and other finds from the site are to form part of an integrated interpretation.

Throughout this report I have been concerned above all with behaviour, whether observed or inferred. The exercise of compiling it has opened my eyes to the difference between the way that silver coins are lost or abandoned (especially in hoards) and the way that bronze coins are lost or abandoned. It is as if the behaviour of individual economic actors with bronze tells me more about the micro-economy (*i.e.* about their own small-scale actions) while that of actors with silver tells me more about the meso-economy, *i.e.* the behaviour of owners of property and investors at the public or entrepreneurial level, but neither mode of behaviour tells me anything about the behaviour of polities. The activities of the latter in minting and issuing coinages tells me indeed, though with huge margins of uncertainty, how much noble or base metal was devoted to the activity[53], but does not even tell me whether the particular city or kingdom was the beneficial owner of that metal or was merely the minting agent for such owners of bullion as wished, for whatever reason and on payment of an *agio,* to have some or all of their metal supply turned into coin. It is therefore the hoards, and above all the *monnaies de fouille,* that show us where coins were last used, and it is only by devising models of activity to account for such data that we have any hope of making progress.

Underlying this entire paper has been the core question "Can *monnaies de fouille* be made to yield substantive economic information?" In spite of the four warning flags which I have felt compelled to raise, it is possible, in the light of my two extended examples, to offer the more positive answer "Yes, with the right interpretative approaches and practical procedures". That is to say, though the practical procedures involved in cataloguing are obviously essential and primary, they are only the start, for what ultimately matter are the movements of people into, through, and beyond this or that specific site or region: and the absolutely basic drivers of those movements are commodities in the widest possible sense (intangible services as much as tangible objects) and the consequential exchange transactions, private or public. Everything that we can know about a site is therefore likely to be relevant to the process of reconstructing those movements and of locating them within whatever institutional or economic or ideological framework of action one may be impelled to hypothesise. Nor, alas, is it simply a matter of absorbing the contents of the single parts or volumes of a site publication, compiled as they mostly are *katà génos* ("The Inscriptions", "The coins", "The pottery", "The small finds", etc.), since what we need to do is to use them as

52 I thank Dr Zosia Archibald, one of the directors, for helpful conversation. Her news that the 2014 season found precisely *one* coin is almost certainly further evidence of the activities of *clandestini.*

53 With all the fundamental reservations that the practice of recall-and-reminting may provoke.

the script for a single moving picture, itself changing shape and dynamics and locations as the decades and the centuries roll on. The task is plainly difficult, but the examples I have quoted – and one could add others, such as Kroll's *Agora* volume – show us that it is possible. I salute all those numismatists who have engaged in the enterprise with such success, and on behalf of all my economic-history-active colleagues offer them my warmest thanks.

Les monnaies de fouilles au Levant
Une approche régionale[1]

Frédérique Duyrat

Le grand intérêt des monnaies de fouilles est leur association avec un contexte archéologique et leur capacité à donner des éléments d'information sur le site où elles ont été trouvées. Leur état de conservation rend leur identification souvent difficile et elles sont rarement publiées intégralement, jamais avec les photographies qui permettraient de compléter ou d'amender la publication initiale. Par ailleurs, l'absence de règles de publication rend les travaux comparatifs d'un site à l'autre assez difficiles. Cependant, étudiées en masse, elles permettent une approche régionale de la circulation monétaire et une estimation de l'usage de la monnaie. Pour débuter cette étude, il faut au préalable préciser ce que sont ces monnaies de fouilles et estimer la représentativité de l'échantillon utilisé. Il est constitué des publications de monnaies de fouilles de 58 sites archéologiques de Syrie, du Liban, de Jordanie, d'Israël et de la région d'Antioche en Turquie (annexe). Seules les monnaies d'époque perse et hellénistique ont été examinées. Il ne s'agit en rien d'une documentation exhaustive, la masse produite par les dizaines de chantiers ouverts dans la région requérant des dépouillements bien au-delà du périmètre de cet article. Mais ces 58 sites, répartis pour la plupart le long d'une large bande côtière[2], donnent une idée de ce que les monnaies de fouilles datées du VIe au Ier s. a.C. peuvent éclairer de l'histoire de la région. Leur usage requiert néanmoins quelques précautions méthodologiques.

Une source à critiquer

Une source scientifiquement contrôlée ?

Les fouilles archéologiques sont des opérations très codifiées répondant à des normes d'enregistrement et de relevé strictes. De ce fait, et par comparaison avec ce que nous fait connaître le marché de l'art, elles fournissent un matériel monétaire contrôlé, bien localisé et

1 Le corpus qui fonde cette étude est extrait d'un livre à paraître sous le titre *Wealth and Warfare. The Archaeology of Money in Ancient Syria*, American Numismatic Society. La carte a été dessinée par Thomas Faucher, que je remercie vivement de sa contribution, dans le cadre de l'ANR Nomisma dirigé par Marie-Christine Marcellesi (Université Paris-Sorbonne).

2 La monnaie est beaucoup moins fréquente à l'est de la ligne Alep-Antiliban-Jourdain-Mer Morte. Duyrat 2004.

contextualisé. Il ne faut cependant pas exagérer la garantie scientifique de l'échantillon ainsi constitué. Elle a ses limites.

Les fouilles livrent des monnaies isolées en stratigraphie ou en ramassage de surface ainsi que des trésors. En ce qui concerne les trésors, ils constituent une part limitée de ce qui sort de terre, la majorité nous étant connue par le marché de l'art. Un compte rendu de *Coin Hoards* 10, publié par P. Iossif, montre que, entre la publication de *CH* 9 (2002) et celle de *CH* X (2010), la vaste région Asie Mineure – Levant – Orient est marquée par une certaine stabilité des volumes. La proportion de monnaies issues de fouilles légales y passe de 16,4 % à 15,8 % en huit ans[3].

Une telle estimation est impossible à faire pour les monnaies isolées dont nous ne savons pas quelle proportion est captée par le marché de l'art. Leur moindre qualité laisse supposer que l'essentiel est trouvé et conservé dans un cadre légal. Il ne faut cependant pas trop se fier à cette assertion. O. Hoover a ainsi montré que les monnaies de plomb nabatéennes, très rares jusqu'au début des années 2000 (deux exemplaires connus), étaient ensuite apparues en assez grand nombre sur le marché des antiquités israélien[4]. Le marché ne s'intéresse plus uniquement aux monnaies précieuses ou aux exemplaires de très belle qualité, mais aussi aux monnaies à valeur historique, même dans un matériau aussi vil que le plomb. Par ailleurs, il serait illusoire de croire que le produit des fouilles est sans défaut. D'abord parce que les monnaies de petit diamètre échappent souvent aux fouilleurs. K. Butcher rappelle qu'en différentes occasions, le faible nombre de bronzes de petit diamètre sur les sites archéologiques a été pointé. L'usage systématique du tamis par les fouilleurs des souks de Beyrouth a donné des résultats très évocateurs : près de 48 % des monnaies faisaient 12 mm de diamètre ou moins[5] et elles avaient largement été retrouvées à l'occasion d'un tamisage[6]. En outre, les monnaies de fouilles sont elles aussi soumises au marché. Y. Meshorer y insiste à propos des monnaies de la guerre des Juifs contre Rome trouvées à Masada : celles de l'an 4 sont relativement peu nombreuses sur le site car leur haute valeur commerciale en fait une source de profit pour les ouvriers qui les distraient plus volontiers[7]. Cette pratique est attestée sur de nombreux chantiers.

Les facteurs politiques sont aussi fondamentaux et créent des discordances dans l'information. Les guerres dont tous les pays de la région ont été le théâtre depuis les années 1960 ont, soit fait disparaître une partie du matériel archéologique[8], soit, une fois la paix revenue, suscité l'ouverture de vastes chantiers de fouilles sur les zones détruites, avant la reconstruction[9]. Par ailleurs, les politiques archéologiques diffèrent considérablement d'un état à l'autre, de même que les moyens de publication, ce qui fait que les informations

3 Iossif 2011a, 442-443.
4 Hoover 2006.
5 Les fragments de diamètre impossible à déterminer ne sont pas comptabilisés.
6 Butcher 2003, 25. Ces bronzes de petit diamètre dataient surtout de l'Empire tardif, mais toutes les périodes en ont livré.
7 Meshorer 2003-2006, 21.
8 Voir par exemple Donceel 2007, n. 352 sur les fouilles de Khirbet Qumran.
9 Présentation partielle des fouilles du centre ville de Beyrouth dans Perring 1997-1998. Monnaies du quartier des souks de Beyrouth dans Butcher 2003.

issues des fouilles ne sont pas réparties de manière homogène sur l'ensemble de la zone géographique. 31 des 58 sites (53,4 %) étudiés ici sont situés en Israël, ainsi que 25 des 43 trésors (58,1 %) venant de fouilles légales.

Le territoire israélien est qualitativement le mieux documenté, par le nombre de chantiers archéologiques officiels, la qualité et la régularité des publications qui sont l'œuvre de spécialistes internationalement reconnus. La documentation illégale compense partiellement la représentation des autres pays, mais avec une forte déperdition d'information et des incertitudes sur la fiabilité des données.

Du bronze et de l'argent

Les quantités et la nature des monnaies trouvées en fouilles changent selon la période. Ainsi les niveaux d'époque perse ont-il livré 223 monnaies trouvées sur 23 sites (fig. 1), c'est-à-dire moins que le total des monnaies hellénistiques des fouilles de Tell Anafa (243). 158 sont en argent, soit les deux tiers, ce qui fait de la Syrie un cas différent du panorama dressé par F. de Callataÿ pour le monde grec, à partir de l'examen des résultats de 38 sites, et qu'il résume par cette formule : "The absolute preponderance of bronze since the fourth century B.C.[10]".

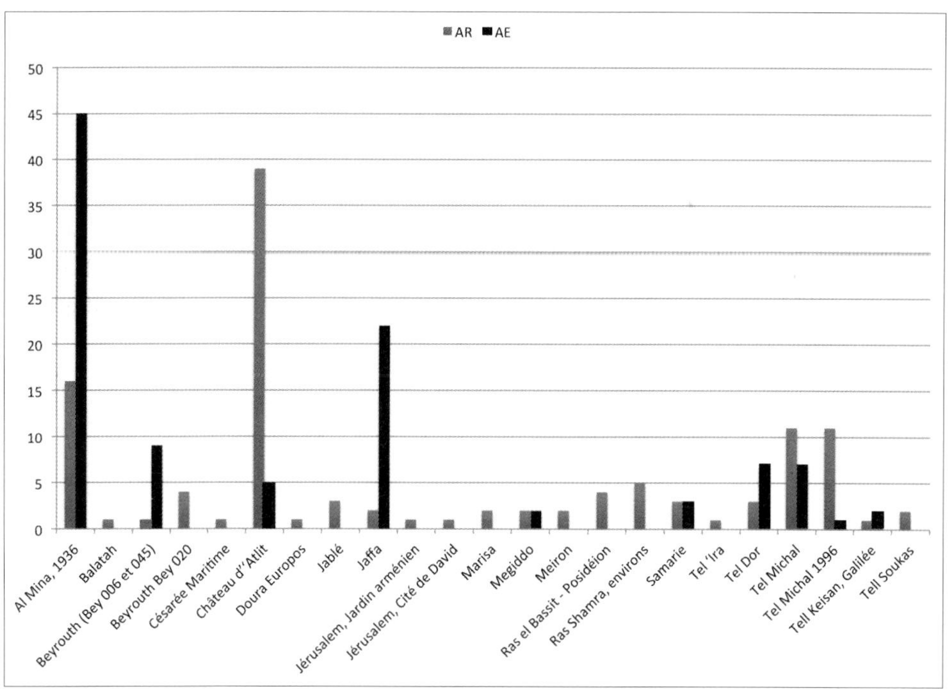

Fig. 1. Monnaies de fouilles d'époque pré-alexandrine.

10 de Callataÿ 2006, 178.

La prépondérance de l'argent avant la conquête macédonienne est directement liée à la production des ateliers de la région, essentiellement dans ce métal, même si le bronze fait son apparition à une date difficile à préciser. Les récents corpus d'époque perse de Tyr et Sidon[11] permettent de dire que ces deux ateliers ont débuté la frappe du bronze probablement peu avant le milieu du IVe s., avec un système élaboré de quatre dénominations à Sidon[12], mais une seule à Tyr[13]. Le fait que les fractions d'argent soient si fréquentes est aussi un reflet des émissions locales. Les sicles, double-sicles et autres tétradrachmes trouvés isolés sont rares, comme partout, la grosse monnaie étant rarement perdue. L'atelier de Sidon est de loin le mieux représenté pour le bronze, en Samarie et en Galilée, où l'influence sidonienne s'exerce directement, ainsi que sur la côte où sa flotte mouille jusqu'à Al-Mina. Ce dernier site livre aussi du matériel aradien en quantité, Arados alimentant la circulation monétaire de Phénicie du Nord dès le Ve s. (tableau 1)[14].

Site	Bronze
Al Mina	45 AE : Cyzique 1 ; Éphèse 2 ; Phygela 2 ; Cos 1; Rhodes 2 ; Kition 1 ; Salamine de Chypre, Évagoras II 3 + 4 ; Arados 12 + 7 + 1 ; Sidon 2 + 1 ; incert. Arados ou Sidon 6
Jaffa	Sidon : 22 AE
Tel Dor	Sidon : 6 AE Philistie : 1 AE
Tel Michal et Tel Michal 1996	Sidon : 7 AE Tyre : 1 AE (0.63 g)

Tableau 1. Détail des trouvailles de bronzes d'Al Mina, Jaffa, Tel Dor et Tel Michal à l'époque perse.

Au contraire, les fouilles ne livrent que très rarement des monnaies en métal précieux d'époque hellénistique. La figure 2 donne le ratio monnaies d'argent/total des monnaies hellénistiques. Observons d'abord que sur les 58 sites étudiés, 38 n'ont livré que du bronze, et que sur les 20 sites restants, 10 ont donné moins de 4 % de monnaies de métal précieux[15]. Parmi les 10 sites restants, 7 ont révélé moins de 30 monnaies ce qui déséquilibre le ratio dès qu'une monnaie précieuse est trouvée. Jablé est un cas particulier : c'est une fouille de nécropole et les pièces ne sont pas perdues mais volontairement placées dans les tombes pour accompagner les défunts, en sélectionnant des monnaies de valeur puisque s'y trouve la seule monnaie d'or répertoriée dans les 58 chantiers étudiés[16] (fig. 2).

Le développement de la production de monnaies de bronze au IIIe et surtout au IIe s. a.C. entraîne l'inversion forte de la présence du bronze dans les fouilles.

11 Le corpus des monnaies d'Arwad d'Elayi & Elayi 2015, n'était pas encore paru au moment de la rédaction de cet article.

12 *Id.* 2004, 349-386.

13 *Id.* 2009, 192-200.

14 *Id.* 1993, fig. 21.

15 Ces proportions sont comparables aux chiffres données par Callataÿ 2006, 180, pour le monde grec.

16 C'est un statère d'or de Ptolémée I assez rare : Svoronos 1904-1908 pl. I, 22-23, *c.* 311. Lorber à paraître.

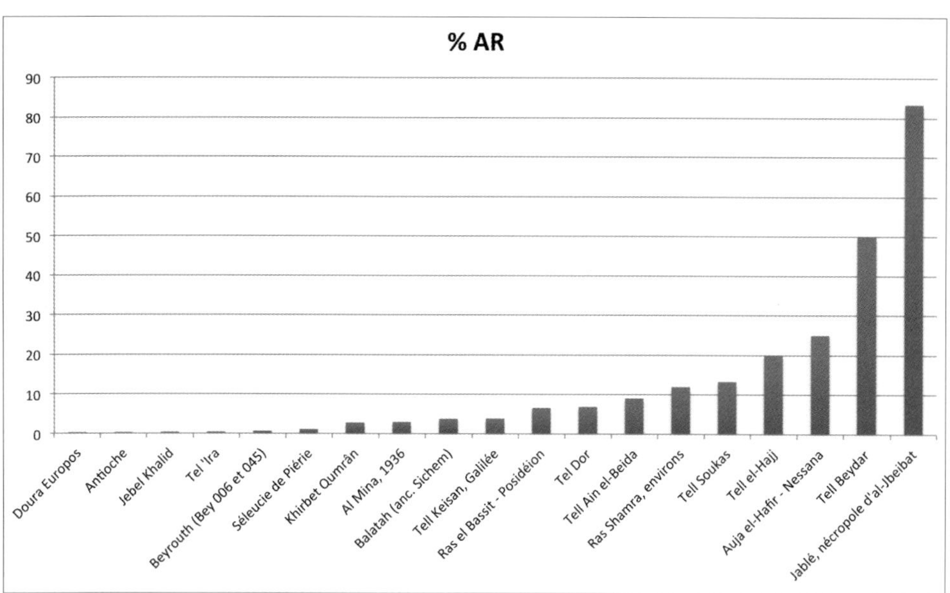

Fig. 2. Monnaies en métal précieux par site archéologique, époque hellénistique (%). Le site de Tel Michal a été supprimé car la description des trésors mêlée à celle des monnaies isolées rend la distinction difficile entre les deux catégories.

Volumétries

Le nombre de monnaies trouvées sur chaque site est un facteur très variable (fig. 3). Sans surprise, Antioche sur l'Oronte et Doura Europos, deux métropoles de l'époque hellénistique, ont livré des quantités importantes de monnaies de cette période (respectivement 1 086 et 1 210). Par comparaison, Gamala est un site beaucoup plus modeste et les quantités de bronze, cinq fois supérieures à celles des deux grandes capitales séleucides, sont frappantes, mais pas surprenantes : il s'agit massivement de bronzes hasmonéens émis en proportion très importantes en particulier sous le règne d'Alexandre Jannée. Gamala ayant été un bastion hasmonéen sans doute dès 129 et jusqu'à la mort d'Alexandre Jannée en 76 a.C. Ils forment une large part des trouvailles hellénistiques de ce site qui a bénéficié de nombreuses campagnes de fouilles (14 à la date de la publication de D. Syon). Marisa, avec près de 1 000 monnaies hellénistiques, est un centre administratif et militaire majeur sous les Lagides puis sous les Séleucides jusqu'à sa destruction par Jean Hyrcan en 108/107[17]. Les palais hasmonéens de Jéricho ont aussi livré de grandes quantités de bronzes de cette dynastie. Ils forment 99 % des trouvailles hellénistiques. À Jérusalem, dans les découvertes faites dans le quartier juif en 2006, les bronzes hasmonéens représentent 97 % des monnaies hellénistiques.

En dehors de ces grands sites, toutes les autres fouilles sont au-dessous de 500 monnaies hellénistiques, sans que cela signifie que l'usage de la monnaie y a été moins répandu durant cette période. En effet, selon la zone fouillée et les niveaux d'occupation qu'elle révèle, telle

17 Barkay 2003-2006.

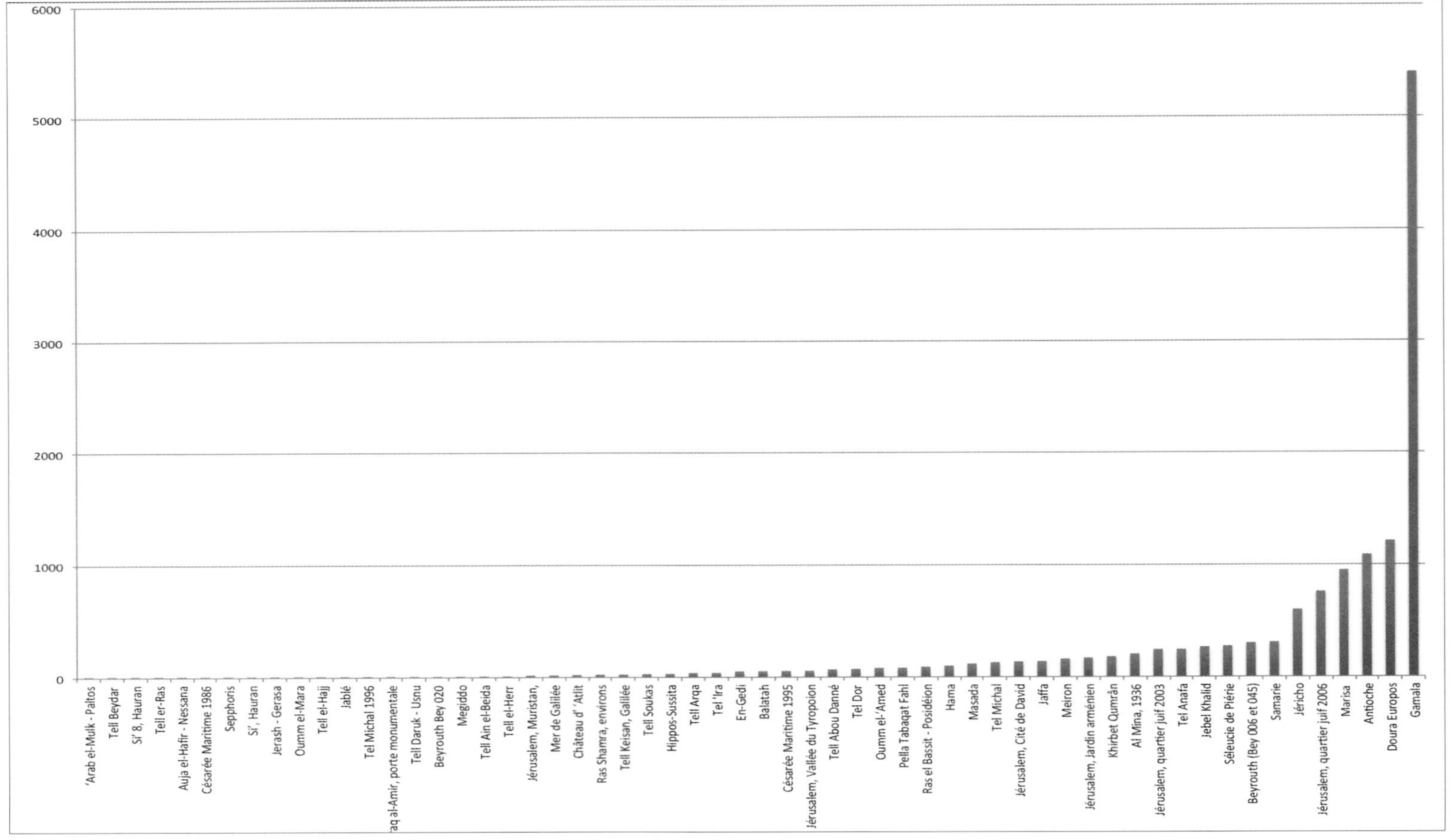

Fig. 3. Nombre de monnaies trouvées sur chaque site.

période sera mieux représentée que les autres. De même, un site rural livrera moins de pièces qu'une agora. Il est cependant notable que les sites autour ou au-dessus de 1 000 monnaies hellénistiques soient tous des centres administratifs et militaires importants. L'usage de la monnaie était très certainement encouragé par la nécessité de payer des troupes ou des taxes en numéraire, alors que les échanges du quotidien n'imposaient pas nécessairement de recours à ce moyen de paiement. Le cas des villes aux mains des Hasmonéens est de ce point de vue le plus illustratif : leur considérable production de pièces de bronze inonde littéralement les fouilles archéologiques.

Domination des bronzes royaux

L'étude globale des monnaies de fouilles donne aussi des indications sur la production monétaire d'une région à une époque donnée. L'histoire économique de la Syrie en est ainsi éclairée avec une précision parfois inusitée. La domination des bronzes royaux aux IIIe et IIe s. ainsi que dans les états hasmonéens au Ier s. en fait des sources particulièrement intéressantes à étudier en masse.

Séleucides et Lagides

Les sites archéologiques du Levant Sud confirment l'étanchéité du système monétaire lagide en dehors de l'Égypte : jusqu'à la conquête de la région par Antiochos III, ils livrent exclusivement des monnaies lagides[18].

La plupart des autres bronzes trouvés sur les sites du Levant Sud viennent des ateliers séleucides après la conquête de la région, avec un pic spectaculaire pour le monnayage d'Antiochos III qui se vérifie sur tous les sites (fig. 4)[19]. À Antioche, Beyrouth et Doura Europos, ces petites monnaies forment respectivement près de 31 %, 59 % et 45 % des bronzes séleucides retrouvés.

C. E. V. Nixon pondère cette observation : dans les fouilles de Jebel Khalid, la surreprésentation du numéraire de ce roi est limitée si on la compare au nombre d'années de règne : Séleucos III est proportionnellement mieux représenté qu'Antiochos III[20]. Ce phénomène était déjà visible dans le corpus des frappes séleucides d'Antioche en or et en argent publié par G. Le Rider[21]. Il montre clairement que la production annuelle de l'atelier reste stable sous Antiochos III : les quantités observées sont liées à la durée du règne[22]. Il n'existe pas d'étude de coins des émissions de bronze mais la longue durée du règne d'Antiochos III doit conduire à pondérer l'impression de masse des chiffres bruts.

18 L'unique exception est un bronze d'Antiochos I trouvé dans les fouilles du quartier du Muristan à Jérusalem.

19 Voir par exemple la courbe comparative établie pour Jebel Khalid par Nixon 2002, 300.

20 *Ibid.*, 301.

21 Le Rider 1999.

22 Tableaux de synthèse dans Duyrat 2002, 413-414, en particulier le tableau de répartition annuelle des frappes qui indique une moyenne de 2 coins de droit de tétradrachmes par an sous Séleucos III, 1,88 sous Antiochos III et 2 sous Séleucos IV.

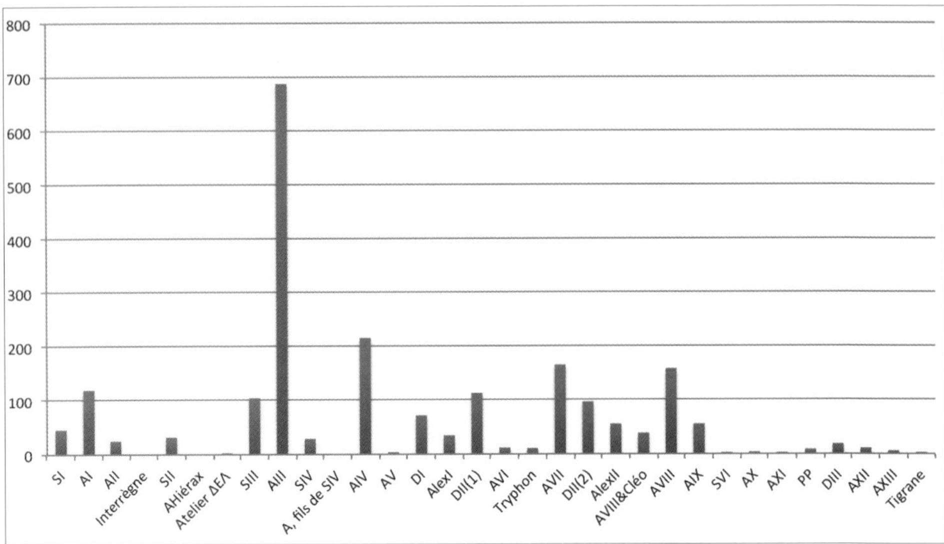

Fig. 4. Monnaies séleucides cumulées sur tous les sites.

Néanmoins, l'importance globale des émissions du règne d'Antiochos III permet de faire face aux besoins des régions qui sont désormais privées du bronze lagide. K. Butcher y voit un signe de la politique de "séleucidisation" conduite par ce roi[23]. Cependant, une explication plus pragmatique pourrait être donnée. À partir du moment où Antiochos III renonçait à changer le système monétaire de ses nouvelles possessions, la région ne pouvait être alimentée que par les stocks déjà en circulation. L'importation de monnaies d'argent d'étalon lagide était nécessaire tant que les Séleucides ne se décidaient pas à produire eux-mêmes le numéraire nécessaire. En revanche, le bronze n'étant pas soumis au problème de l'étalon, il était probablement beaucoup plus simple de le fabriquer sur place, d'autant que les besoins semblent avoir été grands. Que la typologie ait par ailleurs contribué à la diffusion de l'image royale ne fait pas de doute, mais le maintien de l'argent lagide montre que ce n'était pas la vocation primordiale du monnayage, au moins dans ce cas de figure.

Contrairement à ce qu'on observe sous Ptolémée II, les productions de l'argent et du bronze ne semblent pas être corrélées sous Antiochos III. Il a utilisé l'argent lagide mais a émis le bronze en abondance et ce numéraire chasse littéralement celui des Lagides de leur ancienne province de Syrie et Phénicie[24]. En dehors des sites les plus petits, qui ont livré très peu de matériel, le bronze d'Antiochos III est présent partout alors que celui des rois lagides disparaît, à peu d'exceptions près[25]. Le produit des fouilles de Beyrouth montre bien que les monnaies d'Antiochos III sont surtout de petit module (autour de 10 mm), aux types de la tête d'Apollon et d'Apollon debout, et qu'elles sont essentiellement importées du Nord[26]. Au

23 Butcher 2003, 54, n. 6.

24 Ce phénomène avait déjà été observé, notamment par Houghton & Lorber 2000-2002.

25 Pour une autre formalisation de ce changement, voir le tableau publié dans Duyrat 2013, 16-17.

26 Butcher 2003, 47, pour Beyrouth, mais la remarque peut être généralisée aux autres sites.

contraire, celles de ses successeurs proviennent indifféremment des ateliers du Sud ou du Nord.

Bronzes hasmonéens

Les rois hasmonéens n'ont frappé que le bronze, et Alexandre Jannée (103-76) l'a fait dans des proportions remarquables à en juger par l'abondance de sa production dans les trésors comme dans les fouilles. Cette abondance finit par chasser les monnaies séleucides, durant le règne d'Alexandre Jannée probablement[27]. Le nombre inhabituel de moules à flans en calcaire et de flans en chapelets non découpés, voire de flans vierges dans les trésors, qu'ont livrés les fouilles israéliennes témoigne de l'énorme production du règne de Jannée[28]. I. Shachar estime que les bronzes de ce roi représentent 87 % des monnaies hasmonéennes trouvées sur les 44 fouilles ouvertes dans Jérusalem et 52 % de celles de Gamala[29]. Elles ont continué d'être frappées après la mort du roi ; elles ont été imitées en bronze et en plomb[30]. Elles sont tellement abondantes qu'elles peuvent être utilisées pour déterminer les phases d'occupation d'un site, souvent en relation avec une activité militaire.

Enclaves

L'examen des monnaies de fouilles à échelle régionale présente un intérêt particulier pour éclairer des périodes d'occupation temporaire d'une zone donnée. Elles témoignent en effet de l'existence d'enclaves où se développe une pratique monétaire intense et relativement brève à l'échelle de la période étudiée. Deux exemples sont particulièrement bien illustrés par le corpus rassemblé.

Alexandre le Grand

Autant le numéraire d'argent frappé par Alexandre est bien connu, autant le bronze est resté très en marge des recherches (fig. 5). M. J. Price signale cinq ateliers syriens ayant frappé ce métal pour le conquérant : Myriandros, Akè/Tyr, Arados, Byblos et Sidon[31]. Toutes ces émissions sont postérieures à la mort d'Alexandre le Grand. Selon G. Le Rider, il faut sans doute y ajouter l'atelier de Posidéion / Ras el Bassit qui marque sa production des lettres AP. Cette attribution est fondée sur la densité des trouvailles de ces monnaies et sur l'existence de quelques rares monnaies d'argent au nom de Posidéion conservées dans des musées[32]. Aucune de ces séries n'a bénéficié d'une étude de coins. Les témoignages archéologiques peuvent néanmoins donner quelques indications.

27 Meshorer 1982, 47.

28 Shiloh & Ariel 1990, entre autres.

29 Shachar 2004, 10.

30 Fontanille 2007 par exemple.

31 Price 1991, n° 3232 pour Myriandros, 3268 et 3269 pour Akè/Tyr, 3311 et 3334-3335 pour Arados, 3425 et 3427-3428 pour Byblos, 3469 et 3492-3493 pour Sidon.

32 Le Rider 1986.

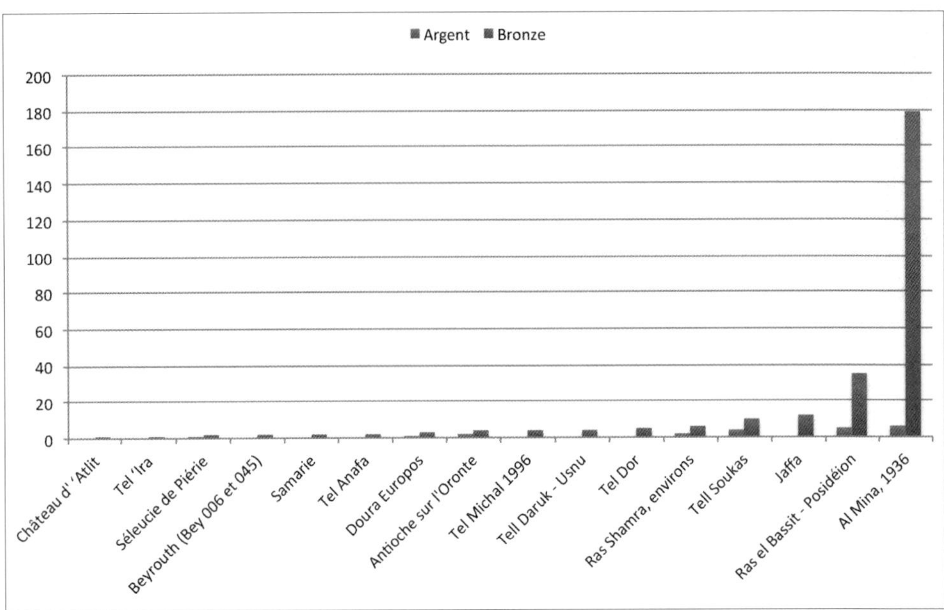

Fig. 5. Monnaies aux types d'Alexandre sur les sites syriens.

La répartition des bronzes est intéressante car elle est très inégale. Les 16 sites qui en ont livré montrent qu'il s'agit d'un monnayage d'empire : il circule partout alors que les monnaies de bronze ont souvent une aire limitée au territoire de la cité émettrice ou de sa zone d'influence. Les quantités sont cependant négligeables : 12 sites sur 16 livrent de un à cinq bronzes d'Alexandre.

Dans ce contexte, la région autour d'Al Mina se distingue par la présence beaucoup plus importante de ces monnaies (fig. 6). Le site d'Al Mina lui-même en a livré un nombre tout à fait exceptionnel : 179 exemplaires venus des ateliers voisins d'Arados, Byblos, Tarse, Salamine de Chypre et Posidéion. Al Mina a été abandonné vers 300. Ces monnaies ont donc été perdues dès le IVe s. ce qui suggère une présence macédonienne intensive sur place, pendant un temps suffisamment long pour que ces monnaies aient été utilisées et perdues. La présence de 5 monnaies de Philippe II, absentes des autres sites étudiés, renforce ce sentiment. Les 30 à 40 fragments illisibles attribués à Arados ou Alexandre sont très certainement aussi des bronzes macédoniens, l'atelier d'Arados n'ayant commencé à émettre ses bronzes autonomes qu'à la fin des années 240[33]. Les autres monnaies livrées par le site sont deux drachmes de Philippe III aux types d'Alexandre, un bronze peut-être frappé par un Diadoque et 12 autres des Séleucides et des Lagides. Les premières années de la présence macédonienne sont donc surreprésentées. En dehors d'Al Mina, seuls Ras el Bassit – Posidéion (40), Jaffa (12),

33 Duyrat 2005, 44. On pourrait émettre l'hypothèse qu'il s'agisse de bronzes aradiens d'époque perse, non attestés en fouilles cependant.

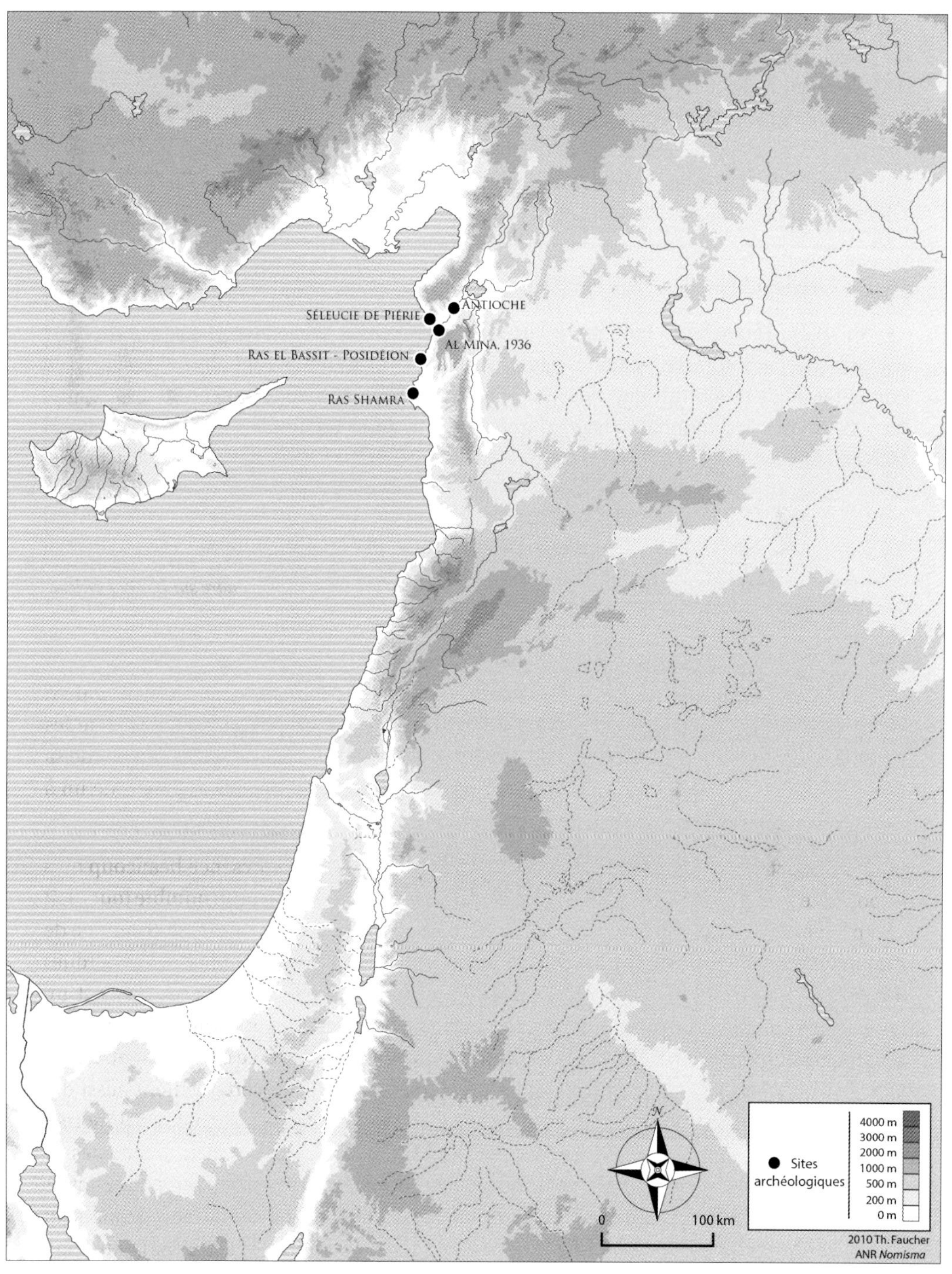

Fig. 6. Enclave lagide du III*e s. en Syrie du Nord (T. Faucher, 2010, ANR* Nomisma).

Ras Shamra (8) et Tell Soukas (10 ou 12[34]) dépassent 5 monnaies de bronze. La localisation de trois de ces sites n'est pas anodine : ils sont tous dans un périmètre rapproché autour d'Al Mina, au Nord de la pérée d'Arados, ce qui laisse supposer que le phénomène observé sur ce site a affecté l'ensemble de la région qui, pendant quelques années, a pu utiliser les bronzes aux types d'Alexandre. Le fait que les armées macédoniennes aient stationné durant l'hiver 333/2 dans la pérée d'Arados, associé à l'importance stratégique de la côte[35], justifie l'installation plus durable de garnisons et l'utilisation plus intense de ces monnaies.

Enclave lagide

Au IIIe s., l'étanchéité monétaire entre les possessions séleucides et lagides de Syrie est presque parfaite[36]. Le système lagide, fondé sur un tétradrachme de poids allégé en comparaison de l'étalon attique, ne laisse pénétrer aucune monnaie étrangère et ne s'exporte pas. Pourtant, des monnaies lagides apparaissent dans les fouilles de Syrie séleucide (tableau 2).

Site	PI	PII	PIII	PIV	PV	Total
Al Mina, 1936	7		1			8
Antioche	1	2	2		1	6
Ras el Bassit–Posidéion		1	7			8
Ras Ibn Hani[37]						Env. 170
Ras Shamra	2					2
Séleucie de Piérie	2	8	9			19

Tableau 2. Sites livrant des monnaies lagides du IIIe siècle.

La concentration de ces bronzes sur la côte a déjà été observée. Les Lagides tiennent la région entre 246 et 219, c'est-à-dire de la troisième à la quatrième guerre de Syrie[38]. Bien que les sources littéraires ne le disent pas, il est évident que les Ptolémées ont occupé non seulement Séleucie, mais aussi un territoire de dimensions inconnues autour[39]. Les limites

34 Les renvois à la *SNG* Cop. de Lund 1986 sont erronés par deux fois : il mentionne deux monnaies d'argent mais la référence donnée dans la collection de Copenhague est celle de monnaies de bronze.

35 Arr. 2.17.

36 Duyrat 2013.

37 Augé 2000, 62.

38 *OGIS* 54 ; Just. 27.1 ; Holleaux 1952, à propos de la troisième guerre de Syrie et de la prise de Séleucie de Piérie et Antioche.

39 Un article de J. Aliquot associe la présence du culte d'Isis à Antioche et Séleucie à la présence lagide au IIIe s. Aliquot 2014.

de cette zone peuvent être précisées grâce aux monnaies des fouilles. À Ras Ibn Hani, près de 170 monnaies lagides ont été exhumées. Ceci place Ibn Hani au premier rang des implantations lagides dans la région. Une stèle portant les noms et les ethniques de vingt-huit mercenaires à la solde des Lagides a été publiée par J.-P. Rey-Coquais : ces hommes se sont très probablement installés là au cours de la première phase de la troisième guerre de Syrie[40]. Sans surprise, Antioche et surtout Séleucie ont livré des témoignages monétaires identiques, comme les textes nous le laissaient déjà entendre. Séleucie a donné des résultats supérieurs à Antioche et cependant modestes au regard de la durée de l'occupation par la garnison ptolémaïque. Ce petit total tient peut-être aux espaces qui ont été fouillés dans la ville[41]. À Al Mina, pourtant abandonné vers 300, huit bronzes des deux premiers Lagides ont été découverts. De même, le site de Ras Shamra – Leukos Limen qui décline et disparaît entre 280 et 250 a livré deux monnaies lagides sur une maigre moisson de ramassages de surface de 25 pièces[42]. Malgré les chiffres très faibles des trouvailles de certains sites, ces bronzes sont significatifs : aucun autre site de Syrie du Nord n'en a livré et leur concentration autour de la zone citée par les textes comme occupée par les Lagides permet d'en dessiner les contours avec plus de précisions. D'autres prospections conduiraient sans doute à préciser encore les limites de cette enclave lagide.

Évolutions de l'usage du bronze

Le bronze semble prendre une place de plus en plus importante dans la circulation monétaire de la région durant l'époque hellénistique si on en juge par sa thésaurisation croissante (fig. 7).

Ces résultats sont cependant en partie déformés par l'importance volumétrique du monnayage hasmonéen qui a été plus thésaurisé que les autres monnaies de bronze produites dans la région. Il faudrait pouvoir comparer ces résultats à la somme des monnaies trouvées en fouilles dans la région. Un dépouillement fin de ces données n'entre pas dans le cadre fixé à cet article. Mais il est possible de travailler sur deux échantillons substantiels : les monnaies des fouilles des souks de Beyrouth et celles d'Antioche (tableau 3).

	IIIe s.	IIe s.	Ier s.
Antioche	522	294	210
Beyrouth	164	99	18

Tableau 3. Monnaies de bronze hellénistiques dans les fouilles d'Antioche et Beyrouth, IIIe-Ier s.

40 Rey-Coquais 1978.

41 La moisson est de toute façon relativement faible à Séleucie, avec au total 275 monnaies hellénistiques dont 4 en argent.

42 Stucky 1983, 54.

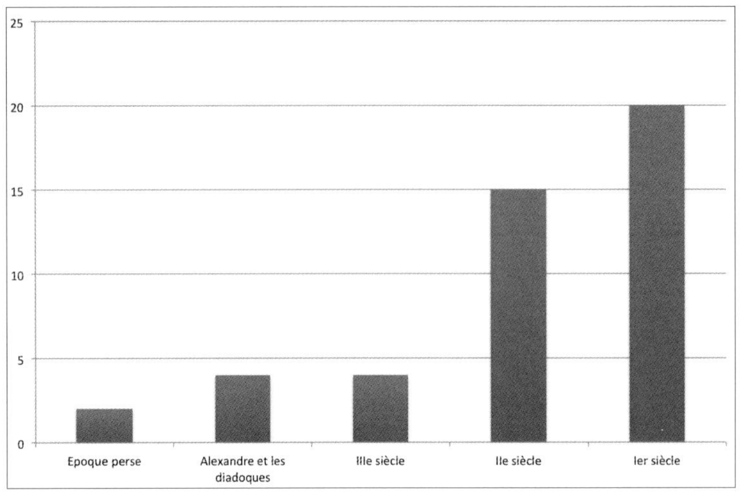

Fig. 7. Trésors de monnaies de bronze par période.

Le cumul des monnaies de bronze hellénistiques trouvées à Antioche et Beyrouth contredit l'impression donnée par les trésors : le nombre de monnaies de cet alliage décroît nettement entre le IIIe et le Ier s. Quelques précautions sont cependant nécessaires avant toute interprétation : le nombre de trouvailles dépend étroitement des niveaux archéologiques fouillés dans chacune de ces cités. Par ailleurs le bronze peut circuler longtemps or ce tableau est fondé sur les dates d'émission des monnaies. La décrue est cependant concordante dans les deux cas. Une analyse plus fine montre que c'est la disparition des monnaies royales séleucides qui explique ce phénomène (tableau 4).

	Séleucides	Lagides	Cités
IIIe s.	609	60	10
IIe s.	327	6	60
Ier s.	35	0	193

Tableau 4. Monnaies de bronzes séleucides, lagides et civiques dans les fouilles d'Antioche et Beyrouth.

Cette observation se confirme avec une courbe cumulative des bronzes séleucides trouvés sur les deux sites (fig. 8). Il n'est pas certain qu'elle donne un reflet exact de la production des différents ateliers concernés, mais elle en est sans doute un écho. Elle met en évidence la plus forte présence des monnaies d'Antiochos I, Séleucos III, Antiochos IV, Démétrios I et surtout les volumes considérables émis sous le règne d'Antiochos III. La baisse est nettement sensible à partir du milieu du IIe s.

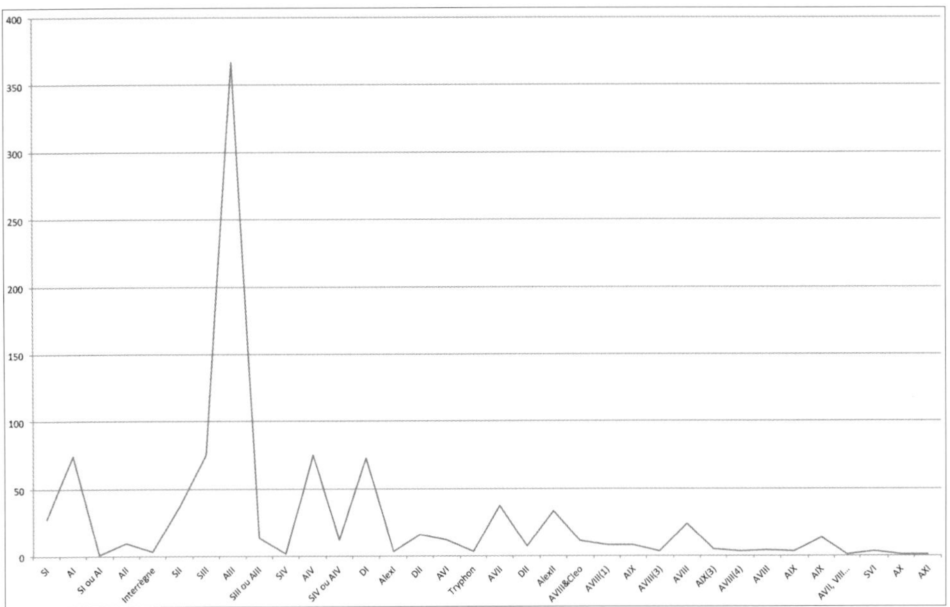

Fig. 8. Monnaies séleucides en bronze dans les fouilles d'Antioche et Beyrouth.

L'exemple d'Antioche et Beyrouth donne l'impression qu'au IIIe s., la monnaie de bronze est plus abondante mais moins thésaurisée qu'aux époques ultérieures. L'extension de ce type de comparaison entre les résultats des trouvailles archéologiques et la thésaurisation serait à n'en pas douter porteuse de nombreuses informations nouvelles. À l'autre extrémité de la période, l'omniprésence du bronze dans la circulation monétaire de l'état hasmonéen en fait une valeur plus fréquemment thésaurisée.

Conclusion

L'examen du produit de 58 sites archéologiques du Levant a été l'occasion de proposer quelques réflexions méthodologiques. Il a aussi permis de mettre en valeur l'intérêt de l'étude régionale du produit des fouilles pour éclairer aussi bien des aspects de l'histoire locale que de la production monétaire et des usages ordinaires de cet alliage. Un examen plus détaillé des découvertes faites en fouilles devrait être un indicateur beaucoup plus précis de l'usage des monnaies de bronze. Il n'est pas possible en l'état actuel du corpus qui ne distingue pas les trouvailles suffisamment précisément. En effet, l'absence de normes de publication, la grande variété des informations données, l'obsolescence des identifications qu'il n'est pas toujours possible de mettre à jour rendent difficile l'exploitation statistique du corpus créé. Cependant, les monnaies de fouilles étudiées à l'échelle régionale donnent un visage de la circulation monétaire différent de celui, mieux connu, tiré des trésors. L'examen parallèle des deux types de sources est aussi fondamental pour reconstituer au plus près les usages de la monnaie, dans toute leur étendue.

Annexe : sites archéologiques étudiés

1. Al Mina, 1936
2. Antioche sur l'Oronte, 1932-1939
3. 'Arab el-Mulk – Paltos
4. Auja el-Hafir – Nessana, Néguev
5. Balatah (anc. Sichem), Drew-McCormick Excavation
6. Beyrouth (Bey 006 et 045)
7. Beyrouth (Bey 020)
8-9. Césarée Maritime
10. Château d''Atlit
11. Doura Europos
12. En-Gedi
13. Gamala
14. Hama
15. Hippos-Sussita
16. Iraq al-Amir, porte monumentale
17. Jablé, nécropole d'al-Jbeibat
18. Jaffa
19. Jebel Khalid
20. Jerash–Gerasa
21. Jéricho
22. Jérusalem
23. Jérusalem, 1961-1967, Jardin arménien, colline Ouest
24. Jérusalem, "Cité de David"
25. Jérusalem, quartier juif 2003
26. Jérusalem, quartier juif 2006
27. Jérusalem, Vallée du Tyropoion, Mont Ophel
28. Khirbet Qumrân
29. Marisa (anc. Maresha)
30. Masada
31. Megiddo
32. Meiron
33. Mer de Galilée
34. Oumm el-'Amed
35. Oumm el-Mara
36. Pella Tabaqat Fahl, areas III, IV, V, XXIII, XXIX, XXXII, XXXIV
37. Ras el Bassit – Posidéion
38. Ras Shamra, environs
39. Samarie, Palestine Exploration Fund, 1931-1933, 1935
40. Séleucie de Piérie, 1932-1939
41. Sepphoris
42. Si' 8, Hauran
43. Si', Hauran
44. Tel Anafa
45. Tel 'Ira
46. Tel Dor
47. Tel Michal
48. Tel Michal 1996
49. Tell Abou Danné
50. Tell Ain el-Beida
51. Tell Arka, 1974-1980
52. Tell Beydar
53. Tell Daruk – Usnu
54. Tell el-Hajj
55. Tell el-Herr
56. Tell er-Ras, Giv'at Yasaf
57. Tell Keisan, Galilée
58. Tell Soukas

Les monnaies grecques des fouilles de l'École française d'Athènes à Argos

Catherine Grandjean

À la mémoire de Mando Oikonomides et de sa philoxénia légendaire

L'École française d'Athènes mène des fouilles à Argos depuis 1902. Après les campagnes de W. Vollgraff intervint une longue interruption liée aux deux guerres mondiales, puis le chantier d'Argos fut rouvert en 1952 par le directeur de l'École, G. Daux, et par son secrétaire général, P. Courbin. Depuis, les travaux ont continué sur différents sites argiens, souvent en collaboration avec les archéologues du service archéologique (4e Éphorie des antiquités préhistoriques et classiques). Les fouilles ont livré plus de 10 000 monnaies de toutes époques, depuis l'archaïsme jusqu'à l'époque contemporaine. Plusieurs personnes les ont inventoriées et étudiées au fil du temps. À partir de 1952 se sont succédés au chevet de ce matériel d'abord J. Bingen et T. Reekmans, J. Servais, Mme Varoucha-Christodoulopoulou, puis T. Hackens, P. Marchetti, O. Picard et moi à partir de 1992. Par la suite, R. Étienne nous demanda, à P. Marchetti, J.-M. Saulnier et moi de publier les monnaies, celles antérieures au règne d'Auguste m'étant alors attribuées.

L'étude d'un matériel trouvé lors de fouilles s'échelonnant sur une très longue durée est évidemment tributaire de l'évolution des pratiques archéologiques et pose des problèmes spécifiques, dont je dirai quelques mots, dans un but historiographique et pour rendre hommage à ceux qui ont exhumé et étudié ce matériel. W. Vollgraff se souciait des monnaies de fouille, qu'il fit envoyer à Athènes au Musée numismatique pour y être conservées. Impeccablement nettoyées à Athènes, elles sont revenues en 2002 au musée archéologique d'Argos dans un bon état de conservation. Mais il n'a laissé aucun inventaire détaillé des trouvailles numismatiques de cette période et les informations sur les lieux de découverte sont rares[1]. Le regard porté sur les monnaies de fouille avait déjà bien changé lors de la reprise des fouilles en 1952. D'emblée, les monnaies furent conservées dans un espace *ad hoc*, toutes dans un sachet séparé, portant numéro d'inventaire par année et mention de la provenance. P. Courbin les utilisait pour dater ses sols, avec le matériel céramique. T. Hackens, chargé du matériel à partir de 1964, se rendait à Argos après chaque campagne pour identifier les

1 Je remercie chaleureusement Marie-Françoise Billot de m'avoir fait parvenir l'inventaire annuel des sites fouillés par W. Vollgraff qu'elle a établi à partir des données disponibles.

monnaies et remettait aux archéologues une fiche dont les indications étaient reportées sur les carnets de fouille. Il dressait un inventaire annuel des monnaies par site, chaque pièce étant dotée d'un numéro distinct de celui des inventaires de fouilles : cela permettait notamment d'éliminer les monnaies trop abîmées et les morceaux de métal. L'étude des monnaies de fouille par T. Hackens avait les deux objectifs classiques qui voient se croiser les préoccupations des archéologues et celles des numismates : contribuer à la datation des contextes archéologiques, en association avec les autres données et matériels disponibles ; nourrir le *corpus* des monnaies argiennes qu'il préparait et que son décès prématuré l'empêcha de mener à bien.

Dans l'état actuel de la recherche, le catalogue des monnaies de fouille est achevé, grâce à l'aide de F. Wojan, S. Berger et d'autres doctorants qui m'ont accompagnée lors des campagnes estivales à Argos. Je remercie aussi H. Nicolet-Pierre et la regrettée Jennifer Warren pour leur aide. J'ai dépouillé tous les carnets et les rapports de fouille, mais il reste encore des points à éclaircir, via des échanges avec les archéologues. Il faut souhaiter en outre que, dans l'avenir, le riche matériel numismatique trouvé par les archéologues de la 4e Éphorie à Argos soit publié et vienne bientôt enrichir un tableau qui est évidemment partiel.

Après une rapide présentation du matériel, j'évoquerai ci-dessous quelques éléments de réflexion sur les informations que sont susceptibles d'apporter les monnaies de fouille sur la circulation, et plus largement sur l'histoire des pratiques monétaires au sein d'une cité.

Présentation du matériel

On compte actuellement 379 monnaies argiennes et 605 monnaies étrangères, soit 984 monnaies grecques identifiées antérieures au règne d'Auguste. Il s'y ajoute 117 monnaies attribuables à la période classique ou hellénistique, le plus souvent brûlées ou très usées, de tous modules. En outre, comme dans beaucoup de sites, une bonne centaine de monnaies est inexploitable et ne peut même pas être datée d'une période en raison de l'usure des flans et du caractère très indistinct des pièces (module, fabrication) qui ne permet même pas de les rattacher à une période de l'histoire monétaire.

Les monnaies argiennes

Monnaies d'argent

Les fouilles ont livré 39 monnaies argiennes classiques et hellénistiques en argent, toutes de faible valeur : 17 hémidrachmes dont 10 saucés (fig. 1-2)[2], 1 diobole (fig. 3)[3], 6 trihémioboles (fig. 4) [4] et 9 oboles (fig. 5)[5] ; il s'y ajoute 6 hémidrachmes du *koinon* achaien, qui avaient cours

2 Voir *BMC Peloponnesus* 9 et 57.

3 Voir *ibid.* 48-49.

4 Voir *ibid.* 84-85.

5 Voir *ibid.* 94.

à Argos, comme dans le reste du Péloponnèse, au IIe s. a.C. (fig. 6)[6]. L'absence de monnaies de forte valeur (statères et drachmes, alexandres à types argiens) n'est pas surprenante. Les monnaies de fouille comprennent en effet rarement de telles pièces, dont les usagers prenaient évidemment grand soin.

Fig. 1. Hémidrachme argien du Ve s., Agora (cl. EfA, P. Collet, échelle 1:1).

Fig. 2. Hémidrachme argien v. 320/270 ?, Thermes A (cl. EfA, P. Collet, échelle 1:1).

Fig. 3. Diobole argien v. 280/260 ?, Secteur delta (cl. EfA, P. Collet, échelle 1:1).

Fig. 4. Trihémiobole argien v. 320/250 ?, Agora (cl. EfA, P. Collet, échelle 1:1).

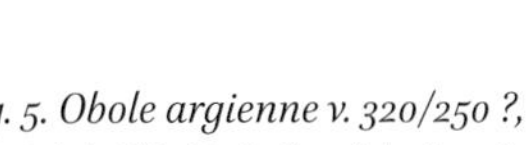

Fig. 5. Obole argienne v. 320/250 ?, Thermes A (cl. EfA, P. Collet, échelle 1:1).

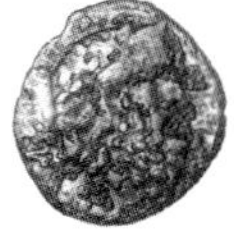
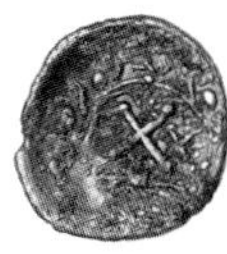

Fig. 6. Hémidrachme du koinon achaien, Tombe 216 (cl. EfA, P. Collet, échelle 1:1).

Il en va en général bien différemment des trésors, lots de monnaies constitués volontairement de monnaies susceptibles de constituer une réserve de valeur. Mais, dans le cas d'Argos, les trésors de monnaies d'argent trouvés localement, de modeste ampleur, comprennent surtout des drachmes, statères et tétradrachmes étrangers, tandis que l'atelier local y est représenté par des fractions. Du point de vue des monnaies locales, il n'y a donc pas de contraste marqué entre trésors et monnaies de fouille. Le trésor d'Argos 2005 (trouvé lors des fouilles de l'*oikopedo* Rentas par Alkestis Papadimitriou), qui doit dater du milieu du Ve s. a.C., comprend ainsi 70 statères et fractions d'Égine[7]. Le trésor d'Argos 1967 (*IGCH* 114) comprend 1 tétradrachme de Philippe Arrhidée, 1 drachme de Corinthe et 6 fractions d'Argos[8]. Son enfouissement a été daté de la fin du IVe s. a.C., mais le "trésor d'Argos 1967 ?" (*IGCH* 131),

6 Voir Thompson 1968, 326-329.
7 Grandjean & Papadimitriou à paraître.
8 Oikonomidou 1968, 12.

pourrait constituer un lot de ce trésor, ce qui inviterait à descendre l'enfouissement de l'ensemble au début du IIIe s. : l'*IGCH* 131 se compose de 4 tétradrachmes d'Alexandre III (Pella, Sicyone, Akè, Babylone) et de 2 tétradrachmes d'Athènes[9]. Le trésor d'Argos 1966 (*IGCH* 130), daté du début du IIIe s., compte au moins 37 monnaies, dont 1 statère Béotien, 3 statères de Sicyone, 1 statère d'Élis, 1 statère de Stymphale et 31 + hémidrachmes argiens[10].

J. H. Kroll notait dans sa publication des monnaies de fouille de l'agora d'Athènes qu'elles provenaient dans leur écrasante majorité de niveaux tardifs et il en va de même à Argos[11]. Dans un certain nombre de cas, il est toutefois possible, via l'étude du contexte, de proposer des hypothèses sur les séquences de dépôt des monnaies, comme le montrera la publication du matériel. Reste que la plupart des monnaies d'argent argiennes ont été trouvées lors des fouilles de W. Vollgraff ou dans des contextes impériaux tardifs : c'est le cas notamment de deux hémidrachmes argiens se rattachant aux premières émissions de la cité.

Monnaies de bronze

Les séries argiennes en bronze les mieux représentées dans les collections publiques et privées sont bien attestées dans les fouilles. Il en va ainsi des chalques à la tête de loup/A (fig. 7)[12] qui sont particulièrement nombreux, bien davantage que ceux aux types de Héra portant le *stephanos*/A surmontant une massue (fig. 8)[13]. Les multiples au type de Héra et du cippe d'Apollon Agyieus (fig. 9-10) [14] sont les mieux représentés dans les fouilles, suivis de ceux aux types d'Apollon et du trépied (fig. 11-12)[15]. Les autres émissions illustrées dans le *BMC Peloponnesus* sont attestées aussi, mais plus faiblement que les précédentes : ainsi, celles à la tête de Héra et au revers figurant le Palladion ne sont représentées que par 7 exemplaires (fig. 13)[16]. Les émissions figurant une tête de loup avec au revers le cippe d'Apollon Agyieus (fig. 14)[17] et de l'émission figurant une tête d'Apollon associé au revers à un loup (fig. 15)[18] sont peu représentées.

Quatre exemplaires de l'émission au type d'Athéna et de Tychè ont été retrouvés lors des fouilles, ce qui donne à penser que l'on peut raisonnablement maintenir son attribution à l'atelier argien, attribution contestée au profit d'un atelier d'Acarnanie (fig. 16)[19]. En revanche,

9 *Ibid.*, 7-8 et 12.

10 T. Hackens (1968, 92 n. 2) indique qu'il faut ajouter à cette liste un hémidrachme du *koinon* achaien et un hémidrachme de Pellène.

11 Kroll 1993, 2.

12 *BMC Peloponnesus* 22, pl. XXVII.

13 *Ibid.* 16, pl. XXVII.

14 *SNG Cop.* 17, 82-83 et *BMC Peloponnesus* 8, pl. XXVIII. Pour l'identification du type de revers, qui a donné lieu à maintes interprétations (principalement : carquois ou fontaine), je remercie Marie-Françoise Billot de ses propos éclairants appuyés sur des indications bibliographiques : Paus. 2.19.2 ; Guarducci 1974, 23-24 ; Marchetti 1994, 148-149 ; *id.* 1995, 437-477.

15 *BMC Peloponnesus* 23, pl. XXVII, *SNG Cop.* 17, 71-74.

16 *BMC Peloponnesus* 4, pl. XXVIII.

17 *Ibid.* 7, pl. XXVIII.

18 *Ibid.* 3, pl. XXVIII.

19 *Ibid.* 24, pl. XXVII. Voir le catalogue de vente *LHS Numismatics* 96, *Coins of the Peloponnesos*, The BCD Collection, 8-9 mai 2006, n° 1119.

Fig. 7. Bronze argien, sondage A (cl. EfA, P. Collet, échelle 1:1).

Fig. 8. Bronze argien, secteur delta (cl. EfA, P. Collet, échelle 1:1).

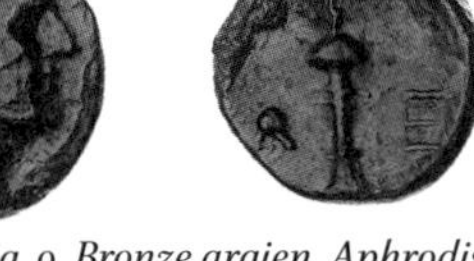

Fig. 9. Bronze argien, Aphrodision (cl. EfA, P. Collet, échelle 1:1).

Fig.10. Bronze argien (cl. EfA, P. Collet, échelle 1:1).

Fig. 11. Bronze argien, secteur delta (cl. EfA, P. Collet, échelle 1:1).

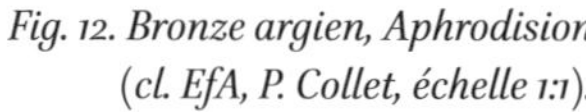

Fig. 12. Bronze argien, Aphrodision (cl. EfA, P. Collet, échelle 1:1).

Fig.13. Bronze argien, sondage 16, zone nécropole sud (cl. EfA, P. Collet, échelle 1:1).

Fig. 14. Bronze argien, Aphrodision (cl. EfA, P. Collet, échelle 1:1).

Fig. 15. Bronze argien, sondage 72 (cl. EfA, P. Collet, échelle 1:1).

Fig. 16. Bronze argien, secteur delta (cl. EfA, P. Collet, échelle 1:1).

aucun exemplaire des autres émissions dont l'attribution à Argos a été contestée n'a été trouvé dans les fouilles françaises[20].

L'étude des rapports et des carnets de fouille apporte déjà des éléments sur la datation de plusieurs séries de monnaies de bronze. La présence de chalques aux types tête de loup/A dans des contextes du IVe s. a.C., comme à Némée, confirme que l'émission du bronze a commencé à Argos bien plus tôt qu'on ne le pensait[21]. Des bronzes de module plus grand que celui des loups ont pu prendre le relais du petit numéraire en argent peut-être dès l'époque de la réforme monétaire évoquée par les tablettes du trésor du sanctuaire de Pallas. Ces tablettes découvertes par les archéologues de la 4e Éphorie des antiquités préhistoriques et classiques qu'étudie C. Kritzas distinguent le *palaion nomisma* de l'*argolikon*[22]. Ce dernier pourrait être le nouveau monnayage au type de Héra avec la légende *ΑΡΓΕΙΩΝ* qui, probablement vers 370, remplaça les drachmes et fractions au loup. Comme à Némée, les bronzes argiens au type d'Apollon n'apparaissent pas dans des contextes antérieurs au IIIe s. a.C.

Les monnaies étrangères

Elles constituent près de 60 % des monnaies grecques identifiées à Argos contre 13 % à Athènes, 37 % à Corinthe et moins de 10 % à Thasos. Il y a là une singularité qu'il convient d'examiner.

Monnaies d'argent

Elles sont très peu nombreuses et proviennent en majorité d'ateliers voisins. On dénombre 1 statère et 2 fractions d'Égine de la fin du VIe s. a.C. et de la 1ère moitié du Ve s. a.C. ; 4 statères corinthiens archaïques, 1 statère corinthien du IVe s., 1 statère à types corinthiens du IVe s d'Anactorion ; 1 obole de Kléonai de la fin du Ve s. ; 1 tétradrachme athénien saucé de la fin du Ve s. ; 4 hémidrachmes classiques et hellénistiques et une obole de Sicyone ; 1 tétradrachme attalide de poids attique ; 1 tétradrachme thasien de la 4e série.

On notera qu'il s'agit en majorité de monnaies de forte valeur, à la différence des monnaies d'argent argiennes trouvées en fouilles. Comme dans les trésors trouvés à Argos, les monnaies étrangères de forte valeur appartiennent surtout à l'époque archaïque et classique.

Monnaies de bronze

Les bronzes étrangers sont en majorité des monnaies de module moyen, comme la majorité des monnaies argiennes trouvées en fouille. Le pourcentage de chalques argiens dans les fouilles est faible, mais il a été impossible d'identifier une quantité importante de monnaies de petit module et le frai a logiquement éliminé une bonne part des plus petites monnaies. Il faudra évidemment attendre le *corpus* monétaire que préparent C. Flament et

20 *Ibid.* n° 1117-1118, 1120 et 1121.1-3.

21 Voir pour une chronologie basse des débuts du bronze monnayé à Argos, Hackens 1976, 83-85 ; pour Némée, Knapp & Mac Isaac 2005, 150-151.

22 Kritzas 2006 ; *id.* 2009.

P. Marchetti pour déterminer si le taux de représentation des émissions dans les fouilles reflète leur importance relative au sein du monnayage.

Les séries représentées appartiennent surtout au nord est du Péloponnèse. Quatre ateliers fournissent à eux seuls plus de la moitié du matériel : les fouilles ont en effet livré environ 200 bronzes de Sicyone, plus d'une centaine de bronzes de Corinthe, une quarantaine de Phlionte et une trentaine de Tégée. Le reste se compose d'exemplaires isolés d'ateliers thraces, macédoniens, thessaliens, béotiens, épirotes et de Corcyre. Chalcis, Athènes, Égine et Mégare sont bien représentées. Il y a en revanche peu de monnaies provenant des ateliers de l'ouest et du sud du Péloponnèse : 20 monnaies au total d'Épidaure et des cités de l'*Aktè* d'Argolide ont été identifiées, ce qui est peu, alors que ces cités sont assez proches d'Argos. Les monnaies des cités arcadiennes, à l'exception de celles de Tégée, toute proche, sont peu nombreuses. Une petite dizaine de monnaies de Kléonai rappelle que cette voisine d'Argos battit monnaie avant d'être absorbée par elle, sans doute à la fin du IVe s.[23]. En dehors de Grèce, il y a des monnaies du Pont, de Samos, de Carie, et de Séleucie du Tigre, mais le seul groupe significatif est constitué par un ensemble de monnaies de bronze de Ptolémée III destinées au Péloponnèse qui fut étudié par Mme Varoucha, puis par T. Hackens[24].

Par sa composition, le matériel est donc assez proche de celui des fouilles de l'École américaine à Némée, si l'on excepte les monnaies de Corinthe, dont la proportion est bien moindre à Argos qu'à Némée.

Comme souvent, on est frappé par le faible reflet, dans les monnaies de fouille, de ce que l'on sait par ailleurs des grands épisodes de l'histoire des cités, notamment des conflits, des sièges ou des phases d'occupation par des puissances étrangères. Les monnaies de Cléomène III et de Nabis sont rares, celles d'Antigone Gonatas et de Pyrrhus aussi.

Monnaies de fouilles et pratiques monétaires

Questions de méthodes

Après cette rapide présentation du matériel, évoquons les informations que sont susceptibles d'apporter les monnaies de fouille sur la circulation et plus largement sur l'histoire des pratiques monétaires au sein de la cité. Il est certes illusoire de prétendre reconstituer la circulation monétaire à partir de l'échantillon dont nous disposons.

> "The coins available for study are only a sample of those that have been found. The coins that have been found are only a sample of those which were lost. These in turn were only a sample of those that had originally been in circulation. Those that had been in circulation in the area for which information is available would be only a sample of the total number of coins issued"[25].

23 Piérart 1982, 119-138.

24 Varoucha-Christodoulopoulou (1944, 171) rapproche ces monnaies de l'envoi de numéraire à Aratos de Sicyone par le roi Ptolémée III (Plu., *Arat.*, 41) ; Hackens 1968 y voit plutôt la trace du numéraire offert par Ptolémée aux Spartiates en 227-223 (Plb. 2.51).

25 Grierson 1965.

Ce constat n'a pas découragé les numismates de terrain celtisants et romanistes qui, depuis quelques décennies, utilisent des outils spécifiques de quantification et de cartographie destinés à l'étude des monnaies de fouille. Ils mettent en série les monnaies trouvées dans de très nombreux sites, à l'échelle parfois d'un pays entier, distinguant des phases chronologiques de 10 à 20 ans dans les arrivées de matériel et considérant aussi les faciès de tel ou tel type de site (militaire, sanctuaire, habitat rural, village, ville, etc.)[26]. Ce type d'approche est susceptible de s'appliquer aux cas pour lesquels on dispose d'une masse de monnaies bien datées provenant de sites nombreux et issues des mêmes ateliers. Dans le monde grec, on pense d'emblée au monde séleucide ou ptolémaïque, ou encore aux colonies grecques au contact de populations barbares, où circulait souvent un type dominant de monnaie grecque, comme à l'ouest de la Sicile ou dans le Pont-Euxin. Il n'est pas évident toutefois que cette méthode puisse donner des résultats fiables pour les autres cités grecques, dont les monnaies sont rarement datées avec précision et où la part des monnaies locales est importante dans la circulation.

En revanche, ce que J.-M. Doyen appelle "l'analyse chronostratigraphique fine" au sein d'un même site est accessible dès lors que les fouilles sont bien conduites : elle permet notamment de distinguer les monnaies résiduelles encore en circulation de celles qui sont mises au rebut et inactives : cela n'est pas sans conséquence pour expliquer la présence si fréquente des monnaies classiques et hellénistiques dans des contextes très tardifs, comme l'a montré K. Butcher pour Beyrouth[27].

L'étude des facies monétaires au sein d'une cité fouillée nous est souvent accessible et gagnerait à distinguer différents types de sites, les nécropoles bien sûr, mais aussi les sanctuaires, les postes militaires, les zones d'habitat et d'artisanat. Cela apporterait des informations sur les pratiques monétaires.

Reste que ce type d'approche requiert des contextes archéologiques précis, notamment pour distinguer les groupes de monnaies des monnaies isolées, les "step-children" (P. Grierson) de la numismatique, ou encore pour connaître la manière dont les contextes archéologiques se sont formés[28].

La plupart des monnaies d'argent de forte valeur des fouilles françaises ont été trouvées lors des fouilles de W. Vollgraff, pour lesquelles les données font défaut. Reste que le reste du matériel autorise bon nombre de réflexions.

26 Voir notamment Reece 2013 ; Doyen 2011.

27 Butcher 2003.

28 T. Hackens indiquait aussi la nécessité, pour une interprétation correcte des monnaies de fouille, de connaître la manière dont les contextes archéologiques s'étaient formés : soulignant qu'en cas de destruction soudaine et violente, l'image de la circulation monétaire est bien différente de ce que l'on observe en cas d'abandon sans précipitation : ainsi en est-il à Délos à l'îlot des Comédiens où une majorité de petits bronzes domine la statistique, les monnaies en argent étant quasi absentes. Dans l'îlot voisin, détruit par la violence, on a retrouvé des monnaies d'argent en plus d'un endroit, car la même sélection n'avait pu s'opérer. Voir Dentzer *et al.* 1975, 217.

Monnaies perdues ou monnaies mises au rebut ?

Un trait frappant du matériel de fouille, à Argos comme ailleurs, est la présence de monnaies saucées, principalement argiennes, mais aussi d'autres ateliers (Athènes, Corinthe). Il s'agit pour la plupart de monnaies isolées, mais un groupe de 16 monnaies saucées, dont 10 au moins sont aux types des hémidrachmes argiens du Ve s. (avant-train de loup/ A dans un carré creux contenant deux petits carrés creux), a été trouvé lors des fouilles menées en 1987. Leurs poids actuels s'échelonnent entre 1 et 2 g et sont donc très inférieurs à ceux d'hémidrachmes de poids éginétique, mais toutes ces monnaies ont été entaillées. Il s'agit donc manifestement d'un ensemble de monnaies mises au rebut [29]. Ce groupe peut être rapproché du lot 1 034 d'un catalogue de vente de la collection BCD[30], constitué d'hémidrachmes contrefaits du Ve s. Or, C. Kritzas indique, dans un de ses articles sur les tablettes trouvées dans le trésor du sanctuaire de Pallas à Argos, que des inventaires évoquent des dépôts de monnaies contrefaites confisquées[31].

On s'accorde souvent à penser que les monnaies étrangères de faible valeur trouvées en fouille sont des monnaies mises au rebut. Dans certains cas, cela n'est toutefois pas si sûr : ainsi, plusieurs monnaies de bronze de Philippe II ont été découvertes sur l'Aspis, là précisément où les récents travaux de Sylvain Fachard sur les fortifications donnent à penser qu'une forteresse macédonienne fut établie vers la fin du IVe ou au début du IIIe s.

Les monnaies surfrappées posent aussi question. Une quarantaine de monnaies surfrappées ont été trouvées à Argos. À l'exception d'un hémidrachme argien surfrappé sur un hémidrachme de Sicyone, toutes ces pièces sont des bronzes. Plusieurs sont des monnaies à types argiens surfrappées sur des monnaies d'autres ateliers, qui sont aussi les mieux représentés dans les fouilles de la cité : Corinthe, Phlionte, Sicyone. Mais la moitié de ce lot est composée de monnaies de Corinthe, Phlionte et Sicyone surfrappées sur des monnaies d'autres ateliers. Ces monnaies ont été découvertes en divers endroits de la ville, le plus souvent isolées. Elles datent surtout des IVe s.- IIIe s., puis du Ier s. a.C., qui correspondent, on le verra, aux phases d'afflux de monnaies étrangères à Argos.

Les monnaies de bronze de Corinthe, Phlionte et Sicyone trouvées à Argos

Les monnaies de ces trois ateliers sont présentes en nombre dans la quasi-totalité des zones fouillées[32]. Elles y ont été trouvées dans les mêmes conditions que les monnaies argiennes, tantôt isolées, tantôt en groupes, associées à des monnaies argiennes et à celles d'autres ateliers étrangers, le plus souvent de modules voisins. La question est évidemment d'expliquer la présence massive de ces monnaies à Argos. Certes, d'autres exemples comparables sont attestés, comme celui des monnaies de Séleucie du Tigre à Suse. G. Le

29 Il n'a pas été possible d'identifier les autres monnaies, en raison de leur piètre état de conservation.

30 Voir le catalogue de vente *LHS Numismatics* 96, *Coins of the Peloponnesos*, The BCD Collection, 8-9 mai 2006; voir aussi les catalogues de vente G. Hirsch 155, 23 sept. 1987, 95 et Spink 90, 16 mars 1992, 761 (lot).

31 Kritzas 2009.

32 Toutefois, celles de Corinthe sont rares sur l'agora, comme celles de Sicyone antérieures au milieu du IIIe s.

Rider avait observé à propos des nombreuses monnaies de Séleucie du Tigre trouvées dans les fouilles de Suse que les arrivages de ces monnaies étrangères connaissaient des fluctuations dans le temps[33]. Ainsi, à Argos, les frappes des trois ateliers étrangers considérés datent surtout de la période antérieure à l'adhésion de la cité au *koinon* achaien, en 229. Les monnaies étrangères frappées entre la fin du IIIe s. et le début du Ier s. a.C. sont rares à Argos, à l'exception des monnaies de bronze de Sicyone, toujours abondantes. Des monnaies grecques étrangères frappées au Ier s. a.C., avant Actium, se rencontrent dans les fouilles, surtout des monnaies de Sicyone et de Tégée.

À en juger par l'étude de monnaies trouvées en contextes classiques et hellénistiques, mais aussi dans des contextes bien plus tardifs, les monnaies étrangères sont souvent associées à des monnaies argiennes, dont rien ne donne à penser qu'elles aient été mises au rebut. Comme l'a écrit K. Butcher, il est bien possible que les Grecs n'aient pas plus prêté attention aux types monétaires que nos contemporains, et/ou que, eu égard de surcroît à leur usure, ils aient prêté avant tout attention aux modules des monnaies[34]. De fait, dans le Péloponnèse, comme dans d'autres régions grecques, les modules des monnaies de bronze des cités étaient assez semblables. La plupart des ateliers frappaient des petites monnaies pesant 1 à 2 g, pour un diamètre de flan rarement supérieur à 13 mm, ainsi que des monnaies un peu plus grosses, d'un diamètre compris entre 13 et 15-16 mm et enfin des monnaies plus lourdes et plus larges. L'étude des inscriptions invite à les désigner comme des chalques et des multiples du chalque[35]. Argos a frappé surtout des bronzes des deux premiers modules. Les monnaies étrangères de Corinthe (fig. 17), Phlionte (fig. 18), Sicyone (fig. 19) ont des modules voisins de celles des argiennes. La proportion des chalques y est plus importante que pour les argiennes, ce qui n'est pas sans intérêt dans la mesure où Argos semble avoir privilégié la frappe des multiples du chalque à partir du IIIe s.

La présence massive des bronzes de l'atelier de Sicyone pendant toute la période n'est pas un phénomène propre à Argos, comme l'a souligné J. Warren pour d'autres sites du Péloponnèse[36]. Tout se passe comme si l'atelier de Sicyone, qui frappa abondamment monnaie avec l'aval de Sparte pour les cités alliées, de la Guerre du Péloponnèse jusqu'à l'époque de la

Fig. 17. Bronze de Corinthe, sondage 71 (cl. EfA, P. Collet, échelle 1:1).

Fig. 18. Bronze de Phlionte, Aspis (cl. EfA, P. Collet, échelle 1:1).

Fig. 19. Bronze de Sicyone (cl. EfA, P. Collet, échelle 1:1).

33 Le Rider 1965, 446-449.

34 Butcher 2003, 24.

35 Voir Tod 1946 ; Psoma 2001, 120-124 ; Grandjean 2003, 44-46.

36 Warren 1985 et 2009.

bataille de Leuctres (371 a.C.) et de l'invasion du Péloponnèse qui s'ensuivit[37], avait continué ensuite à alimenter la circulation dans la région. Son rôle comme atelier du *koinon* achaien a été assez modeste, mais elle semble avoir poursuivi alors de manière concomitante ses frappes à types propres en bronze. Soline Berger, qui examine dans le cadre de sa thèse la part de chaque atelier étranger dans les monnaies des fouilles de l'*American School of Classical Studies* à Corinthe, arrive pour Sicyone à plus 13,3 % du total, soit plus d'1/3 du total des monnaies étrangères, comme à Argos. À Corinthe, le matériel argien ne représente en revanche que 2 % des monnaies grecques, alors que les corinthiennes constituent plus de 10 % des monnaies grecques trouvées à Argos. Phlionte est un peu moins représenté à Corinthe (1,46 %) qu'à Argos (4 %)[38]. G. Le Rider interprétait l'afflux de monnaies de Séleucie du Tigre à Suse en mettant l'accent sur l'adaptation de l'atelier de Suse (qui modulait ses propres frappes en fonction des arrivées) et sur les liens entre les arrivées de monnaies et les fluctuations des échanges commerciaux. Il est encore trop tôt pour formuler une hypothèse concernant Argos, car l'étude des contextes n'est pas terminée, mais je mettrai l'accent sur un point qui pourrait contribuer à expliquer le cas argien, comme les différences que l'on rencontre, selon les sites, dans la composition de la petite monnaie trouvée dans les fouilles archéologiques.

Les tablettes du trésor du sanctuaire de Pallas donnent à penser qu'Argos, comme beaucoup de cités, s'efforçait de contrôler la monnaie d'argent : elles mentionnent 4 mines de monnaies d'argent de Sicile (vraisemblablement hors cours légal) fondues pour faire un brûle-parfum (418) et de l'argent corinthien figure dans le solde des comptes (429)[39]. Mais des données relatives à l'histoire monétaire médiévale et moderne invitent à se demander si le même contrôle s'exerçait sur la petite monnaie en bronze, dès lors qu'il ne s'agissait pas de monnaie saucée.

La spécificité de la "petite monnaie"

Les sources disponibles sur l'histoire monétaire de l'Europe médiévale et moderne attestent en effet que les États ne maîtrisaient pas bien la petite monnaie, le "small change". Cette question a donné lieu à bien des études, car elle a posé en Europe à partir de la réforme carolingienne et jusqu'à la fin du XIXe s. tout une série de problèmes spécifiques, distincts de ceux posés par le denier carolingien d'argent et par les dénominations de forte valeur qui lui ont succédé[40]. Les aspects strictement monétaires sont évidemment différents a priori de ceux qui nous occupent (existence de frappe libre, coexistence de fractions à forte valeur intrinsèque et fiduciaire, importance de la spéculation), mais, *mutadis mutandis*, les

37 Voir les propos de C. M. Kraay (1976, 99). Les Thébais et leurs alliés Argiens et Arcadiens mirent à profit la défaite et l'affaiblissement de Sparte pour édifier, au nord et à l'ouest de la cité, un glacis stratégique, constitué par le *koinon* arcadien, autour de Mégalopolis associée à Messène, affranchie de la domination spartiate.

38 Je remercie Soline Berger de m'avoir communiqué ces chiffres qui confirment la part importante des monnaies de Sicyone dans la circulation monétaire régionale jusqu'au Ier s. a.C., voire au-delà.

39 Kritzas 2006, 418.

40 Sargent & Velde 2002 ; Laurence 1931.

conséquences sociales et politiques des phénomènes affectant la petite monnaie dans ces sociétés préindustrielles à écriture paraissent à considérer.

L'afflux de petites monnaies étrangères pour pallier le manque de monnaies locales paraît avoir été récurrent, sans que les souverains aient été à l'origine de ce mouvement et parviennent à le contrôler. Ainsi, en 1339, le manque de petites monnaies provoqua l'afflux, dû à l'initiative privée, de monnaies étrangères en Angleterre, et le roi Édouard III s'en émut. Il chercha à interdire l'usage de ces monnaies, mais révisa sa politique sous la pression de ses sujets. Car si la petite monnaie était utilisée par tous, elle était la seule monnaie utilisée par les plus pauvres : ils étaient payés en petite monnaie, tandis que les riches l'étaient en monnaie de forte valeur[41]. Les conséquences politiques des phénomènes touchant la petite monnaie pouvaient donc être graves. Ainsi, Florence connut à partir de 1370 un afflux de petites monnaies étrangères qui provoqua une forte inflation dont furent principalement victimes les plus pauvres. Des troubles suivirent, qui provoquèrent en 1378 la prise du pouvoir par le mouvement populaire des Ciompi, mécontents de voir la petite monnaie dévaluée, alors que la monnaie de forte valeur restait stable et que la fiscalité était très lourde[42]. La difficulté du contrôle était certes liée en partie à l'existence de frappe libre, mais aussi au fait que la petite monnaie était utilisée pour des paiements dits horizontaux (entre particuliers), qui n'avaient pas toujours lieu sous le regard des autorités.

Il ne s'agit pas là de chausser les lunettes des économistes *mainstream* pour affirmer que le marché monétaire se régulait naturellement, sans intervention de l'État, via l'afflux de monnaies étrangères. C'est sur un autre plan, celui de la cité et de son équilibre social, face aux risques de *stasis* qu'il convient à mon sens de se placer. Les cités grecques, en évitant la frappe libre et en choisissant de frapper des petites monnaies en bronze et pas en métal précieux, avaient compris d'emblée ce que les États modernes européens ont mis plus de 1 000 ans à réaliser, assurant ainsi la stabilité de la petite monnaie au sein des systèmes monétaires qui associaient monnaies en métaux précieux et en bronze. En revanche, le caractère irrégulier de la plupart de leurs frappes provoquait des périodes de disette de monnaies. Or, Platon lui-même reconnaissait que ces monnaies étaient essentielles pour qu'aient lieu les transactions quotidiennes sur l'agora et que se maintienne la communauté civique[43]. Les arrivées de monnaies étrangères, lorsque la petite monnaie venait à manquer

41 Voir aussi l'anecdote bien connue de l'offrande de 2 piécettes en bronze par la pauvre veuve au Temple de Jérusalem, tandis que des plus riches donnent sans compter des piécettes analogues : "Tous ceux-là ont mis leur superflu, mais elle, de son indigence, a mis tout ce qu'elle possédait, tout ce qu'elle avait pour vivre" (Mc 12.42 ; trad. J. Huby, 1922).

42 Cipolla 1956, 27-37.

43 (Sans monnaie) "Comment les citoyens se feront-il part les uns aux autres des produits de leur travail respectif ? Car c'est précisément pour cela que nous avons fait une communauté (*koinônia*) et fondé une cité. Il est évident [...] que ce sera par vente et par achat. De là la nécessité d'une *agora* et d'une monnaie (*nomisma*), signe de la valeur des objets échangés" (Plat., *Rep.*, 2.371b ; trad. E. Chambry, 1934). "Il ne sera permis à aucun citoyen de posséder tant soit peu d'or ou d'argent, mais seulement de la monnaie pour les échanges quotidiens (*nomisma de eneka allagès tès kath'èmeran*), tels qu'on est presque obligé d'en faire avec les artisans et tous ceux dont on a besoin, pour payer le salaire de pareils services aux mercenaires, esclaves ou étrangers" (Plat., *Lois*, 5.742a-b ; trad. E. Des Places, 1953).

et/ou que la situation sociale se tendait, ne pouvaient-elles pas constituer, pour les cités, un outil parmi d'autres pour limiter les risques de *stasis* ?

Or, Argos a connu à l'automne 370 un massacre de 1 200 riches citoyens (le *skytalismos*), et des tensions sociales très vives sont bien attestées dans le nord-est du Péloponnèse à partir du début du IVe s. a.C. L'accueil enthousiaste réservé à Cléomène III, qui venait d'opérer remise des dettes et partage des terres à Sparte, par de nombreuses cités de la région donne à penser que ces tensions perduraient dans les années 230/220[44].

44 Pour le skytalismos d'Argos, voir Diod. 15.57.3-58 ; Plu., *De Vit. Mor.*, 814B = *Maxime*, 17 ; D.H. 7.66.5 ; Isoc., *Phil.*, 52. Voir aussi Tomlinson 1972, 140, 143 et 193 ; Piérart & Touchais 1996, 59-60 ; Eder 2016.

Les monnaies de fouilles du monde grec : l'apport de Thasos

Olivier Picard

Cette évaluation de l'apport des fouilles de Thasos à notre connaissance de l'usage et de la diffusion de la monnaie dans la cité s'en tiendra aux monnaies de Thasos, sans s'occuper des autres monnaies grecques, ni des monnaies plus récentes, romaines, byzantines et autres[1]. La première constatation est celle de l'abondance du matériel réuni : sur les 8 200 pièces du catalogue des monnaies thasiennes, 6 800 viennent des fouilles. Ce sont presque exclusivement des bronzes, l'argent ne représentant pas 0,5 % du total. Cette masse permet – ce qui est un cas exceptionnel dans notre documentation sur l'antiquité – de dresser un tableau complet des formes institutionnelles qu'a prises la monnaie : les types et valeurs qui sont émis, la forme des monnayages, le système de contrôle des émissions. Cette masse permet aussi dans la plupart des cas – laissons à part les petits modules dont un grand nombre est trop abîmé – d'identifier tous les coins utilisés et fournit donc une image complète de la production des bronzes. Le deuxième apport provient des contextes archéologiques, qui fournissent quantité d'informations chronologiques, que j'utiliserai ici sans les détailler.

L'objectif est d'analyser jusqu'où il est possible de reconstituer la politique monétaire de la cité ainsi que les emplois de la monnaie par les Thasiens. J'emploie le concept de "politique monétaire", bien que sa pertinence ait été contestée, même si le champ de la politique monétaire des cités antiques n'est évidemment pas le même que dans nos sociétés. Mais quels qu'aient été l'extension de ce champ et les formes de la politique monétaire du fait du développement considérable de l'économie monétaire depuis l'antiquité, il n'est pas douteux que, dès le début, dans le monde de la cité, c'est la cité qui décidait des types et des valeurs de la monnaie, du rythme et du volume des émissions[2]. D'autre part, les observations chiffrées auxquelles se prête ce matériel permettent de découvrir un certain nombre de pratiques de l'atelier dans sa gestion du métal. La combinaison des deux sortes d'informations nous incitera à des réflexions sur l'usage de la monnaie de bronze dans l'économie des Thasiens.

1 On trouvera une présentation récente des recherches sur la monnaie thasienne dans Picard 2001a ; *id.* 2011a, *id.* 2011b.

2 Ce pouvoir est propre à la polis, voir Picard 2014 ; *id.* à paraître. Les autres formes d'État (ethnos thraces, empire achéménide, etc.) n'en usent pas de la même manière.

O. Picard, in : *Les monnaies de fouille du monde grec*, p. 65-81

Les institutions : système de contrôle et valeurs mises en circulation

Les systèmes de contrôle : séries monétaires et émissions

Rappelons très brièvement le principe du classement des monnayages thasiens : sont regroupées sous le nom de séries toutes les monnaies qui ont cours légal (qui sont *dokimos*) dans la même période[3]. Chaque série utilise un système de contrôle qui lui est propre et qui change avec la série : ce contrôle permet de reconnaître les émissions, qui regroupent les monnaies frappées sous la responsabilité d'un même monétaire.

La première série, au Silène et à la Ménade, ne nous concerne pas, puisqu'elle ne comporte pas de monnaie de bronze. Seules quelques fractions ont été retrouvées dans les fouilles.

Je commence donc avec la réforme de 390 qui introduit le bronze[4]. C'est la Série 2, que ses types invitent à appeler la Série des "dieux gardiens" par référence aux types monétaires de l'argent, qui inaugure la frappe du bronze. Dans ce métal, le droit a pour type la tête d'Héraclès, barbu sur les chalques et imberbe sur les pièces de valeur plus élevée. Le revers a pour type les armes d'Héraclès : l'arc est toujours représenté horizontalement le bois vers le haut et la massue au-dessous, et non verticalement comme dans certaines séries macédoniennes : l'ajustement des axes, quand il sera pratiqué dans la Série 4, nous indique la bonne manière de regarder cette image[5]. La série compte trois valeurs, que j'identifie comme des chalques (1/12ᵉ d'obole)[6], des dichalques et des hémioboles (fig. 1). La plus petite (le chalque) est la seule à être représentée dans tous les groupes : c'est elle qui nous servira de fil conducteur pour reconstituer le système de contrôle (tableau 1).

Fig. 1. Les trois modules de bronze de la série 2.

3 Sur la définition de ces catégories en numismatique, voir de Callataÿ 2013a.

4 Picard 2001b.

5 La massue est le plus souvent à regarder verticalement sur les monnaies, de même que le foudre comme l'ont montré de Callataÿ & Gerin 1992.

6 Picard 1998 ; Psoma 1998.

Série 2 "dieux gardiens"	ethnique	module	émissions
Groupe 1	ΘΑΣ – ΙΟΝ / carré incus	chalques	sans symbole flèche grappe 1 dauphin 1 canthare 1
Groupe 2	ΘΑΣ – ΙΟΝ / cercle incus	chalques	sans symbole flèche cigale grappe 2 canthare 2 croissant de lune amphore 1 serpent
Groupe 3	ΘΑΣΙΟΝ inversé ΘΑΣΙΟΝ sous massue	chalques dichalques hémioboles	17 émissions thyrse dauphin 2 étoile amphore 2 grappe 3 épi de blé feuille de lierre échassier astragale
Groupe 4	ΘΑΣΙΟΝ Inversé ΘΑΣΙΟΝ entre arc et massue	chalques hémioboles	14 émissions 11 émissions
Groupe 5	positions diverses	chalques + hémioboles	canthare 3 amphore 3 grappe 3
I - Série 2 :	groupes	valeurs	émissions

Tableau 1. Groupes et émissions de la Série 2.

Le contrôle du bronze combine une variation de la disposition de l'ethnique, qui conduit à distinguer cinq groupes, avec un symbole placé dans l'arc pour définir les émissions, dont le nombre est variable selon les groupes. L'ethnique est d'abord coupé en deux : sous la massue ΘΑΣ ION au dessus, dans un carré incus (groupe 1), puis dans un cercle (groupe 2). À partir de 360, quand apparaissent des dénominations plus lourdes, l'ethnique est inscrit en une seule ligne, sous la massue, d'abord dans le sens inverse de l'arc, puis en position verticale. Enfin un cinquième groupe, à partir d'environ 320/15, présente des variantes (fig. 2). Comme

Fig. 2. Le système de contrôle de la série 2 : ethnique (groupe) et symbole (grappe de raisin et amphore).

le montre le tableau, un même symbole (grappe de raisin, amphore etc.) peut être réutilisé d'un groupe à l'autre, mais les contextes archéologiques prouvent que c'est la disposition de l'ethnique – le groupe – et non le symbole qui permet d'établir le cadre chronologique : ainsi le trésor 1971 ne comporte que des chalques du groupe 1 ; les sols superposés des maisons de la Porte du Silène de même que le comblement d'un puits public ont donné des informations très précises sur cette chronologie[7]. Pour identifier le responsable de l'émission, le contrôle combine donc des cycles de durée variable, les groupes qui durent entre 15 et 35 ans, avec les symboles qui renvoient à un responsable. Si un symbole est gravé dans l'arc dès la seconde émission, le système n'a certainement pas été imaginé dans son ensemble dès le début, mais il a dû se développer en fonction de l'histoire politique de la cité (tableau 1).

Vers 310, la Série 2 est abandonnée, ce que marque l'enfouissement du trésor 1952[8] : le système des valeurs est modifié et une nouvelle, l'obole, est introduite. S'ouvre une période de près d'un siècle et demi, où la cité a utilisé cinq monnayages différents, que j'appelle la période des monnayages hétérogènes (fig. 3), qui se situent entre la fin du IVe et le début du IIe s. (tableau 2) :

- les Déméter qui sont les premières oboles, accompagnées de quelques chalques ;
- le retour à Héraclès, qui reprend les types de la Série 2 pour frapper des hémioboles avec quelques modifications qui évitent toute confusion avec les hémioboles précédents ;
- une petite série de chalques, qui réutilise l'amphore dionysiaque des hémihectés de la fin du Ve siècle ;
- un 2e monnayage d'hémioboles avec un second retour à Héraclès, dans une nouvelle variante ;

7 *CH* VIII, 77 ; Picard 1982 ; *id.* 1989. Pour le quartier du Silène, Grandjean 1988.
8 *IGCH* 723 ; Le Rider 1956.

Fig. 3. Les quatre premiers monnayages hétérogènes.

– une émission qui a pour revers une massue dans une couronne et, au droit des hémidrachmes d'argent, la tête de Dionysos, tandis qu'une tête de satyre figure sur les chalques. Cette émission est souvent associée à la fin de la deuxième guerre de Macédoine, quand Thasos retrouve sa liberté, ce qui correspond à l'époque où les données numismatiques et archéologiques permettent de situer ces pièces.

Monnayage	module	types	coins
Déméter / Dioscures	Obole Chalque	Déméter / Dioscures Héraclès barbu / pilos	37 D – 40 R ? - ?
Retour à Héraclès : ΘΑΣΙΟΝ sous la massue	 Hémiobole Chalque	 Héraclès barbu Héraclès imberbe	 42 D – 64 + R 15 D + 29 R
Amphore	Chalque	Amphore / Corne d'abondance	? - ?
2e retour à Héraclès : ΘΑΣΙΩΝ Corne d'abondance	 hémiobole	 Héraclès barbu Armes	 1 D – 3 R
Monnaies à la couronne ΘΑΣΙΩΝ	 AR Chalque	 Dionysos / Massue dans couronne Satyre / Massue dans couronne	 11 D - 14 R 8 D – 10 R

Tableau 2. La période des monnayages hétérogènes.

Ces monnayages isolés n'utilisent pas de marque de contrôle et ne distinguent donc pas d'émissions. Les contextes archéologiques prouvent que les différents monnayages n'ont pas circulé en même temps. Quand un type ancien est repris, on introduit des modifications mineures qui suffisent cependant à empêcher toute confusion avec les emplois précédents, ce qui implique qu'il existe une mémoire monétaire de la cité, que la cité gardait les archives de sa monnaie[9]. C'est ce que montrent les variantes des types des hémioboles : celles des différents retours à Héraclès scandent la récurrence du type à travers les différents monnayages, sans qu'aucune confusion soit possible (fig. 4). Quoique très proches, ces variantes ne se retrouvent jamais dans les mêmes ensembles archéologiques.

9 Picard 2010.

Fig. 4. Les retours d'Héraclès (milieu IVe-fin IIe s.).

Les tétradrachmes à flan large, dont la frappe commence à la veille de la troisième guerre de Macédoine, reprennent les types des dieux gardiens, en les rajeunissant. C'est la Série des dieux jeunes (Série 4), qui s'accompagne de 24 émissions de bronze. Trois modules sont utilisés : des pièces lourdes, aux types d'Artémis au droit et d'Héraclès archer au revers que je considère comme des oboles ; des hémioboles, qui illustrent un troisième retour à Héraclès, avec un nouveau jeu de variantes ; une seule émission de petits bronzes, avec une tête d'Héraclès originale et la reprise de la corne d'abondance. La série utilise un système de contrôle par monogrammes : ils sont au nombre de trois dans un premier groupe de cinq émissions ; il n'y en a plus qu'un dans le deuxième groupe de treize émissions et plus aucun dans les six dernières émissions, que je n'ai pu distinguer que par des critères de style ou de dessin (fig. 5).

Les valeurs monétaires : types et poids

Outre le système de contrôle, l'autre champ de la politique monétaire de la cité porte sur les valeurs, qui sont définies pour l'utilisateur comme pour les gens de métier, par la combinaison des types, des diamètres et des poids. J'ai parlé ci-dessus de chalques, d'hémioboles et d'oboles en place des termes "petits", "moyens" ou "grands" bronzes utilisés traditionnellement dans la littérature scientifique. Ils sont en effet d'une simplicité trompeuse qui cache bien des pièges, comme le montre l'exemple thasien.

Fig. 5. Série 4 : le système de contrôle des bronzes.

Le cas du chalque est le plus simple. Ce module, qui est la valeur la plus faible des monnayages de bronze[10], est aussi la plus ancienne à avoir été frappée à Thasos, à 1/12e d'obole,

10 Marcellesi 2012a.

à en juger par l'échelonnement des poids des valeurs supérieures qui seront frappées dans un deuxième temps. Le chalque est la seule valeur des groupes 1 et 2 de la Série 2. C'est aussi la pièce la plus fréquemment trouvée dans les fouilles.

Les poids des chalques de la première émission de la Série 2 se situent entre 0,8 et 1,6 g (un seul exemplaire), le poids moyen et le poids modal se situant à 1,1 g. Ces chiffres se retrouvent dans les émissions suivantes, jusqu'à la dernière émission du groupe 5, à la grappe de raisin. Ensuite les chalques de l'émission à l'Héraclès des monnayages hétérogènes montrent une légère élévation du poids, entre 0,9 et 2,3 g, le poids moyen se situant à 1,3 et le poids modal à 1,4. Les chiffres sont les mêmes pour l'émission suivante amphore / corne d'abondance (4e monnayage hétérogène). S'agirait-il d'une augmentation sans signification ? Elle va de pair avec un léger changement des types : Héraclès est désormais imberbe. Au revers, l'ethnique est désormais placé entre l'arc et la massue et le symbole qui figure dans l'arc est une grappe de raisin qui a pour correspondant sur les pièces les plus lourdes une amphore. On retrouvera cette amphore sur les hémioboles du 4e monnayage hétérogène et sur celles de la Série 4 : ce n'est donc plus la marque de l'émission et, pour proposer une autre explication, j'y verrais un indicateur de valeur.

Les variations de poids entre la Série 2 et la Série 4 sont plus marquées encore dans les valeurs hautes. Commençons par les "bronzes moyens". G. Le Rider avait rangé sous ce même nom des monnaies de deux sortes dont les types sont les mêmes (la tête d'Héraclès imberbe et les armes du héros), mais qui diffèrent par le diamètre et surtout par le poids, ainsi que par le style et la technique de la gravure. La première sorte, connue par cinq émissions, est présentée dans le *Guide de Thasos* tandis que les deux émissions de la seconde sorte sont présentes dans le trésor de la nécropole, trouvé en 1953[11]. Les poids de la première sorte se répartissent entre 1,6 g et 4 g, pour un poids moyen (et un poids modal) de 2,20-2,40 g : je considère que ce sont des dichalques.

Qu'en est-il de la seconde ? Son poids est de près de 60 % plus lourd. La disposition de la légende est bien curieuse : elle est d'abord inversée, entre l'arc et la massue, présentation qu'elle partage avec la dernière émission d'hémioboles, qui a pour symbole un canthare. Dans l'émission suivante, elle est toujours inversée, mais sous la massue.

Jusque-là, les pièces que je considère comme des hémioboles puisqu'elles pèsent autour de 7-8 g, environ trois fois le poids des dichalques (dans un système de 12 chalques à l'obole), présentaient toujours l'ethnique en position verticale, d'abord sous la massue, puis entre l'arc et la massue. Nous savons que le changement de présentation de l'ethnique jouait une grande importance dans le système de contrôle de Thasos. Nous sommes placés devant une alternative (fig. 6) : alourdissement du dichalque ou allègement de l'hémiobole ?

C'est cette deuxième interprétation que je choisis. Ce poids restera le poids canonique des pièces de même diamètre dans les monnayages hétérogènes et dans la Série 4, jusqu'à l'arrêt de la frappe de ce module, vers la fin du IIe siècle. Je conclus donc qu'il s'agit d'un hémiobole.

11 Le Rider 1956. La première sorte est évoquée par G. Le Rider dans le *Guide de Thasos* (École française d'Athènes 1968, 188 et pl. 38).

Fig. 6. Alourdissement du dichalque ou allègement de l'hémiobole ?

Ces chiffres me paraissent montrer que Thasos passe alors du système de l'obole à 12 chalques à celui de l'obole à 8 chalques, qui est celui du monnayage macédonien (et du monnayage attique). Thasos abandonne la frappe de l'argent après les années 310, ce qui ne veut pas dire que les Thasiens cessent d'utiliser du numéraire d'argent, dont ils ont besoin pour notamment pour leurs exportations de vin qui ne paraissent pas décliner alors[12], tandis que la cité continue sans aucun doute à prélever des taxes douanières et portuaires[13]. Mais la monnaie d'argent de la cité n'est plus utilisée dans les institutions et les *emporoi* et autres gens d'affaire thasiens emploient une monnaie étrangère, sans doute les alexandres et lysimaques posthumes, monnayages dont les chalques valent 1/8e d'obole. Entre-temps, Thasos a créé une nouvelle valeur, l'obole de bronze, sur laquelle nous reviendrons.

Résumons-nous : l'hypothèse des changements de poids par un changement de valeur me paraît offrir l'explication la plus cohérente, car elle ne se contente pas d'évoquer une simple "réévaluation du poids". L'hémiobole ne comptant plus que quatre chalques au lieu de six passes de 7,3 g à 3,8 g (ce qui est un peu faible) et, à la reprise de sa frappe, le poids du chalque est légèrement augmenté.

Quant à la seule émission de pièces légères de la Série 4, elle se situe en marge de la tradition : le droit reprend le type de la tête d'Héraclès, mais sans la léonté, tandis que le revers reprend la corne d'abondance du 3e monnayage hétérogène. La dispersion des poids s'accroît entre 1 et 2,9 g, le poids modal se situant vers 1,6-1,8 g. Nous reviendrons sur le problème financier que pose cette émission unique.

L'obole de bronze est elle aussi une valeur particulière. Elle n'est pas frappée dans la Série 2 et n'apparaît qu'avec la première émission des monnayages hétérogènes. Les types sont tout à fait originaux : la tête de Déméter et les Dioscures. Ils ne seront plus jamais repris

12 C'est l'époque du "timbrage récent", qui commence vers 335/330, tandis que la date d'interruption reste à préciser, voir Grandjean & Salviat, éd. 2000, 190-191. Voir Garlan 1988 ; Debidour 1986.

13 *IG* XII Suppl., 348.

sous aucune forme. Quand l'obole devient une valeur courante de la Série 4, la cité choisira des types nouveaux : la tête d'Artémis Pôlô et Héraclès archer. Les Déméter ont une histoire métallique originale : j'y reviendrai.

Jusque dans les énigmes qu'ils nous posent, nos bronzes sont des monnaies, ce qui veut dire qu'ils appartiennent à un système de valeurs qui, à Thasos, comporte le plus souvent trois niveaux, rattachés à la valeur de l'argent. Ces niveaux sont séparés par des rapports de valeur simples, répondant à des diamètres et à des poids moyens et surtout à des types particuliers. Aucun de ces trois éléments n'est à négliger. Il est erroné de penser, comme on a essayé de le soutenir récemment[14], que la valeur de la monnaie de bronze dépendrait uniquement de la valeur du poids du métal : l'importante dispersion des poids s'inscrit en faux contre cette hypothèse. Ces poids ont évolué au cours du temps en fonction de la politique monétaire de la cité. D'où des difficultés d'identification pour les modernes. Mais la recherche moderne est guidée par une constatation importante : le choix des types des séries successives, du début du IVe s. jusqu'au IIe s., se fait par référence à la tradition monétaire de Thasos, ce qui confirme que la cité conservait la mémoire de sa monnaie.

Techniques monétaires et numismatique

À côté des éléments institutionnels, l'ensemble des monnaies trouvées dans les fouilles permet d'analyser un certain nombre de pratiques de l'atelier, disons des équipes d'ouvriers qui se sont succédé à l'ouvrage, que nous ne connaissons que par les techniques qu'ils ont employées.

Nombre de revers par coins de droit

La première caractéristique analysable est le nombre de coins de revers utilisés par coin de droit. Dans la Série 2, ce rapport ne peut être établi que pour les pièces les plus lourdes, donc les groupes 3 à 5 (tableau 3).

On note combien ce rapport fluctue, même dans des émissions très voisines. Le rapport le plus élevé s'établit à 3 ou 4 revers pour un droit dans les émissions du groupe 3 de la Série 2, les plus anciennes. On retrouve ce chiffre dans certaines émissions du groupe 4 (la rose, la corne d'abondance), et dans l'émission 4 des monnayages hétérogènes. Par la suite, il baisse à 2 pour 1, chiffre que l'on trouve pour les chalques de l'émission 2 des monnayages hétérogènes.

On trouve aussi souvent un rapport 1 / 1 ou à peine supérieur à ce chiffre pour :

- les Déméter et les chalques à la massue "massue dans couronne" des monnayages hétérogènes ;
- la seule émission de chalques de la Série 4 et plusieurs émissions du groupe 3 de cette série.

Dans ces émissions, il n'y a pas de liaison par des revers entre les différents coins de droit.

14 Van Driesche 2009. *Contra*, Picard 2013.

Que tirer de ces chiffres ? D'abord une invitation à la prudence. L'émission de style barbare qui clôt nos monnayages hellénistiques (fin de la Série 4) m'est connue par 174 exemplaires identifiables qui ont utilisé 5 coins de droit et 6 de revers. Mais trois de ces coins ne me sont connus que par une ou deux pièces, les deux autres par 143 et 27 pièces ; on constate la même irrégularité dans l'emploi des revers. Le coin champion a fonctionné avec 2 des 6 revers : prétendre tirer une statistique moyenne de chiffres aussi contrastés est une plaisanterie, tant l'utilisation de chacun atteste une inégalité flagrante. Sous l'Empire, l'émission de Septime Sévère présente un exemple analogue : les 60 exemplaires connus ont utilisé 2 coins de droit, dont un a frappé 59 pièces. Il serait absurde d'invoquer le hasard des trouvailles et ces chiffres apportent la preuve de très grandes irrégularités dans la vie des coins.

Ceci noté, on peut estimer qu'un nombre plus élevé de revers a été employé au début de la frappe du bronze, que le rapport normal est de l'ordre de 1 à 2 revers par droit, sans constituer une règle.

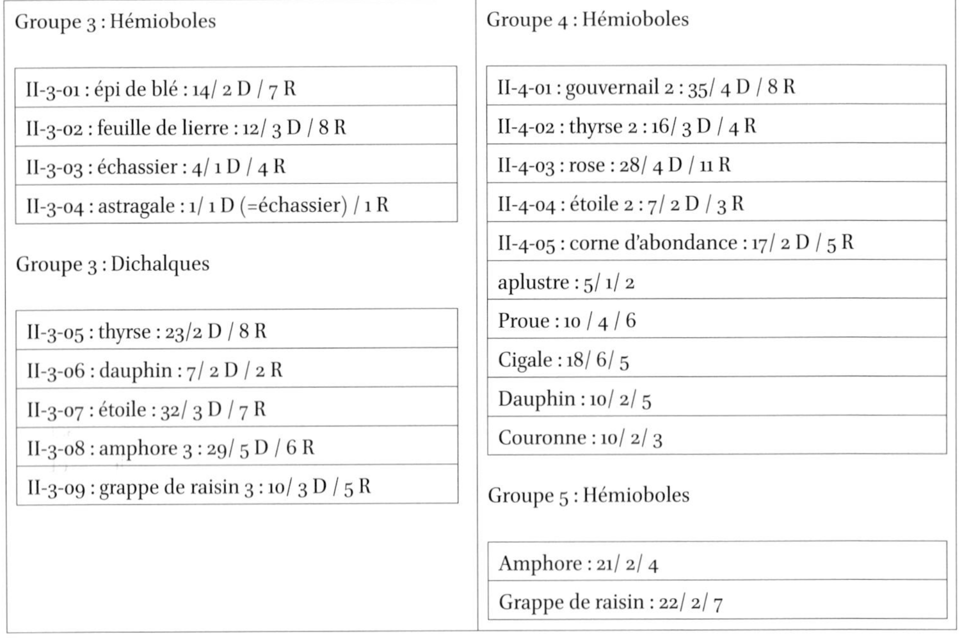

Groupe 3 : Hémioboles

II-3-01 : épi de blé : 14/ 2 D / 7 R
II-3-02 : feuille de lierre : 12/ 3 D / 8 R
II-3-03 : échassier : 4/ 1 D / 4 R
II-3-04 : astragale : 1/ 1 D (=échassier) / 1 R

Groupe 3 : Dichalques

II-3-05 : thyrse : 23/2 D / 8 R
II-3-06 : dauphin : 7/ 2 D / 2 R
II-3-07 : étoile : 32/ 3 D / 7 R
II-3-08 : amphore 3 : 29/ 5 D / 6 R
II-3-09 : grappe de raisin 3 : 10/ 3 D / 5 R

Groupe 4 : Hémioboles

II-4-01 : gouvernail 2 : 35/ 4 D / 8 R
II-4-02 : thyrse 2 : 16/ 3 D / 4 R
II-4-03 : rose : 28/ 4 D / 11 R
II-4-04 : étoile 2 : 7/ 2 D / 3 R
II-4-05 : corne d'abondance : 17/ 2 D / 5 R
aplustre : 5/ 1/ 2
Proue : 10 / 4 / 6
Cigale : 18/ 6/ 5
Dauphin : 10/ 2/ 5
Couronne : 10/ 2/ 3

Groupe 5 : Hémioboles

Amphore : 21/ 2/ 4
Grappe de raisin : 22/ 2/ 7

Tableau 3. Série 2 : rapport nombre de pièces / coins de droit / coins de revers.

Réutilisation du métal et chronologie

L'étude de ces trouvailles fait apparaître un phénomène remarquable : la réutilisation de pièces anciennes pour fournir le métal des émissions nouvelles. On le constate d'abord par les traces de surfrappe. Le phénomène atteint une ampleur considérable pour les oboles à la Déméter. La pièce 80-0421 en offre un bel un exemple (fig. 3) : on reconnaît clairement l'arc d'Héraclès derrière la tête de Déméter tandis que les Dioscures sont pratiquement oblitérés par la tête d'Héraclès ; celle-ci appartenait à l'émission à la rose de la Série 2-4, dont on pourrait presque identifier les coins. D'autres exemples sont incontestables. Notons au passage que ce monnayage a eu un sort mouvementé : la majorité des pièces est surfrappée d'une massue qui évoque le revers aux armes d'Héraclès du monnayage suivant. Les Déméter ont manifestement fait l'objet d'un décri, qui a signifié la perte de leur statut de monnaie légale (*dokimos*).

Sur les 276 exemplaires à la Déméter que je connais, 99 présentent des traces de surfrappe sur des hémioboles au type d'Héraclès de la série précédente, soit plus du tiers. Mais je me demande si le phénomène n'a pas eu une ampleur encore plus grande. Le poids moyen des hémioboles de la Série 2 se situe autour de 7-8 g. 12 exemplaires seulement sur 163 dépassent 10 g, le plus lourd atteignant 11,85 g. Or sur les 256 Déméter dont le poids m'est connu, seulement 30 atteignent ou dépassent 11,90 g, la plus lourde pesant 15,1 g. Seules certaines de ces pièces pèsent plus lourd que les hémioboles de la Série 2, jusqu'à près du double, mais cette augmentation de poids, dûment signalée par le changement de types, ne se constate pas sur les pièces inférieures à 10 g, qui pourraient bien être des surfrappes dans une proportion plus forte qu'un tiers, sans que l'état de conservation de la pièce ait laissé des traces reconnaissables aujourd'hui.

Les surfrappes ne sont pas limitées aux Déméter : j'en ai noté sur plusieurs chalques du troisième monnayage hétérogène (amphore/corne d'abondance) qui sont surfrappés sur des chalques de monnayage 2. Je connais aussi un exemple de surfrappe d'une Artémis du groupe 1 de la Série 4 par une pièce plus récente aux mêmes types.

Il est certain que le phénomène a été très important. La masse des monnaies de fouille permet de confirmer cette conclusion et même de l'amplifier en faisant apparaître, à partir de la comparaison des rapports coins/monnaies, que le taux de conservation d'émissions de la même série sont très différents.

Le tableau 3 montre que, dans la Série 2, le taux de conservation atteint le total de 11 pièces par droit pour les hémioboles du groupe 5, chiffre que l'on retrouve pour deux émissions de dichalques, des pièces qui n'ont pas été surfrappées, ce qui aurait entraîné leur retrait de la circulation. Ce chiffre est nettement plus faible pour les émissions d'hémioboles des groupes antérieurs, dont nous avons montré qu'elles ont fait l'objet d'une surfrappe massive. Autrement dit – et cela paraît tout à fait logique –, le retrait de la circulation des pièces qui ont été surfrappées diminue le taux de conservation des monnaies dans la masse des monnaies de fouille.

L'image est encore plus nette pour les émissions de la Série 4. Le tableau 4 donne, pour chaque émission, dans la colonne 4 le nombre de coins de droit, de revers et de pièces, ainsi que dans la colonne 5 le nombre des pièces trouvées dans des fouilles extérieures à Thasos (Abdère, Maronée, Thessalonique etc.) et le nombre d'exemplaires trouvés à Thasos. Il est curieux de noter que la proportion des pièces extérieures diminue en proportion inverse du rapport coins de droit/monnaie. Nous avons vu que ce rapport, le taux de conservation de l'émission dans la cité, était affecté par le retrait des émissions anciennes destinées à la surfrappe. Ce retrait ne concerne pas les pièces qui y ont été perdues à l'extérieur, en une période qui devait être proche de la date de l'émission.

Le graphique du tableau 5 présente l'évolution du taux de conservation des monnaies de ces émissions de la Série 4[15]. Il confirme un certain nombre d'hypothèses que j'avais formulées d'emblée : ainsi le groupe sans monétaire vient en dernier et l'émission à style barbare se situe tout à fait à la fin. Mais il apporte aussi des indications sur la succession des trois groupes, en montrant qu'il faut placer en tête le groupe à 3 monétaires (émissions 1-5, que j'avais d'abord placées en second) : c'est celui dont le taux de conservation est le plus faible et la part des trouvailles extérieures la plus élevée. Plusieurs arguments m'incitaient déjà à placer l'émission MAK à la fin du groupe à un monétaire. Le graphique les a renforcés. Enfin cette analyse permet de comprendre pourquoi les oboles de style barbare, qui est exécrable, ont cependant gardé un bon poids : elles sont faites de pièces remployées.

Émission	Monétaires	Modules	Dr / R / pièces	Extér. / Thasos
Premier groupe	*3 monétaires*			
IV-1-01	Σ – AMY – HP	Artémis + Héraclès	2/3/3 - 2/5/11	1/4
IV-1-02	Θ – Δ – ΤΡΟΦ-	Artémis	3/4/6	2/3
IV-1-03	K – TH – ΔH	Artémis + Héraclès	4/8/10 - 4/8/21	1/4
IV-1-04	Λ – ΘΕΩ –ΦΡΩΝ	Artémis + Héraclès	2/6/16 - 4/4/16	1/6
IV-1-05	ΘΕΟ – E – N	Héraclès	1/4/9	1/3
Deuxième groupe	1 monétaire			
IV-2-01	EYPY-	Artémis + Héraclès	2/3/5 - 3/5/22	1/3
IV-2-02	ΘΕΟΔΩ-	Artémis + Héraclès	3/4/16 – 1/1/2	1/4
IV-2-03	ΠΑΝΦ-	Artémis + Héraclès	3/4/11 – 4/18/111	1/55
IV-2-04	ΑΝΤΑΓΟΡ-	Artémis	6/13/35	1/7,5
IV-2-05	ΠΑΡΔ-	Artémis	7/15/64	1/16
IV-2-06	ME-	Artémis	6/28/78	1/22
IV-2-07	ΕΥΦΡΙ-	Artémis + Héraclès	3/9/37 – 3/13/71	1/10
IV-2-08	ΠΑΜΦ-	Héraclès	4/10/51	1/15
IV-2-09	TIM-	Héraclès	27/73/204	1/20
IV-2-10	HPAK-	Héraclès	10/26/212	1/19
IV-2-11	ΗΡΑΓ-	Héraclès	9/32/174	1/15
IV-2-12	MAKE-	Artémis + Héraclès	8/29/144	1/12
IV-2-13		Chalque ?	4/17/120 4/7/157	-
Troisième groupe	*o monétaire*			
IV-3-01				
IV-2-02	*Massue*	Artémis	2/ 3/ 110	-
IV-2-03	*Beau style*	Artémis	4/ 6/ 135	1/132
IV-2-04	*Chignon carré*	Artémis	1/ 2/ 30	-
IV-2-05	*Couronne en corne*	Artémis	2/ 3/ 47	1/22
IV-2-06	*Coiffure en côtes*	Artémis	1/ 1/ 18	1/34
	Style barbare	Artémis	5/ 4/ 185	1/65

Tableau 4. Tableau de la série 4.

15 J'ai développé cette analyse dans Picard 2015.

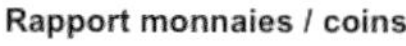

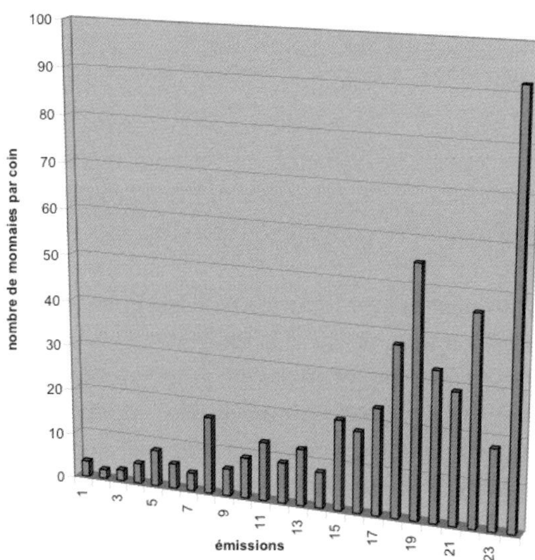

Tableau 5. Série 4 : rapport entre le nombre de coins (en abscisse) et le nombre d'exemplaires (en ordonnée).

Monnaies de bronze et usages économiques

Nous avons présenté quelques apports des monnaies de fouille à l'interprétation des institutions monétaires et de certaines pratiques de l'atelier. Qu'en est-il de leur circulation et de leur utilisation dans les échanges ?

La politique monétaire de la cité : séries à émissions et monnayages hétérogènes

Revenons d'abord sur la distinction faite entre les deux séries à émissions (distinguées par le système de contrôle) et les 5 monnayages hétérogènes. Ces deux sortes de monnayages (que l'on retrouve dans d'autres ateliers, comme à Chalkis[16]) ne se mélangent pas dans les ensembles de fouille, même lorsque les types et les poids sont très proches : je pense en particulier aux quatre versions des hémioboles à l'Héraclès, celles de la Série 2, les deux versions des monnayages hétérogènes et celle de la Série 4 qui ne se retrouvent jamais ensemble dans les contextes de fouille.

Les monnayages hétérogènes ou certaines émissions isolées des séries nous révèlent des comportements financiers à la fois surprenants et révélateurs des rôles que pouvait jouer la monnaie dans les échanges de la cité. Prenons le monnayage hétérogène 3, un des retours d'Héraclès. Les 75 exemplaires connus ont été frappés par un seul coin de droit et 3 revers.

16 C'est le cas des bronzes signés FILIS-AAQ, Picard 1979, 85-89, qui m'avaient intrigué par leur nombre, leur style et divers traits.

Combien de monnaies un coin de droit pouvait-il frapper ? Il est difficile de le dire. À titre d'hypothèse, prenons le chiffre sans doute excessif de 20 000, soit une somme – si j'ai raison d'y voir dans ces pièces des hémioboles – d'environ 1 500 drachmes. Autre opération : les chalques de la seule émission de la Série 4 : 157 monnaies pour 4 coins de droit, soit exactement la même somme ! La cité pouvait donc organiser une frappe pour des sommes aussi faibles ! Par quel système de distribution ces pièces passaient-elles dans le public, quelle part (minime) recevaient les bénéficiaires et pour quelle opération (achat de blé ou autre marchandise exceptionnelle ?) ceux-ci l'utilisaient-ils ? Rien ne nous le dit, mais Thasos nous présente au moins deux exemples d'une émission dotée d'un pouvoir financier très modeste, destinée à un emploi unique. Revenons aux Déméter. Les sommes sont ici plus importantes et pouvaient aller jusqu'à 100 000 drachmes, presque 17 talents. C'est la somme la plus importante des monnayages hétérogènes, mais elle reste au simple niveau d'une fortune privée. Ici encore l'emploi n'a pas été de longue durée. Une grande proportion – sans doute la majorité – des pièces est surfrappée. Elles utilisent donc un métal retiré de la circulation et elles seront elles-mêmes assez vite retirées de la circulation comme le montre la contremarque à la massue qui figure sur beaucoup d'entre elles et surtout leur disparition des contextes de fouille. C'est un trésor qui a fourni la majorité des exemplaires retrouvés : comme souvent pour les trésors de monnaies de bronze, il a été constitué à l'occasion du retrait de ce monnayage.

Les séries monétaires à émissions nombreuses, qui peuvent être réunies dans des groupes distingués par le système de contrôle, représentent un phénomène monétaire d'une tout autre ampleur. La Série 2 dure de 395 à environ 310, la Série 3 d'un peu avant 170 aux années 80 au moins. Les créateurs des deux séries ne pouvaient évidemment pas prévoir le succès de leur monnayage. Mais ce sont des monnayages qui sont organisés pour un usage régulier de la monnaie de bronze par la cité. C'est pourquoi il est important de les signaler aux historiens par un vocabulaire adapté.

Nos sources ne nous donnent que de très rares informations sur leur emploi, si ce n'est le paiement de la taxe au dieu guérisseur Théogénès[17], ou l'indemnité versée aux orphelins des Braves tués à la guerre[18]. Le numéraire de bronze a également servi à payer la partie de la solde versée à la troupe pour leur entretien quotidien[19] lors des guerres que Thasos a mené pendant ces périodes. Mais celles-ci ne semblent pas avoir été permanentes et elles ne peuvent pas tout expliquer. Faut-il chercher cet emploi dans les institutions ? Les tablettes de juges trouvées à Thasos suggèrent l'existence au IVe s. de jurys populaires percevant un misthos[20]. Sur le fonctionnement de l'assemblée, Thasos n'a pas donné de texte comparable à l'Ekklesiastikon d'Iasos. Mais la réconciliation de 395 paraît bien avoir amené la cité à se doter d'institutions proches par certains aspects de celles d'Athènes (qui n'utilise pas le bronze à ce moment). Au IIe s., les institutions de la cité alliée de Rome sont sans doute moins démocratiques (selon notre définition) que celle du IVe s. Mais pour les contemporains,

17 Picard 1990.

18 Fournier & Hamon 2007.

19 Le meilleur exemple du rôle du bronze dans ces transactions est rapporté par le Ps-Arist., *Économiques*, 2.2.23a. Voir Psoma 2000.

20 Grandjean 2010, 65-80. Migeotte 2014, 392. Arist., *Pol.*, 4.9-15.

c'était bien une cité démocratique et l'exemple de Rhodes, rapporté par Strabon[21], montre que des oligarques peuvent se préoccuper de "nourrir le peuple", ce qui, en dehors de son utilisation dans les guerres, était une des raisons de la frappe du bronze[22]. En revanche une bonne partie des dépenses ont dû disparaître avec la fin de la Série 2.

Les trouvailles monétaires : ensembles de fouille et trésors

Une partie du matériel provient de trésors au sens que lui donnent les numismates : un ensemble de monnaies réunies et cachées intentionnellement, que leur propriétaire n'a pas récupéré. La faible valeur du bronze, les risques de démonétisation expliquent que le bronze n'est que rarement thésaurisé. Dans l'Égypte lagide, à Apollonia d'Illyrie[23], les trésors de monnaie de bronze sont constitués d'un numéraire qui vient d'être démonétisé et qui a donc perdu toute valeur financière. C'est le cas à Thasos du trésor de la nécropole[24] ou du trésor de Déméter (qui ne comporte pas de monnaie contremarquée). Mais d'autres trésors ont une composition différente : celui trouvé en 1971 comprenait de l'argent et du bronze[25].

Mais tout aussi importants pour le numismate sont les ensembles de fouilles qui sont recueillis dans des couches d'occupation, par exemple dans les maisons du quartier du Silène ou dans un remblai homogène. On n'y trouve le plus souvent que quelques pièces sans doute perdues par négligence, témoins du numéraire qui circule à ce moment. Mais ces associations sont primordiales pour fixer la chronologie.

À l'issue de ce survol rapide, il faut souligner combien l'étude des monnaies de bronze et des monnayages de Thasos en général aurait été très incomplète sans le matériel fourni par les monnaies de fouille. La cité n'ayant joué qu'à de rares moments un rôle déterminant dans l'histoire de la Grèce, elle n'a guère intéressé les historiens anciens qui nous ont été conservés. Le choix que la cité a fait des documents qu'elle faisait graver sur la pierre et le hasard de ce qui a été préservé ne laissent également qu'une information limitée. À côté, les monnaies offrent le tableau complet des numéraires frappés par la cité et de leur importance respective, elles nous font connaître le déroulement continu de la politique monétaire, y compris dans les périodes où la cité n'a pas frappé monnaie. Elles apportent des indices très importants (parfois ambigus) sur la prospérité de la cité dans les différentes périodes. C'est bien de monnaie que nous parlent ces petits bronzes.

21 Str. 14.2.5. Voir Migeotte 1989 ; *id.* 2014, 291-292.

22 Arist., *Pol.*, 4.9-15. Migeotte 2014, 389-391.

23 Picard *et al.* 2012, par exemple à la fin de la série 5, p. 68-69. Pour Apollonia d'Illyrie, voir Picard & Gjongecaj 2000 ; Gjongecaj 2011.

24 Le Rider 1956.

25 Picard 1982.

Olynthos and Stageira: Bronze Coinage and Political History

Christos A. Gatzolis, Selene E. Psoma

The aim of this paper is to examine the bronze coins excavated at two cities, Olynthos and Stageira. Both cities were situated in the Chalcidic peninsula, were members of the Chalcidian League and were destroyed in late summer of 348 BC by Philip II. Olynthos was the capital of the federal state while Stageira was a member of this state. Olynthos was considered as the largest city in Thrace while Stageira was less significant by far. Olynthos was never re-founded while Stageira was. Excavation coins reveal the political history of the two cities.

Olynthos

The American excavations at Olynthos brought to light a significant number of silver and bronze coins and a number of hoards (table 1)[1].

Thrace[2]		Kersebleptes	4
Abdera	7	*Macedonia*	
Ainos	4	Aineia	5
Alopekonnesos	1	Akanthos	102
Chersonese	11	Amphipolis	125
Kypsela	1	Aphytis	37
Dikaia	1	Apollonia	18
Elaious	2	Argilos	1
Maroneia	2	Berge	1
Islands of Thrace		Bottike	14
Hephaisteia – Lemnos	1	Dikaia	23
Myrina – Lemnos	4	Mende	33
Thasos	24	Methone	1
Kings of Thrace		Neapolis	1
Hebryzelmis	1	Olophyxos	6
Kotys	2	Olynthus	5
Ketriporis	4	Chalcidians	2489

1 The coins were published in *Olynthus* (Robinson 1931, *id.* 1933, Robinson & Clement 1938 and Robinson 1952). For the hoards see full analysis in Robinson & Clement 1938, 161-196; Westermark 1988; Psoma 2001, 154-164 et 166. The hoards found at Olynthos are the following: *IGCH* 356, 359, 366, 367, 372, 373, 374, 375, 376, 377, 378, 379, 380, 383, *CH* VIII 108.

2 Some numbers of the list of coins found at Olynthos have been updated by newly sound evidence. See Hatzopoulos & Psoma 1998-1999 (Dion); Liampi 2005 (Argilos); Psoma 1996 (Chalcidian League); *id.* 1999a (Macedonian kings); *id.* 2002 (Sermylia); Gatzolis & Psoma 2009 (Bottiaeans); *id.* 2012 (Sermylia).

C. A. Gatzolis, S. E. Psoma, in : *Les monnaies de fouille du monde grec*, p. 83-96

Bottiaeans	322
Chalcideans or Bottiaeans	177
Philippi	5
Potidaea	184
Pydna	5
Skapsa	1
Skione	96
Sermylia	15
Torone	74
Thessalonike	4
Tragilos	5
Kings of Macedonia	
Alexander I	4
Perdikkas	44
Archelaos	10
Aeropos	11
Pausanias	8
Amyntas II	2
Amyntas III	114
Alexander II	2
Perdikkas III	47
Philip II	44
Alexander III	28
Anonyma	23
Kassander	3
Antigonos Gonatas	5
Macedonia *post* 168 BC	1
Thessaly	
Dion	1
Herakleia Trachinia	1
Lamia	11
Larisa	6
Phalanna	13
Pharsalos	2
Islands of Thessaly	
Peparethos	10
Skiathos	1
Illyria	
Issa	1
Islands of Illyria	
Corcyra	3
Boeotia	
Thebes	4
Euboea	
Eretria	5

Histiaia	8
Karystos	1
Attica	
Athens	11
Salamis	2
Megaris	
Megara	1
Aegina	2
Corinthia	
Corinth	4
Sicyon	3
The Argolid	
Argos	1
Hermione	1
Arcadia	
Alea	1
Heraia	1
Cycladic islands	
Mykonos	1
Bithynia	
Herakleia Pontica	1
Mysia	
Abydos	1
Kyzikos	4
Lampsakos	4
Plakia	2
Islands of Mysia	
Prokonnesos	2
Troas	
Sigeion	1
Aeolis	
Kyme	1
Pitane	1
Ionia	
Ephesos	3
Magnesia	1
Phygela	2
Islands of Ionia	
Chios	2
Samos	6
Caria	
Iasos	1
Persian Empire	
Satraps?	2
Uncertain	1

Table 1. Coins excavated at Olynthus.

These date mainly from the Classical period. There are also few Hellenistic coins that arrived at its site after the destruction of the city[3]. Life was not abandoned at Olynthos; some people continued to leave among the ruins, while the territories of the city became royal land and were later distributed by the king to his Companions[4]. The "most populous city of Thrace (*polyanthropotate polis Thrakes*) in the 380s became a *kome* of Kassandreia after 316 BC[5].

At Olynthos 3 480 bronze coins were excavated[6]. These coins offer us significant information about the city's life. In a recently published paper we tried to show that Royal Macedonian bronzes from Olynthos narrate the story of the relations of the League with the Argead kingdom, as they served for the payment of *siteresia* in the same way as the few bronzes issued by Timotheus in the area had earlier[7]. The 114 bronzes of Amyntas III and the coins of the same types issued by Pydna, as well as those of Perdikkas III and most of the bronzes of his brother Philip II can be easily explained if we place them in their historical context. Amyntas III asked Sparta to intervene against the League, when the Chalcidians made clear that they intended to remain the main power in the North[8]. Amyntas III collaborated with the Spartans in the war against Olynthos[9]. Perdikkas III together with his ally, the Athenian general Timotheus, campaigned against Olynthos, in their effort to gain Amphipolis for Athens[10]. Philip II at first allied himself with the Chalcidians, then later dissolved the League and sacked Olynthos, when he felt powerful enough to get rid of the federal state, which had been founded following the advice of Perdikkas II and did not stop creating problems for the Argeads by accumulating power[11]. The few bronzes of Alexander III, Kassander and Antigonos Gonatas tell the story of the day after at Olynthos, a ruined site with few inhabitants not far away from the estates of significant Macedonians- its former territories. The total absence until our days at Olynthos of bronzes issued by Ptolemy Keraunos for the Macedonian garrison at Kassandreia (and of bronzes with the legend ΑΠΟΛΛΩΝΟΣ struck on the previous ones) reveal the insignificant character of what remained from the large city (and that these coinages were quite small)[12].

Civic bronzes tell us different stories about the relations of this significant city with the outside world. Sea routes and land routes can be easily revealed by the bronzes that were excavated at Olynthos: from Thasos to the isthmus of the Thracian Chersonese, from the Southern coast of the Propontic Sea to Heraclea Pontica in the Black Sea, from Aeolis

3 Robinson & Clement 1938, 364-368.

4 Hatzopoulos 1996a, II, 195-196 with literary sources and the epigraphic evidence.

5 One recalls that the foundation of this city on the isthmus of the Pallene had the aim to replace the administrative *vacuum* created by the sack of Olynthos and the dissolution of the Chalcidian League. This was the reason Kassander was accused by Antigonos for having re-founded Olynthos: Diod. 19.52.2-3.

6 See Robinson 1931, *id.* 1933, Robinson & Clement 1938 and Robinson 1952.

7 Psoma 2009, 6-8; *id.* 2012, 54-56, Gatzolis 2010 ; 2011.

8 Diod. 15.20.3.

9 Xen., *Hell.*, 5.2.38; 3.9.

10 Psoma 2011, 127-132.

11 See previous note.

12 For these coins see Psoma *et al.* 2008, 217-224.

to Ionia, from Corinth through Megara and Athens, the cities of Euboea, to Skiathos and Peparethos and then to the Chalcidic peninsula.

The bronzes of Corcyra and Issa may have followed old trade routes linking the Adriatic Sea with the Chalcidic peninsula. One of those was followed by Themistokles on his way from Corcyra to Pydna[13], and another was some centuries later replaced by the *Via Egnatia*[14]. The bronzes of Thessaly followed land routes crossing the Temenid kingdom, as the one followed by Brasidas and his soldiers[15], by Thessalian *hippeis* who participated in the Spartan campaign against the Chalcidians in the late 380s trying to become personal friends of the Spartan king Agesipolis[16], and by Pelopidas in the 360s.[17]. Theban Northern policy of the 360s may explain the arrival of the bronzes of the Boeotian cities at Olynthos[18]. These old contacts proved to be useful for the Olynthian *diaspora* in the years that followed the sack of their city.

Excavation coins can also provide information about the political history of Olynthos, *i.e.* its function as the capital of the federal state. To acquire this information we need to trace the frontiers of the League and then turn to the representation of coinages of cities that became members of the League.

The frontiers of the League in the 390s were at Mende, North Bottiaea, Akanthos and Amphipolis[19]. During the 380s Potidaea and Torone participated in the League[20], while Apollonia and Akanthos feared forced participation to the federal state and made an appeal to Sparta[21]. Potidaea was still free during the reign of Perdikkas III, when the city received the *theoroi* of Asklepios, and in 362/361 a.C. asked Athens for a cleruchy to defend herself against the League. The situation changed radically during the early reign of Philip II. Potidaea was captured by the king and delivered to his allies, the Chalcidians of Thrace. Philip did the same with the area of Anthemous[22]. Evidence that derives from the *Philippica* of Theopompus (books 22-25) reveals that some cities of the Western part of the Chalcidic peninsula were incorporated into the federal state of the Chalcidians. The cities and settlements that are mentioned in these fragments are the following: Therma, Chytropolis, Thestoros, Aioleion, Brea, Assera, Skabala and Milkoros. Stageira was also a member of the League[23]. Sinos and Sermylia were also cities of the League, as their territories were later confiscated by Philip II and were distributed to his *hetairoi*[24]. Thus, the territories of the League during the last decade of its history were extended beyond the valley of the Anthemous, in North Bottike

13 Diod. 11.56.3.
14 For the Via Egnatia see now Lolos 2008.
15 Th. 4.78. See also Psoma 2001, 216; Stamatopoulou 2009, 212.
16 Xen., *Hell.*, 5.3.9.
17 For the intervention of Pelopidas in Macedonia see Psoma 2011, 125-126.
18 For this policy see *ibid.*, 124-32 with literary sources, bibliography and discussion.
19 Dittenberger 1915-1924, 135 B10-14. For these cities forming the frontiers of the League in the 390s see Zahrnt 1971, 82; Hatzopoulos 1994, 168; Psoma 1999b, 45; *id.* 2001, 223.
20 Xen., *Hell.*, 5.3.18.
21 Xen., *Hell.*, 5.2.11.
22 Diod. 16.6.3 and 5.
23 Zahrnt 1971, 109-111; Psoma 2001, 243-245.
24 Zahrnt 1971, 225-226; Psoma 2001, 247-248.

with Aioleion, in all the western part of the main body of the peninsula, in a significant part of the central body, in Sithonia and partly in the Pallene.

Deeds of sale sharing common eponymous priests and a common calendar, thus all emanating from cities that participated in the League after 356, come from Olynthos, Spartolos, Stolos, Torone, Arnai, Polichne and Strepsa[25]. The right to acquire properties in the Greek world was restricted to those that were citizens or had the right of *enktesis*. The rights of *enktesis* and *epigamia* were promised to the cities that were willing to join the League in the 380s. With their participation in the League the citizens of Spartolos, *i.e.* the Bottiaeans, Stolos, Torone, Polichne and Strepsa became Chalcidians and thus had the right to buy properties all around the territories of the League. The Olynthian relatives of Aristotle, including Callisthenes, reveal the right of *epigamia* between citizens of different city-members of the League, in this case Olynthos and Stageira[26]. This was mainly a very recent development; these cities, most probably with the exception of Spartolos and Stageira, joined the League only after 357/356 BC.

What about coins? In the well known passage of Polybius[27] describing the function and the success of the Achaean League, the historian from Megalopolis stresses that the members of a federal state have the same laws, weights, measures and coinage, as well as the same magistrates, senate, and courts of justice. In the decrees of *isopoliteia* between the military settlement at Magnesia under the mount Sipylon and the city of Smyrna, there is a special provision which concerns coinage[28]: *...and also in Magnesia the coin of the city* (*sc. of Smyrna*) *should be legal tender*. It is worth mentioning that in Polybius and the decrees of *isopoliteia* the provision about coinage follows the one about the use of common laws.

If we turn now to the coins from the excavations of Olynthos (fig. 1-2), we realize that the most significant currency is that of the Chalcidian League, the federal state that flourished with Olynthos as its capital[29]. The bronzes of the League began to be issued during the last decades of the 5th c. down to 348 BC following the style and the controls of the silver and gold coinage[30]. The historical context of the beginning of this coinage is the Peloponnesian war that the Chalcidians fought opposing Athens. It is also that of the foundation of the League with the *anoikismos* of the small coastal cities of the Chalcidians at Olynthos. The new types, Apollo and his attributes were not a reference to the mother city, Chalkis, as the Olynthian types, but to their common identity as colonists.

The next most numerous coins are those of the Bottiaeans[31]. Their bronzes in three denominations were issued with types similar to those of the Chalcidian League from the last decades of the late 5th c. to 348 BC[32]. There are one hundred and eighty four (184) coins

25 Game 2009, 43-91.

26 Heckel 2006, 76-77 s.n. Callisthenes [1].

27 Plb. 2.37.9-11.

28 *OGIS* 229.II.55; *ISmyrna* 573; voir Cohen 1995, 216-217.

29 The League is represented by 2489 coins, from which 2183 were bronzes: Robinson & Clement 1938, 292-300.

30 *Ibid.*, 292-300.

31 *Ibid.*, 300-304.

32 Psoma 2001, 101-103.

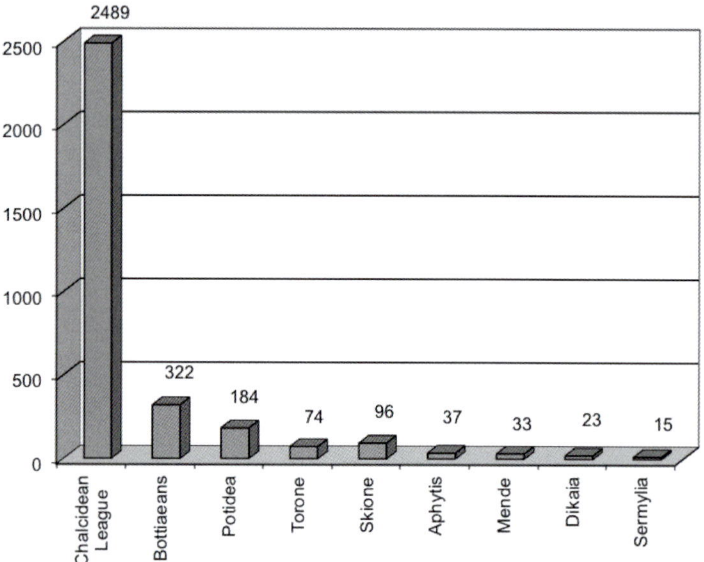

Fig. 1. Bronze coins found at Olynthus.

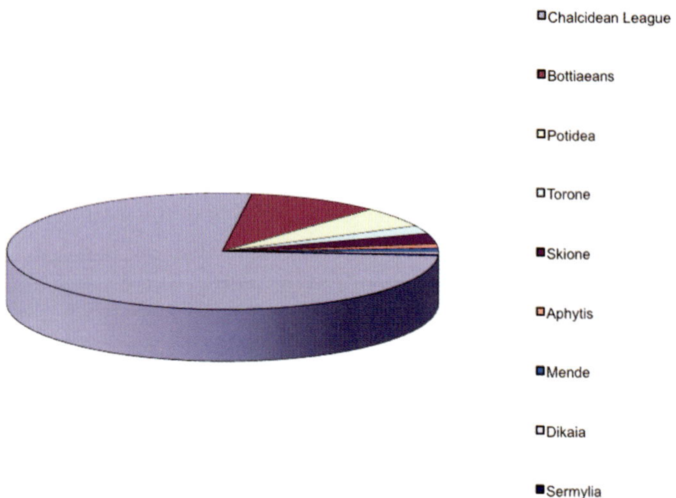

Fig. 2. Bronze coins found at Olynthus.

of Potidaea[33], and seventy four (74) bronzes of Torone[34]. Spartolos and Torone were members of the Chalcidian League after 357/6 BC. This was also the case of Potidaea[35]. We may explain their presence at Olynthos as a result of the participation of these cities in the League and propose the same explanation for the ninety six (96) coins of Skione[36], the thirty-seven coins (37) of Aphytis[37], and the thirty three (33) coins of Mende[38], the twenty three (23) coins of Dikaia[39], and the fifteen (15) coins of Sermylia, an immediate neighbour of Olynthos, which issued very few coins[40]. Their coins may have become federal currency when these cities entered the League by a special agreement as in the decrees of *isopoliteia* between Smyrna and the military settlement at Magnesia on the Mount Sipylos[41].

The arrival of bronzes of Akanthos and Amphipolis in very significant numbers reflects either contacts with the most powerful city of the area or payments of *siteresia* to soldiers involved in operations in the area of Olynthos. For Akanthos this could happen in the late 380s, and maybe also in the late 360s, in both cases against Olynthos. For Amphipolis, whose ties with the Chalcidians are well known, this could be in the 360s when Timotheus was besieging the League's capital in the war for the recapture of Amphipolis.

The coinages that ended with the sack of Olynthos were those of the Chalcidians and the Bottiaeans. All others continued or could have continued as archaeological evidence supported by literary sources reveal[42]. Philip II did not close the mints of the Greek cities[43], but sacked Olynthos, and dissolved the Chalcidian League, his last opponent in Thrace. This is reflected in the restricted number of the excavated coins that date after 348 BC. What Olynthos represented for the Argeads had as a result the systematic refuse of Alexander III to proceed to the re-foundation of the city, a request of Kallisthenes. One recalls that when Kassander founded Kassandreia, was accused by Antigonos for having re-founded Olynthos[44].

33 Robinson & Clement 1938, 305-309.

34 *Ibid.*, 314-316.

35 Stolos, Stageira and Arnai did not have, as far as we know, their own coinages.

36 Robinson & Clement 1938, 310-312. For the history of Skione see Zahrnt 1971, 234-236.

37 Robinson & Clement 1938, 272-274.

38 *Ibid.*, 283-286.

39 *Ibid.*, 280-281. The bronze attributed to Dikaia-by-Abdera (*ibid.*, 335) needs to be attributed to Dikaia in the Chalcidic peninsula: Psoma *et al.* 2008, 11 *ad* PM26.

40 Robinson & Clement 1938, 312-314.

41 See Psoma 2001, 245; Gatzolis 2011, 197. For the decrees of Smyrna see *I.Smyrna* 573 II^2, p. 376, l. 55.

42 Gatzolis 2011, 196-198.

43 See previous note.

44 Diod. 19.52.2-3.

Stageira

Excavations by K. Sismanidis from 1991 to 2000[45] brought to light 1 016 coins[46]. The distribution of coins by issuing authorities is as following (table 2 and fig. 3):[47]

Thrace	
Abdera	2
Ainos	1
Maroneia	1
Thracian Islands	
Lemnos: Hephaistia	1
Thasos	1
Macedonia	
Akanthos	30 (14 AR)
Amphipolis	17
Aphytis	1
Apollonia	1
Berge[47]	1 AR
Chalcidean League and Bottiaeans	40
Mende	1
Philippi	19
Potidaea	3
Sermylia	1
Skione	2 (1 AR)
Stageira	2 AR
Thessalonike	3
Ouranopolis	2

Uncertain Mints (*Incerti*)	2 (1 EL & 1 AR)
Kings of Macedonia	
Amyntas III	6
Perdikkas III	2
Philip II	103 (3 AR)
Alexander III	235 (1 AR)
Kassander	1
Antigonos Gonatas	14 (1 AR)
Philip V	11
Thessaly	
Atrax	1
Larisa	1
Magnetes	1
Pharsalos	1
Euboea	
Chalkis	1
Histiaea	1
Worn	499 (4 AR)
Late Roman	1
Byzantine	5
Ottoman	2 AR
Total number	*1016 (30 AR & 1 EL)*

Table 2.

There is one electron, 30 silver and 985 bronze coins. As these coins are presented here for the first time we will give more details. From the 1 016 coins 517, *i.e.* 51%, could be identified while 499 were completely worn. This very high percentage of corroded coins might be explained by the particular soil conditions of the site of Stagira, which is located in

45 Sismanidis 1990; *id.* 1991; *id.* 1992; *id.* 1993; *id.* 1994; *id.* 1995; *id.* 1996; *id.* 1997; *id.* 1998; *id.* 2003.

46 Gatzolis 2010, 199-212 et 515-519.

47 Psoma 2006.

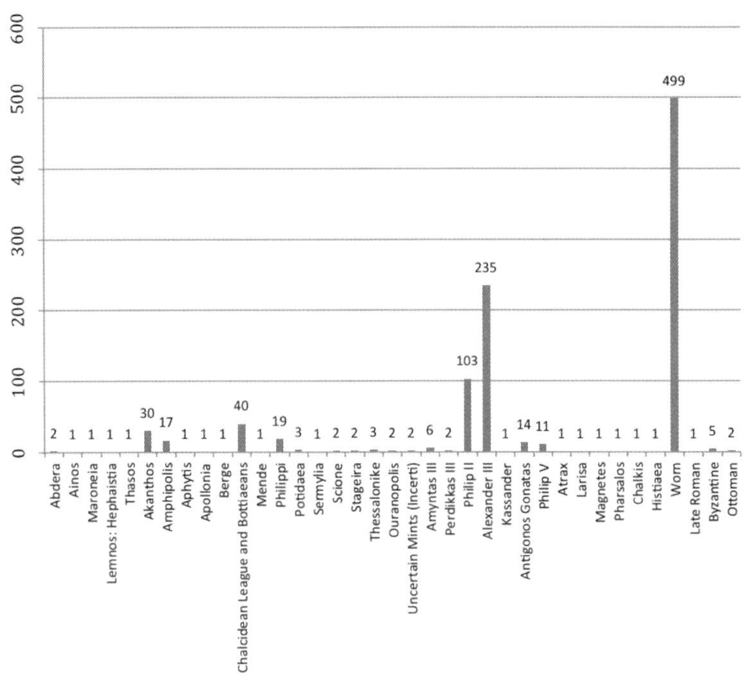

Fig. 3. Stageira. Distribution of coins by issuing authorities.

a small peninsula. As in many other cases, the percentage of precious metal coins was very low, 3%: 30 silver coins and one coin of electron. The silver coins were issued by Akanthos, Berge, Stageira, Skione, Philip II, Alexander III and Antigonos Gonatas. There were also two incerti (fig. 4-5).

The earliest coins date from the 6th c. BC 16 silver coins date down to 424/423 BC: Berge, Stageira, Akanthos and the incerti. From the 3rd c. date 14 coins of Gonatas, 2 of Philip V, one of Chalkis and another of Histiaea. From the 2nd and the 1st c. BC we have (9) bronzes of Philip V, one of Amphipolis, and one of the Magnetes. Between 424 BC and the late 4th c. date the bronzes of Amyntas III (6), Perdikkas III (2), Philip II (103), Alexander III (235), Kassander (1), Akanthos (19), Amphipolis (16), Apollonia (1), Aphytis (1), the Chalcidians and the Bottiaeans of Thrace (40), Mende (1), Ouranopolis (2), Potidaea (3), Sermylia (1), Skione (2), Ainos (1), Abdera (2), Maroneia (1), Hephaistia of Lemnos (1), Thasos (1), Atrax (1), Larisa (1) and Pharsalos (1). *In toto* 461 coins. Size and technic of most of the worn coins point also to 4th c. dates. We have thus *33 issuing authorities for* (509) bronzes from the 6th to the 1st c. BC (fig. 6-7).

The cities of Aegean Thrace, Thessaly and Euboea are represented with one coin each with the exception of Abdera, which is represented with 2 coins: 12 coins or 1% of the excavation coins and 2% of the attributed coins. The royal Macedonian mint is the most significant with (369) specimens, followed by those of the cities with (125) coins. From

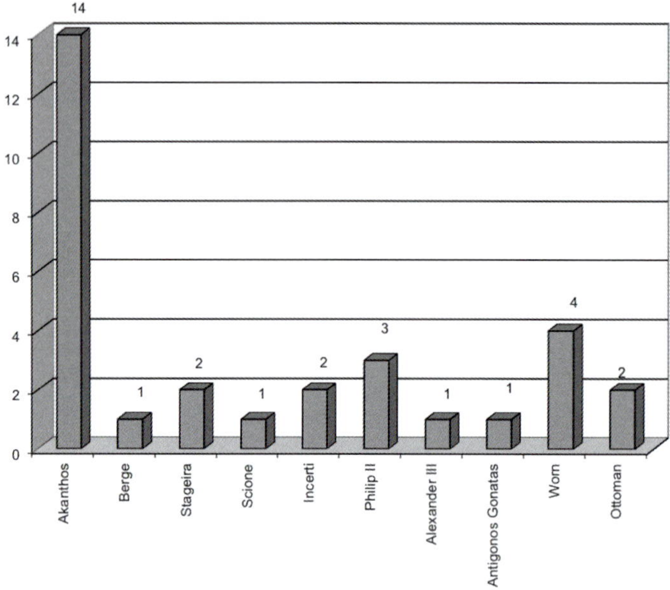

Fig. 4. Stageira. Distribution of precious metal coins by issuing authorities.

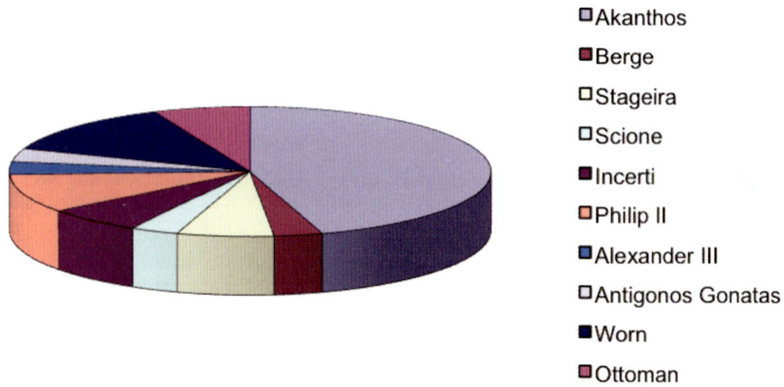

Fig. 5. Stageira. Distribution of precious metal coins by issuing authorities.

the Macedonian kings, the representation of Philip II (103) and Alexander III (325) are the most significant by far: 33% of the excavation coins and 65% of the attributed coins. Very many of the unattributed coins were very probably also issued by these two kings. From the cities of the Chalcidic peninsula and Thrace the Chalcidians and the Bottiaeans are better represented with 40 coins, followed by Akanthos with 30, Philippi with 19 and Amphipolis with 17, Potidaea with 3, Skione with 2 and all others by one coin.

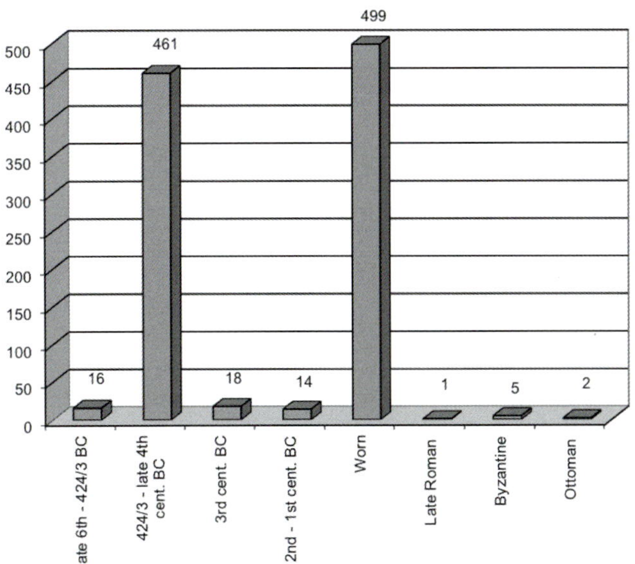

Fig. 6. Stageira. Distribution of coins by centuries.

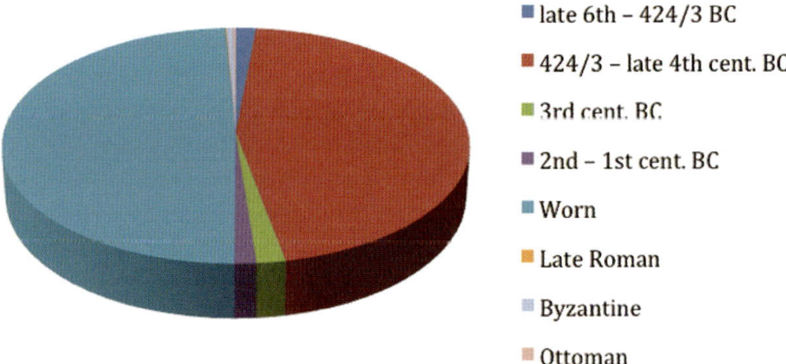

Fig. 7. Stageira. Distribution of coins by centuries.

Two silver fractions were issued by the local mint (a tetrobol and a hemiobol) while the presence of the two incerti points to their attribution to cities of the peninsula. The issuing authority of the electron hekte of 2,53 g. with horse's protome/incuse type is still disputed[48].

48 Close to the hemiekton of 1.37 g (Tzamalis 1999, 16 n° 90), and the electron *hekte* of 2,61 g. (Svoronos 1919, 206 n° 2a, pl. XIV 2).

The presence of a silver coin with roses on the obverse and a weight of 1,32 g might be issued also by the local mint before the *kapros*' series[49].

Following the model of Olynthos and Maroneia we can learn a lot from these coins about contacts of Stageira with the coastal cities of Aegean Thrace through the well known sea-route that brings to Ainos, with the cities of the Pallene, once more by sea, as with Chalkis and Euboea, and also with Thessaly, this time by land. The significance of Amphipolis and Philippi can also be revealed while more could be said about Akanthos, whose silver coinage was the best represented at Stageira. It seems that this coin was in use in this city after 480 BC when Stageira' own coinage came to an end.

The 40 coins of the Chalcidians and the Bottiaeans can be easily explained if we keep in mind that Stageira was a member of the League most probably from 384 BC if not earlier[50]. Stageira might have been one of the cities that accepted to be members of the League in the 380s, when the Chalcidians were offering *enktesis* and *epigamia* to the cities of the Chalcidic peninsula. It is not a coincidence that from all the other cities of the peninsula ambassadors from only Akanthos and Apollonia, *i.e.* Stageira's immediate neigbours, appeared at Sparta[51]. Stageira was a colony of Andros, as Akanthos and Argilos, and her decision to be a member of the League might have been considered as a threat by Akanthos and Apollonia. Independently from the date of the participation of Stageira in the League, the League's coinage was legal tender within the territories of the League, and for this reason it could also circulate at Stageira.

Stageira was besieged by Philip II and also destroyed[52]. The significant number of bronzes of Philip found there reflects his military operations and probably the installation of a garrison after the sack of the city. For Hatzopoulos the sack of Stageira took place "at the heat of the action[53]". Although Stageira was not a permanent threat for the kingdom, Philip II destroyed it and this needs to be explained. Two significant citizens of Stageira lived in the Macedonian royal court: Nicomachus, the physician of Amyntas III, and Aristotle, the teacher of the very promising son of Philip. With two influential *Stageiritai* in the court, Stageira, which was situated far away from the Macedonian frontier, might have received donations and gifts by the two kings. For this reason Philip might have sacked the city, as he did with Olynthos, who by receiving his two half-brothers ignored his benefactions. One recalls that he did the same with his *alma mater* Thebes, that decided to support the Athenians after almost a quarter of a century of close collaboration with the Macedonian king.

49 The second coin weighs 1,32 g and has a pellet in the middle and five roses all around, what called the "Pangaion roses" (*SNG* ANS 729-732 & Svoronos 1919, 126). See also the silver coin Svoronos 1919, 134 n° 24a, pl. XVI 28. These coins depicting roses have been attributed to Stageira by Gaebler 1930. This attribution is supported by the presence of one of these in the excavations of Stageira.

50 One recalls that Stageira were not included in the list of cities that were considered as enemies of the League in the late 390s. See supra n. 17.

51 Xen., *Hell.*, 5.2.11.

52 Diod. 16.52.9; *Vit. Arist.* [fr. 655] Rose.

53 Hatzopoulos 1996a, II, 198.

Direct evidence about the re-foundation of the city by Alexander III derives from literary sources[54]. From Dio we learn that as a request of his teacher Aristotle, the Great Temenid re-founded Stageira. However, the significant number of bronzes of Philip II (100) might add information about the re-foundation of the city already during Philip's reign, most probably as a request of his son, Alexander, to fulfill a promise to his beloved teacher, Aristotle. If we compare the number of bronze coins of Philip II at Stageira (100) with the number of bronzes of the same king from Olynthos (44), this becomes apparent. Zahrnt[55] and Hatzopoulos[56] advanced the hypothesis of a re-foundation of the city by Philip II. This corroborates information found in Plutarch's life of Alexander[57]. Extensive work most probably took place at Stageira under Alexander III. This is revealed by his 234 bronzes excavated on the site.

We do not know if Stageira was re-founded as a Macedonian city but excavation coins reveal that what was legal tender in the city during the last decades of the 4th c. BC, *i.e.* under the last Temenids, was the coinage issued by them. However, the large number of coins of Philip II and Alexander III needs to be explained. It appears that after the city was re-established before the accession of Kassander, a huge number of royal bronze coins entered the city. The only way to explain this is the presence of a military garrison, which was paid on regular basis. The same phenomenon has also been identified in the case of Athens, where a large proportion of bronze coins of Antigonos Gonatas found in excavations – the largest from any other foreign issuing authority – was associated with payments to soldiers in garrisons in the city after 261 BC[58]. A similar thing happened at New Alos (anc. Halos) in Thessaly[59].

Archaeological evidence sheds new light to the re-foundation of the city. The arrangement of the space on the so-called acropolis of the Southern slope has been considered independently by the excavator, Kostas Sismanidis, as serving military needs, and was dated to the Late Classical period[60]. It is thus contemporary with the phase of the wall that dates from Philip's reign[61]. This building seems to have served the needs of a strong garrison overlooking the city. The place of this building opposite the Archaic acropolis of the Northern slope shows that it was built later than the rest and was attached to the external wall of the city. Thus it created space on a higher level than the rest of the city, an ideal place for watching over the city. Building a military camp almost within the city certainly stressed the *dorikteton* and sent messages to Akanthos and the cities of Akte[62].

54 D.Chr. 47.9.

55 Zahrnt 1971, 243.

56 Hatzopoulos 1996a, II, 198.

57 Plu., *Alex.*, 7.2.

58 Lönnquvist 1997, 119-130; Gatzolis 2000, 116.

59 Reinders 2004, 185-206.

60 "Τα δύο εσωτερικά σκέλη του ορθογωνίου τριγώνου "δένουν οργανικά με τον τοίχο του περιβόλου" γεγονός που "φανερώνει το σύγχρονο και ενιαίο της κατασκευής τους": Sismanidis 1994, 280. For a Late classical date contemporary with the wall construction under Philip II see Sismanidis 1992, 453-461; Winter 1999, 286.

61 Sismanidis 2003, 75-76.

62 Gatzolis 2010, 517-518.

The abrupt interruption of the numismatic circulation of the city after its peak during Philip's and Alexander's reign seems very impressive and can only reflect events of historical importance for the region. Discontinuation of monetary circulation indicates interruption of normal life in the city and can only be connected with the foundation of Ouranopolis on the isthmus of the peninsula of Akte[63]. Little is known about the foundation of the city by Alexarhos, but it is likely, as was the case of Kassandreia and Thessalonike, that this was realized through a *synoikismos* of smaller settlements[64]. Stageira was most probably between them. Ouranopolis disappeared perhaps as a result of the Gallic invasion, which had an enormous impact in the North[65].

Coins reappear at Stageira under Antigonos Gonatas (14) and Philip V (11). These bronzes as well as all those that date from the Hellenistic period come from sectors I and III, *i.e.* the North hill and the area between the North Hill and the South Hill. We could eventually associate the presence of the Royal Macedonian issues with the foundation of Stratonikeia by Antigonos[66]. The site of Stageira should be preferred to that of Stratoni, far away from the coast, at a site that presents archaeological remains from the late 4th c. BC, and whose main phase dates between the 1st c. AD and the 4th c. AD[67].

Thus, excavation coins say different things about the political history of these two cities but both reveal this history. One cannot compare life in the significant capital of the League with that in a city member situated on the Western coast of the peninsula, in an area with very few urban settlements and populated by wild animals such as boars. However, there were significant links between these cities, as the wedding of the niece of Aristotle with an Olynthian reveals, and this was a result of the participation of Stageira in the Chalcidian League. They shared the same fate in 348 BC: Olynthos as the capital of the most powerful state in the North that had to be dissolved and leave Philip II master of all Thrace; Stageira was destroyed by Philip II either "at the heat of the action" or because the city showed no gratitude for previous benefactions made by the king and did not take his side (the latter seems more plausible). This was the last point of contact between the two cities. Olynthos would never be re-founded while Stageira was re-founded by the Temenids but only under military supervision. Stageira was never a threat for the Argead kingdom while Olynthos and the League were the main threat to Macedonia in the North.

63 Str. 7.35.
64 Zahrnt 1971, 209-210; Papazoglou 1988, 431-432.
65 Gatzolis 2010, 513-515.
66 *Ibid.*, 518-519.
67 Trakasopoulou-Salakidou 1993, 416-421.

II - TRAITER LES DONNÉES

Coins from a Small Country: How Excavated Coins are Managed in Israel, from the Dig to the Bookshelf

Donald T. Ariel

The region covering Israel and the adjacent disputed territories has been the *situs* of archaeological excavations since 1855. The manner objects from these digs have been treated in the past century-and-a-half have been dictated by many changes in political sovereignty and control, beginning with the Ottoman Turks, through the British Mandate authorities, and now the State of Israel – with yet other authorities controlling the disputed territories, Gaza and the West Bank, during certain periods.

This paper will present the way one set of artifacts – coins – and how they are treated in one of these entities, Israel[1]. The State of Israel is small, roughly 22 000 sq. km, the size of Slovenia. Yet, Israel's archaeological heritage is renowned, and indeed extremely rich.

Thanks to the excellent foundations laid by the British Mandatory Department of Antiquities, and local (Jewish) Palestinian enthusiasm, the nascent State of Israel was in a good position to cope with its multi-faceted archaeology, from shallow prehistoric sites, many multi-layered mounds and patchwork of excavations within historical cities. Israel went on to develop what has become exemplary national archaeological institutions, all the while inculcating high levels of cooperation with local and foreign academic archaeological expeditions.

Over the decades, the Israel Antiquities Authority (IAA; formerly the state-run Israel Department of Antiquities) has developed into the foremost player protecting and developing the nation's archaeological heritage. Like any organization created and funded by a state bureaucracy, there are drawbacks that one may dwell upon, but there is no doubt that today the way the country's archaeological remains is managed is a model to be studied and, at least in part, copied. The IAA Coin Department is but one part of the success story.

Managing a region's archaeological heritage depends not only on good laws, but also firm legal traditions, and a commitment to enforcement. Although not the subject of this paper, there is no doubt that that the country's numismatic heritage has been served by the British Mandate's Antiquities Ordinance of 1929 and subsequent ordinances[2] – and committed civil

1 This article is dedicated to the memory of Levi-Yitzhak Rahmani (1919-2014), indefatigable numismatist, archaeologist and curator active in the Israel Coin Department from 1953 to 1971.

2 Ariel 1998; Kersel 2010.

D. T. Ariel, in : *Les monnaies de fouille du monde grec*, p. 99-111 servants in the archaeological sector[3]. Before I headed up the IAA Coin Department, to my knowledge only three people, Samuel Raffaeli (1920-1923)[4], Charles Lambert (1926-1935)[5] and my immediate predecessor (Marcia Sharabani; from 1971 to 1992), had coins as their only responsibility. The others, Dimitri and Jalil Baramki (1935-1948), Stella Ben-Dor (1950-1951)[6] and Levi-Yitzhak Rahmani (1953-1971)[7], all contributed to the growth of the Department alongside their other archaeological and administrative responsibilities. Upon these not particularly secure foundations the Coin Department in Israel developed.

Development of the Israel National Coin Collection

The Israel national antiquities collection, established in 1948, was not created *ex nihilo*. Artifacts from digs in Ottoman times helped form the nucleus collection of the Mandatory Department of Antiquities but the overwhelming bulk of the antiquities holdings of the Department were registered during the Mandate itself. While most of this material derived from excavations conducted during the Mandate, by foreign expeditions as well as Department-sponsored excavations (primarily digs undertaken in advance of infrastructure development), the mandatory Coin Department grew primarily through purchases by the Department's curators – and not from accession of excavated coins. Only 549 isolated coins (one tenth of the total) came from excavations and 3 000 coins (2 400 of which were provenanced)[8] derived from 23 hoards. The roughly 6 900 coins registered during those years were ultimately accessed into the Israel national coin collection[9].

The Israel coin collection, however, developed in substantially different ways from the British precursor. Broadly speaking, the coins registered in the period of the State of Israel have the opposite proportions of provenanced versus unprovenanced coins[10]. Of the identifiable coins a full 87% are provenanced, making the Israel national collection (administered by the Israel Antiquities Authority) probably the largest national collection of provenanced coins concentrated in one place (fig. 1).

3 The Mandatory Coin Department also benefited from the support of Georges Francis Hill, head of the British Museum's Coins and Medals Department, during the early Mandate (Kool 2000-2002, 260, n. 2).

4 Kool 2000-2002, 261, n. 6; Shay 2009, 469.

5 Weinstein-Evron 2009, 8-19.

6 Barag 1990-1991.

7 Zias & Kloner 2013.

8 Throughout, the word "provenance" is used in its archaeological meaning as "findspot", and not in its curatorial meaning as "collecting history'"

9 The Mandatory coin cabinet was located in the Palestine Archaeological (now Rockefeller) Museum between 1948 and 1967. It came into Israeli hands as a result of the Six Day War. At that time, however, the Israel Department of Antiquities demurred from formally accessing into the national collection any of the antiquities in the Museum – including the coins. The sense then was that the *status quo* of these artifacts should not be changed. The Mandatory coin cabinet was only registered in 1993.

10 The Mandatory Coin Department was undoubtedly budgeted for coin purchases, but from the beginning it seems that the Coin Department of the Israel Department of Antiquities was not budgeted for that. The outcome was and remains a provenanced collection relying on excavated coins and altruistic donations.

Fig. 1. View of Israel National Coin Collection in 2014, with unique storage system for isolated coins to right; hoards stored on back wall.

In the Israel national coin collection 328 780 individual coins are amassed[11]. When the holdings of coins in lumps from large hoards are included, this number grows to over a half-million coins. This imposing number is not as high as the counts of coins at the three major numismatic institutions worldwide (London, Paris and New York)[12], and there would be no expectation that any small country only two-thirds of a century old would have a coin collection as large as any of those collections. What makes the Israel national coin collection so unique is the percentage of provenanced coins in it. Well over three-quarters (124 104 coins; 83,1%) of the identified coins are provenanced. The same proportion of provenanced to unprovenanced coins probably obtains from the total number of coins, identified and unidentified. The breakdown of the coins is given on table 1.

11 Unless otherwise stated, the numbers in this paper are accurate to September 2, 2014.

12 According to their websites, the world's three major coin collections, all surpass a half million objects, presumably mostly coins. The Department of Coins and Medals of the British Museum has about a million objects; the Coins, Medals and Antiques Department of the Bibliothèque nationale de France reports 800,000 coins and medals, and the American Numismatic Society collection amounts to more than 600,000 objects. A certain proportion of these objects are banknotes (e.g., 80,000 in London; Williams 2011, 37) and modern coins, objects which are not held in the IAA. None of the three major coin collections report the percentage of their coins with known provenance. Were these numbers known, the question the reliability of the provenances would also need to be raised, as more often than not, the provenances in these collections derive from marketplace reports.

Category	Subcategory	Accession			
Identified	Provenanced	From excavations:		104,817	
Identified	Provenanced	Not from excavations (kibbutz collections / private donations)[13]	19,287		
Identified	Unprovenanced	Other	5,897		
Identified		Totals (not from excavations):		44,471	
Identified		Totals (identified):			149,288
Unidentified[14]		Turned over by courts after criminal convictions:	46,336		
Unidentified[14]		Unidentified coins:	102,952		
Unidentified[14]		Totals (unidentified):			179,492
		Total number of coins (identified and unidentified):			328,780

Table 1. Numerical breakdown of the coins in the Israel national coin collection according to accession categories.

Composition of the Israel National Coin Collection

What are the identified coins in the collection? What is their breakdown by period? Table 2 presents the numbers of coins in the Israel national coin collection according to major (archaeological, not numismatic) chronological divisions. It must be stressed that the numismatic profile of excavation finds are overwhelmingly composed of low-value coins (bronze/copper). Gold and silver isolated coin finds are rare. Thanks, however, to the large numbers of volunteer-based excavations in the country[15], it seems that more gold and silver

13 In the past quarter century.

14 Does not include coins in lumps from large hoards.

15 In the history of archaeology probably the first well-publicized excavation based primarily on volunteer laborers took place in Israel, at Masada, beginning in 1963. Gamla too was excavated exclusively by volunteers. These are the archaeological sites in Israel with among the largest numbers of isolated high-value coin finds (23 coins + 3 hoards, out of 3,914 identified coins at Masada and 33 coins + 1 hoard, out of identified 6,316 coins at Gamla). No doubt, volunteer participation at these two sites – and in many of the digs in Jerusalem – increases high-value coin finds, but the overarching reason these specific sites yielded so many coins overall is the fact that they (with Jerusalem) were besieged and violently destroyed. Also, Gamla – and to a lesser extent, the other two sites – sifted their excavation debris.

finds than might be expected are found and reported at excavations here, though this has yet to be rigorously established. The numbers on table 2 reflect the relative quantities of coins according to metals. Despite our impression that in the IAA the gold and silver quantities are disproportionately high relative to other countries, overall they are still small compared to the bronze/copper and may nevertheless be discounted. Table 2 may therefore be said to reflect the influences of periods of inflation within the chronological divisions, and the weights and modules of the most popular currencies.

Period (Dates)	Quantity	Percentage
Persian (586-332 BCE)	677	0.61%
Hellenistic (332-64 BCE)	20,811	18.72%
Early Roman (64 BCE-70 CE)	4,211	3.79%
Late Roman (70-324 CE)	19,719	17.74%
Byzantine (324-636 CE)	44,888	40.38%
Early Islamic (636-1099 CE)	8,001	7.20%
Crusader (1099-1291 CE)	4,810	4.33%
Late Islamic (1291-1918 CE)	8,052	7.24%
	111,169[16]	100.00%

Table 2. Numbers of coins[17] in the Israel national coin collection according to major (archaeological, not numismatic) chronological divisions.

Numismatists familiar with the ancient coin profile of the eastern Mediterranean would not be surprised by the breakdown by period of the coins in the Israel collection. A comparison of the percentages of two provenanced databases, the coins in the Israel national coin collection with those noted in the PAS (double Israel's quantities in February 2015) produces the following interesting table (table 3).

<table>
<tr><th colspan="2">IAA (Israel)</th><th colspan="2">PAS (Britain)</th></tr>
<tr><th>Period (Dates)</th><th>%</th><th>%</th><th>PAS period</th></tr>
<tr><td>Persian (586-332 BCE)</td><td>0.61</td><td rowspan="2">17.72</td><td rowspan="2">Iron Age (800 BCE-43 CE)</td></tr>
<tr><td>Hellenistic (332-64 BCE)</td><td>18.72</td></tr>
<tr><td>Early Roman (64 BCE-70 CE)</td><td>3.79</td><td rowspan="2">48.87</td><td rowspan="2">Roman (43-410 CE)</td></tr>
<tr><td>Late Roman (70-324 CE)</td><td>17.74</td></tr>
<tr><td>Byzantine (324-636 CE)</td><td>40.38</td><td rowspan="2">1.40</td><td rowspan="2">Early Medieval (410-1066 CE)</td></tr>
<tr><td>Early Islamic (636-1099 CE)</td><td>7.20</td></tr>
<tr><td>Crusader (1099-1291 CE)</td><td>4.33</td><td>18.47</td><td>Medieval (1066-1500 CE)</td></tr>
<tr><td>Late Islamic (1291-1918 CE)</td><td>7.24</td><td>13.54</td><td>Post-Medieval (1500 CE-present)</td></tr>
</table>

Table 3. Comparison of two provenanced databases.

16 The discrepancy between this number and the total of 149,288 identified coins in the collection is explainable by coins with very large date ranges that were not included, as well as other data entry issues, none of which affect the validity of the proportions.

17 Includes coins from hoards.

Despite the discrepancies in the dates, the comparison of numismatic data on the national level seems a promising pursuit. On the differences between the Israel coin collection and the PAS, see below.

However, when examining the urban sites in Israel which yielded large quantities of coins, the extremely varying quantities of coin finds is not so easily explained. A selection is presented on table 4.

SITE	Coins
`Akko	1,086
Safed (Zefat)	660
Caesarea	5,513
Jaffa (Yafo)	2,320
Modi`in	410
Jerusalem	~20,000
Ashqelon	1,362
Beer Sheba	620

Table 4. Selection of urban sites in Israel with extremely varying quantities of identified coin finds in the IAA.

No doubt, the main reasons for these variations are the different sizes of the ancient settlements underneath these cities, and how much of the settlement was excavated. Another contributing factor is the period of each city's floruit. Safed, for example, may have yielded relatively few coins because the main period of its occupation, the Late Islamic period, was one with less overall currency being lost.

It is also noteworthy that one group of excavated coins in Israel causes the percentages of the different chronological divisions on table 2 to be significantly skewed. These are the coins of the mint of Jerusalem. In the past few years, owing to heightened urban development, the country's capital has been intensively excavated, and more coin finds than from all of the other cities in Israel combined have been generated, and many of these were struck in the Jerusalem mint. It seems to me that the main reason for the huge numbers of excavated coins attributable to this mint are: (1) the preference of the mint for small bronze denominations, (2) the phenomenon of huge issues under the Hasmonean king Alexander Jannaeus (104-76 BC) that can best be understood as inflation, and (3) the many destruction events in that city and in Judea in general during the lifetime of that mint. For this and many other reasons, the mint of Jerusalem receives attention above and beyond its importance in antiquity.

Aware of this, the IAA Coin Department endeavors to relate equally to all of the ancient coins it receives. If there is a bias regarding the material it is definitely towards the fascinating coins from the later periods. Because top scholars of Islamic and Crusader coinages have come to work on coins in the national collection, our local scholars have benefited from those interactions, and have honed their skills in these fields. New publications continue to propel other periods, such as the Persian and Hellenistic (Ptolemaic and Seleucid) to the forefront. The Coin Department is proud to have provided data on site finds from these periods to the authors of those publications.

Research value

It certainly would seem ludicrous to compare the over a half-million coins in the Israel national coin collection – with less than a third identifiable – to the holdings of the major numismatic collections. Worldwide, however, there is a change in attitudes vis-à-vis unprovenanced antiquities and international trade in them[18]. In this environment, the IAA Coin Department has discovered that the collection it manages has much to offer. For example, with most of its coins untainted as regards their authenticity, metallurgical researchers have been drawn to the collection in their investigations. Quantitative analysis is quite applicable to these coins, as they have not undergone sorting of the kind that introduces statistical inaccuracy. This is one collection which allows researchers to learn the extent of culling which the numismatic marketplace inevitably undertakes when preparing its fine and extremely fine coins for auction.

The Israel national collection is also an ideal basis for studies of coin distribution and the movement and longevity of currency. The coins truly derive from all corners of the country, as indicated by the high number of different excavations, represented by discrete license numbers (2 465). This is represented graphically in fig. 2. Throughout the history of the State of Israel, many thousands of excavations have been licensed[19]. Perhaps a quarter of the excavations yielded coin finds. One explanation is that many expeditions excavate in sites with only pre-numismatic strata.

No doubt the Portable Antiquities Scheme (PAS) in Britain has more registered coins (523 000 to date), but they are not stored centrally. The no longer active *Fundmünzen*der römischen Zeit in *Deutschland* (*FMRD*) – with a comparable number of coin finds – and the subsequent national coin-registration enterprises in at least eight other European countries, belong to a model somewhat similar to the PAS[20]. These projects are all not centrally stored and have datasets of variable quality. Also, while an enormous quantity of coins is registered, the overwhelming majority are not from controlled archaeological excavations. The extra layer of micro-contextual information about the coins in the Israel collection bestows upon it invaluable added importance for research.

18 E.g., Elkins 2012.

19 It should also be noted that despite stipulations to the contrary in excavation licenses many foreign expeditions have never turned over their coins to the national collection. I would estimate that there are some 15,000 coins, not to speak of other artifacts, from foreign expeditions that have never been remitted to the IAA.

20 For the PAS, see https://finds.org.uk/, and for the FMRD and some of the other European projects, see http://www.adwmainz.de/index.php?id=425. Generally, see Von Kaenel & Kemmers 2009.

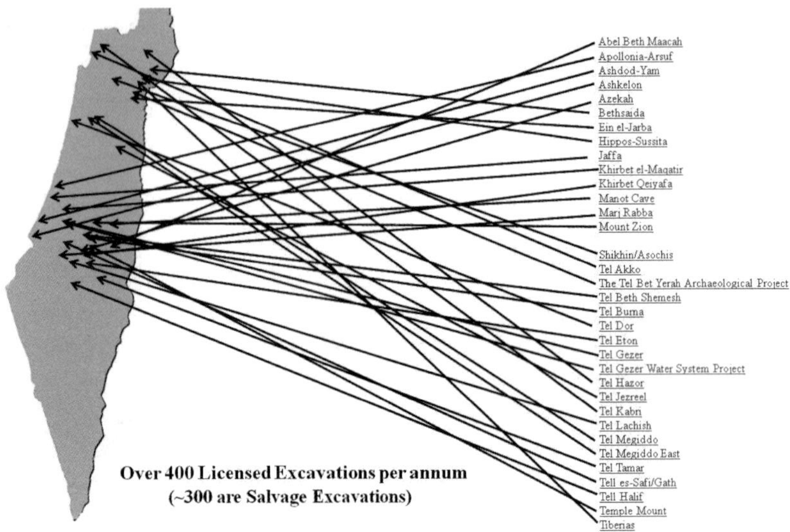

Fig. 2. Graphic depiction of extent of excavations in Israel, detailing the distribution of the approximately 34 excavations using volunteer labor in 2014.

Hoards

Alongside the provenanced coins from the licensed excavations in the national collection there is a much smaller number of provenanced coins *not* from digs, including some noteworthy hoards (table 5).

Period (Dates)	Quantity	Percentages[21]
Persian-Hellenistic (586-64 BCE)	29	10.78%
Early Roman (64 BCE-70 CE)	59	21.93%
Late Roman (70-324 CE)	48	17.84%
Byzantine (324-636 CE)	40	14.87%
Early Islamic (636-332 CE)	33	12.27%
Crusader (1099-1291 CE)	25	9.29%
Late Islamic (1291-1918 CE)	35	13.01%

Table 5. Chronological breakdown of 269[22] provenanced hoards in IAA.

21 Percentages of hoards to the total number of hoards, not percentages of coins in hoards.

22 269 coin hoards are certainly not all the hoards documented from Israel. No estimate of that number is available. For comparison, however, a research project of the Portable Antiquities Scheme has reported at least 3,000 hoards from the Iron Age to the end of the Roman period in Britain, but only 380, or one-eighth of that amount, to date in its database (The Portable Antiquities Scheme Annual Report 2013, undated; p. 14; http://finds.org.uk/documents/annualreports/2013.pdf).

Hoards, of course, are chance finds – as, in essence, are excavated single finds. Nevertheless, with a relatively stable number of coins processed by the Coin Department each year (some 8 000 coins), we can also determine the average number of coin hoards found each year (8). Those hoards do not always come from licensed excavations. Over the years, some are stray finds reported by Good Samaritans, and some have been confiscated by the IAA (and the police) based upon intelligence sources (*e.g.* fig. 3). One of the best aspects of the IAA hoards are that most hoards are completely intact, without coins removed or added, found in their original containers, and in the exact archaeological contexts in which they were deposited. These facts take the 'worry' out of hoard analysis. An example of the value of such comprehensive data is the identification and dating of a phenomenon of unstruck copper flans included in a number of early Byzantine period hoards in the collection[23].

Comparison of the percentages of hoards per period in table 4 to the percentages of coin finds per period (table 2) shows that even within a sample as large as that in the IAA, the behavior of isolated coin losses and the deposition and non-retrieval of hoards are often dissimilar. Explanations can be suggested, but they are beyond the scope of this paper.

Fig. 3. First examination of a hoard of about 4 500 ancient silver coins, soon after its discovery by two Druze farmers in the spring of 1960, not far from the site of the ancient synagogue of 'Isfiya on Mount Carmel.

23 Bijovsky 2012, 129.

The nuts and bolts of managing the Israel National Coin Collection

The archaeologically based coin collection in the IAA presents challenges found neither in a collection deriving from commercial sources, nor in the numismatic assemblage of a single site excavation.

How much to clean[24]

Every dig functions within certain budgetary limitations. As a key member in the post-excavation season analysis, the IAA Coin Department must also contribute to the maintenance of the excavation's budget. In order for us to have the means to fully study the identified coins, and not compromise on the high level of our numismatic research, we agree to lower the numbers of coins cleaned from surface- and non-critical loci.

For small digs, all of the coins are cleaned – in the IAA metals conservation laboratories. For larger digs, however, a selection is made. The coins from critical loci are all cleaned, but a percentage of the coins from much less important contexts – primarily surface finds – are set aside and not cleaned. In the material from the less important contexts, a numismatic selection is also undertaken, and the numismatically more promising coins are returned to the category of coins-to-be-cleaned. None of the uncleaned coins are discarded. They are entered into the computerized database and stored with the coins which were cleaned but not identifiable.

The subject of sorting before cleaning is not without controversy. Archaeologists are trained to sift through enormous amounts of data. In their famous "pottery readings" each day they discard many kilograms of non-indicative potsherds. Numismatists, however, are not accustomed to the idea of selecting coins.

There are three crucial differences between the sifting of pottery and the sorting of coins. First, the pottery is washed and thus identifiable before being thrown away, but the determination that coins are not to be cleaned happens before they can be fully identified. And second, the shards are discarded because there is no place to keep them. But the coins that are not cleaned are never discarded. If there is a need to go back to the coins which were left uncleaned, they are still available for cleaning and identification.

The third and last consideration is our numismatic expertise. The staff of the IAA Coin Department is able to determine the likely dates and types of *uncleaned* coins to a very high degree. My sorting of coins before cleaning is often more accurate than the archaeologists' "pottery reading", and...nothing gets discarded!

24 A related question is, "how much to photograph". The conventional wisdom is that the preservation of excavation coins is generally poor. However, as I hinted above in the discussion on sorting coins, it is more likely the case that coins from digs simply reflect the true proportions of preservation in ancient coins. The IAA coin Department's selection of coins for photography is dictated by fineness of the coins, their numismatic importance, their contextual importance, and the type of publication that is planned. Roughly speaking, the end result is that 5-10% of the isolated coin finds are photographed. In the case of hoards, however, all of the coins are photographed.

Division of labor

The national coin collection administered by the IAA Coin Department is comprised of a staff of three full-time and two part-time employees. Our average of 8 000 coins-per-year workload requires us to be efficient and very practical – even when only about half[25] of the coins ultimately require full treatment.

The amount of work involved in identifying coins from excavations varies. Often, coins from one dig date to many periods. The Coin Department endeavors to assign the coins of individual excavations to only one staff member, this, in order to lower the number of numismatists interacting with each excavator. Research on each excavation's coins is divided among the staff according to two intersecting criteria. The first is geographical. The main groupings of excavation sites in the country have been distributed among the staff.

The second criterion is the different periods of specialization of the Coin Department staff. G. Bijovsky is most fluent with Roman provincial and Byzantine coinage. The sites with many coins in these groups are given to her to identify. My strengths, in the periods from the beginning of coinage to the destruction of Jerusalem in 70 CE, dictate my work on coins from digs in Jerusalem. R. Kool specializes in the Crusader and various Islamic periods, hence his work, for example, on Safed and Jaffa. Our two part-time employees also fill special niches.

This intuitive approach, by which we divide the staff's tasks for researching thousands of coins from hundreds of digs, has proven itself, and has produced publications of very high quality.

How does it work?

Excavators are provided with custom-made paper envelopes before going out to the field. In the excavations they insert the coin finds into the envelopes, one coin per envelope (except for hoards). All of the contextual and administrative information is noted in pen on the envelopes in the field. At the end of the dig, the coins are turned directly over to the laboratories, where the sorting takes place if required. After cleaning, the coins are delivered to the Coin Department, where they are processed, and the unidentifiable ones are separated off. The coins are then divided among the staff according to excavation group.

Each full-time staff member will typically identify 75 excavation groups in one year, from one coin to as many as five hundred coins per group. Reports for only between a quarter and a third of the identified coin groups are then prepared – an average of some twenty reports per staff member per year. The other coins become available, through the IAA database, for publication in the context of other dig reports, especially for distribution studies, die studies, and for research into coin currency.

25 The others are the sorted, uncleaned coins, and the cleaned-but-nevertheless-unidentifiable coins. A third large category of coins is those turned over to the national collection by Israeli courts after criminal convictions. Over the past quarter-century the collection has processed some 46,000 coins in this last category.

According to Israeli Law all archival material becomes available for publication after thirty years. Consequently, the Coin Department has been able to offer 'thirty-year old' coins, and particularly hoards, to outside scholars to publish. The nine-year-old journal, *Israel Numismatic Research*, published by the Israel Numismatic Society, has become a wonderful venue for such reports. In the recently published volume 9 exactly half of the articles are reports of coin hoards, most from the national collection.

Most of our publications, however, are in the IAA's three in-house publication platforms. In *Hadashot Arkheologiyot*, a web-based platform for small reports, the coins are described within the stratigraphic narrative. In *'Atiqot*, for publishing medium-sized reports, and *IAA Reports*, the monograph series, the coin reports merit separate chapters, which appear alongside other appendices. The coins are fully described in large catalogues in tabular format. The analysis of the coins focuses on: (1) the coin finds in well-stratified contexts, (2) coins of numismatic interest (variants, countermarks, overstrikes, and technological curiosities), and (3) the site's coin-currency profile which includes coins from all excavations in the site or nearby. Not resting on its laurels, the staff of the Coin Department, has also engaged in synthetic research. All have conducted doctoral dissertations, and published them. The wonderful finds in the Israel coin collection have provided many scholars, including the staff, with an excellent dataset for research topics that emphasize coin-currency and the intersection between stratigraphy and numismatics.

Accessibility

Above I noted that foreign scholars come to do numismatic research in Israel. They do so because the level of services they receive in Israel, and the ease of accessibility to the numismatic material, is much better than in the countries contiguous with Israel. Israel has not only become a place to study locally minted coins, but also a magnet for research on locally provenanced coins minted in adjacent regions.

The just-mentioned accessibility to coin collections, first among them the national coin collection, is the direct outgrowth of the presence of highly motivated local scholars interested in cross-fertilization with outside researchers.

Computerization

The coin collection is computerized, in a database powered by a customized software package (Oracle 10.2; forms 6-I). This database is integrated in the dataset of over 178 000 fully registered non-coin artifacts (with 46% coins and 54% non-coin artifacts). Unfortunately the disadvantages of the program outweigh the advantages. I will begin with the advantages. Numismatists may identify stratigraphic relationships between the coins that would not normally be found in a purely numismatic registration system. Numismatists may also examine large quantities of provenanced material according to geographic parameters, and thus be able to make reliable statements about coin currency.

The main disadvantages are twofold. First, as a database for both coins and non-coins, special features relating to coins were customized with great difficulty. In other words, it takes many, many "clicks" to enter the information, and just as many to retrieve it.

The second main drawback is that the bi-lingual (Hebrew/English) database does not support other character sets. Especially without Greek and Arabic, the Coin Department continues to compose its identifications on heavy paper cards, with pen and pencil, and is thus the only department in the IAA to retain such "old technology". As a result, for example, while one may search the database according to numismatic categories such as ruler, date, mint, material, denomination, not to speak of archaeological and technical information (*e.g.*, weight, diameter, axis etc.), one cannot search by inscription. Another problem is the duplication involved in the preparation of catalogues. Finding solutions to this critical issue will be the main challenge of the Coin Department in the coming decade.

Publication

In the Department a high priority is given to the publication of coins from excavations in Israel. While some reports are as long as 90 pages, the large majority are reports on small numbers of coins – often less than a dozen – from salvage excavations, the bread-and-butter of the IAA.

However, and here is one of the drawbacks in the system, we must wait until the excavators have finished their stratigraphic reports before our coin chapters can be published. So although an average of 24 reports have been prepared each year in the past quarter century, much less have yet seen the light of day. From the Mandatory period until today, over 30 000 coins have nevertheless been fully published. These successes fortunately lower the frustration of the Coin Department's staff with unnecessarily long delays in publication.

Conclusion

This description of Israel's national coin collection provides a glimpse into the large policies and smaller strategies and protocols one small country has employed in order to build and maintain its numismatic heritage. It would be especially interesting to compare notes with other countries, learning of the successes and failures with regard to their national coin collections. How are their excavated or locally-struck coins managed? Are there policies for accession, for registration, for storage? Has progress been made in computerization and publication? And, perhaps most importantly, how strong are the countries' commitments to fostering numismatic research in the future?

It is hoped that this survey throws light on how archaeological numismatics oftentimes differs from single-site numismatics. The perspectives are broader, which is the way today's numismatic research seems to be going.

Cartographie des monnaies de fouilles (1950-2050)

Thomas Faucher

Même si des cartes associées à des monnaies existaient déjà[1], la cartographie en tant que science (associée ou non aux sciences humaines) est en fait relativement nouvelle. Le terme lui-même – cartographie – n'apparaît que vers le milieu du XIXe s.[2]. C'est principalement la seconde guerre mondiale qui a fait prendre conscience d'abord aux militaires, puis aux civils, de l'importance de représenter la réalité en la géolocalisant[3]. Mais alors que la croissance exponentielle du nombre de cartographes après-guerre s'est ralentie au cours des années 90, l'utilisation des cartes n'a jamais été aussi répandue. Il faut noter que l'utilisation systématique de cartes dans les articles de numismatique, et au-delà dans les articles de sciences humaines, est relativement récente. De sorte qu'un article publié en 1959 intitulé : "Un Problème cartographié : le bois dans la Méditerranée musulmane (VIIe-XIe s.)[4]", ne comporte aucune carte ! Il serait intéressant de développer des considérations sur le besoin de représentation graphique lié aux capacités d'apprentissage accrues par l'image ; il serait également possible d'aborder le sujet de la représentation du réel, intimement liée à l'éducation d'une part, et aux expériences vécues de l'autre. Ces sujets, bien que passionnants, ne peuvent pas être traités ici. Toutefois, ils amènent une première question.

Quel est l'objectif de la carte ?

Une carte doit permettre de répondre aux questions posées, d'offrir une perception immédiate de l'information et doit en faciliter la mémorisation[5]. Pour cela, il faut respecter un certain nombre de codes pour que chaque lecteur puisse interpréter une même information de la même manière.

Les monnaies de fouilles sont des objets qui peuvent être géo-localisés et donc, dont la représentation graphique est possible. Il existe deux types de cartes de monnaies de fouilles. Le premier type concerne les monnaies d'un seul site. Il s'agit alors de représenter sous forme graphique la dispersion des monnaies sur l'ensemble ou la partie d'un site archéologique ou d'une zone de *survey*. Le second type est la représentation spatiale des monnaies trouvées en fouilles dans une région donnée.

1 http://gallica.bnf.fr/ark:/12148/btv1b84928265.
2 Un universitaire portugais, Viscount de Santarem, l'a utilisé le premier en 1839 : Cosgrove 2008, 170.
3 Robinson *et al.* 1977, 3-18.
4 Lombard 1959, 234-254.
5 http://cartographie.sciences-po.fr/.

Si ces deux types de cartes offrent des possibilités différentes, certaines normes existent, issues de la cartographie. On s'intéressera donc dans un premier temps à ces différents modèles de représentations et aux normes qu'il est souhaitable d'adopter. Mais la représentation graphique des données en archéologie n'est maintenant plus l'affaire d'un seul site archéologique, ni même d'une discipline. Là où le chercheur répondait autrefois à une question en proposant à son lecteur l'interprétation d'une série de données, maintenant, l'association des bases de données connectées (*Linked Data*) a fait s'inverser le mouvement. C'est dorénavant au lecteur de trier l'information pour obtenir la réponse à la question qu'il se pose, le chercheur étant principalement un fournisseur d'informations inventoriées, triées et classées. Il s'agira plus tard dans cet article d'indiquer comment participer à cette deuxième démarche.

Cartographie et monnaies de fouilles

Il existe donc deux types de cartes de monnaies de fouilles, celle à l'échelle d'un site (où seules les monnaies d'un seul site sont répertoriées) et celle à l'échelle d'une région, où l'information vient, soit des monnaies trouvées sur le site en question, soit de l'accumulation de données provenant de différents sites. Ces deux types répondent régulièrement à des questions différentes.

Le premier permet de s'interroger plus particulièrement sur la vie d'une cité en s'attachant à comprendre les différentes phases d'occupation du site ou bien à définir les types d'activité qu'a pu connaître tel ou tel quartier. Les monnaies deviennent en ce sens un marqueur chronologique ou social et le matériel numismatique doit alors être comparé au reste du matériel archéologique (production locale/importations de céramique, de verre, etc.). Malheureusement, il est peu de fouilles où la localisation précise d'une monnaie a été enregistrée ; l'information géographique se limite le plus souvent à l'unité stratigraphique dans laquelle la monnaie a été trouvée. En Égypte, très peu d'équipes d'archéologues notent consciencieusement les coordonnées de chaque monnaie (les fouilles sous-marines, plus promptes à répertorier ce type de données, le font plus naturellement). Il faut toutefois noter que l'enregistrement des monnaies dans une US donnée offre tout de même des informations précises, ne serait-ce que par l'intermédiaire de l'altitude. Mais il est alors difficile pour le cartographe d'offrir une représentation précise des trouvailles. Et même lorsque c'est le cas, le résultat n'est pas toujours heureux et l'information pas toujours lisible. Il faut préciser que ces cartes sont à la fois très peu employées et que leur emploi est tout à fait récent. Il faut attendre le début des années 1990 pour voir apparaître ce type de représentations (exemple des fouilles de Risan[6] (fig. 1), d'Egira[7], Tell Athrib[8] et de Némée[9]).

6 Ujes 1993, 142, fig. 1.

7 Hainzmann 1997, 42, fig. 2.

8 Krzyżanowska & Myśliwiec 2009.

9 Knapp & Mac Isaac 2005.

Fig. 1. Vestige des murs et position des monnaies de Ballaios, fouilles de Risan (*Ujes 1993, fig. 1*).

Les éditeurs des fouilles de Karanis ont jugé bon de représenter la localisation des différents trésors trouvés sur le site[10]. Si ce type de représentation peut avoir un sens pour l'archéologue, elle n'a que peu d'intérêt pour le numismate. Imprimée en 1964, la publication des monnaies de fouilles de Karanis représente pourtant un modèle du genre[11]. Le cas général veut que ce type de carte, ou de plan, n'existe pas. Les seules cartes ou plans imprimés dans les publications de monnaies de fouilles sont généralement des plans des différents secteurs fouillés pour que le lecteur puisse se repérer quand des informations liées au contexte archéologique sont fournies. C'est le cas des monnaies de fouilles de l'agora d'Athènes[12], ou de Sardes[13] par exemple, mais également de la vaste majorité des publications de monnaies de fouilles comme celle de K. Butcher et des fouilles de Beyrouth, où deux plans sont publiés[14]

10 Je me suis appuyé pour ces recherches sur le *conspectus* établi par F. de Callataÿ dans le volume en l'honneur de J. Kroll : de Callataÿ 2006, 177-201.

11 Haatvedt & Peterson, éd. 1964.

12 Kroll 1993, pl. 35-36.

13 Buttrey *et al.* 1981.

14 Butcher 2003.

ainsi que des monnaies de fouilles d'Alexandrie[15]. Dans la publication de K. Butcher, deux cartes illustrent les ateliers représentés par les monnaies des fouilles ainsi que les autres sites archéologiques mentionnés dans le texte. D'autres publications vont plus loin. C'est le cas de Némée où les plans sur lesquels apparaissent les monnaies de fouilles représentent l'origine et le nombre de monnaies trouvées et répertoriées. Mais ce type de représentation ne s'est répandu que récemment dans les publications – la première trace d'une carte de ce type apparaît dans la publication des monnaies des fouilles d'Olynthe par Robinson[16] – mais ce n'est pas avant le début des années 1990 en fait où elles apparaissent régulièrement dans des publications comme celle des monnaies de fouilles d'Olympie[17] ou de l'antre Corycien[18] (fig. 2).

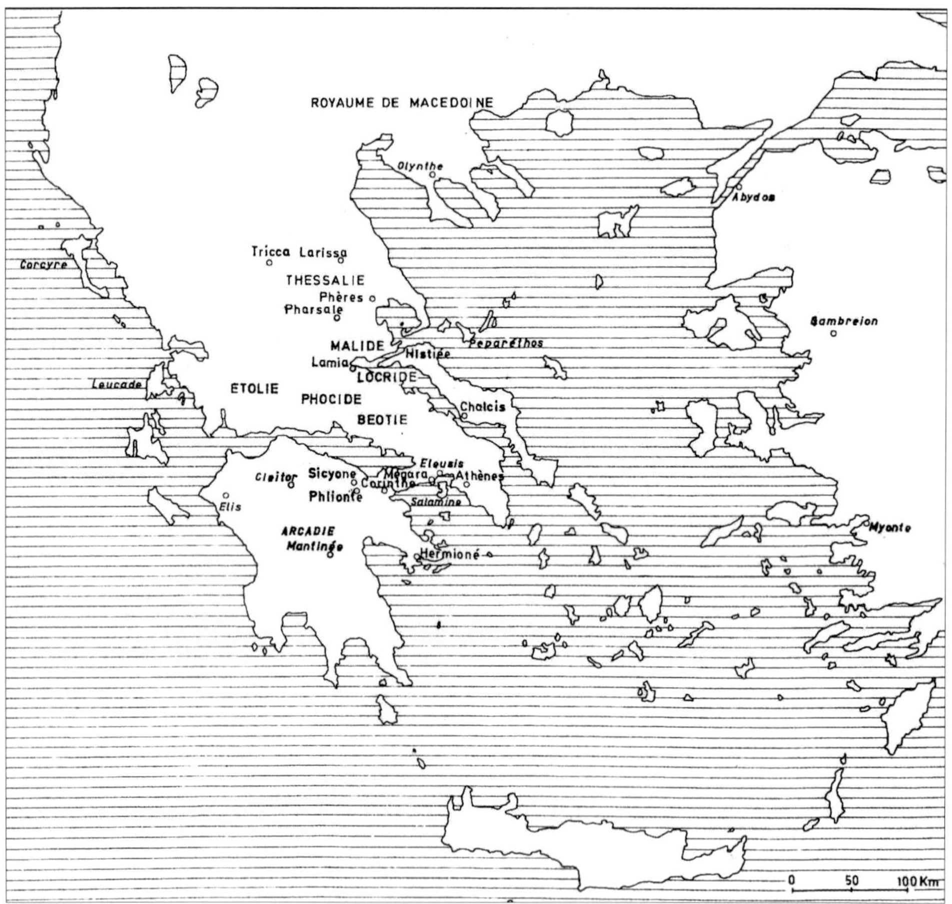

Fig. 2. Origines des monnaies trouvées dans l'antre Corycien (Picard 1984, fig. 1).

15 Picard 2012.
16 Robinson 1931, fig. 1.
17 Moustaka 1999, 154, fig. 109.
18 Picard 1984, 282, fig. 1.

De manière générale, la carte non interactive devrait se limiter à un objectif simple : répondre à une question donnée. Il est extrêmement délicat de multiplier les informations sur une seule et même carte sans perdre en lisibilité. Dans tous les cas, il serait préférable de se limiter à trois types de représentations, que ce soit en forme, en taille ou en couleur. Il serait également préférable de limiter les informations sur la carte. On préférera par exemple les numéros aux lieux en toutes lettres (cela dépend évidemment du nombre) avec un renvoi à un tableau en annexe. Les données sont d'autant plus facilement utilisables qu'elles sont sous forme de tableaux.

En ce qui concerne les fonds de carte, il faudrait préférer des fonds de cartes simples, mais où les informations sont claires et lisibles (pas de relief ombré par exemple) pour que l'information ressorte mieux. Le relief ainsi qu'une hydrographie minimale sont indispensables, surtout lorsqu'il s'agit de comprendre les échanges entre tel ou tel peuple ou cité. Les trouvailles, comme les cités, auront tendance à se trouver près de cours d'eaux. Dans un certain cas, la représentation de routes antiques peut être souhaitable mais il est difficile d'avoir des informations fiables, en tout cas sur l'ensemble de la carte, de même qu'il est sera délicat d'obtenir des informations pertinentes quant à l'époque représentée.

À l'heure actuelle, et compte tenu des moyens à disposition, deux types d'information sembleraient utiles à représenter sur une carte :

1. La localisation de trouvailles quelles qu'elles soient. Il s'agit de mettre en évidence des tendances, un seul ou plusieurs foyers de trouvailles (la localisation de la provenance des monnaies d'une fouille par exemple).
2. La localisation différenciée de deux, ou trois groupes de monnaies. Soit par types, soit par périodes.

Pour l'interprétation des données, on peut se référer à l'article de J. Collis[19].

Il existe plusieurs difficultés à dépasser lors de l'élaboration de la carte. La représentation d'un point est une combinaison de deux coordonnées, X et Y (trois lorsque l'on veut une représentation spatiale en trois dimensions : on ajoute Z). Mais quelle est la précision de ce point ? Il est presque impossible de répondre à cette question : presque tout est question d'échelle[20]. Mais pas seulement. Si le point représente un espace, il est logique de faire figurer ce point au centre de l'espace. Si cela semble se justifier pour un certain nombre d'espaces : Chypre, le Delta du Nil, la Sicile ; il est au contraire moins pertinent que ce point soit central dans des cas comme la Turquie ou la Syrie qui sont des pays ou une grande majorité de la population vie dans des zones excentrées. Mais si l'information est essentielle, elle nécessite peut-être d'être tout de même représentée, s'il s'agit d'un cas unique et bien attesté par exemple. Par contre, ajouter une monnaie trouvée dans le Delta à une représentation des monnaies de fouilles égyptiennes n'aura la plupart du temps pas de sens.

19 Collis 1981.
20 Moins de 1/10 000 : plan ; plus de 1/10 000 : carte.

D'autres problèmes surgissent pour la représentation des points ; le degré de certitude de l'information[21]. Comment par exemple représenter une notice : "Jérusalem ?". La monnaie ne vient peut-être pas de Jérusalem, mais elle provient très certainement d'Israël, en cela l'information est intéressante et peut-être fiable. Le problème est d'autant plus complexe que l'incertitude ne vient pas forcément uniquement du degré de précision de l'information spatiale, elle peut également toucher le contenu. Par exemple, dans la représentation d'une émission particulière, l'identification de certaines monnaies pose régulièrement problème. Dans ce deuxième cas, il semble plus simple d'évacuer de la carte les données dont l'information n'est pas assurée. Si ce n'est pas le cas, il est possible de représenter le point d'une manière différente, grise ou floutée (foyer dont les contours sont estompés) par exemple, qui sera explicitée dans la légende.

Pour réaliser des cartes, il existe principalement deux solutions, soit les faire soi-même, soit faire appel à un cartographe qui sera chargé d'effectuer le travail. Alors qu'il y a quelques années, les outils des cartographes étaient presque inaccessibles aux chercheurs non spécialistes, comme l'emploi d'*Illustrator* par exemple, toute une série d'outils didactiques ont, depuis quelques années, fait leur apparition. Je n'entrerai pas ici dans les détails de ce qui peut être fait soit à partir de logiciels de SIG, tel *ArcGis*, puisqu'une présentation des possibilités offertes par le SIG est faite dans cet ouvrage[22], ni non plus sur l'utilisation d'*Illustrator*. Mais il est dorénavant possible d'effectuer des cartes de travail et de faciliter grandement le travail des cartographes dans le cas où le recours à un spécialiste serait nécessaire.

Une carte n'est en fait qu'une série de données. Un tableau, dans lequel un certain nombre d'informations auront été renseignées, est donc nécessaire. Deux données sont indispensables à l'établissement d'une carte, il s'agit de la longitude et de la latitude. Elles peuvent être présentées sous deux formes, soit sexagésimale (appelée plus couramment "degré minute seconde"), soit décimale. Il est préférable d'utiliser la seconde puisqu'elle ne contient que du numérique, ce qui facilite la compréhension par l'ordinateur (il existe des convertisseurs en ligne). Ces coordonnées représentent soit l'endroit précis de la trouvaille, soit l'atelier d'où provient la monnaie. Il est fait mention plus bas des différentes possibilités de se procurer ces coordonnées.

Google Maps offre une solution pour représenter les éléments. Après avoir créé une carte, il est possible d'importer les données directement d'un tableur. Grâce aux coordonnées enregistrées dans le tableau, la localisation des ateliers (leur représentation graphique) s'effectue automatiquement. Une série d'outils permet de sélectionner les données qu'il est possible d'afficher, ainsi que de créer une palette de couleur en fonction du type d'informations recensées dans le tableau. Ces données sont exportables soit en fichier .xml, soit en fichier .kmz, ce qui permet de les utiliser dans d'autres logiciels comme *ArcGis* ou *Google Earth*. Cette base permettra au cartographe d'utiliser les données pour créer rapidement une carte. Au bout du compte, l'étape la plus prenante lors de l'élaboration de la carte est la recherche des différentes coordonnées géographiques des lieux concernés.

21 Arnaud & Davoine 2009.
22 Voir Fadin & Chankowski, sur le SIG de Délos, dans ce volume.

Cartographie, monnaies de fouilles et données connectées

Il est clair que la représentation spatiale des monnaies de fouilles est difficile à normaliser et pose un certain nombre de problèmes qui sont malaisés à résoudre. Il semble important de militer pour la mise en commun des informations.

La carte est la représentation spatiale d'une série de données[23]. Les coordonnées vont permettre de localiser le point alors que les autres données mettront ce point en forme, en taille ou en couleur. La réunion de ces bases de données permet de normaliser l'information et sa représentation. La raison de la volonté de normalisation des représentations est simple : être capable de comparer les données. Cela n'effacera pas les biais historiques ou archéologiques qui peuvent être nombreux, mais la normalisation permettra de représenter des données comparables de manière similaire.

Dans un but de normalisation, et pour améliorer la facilité d'utilisation, il est nécessaire de travailler sur des données communes, et notamment sur les données géographiques. Dans une base de données de monnaies de fouilles, il serait important de faire figurer le géoréférencement des données. Pour retrouver une cité ou bien un lieu de trouvaille, soit les coordonnées géographiques sont exactement connues soit il est nécessaire de les chercher. Chaque localisation devrait donc être accompagnée des coordonnées géographiques (latitude et longitude). Cela est particulièrement souhaitable lorsque les sites peuvent avoir des noms équivoques, comme des cités dont le nom est régulièrement utilisé autour de la Méditerranée (Alexandrie, Arsinoé, etc). Il existe deux sites de référence pour retrouver les sites antiques : le premier est *GeoNames*[24] qui recense quelque 9 millions de localités modernes, mais aussi anciennes. On notera aussi la mise en ligne récente du *Thesaurus of Geographic Names* du Getty Museum[25]. Le second est *Pleiades*, qui recense les sites antiques[26]. Ce dernier site est une prolongation du *Barrington Atlas*[27]. Fort de presque 35 000 sites antiques, le site web, après une période d'arrêt, est mis à jour très régulièrement, ce qui permet aux sites archéologiques, même les plus humbles ou les plus récemment découverts, d'être répertoriés.

C'est l'American Numismatic Society qui a fait le plus gros du travail ces dernières années en utilisant les compétences de S. Heath d'abord puis d'E. Gruber dorénavant, sous l'impulsion d'A. Meadows. Un premier travail avait été effectué par l'intermédiaire du projet Nomisma, programme ANR dirigé par M.-C. Marcellesi[28]. Le travail a d'abord porté sur la localisation des trésors de monnaies grecques issus de l'*IGCH*. Depuis, les recherches ont

23 L'apparition des ordinateurs et la puissance de calculs développée par ces derniers ont apporté des modifications fondamentales dans le traitement des cartes : “the storage capacity of modern computers means that the data bases are separate from actual maps that display the data they hold, allowing the latter to be customized in content and design”, Cosgrove 2008, 170-171.

24 http://www.geonames.org/

25 http://www.getty.edu/research/tools/vocabularies/tgn/

26 http://pleiades.stoa.org/

27 Talbert & Bagnall 2000. Travail repris par l'Ancient World Mapping Center, situé à l'université North Carolina à Chapel Hill : http://awmc.unc.edu/wordpress/

28 Faucher 2012.

considérablement évolué. Le but n'est pas ici de présenter les *Linked Data*[29] mais plutôt de montrer leurs possibles apports en termes de cartographie des monnaies de fouilles.

Comme le prévoyaient déjà certains géographes dans les années 70, la carte est passée ces dernières années de la main du cartographe à celle de l'utilisateur de la carte[30]. À l'ère du Web 2.0, puisque c'est de cela dont il s'agit, l'utilisateur de la carte doit pouvoir interagir sur son contenu. Des débats existent encore sur le rôle du chercheur et sur sa plus-value en matière d'analyse des données ; il s'agit ici de montrer les différentes possibilités offertes au chercheur, non seulement de proposer à une communauté la plus large possible le fruit de son travail, mais également de disposer des données d'autres groupes de chercheurs pour satisfaire à sa propre recherche.

La première partie de cet article montre clairement que le nombre et le type d'informations représentables sur une carte sont limités. Cela amène souvent au fait que, lors d'une publication, faute de place, il soit nécessaire de limiter le nombre de cartes. Pourtant, même pour une base de données relativement simple (date, type, géolocalisation) il est possible d'effectuer des dizaines de cartes différentes. La mise en ligne permet à l'utilisateur de choisir les données qui lui conviennent et non celles que le chercheur aura cru bon de montrer pour développer son propos.

Pour être capable d'offrir ces données et que ces données s'ajoutent elles-mêmes à un ensemble de données, il est nécessaire de respecter une certaine mise en forme, laquelle sera la plus à même de s'adapter à un système global, certains y travaillent. Pour les monnaies grecques, des projets sont en cours pour normaliser la description des monnaies et surtout leur classification. Avec l'utilisation d'URI fixes, les références aux cités antiques seront normalisées. L'idée est bien sûr d'offrir à chaque donnée une identité propre, inamovible, qui ne pourra donc pas être confondue avec une autre donnée. Cela évite également la répétition des informations. Selon que l'on utilise *Pleiades*, ou *Nomisma*[31], chaque identité est à la fois unique mais également mise en relation avec une autre entité identique.

Corinthe sera ainsi l'endroit 570182 de *Pleiades*[32] ainsi que l'endroit dénommé "Corinth" dans *Nomisma*[33], où y est ajoutée une description : "The mint at the ancient site of Corinth in Peloponnesus". Des liens *hypertext* permettent déjà de naviguer d'une page à l'autre. Il est déjà possible de naviguer entre ces différentes pages en tapant Corinth en anglais, français, espagnol, allemand, grec... L'information est donc à la fois normalisée et pérenne.

L'un des avantages de la mise en commun de ces données est la création de puissants outils d'analyses. La cartographie bénéficie pleinement de l'évolution de cette démarche. Il s'agit en quelque sorte d'une mutualisation des moyens poussée à l'extrême, où un seul, ou plusieurs cartographes ou informaticiens travaillent pour un collectif de nombreux chercheurs. Si l'on prend l'exemple de la représentation dynamique des cartes, lorsqu'en 2010, lors du colloque Nomisma, dans le cadre d'une communication l'évolution de la distribution des monnaies

29 Meadows & Gruber 2014.
30 Robinson *et al.* 1977.
31 http://nomisma.org
32 http://pleiades.stoa.org/places/570182
33 http://nomisma.org/id/corinth

en Égypte lagide, il était nécessaire de disposer à la suite plusieurs cartes au même format et de les faire défiler, pour avoir l'impression visuelle de se déplacer dans le temps. Aujourd'hui, cinq ans plus tard, ces outils sont déjà utilisés par des bases de données. C'est le cas d'OCRE[34] et CHRR[35], bases de données hébergées par l'ANS (fig. 3). Il est possible, en choisissant un type de monnaie, de déplacer le curseur pour voir défiler dans le temps l'enfouissement des découvertes. Nul doute que ces outils vont devenir de plus en plus puissants, permettant à chacun d'utiliser les données disponibles et de les faire parler.

Ajouter ses données à l'ensemble des données existantes présente deux intérêts. Le premier est la visibilité du matériel. Dans un outil libre d'accès, que le chercheur aura l'occasion de plus en plus de consulter puisque de plus en plus de données seront disponibles, les informations seront plus visibles et donc plus consultées. Il n'existe pas de chiffres pour les monnaies de Corinthe ou celles de l'agora d'Athènes désormais mises en ligne[36]. Mais pour le matériel des fouilles américaines de Pétra, dans lequel figurent 760 monnaies, les

Fig. 3. Provenance des monnaies trouvées dans un trésor à Nice (RRCH online).

34 Online Coins of the Roman Empire : http://numismatics.org/ocre/

35 Coin Hoards of the Roman Republic : http://numismatics.org/chrr/

36 http://ascsa.net/research?v=default

pages ont été consultées 4 583 876 fois[37]. Le second est l'assurance de bénéficier, à très court terme, d'outils cartographiques que le meilleur cartographe à votre disposition ne pourra pas fournir. Tout simplement parce que la mutualisation des moyens permet la mise à disposition de technologies novatrices qui, par la suite, peuvent être de nouveau mutualisées, il s'agit d'un cercle vertueux.

Conclusion

La cartographie a fait d'immenses progrès ces cinquante dernières années, à tel point qu'elle est devenue un outil commun des recherches numismatiques. Si certaines normes doivent être suivies pour l'édition de cartes, qui orneront encore un certain temps les ouvrages imprimés, la mise en ligne des bases de données connectées offre des possibilités presque infinies, à la fois pour le lecteur mais aussi pour le chercheur.

37 http://opencontext.org/projects/A5DDBEA2-B3C8-43F9-8151-33343CBDC857

Monnaies de fouilles et SIG : l'exemple de Délos

Lionel Fadin, Véronique Chankowski

Les monnaies constituent, du point de vue de la fabrication et de l'usage d'un SIG, des objets comme les autres. Elles ont la particularité, du point de vue du numismate, de pouvoir entrer dans des mises en séries qui sont de nature à permettre le développement d'une analyse statistique ou du moins d'une analyse proche de méthodes statistiques par les résultats quantitatifs que l'on peut espérer obtenir.

De nombreuses publications de numismatique ont certes fait un usage développé de la cartographie dans l'analyse des trésors monétaires et dans l'étude de la circulation d'un monnayage sur un territoire donné. Le travail consiste alors à repérer les trouvailles monétaires en les identifiant sur une carte sous la forme d'un point, ce qui permet ensuite d'établir une carte de diffusion des monnaies d'une cité dans un périmètre plus ou moins étendu. Inversement, à partir d'un trésor localisé en un point donné, on détermine l'origine des différentes monnaies qui le composent pour établir une carte de provenances sous la forme d'un faisceau de points.

L'enjeu de la relation entre les données numismatiques et le SIG va bien au-delà d'une simple cartographie puisque le SIG permet de travailler à l'échelle d'un site, en exploitant les données matérielles et textuelles disponibles en fonction de différents paramètres que le chercheur peut définir, et en les intégrant à un cadre spatial. Il devient ainsi possible de visualiser la répartition des trouvailles à l'échelle d'un site et de faire apparaître des profils monétaires en fonction de différents secteurs du site. De ce point de vue, le géo-référencement apporte un bénéfice considérable à l'étude numismatique, dans le cas de sites pour lesquels il est possible de construire une analyse associant plusieurs espaces du territoire. C'est globalement le cas pour toute cité grecque, mais Délos présente l'avantage d'être, là encore, un site particulièrement bien documenté.

Le matériel numismatique issu des fouilles de Délos consiste à la fois en trésors (32 trésors qui comportent à la fois des tétradrachmes et drachmes stéphanéphores d'Athènes et des petites dénominations de bronze datant surtout de l'époque de la seconde domination athénienne) et en monnaies de fouille (près de 5 000 monnaies, en grande majorité de petites dénominations de bronze). Pour chacune de ces catégories, nous sommes dépendants d'informations tirées des archives des fouilles anciennes (publications et archives de l'EfA pour les fouilles françaises, publications de J. Svoronos dans le *Journal international d'archéologie numismatique* pour les trouvailles du service archéologique grec), qui sont d'une précision très variable, et de données plus récentes de fouilles et sondages dont les rapports présentent

L. Fadin, V. Chankowski, in : *Les monnaies de fouille du monde grec*, p. 123-130

plus fréquemment, pour les trouvailles monétaires, des informations sur une triangulation[1]. La base informatisée inventoriant les trésors et les monnaies de fouilles découverts à Délos est aujourd'hui quasiment achevée. Elle rassemblera les données disponibles (photographie, description, identification, lieu et contexte de découverte), afin d'être progressivement intégrée dans le SIG de Délos développé par l'École française d'Athènes sous la responsabilité de L. Fadin, et de permettre une analyse spatiale des données.

Le Web SIG de Délos : histoire de son développement

Le projet d'un atlas archéologique de l'île de Délos est né en 2003. Les missions de terrain se sont achevées en 2011 et il est publié au format papier dans la collection des volumes de l'Exploration archéologique de Délos au premier semestre 2015[2]. Il est composé de trois planches au 1/5000e, une planche 1/2000e, quatre planches au 1/1000e, de trente-sept planches au 1/200e et de cinq planches regroupant 13 coupes topographiques au 1/200e.

Toutes ces données graphiques ne pouvaient pas simplement rester figées sur le papier mais devaient pouvoir constituer la base cartographique archéologique composant le fond de plan d'un Système d'information géographique (SIG) accueillant les bases de données archéologiques des chercheurs.

En 2012, le choix de diffuser ces données à travers un Web SIG est apparu comme la meilleure des solutions, qu'elles soient techniques, pratiques ou encore financières. En effet, notre Web SIG est uniquement composé d'éléments informatiques Open Source[3] développés et mis à jour régulièrement par une communauté d'utilisateurs et de développeurs très actifs à travers le monde.

Présentation de l'environnement du Web SIG de Délos

Le Web SIG de Délos propose aux chercheurs une application web complète et fonctionnelle, disposant de fonctions caractéristiques d'un SIG : acquisition, affichage, abstraction, analyse et archivage des données géoréférencées.

C'est un outil universel, qui peut être utilisé par n'importe qui depuis n'importe quel appareil connecté à Internet (ordinateur : PC ou Mac, tablette, smartphone, etc.). Son environnement se veut convivial et simple d'accès comme peut l'être Google Map.

La fenêtre du navigateur Internet se décompose en quatre parties distinctes. Sur la gauche, trois cadres se superposent. Le cadre supérieur est réservé à une *mini carte* qui représente la position du niveau de zoom de la fenêtre carte principale. En dessous, le cadre des *thèmes actifs* regroupe seulement les couches actives. Il est possible à l'aide des flèches ou d'un

1 Voir la présentation de la documentation dans Bruneau & Ducat, éd. 2005, 153-158.

2 Moretti *et al.* 2015.

3 La désignation *open source*, ou "code source ouvert", s'applique aux logiciels dont la licence respecte des critères précisément établis par l'Open Source Initiative, c'est-à-dire les possibilités de libre redistribution, d'accès au code source et de création de travaux dérivés.

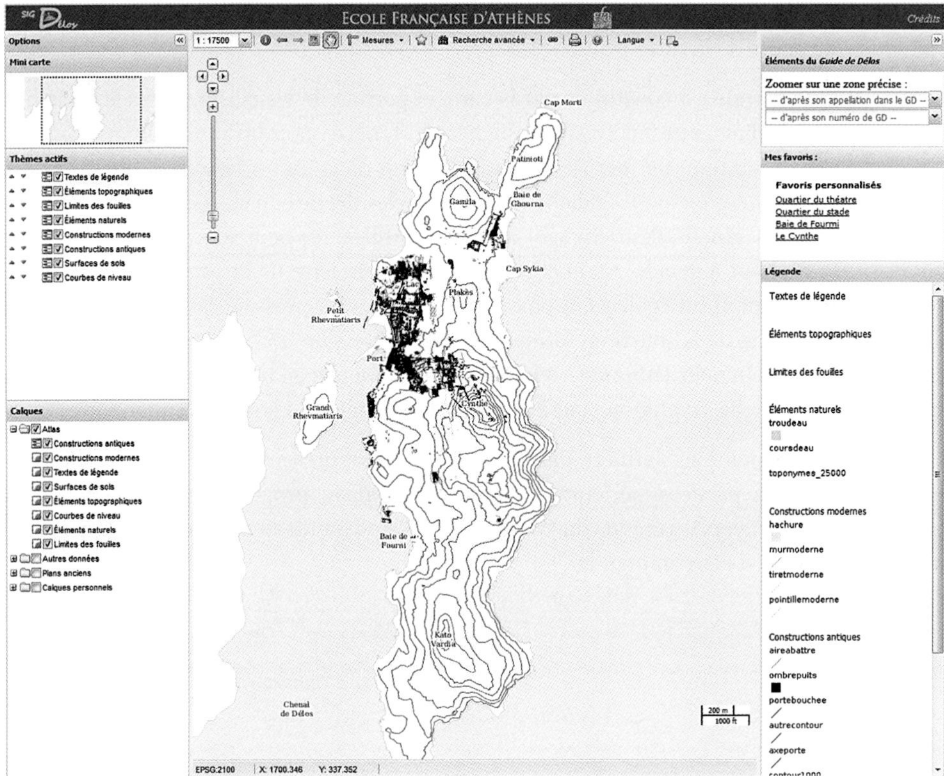

Fig. 1. Page d'accueil du Web SIG de Délos.

glisser/déposer de changer l'ordre d'affichage de ces couches. De plus, à l'aide du clic droit de la souris sur l'une de ces couches, trois fonctions sont accessibles. L'option *information sur la couche* donne accès aux métadonnées de la couche avec notamment son nom dans la base de données, son système de coordonnées natif, son style et des remarques pouvant recevoir des informations sur l'origine de la couche. La fonction de *zoom sur l'emprise de la couche* affiche et centre dans la fenêtre carte l'emprise de la couche. La *modification de la transparence* fait apparaitre une nouvelle fenêtre avec un curseur que l'on peut déplacer le long d'une échelle graduée de 0 à 100 %. Le dernier cadre est réservé à l'ensemble des couches disponibles dans le Web SIG. Des dossiers principaux renferment des couches thématiques, cette *arborescence* permet de rendre actif une ou plusieurs nouvelles couches ou un dossier complet.

Sur la droite de la fenêtre, le cadre supérieur permet de zoomer sur un monument choisi par son nom ou par son numéro de guide et d'afficher les données liées au guide de Délos. Un lien vers la notice du guide est également disponible à partir de cette nouvelle fenêtre. Le cadre central nous offre un accès vers des *favoris*, où des vues préréglées nous amènent vers nos affichages préférés. Le cadre inférieur présente la *légende* de la fenêtre centrale de la carte. Si une couche est désactivée, sa légende disparaît automatiquement et inversement.

Les panneaux droits et gauches peuvent se rétracter afin de laisser plus d'espace à l'affichage du cadre de la carte.

La fenêtre centrale est constituée par la carte et permet de visualiser toutes les couches actives, c'est aussi dans cette fenêtre que s'affichent les fenêtres pop-up lors des interrogations. Un clic gauche maintenu permet de déplacer la carte dans toutes les directions. Mais les flèches directionnelles en haut à gauche de l'écran ou les flèches du clavier permettent aussi ces types de déplacement. Pour changer d'échelle, l'utilisateur peut soit utiliser la barre de zoom située en haut à gauche ou encore actionner la molette de la souris ou les touches "+" et "–" du clavier. Il est également possible de zoomer en pressant la touche majuscule et le bouton gauche de la souris en formant un rectangle autour de la zone sur laquelle on souhaite zoomer. L'échelle courante est lisible en permanence en bas à droite de l'écran sous la forme d'une échelle graphique mais aussi dans une fenêtre du bandeau supérieur.

Enfin, la quatrième et dernière partie du Web SIG se présente sous la forme de deux bandeaux dans la partie supérieure. Le premier bandeau propose un lien vers le site Internet de l'EfA et vers les crédits du Web SIG. Le second bandeau est composé de boutons permettant l'accès à des commandes.

Fig. 2. Bandeau des boutons de commandes.

La première commande propose des échelles d'affichage préréglées qui mettent en évidence l'affichage ou la disparition de certaines couches à certaines échelles. Le bouton "i" permet d'interroger les couches au clic. Cette fonction affiche les informations des couches situées sous le pointeur de la souris. Les flèches permettent de reculer ou d'avancer vers le zoom précédent ou suivant. Le bouton suivant offre la possibilité de zoomer sur des coordonnées particulières à saisir. Les outils de mesures offrent la possibilité de mesurer des distances, des surfaces et des azimuts. L'étoile permet de créer ses propres vues favorites et de les ajouter dans le menu *Mes favoris*. Le bouton recherche avancée offre la possibilité de trois recherches différentes : par zone de recherche, par jointure spatiale, par une requête personnalisée. Le module d'impression permet de choisir le format de sortie (A4 ou A3, paysage ou portrait), la résolution (de 75 à 600 dpi), de saisir un titre et un commentaire, de choisir son format d'impression numérique parmi les formats classiques (bmp, pdf, jpg, gif, png, tif), de choisir la surface à imprimer directement sur la carte, de choisir son échelle de sortie ou encore l'angle de rotation de la zone d'impression. Le bouton d'aide ouvre une nouvelle fenêtre dans le navigateur avec l'aide en format pdf. Une seule langue est pour le moment disponible mais le grec et l'anglais sont prévus. Le dernier bouton permet de désactiver toutes les couches actives.

Présentation de ses avantages

Cet outil nous offre de nombreux avantages comparés à des solutions bureautiques propriétaires classiques: des avantages d'ordre structurel mais aussi fonctionnel. Tout d'abord, il est universel et multiplateforme, et des accès différents peuvent exister suivant les privilèges des utilisateurs. Les données sont compatibles avec la majeure partie des logiciels de SIG qu'ils soient Open Source ou propriétaire. L'EfA, et non pas l'utilisateur, assure les sauvegardes et la maintenance et toutes les données sont centralisées au même endroit. Elles sont stockées sur un ordinateur très puissant diminuant ainsi le temps de calcul. L'accès aux informations peut se faire partout à la seule condition d'avoir une connexion Internet et un navigateur internet à jour. Le contrôle des données et leur accès sont gérés par l'EfA.

Le système tel qu'il est construit apporte aussi des bénéfices à son utilisateur qui n'a pas besoin d'installer ou de mettre à jour de logiciel. Le système étant indépendant du support et du système d'exploitation, le client peut utiliser un ordinateur de faible puissance pour accéder aux données.

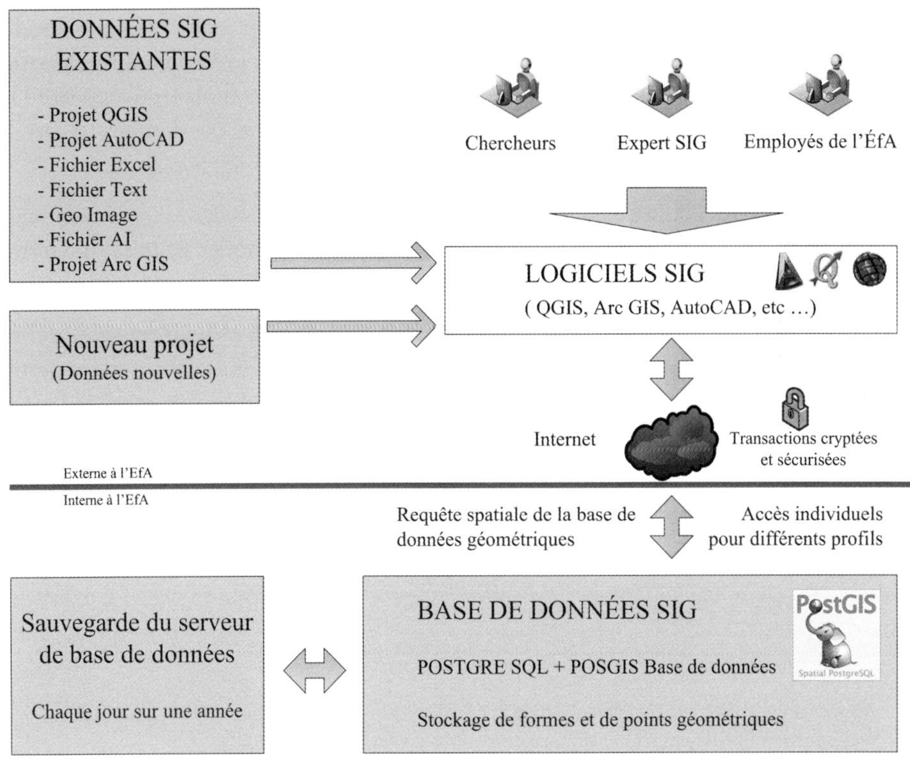

Fig. 3. Architecture du système.

Intégration de la base de données des trésors déliens

Les données de départ étaient stockées dans un logiciel de type tableur composé de huit champs et d'une trentaine de lignes. Après harmonisation et normalisation, le fichier a été encodé en UTF8[4] afin d'être importable dans le logiciel QGIS[5].

Les champs descriptifs retenus tenaient compte de la nature des données disponibles dans les archives (référence *IGCH*, date et lieu de trouvaille, lieu de conservation, date d'enfouissement, contenant, composition du trésor, références de publications le cas échéant).

L'une des difficultés posées par la spatialisation des données était en effet la précision inégale des informations recueillies dans les archives au sujet de la localisation des trésors et des trouvailles monétaires. Une fois la base ouverte sous QGIS, l'étude des données de localisation a permis de définir une nouvelle colonne correspondant à un indice de fiabilité de la localisation des trésors monétaires lors de leur découverte.

L'indice 1 représente une localisation certaine de type ponctuel, par exemple, l'un des trésors de la Maison des Sceaux se trouve sur le seuil entre les pièces χ et μ. L'indice 2 représente une localisation certaine de type surfacique, par exemple, un trésor a été localisé à l'étage de l'habitation II dans la Maison des Bijoux. L'indice 3 représente une localisation incertaine de type surfacique, par exemple, un trésor a été décrit comme trouvé au Nord Est du Lac. Enfin, l'indice 4 indique une absence de localisation connue. Ces derniers trésors ont été placés arbitrairement sur la représentation du musée de Délos sur le plan.

Les indices et les choix de styles de représentation des indices sont bien évidemment paramétrables dans les limites techniques des outils informatiques utilisés qui restent cependant très vastes.

Dans QGIS, il est possible de tracer les géométries propres à chaque trésor et de leur donner comme clé primaire le numéro attribué dans l'*IGCH*. Cette clé primaire permet la géocodification de la base de données c'est-à-dire la création d'un lien entre la base de données attributaires et les géométries.

Après la géocodification, la table des données et les géométries sont importées dans PostgreSQL[6] et son applicatif géographique Postgis[7] à partir de QGIS. Les styles graphiques sont ensuite exportés vers le Web SIG par l'intermédiaire de GeoServer[8].

4 Abréviation de l'anglais : Universal Character Set Transformation Format – 8 bits, codage conçu pour coder l'ensemble des caractères du répertoire universel de caractères codés.

5 QGIS, ou Quantum GIS, est un logiciel SIG libre multiplateforme publié sous licence GPL.

6 PostgreSQL est un système de gestion de base de données relationnelle et objet.

7 PostGIS est une extension de PostgreSQL, qui active la manipulation d'informations géographiques sous forme de géométries (points, lignes, polygones), conformément aux standards établis par l'Open Geospatial Consortium.

8 GeoServer est un serveur informatique Open source et libre écrit en Java qui permet aux utilisateurs de partager et modifier des données géographiques. Conçu pour l'interopérabilité, il publie les données de toutes les sources principales de données spatiales utilisant des normes ouvertes.

Dans l'interface Web SIG, l'affichage de ces données est rendu possible grâce à une nouvelle ligne de l'arborescence. À partir de ce moment, les trois outils de recherches avancées du Web SIG sont disponibles pour l'utilisateur et les recherches peuvent alors commencer. Par *zone de recherche*, il faut d'abord sélectionner la couche d'informations à interroger puis sélectionner des objets vectoriels à l'aide du pointeur de la souris, ce qui équivaut à tracer un cadre de sélection et à ouvrir la table attributaire sous un logiciel de SIG. La recherche *par jointure spatiale* permet de rechercher les éléments d'une couche qui sont en interaction avec une autre couche selon un opérateur logique et selon une zone de recherche. La recherche par une *requête personnalisée* permet de construire une requête SQL[9] de manière graphique à partir d'une ou plusieurs requêtes croisées. Elle correspond à l'interrogation de la table attributaire d'une couche sur un ou plusieurs champs.

Pour chacune des trois recherches on peut obtenir un tableau complet des résultats inclus dans la zone de sélection. Ce tableau peut aussi présenter en détail les résultats un à un. Ceux-ci peuvent être exportés vers un fichier compatible avec les formats standards du marché (xls, csv, GML, GeoJSON, WKT).

Conclusion

Le matériel numismatique ainsi intégré dans le Web SIG pourra être étudié en fonction de différents paramètres. Le plus intéressant du point de vue de la numismatique sera de faire apparaître des profils monétaires en fonction de différents secteurs du site de Délos[10].

La localisation des trésors fait d'ores et déjà apparaître qu'ils sont massivement enfouis dans les zones d'habitat (le Quartier du Théâtre et Skardhana) et non dans le *hieron* : ce n'est donc pas la protection des dieux que recherchait d'abord leur propriétaire, et c'est là un indice non négligeable sur la nature de ces dépôts. Comme c'est le cas pour les trouvailles de la Maison des Sceaux[11], il est probable que dans bien des cas, ces trésors doivent être interprétés comme de la trésorerie, en lien avec l'implantation des activités marchandes et le développement des boutiques et lieux de stockage dans les quartiers[12]. Dans la majorité des cas, on a donc sans doute moins affaire à de la thésaurisation qu'à de l'encaisse. Cette observation, permise par la géo-localisation, contribue à lever le cloisonnement habituel de l'étude des monnaies, partagée entre trésors monétaires et monnaies de fouilles. L'implémentation des données numismatiques dans le SIG atténue la valeur de cette

9 SQL (Structured Query Language) est un langage informatique normalisé servant à exploiter des bases de données relationnelles. La partie langage de manipulation des données de SQL permet de rechercher, d'ajouter, de modifier ou de supprimer des données dans les bases de données relationnelles.

10 Les résultats complets de cette étude seront publiés à partir de Chankowski 2011.

11 La publication du matériel des fouilles de la Maison des Sceaux est en cours et comportera un chapitre consacré aux monnaies.

12 Le programme ANR *Entrepôts et lieux de stockage dans le monde gréco-romain antique* (http://www.entrepots-anr.fr) a permis de montrer l'important développement des activités de stockage au cœur des quartiers : voir en particulier Karvonis & Malmary 2012.

distinction au profit de la mise en évidence de zones ou de secteurs qui correspondent à des profils monétaires.

On voit également apparaître une différence nette entre le secteur portuaire, dans lequel on trouve des monnaies étrangères en grand nombre, et les quartiers dans lesquels les petites dénominations de bronze sont majoritaires à l'époque de la seconde domination athénienne. On peut ensuite affiner l'analyse selon les quartiers : le quartier du théâtre, plus ancien et plus directement lié aux activités artisanales et aux entrepôts du front de mer, n'a pas non plus tout à fait le même profil monétaire que le quartier de Skardhana, plus résidentiel et comportant des boutiques destinées à l'alimentation de proximité. Ainsi, à la suite du premier panorama de la circulation monétaire délienne et égéenne qu'a permis de dresser l'étude, par T. Hackens, des monnaies découvertes lors du grand programme de fouilles de l'Îlot des Comédiens, sous la direction de P. Bruneau[13], le géo-référencement permet aujourd'hui d'apporter des précisions non négligeables pour la compréhension des usages monétaires.

Le bénéfice de l'introduction du matériel numismatique dans le SIG de Délos sera en premier lieu de permettre de visualiser avec une plus grande netteté ces différences d'usage des instruments monétaires. On peut espérer ainsi faire progresser, en particulier, le débat sur l'utilisation des petites dénominations de bronze et, en regard, la question de la politique monétaire des autorités portuaires.

13 Hackens 1970.

III - FACIÈS

Coins from Underwater Excavations. The Case of Thonis-Herakleion

Andrew Meadows

The organisers of the conference from which this volume springs invited me to contribute some thoughts on the methodological problems and possibilities arising out of working with coins from an underwater excavation. As will become clear, such coins are far from the most attractive to survive from antiquity, but they can certainly be among the most interesting. However, I should begin with a disclaimer: I do not personally dive. The coins under discussion here have been excavated by the extraordinary group of divers of the Institut européen d'archéologie sous-marine, under the direction of F. Goddio, and with the generous sponsorship of the Hilti Foundation[1]. I cannot, therefore, offer any firsthand account of the process of excavation. My knowledge in this area comes solely from discussion with the excavation director and divers, and from my own inferences from the material I study. This material, once excavated, is first conserved at the laboratory of the Maritime Museum in Alexandria, before being registered and organised within the storerooms there[2]. My procedure in examining these coins has been to work through them in a continuous sequence as they have been registered. This means that I have essentially worked through the coins in the order that they were discovered. There will, therefore, be a bias in the provisional picture of finds that I present here, as a result of the focuses of excavation and survey in the first six years of work. The exception to this pattern has been in the work on hoards from the site. When they were available to me for study, I have prioritized work on such assemblages. In presenting data regarding overall patterns of coin deposition across the site I have sought to negate this bias, as well as the tendency of hoards to skew proportions of coins, by excluding them from the figures quoted and distribution maps presented.

A final caveat concerns the site itself. If there is such a thing as a typical underwater site or excavation, Thonis-Herakleion is most definitely not it. This statement may best be explained by consideration of the discovery of the site, and the picture that may be obtained so far of its nature. The site in question is Thonis Herakleion, which was located during the summer

1 I must here express my admiration for the divers for the remarkable job they do in retrieving and accurately recording their finds, to F. Goddio for the initial invitation to work on this material, and continuing support and help in understanding the site, and to the Hilti Foundation for the funding that makes my work possible.

2 Conservation of the coins I have thus far studied has been the work of O. Berger and M.-A. Coingnard. Registration and organisation of the material (including preparing it for my study) has been the work of Abd el-Hamid and Youssria el-Gandour. To all I am extremely grateful.

A. Meadows, in : *Les monnaies de fouille du monde grec*, p. 133-145

of 2000 by the archaeological expedition of the IEASM. It lies on the sea-bed *c.* 6,5 km off the coast of Egypt, to the East of the modern town of Aboukir. Survey and excavation of the site has proceeded on an annual basis – political and military circumstances permitting[3]. The main part of the city, with its great temple of Amun-Gereb was situated at the tip of a peninsula. To the east of this peninsula were a series of interconnecting basins that were separated from the main Canopic branch of the Nile by large sand dunes pierced by channels permitting communication, via the basins, with the city and its ports. To the west of the peninsula lay a lake, which was connected to the eastern basins by a large "Grand Canal". The general effect of modern artistic reconstructions of this landscape is not so very different from the impression we receive from the famous 1st c. BC Palestrina mosaic (fig. 1).

Perched at the northern tip of the Canopic Branch of the Nile, Thonis-Herakleion constituted the entrance to Egypt from the Mediterranean[4]. The existence of the city of Herakleion was long known from Strabo and later writers[5], along with its temple of Herakles, ancient, it seems, even in Herodotus' day[6]. The identity of this city with the Thonis also mentioned by Strabo[7] was strongly suggested by the Canopus Decree which refers in Greek to the temple of Herakleion[8] and in hieroglyphics to (ll. 25-6) "the temple of Amun-Gereb in the mouth of the Hone[9]". These names and identity of the city discovered by the IEASM were stunningly confirmed in 2001 by the discovery of the second copy of the Sais (Naucratis) stele, set up at Herakleion, which provides for its erection "in a town called the Hone-of-Sais[10]".

But in this image, we encounter one of the primary difficulties faced in working with material from such a site. This is an entire town underwater. It had temples, houses, canals, streets, harbours and all the variety of buildings and public spaces we might expect of an urban centre in antiquity. And all are completely invisible from the surface (fig. 2). It is impossible to gain a physical overview of the site as we might for a site on land. We can add a further layer of complexity to this by noting the maritime/riverine nature of this city means that there are archaeological contexts that were under water even in antiquity. Thus we are dealing sometimes with objects from areas that were above water when they were deposited, and sometimes with objects that have been recovered from locations that were under water when they were lost or deposited.

3 For a full account of the history of the discovery and the initial years of excavation see Goddio 2007, 69-130. Further accounts of the excavation and finds from Herakleion can be found in Goddio & Fabre 2006.

4 According to Herodotus there was a time (perhaps from the time of Amasis onwards) at which the Canopic branch was the only legal point of entry. See Hdt. 3.179 with Lloyd 1988, 229-230 (cf. Asheri *et al.* 2007, 376 on the chronology).

5 Str. 17.1.18, C801. For other sources see Radt 2009, 439-440.

6 Hdt. 2.113. See further Lloyd 1988, 48 and Radt 2009.

7 Str. 17.1.16, C800.

8 *OGIS* 56, 55.

9 See Bomhard 2012, 7-8. For the identity of hone and Thonis: Yoyotte 1958, 414-430.

10 Now published by Bomhard 2012. The publication provision is in col. 14; *ibid.* 88-89.

Fig. 1. Image of Palestrina Mosaic (https://commons.wikimedia.org/wiki/File:NileMosaicOfPalestrina.jpg).

Fig. 2. Photo of site from boat (by the author).

And indeed the process of identifying the basic topography of the town in what survives on the seabed today has proven challenging and has had to be built up from a combination of survey methods (sonar and magnetometry), as well as core-sampling, spot-cleaning and basic physical examination[11].

Matters are still further complicated by the processes by which the city came to be under water. On the one hand there is evidence to suggest that the sea-level has been rising since antiquity with respect to this part of the coast at a rate of *c.* 2 mm per annum. But this by itself is not sufficient to account for the depth of the city at around 6 m below sea-level today. Geological investigation has suggested that the additional sinking must be the result of substrate failure, some of it probably sudden. The precise cause remains elusive: there may not have been one massive event such as an earthquake, but perhaps a series of smaller shocks or high Nile floods. But Herakleion was clearly a disaster waiting to happen: "This geoarchaeological analysis illustrates extreme consequences that occur when carefully implemented protection measures related to coastal sites and associated environmental conditions are overlooked. In the examples presented here, the Greeks and subsequent inhabitants built and maintained their sites on unstable wetland sediment, without foundations and pilings, at distributary mouths that experienced powerful annual Nile floods. Given the remarkable Greek and Roman building and engineering tradition, it is difficult to fully comprehend the decisions that led to emplacement of large, monumental

11 For a summary see Goddio 2007, 69-72, n. 3

structures directly on underconsolidated and unstable sediment prone to soil instability and associated geohazards[12]". The city was thus doomed to disappear beneath the waves, and this may have happened in a series of stages. Moreover, the sheer instability of land on which the city was built should prepare us for the possibility of a number of possible minor or major disaster-events before the city finally vanished. The date of this final submergence remains unclear. The last writer to describe the landscape between Canopus and Thonis-Herakleion is St Sophronius, who lived in the region from the late 6th to early 7th c. AD. So far, the latest coins to be found at the similarly submerged site of East Canopus belong to the first half of the 8th c. One possibility is that the final event that led to the complete submergence of this area was the abnormally high Nile flood attested for 741 or 742 AD[13]. It is probable, therefore, that Herakleion has been under water for more close to 1 300 years.

This fact of long submergence brings with it one obvious benefit, of course. The site has been immune to casual gleaning or systematic plundering by treasure hunters. This should mean that we have the opportunity to explore the monetary history of the town at its various points of destruction (the plural is important here). But equally, the submerged nature, as for any underwater site, creates a very basic problem for the numismatist, and indeed for anyone working on or visiting the site, in that it is extremely difficult to obtain an overview of the contexts in which objects are found. However, the excavation's response to this problem has created a huge opportunity, to which I will return.

But first I should outline some of the difficulties in dealing with the numismatic material that has been found at Herakleion. Some of these difficulties are not specific to an underwater site, of course. First there is the sheer number of coins that are emerging. As we have noted, one obvious characteristic of a site that has been underwater for over a millennium is that it has not been metal detected or otherwise robbed of its monetary finds. What we have from the site, potentially, is everything that was in the city when a particular phase of occupation was brought to an end by disaster and/or when it disappeared under the waves, apparently in the 8th c. AD. Excavation continues on the site, so we do not yet have final numbers. The material I will drawn on for this paper consists of some 2 200 coins, of which approximately 1 400 have proven identifiable in some respect.

Second there is the problem of context. The site of Herakleion preserves the fallen remains of a city, and beneath those remains lies a context that resembles that which we might find on a site of dry-land: an "archaeological layer" subject to excavation and a process of stratigraphic analysis. Within this layer, with a characteristic clay-like texture, hoards and other single finds have been excavated. However, on top of this intact context the entire site is covered by a layer of mobile silt (dubbed '*tout venant*' by the archaeologists), the depth of which varies, but can be measured in the 10s of centimetres. While this might, at first sight, appear problematic, in fact it seems that the reverse might be true. Coins are never found in the *tout venant*. Rather they rest beneath it, and they rest there in large numbers.

12 Stanley *et al.* 2004, 9. Cf. Stanley 2007, 54-57.

13 Stanley *et al.* 2001.

However, it is important to stress that the context of these coins is not securely that of their original deposition in antiquity. What seems to have happened is that at the point of substrate failure, coins buried or otherwise close to the ancient surface were dislodged from their original context and gently scattered. However, after this initial point of scattering, they have remained in place, and subsequently have been covered by the *tout venant*.

An example may serve to illustrate the point. By good fortune we have evidence of one undoubted hoard that bears witness to the extent of this initial movement, while suggesting the relative immobility that follows. This find consists of a group of gold quarter staters of Ptolemy I (*EH* 1.153)[14]. Gold coins are not common, needless to say, among the finds from Thonis-Herakleion. Thus, to find five gold coins of identical type within a single area of the site is as sure an indication that there can be that these coins were deposited together. That said, these coins were not excavated from the clay-like layer beneath the *tout venant*, but were found on top of it during survey work around the main temple area. A map (fig. 3) of their distribution thus reveals not a single find, but rather a scatter.

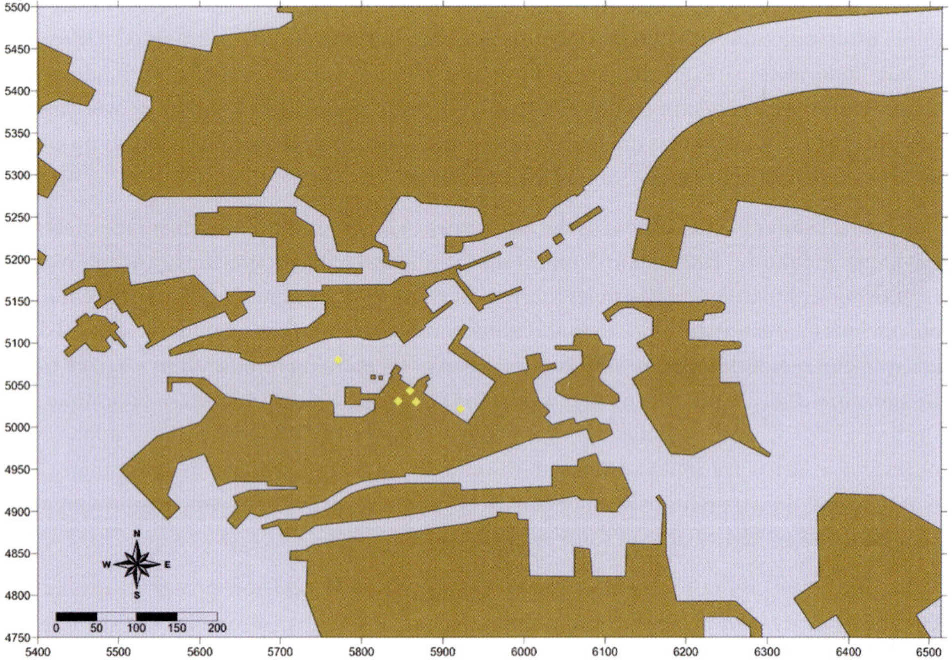

Fig. 3. The Gold hoard from Thonis-Herakleion.

14 H4536, SCA 318; H4504, SCA 313; H4160, SCA 312; H3578, SCA 304; H3642, SCA 307. Goddio & Fabre 2006, 269-271, n° 320, 319, 318, 317 and 328.

This might, at first sight, appear alarming: the hoard has become dispersed. But it is at least clear that they seem to cluster around an original point of deposit, probably within the precinct of the main temple of Herakles (H1)[15], and have not been carried from one side of the site to another. During a decade of prior and subsequent survey and excavation work no further specimen of this type has been found. This suggests that, while we should be aware that coins did move at the time of catastrophic substrate failure, this movement is limited, and that it is, therefore, worthwhile examining the distribution of coins from this layer for general patterns of deposit.

But there is one important way in which this gold hoard is misleading: the state of preservation of these coins is wholly unrepresentative of the finds from the site in general. A few illustrations will make the key points about the nature of the finds (fig. 4, 1-4). The vast majority, over 95% of the total finds, are of bronze. Bronze, unlike gold, does not respond well to 1200+ years of immersion in sea-water. The result is that 36% of the coin finds cannot be identified beyond saying that they were definitely once coins. And when I claim 64% as identifiable in some way, by this I mean that they can securely be assigned to one of the following four categories: Greek (*i.e.* pre-Roman and non-Ptolemaic), Ptolemaic, Roman (exclusively so far from the mint of Alexandria) and Byzantine (this last category consists exclusively of the local production of dodecanummi).

Fig. 4.1. Bronze coin of 'Kition', 2nd half of 4th c. BC. Maritime Museum inv. 1386. H4097. 0.73g. 7mm. scale 2:1.

Fig. 4.2. Ptolemaic bronze diobol of Series 2, c. 301-261 BC. Maritime Museum inv. 1527 5; H3721 5. 11.07g. 22mm. scale 1:1.

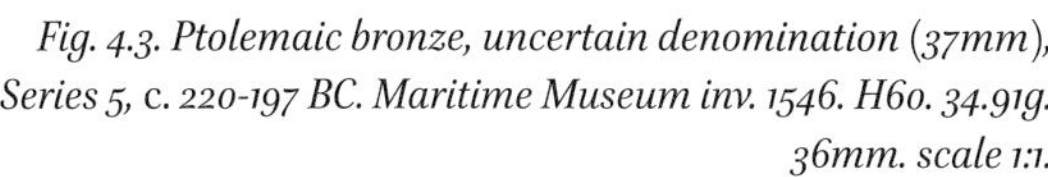

Fig. 4.3. Ptolemaic bronze, uncertain denomination (37mm), Series 5, c. 220-197 BC. Maritime Museum inv. 1546. H60. 34.91g. 36mm. scale 1:1.

Fig. 4.4. Byzantine bronze dodecanummium, c. 7th c. AD. Maritime Museum inv. 2338 12. H9741 12. 4.30g. 17mm. scale 1:1.

15 On the topography nature and finds from this area see Goddio 2007, 75-100.

A serious deficiency resulting from the condition of coins from underwater excavation is the amount of weight-loss they have suffered as a result of long immersion. The effect of this can be most easily seen by comparing the average weights of some specimens from Herakleion with the average recently published by Wolf for coins that in all probability have not been so corroded. Table 1 presents the mean weights identified by Wolf for the diobols of seven subseries of Series 2[16]. The range is from 14,38 g to 15,99 g. The 28 coins of Series 2 recorded so far from Herakleion range from 3,21g-14,46 g, with a mean weight of 9,31 g (fig. 6). Herakleion coins weigh, on average, a little over half of their original weight, it seems.

Series	**Mean weight (g.)**
2 Di	15.48
2 Dii	15.58
2 Diii	15.99
2E	14.44
2F	15.77
2G	14.91
2H	14.38
All subseries combined (249 specimens)	15.71

Table 1. Mean weights of Series 2 Diobols (Wolf 2013).

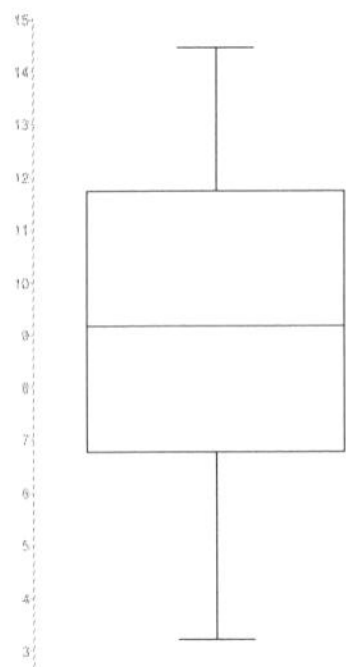

Fig. 5. Series 2 Diobols from Herakleion.

It is immediately clear that the weight loss is substantial. This has two corollaries. First it means that the Herakleion coins are not useful for metrological study, since their weights bear no clear relation to that at which they were struck. Second, it means that weight cannot be used as a reliable guide to denomination. Thus if a coin is illegible, or only partially legible, its weight cannot be used to deduce its identity.

Illegibility, of course, is a significant problem. The coins illustrated in fig. 4 are entirely representative of the material at large. For the earlier coinages where types alone may suffice to attribute the coin to a mint, then such an attribution is possible so long as the types are

16 Wolf 2013, 59 and, with tables, 89-93.

clear. But when issues begin to be marked by variations in monogram, symbol or legend, it is almost impossible to subdivide identifications along these lines, for these subtleties of identifier are rarely if ever legible. So it might be possible to identify a Ptolemaic bronze by type and module, but it is generally impossible to read the letters that identify issues in the third century coinage. An issue of Roman Alexandria may be attributable to an emperor, and the reverse type may be discernable, but it is rare that the year of issue will be clear enough to complete the identification.

Again, this will be a familiar problem to colleagues who work on dry-land sites, but I suspect that the problem is more severe for underwater material. Happily, however, this limitation of the evidence is not necessarily an impediment to what the numismatic material may offer at an interpretative level. In many contexts, it rarely matters to anyone other than the numismatist whether a coin was part of issue E or A, if that distinction in issue cannot be translated into one of clear chronological, economic or political implication. And it often cannot.

In this respect, however, the location of the site in question, and the coinage it is likely to yield, is obviously a major factor in determining the usefulness of partially illegible material. Herakleion, of course, is in Egypt, and this fact brings with it a distinct set of challenges in terms of the material that is found; but also some obvious potential in terms of illuminating monetary practice in – dare one say – an exceptional part of the world. This potential has been very much enhanced recently by the work of C. Lorber, O. Picard and T. Faucher through their recategorization of Ptolemaic bronze, and the publication of an important body of excavation material from the CEA excavations in Alexandria[17]. This categorization, and the recognisability of Ptolemaic issues through a clear iconographic programme and differentiation by module, means that it is possible to place even badly corroded coins within the new Series into which these three scholars have now organized the bronze (table 2).

Series	N° of Denominations	Reigns	Approx Dates
1	2	Ptol. 1	315-301 BC
2	4	Ptol. 1 and 2	301-261 BC
3	6	Ptol. 2 and 3	261-240 BC
4	7	Ptol. 3 and 4	240-220 BC
5	8	Ptol. 4 and 5	220-197 BC
6	8	Ptol. 5 and 6	197-163 BC
7	6	Ptol. 6 and 8, Cleo. 2	163-115 BC
8	2	Ptol. 9	115-113 BC
9	2	Ptol. 10-14	113-44 BC
10	2	Cleo. 7	44-30 BC

Table 2. The Ptolemaic Bronze coin series as defined in Picard & Faucher 2012.

17 For important preliminary studies see Lorber 2000; *ead.* 2005; Huston & Lorber 2001; Lorber & Faucher 2010. For Alexandria, Picard & Faucher 2012 with a summary in Meadows 2014a, 229-239.

This new categorization offers the prospect both of new forms of analysis of coin use and deposition within an individual site and of comparison of deposition across multiple sites. The latter is not specific to underwater sites, but it does make it possible to compare the coin finds from different types of excavation. I have discussed this possibility at greater length elsewhere[18], so I confine myself to reproducing a chart (fig. 6) that summarises the coin finds from four sites in relatively close proximity to one another: Thonis-Herakleion, Naucratis, Athribis and Alexandria[19].

While the resulting pattern is interesting, and perhaps suggests different patterns of occupation at the different sites, the important point from our point of view is that the poorly preserved specimens from underwater excavation still have comparative value with better preserved coins from land-based excavations.

Finally there is one last element of an underwater site, or at least of this particular underwater site, that makes a fundamental difference to the way in which we can use the numismatic evidence to enhance our interpretation. An underwater site, as we have noted, is invisible. All of our interpretation must take place through the use of maps and precisely recorded contexts. Here we are very fortunate that the working methods of the excavators at Herakleion have been precise and careful from the very beginning. On the one hand a picture of the topography of the site has been built up through electronic means. So we have base maps on which we plot the coins. But we also have the precise find-spots of the coins. Goddio and the IEASM have been pioneers in the use of underwater GPS systems. Every object found has its find-spot accurately recorded, and is therefore individually mappable. This creates enormous potential for tracing patterns of deposition over time, as the following series of maps (fig. 7-10) demonstrates.

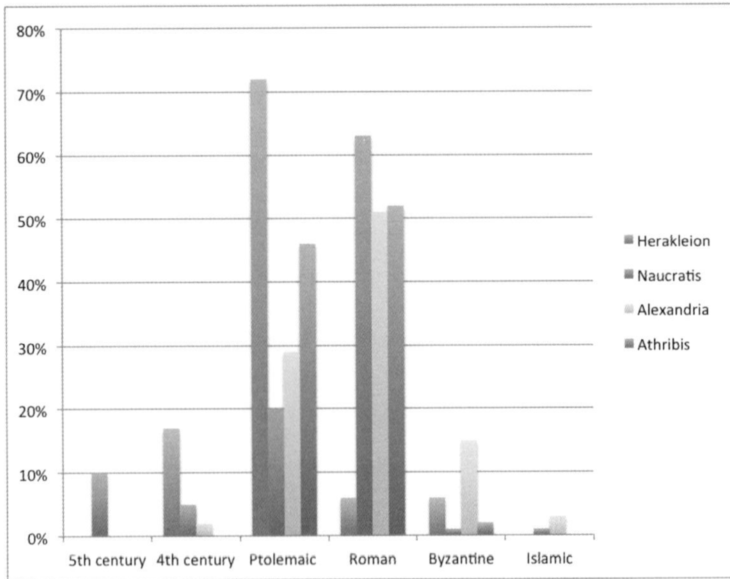

Fig. 6. Comparison of sites by broad period.

18 Meadows 2014b.

19 Alexandria: Picard *et al.* 2012 (3 529 coins). Athribis: Krzyżanowska & Myśliwiec 2009 (1 682 coins). Naucratis (740 coins): published twice by Head 1886a and 1886b.

The distribution of finds appears to tell a story. Relatively intense deposition of coins centered predominantly on the Temple of Ammon-Gereb at the centre of the site in the late 4th c. (fig. 7) gives way to a broader distribution and period of largest number of coin deposits in the Ptolemaic period down to the mid 2nd c. BC (fig. 8). There then follows abrupt fall off in quantity of coins deposited, and a confinement of them across the site in the following 150 years down to the Roman period (fig. 9). Finally, the Byzantine finds attest to a relatively narrow zone of deposit based on the central island of the city (fig. 10). This deceptively cursory account of the coin finds across a site belies the vast amount of work that has gone into creating it. Hours of diving and careful recording of provenance combine with hours spent identifying coins in appalling condition. Sadly, few sites have this amount of care lavished on them. And fewer still are published in a way that the story can be told. But if it is possible under water, then surely it must be possible on land too.

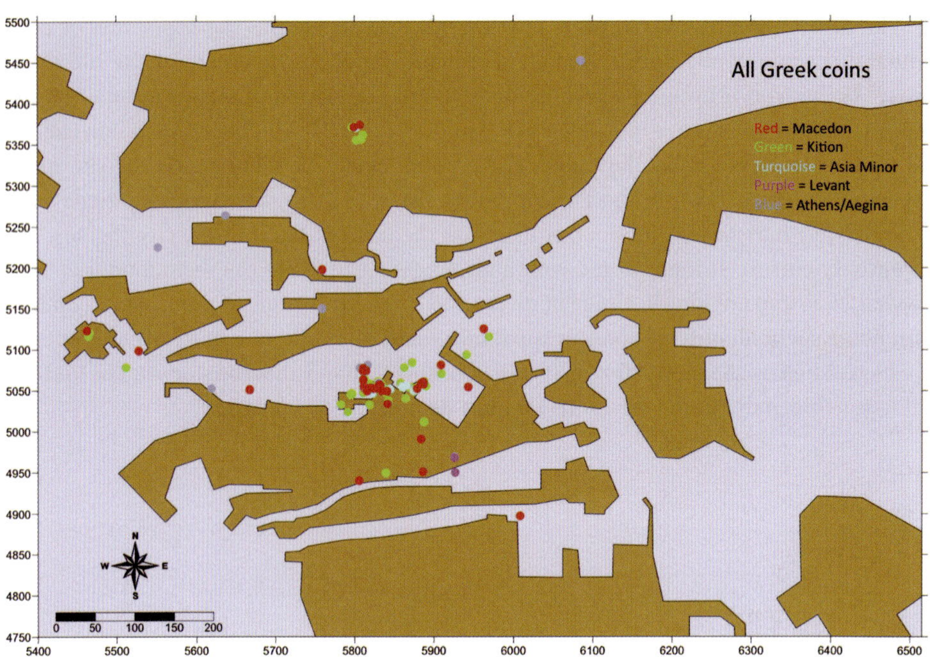

Fig. 6. Distribution of pre-Ptolemaic Greek coins (©F. Goddio/IEASM).

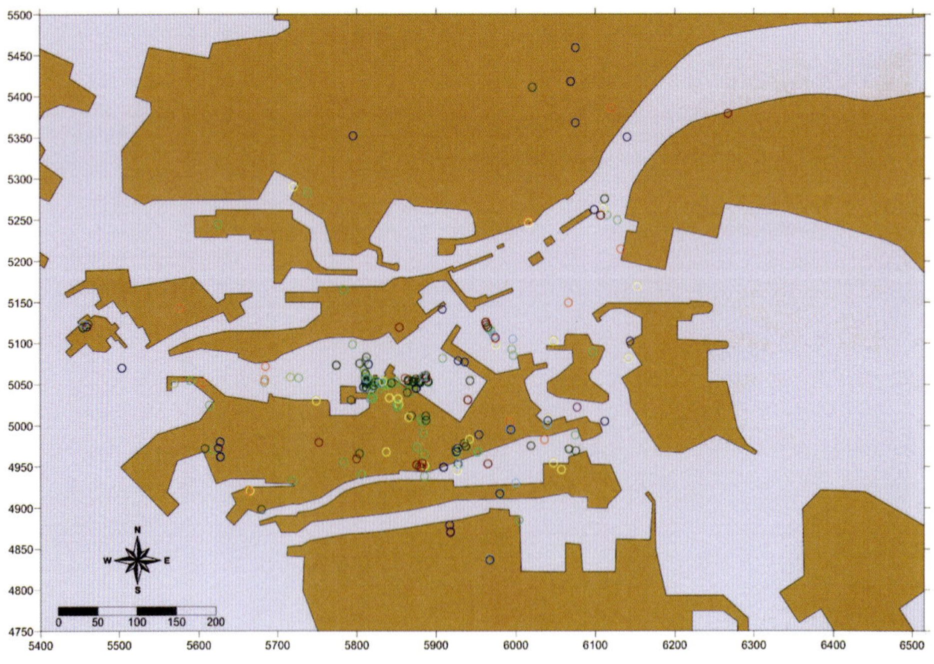

Fig. 7. Distribution of Ptolemaic coins of Series 1-7 (©F. Goddio/IEASM).

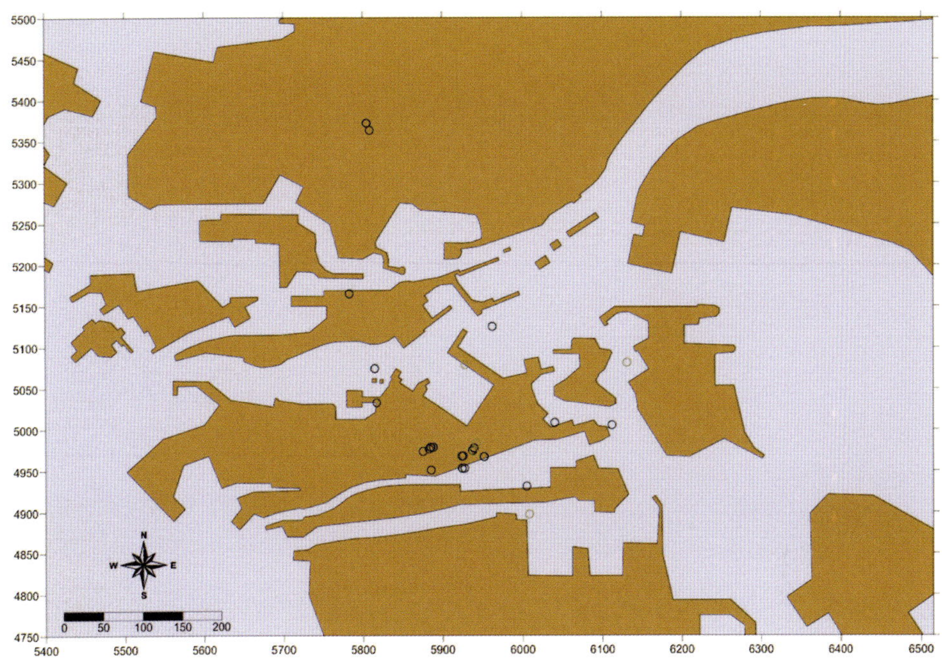

Fig. 8. Distribution of Ptolemaic coins of Series 9-10 (©F. Goddio/IEASM).

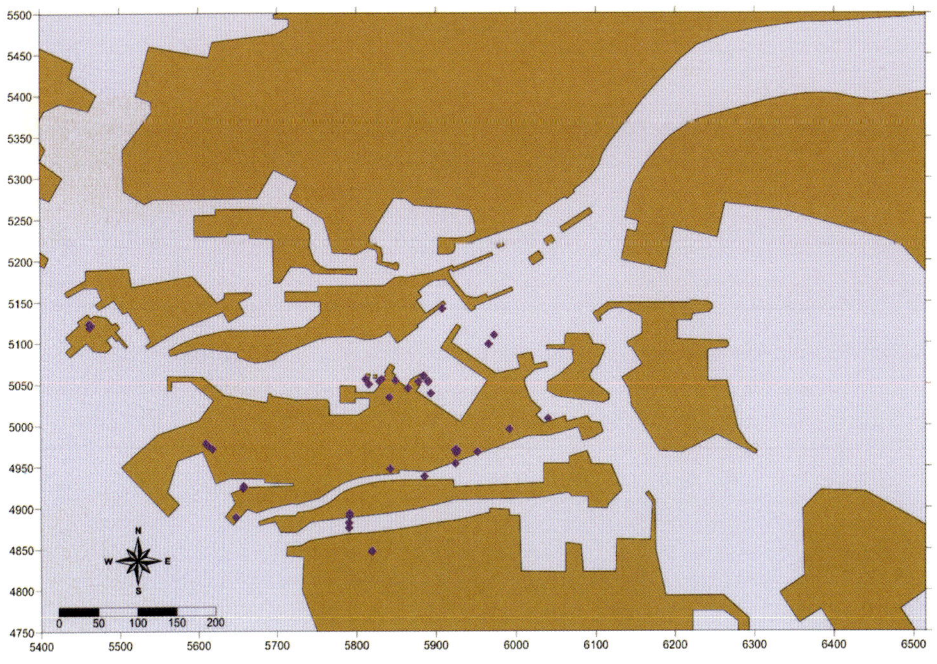

Fig. 9. Distribution of Byzantine coins (©F. Goddio/IEASM).

Treasures from the Deep: Coins from Hellenistic and Roman Republican Shipwrecks[1]

Panagiotis Tselekas

The present paper surveys the shipwrecks dated to the Hellenistic and Roman Republican era – namely from late 4th to late 1st c. BC – that have been reported to have yielded coins[2]. The hundreds of sites recorded over the years are only a sample of the many thousands of ships which must have put to sea in ancient times, but nonetheless it is a sample which contains a good deal of information about ancient trade. Long-distance trade was primarily conducted by merchant ships over the waters of the Aegean, Mediterranean and Black Sea. Evidence from ancient authors as well as shipwrecks indicates that overseas trade developed into a specialized and important sector of the economy. Many of the goods traded included luxury items, such as jewelry, fine pottery and pieces of art as well as specialty agricultural products like wine and honey. Necessities were also traded, however, for without long-distance trade many areas would not have been able to obtain corn, metals, timber, and slaves[3].

The aim is, by presenting certain examples, to examine the potential of the coins to date the shipwrecks as well as to reconstruct ancient maritime trade routes.

The nature of the evidence

Shipwrecks are examined by the appropriately-called "shipwreck archaeology", a branch of the maritime and underwater archaeology[4].

A unique characteristic of the shipwreck sites is that they happen to be catastrophic sites – that is, sites created within minutes by some disaster that preserves various materials

1 Special thanks are due to Professor Catherine Grandjean, Director of Centre Tourangeau d'Histoire et d'études des Sources, Université François-Rabelais and Dr Frédérique Duyrat, Director of the Département des Monnaies, médailles et antiques, Bibliothèque nationale de France, for inviting me to participate in the conference on *Les monnaies de fouille du monde grec*, as well as the École française d'Athènes for its hospitality. The topic on coins found in shipwrecks first caught the author's attention in 2011, when – as a curator at the Athens Numismatic Museum – he was asked to study the coins from the "Antikythera" shipwreck. The coins were to be displayed in the most successful temporary exhibition "The Antikythera Shipwreck. The Ship, the Treasures, the Mechanism" at the Athens National Archaeological Museum from 5 April 2012 to 28 April 2013.

2 The data have been gathered from Parker 1992 and Strauss 2013.

3 For a comprehensive presentation, see Bouyia 2012.

4 On the archaeology of shipwrecks, see Muckelroy 1978, 157-214 and Gibbs 2006, 4-19.

and the cultural context. These destructive sites offer valuable information on the study of ancient marine technology, maritime trade routes, transportation of people and goods, etc. A group of items from an archaeological site such as a shipwreck is found in a state that reflects a specific moment in the past. Such closed groups occur also in burials or in votive deposits, with the difference that in those cases the objects selected were intended to be used for the last time. In the case of ships, as of material remains revealed in constructions ruined during a physical devastation, like a volcanic eruption or an earthquake, the artefacts found allow a glance into the regular every-day life aboard a vessel[5].

Regarding the hundreds of shipwrecks dated to the Hellenistic and Roman Republican era coins comprise one of the least abundant types of material preserved. On the evidence provided in Parker 1992, there are 403 shipwrecks dated from the 3rd to late 1st c. BC only 27 have yielded coins (table 1). Although there have been new finds over the past decades recorded in Strauss 2013, the figure and percentage of the sites where coins have been found has not changed significantly. The nature and quality of the evidence are highly variable, ranging from isolate unidentifiable specimens to large hoards (table 2).

Centuries a.C.	Shipwrecks catalogued	Shipwrecks with coins	%
IIIrd	64	1	1,6%
IInd	155	14	9,0%
Ist	184	12	6,5%

Table 1. Shipwrecks of the 3rd- 1st c. BC (based on Parker 1992, 10-12 with modifications).

Shipwreck	Site	Wreck date (BC)	Coins reported	References
Kyrenia	Cyprus: N coast; 27 m depth.	early 3rd c.	7 AE, mainly issues of Demetrios I Poliorketes.	Parker 1992, n° 563; Strauss 2013, n° 118.
Sanguinaires	France: Near Ajaccio, Corsica; 18 m depth.	late 3rd c.	1 AE of Ptolemy III Euergetes or Ptolemy IV Philopator.	Strauss 2013, n° 190.
Grazel A	France: At Gruissan; in a sanded-up channel.	200-150	1 AE of Ampurias.	Parker 1992, n° 482; Strauss 2013, n° 7898.
La Chrétienne C	France: Near Agay/Anthéor; W of La Chrétienne; 35 m depth.	175-150	1 denarius (210-200 BC).	Parker 1992, n° 304; Strauss 2013, n° 7724.
Le Formiche di Capraia	Italy: N tip Capraia Island, Tuscany; 18 m depth.	175-125	1 Roman ass (200-150 BC).	Strauss 2013, n° 8919.
Capo Graziano A	Italy: SE of the Secca di Capo Graziano; 33-43 m depth.	160-140	4 Roman asses.	Parker 1992, n° 233; Strauss 2013, n° 7656.

5 Parker 1992, 3; Gibbins 2001, 205.

Isla Pedrosa	Spain: At Cala Pedrosa, near L'Estartit; 36-40 m depth.	150-140	2 AE of Kaiantolos; 1 AE of Rome; 6 AE of Massalia; 1 AE of Neapolis; 6 unidentifiable AE.	Parker 1992, n° 520; Strauss 2013, n° 7934.
Apollonia A	Libya: In the harbour of Apollonia; 9 m depth.	150-120	2 AE (2nd c. BC).	Parker 1992, n° 47; Strauss 2013, n° 128.
Punta Scaletta	Italy: At the N point of Giannutri island; 33 m depth	140-130	1 AR and 3 AE of Neapolis, 1 victoriate, 1 AE of Ptolemy VI Philometor.	Parker 1992, n° 960; Strauss 2013, n° 8342.
Pointe du Brouil	France: Off Pointe du Brouil, Cavalaire bay; 32 m depth.	140-130	2 Roman asses.	Parker 1992, n° 844; Strauss 2013, n° 8233.
La Chrétienne A	France: Near Agay/Anthéor; E of La Chrétienne beacon; 21-25 m depth.	150-100	1 AE of Cossura (2nd c. BC).	Parker 1992, n° 302; Strauss 2013, n° 7722.
Spargi	Italy: Maddelana Island, NE Sardinia; 17-18 m depth.	120-100	2 unidentified AE.	Parker 1992, n° 1108; Strauss 2013, n° 169.
Atlit North Bay I	Israel: Off N bay of Atlit; 5 m depth.	late 2nd c.	Dozens of small Ptolemaic AE.	Strauss 2013, n° 8942.
Naham Norem	Israel: Off N bay of Atlit; 5 m depth.		Ptolemaic AR.	Strauss 2013, n° 8943.
Neve Yam	Israel: Off Neve Yam shore; 3,5 m depth.	late 2nd c.	Several Ptolemaic AE.	Strauss 2013, n° 8846.
Bagaud B	France: On the N side of Bagaud island; 18 m depth.	110-100	1 AE of Massalia.	Parker 1992, n° 77; Strauss 2013, n° 7508.
Kizil Burun Column	Turkey: SW of Izmir; 50 m depth.	late 2nd- 1st c.	1 worn and corroded AE.	Strauss 2013, n° 12
Grand Bassin B	France: At Gruissan; 2-4 m depth.	110-90	4 AE of Cese-Tarraco.	Parker 1992, n° 469; Strauss 2013, n° 7885.
Mahdia	Tunisia: NE of Ras Mahedia; 40 m depth.	110-90	4 AE.	Parker 1992, n° 621; Strauss 2013, n° 132.
Cap Taillat	France: In Bon Porté bay; 33 m depth.	100	1 illegible AE.	Parker 1992, n° 200; Strauss 2013, n° 7623.
Cavalière	France: At the mouth of the Cavalière bay, near Le Lavandou; 43 m depth.	100	5 AE of Massalia, 5 AE of Numidia, 1 AE of Carteia.	Parker 1992, n° 282; Strauss 2013, n° 133.
Megadim A	Israel: Off Nahal Megadim, near 'Atlit; shallow.	early 1st c.	A hoard of 55 Ptolemaic AE; a hoard of 19 Ptolemaic tetradrachms; a hoard of 7 Lycian, Ptolemaic and Seleucid AE.	Parker 1992, n° 689; Strauss 2013, n° 60.
Cap Sicié	France: Near Les Deux Frères in the anchorage of Le Bruse; 40 m depth.	75-70	A hoard of 20 denarii.	Parker 1992, n° 198; Strauss 2013, n° 7621.
Cap Camarat B	France: At Cap Camarat, near Saint Tropez; 41 m depth.	75-25	Roman asses.	Parker 1992, n° 180; Strauss 2013, n° 187.

La Madrague de Giens	France: Off the N side of the Giens promontory; 18-21 m depth	70-50	20 AE, 15 denarii.	Parker 1992, n° 616; Strauss 2013, n° 8023.
Antikythera	Greece: NE side of Antikythera; 50-60 m depth.	60	A hoard of 36 cistophoric tetradrachms; 2 AE of Katane, 1 AE of Panormos, 1 AE of Knidos, 2 AE of Ephesos, 34 unidentifiable AE.	Parker 1992, n° 44; Strauss 2013, n° 69.
Haifa	Israel: Off the Haifa shore.	mid 1st c.	A hoard of Ptolemaic tetradrachms (approximately 40 kg).	Strauss 2013, n° 59.
Le Grotticelle	Italy: Between Ventotene and S. Stefano, Pontine Islands; 42-45 m depth.	mid 1st c.	Some specimens.	Parker 1992, n° 486; Strauss 2013, n° 9.
Dramont A	France: In Saint Rafael bay, SW of Île d'Or; 36 m depth.	mid 1st c.	1 Roman ass, 1 denarius (82 BC).	Parker 1992, n° 371; Strauss 2013, n° 7789.
Plane A	France: Between the islands of Plane and Riou; 20 m depth.	50	1 AE of Cese-Tarraco.	Parker 1992, n° 819; Strauss 2013, n° 8209.
Le Titan	France: Off the E tip of Île du Levant; 27-29 m depth.	50-45	2 Roman semiunciae.	Parker 1992, n° 1149; Strauss 2013, n° 8525.
Fos A	France: 1 km off Fos-sur-Mer; 8-10 m depth.	50-25	1 Roman ass.	Parker 1992, n° 422; Strauss 2013, n° 7839.
Le Grand Radeau	France: On the beach of Le Grand Radeau, S/SE of L'Étang d'Icard.	45-35	1 denarius (Gn. Pompeius, 46/45 BC).	Parker 1992, n° 475; Strauss 2013, n° 7891.
Capo Rasocolmo A	Italy: W of Capo Rasocolmo, Sicily; 8m depth.	36	34 denarii, asses, semisses (42/40-mid 30s BC).	Parker 1992, n° 247; Strauss 2013, n° 7670.

Table 2. Shipwrecks of the 3rd-1st c. BC where coins have been reported.

The condition of the coins

Usually, coins uncovered from shipwrecks are not in the best of condition. Unless circumstances are exceptional, coins – especially those of base metal – would succumb to the ravages of marine environment. To the above, it should be added in certain cases the effect of the cleaning process at the laboratory. It is not uncommon in the cases of groups of coins, the latter to be found in masses with corrosion products and incrustations.

When the "Sophikon, 1893" hoard (*IGCH* 179) was discovered by sponge divers in the sea area of Sophiko – ancient Solygeia – in Northeastern Peloponnese, its coins were stuck together forming a solid heavy bulk[6]. In addition to the corrosion caused by the marine environment, coins had undergone chemical cleaning as well in order to separate them and study them further[7]. This procedure altered their initial weight.

6 Svoronos 1899, 289-290.

7 *Ibid.*, 295; *id.* 1907, 35.

Similarly, the coins from the "Antikythera" shipwreck, that were retrieved during the 1976 supplementary investigation carried out by the Greek Archaeological Service and J.-Y. Cousteau's oceonographic "Calypso", were accumulated in masses with corrosion products and incrustations. After they were separated and cleaned at the National Archaeological Museum, it was determined that they included a hoard of 36 silver cistophoric tetradrachms and more than 40 bronze coins. Most of the silver coins are in an advanced state of corrosion, some to such a degree that they present extensive wear on their surfaces and/or loss of material around their circumference, or have been broken. Their corrosion, together with the effects of chemical cleaning, has resulted in the reduction of each coin's initial weight. Moreover, the number of bronze coins cannot be determined with greater precision since there are still some small bronze lamps of coins that could not be broken apart. In addition, most are in an advanced state of corrosion or mineralized, making it impossible to identify only but a very few[8].

The "Pantelleria, 2013" hoard was found in Cala Tramontana at 13 m depth and about 50 m southwest of a shipwreck site. Its 3,471 bronze coins were dispersed fairly evenly over an area of 4 x 4 m and had a thick, green, grainy encrustation characteristic of bronze oxidation. Following their recovery and delivery to a conservation laboratory at the Soprintendenza dei Beni Culturali di Trapani, on-site analysis revealed that their average weight seemed to be slightly reduced, probably due to the loss of material by oxidation[9].

The coin evidence for dating

In general, coins are considered to function as a fairly reliable tool for dating archaeological assemblages, when all the details of numismatic testimony are taken into account. One of these concerns the date of issue of the latest coins, that forms a *terminus post quem*, with the period of their circulation marked by their date of issue and the date of their deposit in an archaeological assemblage. It should be always born in mind that the potential for this particular means of dating is limited in the cases where the numismatic material is corroded. The corrosion does not allow one to determine the degree of wear on the coins, which would be suggestive of their having circulated over a shorter or longer period. The chronology of a wreck becomes less difficult if there were coin hoards on board and/or the cargo of the ship contained well-dated artefacts, then the proposed dating of the wreck should be deduced by combining all the evidence.

8 Tselekas 2012, 216-217.

9 Abelli *et al.* 2014,349.

There are certain examples indicative of the above.

The "Kyrenia" shipwreck produced a few corroded bronze coins. Among them there are issues of Demetrios I Poliorketes (306-283 BC), which indicates that the ship sank in the early 3rd c. BC[10].

The "Punta Scaletta" shipwreck produced 13 coins, which included 1 silver and 3 bronze specimens of Neapolis, 1 bronze victoriate and 1 bronze of Ptolemy VI Philometor (181-146 BC). The numismatic evidence supports the dating of the pottery found at the site in the 130s BC thus indicating a date 140-130 BC for the wreck[11].

The "Megadim A" shipwreck[12] revealed three hoards: one of 55 Ptolemaic bronze coins, mainly issues of Cleopatra III and Ptolemy IX (116-107 BC)[13]; one of 19 Ptolemaic silver tetratrachms, containing issues of Ptolemy VIII Euergetes II (145-116 BC), Cleopatra III and Ptolemy IX, and Ptolemy X Alexander I (101-88 BC)[14]; and one of 7 bronze coins, with 1 Lycian, 4 Ptolemaic and 2 Seleucid issues[15]. The latest identifiable coin from the three hoards, a tetradrachm of Ptolemy X issued in 100/99 BC, places the shipwreck in the beginning of the 1st c. BC[16].

The "Cap Sicié" shipwreck produced a hoard of 20 Roman Republican denarii. The latest denarius is an issue of L. Rutilius Flaccus (77 BC), which supplies a *terminus post quem* for the ship's final voyage[17].

In the case of the "Antikythera" shipwreck the "Antikythera, 1976" hoard (*CH* VIII [1994], 521) of 36 cistophoric tetradrachms offers the most secure dating indication for the shipwreck, as far as numismatics is concerned. Thirty-two specimens issued between 104 and 67 BC come from the mint at Pergamon. The other 4 are from the Ephesos mint, and are dated between 94/93 (or 89/88) and 82/81 (or 77/76) BC[18]. The fact that, on one hand the latest issues included are from the years 76-67 BC, and on the other that it contains no issues from the years 59-49 BC, suggests that the group was probably closed prior to 60 BC. However, the absence from the hoard of issues containing the names of Roman proconsuls may be entirely accidental. In this case, one should not rule out the possibility that the group

10 A certain ambiguity is observed with regards to the coins discovered in the "Kyrenia" shipwreck. In Katzev 1970, 8-9 is reported that four coins were found, "One of these was minted during the reign of Antigonos Monopthalmos (316-301 BC) and the other struck in the reign of his son, Demetrios Poliorketes (306-294)". Katzev 2005, 78 mentions that "only seven bronze coins minted 306 to 294 were found".

11 Parker 1992, 359.

12 *Ibid.*, 273.

13 Syon *et al.* 2013, 4-5, n° 1-55.

14 *Ibid.*, 5-6, n° 56-74.

15 *Ibid.*, 6-7, n° 78-84.

16 *Ibid.*, 3. An earlier examination of the numismatic material concluded that the latest coins belong to the 130s BC so the wreckage might have happened soon after that; see Raban & Galili 1985, 353.

17 Parker 1992, 106.

18 Tselekas 2012, 216 and 220-225.

was formed even later than 60 BC, made up from earlier cistophori that had remained in circulation at the same time as the proconsular issues[19].

THE COIN EVIDENCE FOR SHIP VOYAGES

In addition to their use as chronology tools, the study of coins provides valuable information regarding ship voyages. The presence of issues from various regions in a shipwreck demonstrates the ship's wide sailing range. This is nicely indicated by the bronze coins, which were intended to facilitate a large number of small-scale financial transactions and were normally circulated within the territory of their issuing authority and neighboring regions. The coins found on the ship probably suggest the place of origin of persons on board and/or were connected with transactions carried out at inns, taverns and on the docksides of various Mediterranean ports.

The "Isla Pedrosa" shipwreck produced 16 bronze coins, of which 2 of Kaiantolos (late 2nd-early 1st c. BC) of the Longostaletes, 6 of Massalia, 1 uncial as of Rome, 1 of Neapolis and 6 unidentifiable specimens which might be of Syracuse and Tarentum. According to the numismatic evidence, the ship should have travelled in Western and Central Mediterranean calling at places in Southern France, Italy and Sicily[20].

The "Cavalière" shipwreck produced 12 bronze coins, of which 1 of Carteia, 5 of Massalia and 5 of Numidia. According to the numismatic evidence alone, the ship, before her loss in the late 2nd c. BC, had visited among other places North Africa and Southern France[21].

The "Grand Bassin B" wreck, dated in 110-90 BC, yielded 4 bronzes of Cese-Tarraco. The coins as well as few other items on board show that the ship had Spanish connections[22].

In the case of the "Antikythera" shipwreck the numismatic evidence is quite suggestive for the ship's last trip. From the 6 identifiable out of 40 bronze coins, 3 are from Sicily and 3 from Asia Minor. The Sicilian coins include 2 of Katane and 1 of Panormos. The Asia Minor coins include 1 of Knidos and 2 of Ephesos.[23] Furthermore, the composition of the "Antikythera, 1976" hoard – with silver issues exclusively circulated in Asia Minor – suggests that some port in the province of Asia must have been one of the ship's final stops before it sank. It has been maintained that since the majority of the hoard's tetradrachms were struck at the Pergamon mint, the most important port on the ship's final voyage has to be sought in that region[24]. That is not necessarily true. Pergamon (together with Ephesos) was the main mint for cistophori; hence, it's reasonable that the size of its numismatic production would be represented in relevant proportion in hoards with cistophoric coins. More indicative in this case is the presence of the 2 bronze issues from Ephesos, which are probably contemporary

19 *Ibid.*, 217-218.

20 Parker 1992, 217-218.

21 *Ibid.*, 133-134.

22 *Ibid.*, 198-199.

23 Tselekas 2012, 217 and 216.

24 Yalouris 1990, 136.

with the hoard's latest tetradrachms. Their more limited circulation vis-à-vis the cistophori demonstrates that the ship had most likely docked at Ephesos before it went under[25].

The chronological and geographic range of the coins from a ship that was transporting goods and passengers to and from different destinations corresponds with the nature of numismatic finds from a large harbour and important commercial center. Such a case is the island of Delos, which after its incorporation into the Athenian realm and its proclamation as a free port in 168 BC became a place of permanent or temporary residence and activity for thousands of people from many parts of the ancient world. In addition to Athenian cleruchy issues, many bronze coins from most of the regions in the central and eastern Mediterranean as well as the Black Sea were found on the island[26].

Similar conclusions are drawn from the "Ascalon, 1988" hoard (*CH* IX [2002], 548) found during excavations. It consists of 47 coins, 1 diobol and 46 bronzes, dated from the end of the 5th to the end of the 2nd c. BC and minted at Teos, Samos, Kos, Knidos, Rhodes, Lycia, Side, Paphos, Antioch and Tyre. All of these places are located along a geographically seafaring route and where remnants of ancient harbours can be traced. Thus, it has been suggested that this hoard may have been gathered by a sailor during his travels[27].

Could there be more coins?

It goes without saying that this is a period when many areas of the Mediterranean were heavily monetized. In those centuries, coins played a most prominent role in transactions. It is expected, in sites such as wrecks, which have a distinctly commercial nature, coins would be in abundance. Yet, there seems to be a discrepancy between the probable and the reality of evidence. What might be the reason behind it?

Most of the shipwrecks are not fully excavated. A grand majority of them have been spotted because of their largest artefacts carrying in their hulls. Many shipwrecks of antiquity are typified by their amphoras manufactured in various places and used for storing and transporting goods[28]. Coins due to their size as well as the marine environment are normally less easily spotted in a non-systematic and appropriately equipped excavation.

When coins are in fact found in a shipwreck, there is no certainty that those were the only ones kept there before the sinking. Absence of coins and valuables suggest that the crew and/or the passengers had time to collect their most precious possessions – or at least some of them – and then abandon ship. Coins could easily be carried away by the escaping people. Consequently, it is very plausible that those coins left behind might well be those their owners had no time to collect or did not think of taking with them or sadly went down with them.

25 Tselekas 2012, 218.
26 Hackens 1970; Hadjidakis 1997, 306.
27 Gitler & Kahanov 2002, 259-268.
28 Parker 1992, 31-35; Gibbins 2001.

Even so, it should be stressed that the general picture might be misleading. It cannot be excluded that in cases where the ships sank near the shore, and their remains rested in water sufficiently shallow for breath-holding divers, salvage operations would most probably been carried later in order to recover the most valuables. The "La Madrague de Giens" shipwreck dated in the second quarter of the 1st c. BC, comprises such a case. Many of the shipboard objects and part of the cargo were salvaged in antiquity by divers, as it is evidenced by their stones lay abandoned in the upper layers of the wreck. Apparently 35 coins were found, 20 bronzes and 15 silver, of which the latest is a denarius of *L. Farsuleius Mensor* (75 BC)[29].

Apparently, this was commonplace as suggested by the silver hoards found in a few shipwreck sites.

One example constitutes the "Sophikon, 1893" hoard (*IGCH* 179). It consists of 945 silver drachms, didrachms and tetradachms and weights more than 6 kg. There are issues of Alexander III (336-323 BC), Philip III Arrhidaios (323-317 BC), Demetrios I Poliorketes (306-283 BC, Antigonos II Gonatas (276-239 BC), Lysimachos (306-281 BC), the Aetolian League, the Boeotian Confederation, Athens, Sparta, Rhodes, Attalos I (241-197 BC), Seleukos I Nikator (312-281 BC), Antiochos I Soter (281-261 BC), Antiochos II Theos (261–246 BC), Seleukos II Kallinikos (246-226/225 BC), Ptolemy I Soter (305-283/282), Ptolemy II Philadelphos (285-246 BC) and Ptolemy III Euergetes (246-222 BC)[30]. The hoard may be connected with a shipwreck occurred in the last decades of the 3rd c. BC in the busy sea-route along the coast of the Argo-Saronic Gulf.

Another is the "Haifa, 1994" hoard, discovered off the Haifa shore and consisted of thousands of silver Ptolemaic tetradrachms. The coins must have been placed in vessels or sacks and over the centuries the bulk of them conglomerated into a lump of more than 23 kg while the rest 1 500-1 700 remained separated. A preliminary assessment of the material has shown that there are issues of Cleopatra III and Ptolemy IX (116-109 BC), Ptolemy X Alexander I (88-80 BC) and Ptolemy XII Neos Dionysos (80-58 BC) minted in Paphos and Alexandria and has suggested that the hoard should have closed in c. 63 BC[31].

A third example concerns the "Antikythera, 1976" hoard. Despite its modest size compared to other hoards, its significance lies in its being the only one discovered to date that consists exclusively of cistophori, whether Attalid or Roman issues, and to have been found outside Asia Minor. It has been argued that this may be related to possible commercial practices. It is likely that some merchants who were making trips back and forth to the Roman province of Asia took cistophori with them upon sailing from some Asia Minor port, in the expectation that they would use them on their next trip back. In this way, they would avoid the services of bankers active in the area who exchanged the coins of other issuing authorities for cistophori charging a commission for doing so[32]. The renewed research at the site inaugurated in Autumn 2014 will demonstrate whether the hoard constitutes the whole or a part of a larger assemblage.

29 Parker 1992, 198-199.

30 Svoronos 1899, 291-296; *id.* 1907.

31 Galili & Sharvit 1999, 17; Ariel & Sokolov 2003, 16.

32 Tselekas 2012, 217-218.

A case of an intentional concealment of coins in the sea in the hope to be retrieved later might be the "Pantelleria, 2011" hoard, which consists of Carthaginian bronzes minted in Sardinia during the First Punic war (264-241 BC). The hoard was found in the middle of the Cala Tramontana bay about 100 m from the shore in shallow depth. Apart from a large, trapezoidal lithic anchor at a distance of 1m, no other artefacts have been found that can associate the coins with a shipwreck. On the above evidence, it has been argued that the coins were carried on a Carthaginian ship headed to Sicily in the course of the First Punic War. As a result of an imminent danger, such as an approaching enemy fleet, the people on-board decided to hide the treasure on the bottom of the sea in relatively low waters. The anchor probably served as a marker to easily locate the spot from the surface and the shallow depth would allow free divers to easily access the hoard[33].

Conclusions

The coins recovered from Hellenistic and Roman Republican shipwrecks constitute an important piece of evidence for the maritime record of that era. Although the number of wreck sites that yielded coins is rather modest, the existed evidence indicates that coinage was carried on board as personal cash of the crew and the passengers as well as for military and trading purposes. The scarcity of coin finds is due to a variety of reasons associated with the very nature of coinage. Coins, due to their small size and value, must have been among the objects first taken by the people abandoning a sinking vessel and must have also been of the high priority material to be recovered during salvage operations. Furthermore, when coins remain at wreck sites for many centuries are affected by the marine environment and are less easily spotted compared to artefacts of larger size in a non-systematic research. Those found – whether isolate specimens or hoards – can offer alongside pottery and other datable artefacts valuable information on the dating of wrecks as well as indications for the possible ship traveling routes.

33 Abelli *et al.* 2014, 349-350.

Aigeai and Amphipolis: Numismatic Circulation in two Major Macedonian Cities

Sophia Kremydi, Katerina Chryssanthaki-Nagle

The study of the numismatic finds of Aigeai and Amphipolis has been incorporated in the Research Programme: "Inscriptions and Coins: New documents from ancient Macedonia (InCoMac)" realised by the Section of Greek and Roman Antiquity of the Institute of Historical Studies, and has been funded by the "Aristeia" Program for the period 2012-2015. In addition to the study of the numismatic finds of the two cities, this collaborative research project also includes the publication of a monograph on the coinage of the Macedonian *ethnos* and regions during the Hellenistic period, the publication of the *corpus* of the inscriptions of western Macedonia (the area known since antiquity as the third Macedonian district), as well as the creation of a digital archive on the inscriptions of central Macedonia (second Macedonian district), with the exception of those of Thessalonike, prepared for publication in the series *Inscriptiones Grecae*[1].

Studies of numismatic circulation have multiple aims: they provide an indication concerning the type of currency that was legal tender within a certain city, but also inform us about the movement of people to and from the city being studied. The percentage of "local" *versus* "foreign" coins is important for the discussion on whether "foreign" coins could actually be accepted for use in local transactions. Furthermore, the study of numismatic finds and of their chronological and geographical dispersion may highlight various aspects of the history of the city and add valuable information concerning the dating and function of public or private buildings. The difference of circulation patterns within different areas of a city may also be revealing regarding the use of coinage.

Aigeai and Amphipolis were two important cities in Macedonia with a different historical background. Aigeai, a community taken over by the Temenids at an early date, was a Macedonian city *per excellence*. Amphipolis, on the other hand, was a 5th c. Athenian colony that surrendered to Philip II in 357 and gradually became an important Hellenistic center. A

1 The project has been funded by the Operational Program "Education and Lifelong Learning" (Aristeia) of the Ministry of Education, Lifelong Learning, and Religious Affairs, in the framework of the NRSF 2007-2013 and is being directed by S. Kremydi. Participants include: P. Paschidis, D. Adrianou, M. Kalaitzi (KERA, IHR), K. Chryssanthaki-Nagle (Paris Ouest, Nanterre), S. Psoma (Kapodistrian University of Athens), A. Iakovidou and E. Gondalez-Martin (Post-doc collaborators). The former director of the KERA and member of the Academy of Athens, Prof. M. Hatzopoulos is also a member of the research team.

comparative study of the coinage circulating in these two major cities is of obvious interest for the study of ancient Macedonia.

Our present paper on the numismatic finds at Aigeai and Amphipolis aims at presenting the preliminary results of our research on the coin finds of the two cities. The study is far from complete, a full catalogue has not yet been composed and parts of the material require further study. However, this conference seemed like the ideal occasion to present our first thoughts and open the discussion. The material of Amphipolis has been studied by K. Chryssanthaki-Nagle whereas that of Aigeai by S. Kremydi. The contribution of A. Iakovidou has been essential for the identification of the coins and their entry in the database.

Aigeai

Aigeai had been the usual seat of the Temenids from the foundation of the kingdom until the early 6th c. BC. The city was situated on the foothills of the Pierian mountains and controlled the passages to the central plain of Pieria, as well as the crossing of the Haliakmon river[2]. The establishment of the Macedonians at Aigeai must have occurred between the end of the eight and the first half of the 6th c. BC, but the precise date cannot be established since existing evidence relies exclusively on the literary tradition recording ancient myths[3]. The placement of the ancient city of Aigeai on the site of the modern villages of Vergina-Palatitsia was first proposed by Nicolas Hammond in 1968[4], an hypothesis that has been confirmed by archaeological evidence[5].

The ancient city was first visited by L. Heuzey in 1855. Heuzey anticipated the importance of the city for the history of ancient Macedonia and returned for a second mission with Henri Daumet in 1861, in order to conduct excavations in the "Propylon", a building that was proven to be a Palace. In their joint publication Heuzey proposed the identification of the city with Balla, and Daumet provided all the details and drawings of the monumental building[6]. Archaeological fieldwork began once again after the incorporation of Macedonia into the modern Greek state in the 20th c. Excavations have brought to light an important part of the ancient fortification, whose earlier phases date from the 5th c., new evidence regarding the monumental Palace, built on the middle slope of the hill, and have revealed a theater just below. Less is known concerning the city, situated in the plain to the north of the Palace. Two important sanctuaries, that of Eukleia with offerings of queen Eurydike and that of the Mother of the Gods, have been excavated and studied; both lie within the fortifications of

2 Hammond 1972, 156.

3 Diod. 7.16, records a Delphic oracle for the foundation of the city. For full discussion of this and other literary sources see: M. Hatzopoulos, in: M. Hatzopoulos, L. Loukopoulou, P. Paschidis, *Ἐπιγραφές Κάτω Μακεδονίας*, τόμος Β', Athens, 2016.

4 Hammond 1970, 64-67.

5 Andronikos 1991, 55-85. Also Hatzopoulos 1996b, 264-269. For a recent overview of the long discussion on the location of the city and all the objections that have been raised see: M. Hatzopoulos in: M. Hatzopoulos, L. Loukopoulou, P. Paschidis, *Ἐπιγραφές Κάτω Μακεδονίας*, τόμος Β', Athens, 2016.

6 Heuzey & Daumet 1876, 175-238.

the city. The part of the city, however that has received most attention is the cemetery. Apart from the monumental Macedonian tombs, several of which are undoubtedly royal, earlier monumental cist burials have also been discovered not far from the Great Tumulus, as well as a large number of simple pit graves that have provided a considerable number of coins[7].

The ancient city of Aigeai is actually being excavated by the University of Thessalonike and the Ephorate of Antiquities of Emathia[8]. The numismatic material we are studying includes the finds held at the Ephorate of Antiquities that derive from recent excavations of the last few decades from the cemeteries, the city and the Palace, as well as earlier finds from excavations that took place in the 1950s and 1960s, mainly at the Palace. For the purpose of the present contribution we have added the few coins from the Sanctuary of the Mother of the Gods published by I. Touratsoglou and S. Drougou[9], as well as the coin finds from the Sanctuary of Eukleia discussed by A. Donas[10].

The general pattern of the coin finds

The main bulk (84%, 410 specimens) of the securely identified coins found at Aigeai belong to the period between the reign of Perdiccas II (451-413 a.C.) and the Julioclaudians (fig. 1). After that we only have fifteen Roman and Roman Provincial coins that date to the 2nd and 3rd c. AD. The late Roman coins are more abundant: thirty seven date to the 4th and early 5th c. AD. For the period between the 5th and the 19th c. we only have eleven Byzantine coins. Finally for the 19th and 20th c. we count eleven Ottoman, one Italian and seven contemporary Greek coins. This general pattern is in accordance with archeological and other evidence on the history of the site. Archeological research has shown that the city suffered a violent landslip which destroyed its buildings in the beginning of the 1st c. AD. and was thereafter abandoned[11]. Epigraphic evidence has shown that the community continued to exist in the imperial period, most probably as a *kome* dependent on the prosperous city of Beroia[12]. In the early Christian period the settlement was transferred and a small basilica, built from ancient material was erected to the northeast of the old cemetery[13]. The late Roman coins which have come to light at Aigeai are certainly connected with the pillaging of the ruins that were used as building material for the new settlement and its church. Between the 6th and the 19th c., visit to the ruins must have been random, as shown by the very small

7 For an overview of the archaeological finds at Vergina and selective bibliography see Drougou 2011. In the same volume also see Kottaridi 2011 and Saatsoglou-Paliadeli 2011. More extended bibliography including references to the archaeological reports may be found in Drougou & Saatsoglou-Paliadeli 2005, 312-315.

8 Professors S. Drougou, C. Paliadeli and P. Faklaris from the University of Thessaloniki and Dr A. Kottaridi, director of the Ephorate of Antiquities of Emathia (former 17th Ephorate of Prehistoric and Classical Antiquities) continue the work of the late Prof. M. Andronikos.

9 Touratsoglou & Drougou 2000.

10 Donas 2008

11 Kottaridi, ed. 2009, 21. The same has been shown for the acropolis of the city: Faklaris 1996, 74-75.

12 The ethnic and the name of the city are mentioned in two inscriptions dating to the imperial period: Petsas *et al.* 2000, n° 73 and 103.

13 Kottaridi 2006, 778.

number of Byzantine coins found on the site. Finally the 19th and 20th c. specimens could be connected to the revived interest in the antiquities, and to the foundation of the modern village in 1922. These few remarks are aimed at showing that the general pattern of the coin finds is in accordance with other evidence on the history of the site and can therefore be used as a reliable source.

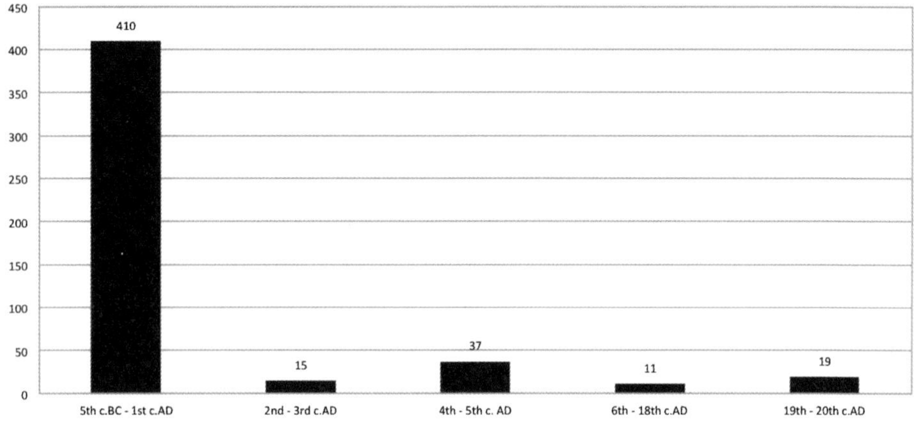

Fig. 1. General pattern of circulation at Aigeai

The currency circulating in the ancient city of Aigeai

As a city that belonged to the Macedonian kingdom, Aigeai never had a coinage of its own. The goat staters, once connected to this city because of their iconography may now be attributed to a mint in the region of the Pangaion[14]. As for the suggestion of Martin Price that Aigeai could have been the seat of a third royal mint, this is unlikely and, in any case, very hard to prove[15].

As shown by the coin finds and as one would certainly expect, the main currency that circulated in the city was the local coinage. Macedonian coins form the vast majority (92%) of our material and include the regal issues down to Perseus, the bronzes in the name of the Macedonians, the Amphaxians and the Botteatai, those minted under the Roman administration and finally the coins of the cities of Thessalonike, Pella and Amphipolis, that

14 Psoma 2003.

15 Price 1991, 109-111, tentatively attributed part of the "eagle coinage" to a mint that worked for a limited period at Aigeai. Troxell 1997 accepted the traditional identification of Amphipolis for the main Macedonian mint but noted, p. 19: "This name (Amphipolis) is used with great reluctance, for I have no confidence that this city, rather than Pella or perhaps Aegae or Philippi, was the source of this enormous output". Aigeai, however, seems a highly improbable location for the royal mint because of its large distance from the source of silver and its unfavourable position for the distribution of coins towards the east.

are found in considerable numbers. To these we should also add the Roman Provincial coins which are all Macedonian (fig. 2).

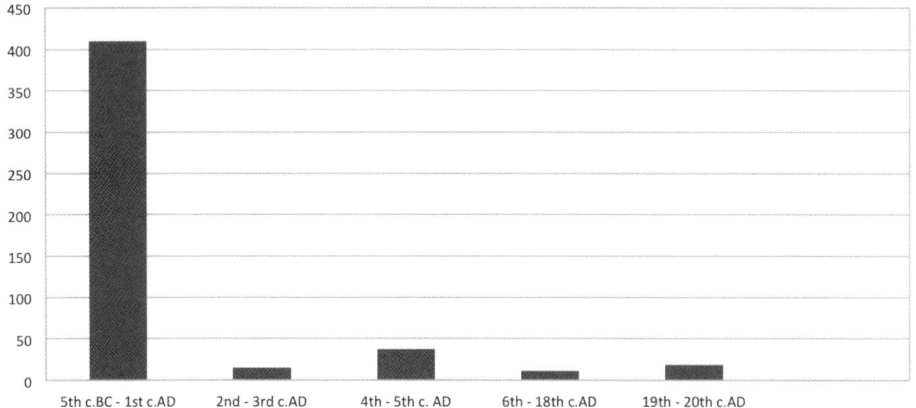

Fig. 2. Aigeai: Macedonian coins.

The earliest coins found at Aigeai are three light tetrobols of Perdiccas II and an hemiobol of Archelaos, the latter found as a votive offering in a tomb. The absence of heavy tetrobols of Pediccas II confirms their circulation outside the borders of the Macedonian kingdom. Bronzes of Archelaos' successors, Aeropos, Amyntas II and Pausanias are present in very small numbers. As in most sites in Macedonia, bronzes at Aigeai become abundant under Amyntas III. Only one specimen of this ruler belongs to the early Herakles / forepart of boar issue, whereas the other twenty four are of the very common Herakles / eagle devouring snake type that dates to the latter part of Amyntas reign. This is an abundant coinage that has been found in considerable numbers, not only in Macedonia but also in the Chalkidike. The excavations at Olynthos have brought to light an important number of these coins which probably arrived in the region during the war between the Spartans and the Chalkidians between 382 and 379, in which Macedonia supported the Spartans[16]. As we shall see below, such coins were also found at Amphipolis. The two coins of Pydna from the sanctuary of Eukleia copied the types of Amyntas, and could have easily circulated at Aigeai since they could hardly be distinguished from the royal coins[17]. During the reign of Amyntas III, Macedonia was ravaged both by the Illyrians in 393 and by the Chalcidians in 383 that invaded from the east "freed" the Macedonian cities and reached Pella[18]. This episode was probably the reason behind the creation of a second royal center at Pella by Amyntas, who realised that he needed a strong bases further east in order to protect his kingdom[19]. But

16 Psoma 2011.

17 For the coinage of Pydna see Tselekas 1996a and Gatzolis 2010, 408-410.

18 Xen., *Hell.*, 5.2.12-13.

19 First suggested by M. B. Hatzopoulos in Hatzopoulos & Loukopoulou 1987, 42-44.

the creation of the second capital did not mean that Aigeai were abandoned. Neither the literary sources nor the archaeological finds, including coins, show any such sign. In fact the majority of royal coins found at Aigeai belong to the 4th c. and are mainly coins of Philip II and Alexander III. A few specimens in precious metal make their appearance amongst these issues: A gold fraction of Philip II from the mint of Pella, the only gold coin in our sample, a fifth of the tetradrachm of the same ruler, and ten drachms of Alexander, eight of which belong to a small hoard that was discovered in the destruction layer of a private residence situated just outside the city walls. The coins of the hoard date between 328 and 301 BC and come from mints in Asia Minor[20] (fig. 3-10). Coins of Cassander belong to the period both before and after he resumed the royal title. In total we count 234 regal coins dating to the 4th c., that is to the period from the death of Archelaos to the reign of Cassander.

Coins of the IIIrd c. are much less abundant. Between Demetrios Poliorketes and Antigonos we only have 61 specimens, all of them bronze. Most of the coins of Demetrios belong to issues of the shield / helmet type that bear the monogram of the king for which attribution to Macedonia is certain. However, we also find one specimen of the crested male head / prow type, attributed by Newell to eastern mints, for which Thessalian and Peloponnesian provenances have also been attested[21]. Another two specimens belong to the Poseidon / prow issues, attributed by Newell to mints in Asia Minor or Caria; a coin of this type has also been found in a hoard from Athens[22]. The attributions of bronze coins of Demetrios Poliorketes therefore needs to be reconsidered in the light of new evidence on their circulation. The most abundant 3rd c. royal coins found at Aigeai are the bronzes in the name of Antigonos, and especially the Athena / Pan coins. These are abundant issues with interesting circulation patterns. They are found in large numbers, not only in Macedonia, but also in areas under Macedonian control and are often countermarked. Their circulation shows that they most probably served as garrison payments[23]. On the whole, the Macedonian coins of the 3rd c. found at Aigeai are much more limited in numbers than those of the fourth (fig. 11). Is this the result of chance, because of the sectors of the city that have been excavated, or should it be taken as an indication that the production of bronze coinage was more limited during the 3rd c.? Die studies could answer this question, but it is worth noting that a similar pattern is repeated both at Amphipolis and at Pella[24]. It is therefore not improbable that the very large quantities of bronzes, especially those in the name Philip and Alexander, continued to circulate within the 3rd c. and covered, to a certain extent, the needs for local coinage.

The percentage of coins of Philip V and Perseus is relatively high. The coins of Philip V include ten specimens that were struck before Kynoskephalai and should therefore be added to our 3rd c. column. But still the *equilibrium* with the 4th c. material remains practically

20 The coins were found in 2013, during the excavations realised for the construction of the new Museum of Vergina, just outside the modern village. Two are from Lampsakos (Price 1382, 1406), three from Abydos (?) (Price 1528, 1541), one from "Teos" (Price 2285), one from Asia Minor (?) (Price 1501 or 1503) and one is uncertain.

21 Weir 2007, 17.

22 *IGCH* 157; Kroll 1979, 152.

23 See *id.* 1993, 166.

24 See below for Amphipolis and the paper of N. Akamatis in this volume for Pella.

Fig. 3. Drachm of Alexander III, BM 5905.

Fig. 4. Drachm of Alexander III, BM 5906.

Fig. 5. Drachm of Alexander III, BM 5907.

Fig. 6. Drachm of Alexander III, BM 5908.

Fig. 7. Drachm of Alexander III, BM 5909.

Fig. 8. Drachm of Alexander III, BM 5910.

Fig. 9. Drachm of Alexander III, BM 5911.

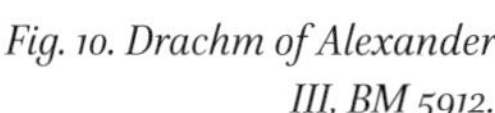

Fig. 10. Drachm of Alexander III, BM 5912.

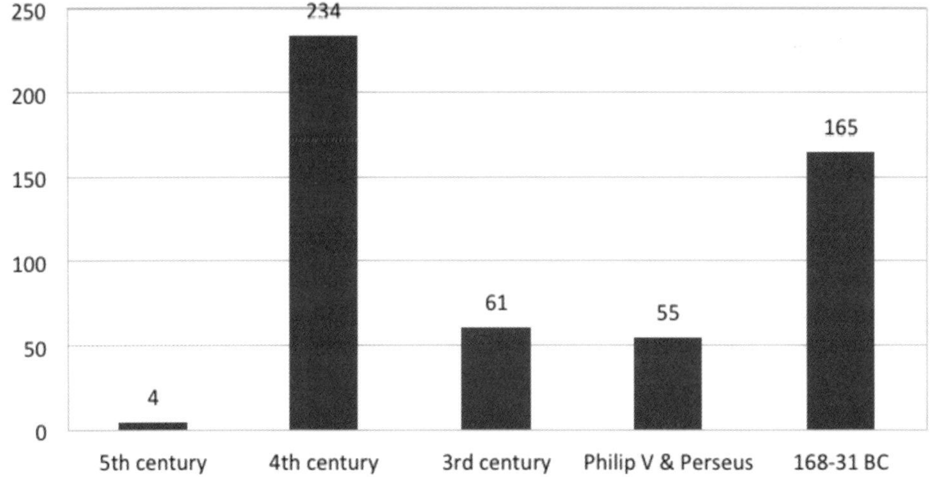

Fig. 11. Aigeai: Macedonian coins per period.

unchanged. The relatively large number of coins of Perseus found at Aigeai, fifteen specimens for only seven years of reign, could reflect the unsecure conditions that prevailed in the city during the third Macedonian war.

Coins of the cities of Thessalonike, Amphipolis and Pella were found in large numbers at Aigeai. The material presented in this paper includes 104 specimens of this type; to this we could add a hoard of 54 coins of the three cities discovered in the Acropolis in 1993[25], as well as the 41 coins of the cities found in the "Hellenistic house" excavated by Bettina Tsigarida in the 1980's and 1990's[26]. The correct dating of these coins, discovered in large numbers in Macedonia, is of crucial importance, not only for the history of the coinage, but also for our understanding of the history of the cities after the Roman conquest. The proposal for their dating between 187 and 168[27] has not been confirmed by hoard evidence and although their inauguration date cannot yet be established with certainty, they were certainly issued and circulated in large numbers after the fall of the monarchy, in the second half of the second and the first half of the 1st c. BC[28]. The relatively large number of these coins found at Aigeai, to which we should add the few bronzes of the Roman quaestors, as well as the Roman Republican specimens, shows an important monetary circulation in the city after the battle of Pydna and the fall of the monarchy.

Foreign coins at Aigeai

The non Macedonian coins discovered at Aigeai are a small percentage of the total currency found on the site and form less than 8% of the total material examined. Their geographical range is limited to neighbouring areas with close ties to Macedonia. From Thessaly we have individual specimens from the mints of Larissa, Pharsalos, Gomphoi, Pelinna and perhaps Gyrtone dated to the 4th and 3rd c., as well as specimens of the Magnetes and the Thessalian League dated to the 2nd or 1st c. BC. From the regions east of Macedonia we have two coins of the Chalkidian League, one of the Bottiaioi and one of Poteidaia, all issues dating before the time of Philip II, and across the Strymon, two coins of Neapolis and three of Philippi. The mint of the four coins of Lysimachus with the Athena / lion types is not certain, but they could have been considered legal tender since Lysimachus ruled Macedonia for a short period. From the areas west of Macedonia we count one coin of the Chaones, two probably from Ambrakia, two of the Akarnanian League and two from Dyrrhachium. We may also mention one tetrobol and one bronze of Histiaia, one Athenian tetradrachm and two Corinthian staters. Finally a few Republican bronzes and denarii have been discovered, the earliest silver dating to 120 BC. The only Greek coin to come from a distant region is a silver obol from Taras, dated to *c.* 325-280 BC (fig. 12)[29]. The only possible explanation for this

25 *CH* IX, 229. Faklaris 1993, 63, pl. 20-21.

26 The finds of this excavation sector are included in Gatzolis 2010, 65-74. Out of the 111 coins discovered in this building, 41 (37%) belong to issues of the three cities.

27 Touratsogou 1987, 55. See also Touratsoglou 1993, 38-41 and Drougou & Touratsoglou 2012.

28 Gatzolis 2010, 361-373. Kourempanas 2011a and 2011b.

29 Rutter 2001, 979.

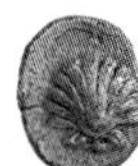 

Fig. 12. Obol of Taras, BM 2812.

unusual find could be that it was brought by the soldiers of Pyrrhos when they returned from their expedition in southern Italy after a demand of the Tarantines in 281 BC[30].

It is obvious that both the number and the geographical range of the foreign coins found at Aigeai is limited. The only foreign coins dating before the reign of Philip II and the expansion of the Macedonian kingdom are the few specimens from the Chalkidike that reflect the relations between Macedonia and the Chalkidian League during the reign of Amyntas III[31]. The rest of the finds come, mostly, from Thessaly, a region that was annexed to the Macedonian kingdom in the period between the reign of Philip II and the end of the 2nd c. BC, as well as from Ambrakia, Akarnania and Histiaia, close allies of the Macedonians during the 3rd c. BC. The presence of the foreign coins at Aigeai, therefore, may be explained by the close relations the Macedonians had to these cities or regions, and these coins must have been brought to Macedonia by soldiers or other officials that had visited them. Non-Macedonian coins were never found as grave offerings in tombs, a fact that shows that the citizens of Aigeai did not consider them as "their" coins. One should note that no coins of Hellenistic rulers, Seleucids or Ptolemies, no coins from the Peloponnese, apart from the Corinthian staters, and no coins from Asia Minor have been included in the material we have studied.

Numismatic evidence for the royal Palace at Aigeai

The ruins of the palace at Aigeai were first visited by L. Heuzey in 1855. Heuzey was impressed by the remains of the palace and compared it to Periclean buildings. In a second mission a few years later, the French archaeologist, accompanied by the architect H. Daumet, began a short excavation whose results were soon published. Since the city had not been correctly identified, the building was interpreted as a prytanée royale and was dated to the second half of the 5th c.[32]. Further excavation of the building began in 1937 under the direction of K. Romaios, Professor at the University of Thessaloniki, but this was interrupted by the war. Research was resumed again in the late 1950's by Prof. C. Makaronas, G. Bakalakis and M. Andronikos. After the retirement of G. Bakalakis in 1975, M. Andronikos took over and focused his research on the excavation of the Great Tumulus. The result of his outstanding finds was the identification of the city with Aigeai and, subsequently, the identification of the monumental building as the seat of the kings. After the passing of Andronikos in 1992, sections of the Palace were excavated once more by his collaborators, Prof. C. Paliadeli and

30 Hammond & Walbank 1988, 246.

31 Psoma 2011, 120-124.

32 Heuzey & Daumet 1876, 203-212 and 224-225.

S. Drougou[33]. In 2007 the 17th Ephorate of Antiquities, under the direction of Dr A. Kottaridi, inaugurated a large project of restoration and reconstruction that provided the opportunity for further excavation and study of this important monument[34].

The extensive number of excavations and the few systematic studies of parts of this important building have led to various proposals regarding its dating. After the initial dating of the *prytaneion* to the time of Archelaos, it was subsequently considered a summer residence of Antigonos Gonatas and was dated accordingly. A coin of Lysimachos, found in what was believed to be a foundation trench, was used by Andronikos to corroborate this dating[35]. This dating was reconsidered by Makaronas in 1971, who suggested the end of the 4th c., a dating also accepted by Andronikos in 1991[36]. Based on the study of architecture, scholars today agree to date the Palace to the second half of the 4th c., although opinions on a more precise dating may differ[37]. Since, however, the dating of the Palace to the reign of Alexander would be highly improbable for historical reasons, dates during the reign of Philip II[38] or Cassander[39] have been proposed. Systematic research on its architectural fragments, such as column capitals and entablature, corroborated by the evidence of a few ceramic finds realised in the context of a large restoration project, has led A. Kottaridi to propose that the construction of the Palace had begun around the middle of the 4th c. BC, or somewhat later, and was accomplished by the time of the death of Philip in 336 BC. She maintained that the Palace, together with the theater just below, the sanctuary of Eukleia a little further north and the second phase of the fortifications (fig. 13) were part of a larger plan of Philip II for the renovation of the ancestral capital. She also confirmed that the whole complex of the Palace, including the smaller *peristylion* to the west, belonged to one architectural phase and furthermore, that no traces of earlier buildings have survived underneath[40].

Since the coins found at the Palace have never been studied, our aim is to isolate them from the rest of the numismatic finds of the city and trace their contribution to the question of the dating of this monumental building. The material we have examined derives from excavations held in 1956 and in the early 1960s, as well as those from the recent excavations held after 2007. All in all we have examined 175 coins, not a very large number; a number however, that allows a pattern to evolve. Out of these we have identified 119 Greek coins, 2 Roman (a denarius dated to 120 BC and an as of Trajan), seven Roman Provincial from Macedonian mints, mainly of the 1st c. AD, 15 Roman, 13 Ottoman, 6 Byzantine and 1 modern coin, whereas 12 remain uncertain. Out of the 119 Greek coins ten belong to non-Macedonian

33 For the history of the excavations of the Palace and an extensive bibliography and discussion see Paliadeli 2007.

34 The first results of this project see Kottaridi, ed. 2009 and especially the chapter by A. Kottaridi with the archaeological results.

35 Andronikos *et al.* 1961, 29-30. This view was repeated by Errington 1993, 165 and n. 17 (translation of a book published in German in 1986).

36 Andronikos 1991, 39. I have not been able to find the publication of Makaronas quoted, without a reference, by Andronikos.

37 Nielsen 1999, 81-88 proposes the second half of the 4th c.

38 Miller 1970, 95-99, esp. 98. Hoepfner 1996, 9-17; Hoepfner 2002, 423 sq.

39 Heermann 1980, esp. 313 sq.; Pandermalis 1987, 579-605.

40 Kottaridi 2009 and *id.* 2011.

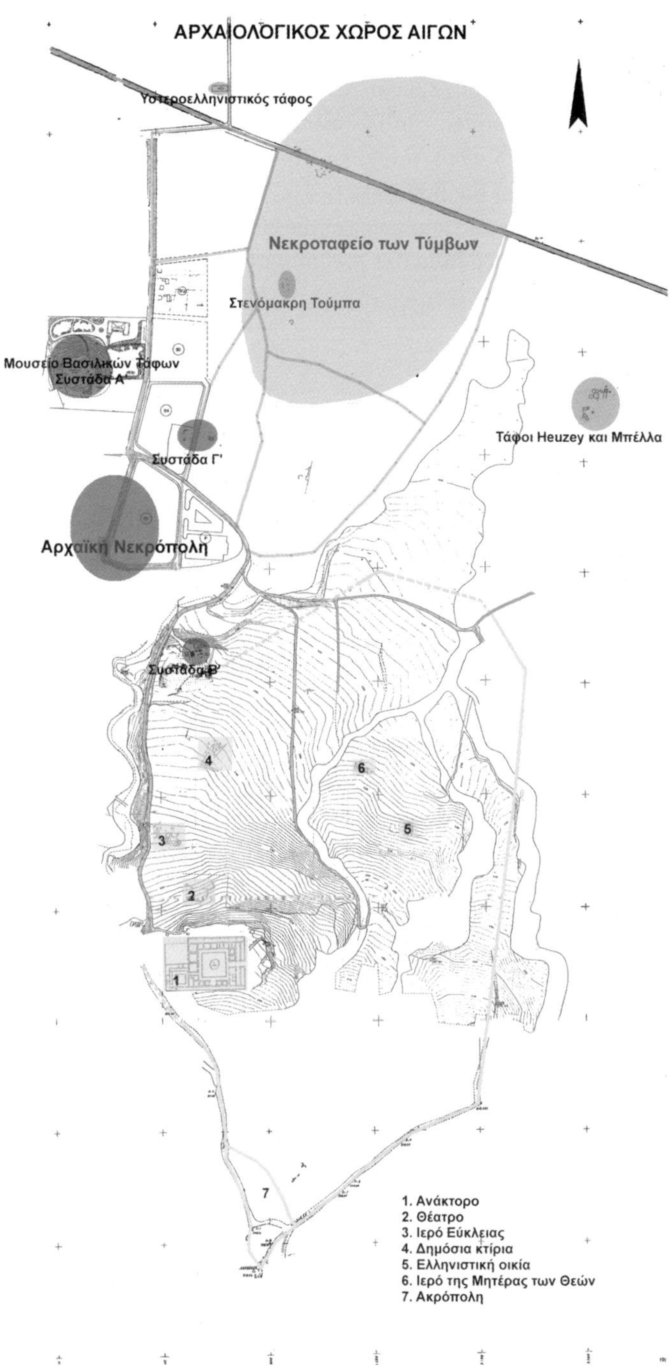

Fig. 13. Plan of Aigeai.

mints such as Corinth, Histiaia, Larissa, Phtiotides Thebai, Akarnania and Athens. All of them are dated before 168 BC. The Macedonian coins are mostly royal (fig. 14). Securely identified royal coins include: 4 specimens of Amyntas III, 1 of Perdiccas III, 12 of Philip II, 10 of Alexander, 6 of Cassander, 3 of Lysimachus, 2 of Demetrios Poliorketes, 2 of Pyrrhos, 1 of "Ptolemy Keraunos" (?), 28 of Antigonos Gonatas, 3 of Philip V and 5 of Perseus. To these one should add one coin of the Botteatai, two of the Macedonians, one bronze struck under the Roman administration and four coins of the cities (Pella 2, Thessalonike 1, Amphipolis 1). Some first conclusions derive from this preliminary list.

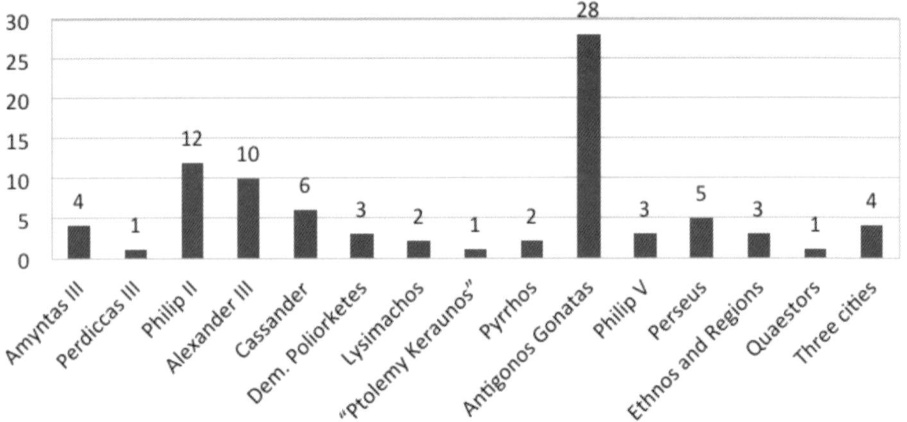

Fig. 14. The Palace: Macedonian coins.

First conclusion: More than 30% of the Greek coins that we have studied from the Palace date to the 4th c. BC, between *c.* 380 and *c.* 300 BC (fig. 15). Their number is high and proves that the initial hypothesis for the construction of the Palace under Antigonos Gonatas was correctly abandoned. Furthermore, the earliest 4th c. coins discovered at the Palace are the bronzes of Amyntas III and Perdiccas III, the father and the elder brother of Philip II. Hoard evidence concerning these coins is straightforward: both the silver and the bronze issues of these two kings circulated and are found in hoards that date down to the reign of Philip II at the latest; they are never found in the same context with coins of Alexander and, even less, of Cassander. Under the condition that these coins derive from stratigraphical layers that belong to the period of use of the building, their presence is strongly in favour of a construction of the Palace under Philip II. To conclude therefore, the numismatic evidence confirms the fact that the palace was constructed in the second half of the 4th c. BC, and points, more specifically, towards the direction of the middle of the century.

Second conclusion: The number of coins of Antigonos Gonatas found at the site of the Palace is surprisingly high. We count 28 coins of Gonatas out of a total of 77 royal coins, which is a percentage of nearly 37%. In the rest of the city (excluding the Palace) we count 17 coins of Gonatas out of a total of 264 royal coins, which is a percentage of 6,5%. The relatively large number of the bronzes of Gonatas found at the Palace, therefore, points at

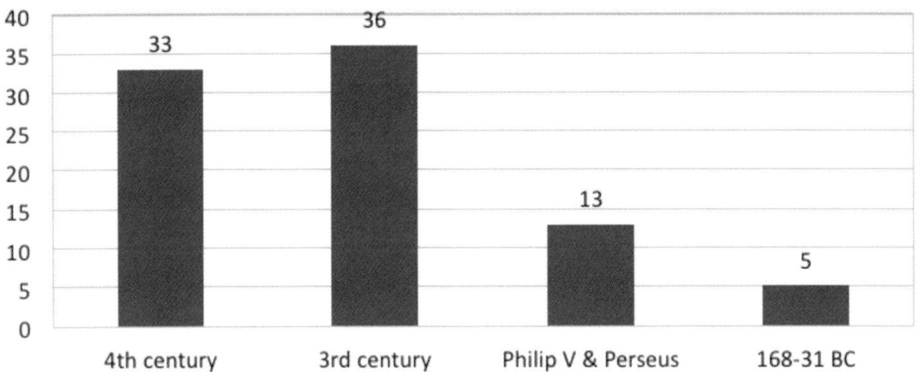

Fig. 15. The Palace: Macedonian coins per period.

a loss rate of coins which was much higher than usual, a fact that must reflect some special circumstances. A high loss rate of coins, together with hoarding, is often related to conditions of insecurity and war. We know that Aigeai, and especially its cemetery, were plundered by the Gauls that Pyrrhuos left as garrisons at the city after taking it over in 274/273 BC[41]. Although the bronze Athena / Pan issues have not been systematically studied, they are usually considered to have been struck later on in his reign. A date only three years after he was established on the throne is perhaps too early for these issues, that – unlike the Herakles / rider and shield / helmet issues – introduce a new iconographic type. The finds of the Palace, therefore, must probably be related to events that took place somewhat later. We know that sometime after the destruction, Gonatas built the Great Tumulus that covered the royal tombs of his ancestors in order to pay tribute to the deceased, to protect their tombs from eventual looting in the future, but also as a landmark of his own power. This was a great enterprise in itself and one could imagine that other public works could have also taken place in the city. Recent research at the Palace has shown that additions to and ameliorations of its structure had taken place during the Hellenistic period[42]. These coins therefore could possibly be connected to a renovation of the Palace at the time of Antigonos Gonatas.

Third conclusion: The coins from the Palace which can be dated after Pydna are extremely scarce. We only have six coins, one bronze of the Macedonians under the Roman administration, four bronzes of the cities and one denarius dated to *c.* 120 BC. As has been stressed above, this is in complete discordance with the evidence from the city as a whole (see fig. 2 and 11). There, the number of coins dating after the fall of the monarchy is high and shows that the city survived and continued to live after the victory of the Romans and the fall of the monarchy, probably in decline, until the physical disaster of the 1st c. BC. The Palace, however, was abandoned after the fall of the last Antigonid king.

41 Plu., *Pyrrh.*, 26.6.
42 A. Kottaridi in : Kottaridi, ed. 2009, 18.

To resume, therefore, numismatic evidence corroborates other archaeological sources for dating the construction of the Palace to the second half of the 4th c. and leaves no doubt that it was abandoned after the battle of Pydna. The end of the 4th c. however, seems to be somewhat late according to our coins. The percentage of the 4th c. coins as a whole is quite high for a monument that was constructed at the end of this century and a certain number of specimens date before Philip and do not circulate after his reign.

The correct dating of the construction of the monumental Palace at Aigeai is of obvious importance for the history of the Kingdom. The theater just below the Palace was discovered in 1981 and was excavated systematically. In 1991 Manolis Andronikos wrote: "It is not easy to put an exact dating on this theater. However, from such evidence as we have I believe that it can be dated to the 4th c. BC. It is worth noting that, aside from its exact date, we may be certain that it was the theater that Philip was murdered in 336 BC since the site of the theater did not change from one period to another. This alternation would not have been possible, firstly because there was no other area easily available which was suitable for the construction of such a building, and secondly because the site of a theatre was endowed with a certain sanctity linked with the worship of Dionysos"[43]. In her subsequent publications, S. Drougou, who had been responsible for the excavation of the site all along, has proposed a dating under Philip II[44]. The very reasonable suggestion that the theater and the Palace belonged to the same architectural plan is another strong indication for the dating of the Palace under Philip II.

Amphipolis

Amphipolis, an important Greek city-state since her foundation by the Athenians in 438/437 and a major Macedonian city after her surrender to Philip II in 357, was founded in a prosperous region, rich in natural resources such as the precious metal mines and the dense forests that provided timber for shipbuilding. Her strategic location enabled the control of the trade route between the Aegean coast and the Thracian hinterland, as well as the routes connecting the lower Strymon valley, with Macedon to the west and Thrace to the east. Athenians, Spartans, the Chalcidian League, the Macedonians and finally the Romans showed a permanent interest in Amphipolis, intervened and took possession of the city during different moments of her long history. The well fortified city, located on a group of hills south of the earlier settlement of Ennea Hodoi (Hill 133) acted as a military base for the Athenian operations in the north Aegean and developed into a naval base for the Macedonian royal fleet of Alexander III before his campaign in Asia. The inclusion of the temple of Artemis Tauropolos at Amphipolis in Alexander's building project illustrates the importance accorded to the city by the Macedonian king[45]. The archaeological evidence,

43 Andronikos *et al.* 1961, 49.

44 In an early publication Drougou 1989, 18, mentioned that the sherds found in the foundation trenches of the seats of the theater date "certainly before the end of the fourth century". See also *id.* 1997. Later on, *id.* 2011, 248 and Drougou & Saatsoglou-Paliadeli 2005, 130 proposed the dating of the theater to the time of Philip II.

45 Diod. 18.4.

mainly epigraphic documents, funerary monuments, ceramics and sculpture, all attest the cosmopolitan character of the city which housed a mixed population since its foundation as an Athenian colony, as well as the artistic and cultural links of Amphipolis with Attic art, local Ionic tradition and the high quality Hellenistic art that flourished in Macedonia[46].

Amphipolis is a "successful" example of the incorporation of a Greek city state into the Macedonian kingdom and probably served as a model for the new cities that Philip founded in the "New Lands" of his kingdom. The numismatic history of Amphipolis completes the epigraphic[47] and archaeological documentation[48] for the period of political and institutional turmoil following the surrender of the city to Philip and its transformation into a Macedonian city. One of the main results presented in the study of the silver and gold civic coinage conducted by C. C. Lorber was that Amphipolis continued to issue her silver autonomous coinage some years after Philip's siege and that the end of the civic coinage and the inauguration of a royal mint was due to an administrative reform by the Macedonian king rather than to a brutal cessation of civic coinage as an expression of Philip's sovereignty[49]. According to O. Picard, the bronze coins of Amphipolis continued to be issued during a short period after his capture of the city in 357 and its annexation in the Macedonian kingdom, as is demonstrated by a limited series of bronze coins of Amphipolis found in the excavations of Thasos[50]. If we follow these scholars, after entering her alliance with the Macedonian king, Amphipolis continued her civic coinage for a short period maintaining the same types for the silver issues and introducing new ones for the bronze ones.

The study and publication of the coin finds of Amphipolis discovered during the excavations of the Athenian Archaeological Society since 1956, under the direction of the late D. Larazidis, and those of the Greek Archaeological Service is an important research project which will shed new light into the monetary history of Amphipolis and will complete, and certainly clarify, the archaeological and epigraphic data. 500 of these excavation coins have been cleaned, restored and included in the current research project.

The coins were found in excavation trenches of the important fortification walls of the city, mainly from gates A, B, C, D and E, from buildings situated outside and near the north city walls, from the sector of the Acropolis and of the region inside and outside the south of part of the east fortification wall (nearby the open air sanctuary of Cybele and Attis) and from the sector underneath the modern archeological museum, within the ancient city where the suggested heroon of Brasidas was localized (fig. 16).

Apart from the few silver coins (8 for the moment), the rest of the coins studied are bronze (Greek, Roman provincial – mainly issues of Amphipolis and Philippi –, Roman imperial, Early Christian and Byzantine and Ottoman) (fig. 17).

46 Lazaridis 1972; *id.* 1997; Koukouli-Chrysanthaki 2011.

47 Hatzopoulos 1991.

48 Lazaridis 1997; Koukouli-Chrysanthaki 2002.

49 Lorber 1990. In her study on Olynthus, S. Psoma proposed the end of a part of the autonomous civic coinage (silver tetradrachms) at 357 BC instead of 354 proposed by Lorber & Psoma 2001, 185-187.

50 Picard 1994a.

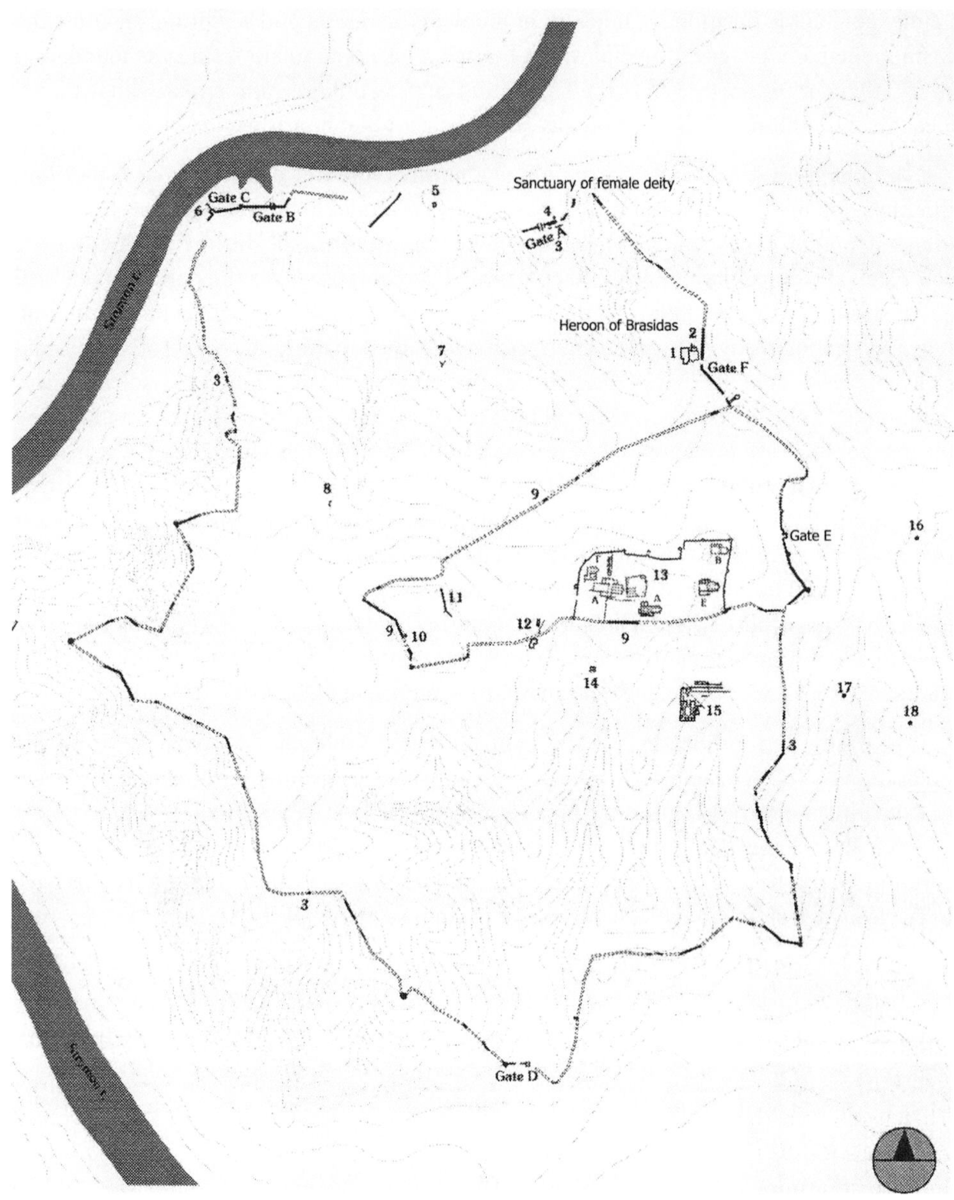

Fig. 16. Plan of Amphipolis.

The material unfortunately does not help to illuminate the earliest phases of the history of the city of Amphipolis, especially the first years of the Athenian colony and the difficult period of the Peloponnesian war, since early numismatic material is absent from our finds. A very interesting question is the circulation of Athenian coins in the colony. For the moment the presence of the 5th c. Athenian coins is only attested by rare random finds from the nearby region. All coins found in the selected excavated sectors date from the beginning of

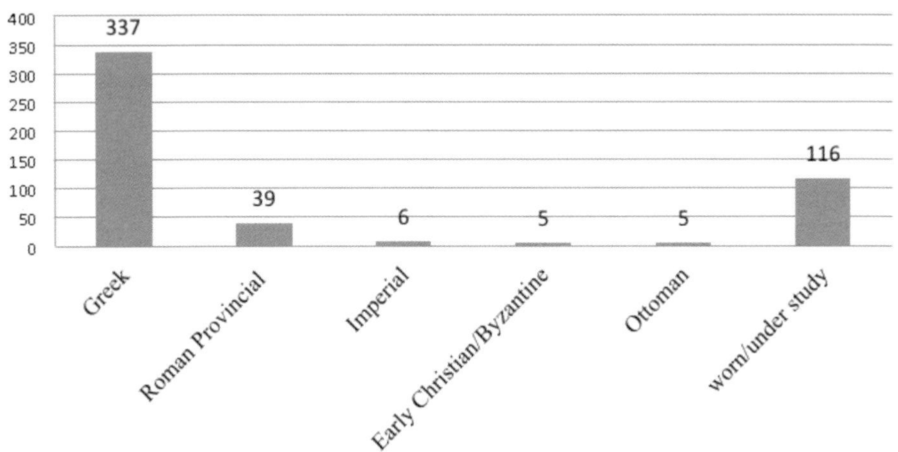

Fig. 17. Amphipolis: Coins incorporated in the current study.

the 4th c. BC and beyond. For example, the trenches on the north side of the fortification wall, as well as those from Gates B and C that lead to the famous wooden bridge of Amphipolis[51], one of the successive phases of which was dated by the archaeologists to the end of the 5th c. BC and associated to the first fortification built by the Athenian general Hagnon on the occasion of Brasidas' intervention between 424 and 422, did not provide any numismatic finds which would corroborate this hypothesis. On the contrary, the numismatic finds can be associated to the extensive reparations of the northern walls at the end of the fourth and the beginning of the third centuries after Philip's siege and a well known flood incident which led to the reconstruction and the raising of the level of gate A[52] (fig. 18).

Coins from the small sanctuary of a female deity[53] and from the constructions located under the foundations of the northern wall[54], near Gate A and B cannot, for the moment, clarify the topographical relationship between Amphipolis and the so-called *proasteion* or the first Athenian colony of Ennea Hodoi, which Thucydides placed at the site of Amphipolis[55]. They testify that the small extra-urbain sanctuary did not function during the 4th c., they contribute mostly to the reconstruction of the monetary circulation of Amphipolis after her incorporation into the Macedonian kingdom and testify to the dominance of the Macedonian royal bronze coinage after 357. Finally, the sector of the so-called Brasidas heroon revealed coins mainly of the second half of the 4th c. that correspond to the period when the heroon was demolished and replaced by a new building complex and when a new urban planning, probably hippodamian, was adopted for the city after the siege of Amphipolis by Philip II.

51 Maniatis *et al.* 2010, n° 1; Lazaridis 1997, 32-36 and fig. 17-18.
52 Lazaridis 1997, 21-26, fig. 8; Koukouli-Chrysanthaki 2011.
53 Lazaridis 1975, 63-65, fig. 2, pl. 51-56; *id.* 1997, 26-29 and fig. 10-12.
54 *Id.* 1997, 30-31.
55 Salviat 2013, 63-78.

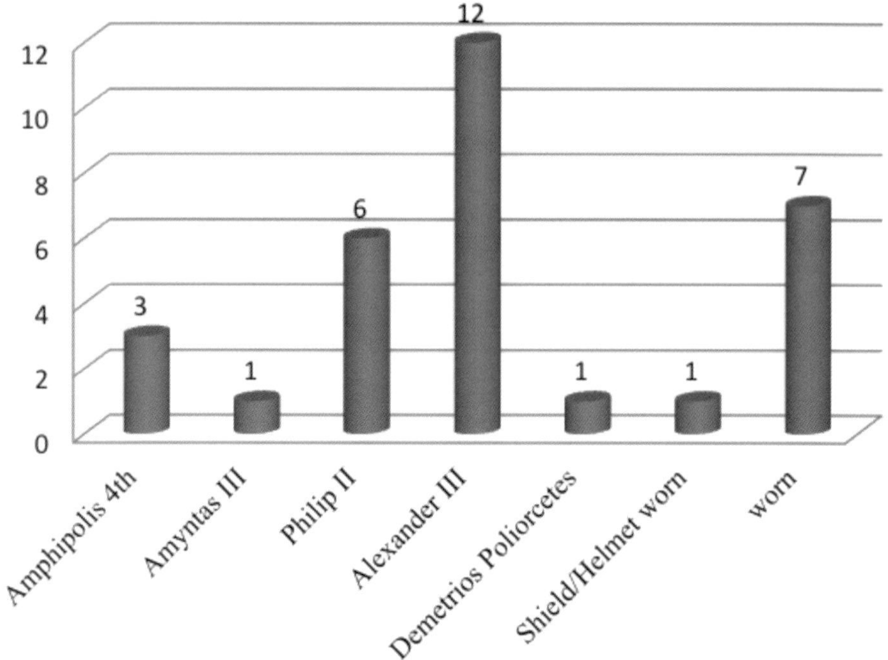

Fig. 18. Amphipolis: Coins from Gate A.

For the moment, the earliest coins (Ainos, Acanthus, Neapolis, Thasos) found at Amphipolis, come from the eastern cemetery of the city[56]. Therefore, the first results of our preliminary study contribute to the reconstruction of the circulation pattern in the city of Amphipolis mainly during the second half of the 4th and the beginning of the 3rd c. BC, in other words during the Macedonian period of the city. Apart for the Amphipolitan bronzes belonging to the first issues of the mint dated before 357, the earliest coins from the sample studied so far include a few specimens of Pausanias, Amyntas III and the Chalcidian League dating to the first half of the 4th c. These coins illustrate the existing alliances between Amphipolis and these leading political powers in the north Aegean during this period and are certainly connected to the presence of Chalcidian settlers and to the political role of the Macedonian royal house in the region of Amphipolis. The absence, for the moment, in the city and the limited presence in the eastern cemetery of coins of Perdiccas III show that the Macedonian garrison in Amphipolis established during his reign left few traces in the numismatic circulation of the city.

The royal Macedonian bronzes arrived massively in the city after 357 and dominated the coin circulation until the end of the Macedonian reign. Bronze coins of Philip II and Alexander III issued during and after their reigns are the most numerous currency found at Amphipolis. It is interesting to underline the important presence of the bronze coins in the

56 Kosmidou 2006.

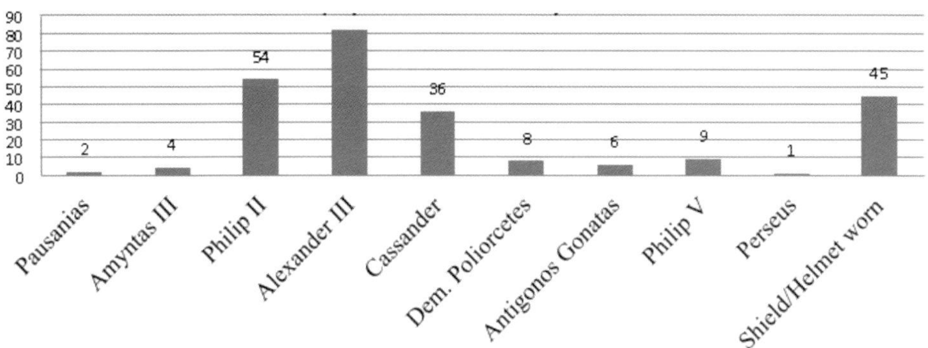

Fig. 19. Macedonian Royal Coins.

name of Alexander III bearing the young diademed head on the obverse and the galloping horse on the reverse which are now associated to Cassander[57]. These issues are followed by the coins of Cassander, the Macedonian shield/ helmet royal bronzes, mostly issues of Demetrios Poliorketes, and the coins of the Macedonian city of Philippi. Later issues of Antigonos Gonatas, Philip V and Perseus are more scarce in our sample. Their limited presence is certainly due to the choice of the excavations sectors (fig. 19).

The cosmopolitan character of Amphipolis, as illustrated by her artistic production and the archeological finds, is not reflected in the numismatic documentation during the late classical and Hellenistic periods since only some isolated foreign coins were found. Coins of Orthagoreia, Maroneia, Abdera, Thasos, Tragilos, Thessaloniki, Pella, Larissa, the Thessalian League, Amphaxitis and Paroreia were present in the city of Amphipolis, whereas few of them dated to the 3rd, 2nd or 1st c. BC.

The image drawn from the coin circulation in the city seems to be confirmed by the coins found in the eastern cemetery of Amphipolis which is the most important cemetery of the late classical and Hellenistic period. The coins used as Charon's fee are mostly royal Macedonian issues of the second half of the 4th and the early 3rd c. BC whereas very few coins date to before or after this period[58]. As for the finds of the imperial period, the main currency found in the burial hoards are the provincial issues of Amphipolis with the addition of very few foreign issues, mainly those of the Roman colony of Philippi.

Finally, an important question which needs to be reconsidered is the date of the beginning and mainly the date of the end of the first phase of the bronze Amphipolitan coinage issued in three denominations before 357, and its eventual circulation after Philip's capture of the city. The beginning of these issues was traditionally placed at the end of the 5th c.[59] and, more recently, to the first decades of the fourth or the second quarter of the 4th c.[60]. It has

57 Gatzolis 2012; *id.* forthcoming.

58 Kosmidou 2006.

59 Gaebler 1935, 32-33, pl. VIII, n° 17-22.

60 Westermark 1987; Psoma 2001, 110.

been proposed by U. Westermark that the bronze coinage of Amphipolis was inaugurated with the B and C denominations bearing the young male diademed head on the obverse and the torch within or without a linear square on the reverse and that the large module (A denomination) with laureate Apollo head was added later, around 370 BC. S. Psoma argued that the three modules were introduced at the same time[61].

Among the sample already studied, the bronze coins of Amphipolis belong to denominations B and mostly C which is more numerous and stylistically more varied. The large denomination, A, is for the moment absent from our sample, testifying that this module was not continued, at least later than 357. However, our preliminary study clearly showed that the last silver obols of Amphipolis bearing the young head with taenia and the medium (denomination B) and mostly the small (denomination C) module bronzes of Amphipolis circulated side by side with the bronze coins of Philip, of Alexander III and of Cassander, as well as with bronze coins of Philippi, since they have been found in the same archaeological strata of the 4th c. BC. As C.C. Lorber has already proposed for the last issues of silver tetradrachms, we can formulate the hypothesis that Amphipolis continued to issue her bronze coinage after Philip's capture of the city in 357 BC and that the small C denomination, identified with the chalkous, circulated side by side with the Macedonian royal bronze coins and completed the royal bronze denominations which were imposed in the internal economic transactions.

For the moment, none of Amphipolis' bronze issues found at Thasos bearing a young head of Heracles on the obverse and a boar or a lion on the reverse have been attested amongst the 500 coins studied. This can be explained if we accept the new date proposed for these coins by S. Psoma, who places these issues bearing a similar iconography with the bronze royal coins of Perdiccas III during the reign of this king and associates them with his Macedonian royal garrison in Amphipolis[62].

To conclude, the partial study of the numismatic documentation of Amphipolis has provided material which dates mostly to the fourth and third centuries and shows that the important Athenian stronghold in Aegean Thrace was successfully transformed into a Macedonian city comparable to the old Macedonian capital of Aegeae. After Philip's siege, Amphipolis, with a new urban plan, received Macedonian population, adopted Macedonian institutions and finally used the Macedonian currency which gradually replaced its own civic coinage.

61 Westermark 1987, 181; Psoma 2001, 110.
62 Psoma *et al.* 2008, 98.

Numismatic Circulation in the Macedonian Kingdom. The Case of Pella

Nikos Akamatis

Excavation over the past decades at Pella has brought to light many aspects of the city's public and domestic life[1]. Monumental complexes, such as the palace and the Agora, public buildings, houses, sanctuaries and cemeteries have been unearthed[2]. An especially interesting find is the city's north wall of the classical period, which was built in the late 4th c. BC and was probably related to the transfer of the Macedonian capital from Aegae to Pella. This fortification was abandoned in the last quarter of the 4th c. BC, because of the city's expansion during the reign of Cassander[3]. In this paper, numismatic material from the south part of Pella, south of the Classical wall, is going to be presented. This material is very important, since it derives from the city of both Classical and Hellenistic periods.

Numismatic material under study comes from three major excavation areas (fig. 1). First, the new entrance of the archaeological site, where came to light three town blocks, in which public buildings, such as a bath, but also pottery and metal workshops have been found[4]. Second, the area of the sanctuaries, where the sanctuary of Darron, a local healing god of the Macedonians, as well as a circular building probably related to a hero cult and other buildings that presumably served cult needs have been excavated[5]. Third, the area of Phacus, the

1 I am grateful to the Honorary Curator of the IZ′ Ephorate of Prehistoric and Classical Antiquities (now Ephorate of Antiquities of Pella) Dr. Maria Lilimpaki-Akamati, for the permission to study the numismatic material from Pella. I also wish to thank Professor Aliki Moustaka of the Aristotle University of Thessaloniki for the interest she has shown in my work, and Professor Ioannis Akamatis of the Aristotle University of Thessaloniki, for reading my text and for his useful comments. My research was partly supported by the Alexander S. Onassis Public Benefit Foundation.

2 For the latest archaeological research at Pella and the history of the city in general see indicatively Papakonstantinou-Diamantourou 1971; Lilimpaki-Akamati & Akamatis, ed. 2003, 11-101; Akamatis 2011; Lilimpaki-Akamati & Akamatis 2012.

3 For the dating of the wall of the Classical city and the location of the cemeteries of the 5th c. BC see Lilimpaki-Akamati & Akamatis 2009. For the Classical city see Lilimpaki-Akamati & Akamatis 2012, 11-16.

4 From this area around 977 coins were studied. For the archaeological research at the new entrance to the site of Pella see Lilimpaki-Akamati 2000a; Lilimpaki-Akamati & Akamatis 2007; *id.* 2008; Lilimpaki-Akamati 2011; *id.* 2013. For a preliminary study of the coins from the bath and the pottery workshop of the "Enimerosis" block see Akamatis 2013a.

5 Excavation at the area of the sanctuaries brought to light around 660 coins. For this specific part of Pella see Lilimpaki-Akamati 1996; Akamatis 2009.

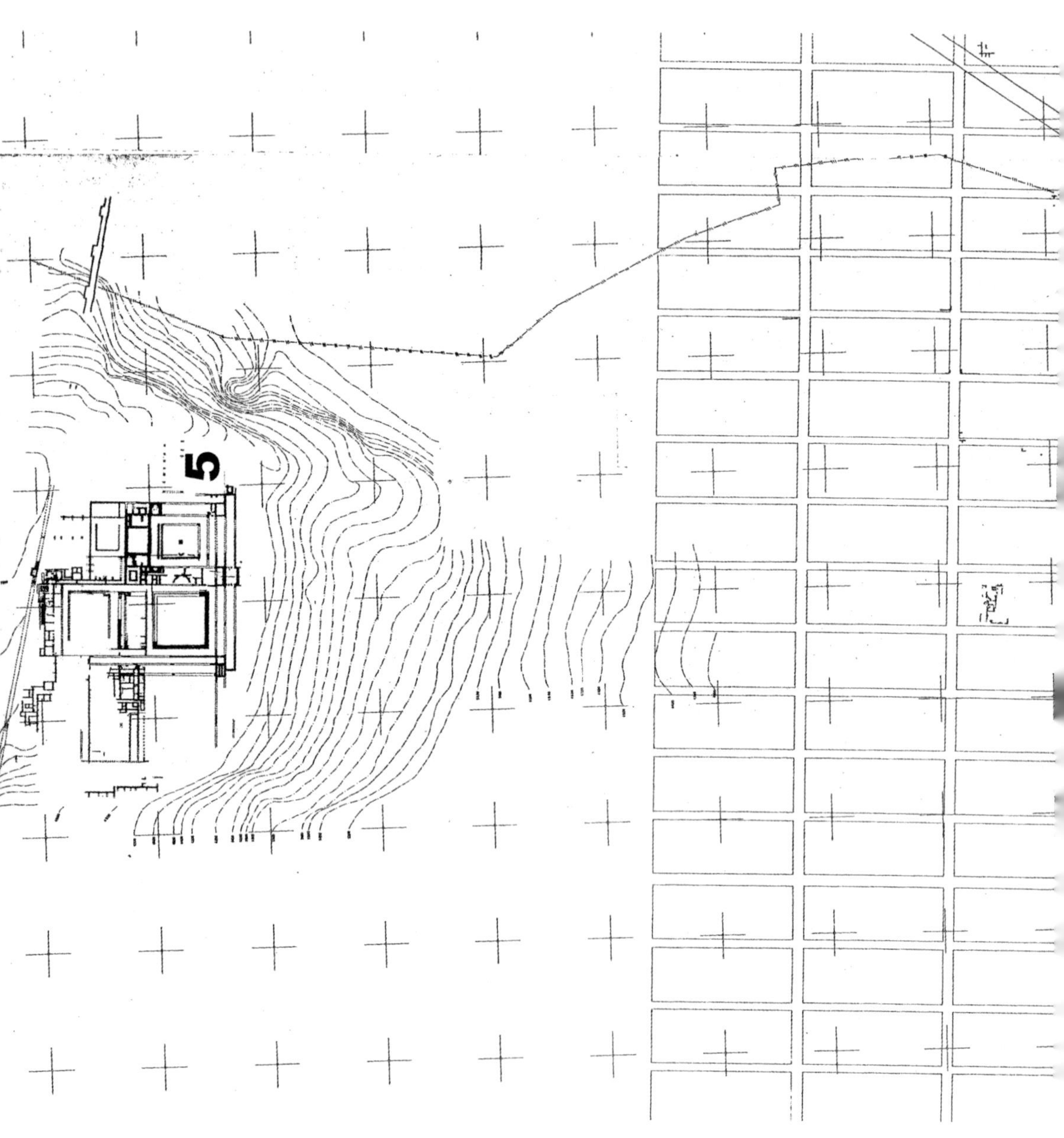
5

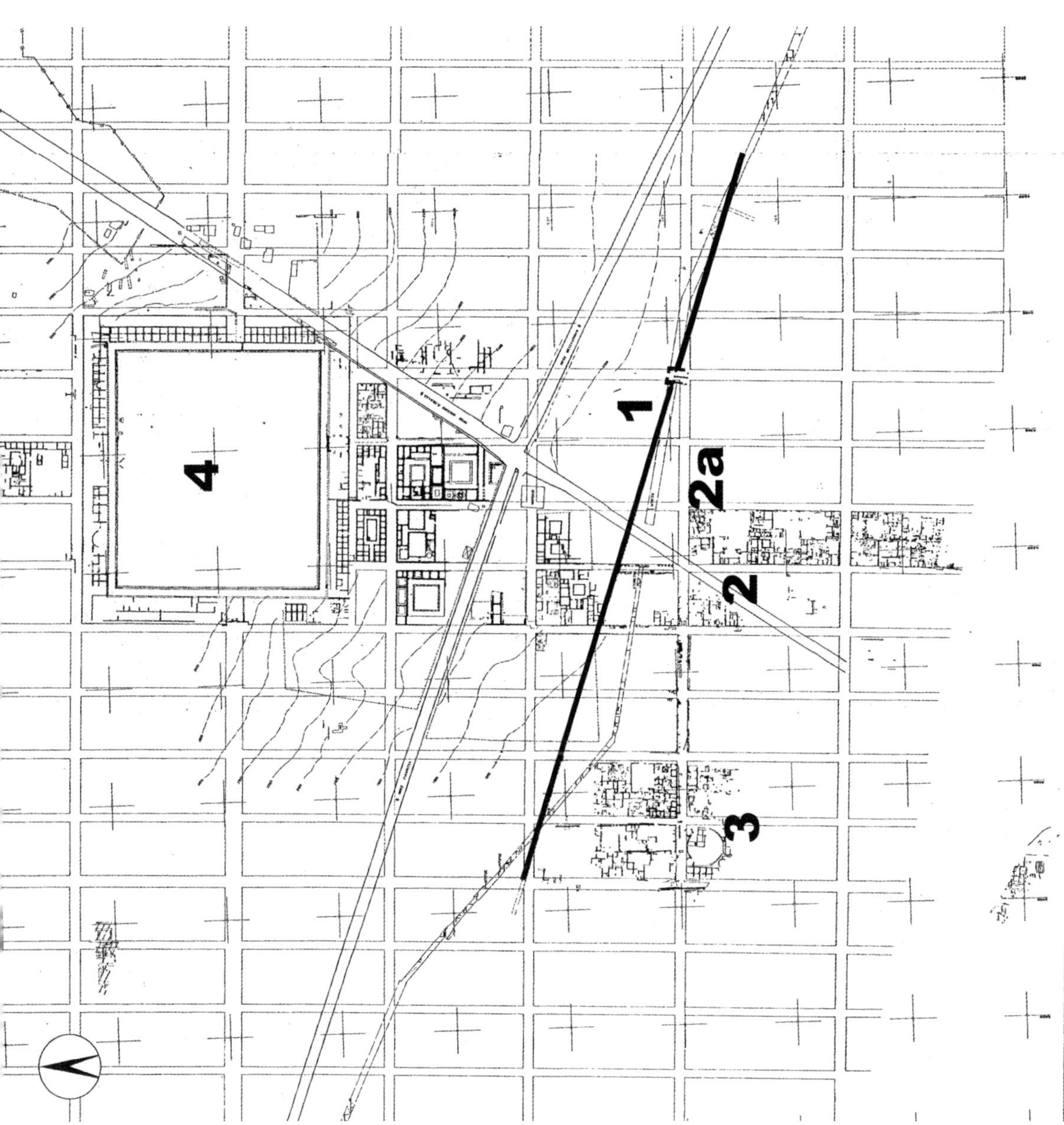

Fig. 1. Plan of Hellenistic Pella with restoration of the north wall of the Classical period. North wall of the Classical period. 2. Area of the new entrance of the archaeological site. 2a. The public bath. 3. Area of the sanctuaries. 4. Agora. 5. Palace.

fortified island inside the river Loudias, where the city's treasury and harbor were located, as Titus Livius informs us when describing the events of the third Macedonian war[6]. Finally, at plots between these areas parts of buildings, mainly houses, have also been unearthed[7].

From the aforementioned areas around 2 400 coins were studied. 264 coins were worn, so it was not possible to attribute them to any issuing authority. 353 of the coins were silver, while the rest were bronze. The relatively large quantity of silver coins is due to a coin hoard, numbering 307 Rhodian and pseudo-rhodian drachms, as well as tetrobols in the name of the "Macedonians" and Histiaia[8]. Without taking this hoard into account, silver coins, as one would expect, are relatively few[9]. Numismatic material form Pella can be divided in three major categories according to issuing authority; a) regal coins b) issues of the Macedonian cities and the "Macedonians" c) coins from areas outside Macedonia. Finally, the find of 17 flans and parts of bronze rods used for minting must be mentioned.

Regal coins

Regal issues represent the largest category of coins from the Pella excavations. In total, 1 279 coins came to light or 59,9% of the identified numismatic material (fig. 2-3). The earliest issues belong to Alexander I (498-454 BC), the first Macedonian king who struck coins in the first half of the 5th c. BC[10] (fig. 9a-b). Furthermore, at the Pella excavations were found 3 coins of Perdiccas II (454-413 BC, fig. 9c-d)[11], 2 of Archelaus (413-399 BC, fig. 9e)[12], 20 of Aeropus

6 125 coins from Phacus were studied. For the excavation of this area see Lilimpaki-Akamati 2003; *id.* 2005, 400-402. For Phacus see also Liv. 44.6.1-2 and 44.46.4-11.

7 From other excavation sectors, such as the trench that supplied fresh water from the Aravyssos springs (O.Y.Θ. trench), the area where the new road that connects Thessaloniki with Edessa was constructed, the Karavasilis and the Bourakis plot, 638 coins were examined.

8 For this find see coin hoard n° 4 bellow.

9 Silver coins constitute 14,7% of the total amount of coins under study. Without the hoard this percentage falls to 1,9%.

10 4 silver coins of Alexander I came to light. They belong to the following types: a) Head of horse/incuse square with dots (hemiobols, 2) b) Standing horse/incuse square (trihemiobol, 1) c) forepart of horse/incuse square (diobol, 1). For the coinage of Alexander I see indicatively Raymond 1953; Kremydi-Sisilianou 1999; Psoma 1999a.

11 These coins represent the following types: a) Walking horse/helmet within incuse square (tetrobol, 1) b) Galloping horse/ helmet within incuse square (light tetrobol, 1) c) forepart of horse/incuse square with dots (hemiobol, 1). For the coinage e of Perdiccas II see indicatively Raymond 1953; Psoma 1999a; Lykiardopoulou & Psoma 2000.

12 The types Horse/eagle in incuse square (obol) and Heracles/forepart of wolf in incuse square (hemiobol) of Archelaus were identified. For the coinage of Archelaus see Westermark 1989, 303-304; Psoma 2000; Gatzolis 2013, 125.

(396-392 BC)[13], 6 of Amyntas II (392-390 BC)[14], 2 of Pausanias (390-389 BC)[15], 72 of Amyntas III (389-369 BC)[16], 1 of Alexander II (369-368 BC)[17], 24 of Perdiccas III (364-359 BC)[18], 299 of Philip II (359-336 BC.)[19], and 331 of Alexander III (336-323 BC)[20], in whose name the majority of regal coins was struck. Also, came to light 1 coin of Philip III (323-316 BC)[21], 176 coins of Cassander (316-297 BC)[22], 83 of Demetrius Poliorcetes (306-283 BC)[23], 16 probably of Ptolemy

13 Coins of Aeropus are all bronze and belong to the types a) Male head/forepart of lion (13) b) Male head/forepart of lion gnawing bone (2) c) Male head/horse (5). For the coinage of Aeropus see Westermark 1989, 304-305.

14 The coins of Amyntas II belong to the types: a) Male head/helmet (4) b) Male head/forepart of wolf (2). For the coinage of Amyntas II see Westermark 1989, 305-306.

15 Both coins are of the type Male head/forepart of boar. For the coinage of Pausanias see Westermark 1989, 306.

16 The following types were identified: Silver: a) Heracles/horse (staters, 2). Bronze: a) Heracles/eagle devouring serpent (58) b) Heracles/forepart of boar (10) c) Heracles/club (2). For the coinage of Amyntas III see Westermark 1989, 307-308; Lykiardopoulou & Psoma 2000; Gatzolis 2010, 274-275 and 397-410.

17 This is of the type Male head/horse. For the coinage of Alexander II see Westermark 1989, 308.

18 Almost all are bronze coins of the type Heracles/lion gnawing bone, denomination A. Only two represent denomination AA. For the coinage of Perdiccas III see Westermark 1989, 308-309.

19 The following coins came to light: Silver: a) Zeus/horseman (plated tetradrachm, 1) b) Male head/horseman (tetrobols, 2). Bronze: a) Male head/horseman (denomination A, 194) b) Heracles/club (59) c) Heracles/thunderbolt (21) d) Male head/horseman (denomination AA, 14) e) Heracles/horseman holding whip (7) f) Heracles/horseman (1). For the coinage of Philip II see Bellinger 1964, 29-52; Le Rider 1977; Price 1979; Portolos 1996; Touratsoglou 2003.

20 The following coins were examined: Silver: a) Heracles/enthroned Zeus (drachms, 10) b) Heracles/thunderbolt (obol, 1). Bronze: a) Heracles/ΑΛΕΞΑΝΔΡΟΥ, ΒΑ or ΒΑΣΙΛΕΩΣ between club and bow in case (137) b) Male head/horse (123) c) Macedonian shield with thunderbolt in centre/Macedonian helmet (45) d) Heracles/eagle (13) e) Appolo/thunderbolt (1) f) Macedonian shield with axe in centre/Macedonian helmet (1). For the coinage of Alexander III see indicatively Price 1991; Liampi 1998a; Gatzolis 2012.

21 This is a drachm of the type Heracles/enthroned Zeus. For the coinage of Philip III see Price 1991.

22 These belong to the types: a) Heracles/horseman (109) b) Heracles/seated lion (32) c) Apollo/tripod (25) d) Heracles/lion breaking spear (10). For the coinage of Cassander see Oikonomos 1918; Ehrhardt 1973; Valassiadis 2005; Gatzolis 2012.

23 The coins of Demetrius Poliorcetes are all bronze and follow the types: a) Macedonian shield with monogram [monogram]/helmet (59) b) Demetrius/prow (24). For the coinage of Demetrius Poliorcetes see Newell 1927; Liampi 1998b, 105-106.

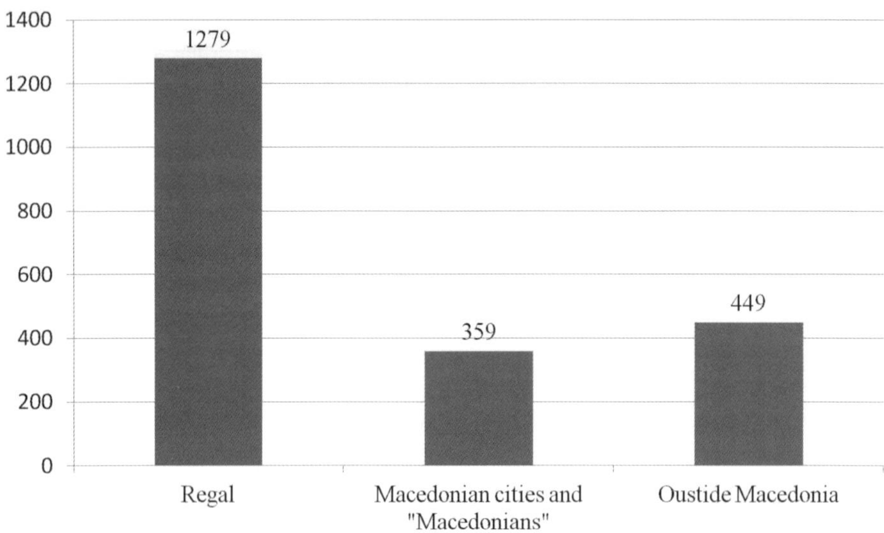

Fig. 2. Categories of coins from Pella.

Keraunos (281-279 BC, fig. 10)[24], 147 of Antigonus Gonatas (277-239 BC)[25], 62 of Philip V (220-179 BC)[26], and 30 of Perseus (178-168 BC)[27] (fig. 3).

The large quantity of regal coins found at Pella is justified, because the city was one of the most important in the Macedonian kingdom and seat of the Macedonian kings. The royal mint during the Hellenistic period was probably located on the palace hill, presumably in building IV, where parts of bronze rods and a number of flans came to light[28]. But it cannot be excluded that some coins were also struck in block I/3, south of the Agora, where a mint was also unearthed[29]. Furthermore, it must be noted, that 17 flans and parts of bronze rods

24 These are the coins with the monogram ΑΡ on the reverse. The following types were found: a) Zeus/eagle standing on thunderbolt (denomination B, 8) b) Zeus/eagle standing on thunderbolt, reverted head (denomination A, 5) c) Zeus/thunderbolt (3). For these coins see Psoma *et al.* 2008, 217-224 with earlier bibliography.

25 The following bronze coins were discovered: a) Athena/Pan erecting trophy (86) b) Macedonian shield with monogram N/helmet(40) c) Heracles/horseman (23). For the coinage of Antigonus Gonatas see Furtwängler 2004; Poulios 2001.

26 The bronze coins of Philip V are represented by a variety of types: a) Heracles/horseman (16) b) Zeus/Athena (16) c) Heracles/two goats (12) d) Perseus/eagle (4) e) Perseus/harpa (3) f) Poseidon/prow (3) g) Macedonian shield, in centre Perseus/helmet (3) h) Zeus/horseman (2) i) Helios/thunderbolt (2) j) Heracles/club (1). For the coinage of Philip V see Mamroth 1935; Gatzolis 2010, 479-492 with relevant bibliography. The types Helios/thunderbolt and Heracles/club have been attributed to Philip VI by T. Kourempanas. See Kourempanas 2010.

27 The following types were identified: a) Perseus/eagle (25) b) Macedonian shield, in centre whirl/harpa (5). For the coinage of Perseus see Mamroth 1928; Franke 1957.

28 For the finds from the palace see Chrysostomou 1996, 114; *id.* 2008.

29 For this mint see Oikonomidou 1989; Oikonomidou & Kourempanas 2007; Kourempanas 2012.

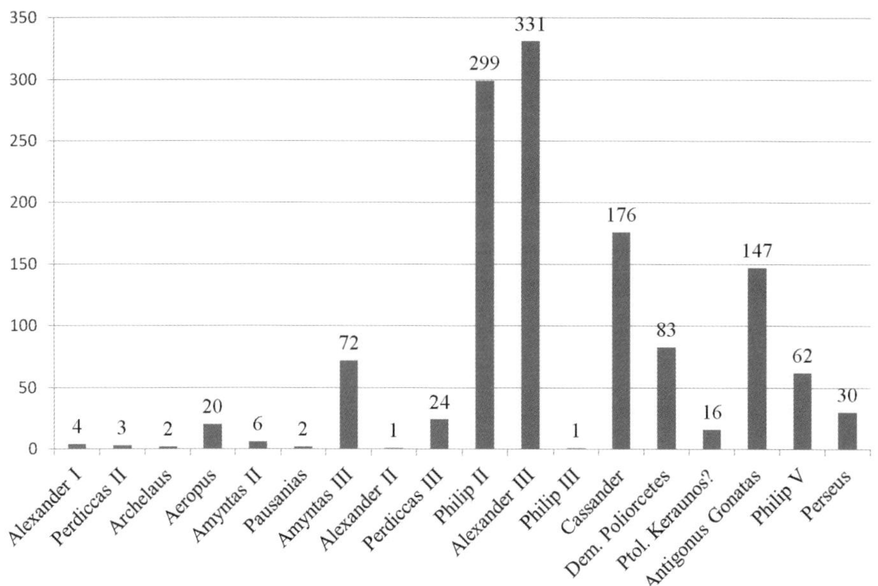

Fig. 3. Regal coins per king.

were found in areas south of the Classical wall, perhaps indicating the process of minting as well[30].

Regal coins of the 5th c. BC are fewer than those of the 4th c. (fig. 3). This is to be expected, because silver coins of the 5th c. were neither struck in great numbers nor did they circulate much[31]. Although Archelaus was the first Macedonian king who struck bronze coins, none of his bronze issues were found at Pella so far, thus strengthening the opinion stated by U. Westermark, according to whom this king issued mainly silver coins and that his bronze coins were struck in small quantities during the end of his reign[32].

During the 4th c. BC, the first king in whose name bronze coins appear in some quantity is Aeropus, who is represented by 20 issues (fig. 3). Coins of the rest of the Macedonian kings of the first half of the 4th c. BC are rather limited, excluding those of Amyntas III. The large quantity of Amyntas' coins, in total 72, is due to his longer period of reign, which exceeded 20 years, as well as his extended military needs[33].

30 Parts of bronze rods and flans were found at the new entrance of the archaeological site (4), at the area of the sanctuaries (3), at Phacus (3), and in other sectors of the city (7).

31 Regal coins of the 5th c. BC number only 9 issues, in contrast to around 900 regal issues of the 4th c. BC

32 Westermark 1989, 304.

33 It must be noted that from the material under study 27 coins of the type Heracles/eagle devouring snake, had an illegible legend, so they could be attributed either to Amyntas III or Pydna. For the coins of Pydna see below, n. 49.

From the time of Philip II bronze coins appear in greater numbers, and thus seem to play a more important role in everyday economy, as has recently been supported by H. Gatzolis[34]. The largest quantity of regal issues from Pella was struck during the second half of the 4th c. BC in the name of Alexander III, Philip II, and Cassander[35] (fig. 3). This fact is probably not accidental, and must be related firstly to the influx of wealth in the royal coffers after the campaign of Alexander III, and secondly to the intense building activity that took place in Pella during the last quarter of the 4th c. BC, when the city expanded to a large degree[36].

Apart from the kings mentioned above, a fair number of coins (83) were struck by Demetrius Poliorcetes (fig. 3). These are mainly issues of the type Macedonian shield with monogram ΗΑΡ/helmet. The attribution of this type to Demetrius Poliorcetes that has been proved by recent research is further supported by the finds from Pella, since this type is connected to archaeological strata of the first half of the 3rd c. BC[37]. Most of these coins are small bronze denominations that weigh around 3-5 grams, but also 3 coins weighing no more than 1 gram were found. It is highly possible that these coins were minted primarily in order to cover everyday needs.

Especially interesting is the find of 16 issues bearing the monogram ΑΡ on the reverse (fig. 3 and 10). These coins were attributed to the mint of Paroreia by H. Gaebler and were dated in the 2nd c. BC[38]. According to S. Psoma, they can be attributed to the Macedonian king Ptolemy Keraunos, and should be dated in his short period of reign (281-279 BC). This opinion is strengthened by iconographic and metrological comparison of the aforementioned coins with those of the Ptolemies and Pyrrhus of Epirus[39]. The find of coins with the monogram ΑΡ in a well dated stratum of the 3rd c. BC at a pottery workshop in Pella strengthens Psoma's opinion, at least regarding the dating problem. In one particular case, a coin of the type Zeus/eagle standing on thunderbolt (denomination A) was found with an issue of Cassander[40].

The 147 coins in the name of Antigonus Gonatas represent around 11,5% of the regal coins that were found at Pella (fig. 3). This quantity of coins is justified considering the long period of Antigonus' reign. The majority of coins belong to the types Athena/Pan erecting trophy (86) and Macedonian shield with monogram/helmet (40), while some issues of the type Heracles/horseman (23) were also found. According to A. Furtwängler, many of these issues, especially those of the type Heracles/horseman, should be attributed to Antigonus III

34 Gatzolis 2010, 531 and 537. It must be noted that some of the coins in the name of Philip II were struck after his death. Still, according to our knowledge so far, it is not easy to distinguish the issues that were minted during Philip's lifetime from his posthumous issues. Regarding the posthumous issues of Philip II see Touratsoglou 2003, 100-101.

35 The coinage of these three kings represents around 63% of the regal coins that were found at Pella.

36 For Pella's expansion during the second half of the 4th c. BC see n. 2.

37 For the attribution of the type Macedonian shield with monogram ΗΑΡ/helmet to Demetrius Poliorcetes see Liampi 1998b, 105-106.

38 Gaebler 1935, 5-6.

39 For the arguments that connect the coins with Ptolemy Keraunos see Psoma *et al.* 2008, 217-224.

40 The coin of Cassander belongs to the type Apollo/tripod. For the dating of the pottery of the workshop see Lilimpaki-Akamati & Akamatis 2008, 153.

Doson[41]. Instead, V. Poulios supported the opinion that only coins of Antigonus Gonatas with countermarks should be ascribed to his successors[42]. At Pella, 11 countermarked coins of Antigonus Gonatas were identified, which represent around 7,5% of his coinage. These mainly follow the type Athena/Pan erecting trophy and bear various countermarks, such as the head of Heracles (4), the head of Pan (2), the symbol ⅋ (2), and others that are indiscreet (3)[43]. Unfortunately, excavation data from Pella cannot contribute decisively to the dating of the coins of Antigonus Gonatas and his successors, because these coins were used for a long period of time, even in the 2nd c. BC[44]. Finally, extremely interesting is the discovery of a barbaric imitation of Gonatas' type Athena/Pan erecting trophy[45].

In contrast to the coinage in the name of Antigonus Gonatas, the 62 coins that are attributed to Philip V represent a rather small number (fig. 3). This fact disagrees with Philip V's long period of reign that exceeded 40 years. Furthermore, during his lifetime Philip practiced warfare allover Greece, and fought against Rome as well. In addition, a great number of coin types have been ascribed to his mints. Taking these facts into account, a much greater quantity of coinage should be expected in order to cover local economy as well as military needs. In this specific case, the opinion stated by I. Touratsoglou, that the Romans reminted the coins of the last two Macedonian kings, Philip V and Perseus, seems highly plausible[46]. This opinion also comes to an agreement with the relatively small number of coins (30) from the Pella excavations that are attributed to Perseus[47].

Issues of the Macedonian cites and the "Macedonians"

Issues of the Macedonian cities and the "Macedonians" represent the second largest category of coins that were found at the Pella excavations, without taking into account coin hoard n° 4[48]. The 359 coins that were identified represent around 16,8%, of the identified numismatic material (fig. 2). These can be classified to two categories of issues; those of the 4th c. BC, which are represented by Pydna and Philippoi, and those of the second and 1st c. BC that were struck by Pella, Thessaloniki, Amphipolis and the "Macedonians".

From the end of the first quarter of the 4th c. BC the city of Pydna at Pieria struck bronze coins using the iconographic type Heracles/eagle devouring snake of Amyntas III, thus

41 See Furtwängler 2004 with related bibliography.

42 Poulios 2001, 281-293.

43 10 coins of the type Athena/Pan erecting trophy and only one coin of the type Heracles/horseman were countermarked. For countermarks on the coinage of Antigonus Gonatas see Poulios 2001, 281-286.

44 Most of the coins in the name of Antigonus Gonatas show traces of ware that prove their long-term circulation. For the use of this king's coinage in the 2nd c. BC see coin hoard n° 5 below.

45 Inv. n° 77/1260. This coin copies a small denomination (AE2) of the type. On the obverse the eye of Athena is disproportional to the rest of the face, and the helmet compact. On the reverse the figure of Pan and the trophy are rendered without details and the inscriptions are obscured.

46 Touratsoglou 1993, 33 n. 6.

47 Worth mentioning is the case of a rare coin of Perseus of the type Perseus/eagle with a countermark, probably an owl (inv. n° 77/1300).

48 Most of the pseudo-rhodian coins of this hoard must have been minted in Macedonia.

showing its dependency on the Macedonian kingdom. At the Pella excavations only 4 coins of Pydna were identified. Half of them follow the type of Amyntas' coinage, while the others are represented by the type female head/owl that is influenced by Athenian models[49].

The city of Philippoi, in eastern Macedonia, during the second half of the 4th c. BC struck significant quantities of coins that regularly appear in coin hoards with issues of Philip II and Alexander III. At the Pella excavations were found 18 bronze coins of Philippoi, all of the type Heracles/tripod. Their relatively large number confirms that these issues circulated to an extent within the Macedonian kingdom[50].

Coins of the 2nd c. BC that were struck by the Macedonian cities and the "Macedonians" are much more numerous than those of the fourth century and are related to a tantalizing dating problem. According to earlier opinions, the right to strike coins to the cities of Pella, Thessaloniki and Amphipolis, as well as the "Macedonians", was given by the last two Antigonid kings, Philip V and Perseus, in order to strengthen local economy[51]. But according to most recent views, while coins of the "Macedonians" could be dated to the time of the kings mentioned above, those of the cities were struck after the roman conquest of Macedonia, specifically after the battle of Pydna (168/167 BC) or after the formation of the roman province of Macedonia (148 BC)[52].

Excavation finds and coin hoards from Pella and other Macedonian cities seem to favor the dating of the autonomous city coinage after the roman conquest. Specifically, at Pella these issues appear in strata of the second half of the 2nd c. BC, or those of the early 1st c. BC. For example, at trial trenches dug underneath the third architectural phase of the public bath, coins of Pella and Thessaloniki were found with pottery of the second half of the 2nd c. BC[53] (fig. 11-12). Furthermore, in coin hoards when coins of the cities appear in great numbers, those of Philip V and Perseus are extremely few or nonexistent[54]. Characteristic is the example of three coin hoards (n° 5-7) that were found at Pella. These hoards consist almost exclusively of autonomous city issues and completely lack regal coins of the last two kings of Macedonia[55].

As is expected, most of the autonomous city coins from the numismatic material under study can be attributed to the mint of Pella. The 152 coins of Pella represent around 53,9% of the total amount of 2nd and 1st c. BC Macedonian civic issues (fig. 4). Most of the coins belong

49 For the coinage of Pydna see Tselekas 1996a; Psoma 2001, 114-115. It must be noted, that 27 coins from the material under study were of the type Heracles/eagle devouring snake, but since their inscription was illegible, they could be attributed either to Amyntas III or Pydna.

50 For the coinage of Philippoi see Bellinger 1964, 29-40; Poulios 1982, 197-202; Lazaridis *et al.* 1992, 50-52.

51 For the dating of the above mentioned coins during the reign of Philip V and Perseus see Gaebler 1935, 1-50; Crawford 1985, 128-131; Touratsoglou 1987; Mørkholm 1991, 164-167; Touratsoglou 1993, 33 and 36-37.

52 For the dating after the roman conquest see Psoma *et al.* 2008, 37, 99 and 101; Kourempanas 2011b, 251; Gatzolis 2010, 369-373; Kourempanas 2011a.

53 Lilimpaki-Akamati & Akamatis 2007, 105.

54 For coin hoards of the 2nd and 1st c. BC from Macedonia see Touratsoglou 1993, 47-55.

55 For these coin hoards see below. From a total of 84 coins of the three coin hoards only one issue was regal, struck in the name of Antigonus Gonatas (coin hoard n° 5).

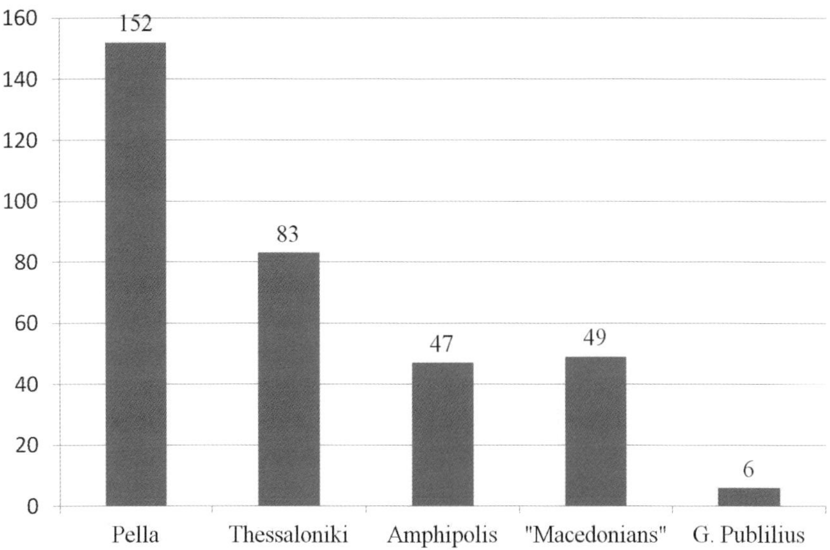

Fig. 4. Issues of the Macedonian cities and the "Macedonians".

to the types Athena/grazing cow (54), Pan/Athena (38), Apollo/tripod (24), and Poseidon/bull (20)[56]. These seem to be the main types of Pella's coinage as is deducted by their frequent appearance in coin hoards as well. The mint of Pella was probably located in building I/3, south of the Agora, where a metallurgy kiln, as well as metal rods and flans were found[57].

The coins of Thessaloniki and Amphipolis are fewer than those of Pella, however they are represented by a fair amount of issues. From the numismatic material under study 83 coins of Thessaloniki and 47 of Amphipolis came to light[58] (fig. 4). Coins of Thessaloniki belong mainly to the types Artemis/quiver and bow (18), Zeus/two goats (16), Dionysus/goat (14), and Zeus/bull (14), while those of Amphipolis principally follow the types Artemis/two goats (17), Poseidon/club (13), and Poseidon/horse (6). Apart from the aforementioned coins, many more issues of the two cities came to light[59]. The large quantity of civic issues testifies that these coins circulated freely within Macedonia during the 2nd and 1st c. BC. Coins of Pella and Thessaloniki primarily appear in central and west Macedonia, while those of

56 The other coins of Pella that were identified are of the types Apollo/cithara (6), Athena/biga (3), Zeus/eagle (2), Zeus/bull (2), Pan/two goats (1), Roma/ΠΕΛΛΗΣ within wreath (1), Zeus/thunderbolt (1).

57 For this mint see n. 29. After the roman conquest the mint of the palace must have stopped to operate.

58 Coins of Thessaloniki represent around 29,4%, while those of Amphipolis around 16,6% of the total amount of civic issues.

59 The other coins of Thessaloniki that were identified follow the types Athena/horse (4), Dionysus/grapes (3), Dionysus/Pegasus (2), Zeus/eagle (2), Poseidon/prow (2), Janus/Dioscuri (2), Janus/two Centaurs (2), Heracles/club (1), Pan/Pan (1), Apollo/tripod (1), Roma/ΘΕΣΣΑΛΟΝΙΚΗΣ within wreath (1). The other coins of Amphipolis are of the types Artemis/corn-ear (4), Janus/two Centaurs (2), Zeus/two goats (1), Roma/ΑΜΦΙΠΟΛΙΤΩΝ within wreath (1), Artemis/quiver and bow (1), Zeus/bull (1), Artemis/Tauropolos (1).

Amphipolis mainly in east Macedonia, Thrace and southwest Bulgaria[60]. From the sequence of issues and their iconography, it seems that the three Macedonian cities had to a large extent a common economic policy.

Apart from the civic issues, at the Pella excavations 49 coins in the name of the "Macedonians" were identified (fig. 4). 27 silver tetrobols were part of hoard n° 4 and 22 bronze coins were solitary finds[61]. The bronze coins belong mainly to the types Zeus/thunderbolt (8) and Heracles/club (4), but other types were identified as well[62]. According to most scholars, the minting of coins in the name of the "Macedonians" began towards the end of Philip V's reign or the beginning of Perseus' and continued after the roman conquest as well[63].

From the Pella excavations also came to light 6 coins in the name of Gaius Publilius, which belong to the type Athena/grazing cow (fig. 4). The existence of the same numismatic type in the coinage of Pella and Bottiaia possibly testifies to the minting of the specific Publilius coins by the mint of Pella too[64]. Characteristic of these issues is their relatively large weight (approximately 10-12 grams) in contrast to most Macedonian civic issues of the 2nd and 1st c. BC, as well as earlier regal coins. Most scholars believe that coins in the name of Gaius Publilius were minted shortly after the battle of Pydna in 168/167 BC[65], but others relate them to the period after the formation of the roman province of Macedonia in 148 BC[66].

Coins from areas outside Macedonia

Issues from areas outside Macedonia form the third category of the numismatic material under study. The 449 coins that were identified represent around 21%, of the identified numismatic material (fig. 2). This relatively large number is due to the existence of the 276 rhodian and pseudo-rhodian drachms of hoard n° 4. Without this hoard, the 173 coins from areas outside Macedonia represent only around 8,1% of the identified numismatic material. Although relatively few in number, these coins show great variety. The majority is dated to the 4th and 2nd c. BC, while some issues belong to the 3rd c. BC.

60 See indicatively Touratsoglou 1993, 47-55; Adam-Veleni 2000, 128-133; Kosmidou 2006, 419-420; Ivanov 2011; *id.* 2012.

61 For coin hoard n° 4 see below.

62 The other bronzes in the name of the "Macedonians" follow the types Heracles/horse (2), Pan/two goats (2), Apollo/tripod (2), Dionysus/goat (1), Macedonian shield/helmet (1), Macedonian shield/ΜΑΚΕΔΟΝΩΝ within wreath (1), Strymon/trident (1).

63 See Touratsoglou 1987, 55; Kremydi-Sisilianou 2007; *id.* 2009, 193.

64 See Gaebler 1935, pl. 12 fig. 16 and pl. 19 fig. 4.

65 According to P. MacKay, G. Publilius was the first quaestor of Macedonia after the battle of Pydna (Mackay 1968). See also Boehringer 1972a, 114; Touratsoglou 1987, 56; Papazoglou 1988, 63; Touratsoglou 1993, 37; Psoma *et al.* 2008, 107.

66 Gaebler 1935, 8-9; *SNG* Cop. 1318-1326; Kourempanas 2011a, 200.

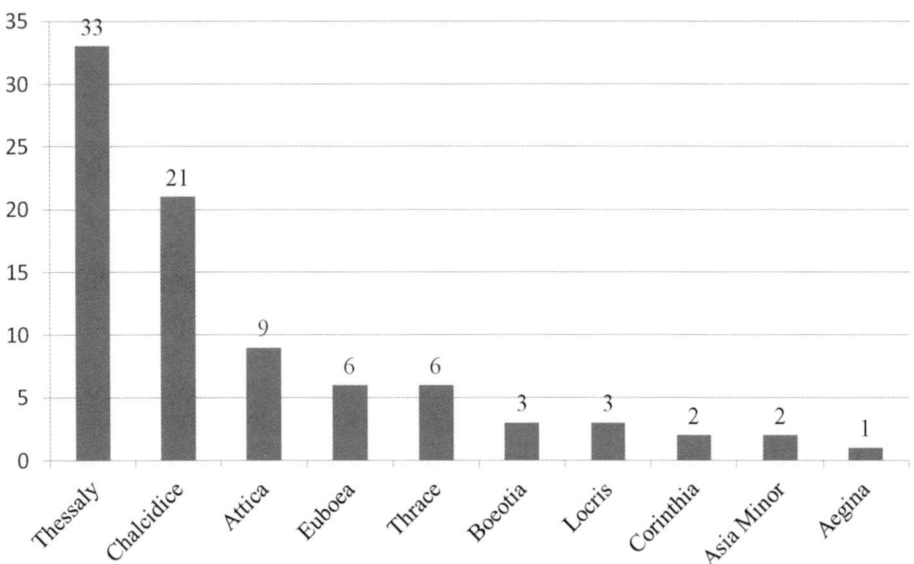

Fig. 5. 4th c. BC non-Macedonian coins per region.

Coins of the 4th c. BC mainly come from Thessaly (fig. 5). Most of them, 17, were struck by Larissa, the most important Thessalian mint and city[67]. In contrast to Larissa's coins, those of the other Thessalian cities are represented by only one to three issues. Specifically, at Pella came to light 3 coins from Phalanna[68] and Gyrton[69], 2 from Pharsalus[70], Meliboea[71] and Lamia[72], and 1 form Pelinna[73], Gomphi[74], Sciathus[75] and Peparethus[76].

Apart from Thessaly, relatively large is also the number of coins from the Chalkidice (fig. 5). The majority of these belong to the Chalcidian League (11)[77]. Furthermore, at Pella

67 Coins of Larisa are all bronze. The following types were identified: a) Nymph/horse feeding (11, *SNG* Cop. 142) b) Nymph facing/horse (3, *SNG* Cop. 136-139) c) Nymph facing/horseman (3, *SNG* Cop. 140-141).

68 These belong to the type Male head/Nymph (*SNG* Cop. 203-205).

69 They are all of the type Zeus/horse (*SNG* Cop. 60).

70 The coins from Pharsalus are represented by the following types: a) Athena/horse's head (hemidrachm, *SNG* Cop. 222-223) b) Athena/horseman (*SNG* Cop. 230-231).

71 They both follow the type Nymph/grapes (*SNG* Cop. 171).

72 Coins of Lamia belong to the types Nymph/Philoctetes seated on rock and Athena/Philoctetes standing and shooting birds (*SNG* Cop. 82 and 87-88).

73 The coin of Pelinna belongs to the type Mantho/horseman (*SNG* Cop. 191).

74 This is of the type Hera facing/Zeus seated on rocks (*SNG* Cop. 50).

75 It follows the type Apollo/caduceus (*SNG* Cop. 366).

76 The coin of Peparethus is of the type Dionysus/cantharus (*SNG* Cop. 359-360).

77 Coins from the Chalcidian League are represented by the types: a) Apollo/cithara (9, *SNG* Cop. 246) b) Apollo/tripod (2, *SNG* Cop. 247-249).

were identified 3 coins of Potidaea[78], and 2 of Scione[79], Aphytis[80] and Bottice[81]. A coin of Tragilus must also be added to the group of coins from north Greece[82].

4th c. coins from southern Greece, Thrace and Asia Minor are relatively few (fig. 5). Most of the coins from south Greece came from Attica, mainly Athens. Specifically, at Pella seven Athenian tetradrachms were found in hoard n° 2, and also 2 coins from Eleusis came to light elsewhere[83]. Worth noting is also the number of coins from Euboea, and specifically Chalkis (5) and Histiaea (1)[84]. Furthermore, 3 coins were minted in Locris[85] and in Boeotia[86], 2 in Corinthia[87] and 1 in Aegina[88]. Only 6 coins from Thrace, all bronze, came to light. These were minted by Thasos (2)[89], Abdera (1)[90], Maroneia (1)[91], Cypsela (1)[92] and Cetriporis (1), ruler of the Odrysians[93]. Finally, single coins of Assus and Ephessus possibly belong to the time period under study[94].

In contrast to 4th c. non Macedonian coins, which were struck by the Greek cities, those of the 3rd c. BC were mainly minted by the Hellenistic rulers (fig. 6). The 21 issues of Lysimachus (306-281 BC) are probably related to the period when he ruled the Macedonian kingdom[95]. This was probably also the case for the coins of Pyrrhus (295-272 BC), although only 4 of his issues came to light[96]. Furthermore, at the Pella excavations came to light 2 coins of Seleucus I

78 They all belong to the type Athena/trident (Gaebler 1935, pl. 2 fig. 4).

79 Both coins follow the type Aphrodite/two doves (*SNG* Cop. 323-324).

80 The coins of Aphytis are of the types Zeus Ammon/eagle and Zeus Ammon/two eagles (*SNG* Cop. 129-132). For the dating of these coins in the 4th c. BC see Gatzolis 2011, 196-198.

81 The coins from Boticce follow the types Apollo/lyre (*SNG* Cop. 140-144) and female head/butting bull (Gaebler 1935, pl. 20 fig. 28).

82 It belongs to the type Hermes/TPAI in the four quarters of the field (Gaebler 1935, pl. 24 fig. 35).

83 For coin hoard n° 2 see bellow. For the coins from Eleusis see *SNG* Cop. 414-419 (Triptolemos/pig).

84 Coins from Chalcis follow the type Hera facing/eagle devouring snake (*SNG* Cop. 443-446). The coin from Histiaea belongs to the type Maenad/bull (*SNG* Cop. 510-511).

85 All belong to the type Athena/grapes (*SNG* Cop. 65-71).

86 The following coins from Boeotia came to light: a) hemidrachm of the federal mint (Boeotian shield/cantharus, *SNG* Cop. 173-175) b) bronze coin of the federal mint (Boeotian shield/trident, *SNG* Cop. 179-181) c) hemidrachm of Thespiae (Boeotian shield/Aphrodite, *SNG* Cop. 403-404).

87 Two Corinthian staters of the type Pegasus/Athena were identified (*SNG* Cop. 48 and 93-100).

88 The bronze coin of Aegina is of the type A between two dolphins/incuse square (*SNG* Cop. 533-536).

89 The two bronze coins from Thasos are of the type Heracles/club and strung bow (*SNG* Cop. 1050).

90 This follows the type Griffin/quartered square with four pellets (*SNG* Cop. 371-373).

91 This is of the type horse/vine (*SNG* Cop. 630).

92 The coin form Cypsela is of the type Hermes/cup (*SNG* Cop. 532).

93 This is of the type Dionysus/cantharus (*SNG* Cop. 1068-1069).

94 The coin of Assus follows the type Athena/bucranium (*SNG* Cop. 243-244). The coin of Ephessus is of the type Bee/stag (*SNG* Cop. 245-246).

95 Coins of Lysimachus are represented by the following types: a) Athena/lion (18, *SNG* Cop. 1150-1157) b) Athena/forepart of lion (2, *SNG* Cop. 1159-1163) c) Head in Phrygian helmet/trophy (1, *SNG* Cop. 1164-1167).

96 The coins of Pyrrhus belong to the type Macedonian shield with monogram ΠΡ/helmet (*SNG* Cop. 1195-1197).

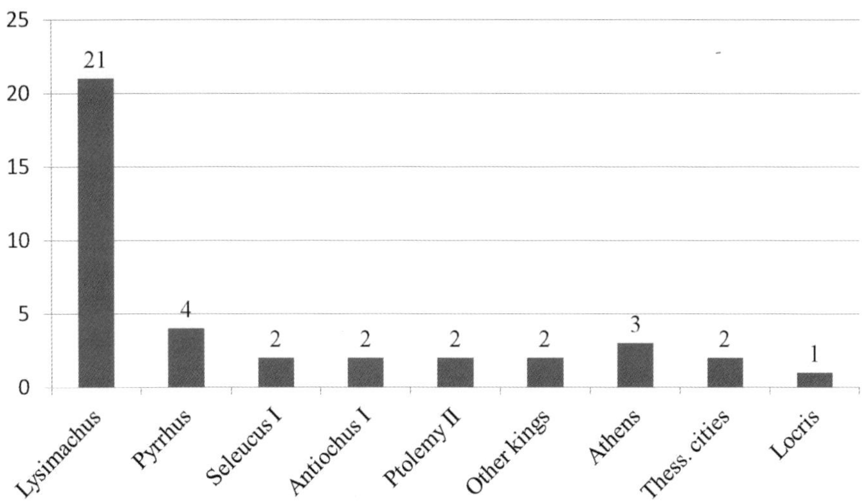

Fig. 6. 3rd c. BC non-Macedonian coins.

(305-281 BC)[97], Antiochus I (281-261 BC)[98] and Ptolemy II (285-246 BC)[99], as well as single coins of Philetaerus (284-263 BC)[100] and Dropion (*c.* 250-230 BC), ruler of the Paeonians[101].

Coins of the 3rd c. BC that were not minted by the Hellenistic rulers are very few (fig. 5). At the Pella excavations came to light 3 bronze coins of Athens[102] and single issues of Larissa Cremaste[103], Halus[104] and the Locri[105] that belong to the time period under study. Moreover, 3 coins of the Epirote Republic, 2 of the Acarnanian League, and 1 probably from Elis can be dated either in the 3rd or in the 2nd c. BC[106].

97 These belong to the type Medusa/bull (*SNG* Cop. 36-37).

98 The coins of Antiochus I follow the types Apollo/tripod (*SNG* Cop. 71-72) and Apollo/Apollo (*SNG* Leipzig, 1330).

99 Coins of Ptolemy II belong to the types Apollo/eagle (*SNG* Leipzig 1427) and Alexander in elephant's skin/eagle (*SNG* Leipzig 1418-1419).

100 The coin of Philetaerus belongs to the type Athena/bow (*SNG* Cop. 348-350).

101 The coin of Dropion is of the type Athena/thunderbolt. It is interesting to note that coins of Dropion usually bear the inscription ΠΑΙΟΝΩΝ and the monogram of the king above and below the thunderbolt on the reverse, while on the coin from Pella the inscription ΔΡΟ/ΠΙΩΝ can be read. For the coinage of Dropion see Pavlovska 2011.

102 All Athenian coins belong to the type Athena/owl (*SNG* Cop. 94-99).

103 Nymph/harpa in wreath (*SNG* Cop. 152).

104 The coin from Halus is of the type Zeus/Phryxus (*SNG* Cop. 63).

105 The coin of the Locri was found in hoard n° 3, which is analyzed below. It is of the type Athena/grape (*BCD* Locris 131).

106 The coins of the Epirote Republic belong to the types Zeus/thunderbolt (*SNG* Cop. 129), Dione/tripod (*SNG* Cop. 132) and Artemis/spear-head (*SNG* Cop. 135-137). The coins of the Acarnanian League both follow the type Heracles/Achelous (*SNG* Cop. 421-422). The coin from Elis is of the type Apollo/Zeus (*SNG* Cop. 435-437).

A number of coins from areas outside Macedonia found at Pella can be dated in the 2nd c. BC. Most of these were Rhodian and pseudo-rhodian drachms (276) that comprised the greater part of hoard n° 4[107]. Others belong to mints from mainland Greece and the islands of the Aegean, Rome, the Illyricum and Asia Minor (fig. 7). Specifically, were identified 11 coins from Histiaia[108], 5 from Thessaly[109] and 1 from Delos[110]. Also, at the Pella excavations came to light 2 victoriates of Apollonia[111] and single bronze coins of Dyrrachium[112], Magnesia ad Maeandrum[113], Miletus[114] and Apameia[115].

The 19 issues of Rome constitute a great part of the 2nd c. BC coins from Pella. Most of these are asses (9)[116], but also 3 denarii[117] and other denominations came to light[118]. It is interesting to note that most of these coins were minted before the roman conquest. Although they could have arrived at the Macedonian capital through a Roman embassy or trade, the signs of wear on most of them lead us to the conclusion that they were in use for a long period of time, possibly after the battle of Pydna in 168/167 BC. The latest issue, a plated denarius minted by MN. FONTEI C.F, probably in 85 BC, was found at the area of Phacus, where human presence can be traced after the destruction Pella in the first decade of the 1st c. BC[119].

To sum up, coins from mints outside Macedonia do not necessarily testify to the existence of systematic trade, but moreover to the movement of sole persons[120]. Exception are some silver coins, especially those of the 2nd c. BC like rhodian and pseudo-rhodian drachms, Histiaiean tetrobols and roman denarii. These coins, along with "new style" Athenian

107 For this hoard see below.

108 At Pella came to light 7 tetrobols of the type Maenad/Nymph seated on stern (*SNG* Cop. 517-536) and 4 bronze issues of the type Maenad/forepart of bull (*SNG* Cop. 538-543).

109 4 bronze coins belong to the Thessalian confederacy, all of the type Athena/horse (*SNG* Cop. 324-328), and 1 to the Magnetes (type: Zeus/Centaur, *SNG* Cop. 160).

110 This coin was struck by the Athenian Cleruchs in Delos. It is a small denomination of the type Artemis/quiver and bow (*SNG* Cop. 440).

111 Both coins belong to the type cow standing/floral pattern within double linear square (*SNG* Cop. 371-398). One of them is plated.

112 This belongs to the type Zeus/tripod (*SNG* Cop. 506).

113 The coin form Magnesia is of the type Stag/statue of Artemis (*SNG* Cop. 853).

114 The coin of Miletus follows the type Apollo/lion (*SNG* Cop. 994-1000).

115 This coin is of the type Athena/eagle (*SNG* Cop. 163-168).

116 The following issues were identified: a) Anonymous (2, Crawford 1974, 56.2, after 211 BC) b) Bird and TOD (Crawford 1974, 141.2a with legend TOD, 189-180 BC) c) Caps of the Dioscuri (Crawford 1974, 181.1, 169-158 BC). Apart from these, 5 asses were worn beyond identification.

117 The denarii are represented by the following types: a) Roma/Luna in biga (Crawford 1974, 161.1, TAL, 179-170 BC) b) Roma/Dioscuri (Crawford 1974, 237.1a, CN. LVCR TRIO, 136 BC) c) Apollo/Cupid on goat (Crawford 1974, 353.1a, MN. FONTEI C.F, 85 BC).

118 From the material under study were identified 2 victoriati of the type Jupiter/Victory crowning trophy (Crawford 1974, 168.1, 179-170 BC), 1 double litra of the type Heracles/Pegasus (Crawford 1974, 27.3, 230-226 BC), 1 sextans of the type Mercury/prow (Crawford 1974, 69.6, 211-208 BC), 1 triens of the type Minerva/prow (Crawford 1974, 120.5, 206-195 BC) and 2 very worn quadranses of the type Heracles/prow.

119 The denarius is of the type Apollo/cupid on goat (Crawford 1974, 353.1a).

120 Regarding this issue see Gatzolis 2010, 303 with related bibliography.

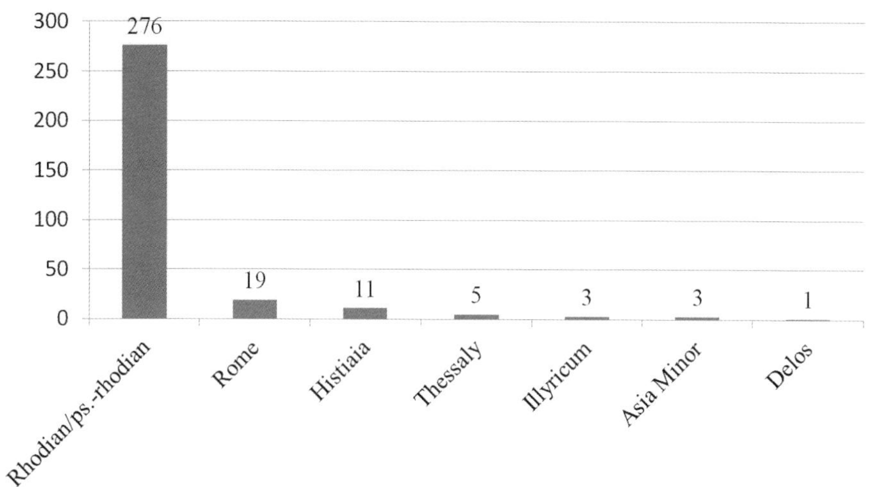

Fig. 7. 2nd c. BC non-Macedonian coins.

tetradrachms, arrived systematically in Macedonia during the 2nd c. BC in order to cover economic needs[121].

Coin hoards

Apart from single coins that were found in different archaeological layers, at the excavation areas south of the Classical fortification of Pella came to light seven coin hoards (fig. 8):

1) Hoard of seventeen bronze coins. 1 is attributed to Amyntas III (Heracles/eagle devouring snake type), 4 to Perdiccas III (all Heracles/ lion gnawing bone type), 11 to Philip II (types: 2 Heracles/horseman holding whip, 8 Male head/horseman, 1 Heracles/horseman) and 1 to Cetriporis (Dionysus/cantharus type). The hoard, which came to light in 1998, was concealed inside a black-glaze skyphos underneath the earthen floor of a building at the "Enimerosis" block, which is located at the new entrance of the archaeological site of Pella.

2) Hoard of 7 Athenian tetradrachms (Athena/owl type), 2 silver drachms of Alexander III (Heracles/enthroned Zeus type) and gold jewelry. It was found in 1996 in a building complex located east of the sanctuary of Darron.

3) Hoard of 6 bronze coins. 2 of these were highly oxidized, 3 were struck by Antigonus Gonatas (types: 1 Macedonian shield with monogram N/helmet, 2 Athena/Pan erecting trophy) and 1 by the Locri (Athena/grapes type). The hoard was found in 2008 underneath the earthen floor of a room at a pottery workshop located in the "Enimerosis" block.

121 See Touratsoglou 1993, 35-37. Although no "new style" Athenian tetradrachms were found in the numismatic material under study, their existence is testified in Pella. This is deducted from a coin hoard numbering 101 coins of this type, as well as their appearance in different sectors of Pella's Agora.

4) Hoard of 307 silver coins. It comprises 276 Rhodian and pseudo-rhodian drachms, 27 tetrobols in the name of the "Macedonians" and 4 tetrobols of Histiaia. The hoard was found inside a chytra in a house located at the southwest corner of block IV/2 in 1976.

5) Hoard of 77 bronze coins. It comprises 1 coin of Antigonus Gonatas (Athena/Pan erecting trophy type), 2 of the "Macedonians" under Gaius Publilius (Athena/grazing cow type), 36 of Pella (types: 16 Pan/Athena, 11 Poseidon/bull, 6 Athena/grazing cow, 2 Zeus/eagle, 1 Athena/biga), 22 of Thessaloniki (types: 7 Zeus/two goats, 7 Zeus/bull, 4 Dionysus/goat, 2 Janus/Dioscuri, 1 Dionysus/Pegasus, 1 Poseidon/prow) and 16 of Amphipolis (types: 8 Artemis/two goats, 6 Poseidon/club, 1 Zeus/bull, 1 Janus/two Centaurs). This hoard was found in 1996 inside a closed black-glaze vase, probably a lekythos or oinochoe, hidden beneath the threshold of a building complex east of the sanctuary of Darron.

6) Hoard of 4 bronze coins. 3 were struck by the mint of Thessaloniki (types: 1 Dionysus/goat, 1 Zeus/bull, 1 Artemis/quiver and bow) and 1 by Amphipolis (Poseidon/club). This hoard was found in 2007, concealed between the walls of two bathtubs of the public bath in the "Enimerosis" block at the new entrance of the archaeological site.

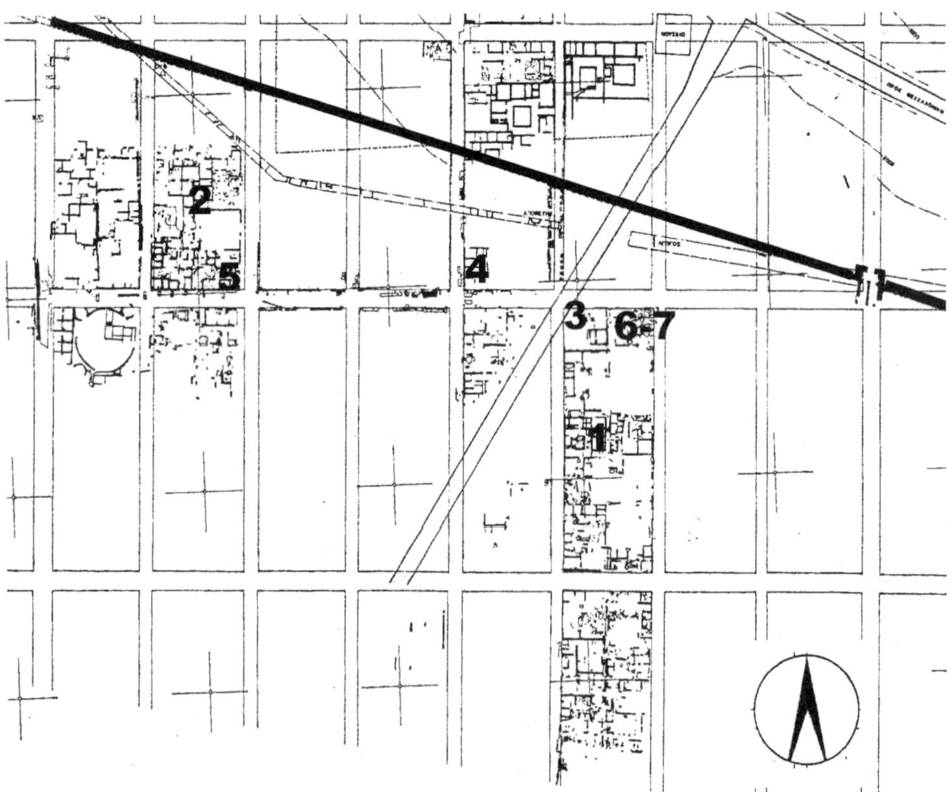

Fig. 8. FIndspot of coin hoards.

7) Hoard of 3 bronze coins of Amphipolis (types: 2 Poseidon/horse, 1 Artemis/two goats). This hoard was found in 2008 during the excavation of the north wall of the "Enimerosis" block.

The hoards mentioned above can be dated from the middle of the 4th until the beginning of the 1st c. BC. Hoard n° 1, which is the earliest, is especially interesting, because it constitutes one of the few cases of numismatic concealment during the lifetime of Philip II. It is interesting to note that the majority of Philip's coins lack symbols, monograms and letters, which frequently appear in posthumous issues of this king. Only two coins of Philip II from the Pella hoard bear the thunderbolt symbol. The existence of coins attributed to Philip's predecessors (Amyntas III, Perdiccas III), the appearance of Philip's early type (Heracles/ horseman holding whip), the lack of symbols apart from the thunderbolt and the absence of monograms and letters from Philip's issues, the coin of Cetriporis (357-352 BC) and the shape of the skyphos, in which the hoard was concealed, allow us to date the coins' concealment around the middle of the 4th c. BC[122].

Hoards n° 2-3 are also interesting because of the appearance of non Macedonian coins with regal issues. The Athenian coins of hoard n° 2 testify to the relations between Attica and Macedonia, which are attested by the trade of attic pottery from the last quarter of the 6th c. BC. In both cases the regal issues help us to date hoard n° 2 in the late fourth or the early 3rd c. BC and hoard n° 3 shortly after the middle of the 3rd c. BC[123].

Although hoard n° 4 is one of the best known from Pella, it has not yet been fully published. The find is related to the circulation of Rhodian and pseudo-rhodian drachms throughout the Aegean and the hoard's synthesis is similar to that of others from Macedonia and Thessaly. Various dates have been proposed for its concealment from 175 until 168 BC[124].

Hoards n° 5-7 have a similar synthesis, since the majority of their coins was struck by the Macedonian cities of Pella, Thessaloniki and Amphipolis. All of these hoards can possibly be dated after the roman conquest of Macedonia as has been mentioned above. Hoards n° 6-7 can be placed in the second half of the 2nd c. BC and hoard n° 5 possibly in the early 1st c. BC.

Dating the buildings. The case of the public bath

Apart from the information regarding economy, coins from Pella also contribute drastically to the dating of the buildings, in which they were found. Characteristic is the example of the public bath at the area of the new entrance of the archaeological site. This building is very important, because it is the earliest known bath complex that has been found in Macedonia so far. Furthermore, it is representative for Pella south of the Classical fortification as a whole, because here have been traced architectural phases dating from the late 5th until the early 1st c. BC, as is usually the case in this part of the ancient city.

122 For the publication of coin hoard n° 1 see Akamatis 2014a.

123 For hoard n° 2 see M. Lilimpaki-Akamati 2000b. For hoard n° 3 see Akamatis 2013a.

124 For this coin hoard see *CH* VI, 46; *CH* VII, 96; *CH* VIII, 420; Touratsoglou 1993, pl. IIa; Chrysostomou 1993, 630-631; Apostolou 2004, 263.

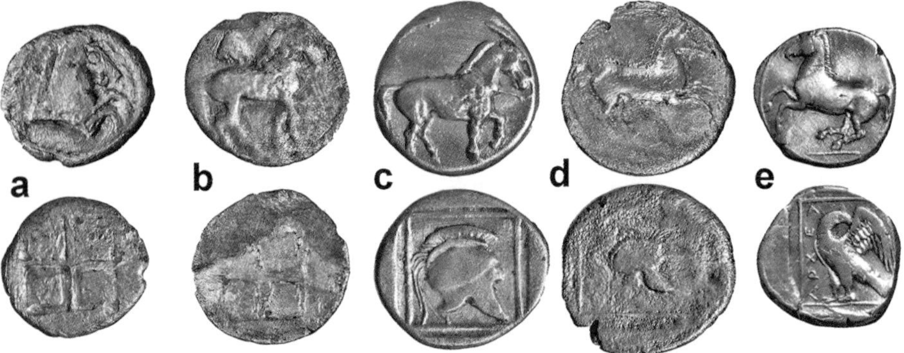

Fig. 9. 5th c. BC regal coins (photo author).

Fig. 10. Coins with the monogram ΑΡ (photo author).

A silver hemiobol from the reign of Perdiccas II, along with attic pottery of approximately the same period from the foundation layer of the N-S wall that separates the "Enimerosis" town block, in which the bath was located, in two sectors, allow us to date its construction in the late 5th c. BC[125]. Moreover, coins of Aeropus, Amyntas III and Perdiccas III, as well as black glaze and red-figure pottery of the same period testify to the existence of 4th c. buildings, of which few architectural remains have come to light[126].

Better preserved are the remains of the early Hellenistic bath. During this period a large open courtyard with rooms on four sides, a swimming pool at the west part of the building, as well as a clay water pipe that ran through the complex was built. The find of coins of

125 Akamatis 2014a, 68.

126 For the Classical age pottery from the public bath see Akamatis 2008; Akamatis & Aamodt 2015.

Philip II and Alexander III in stratigraphical trenches underneath the limestone chips of the walls and the earliest floors lead us to the dating of this architectural phase in the last quarter of the 4th c. BC, which concurs with the reign of Cassander and the intense building activity that took place in Pella during that period.

During the second and third architectural phases the plan of the bath and the use of the rooms were more clearly defined, consisting of rooms with bath tubs for warm and hot baths, an underground heating system with an underground furnace and an air shaft, as well as a number of secondary rooms with floors made of plaster. Furthermore, the large swimming pool remained in use for the cold bath. The second architectural phase of the bath is marked by coins of Cassander and Demetrius Poliorcetes, as well as black glaze and "west slope" pottery of the first quarter of the 3rd c. BC. Finally, the find of autonomous civic issues of Pella and Thessaloniki along with mould-made pottery, oil lamps and unguentaria underneath the floors of the various rooms allow us to date the third architectural phase in the last quarter of the 2nd c. BC[127] (fig. 11-12).

The destruction of the public bath, probably by an earthquake, can be placed in the early 1st c. BC as the majority of the buildings in Pella[128]. A coin of Thessaloniki of the type Agonothesia/ANT KAI within wreath, which is probably dated shortly after the battle of Philippoi[129], is the latest issue and testifies to the limited human presence at least during the 3rd quarter of the 1st c. BC[130].

Conclusions

Besides dating, the study of coins provides valuable information regarding the numismatic circulation at Pella and the Macedonian kingdom in general during the Classical and Hellenistic periods. Although the sample under study does not cover the great quantity of coins that has been found at Pella as a whole, it can be considered representative to a large degree. A fact that must be noted from the 5th c. until 168 BC is the large quantity of regal coins that constituted the economic medium of this period. After the roman conquest, the place of regal issues, which ceased to exist, was taken by the autonomous civic issues of Pella, Thessaloniki and Amphipolis and by the coins of the "Macedonians".

Although Vth c. coins from the numismatic material under study are very few, they possibly reflect Pella's economic dependency to the Macedonian kings (fig. 3 and 9). This fact can also be deducted from the large quantity of regal issues that constituted the greater part of a coin hoard found in the area of the east cemetery of Pella[131]. It is also interesting

127 For the architectural phases of the public bath see Lilimpaki-Akamati & Akamatis 2007.

128 For the destruction of Pella see indicatively Akamatis 1993, 345-346; Lilimpaki-Akamati 2000c, 200-201; Akamatis 2012.

129 Gaebler 1935, 121, pl. 24 fig. 3; *SNG* ANS 819-822 (41/40 BC).

130 For the limited human presence at Pella after the first decade of the 1st c. BC, see Akamatis 1989; Lilimpaki-Akamati 2008.

131 The aforementioned hoard numbers 336 silver issues of the following issuing authorities: a) Alexander I (81) b) Perdiccas II (220) c) Archelaus (22) d) Amyntas III (1) e) Chalcidian League (8) f) Acanthus (4). For the hoard see Chrysostomou 1993.

Fig. 11. Coins of Pella and Thessaloniki from the third architectural phase of the bath of Pella (photo author).

Fig. 12. Pottery from the third architectural phase of the bath of Pella (photo author).

to note, that most of the 5th c. coins under study came from the area of Phacus, the small island inside river Loudias[132]. According to current evidence, Pella appears to have started off as a small town around Phacus, where the ancient harbor was situated approximately 800 m south of the later Agora, and gradually began to expand to the north possibly during the reign of Archelaus, when the north fortification wall was built. This notion is also proven by the pottery and other finds of Phacus that date from the Bronze Age and by the writings of Herodotus and Thucydides, who mention Pella's proximity to the Thermaic gulf in the 5th c. BC[133]. Moreover, at Phacus part of the island's independent fortification has come to light, as well as buildings dating to the end of the 5th or the beginning of the 4th c. BC[134].

In contrast to the small number of 5th c. coins, those of the first half of the 4th century are much more numerous. Apart from regal issues, which represent the majority, the appearance of coins from Pydna, Thessaly and south Greece affirms the movement of people from these territories (fig. 3 and 5). The coins from the Chalcidice, especially those of the Chalcidian League, can perhaps be related to the period of warfare between the Macedonians and the Chalcidians during the reign of Amyntas III, when the latter possibly captured Pella for a short period of time[135]. Although the period under examination is characterized by political instability and warfare, Pella's economy must have developed due to the city's proximity to the sea. Xenophon characteristically mentions Pella as "μεγίστη τῶν ἐν Μακεδονίᾳ πόλεων[136]". It is worth noting that during the second half and especially in the second quarter of the 4th c. BC the import of attic pottery, especially red-figure, rises drastically[137].

During the second half of the 4th c. BC regal bronze coins appear in greater numbers and must have played an even more important role in everyday transactions (fig. 3). Moreover, the find of 15 silver coins, mostly drachms in the name of Alexander III, testifies to the systematic issuing of silver coinage as well[138]. The intense minting of this period must be related to the immense wealth that arrived in the Macedonian treasury after Alexander III's campaign in the East. This wealth probably led to the expansion of Pella during the reign of Cassander, although the city's size must have increased from the lifetime of Philip II[139]. During the second half of the 4th c. apart from regal issues, those of Philippoi must have circulated within the Macedonian kingdom and possibly some coins from Thessaly and Chalcidice. The case of hoard n° 2 testifies to the fact that silver issues from areas outside Macedonia, such as Athenian tetradrachms, were concealed in order to cover future economic needs[140]. In the period under examination, although the trade of attic pottery continued to a smaller degree,

132 Specifically, 5 of the 9 silver regal coins under study came from Phacus.

133 Hdt 7.123; Thc. 2.99,3-4.

134 For the excavation at Phacus see n. 6.

135 For these events see Hammond & Griffith 1979, 175-178; Hammond 1992, 79-80; Errington 1993, 30-34.

136 Xen., *Hell.*, 5.2.13.

137 See Akamatis 2008, 72-73.

138 Apart from the 10 drachms in the name of Alexander III, an obol of the same king was identified, as well as 1 tetradrachm and 2 tetrobols in the name of Philip II, and 1 drachm of Philip III. For the wealth of the Macedonian kingdom after the death of Alexander III see I. Touratsoglou 2010.

139 Str. 7a.1.23.1-2.

140 For coin hoard n° 2 see above.

local pottery workshops intensified their production manufacturing plain pottery, as well as black-glaze and red-figure vases, thus contributing to the city's economy[141].

Pella remained one of the most prominent Macedonian cities in the 3rd c. BC. During the reign of Antigonus Gonatas many buildings were repaired, while others were architecturally transformed. Bronze regal coins, although fewer than those of the second half of the 4th c. BC, were still much more numerous than those of other issuing authorities. Regarding this period, the lack of silver coinage must be noted. Apart from the numismatic presence of the Macedonian kings, that of other Hellenistic rulers is attested, as well as some issues from south Greece testifying to the movement of people from the areas where the aforementioned coins circulated (fig. 6). During the 3rd c., Pella's local workshops continued to produce pottery, figurines, metal objects, but also to import goods from other areas outside Macedonia[142].

In the 2nd c. BC, the coins of the last two Macedonian kings, Philip V and Perseus, appear to be very few in contrast to those of their predecessors (fig. 3). This must have been due to the reminting of their coins by the Romans. Apart from regal issues, during the last years of Philip's reign and the reign of Perseus economic needs were also possibly covered by bronze and silver coins in the name of the "Macedonians", which were struck in rather small quantities and probably continued to be issued after the roman conquest (fig. 4). Furthermore, the circulation of Rhodian and pseudo-rhodian drachms, as well as Histiaiean tetrobols within Macedonia should be noted (fig. 7).

After the roman conquest, an important economic change must have occurred; the transition from regal coinage to the civic issues of the Macedonian cities (fig. 2 and 4). Specifically, the cities of Pella, Thessaloniki and Amphipolis struck significant quantities of coins and used a great number of coin types. During this period of relative instability mainly due to barbaric invasions, which the roman authority had difficulty to confront, cases of hoarding become more common in Macedonia, and specifically Pella[143]. Apart from civic issues, possibly coins of the "Macedonians" were still in use during this period, as well as roman coins, mainly asses and denarii. Few coins from other areas of Greece, Asia Minor and the Illyricum have been identified (fig. 7). Economic needs in silver were covered by roman denarii and Athenian "new style" tetradrachms. Although the time after the roman conquest was not a period of prime for Pella in comparison to the former rule of the kings, the city remained an important Macedonian civic centre. This is also deducted from the quantity of Pella's civic issues and their appearance in hoards all over Macedonia, as well as the city's trade and manufacturing, mainly of pottery and figurines[144]. Most of Pella's buildings were abandoned in the beginning of the 1st c. BC because of a large scale earthquake. However, a small number coins that were found in various areas testify to the limited human presence throughout the 1st c., even after the foundation of the Roman Colony of Pella around 1,5 km west of the Hellenistic city.

141 For the pottery production of Pella during the second half of the 4th c. BC see Akamatis forthcoming. For the red-figure vases specifically see *id.* 2013b and 2014b.

142 For the trade of Pella during the Hellenistic period see Akamatis 1995, 100; *id.* 2012, 53-55.

143 Hoards n° 5-7 belong to the period under discussion. For these hoards see above.

144 For Pella's pottery and figurine production during the 2nd c. BC see indicatively Akamatis 1993; Lilimpaki-Akamati 1993; Akamatis 2012, 53-54.

Περιληψη

Σε αυτό το άρθρο, παρουσιάζεται το νομισματικό υλικό από το νότιο τμήμα της Πέλλας, νότια του τείχους των Κλασικών χρόνων. Το υλικό αυτό είναι ιδιαίτερα σημαντικό, γιατί προέρχεται από την πόλη, τόσο των Κλασικών, όσο και των Ελληνιστικών χρόνων. Εξετάστηκαν περίπου 2400 νομίσματα από τρεις κυρίως ανασκαφικές περιοχές: 1) Την περιοχή της νέας εισόδου του αρχαιολογικού χώρου, όπου ήρθαν στο φως τρία οικοδομικά τετράγωνα με δημόσια οικοδομήματα, όπως το λουτρό, καθώς και εργαστήρια κεραμικής και μεταλλοτεχνίας. 2) Την περιοχή των ιερών, όπου αποκαλύφθηκε το ιερό του Δάρρωνος, τοπικού θεραπευτή θεού των Μακεδόνων, καθώς και άλλα οικοδομήματα που συνδέονται με λατρευτικές δραστηριότητες. 3) Τον Φάκο, την οχυρή νησίδα στο εσωτερικό της λιμνοθάλασσας του ποταμού Λουδία, όπου βρισκόταν το λιμάνι και το θησαυροφυλάκιο της πόλης. Επιπλέον, μελετήθηκαν νομίσματα και από άλλες σωστικές ανασκαφές της εξεταζόμενης περιοχής. Εκτός από μεμονωμένα νομίσματα παρουσιάζονται και επτά νομισματικοί θησαυροί. Σύμφωνα με την εκδίδουσα αρχή, τα νομίσματα της Πέλλας είναι δυνατό να ενταχθούν σε τρεις κατηγορίες: 1) βασιλικές κοπές 2) νομίσματα των μακεδονικών πόλεων και των "Μακεδόνων" 3) νομίσματα περιοχών εκτός της Μακεδονίας. Τα συγκεκριμένα ευρήματα παρέχουν χρήσιμες πληροφορίες για την οικονομία και τη νομισματική κυκλοφορία κατά τους Κλασσικούς και Ελληνιστικούς χρόνους, καθώς και για τη χρονολόγηση των οικοδομημάτων, στα οποία βρέθηκαν.

Territoire, institutions et rayonnement de Pergame : l'apport des monnaies de fouille

Marie-Christine Marcellesi

Les monnaies mises au jour dans les fouilles de Pergame ont donné lieu à différentes publications et constituent un ensemble documentaire important[1]. Leur analyse permet d'éclairer, à travers un élément concret, l'histoire du territoire, des institutions et du rayonnement de Pergame. En effet, les fouilles menées depuis la fin du XIXe s. par l'Institut archéologique allemand ont concerné différents secteurs de l'acropole – zones d'habitat ou zones monumentales –, le sanctuaire extra-urbain de l'Asclépieion dans la plaine, enfin des sanctuaires distants de quelques kilomètres ou dizaines de kilomètres. On peut se demander si les trouvailles monétaires dans ces différents secteurs présentent le même faciès et tenter d'expliquer les différences constatées entre différentes zones du territoire civique et/ou attalide. Pergame, cité relativement obscure à l'époque classique, devient à l'époque hellénistique le siège de la dynastie attalide et une capitale royale mais la cité garde une existence institutionnelle, bien attestée par les inscriptions. La dynastie attalide atteint son apogée au IIe s. a.C. et la ville de Pergame demeure ensuite l'une des cités les plus importantes de l'Asie sous domination romaine. On se demandera comment cette histoire politique et institutionnelle se traduit dans le monnayage de bronze et quel est l'apport des trouvailles des fouilles. Enfin, Pergame a connu un rayonnement important avec l'apogée de la dynastie attalide. L'analyse de l'origine des monnaies "étrangères" (ni pergaméniennes ni attalides) trouvées dans les fouilles permettra d'en mesurer l'évolution et la portée.

Nous commencerons par présenter les différentes publications de monnaies de fouille de Pergame ou de sites proches, en signalant les rares ensembles clos, et nous en dégagerons les apports généraux. Nous consacrerons ensuite un long développement à la chronologie des monnaies de bronze de Pergame. En effet, récemment, une nouvelle chronologie des monnaies de bronze a été proposée par J. Chameroy, qui affirme se fonder principalement sur l'apport des fouilles, notamment sur du matériel nouveau, et s'éloigne sur plusieurs points de la chronologie proposée par les études antérieures et par moi-même[2]. Je ne suivrai pas J. Chameroy dans ses propositions et il convient donc de revoir en détail l'apport du matériel

1 Voir déjà Marcellesi 2012b, 41-42, 74, 83-84, 99-102 et 160-161. Je tiens à préciser que, alors que j'ai publié ou que je prépare actuellement la publication de gros ensembles de monnaies de fouille, dans le cas de Pergame je n'ai jamais travaillé directement sur le matériel des fouilles et je n'ai pas d'information sur le matériel encore inédit. Les réflexions qui suivent sont fondées exclusivement sur les publications existantes.

2 Chameroy 2012, paru quelques mois seulement après Marcellesi 2012b.

M.-C. Marcellesi, in : *Les monnaies de fouille du monde grec*, p. 203-222 des fouilles, ancien et nouveau, à la chronologie du monnayage de bronze pergaménien et attalide. Enfin, nous analyserons les monnaies "étrangères" trouvées à Pergame et les comparerons aux trouvailles faites dans le sanctuaire de la Mère des Dieux à Mamurt Kale.

Une publication dispersée

Les trouvailles monétaires provenant des fouilles menées à Pergame et dans les environs par l'Institut archéologique allemand, sont réparties dans plusieurs ouvrages, qui s'étendent sur un siècle et témoignent de l'évolution des normes de publication de cette catégorie de matériel.

Les trouvailles monétaires des premières fouilles

La plus ancienne publication reste aussi la plus importante pour le nombre de monnaies publiées : K. Regling a dressé le catalogue de 3 485 monnaies, trouvées dans les premières fouilles menées à Pergame à la fin du XIXe s. et au début du XXe s.[3]. Malheureusement, les informations sur les contextes n'avaient pas été conservées[4]. Aucun trésor n'est signalé. Le catalogue, qui tient en une dizaine de pages, est présenté de manière sommaire, en particulier pour les monnaies "étrangères". Les monnaies antérieures à Auguste, qui retiendront ici notre attention, sont au nombre de 631, soit 18 % du total.

Le volume consacré aux trouvailles monétaires de la "Stadtgrabung"

Sans suivre l'ordre chronologique des publications, j'évoquerai tout de suite l'autre grand ensemble de monnaies, publié par H. Voegtli en 1993[5]. Il se compose de deux parties : la première offre le catalogue ("Katalog") des monnaies trouvées de 1973 à 1981 dans les fouilles appelées "Stadtgrabung", menées dans une zone de l'acropole située au Nord du sanctuaire de Déméter, du sanctuaire d'Héra et du gymnase supérieur et les surplombant. Il s'agit d'une zone d'habitat. Le catalogue enregistre au total 1 093 monnaies, dont 344 antérieures à Auguste (soit 31 %). La seconde partie du volume enregistre des monnaies découvertes fortuitement et hors contexte ("Streufunde"), dont le total s'élève à 174, dont 58 monnaies antérieures à Auguste, soit 33 % du total.

Les deux catalogues sont ici très détaillés. Pour les monnaies trouvées dans la "Stadtgrabung", les contextes sont connus ; malheureusement, H. Voegtli indique qu'on ne peut en tirer aucune information sur la chronologie des monnaies – ni absolue ni même relative – étant donné les nivellements, terrassements et destructions importants constatés dans toutes les phases de construction et dus à la situation topographique du chantier[6]. H. Voegtli signale que certaines monnaies proviennent de citernes où elles ont été jetées sans doute comme des offrandes, peut-être destinées à la réalisation d'un vœu ; elles se

3 Regling 1913.
4 *Ibid.*, 331.
5 Voegtli *et al.* 1993.
6 *Ibid.*, 6.

distinguent donc des autres monnaies qui ont été simplement perdues, mais le catalogue ne signale pas ces monnaies trouvées dans des citernes. En revanche, sont signalées en note les quelques monnaies hellénistiques trouvées dans des tombes byzantines, sans que l'on puisse savoir si cela résulte d'un accident ou d'un dépôt intentionnel[7]. Enfin, H. Voegtli explique le grand nombre de monnaies non identifiables d'une part par leur durée de circulation, d'autre part par l'agressivité du sol de Pergame.

Les autres trouvailles monétaires de la "Stadtgrabung"

Le volume de H. Voegtli ne concerne que la première partie des monnaies trouvées dans la "Stadtgrabung" puisque celle-ci, démarrée en 1973, s'est poursuivie jusqu'en 1993[8].

H. Voegtli lui-même a publié deux trésors mis au jour dans ces fouilles[9]. Le plus important[10], découvert en 1987 dans une grande maison hellénistique à péristyle et contenu dans un vase fermé, réunit 65 cistophores ; il a été enfoui vers le milieu du Ier s. a.C. L'autre[11] est un petit ensemble trouvé en 1988 sur la terrasse du théâtre, constitué de 2 monnaies de bronze au nom d'Athéna Niképhoros et de 25 flans ; il pourrait s'agir du trésor d'un faussaire.

La "Stadtgrabung" a par ailleurs donné lieu à la publication de 5 volumes dans la série des *Altertümer von Pergamon*. Dans l'un d'eux, 37 monnaies sont publiées, presque toutes de l'époque impériale, à l'exception d'une monnaie hellénistique d'Élaia[12].

Enfin, J. Chameroy a publié un ensemble de 63 monnaies de bronze, la "trouvaille du canal" ("Kanalmünzfund"), trouvées dans la "rue du canal", dans les interstices des pierres qui constituent la couverture du canal, certaines monnaies ayant été trouvées au-dessus, d'autres en dessous[13]. L'accumulation de monnaies à cet endroit s'explique par le passage d'une pente abrupte à une pente plus douce ; les monnaies ont donc été charriées par les eaux du canal. J. Chameroy croit pouvoir déduire de la présence de débris d'objets en métal (or, fer, bronze) trouvés avec les monnaies et de trous dans la terre sur le terrain en amont, l'existence d'une réserve de métal, d'où proviendrait une partie au moins des monnaies, si bien qu'on aurait affaire à un lot homogène et non à un ensemble disparate. Cette hypothèse ne paraît guère fondée[14] et je crois qu'il faut reconnaître dans ces monnaies charriées par les eaux du canal un ensemble hétérogène. Seules 39 monnaies ont pu être identifiées, soit un peu moins des deux tiers ; 36 datent de l'époque hellénistique, 3 de l'époque impériale (jusqu'à Tibère).

7 *Ibid.*, 6, n. 12.
8 Radt 2006.
9 Voegtli 1990.
10 *CH* IX, 568 (= *CH* VIII, 536).
11 *CH* IX, 502.
12 Schwarzer 2008, 194-197 ; monnaie d'Élaia : 195 n° 20.
13 Chameroy 2012, catalogue 162-164 ; sur le contexte 148-150, où la date de *c.* 30 p.C. est proposée pour l'enfouissement supposé d'une partie des monnaies.
14 Chameroy 2012, 148-149, signale lui-même que ce n'est pas l'hypothèse retenue par l'archéologue.

Autres trouvailles sur l'acropole

Pour ce qui est des autres trouvailles monétaires faites sur l'acropole, deux publications sont à signaler. Dans la fouille des maisons à péristyle à l'ouest de l'agora du bas, qui a dégagé des demeures d'époque hellénistique et impériale, 15 monnaies ont été mises au jour, dont 6 antérieures à Auguste (soit 40 % du total)[15].

Enfin, un sondage dans les fondations du Grand autel a livré une monnaie de bronze au nom de Philétaire, qui serait donc antérieure au début de la construction que les archéologues proposent de dater des années 170[16].

Les trouvailles de l'Asclépieion

Les travaux à l'Asclépieion ont commencé en 1928 (1934 pour les fouilles proprement dites) et donné lieu à la publication de cinq volumes. Au départ, le projet de publication prévoyait de consacrer d'abord deux volumes aux bâtiments de l'époque hellénistique et du début de l'époque impériale, puis deux volumes aux bâtiments relevant du grand réaménagement entrepris dans le sanctuaire à l'époque d'Hadrien. Dans ce projet, la publication des objets trouvés en contexte bien défini devait accompagner celle des bâtiments eux-mêmes, tandis que les objets mis au jour dans des contextes non datés devaient être publiés dans un cinquième volume. Les premiers volumes, consacrés aux bâtiments de la première phase de l'histoire du sanctuaire, se sont conformés à ce projet, mais, par la suite, le plan de publication a évolué, si bien que le volume qui devait comprendre l'ensemble des objets trouvés dans des contextes non datés n'a jamais vu le jour. Aussi ne connaît-on, pour les niveaux les plus anciens, que les trouvailles en contexte bien daté.

Dans le premier volume des fouilles de l'Asclépieion, consacré à la partie méridionale du sanctuaire à l'époque hellénistique et au début de l'époque impériale, C. Boehringer a publié 2 trésors monétaires, ainsi que 2 monnaies trouvées isolément dans un contexte bien daté[17]. Le premier trésor, *IGCH* 1296, est un petit lot de monnaies de bronze, trouvé dans le bâtiment à mosaïque, dans la phase de construction n° 5, datée du deuxième tiers du IIIe s. d'après le style et la technique de la mosaïque. Parmi les 16 monnaies de bronze, 13 ont été frappées à Pergame, 2 par d'autres ateliers, la dernière n'est pas identifiée. L'autre trésor, *IGCH* 1303, a été découvert dans une cruche, dans le mur d'un portique. Le contexte est la phase de construction n° 9, datée de *c.* 200-191 d'après le trésor monétaire et la céramique. Le vase contenait 22 tétradrachmes d'argent d'étalon attique (alexandres, philétaires, autres monnaies royales, Sidé) et l'enfouissement se situe *c.* 201. Les 2 monnaies isolées proviennent

15 Boehringer 1984. Malgré un dépouillement attentif des publications des fouilles de Pergame, cette publication n'est pas citée par Chameroy 2012.

16 Chameroy 2012, 144. de Luca & Radt 1999, 119, n° 622 et 120-125 sur la chronologie du monument : les auteurs se fondent principalement sur une datation proposée pour les tétradrachmes aux types et au nom d'Eumène II, mais il faut souligner que celle-ci est elle-même bien incertaine. Voir Marcellesi 2012b, 123-125.

17 C. Boehringer in : Ziegenaus & de Luca, éd. 1968, 110-111 (*IGCH* 1296), 132-134 (*IGCH* 1303), 114 (2 monnaies isolées, catalogue n° 145-146 ; ces deux monnaies m'avaient échappé lorsque j'ai préparé mon livre sur Pergame, de même que celle citée dans la note précédente).

d'un contexte correspondant à un réaménagement des bâtiments d'incubation dans la phase de construction n° 7, datée du dernier tiers du IIIe s. (d'après la chronologie relative générale). Elles appartiennent toutes les deux à la série au nom de Philétaire.

Dans le deuxième volume, consacré à la partie septentrionale du sanctuaire, toujours dans la première phase de son histoire (époque hellénistique et début de l'époque impériale), A. Furtwängler a publié 23 monnaies, dont 2 seulement antérieures à Auguste[18].

Le troisième volume est consacré aux bâtiments cultuels de l'époque romaine dans la partie orientale du sanctuaire et ne concerne que l'architecture et la sculpture ; aucune monnaie n'y est publiée[19].

Dans le quatrième volume, qui s'éloigne du projet de publication initial, c'est l'ensemble du matériel numismatique, que les monnaies aient été trouvées dans des contextes bien datés ou non, qui est publié par H. Voegtli[20]. Sur un total de 483 monnaies, de l'Antiquité et de l'époque byzantine, 61 sont impossibles à identifier (12 %). Les monnaies antérieures à Auguste sont peu nombreuses – 9 en tout (moins de 2 %). Cela s'explique sans doute par l'histoire du secteur – partie de la voie sacrée la plus proche du sanctuaire, dans laquelle on distingue deux tronçons, la Via tecta et la voie des portiques ("Hallenstraße"). Le cinquième tome porte sur des questions d'architecture et de topographie[21].

Les environs de Pergame

En dehors de la ville même et de l'Asclépieion, grand sanctuaire extra-urbain, le sanctuaire rupestre de Kapıkaya, à 2 km au Nord de la ville de Pergame, a fait l'objet de fouilles qui ont livré 12 monnaies, dont 6 antérieures à Auguste (soit la moitié)[22].

Un autre sanctuaire, plus éloigné, a fait l'objet de fouilles : il s'agit du sanctuaire de la Mère des Dieux découvert dans le lieu-dit Mamurt Kale et identifié avec celui évoqué par Strabon dans le massif de l'Aspordènè (act. Yünd Dağ), au Sud du Caïque et à l'Est d'Élaia, à 30 km de Pergame environ[23]. Ce sanctuaire faisait partie du territoire attalide mais on discute pour savoir s'il faisait partie du territoire d'une cité – Pergame ou une autre cité ? – ou de la terre royale[24]. Les fouilles menées par l'Institut archéologique allemand ont mis au jour 50 monnaies qui ont été publiées par K. Regling, parmi lesquelles 26 sont antérieures à Auguste (un peu plus de la moitié)[25].

Enfin, dans une nécropole située sur le mont Maymun Sekisi, à 13 km environ au Nord-Est de Pergame, des fouilles turques ont mis au jour 30 monnaies de bronze, presque toutes

18 Furtwängler 1975.
19 Ziegenaus, mit einem Beitrag von de Luca 1981.
20 Voegtli 1984.
21 Hoffmann 2011.
22 Furtwängler 1978.
23 Str. 13.2.6.
24 Sur ces questions, Schuchhardt 1912, 69-70, 95 et 105-108, carte 64. Sur le territoire de Pergame, ses limites et son évolution au cours du temps, voir Sommerey 2008, 135-150, spéc. 146-147 sur la région du Yünd Dağ.
25 K. Regling in : Conze & Schazmann 1911, 41-43.

de l'époque impériale, à l'exception d'une monnaie hellénistique de Pergame (série avec l'ethnique des Pegaméniens)[26].

Premières conclusions

Dans le cas de Pergame, on se trouve donc dans une situation favorable dans la mesure où un nombre important de monnaies trouvées dans les fouilles a été publié. Parmi elles, les monnaies antérieures à Auguste, qui nous occupent dans le cadre de ce colloque, sont au nombre de 1 202 pour Pergame, l'Asclépieion, Kapıkaya, la nécropole de Maymun Sekisi, chiffre auquel viennent s'ajouter les 26 monnaies de Mamurt Kale. Néanmoins, très peu de monnaies ont été trouvées dans des contextes bien datés, permettant une exploitation pour la chronologie des monnaies elles-mêmes.

La part des monnaies antérieures à Auguste varie considérablement d'une publication et d'un site à l'autre. Elle est liée à l'histoire de la zone et aux objectifs de la fouille, en particulier dans l'Asclépieion. En effet, à l'Asclépieion, les monnaies semblent peu nombreuses pour l'époque hellénistique. Cela s'explique en partie par le fait que le sanctuaire a été largement remanié à l'époque d'Hadrien. Cependant, toutes les monnaies des secteurs les plus anciens n'ont pas été publiées. On ignore donc le nombre total de monnaies trouvées dans l'ensemble de l'Asclépieion pour la période héllenistique. De ce fait, il s'avère difficile de comparer les trouvailles monétaires de l'Asclépieion avec celles de l'acropole car les choix de publication ne sont pas les mêmes.

En l'état actuel des publications et pour l'époque antérieure à Auguste, on ne peut donc guère comparer les différents espaces (sanctuaire extra-urbain / centre urbain monumental / habitat) pour ce qui est des trouvailles monétaires, contrairement à ce qu'on aurait pu espérer au début de cette enquête[27]. Même dans la ville, il est plus aisé de mettre en relation le faciès des trouvailles monétaires avec l'histoire de la zone fouillée qu'avec la nature de l'occupation.

Mis à part deux trésors de monnaies d'argent[28], la part des monnaies d'argent est tout à fait négligeable, comme souvent dans les trouvailles des fouilles. Avant l'époque impériale, on en compte 8 parmi les trouvailles isolées : 5 monnaies royales ou étrangères proviennent des premières fouilles de Pergame[29], 3 cistophores pergaméniens ont été mis au jour dans la "Stadtgrabung"[30]. Ces monnaies ne présentent pas d'intérêt particulier pour notre propos. Nous évoquerons donc exclusivement, dans les pages qui suivent, le monnayage de bronze.

Outre les deux trésors de monnaies d'argent mentionnés ci-dessus, les fouilles de Pergame ont livré deux trésors de monnaies de bronze. La trouvaille de l'Asclépieion, *IGCH* 1296, est la seule qui apporte une information sur la chronologie des monnaies ; nous y

26 Yaraş & Lenger 2009, monnaie pergaménienne : 402, n° 1.

27 Les choses sont sans doute différentes pour l'époque impériale.

28 *IGCH* 1303, mis au jour dans l'Asclépieion (22 tétradrachmes d'étalon attique) ; *CH* IX, 568 (= *CH* VIII, 536), qui provient de la "Stadtgrabung" (65 cistophores).

29 Regling 1913, 356-358 : un alexandre, une monnaie lagide, monnaies de Thasos et Érythrées, une monnaie non identifiée.

30 Voegtli *et al.* 1993, Katalog n° 32-34.

reviendrons. L'autre lot (*CH* 9, 502), qui provient de la "Stadtgrabung", a livré deux monnaies de la même série ; il est intéressant surtout par la présence de flans, mais on ne peut en tirer aucune information sur la chronologie des bronzes de Pergame. Quant à la "trouvaille du canal", comme nous l'avons indiqué ci-dessus, elle doit selon nous être considérée comme un ensemble disparate et non comme un trésor.

Les monnaies de bronze frappées à Pergame

Les fouilles menées à Pergame et dans les environs ont livré 833 monnaies de bronze au nom de Pergame, de Philétaire ou des divinités Athéna Niképhoros et Asclépios Sôter, auxquelles s'ajoutent 6 exemplaires trouvés à Mamurt Kale. À titre de comparaison, les dépouillements que j'avais effectués lors de la rédaction de mon livre dans les différents catalogues de collections, dépouillements qui ne sont peut-être pas exhaustifs, m'avaient permis de rassembler dans une base de données un total de 755 bronzes pergaméniens ou attalides, soit un nombre proche de celui des fouilles. Cette situation est différente de celle qu'on rencontre dans de nombreuses cités où les bronzes trouvés dans les fouilles sont de très loin majoritaires[31]. De fait, on constate que l'image générale donnée du monnayage de bronze à Pergame par H. von Fritze avant les publications des fouilles n'a pas été modifiée fondamentalement par la suite[32]. S. Ziesmann m'a signalé récemment des types inédits dans la collection de Berlin, dont elle prépare la publication[33] ; il y a peut-être plus à attendre de la publication de cette collection que des trouvailles des fouilles. Quel est néanmoins l'apport des trouvailles des fouilles ?

Les séries du IVe s.

D'après l'état actuel de la documentation[34], les premières monnaies de bronze au nom de Pergame présentent une tête d'Apollon au droit, deux têtes de taureau affrontées au revers[35]. Elles s'insèrent dans la première série de Pergame, composée de monnaies d'argent et de ces monnaies de bronze et tout entière caractérisée par une tête d'Apollon au droit. Viennent ensuite des monnaies de bronze avec une tête d'Héraclès au droit, d'Athéna au revers[36]. Elles font partie de la deuxième série du monnayage pergaménien, caractérisée par une tête d'Héraclès au droit sur presque toutes les dénominations et l'émission de monnaies d'argent, de bronze mais aussi d'or. L'accord s'est fait désormais sur la datation de ces deux séries

31 C'est le cas notamment à Thasos, dont O. Picard traite dans le présent volume.

32 Fritze 1906 ; *id.* 1910.

33 Ziesmann 2016.

34 Le travail en cours de S. Ziesmann apportera peut-être des modifications mineures dans ce schéma général.

35 Marcellesi 2012b, 31-32 et annexe 1 n° 4, ill. pl. 1.

36 *Ibid.*, 43-44 et annexe 1 n° 8, ill. pl. 1.

qui se succèdent au cours du IVe s., la première série se situant dans la première moitié, la deuxième série dans la seconde moitié de ce siècle (tableau 1)[37].

	Boehringer 1972b	Westermark 1991 et 1995	Voegtli *et al.* 1993	Marcellesi 2012b	Chameroy 2012
1ère série, tête d'Apollon	1ère moitié du IVe s.		400-350	1ère moitié du IVe s.	*c.* 400-350 ?
2e série, tête d'Héraclès	1ère moitié du IIIe s.		306-280	2e moitié du IVe s.	fin du IVe-début du IIIe s.
3e série, tête d'Athéna / ethnique abrégé	1ère moitié du IIIe s.	280-230/225	300 -250	*c.* 300-*ca* 200 ?	1er tiers du IIIe s.
Série au nom de Philétaire	*c.* 240-170	*c.* 260-début du IIe s.	200-133	à partir des années 270-début du IIe s. ?	2e tiers du IIIe s.-133
Série au nom d'Athéna Niképhoros	*c.* 190-Ier s.	181-133	200-133	181-début du Ier s. ?	*c.* 130-10
Série au nom d'Asclépios Sôter	*c.* 190-Ier s.		200-133	années 160-début du Ier s. ?	après 133-début du Ier s.
Série au nom des Pergaméniens	*c.* 190-Ier s.		200-133	début du IIe-début du Ier s. ?	Ier s.

Tableau. 1. Les différentes datations proposées pour les séries de bronze de Pergame.

Ces deux premières séries de bronze sont faiblement représentées dans les trouvailles des fouilles. On en a déduit généralement qu'elles avaient été produites en faible quantité, surtout par rapport à des séries plus tardives[38]. C'est probable. Néanmoins, il ne faut pas négliger le rôle de l'histoire du site dans cette répartition. L'épigraphie nous apprend que la ville de Pergame a été déplacée, à l'initiative du satrape Orontès, peu avant le milieu du IVe s. de la plaine vers l'acropole[39]. On ne connaît pas le site occupé avant cette date ; il est probablement recouvert par la ville moderne de Bergama. L'acropole n'a été réoccupée[40] qu'à partir du milieu du IVe s. Il est donc normal de ne pas trouver beaucoup de monnaies antérieures. Par ailleurs, les terrassements importants de l'époque hellénistique ont généralement fait disparaître les couches d'occupation les plus anciennes.

37 La datation de cette deuxième série a évolué au cours des dernières décennies en même temps que la datation des statères d'or : les statères ont d'abord été placés à l'époque de Lysimaque, mais la révision du trésor de Saida, qui en contenait deux exemplaires, par Westermark 1979-1980, l'a conduite à les placer dans le troisième quart du IVe s. Voir Marcellesi 2012b, 46-47. À la lumière de trouvailles récentes, Callataÿ 2012a, a proposé de les mettre en relation avec la conquête d'Alexandre. Cette datation très précise reste très hypothétique.

38 Regling 1913, 361.

39 *OGIS* 264, l. 4-9. Marcellesi 2012b, 25-26.

40 On sait qu'il y avait eu une première occupation à une date beaucoup plus ancienne.

Les séries du IIIe s. et du début du IIe s.

La série à la tête d'Athéna et à l'ethnique abrégé

La troisième série se situe dans le prolongement de la précédente, avec une tête d'Athéna au droit, une ou deux têtes de taureau au revers (et, plus tard semble-t-il, deux étoiles) et, en légende, l'ethnique abrégé ΠΕΡΓΑ[41]. Le début de la frappe se déduit de la datation de la série précédente, à laquelle celle-ci succède, au début du IIIe s., datation sur laquelle l'accord s'est fait (tableau 1). La question est de savoir quand s'arrête cette série et si elle a été frappée, en partie au moins, en même temps que la série au nom de Philétaire. En effet, une série de bronze a été frappée au nom de Philétaire, qui présente différents types (tête d'Athéna, Apollon ou Asclépios au droit, types variés au revers)[42].

Le trésor de l'Asclépieion, *IGCH* 1296, comporte des exemplaires des deux séries. On trouve en outre un exemplaire de chacune dans un trésor trouvé dans l'antique Smyrne et daté de la fin du IIIe s.[43]. Ces deux trésors indiquent que les deux séries, la série civique et la série dynastique, ont circulé ensemble au cours du IIIe s. Les données des fouilles permettent-elles de préciser la chronologie ? Dans les trouvailles des fouilles de Pergame, la série à la tête d'Athéna et à l'ethnique abrégé ΠΕΡΓΑ est faiblement représentée par rapport à la série au nom de Philétaire (tableau 2). On peut se demander si cette répartition est le résultat de la durée respective de la frappe de chacune des deux séries ou du volume de production.

	Regling 1913		Voegtli *et al.* 1993 Katalog		Voegtli *et al.* 1993 Streufunde	
	Nb	%ge	Nb	%ge	Nb	%ge
1ère série, tête d'Apollon	2	0,5 %	6	2 %		
2e série, tête d'Héraclès	3	0,5 %	6	2 %	1	2 %
3e série, tête d'Athéna / ethnique abrégé	16	4 %	19	7 %	7	16 %
Série au nom de Philétaire	117	26 %	77	29 %	16	36,5 %
Série au nom d'Athéna Niképhoros	45	10 %	19	7 %	3	7 %
Série au nom d'Asclépios Sôter	115	26 %	63	24 %	9	20,5 %
Série au nom des Pergaméniens	145	33 %	76	29 %	8	18 %
Total	**443**	**100 %**	**266**	**100 %**	**44**	**100 %**

Tableau. 2. Répartition des monnaies de bronze pergaméniennes antérieures à Auguste dans les publications les plus importantes des fouilles de Pergame.

41 Marcellesi 2012b, 73-77, 92-94 et annexe 1 n° 4-17, 21, ill. pl. 2.

42 *Ibid.*, annexe 1 n° 18-20, 22-25, 33-41, ill. pl. 2-4. Un exemplaire anépigraphe aux types tête d'Athéna / serpent, proche des monnaies de mêmes types au nom de Philétaire (Marcellesi 2012b, n° 18) a été publié récemment par Barbara 2014. Cet exemplaire se caractérise par l'absence de légende mais aussi par la présence de monogrammes que l'on retrouve sur des exemplaires de la série au nom d'Athéna Niképhoros. Cette nouvelle émission pourrait dater de la fin de la série au nom de Philétaire, dans une période de transition avec les séries au nom de divinités qui commencent sous le règne d'Eumène II ; c'est la datation proposée par Barbara 2014, 52 : elle me paraît la meilleure pour cette monnaie, tout comme l'attribution à Pergame.

43 *CH* VIII, 343 (= *IGCH* 1313).

Le trésor *IGCH* 1296 constitue une exception notable : on y trouve 10 exemplaires de la série à la tête d'Athéna et à l'ethnique ΠΕΡΓΑ contre 1 seul exemplaire de la série au nom de Philétaire. On a déduit de cette répartition qu'il y avait sans doute un décalage chronologique entre les deux séries. La série au nom de Philétaire ne faisait que commencer lorsque le trésor a été enfoui, vers le milieu du IIIe s., tandis que la frappe de la série civique était déjà bien avancée. Pour autant, on ne peut pas affirmer que la frappe de cette dernière était achevée : elle a pu se poursuivre après la période de l'enfouissement du trésor et, donc, les deux séries ont pu être frappées, en partie au moins, de manière simultanée. C'était déjà l'hypothèse de U. Westermark, que j'ai reprise dans mon livre[44]. Au contraire, C. Boehringer, H. Voegtli, J. Chameroy préfèrent supposer une frappe successive et non simultanée des deux séries (tableau 1)[45]. Néanmoins, l'épigraphie atteste le maintien de l'existence institutionnelle de la cité sous les Attalides ; la cité désignait des magistrats, avait à effectuer des petits paiements pour rémunérer telle ou telle fonction[46]. Rien n'oblige à supposer un arrêt de la frappe monétaire au nom de la cité très tôt dans le IIIe s. En tout état de cause, la présence d'exemplaires des deux séries dans *IGCH* 1296 montre qu'elles ont circulé ensemble à Pergame et que la frappe de la série dynastique n'a nullement entraîné le décri de la série civique.

Les fouilles n'apportent donc pas d'élément déterminant pour dater la fin de la série à la tête d'Athéna et à l'ethnique abrégé ΠΕΡΓΑ. Les datations proposées dépendent de l'image que l'on se fait du fonctionnement institutionnel de la cité et de la dynastie et des relations entre elles. La datation large que j'ai proposée dans mon livre, où j'ai suggéré qu'une partie de la série civique avec l'ethnique abrégé avait été frappée dans la seconde moitié du IIIe s. (après l'enfouissement de *IGCH* 1296), sans autre précision, vise à souligner l'incertitude dans laquelle on se trouve et à montrer que l'intervalle entre cette série et la série ultérieure au nom des Pergaméniens a peut-être été moins long que ne le laissent entendre les datations proposées auparavant. Il est bien entendu que la frappe n'a pas été continue.

La série au nom de Philétaire

En ce qui concerne la série au nom de Philétaire, le début de la frappe se situe avant le milieu du IIIe s. comme l'atteste le trésor de l'Asclépieion *IGCH* 1296. Est-il possible de préciser les choses et de déterminer si la série a commencé du vivant de Philétaire ou seulement après sa mort ?

Un petit lot de 5 monnaies de bronze trouvées dans l'Est de l'Attique (*CH* IX, 170), daté de la guerre chrémonidéenne (*c.* 267-262) contient un bronze au nom de Philétaire, ce qui invite à placer le début de la série du vivant du dynaste. Cette nouvelle datation est conforme à la datation des tétradrachmes d'argent au nom de Philétaire proposée par G. Le

44 Westermark 1991, sp. 154. Marcellesi 2012b, 74 et 92-94.

45 Boehringer 1972b, M 10-12 (série à l'ethnique abrégé), M 32-35 (série dynastique) ; Chameroy 2012, 139-147 et 154. Nous retenons ici l'ouvrage de C. Boehringer, bien qu'il s'agisse d'un catalogue d'exposition, car il présente l'intérêt d'offrir une vision d'ensemble du monnayage émis à Pergame. Il n'est pas cité par Chameroy 2012.

46 Marcellesi 2012b, 96-102.

Rider d'après le trésor de Meydancıkkale, selon laquelle le groupe II, montrant le portrait diadémé de Philétaire au droit, Athéna et le nom du dynaste au revers, aurait été frappé du vivant de Philétaire et non après sa mort comme on le pensait auparavant[47]. Si l'on admet que Philétaire a pu frapper des monnaies d'argent à son nom et avec son portrait de son vivant, il n'y a aucune raison de penser qu'il n'ait pas pu frapper aussi des bronzes à son nom.

J. Chameroy a cru pouvoir mettre en cause la fiabilité du trésor *CH* IX, 170 ainsi que le lien que l'on peut établir entre les monnaies d'argent et les monnaies de bronze[48]. Je crois qu'il se trompe dans les deux cas. Le lieu de trouvaille précis du petit lot *CH* IX, 170, certes, n'est pas connu mais c'est le cas d'un très grand nombre de trésors. Contrairement à de nombreux trésors d'argent passés par voie commerciale, il n'y a aucune raison, dans le cas de ce petit lot de monnaies de bronze sans grande valeur, de suspecter qu'il ait été divisé en plusieurs parties et qu'on n'en connaîtrait pas la composition complète. Ce trésor paraît plus fiable qu'un grand nombre de ceux qui sont utilisés pour dater bien des séries monétaires. De même, on a montré depuis longtemps le lien qui existait, attesté par les marques de contrôle et parfois par des identités de coins, entre monnaies de bronze et monnaies d'argent dans de nombreux États – cités ou royaumes. À Pergame, on rencontre plusieurs cas de lettres, symboles et monogrammes communs aux deux séries[49]. On voit en outre le système évoluer : après une période caractérisée par des symboles et/ou lettres seules, le rôle des monogrammes se développe, ceux-ci devenant eux-mêmes de plus en plus complexes[50]. Donc, je crois qu'on peut, d'après le trésor *CH* IX, 170, placer le début de la série au nom de Philétaire du vivant du dynaste. Cette datation haute conforte l'idée d'une frappe parallèle entre la série civique et la série dynastique.

Comme pour les monnaies à l'ethnique abrégé, il est plus difficile de dater la fin de la série. Là encore, il paraît logique de la placer à peu près en même temps que la fin des tétradrachmes au nom de Philétaire, c'est-à-dire au début du IIe s. Cette datation est celle qui a été proposée par C. Boehringer, U. Westermark et moi-même[51]. H. Voegtli indique dans son catalogue une datation de *c.* 200 à 133, sans explication[52]. J. Chameroy, à son tour, croit pouvoir faire durer la série jusqu'à la fin des Attalides en 133. Son argumentation se fonde principalement sur les trouvailles monétaires faites à Atarnée, cité côtière à l'Est de Pergame, lors de prospections effectuées sur le site entre 2006 et 2011. Ces monnaies ne sont pas encore publiées en détail, mais J. Chameroy en donne la composition dans un tableau suffisamment précis[53]. Parmi les 47 monnaies isolées qui ont été recueillies, 22 proviennent de Pergame ; parmi elles, l'écrasante majorité (20 monnaies sur 22) est constituée par la série au nom de

47 Sur la chronologie des philétaires, voir principalement Davesne & Le Rider 1989, 333-339 ; Marcellesi 2012b, 89-92.

48 Chameroy 2012, 135-138 sur les monnaies d'argent et 144 sur le trésor *CH* IX, 170. Sur ce trésor et sa provenance, Lagos 1996.

49 Voir déjà Imhoof-Blumer 1884, 20 et 38. Les monogrammes ne sont pas pris en compte dans les tableaux de Chameroy 2012, 176-177, sans que cette absence soit expliquée.

50 Sur l'évolution des marques de contrôle à l'époque hellénistique, de Callataÿ 2012b.

51 Boehringer 1972b, M 32-35 ; Westermark 1991, 151-157 ; Marcellesi 2012b, 92-94.

52 Voegtli *et al.* 1993, Katalog n° 193-269, Streufunde n° 31-46. Cette datation a été reprise par de Luca & Radt 1999, 119, n° 622.

53 Chameroy 2012, 141-144 et tableau 170-173.

Philétaire. En outre, on a trouvé un lot de 8 monnaies qui constituaient le contenu d'une bourse : parmi ces monnaies qui sont toutes pergaméniennes, 7 appartiennent à la série au nom de Philétaire. Le site d'Atarnée ayant été abandonné au début du Ier s. a.C., J. Chameroy croit pouvoir déduire de ces données que les monnaies de bronze au nom de Philétaire ont été frappées jusqu'à la fin de la dynastie.

Cependant, l'abandon du site d'Atarnée ne donne qu'un *terminus ante quem* et les monnaies trouvées lors des prospections ne peuvent pas être traitées comme un lot homogène. On sait que les monnaies de bronze circulent parfois très longtemps[54] ; c'est une donnée négligée par J. Chameroy. Enfin, l'image donnée par les prospections faites entre 2006 et 2011 est sensiblement différente de celle que l'on peut tirer des monnaies trouvées dans les fouilles anciennes menées à Atarnée : d'après la description succincte qui en a été donnée[55], les monnaies de bronze "royales", c'est-à-dire appartenant à la série au nom de Philétaire, sont au nombre de 3 contre 15 monnaies qualifiées de "civiques", appellation sous laquelle sont englobées à la fois des monnaies avec ethnique du IIIe s. et les différentes séries du IIe et du début du Ier s.

Un autre ensemble, publié par J. Chameroy lui-même mais qu'il n'invoque pas dans cette discussion, me paraît aller dans le sens d'une datation haute pour l'interruption des bronzes au nom de Philétaire. Il s'agit de la "trouvaille du canal", qui ne contient pas de bronzes au nom de Philétaire, mais seulement des séries postérieures. Comme nous l'avons indiqué, il ne s'agit pas d'un ensemble homogène[56], mais l'absence totale de monnaies du IIIe s. s'explique par l'occupation du secteur : la "rue du canal" a été percée au IIIe s. Il est logique d'y trouver surtout un matériel postérieur. L'absence totale de monnaies de bronze au nom de Philétaire, par ailleurs courantes dans les trouvailles des fouilles de Pergame, me paraît plaider en faveur d'un arrêt de la série peu de temps après le percement de la rue, c'est-à-dire vers le début du IIe s., ce qui coïncide avec la fin des philétaires d'argent.

U. Westermark puis J. Chameroy ont tenté de préciser la chronologie relative d'après les rares données des trésors et des fouilles[57]. Cette tentative me paraît très hasardeuse, étant donné le très petit nombre de monnaies trouvées en contexte bien daté.

54 Voir par exemple Knapp & Mac Isaac 2005, 21.

55 Schazmann & Darier, 342-343. Voir Chameroy 2012, 142. La nomenclature est celle de Regling 1913 auquel est due l'identification des monnaies trouvées à Atarnée.

56 Contrairement à l'hypothèse de Chameroy 2012, 149-150.

57 Westermark 1991, 151-157 ; Chameroy 2012, 140-147.

Les séries du IIe et du Ier s.

À la basse époque hellénistique, trois grandes séries de bronze ont été frappées à Pergame, l'une au nom d'Athéna Niképhoros[58], l'autre au nom d'Asclépios Sôter[59], la troisième au nom des Pergaméniens (l'ethnique étant le plus souvent complet)[60]. C. Boehringer, H. Voegtli et moi-même avons proposé pour ces trois séries une datation large, couvrant une grande partie du IIe s. et du début du Ier s.[61] ; dans mon livre paru en 2012, j'ai volontairement employé une expression floue "début du Ier s.", qui doit être entendue dans un sens très large, pour la fin de ces séries car elle est en réalité très difficile à situer[62]. U. Westermark ne s'est intéressée qu'à la série au nom d'Athéna et préfère l'arrêter à la fin de la dynastie attalide[63].

J. Chameroy se distingue de tous ses prédécesseurs, en proposant une datation après 133, qui découle de celle qu'il propose pour les monnaies de bronze au nom de Philétaire. Il croit pouvoir en outre tirer des données des fouilles une chronologie relative des trois séries (même s'il considère qu'elles sont frappées en partie de manière parallèle) : la série la plus ancienne serait celle au nom d'Asclépios, suivie par la série au nom d'Athéna et, enfin, par

58 Marcellesi 2012b, 127-128 et annexe 1 n° 53-57, ill. pl. 6.

59 *Ibid.*, 128-130 et annexe 1 n° 59-61, ill. pl. 6. Pour notre n° 60 bis (aux mêmes types que le n° 60, à savoir tête d'Asclépios/serpent enroulé autour du bâton, mais sans légende et avec les lettres A à Γ sur certains exemplaires), Butcher 2004, 229 et 405 n° 12 a proposé une attribution à Antioche-sur-l'Oronte en raison des trouvailles faites sur le site même de la cité (5 monnaies), à Séleucie-de-Piérie (2), enfin de 4 exemplaires conservés au musée d'Antakya ; il met ces monnaies en relation avec un temple d'Asclépios construit à Antioche à l'époque de Domitien et propose de les placer sous le règne d'Hadrien car des lettres semblables apparaissent sur les bronzes antiochéens de cette époque. Cette réattribution m'avait échappé à l'époque où je préparais mon livre. En l'état actuel de la documentation, elle paraît acceptable : l'argument des lieux de trouvaille est solide ; à Pergame, on a trouvé un grand nombre de monnaies aux types tête d'Asclépios/serpent enroulé autour du bâton avec la légende Ἀσκληπιοῦ Σωτῆρος, mais on n'a pas identifié de monnaies aux mêmes types sans légende. Voir aussi Mac Alee 2007, 85.

60 Marcellesi 2012b, 130-131 et annexe 1 n° 63-67, ill. pl. 6. Je n'évoquerai pas ici les rares monnaies au nom d'Athéna Areia, ni celles au nom d'Asclépios et Hygie (*ibid.*, annexe 1 n° 58 et 62, pl. 6), dont on n'a pas trouvé d'exemplaires dans les fouilles de Pergame. Un exemplaire de la série au nom d'Athéna Areia a été découvert dans un sanctuaire rupestre à Priène : Weisser 2014, 663, n° 17. L'attribution à Pergame des monnaies au nom d'Athéna Areia a été récemment mise en cause par Chameroy 2013, 715 mais, en l'état actuel de la documentation, elle me paraît justifiée en raison de l'attestation du culte d'Areia à Pergame (Marcellesi 2012b, 128, spéc. n. 53) et de la parenté avec les monnaies d'Athéna Niképhoros. Contrairement à J. Chameroy, je ne crois pas que la trouvaille d'un exemplaire à Sardes, cité qui a été attalide après 188, et à Priène, cité voisine du royaume, soit un élément suffisant pour supposer une frappe plus méridionale. Un exemplaire de la série au nom d'Asclépios et Hygie a récemment été découvert à Allianoi en Phrygie : Tekin & Erol-Özdizbay 2012, 350, n° 6.

61 Voegtli *et al.* 1993, s'il reprend dans son catalogue la datation proposée par F. Imhoof-Blumer et H. von Fritze entre 200 et 133, la nuance dans le commentaire (p. 6) en précisant qu'il n'exclut pas que la frappe ait pu se poursuivre jusqu'au début du Ier s. Boehringer 1972b, M 43-50 ; Marcellesi 2012b, 127-132.

62 C'est le cas en particulier pour la série à l'ethnique long des Pergaméniens qui se prolonge à l'époque impériale avec une iconographie qui évolue : Marcellesi 2012b, 131-132. Signalons que, pour certains de ces bronzes (Marcellesi 2012b, n° 66-67), une datation plus tardive, à l'époque impériale, a été proposée : Chameroy 2013, 715-716.

63 Westermark 1995, 32.

celle au nom des Pergaméniens. L'examen des différentes données montre une fois encore que l'argumentation de J. Chameroy est très discutable.

La série au nom d'Athéna Niképhoros est faiblement représentée dans les trouvailles des fouilles par comparaison avec celle au nom de Philétaire d'une part, au nom d'Asclépios et au nom des Pergaméniens d'autre part. Parmi les monnaies de bronze de Pergame antérieures à Auguste, la série au nom d'Athéna Niképhoros représente 10 % dans la publication de K. Regling contre 26 % à 33 % pour les séries au nom de Philétaire, d'Asclépios Sôter et des Pergaméniens. Dans le volume de H. Voegtli, on compte 7 % de monnaies au nom d'Athéna Niképhoros contre 18 à 36,5 % pour les trois autres séries[64]. Cette faible représentation résulte-t-elle de la durée de la frappe, qui aurait été plus brève pour cette série, ou d'un volume de production plus faible ? Une fois encore, c'est une question à laquelle il est difficile de répondre.

Les trois séries sont représentées dans la "trouvaille du canal" publiée par J. Chameroy. Cependant, on a vu qu'il ne s'agissait pas d'un lot homogène et il est bien difficile d'en tirer des informations sur la chronologie relative et, plus encore, absolue. En faveur d'une datation des trois séries après 133, J. Chameroy se fonde principalement sur les trouvailles monétaires d'Atarnée, une monnaie trouvée à Aizanoi, des analyses métalliques. À Atarnée, dans les prospections menées entre 2006 et 2011, on n'a trouvé qu'un seul exemplaire de la série au nom d'Asclépios et aucun exemplaire des deux autres séries. Étant donné qu'il s'agit de trouvailles de surface, il est bien difficile d'en tirer une information chronologique. Pour les trouvailles des fouilles anciennes, le détail n'est pas connu, comme on l'a vu.

À Aizanoi, un exemplaire de la série au nom d'Athéna Niképhoros a été découvert dans la couche de destruction d'une maison hellénistique dans la seconde moitié du IIe s., que l'on a proposé de mettre en relation avec la révolte d'Aristonicos[65]. J. Chameroy croit pouvoir en déduire une datation vers 130 pour le début de la série d'Athéna Niképhoros mais on peut lui faire plusieurs objections : le lien avec la révolte d'Aristonicos n'est qu'une hypothèse ; la date de destruction de la maison n'offre qu'un *terminus ante quem* pour le matériel qui y a été découvert et pas une date absolue ; surtout, la monnaie est un des éléments ayant permis aux archéologues de dater la couche de destruction, il faut donc prendre garde à ne pas tomber dans le piège d'un raisonnement circulaire.

Des analyses métalliques récentes indiqueraient que certaines monnaies au nom d'Athéna Niképhoros et au nom des Pergaméniens sont en laiton et on en a déduit une datation dans les années 80 a.C., à l'époque de la première guerre mithridatique, en rapprochant ces résultats de ceux obtenus pour des monnaies royales du Pont[66]. Le problème est que les analyses effectuées sont des analyses de surface (fluorescence X) or cette méthode ne va pas sans poser problème pour des monnaies frappées dans un alliage cuivreux ; les résultats

64 Voir tableau 2, où l'on trouvera les chiffres absolus à côté des pourcentages.

65 Mention succincte de la monnaie par von Mosch 2000, 119, n. 25 ; Rheidt 2001, 262, où la monnaie est citée parmi les éléments permettant de dater la couche de destruction ; Atik & Rheidt 2004, 379. Voir aussi, sur le lien supposé avec les événements qui suivent la fin des Attalides, Lochner 2010, 35-36 ; Berges 2010, 38-43.

66 Smekalova 2009.

doivent donc être abordés avec prudence[67]. Si certains exemplaires de ces séries semblent être en laiton, d'autres paraissent bien être en bronze. Enfin, les derniers travaux sur ces questions invitent à réviser l'opinion traditionnelle selon laquelle le laiton et le cuivre pur n'auraient été utilisés qu'à l'époque impériale[68]. Il me semble que la conclusion à tirer de ces différentes données est que ces séries ont pu être frappées pendant une période assez longue au cours de la basse époque hellénistique, ce qui nous ramène à une datation large au IIe et dans les premières décennies du Ier s.

Je ne crois pas que les données des fouilles permettent de préciser davantage la chronologie. En revanche, le lien avec les monnayages d'argent (tétradrachmes d'Athéna Niképhoros et rares subdivisions, cistophores de l'époque attalide), l'épigraphie et l'histoire des fêtes religieuses à Pergame apportent des éléments à ne pas négliger. En l'état actuel de la documentation, il paraît raisonnable de situer le début de la série au nom d'Athéna Niképhoros (argent et bronze) à l'époque de la refondation des Niképhoria en concours panhelléniques en 181[69], le début de la série au nom d'Asclépios à l'époque de la refondation des Sôteria et Hérakleia en 165[70]. On n'a pas de point de repère pour le début de la série au nom des Pergaméniens mais le maintien institutionnel d'une cité de Pergame, mise en valeur par la dynastie attalide comme l'attestent de nombreuses inscriptions, autorise à penser que le début de la série a pu être antérieur à la fin de la dynastie. D'autre part, comme dans le cas des séries du IIIe s., il paraît important de souligner que ces trois séries ont circulé ensemble à Pergame.

La diffusion des monnaies frappées à Pergame éclaire leur fonction[71]. Les monnaies de bronze au nom de Philétaire, d'Athéna Niképhoros et d'Asclépios Sôter se sont largement diffusées. Au contraire, les monnaies au nom des Pergaméniens ne se rencontrent que dans une aire géographique réduite à des cités ayant fait partie du royaume attalide au IIe s. – Sardes[72], Éphèse[73] et probablement Hadrianoutherai (mod. Balıkesir, dans l'intérieur de la Mysie)[74] – ou dans des cités voisines comme Kymé[75]. Cependant, elles y sont généralement en nombre beaucoup moins important que les monnaies au nom de divinités. En dehors de cette zone, on en trouve à Athènes[76] et Cos[77] qui sont des cités avec lesquelles Pergame entretient des relations exceptionnelles, Athènes en raison de son rayonnement dans

67 J'ai proposé au centre Ernest Babelon d'Orléans un programme d'analyse par activation de ces bronzes mais ce programme est impossible à réaliser pour le moment à cause du déménagement du Cabinet des médailles de Paris.

68 Des analyses récentes ont montré que des monnaies de cuivre pur de la cité d'Élis semblent bien devoir être datées du IIIe s. a.C. : Wojan 2016.

69 C'est le choix fait par Westermark 1995, 29-35. Voir Marcellesi 2012b, 117, 121-122 et 125-128.

70 Marcellesi 2012b, 124, 129 et 159-160.

71 Sur ce sujet, Marcellesi 2012b, 101-102 et 160-161 ; Chameroy 2012, 164-167 et carte 179. Les données de J. Chameroy ne sont pas exactement les mêmes que les miennes, certaines informations ayant été prises en compte par l'un et pas par l'autre, et vice-versa, mais le tableau général n'en est guère modifié.

72 A. Johnston, in : Buttrey *et al.* 1981, n° 41-42 (4 monnaies).

73 Milne 1925, 389, n° 29 (fouilles de l'Artémision).

74 Delrieux 2011, 291-292, n° 230 sur le lieu d'acquisition et, probablement, de trouvaille.

75 Ünal 2009, 408 n° 3.

76 Kroll 1993, n° 873-876.

77 Stefanaki 2012, 317 n° K358. Sur cet ouvrage, voir Marcellesi 2014.

l'ensemble du monde hellénistique, Cos en raison de la présence du sanctuaire d'Asclépios. En dehors de ces exceptions qui confirment la règle, la série portant la forme longue de l'ethnique se caractérise donc par une diffusion très restreinte qui rappelle celle des monnaies portant l'ethnique abrégé au IIIe s.

Cette différence avec les séries contemporaines au nom de divinités me paraît confirmer l'hypothèse que j'ai suggérée[78], à savoir que la série au nom des Pergaméniens prend la suite de la série à l'ethnique abrégé, après une interruption dont la durée est difficile à préciser, tandis que les séries au nom de divinités prennent la suite de la série au nom de Philétaire et doivent être considérées, au moins dans les premières décennies de leur frappe, comme des monnaies royales. Après la fin de la dynastie attalide, elles continuent probablement d'être frappées et leur large diffusion est sans doute à mettre en relation avec le rayonnement des panégyries auxquelles elles sont associées, même s'il s'agit alors selon moi de monnaies civiques[79].

Les monnaies "étrangères"

Après avoir analysé les monnaies pergaméniennes et attalides trouvées dans les fouilles, nous pouvons passer à l'analyse des autres numéraires, les monnaies "étrangères", pour en tirer des informations sur la portée et l'évolution du rayonnement de Pergame.

La part des monnaies "étrangères"

Quelle est la part des monnaies "étrangères" antérieures à l'époque d'Auguste dans les différentes publications ?

Commençons par les ensembles relativement importants pouvant donner lieu à des mesures statistiques : on compte 188 monnaies "étrangères" (soit 30 %) dans la publication de K. Regling, 59 (soit 17 %) dans la rubrique "Katalog" du volume de H. Voegtli et 14 (24 %) dans la rubrique "Streufunde"[80]. Dans les ensembles plus petits mis au jour sur l'acropole, on compte 2 monnaies "étrangères" sur 6, soit le tiers, dans la fouille des maisons à péristyle à l'Ouest de l'agora[81], 5 sur les 36 monnaies identifiées antérieures à Auguste (soit 14 %) parmi celles provenant du canal de la "Stadtgrabung"[82] ; dans un autre secteur de la "Stadtgrabung",

78 Marcellesi 2012b, 158-161.

79 La notion de "monnaies de sanctuaire" me paraît devoir être bannie, étant donné ce que l'on sait des institutions des cités grecques. Voir Robert 1966 ; Le Rider 1973, 76 n. 1. L'expression "Tempelmünzen" a récemment été employée, à propos des monnaies pergaméniennes au nom de divinités : Schultz 1996, 19 ; Chameroy 2012, 147-156 ; enfin Nollé 2014, spéc. 299-309 à propos de Pergame. Nous ne pouvons discuter ici en détail de ces questions, qui dépassent le cadre du présent colloque.

80 Regling 1913, 356-358 ; Voegtli *et al.* 1993, Katalog n° 414-420, 456, 458-464, 466-469, 471, 473-488, 490, 493-502, 506-508, 510-512, 516 et 520-524 ; Streufunde n° 2, 78, 85, 87-91, 93-95, 97 et 100-101. Nous ne prenons pas en compte ici les monnaies dont la datation s'étend à l'époque impériale (par exemple Ier s. a.C.-Ier s. p.C.).

81 Boehringer 1984, 163, n° 5-6.

82 Chameroy 2012, 163, n° 35-39.

la seule monnaie hellénistique est une monnaie d'Élaia[83]. À l'Asclépieion, parmi les trouvailles isolées, elles-mêmes rares, on ne rencontre de monnaies "étrangères" que dans le secteur de la Via Tecta et la voie des portiques, au nombre de 5 sur 9, soit un peu moins de la moitié[84]. Dans le trésor de monnaies de bronze *IGCH* 1296, mis au jour dans la partie méridionale du sanctuaire, les monnaies "étrangères" identifiées sont au nombre de 2 sur un total de 16, soit 12 %[85].

Les deux trésors de monnaies d'argent relèvent d'une autre circulation. Dans le trésor de l'Asclépieion contenant 22 tétradrachmes d'étalon attique (*IGCH* 1303), les monnaies frappées dans d'autres ateliers que Pergame sont très largement majoritaires (19 monnaies, soit 86 %) ; cette forte proportion illustre le choix fait par les Attalides d'un système monétaire ouvert jusqu'au début du IIe s. a.C.[86]. Dans le trésor de 65 cistophores du Ier s. a.C. mis au jour dans la "Stadtgrabung" (*CH* 9, 568), 48 sont des cistophores pergaméniens, 17 sont éphésiens (soit 26 %).

Enfin, dans les trouvailles monétaires faites dans les environs de Pergame, on n'a pas mis au jour de monnaies "étrangères" à Kapıkaya ni dans la nécropole de Maymun Sekisi[87]. Dans le sanctuaire de Mamurt Kale, aux confins du territoire de différentes cités, les monnaies non pergaméniennes sont au nombre de 14 sur 20 monnaies identifiées (soit 70 %)[88]. Nous reviendrons plus loin sur ce cas particulier.

Pour le reste, on peut exclure les ensembles trop restreints pour pouvoir donner lieu à une quelconque interprétation. Si l'on s'en tient aux grands ensembles, au total la part des monnaies "étrangères" sur le territoire de Pergame est relativement faible. La publication de K. Regling a pu donner une image un peu faussée de la réalité : on y compte 30 % de monnaies "étrangères", ce qui a pu faire croire qu'elles étaient intégrées à la circulation locale[89] mais les publications ultérieures en comportent beaucoup moins ; seules les "Streufunde" de l'ouvrage de H. Voegtli offrent un chiffre qui s'approche de celui de K. Regling ; dans les deux cas, on peut se demander si certaines monnaies "étrangères" apportées aux archéologues et réputées provenir de Pergame ne proviennent pas en fait de territoires plus éloignés. En tout état de cause, la part des monnaies "étrangères" est, au total, très minoritaire, et inférieure à celle qui se rencontre dans d'autres cités d'Asie Mineure[90].

Encore faut-il distinguer dans cet ensemble les bronzes royaux qui ont pu avoir cours à Pergame à certaines époques, donc ne sont pas à proprement parler des monnaies "étrangères" : il s'agit des monnaies royales macédoniennes (au nom d'Alexandre, de Philippe, bronzes anonymes aux types du bouclier et du casque macédonien), des monnaies

83 Schwarzer 2008, 195 n° 20.

84 Voegtli 1984, 63-64, n° 1, 26, 28-30 ; il n'y a pas de monnaies "étrangères" dans les trouvailles isolées publiées dans les autres volumes des fouilles de l'Asclépieion (supra p. 207-208).

85 C. Boehringer in : Ziegenaus & de Luca, éd. 1968, 110-111, n° 73-74.

86 Marcellesi 2012b, 102-109, où l'on trouvera la bibliographie antérieure. Voir aussi Meadows 2013 ; de Callataÿ 2013b.

87 Voir supra p. 207-208 et n. 22 et 26.

88 K. Regling, in : Conze & Schazmann 1911, 42.

89 Regling 1913, 361 ; Westermark 1991, 157.

90 Par exemple à Priène : voir en dernier lieu Weisser 2014, 666-667.

de Lysimaque et des Séleucides. Ces monnaies sont particulièrement nombreuses dans la publication de Regling, qui en signale 18, soit 10 % du total des monnaies "étrangères"[91]. La proportion est de 8 % pour l'ensemble des fouilles de Pergame[92].

Au contraire, les monnaies émises par des cités autres que Pergame n'avaient pas cours officiellement à Pergame, selon nous[93]. Leur présence s'explique par des voyages d'une cité à l'autre et des pertes fortuites à Pergame ; il n'est pas exclu que certaines monnaies de types et de module proche des monnaies frappées à Pergame aient pu se fondre dans la circulation locale, que cela ait échappé ou non à leur propriétaire, mais en tout cas de manière illégale.

L'origine des monnaies de cités "étrangères"

L'origine des monnaies "étrangères" mises au jour dans les fouilles de Pergame a fait l'objet d'une analyse globale par Z. Çizmeli-Ögün et moi-même[94]. Dans mon livre de 2012, j'ai proposé de distinguer différentes phases chronologiques, d'après les datations des monnaies indiquées dans les publications[95]. La publication récente des monnaies de la "trouvaille du canal" par J. Chameroy ne modifie pas les résultats de ces enquêtes.

Il ressort de ces études que les cités les mieux représentées à Pergame sont celles du Nord de l'Égée (Thrace et îles proches), de la côte méridionale de la Propontide, de Troade, du golfe d'Adramyttion et de Lesbos, de la vallée du Caïque et du golfe d'Élaia, d'Ionie. La Carie, qui n'a jamais été sous domination attalide, est absente des fouilles de Pergame.

La vallée du Caïque apparaît comme un axe de circulation et d'échanges important entre la côte et l'intérieur, du IVe s. au début de l'Empire romain. Les relations avec le Nord de l'Égée semblent plus importantes au IVe s. qu'à l'époque hellénistique. Au contraire, les relations entre Pergame et l'Ionie, la Lydie ou la Phrygie se développent à partir du milieu du IIIe s., ce qui reflète l'histoire et l'extension du royaume attalide.

91 Regling 1913, 356 et 358. Détail : 1 drachme et 6 bronzes aux types d'Alexandre, 3 bronzes royaux macédoniens aux types bouclier/casque, 2 bronzes de Lysimaque, 6 bronzes séleucides.

92 Après la publication de Regling 1913 on a mis au jour à Pergame 4 monnaies séleucides (Voegtli *et al.* 1993, Katalog 521-522 et Streufunde 100-101) et 1 monnaie de Démétrios Poliorcète (à l'Asclépieion, dans le trésor *IGCH* 1296 : C. Boehringer in : Ziegenaus & de Luca, éd. 1968, 111 n° 74).

93 Je me distingue sur ce point d'une tendance récente chez les numismates. Voir notamment Knapp & Mac Isaac 2005, 36-49, qui ont émis l'hypothèse selon laquelle les bronzes étrangers avaient pu être acceptés dans les cités, au prix le plus souvent de l'acquittement d'une taxe, voire sans taxe dans les sanctuaires à l'occasion des fêtes panhelléniques. Cette hypothèse me paraît contraire à ce que nous apprend l'épigraphie, pour l'époque hellénistique du moins.

94 Çizmeli-Ögün & Marcellesi 2011, 306-310 et cartes 332-333, fig. 5 et 5a (détail de la précédente). Nous prenions en compte l'ensemble des données des fouilles. Seule la monnaie d'Élaia publiée par Schwarzer 2008, 195 n° 20 nous avait échappé. La "trouvaille du canal" n'avait pas encore été publiée. Les différences entre les chiffres donnés dans notre article de 2011 et ceux indiqués ici viennent de ce que je prends en compte ici les monnaies non identifiées, ce qui n'était pas le cas dans notre article de 2011, l'objectif poursuivi étant légèrement différent.

95 Marcellesi 2012b, n. 1 ; cartes 6 à 8 ; 281-282 (légendes) ; 31, 41-42, 54, 84 et 161 (commentaires). Les cartes ont été établies à partir des mêmes données que dans l'article cité dans la note précédente ; seule la publication de Regling 1913 n'a pas pu être prise en compte dans les cartes car la date des monnaies n'y est généralement pas précisée.

Ainsi, l'élargissement de l'origine des monnaies de cités "étrangères" coïncide avec l'apogée de la dynastie attalide, l'agrandissement du royaume et, plus généralement, la basse époque hellénistique où le rôle de Pergame comme métropole régionale se maintient, après la fin de la dynastie attalide, au sein de la province romaine d'Asie.

Le cas du sanctuaire de Mamurt Kale

La proportion des monnaies "étrangères" trouvées à Mamurt Kale est beaucoup plus importante que dans les fouilles de Pergame et des proches environs (70 %)[96]. Les 14 monnaies "étrangères" bien identifiées se répartissent comme suit : 4 monnaies macédoniennes ou des Diadoques et 10 monnaies de cités – cités de la vallée du Caïque, du golfe d'Élaia et Sardes[97].

On a vu que le sanctuaire ne faisait peut-être pas partie de la *chôra* de Pergame, si bien que le fait que les monnaies pergaméniennes ne soient pas majoritaires n'étonne guère. En revanche, le sanctuaire de la Mère des Dieux à Mamurt Kale est intimement lié à la dynastie attalide, comme l'attestent la dédicace du temple par Philétaire[98] et la dédicace d'une prêtresse à un roi Attale (probablement Attale Ier)[99] ; il a fait partie du domaine attalide pendant une grande partie de l'histoire du royaume. Or les cités représentées dans les trouvailles monétaires ont été sous domination attalide.

On remarque une présence relativement importante de monnaies macédoniennes ou des Diadoques d'une part, de monnaies de cités qui sont le siège de garnisons attalides dans la haute vallée du Caïque d'autre part – Apollonis et Thyatire, peu représentées par ailleurs dans les fouilles de Pergame. On peut se demander si ce sanctuaire n'a pas été fréquenté particulièrement par des soldats au service des Attalides.

Au contraire, dans le sanctuaire rupestre de Kapıkaya, tout proche de la ville de Pergame, consacré à Cybèle et à Mithra, on n'a pas trouvé de monnaies "étrangères".

Conclusion

La distinction institutionnelle entre la cité de Pergame d'une part, les dynastes puis les rois d'autre part, bien attestée par les inscriptions, trouve sa traduction dans le domaine monétaire avec des séries civiques d'une part, d'autre part une série dynastique au nom de Philétaire et les séries au nom de divinités qui semblent avoir été frappées d'abord sous l'autorité des rois avant de se poursuivre vraisemblablement après la fin de la dynastie attalide dans un cadre civique.

Bien que, depuis un siècle, les trouvailles monétaires des fouilles menées à Pergame aient fait l'objet de différentes publications qui donnent une bonne idée de l'ensemble, l'apport des fouilles à la chronologie relative et absolue des monnaies de bronze est relativement limité

96 Supra p. 208.

97 Tableau détaillé dans Çizmeli-Ögün & Marcellesi 2011, 310-311. Voir aussi Marcellesi 2012b, 100-101 et 160.

98 Φιλέταιρος Ἀττάλου Μητρὶ Θεῶν. Conze & Schazmann 1911, 10 ; Bringmann & Steuben, éd 1995, n° 256.

99 Βασιλεῖ Ἀττάλωι Σωτῆρι Μητρεῖς ἡ ἱέρεια. Conze & Schazmann 1911, 6-7.

dans le cas de Pergame, où les ensembles clos sont rares. En revanche, pour la chronologie du monnayage de bronze, on peut s'appuyer sur le monnayage d'argent qui est bien connu et relativement bien daté et sur l'épigraphie qui permet de bien connaître l'histoire de la cité et de la dynastie. Néanmoins, l'image que l'on peut se faire de cette chronologie dépend largement de celle qu'on se fait des relations entre cité et dynastes.

De même, si les fouilles menées par l'Institut archéologique allemand à Pergame ont porté sur des secteurs très différents de la ville et du territoire – habitat urbain, espaces monumentaux dans le centre urbain, grand sanctuaire extra-urbain, petit sanctuaire rupestre –, les choix de publication, l'histoire des fouilles et celle du site lui-même rendent difficile l'exploitation des données dans une perspective topographique. Néanmoins, on a souligné l'intérêt des trouvailles du sanctuaire de Mamurt Kale, qui se distinguent nettement de celles faites dans la ville et ses abords, ce qui s'explique sans doute par son statut de sanctuaire des confins, fréquenté par des gens venus de différentes cités et de garnisons attalides.

L'examen des monnaies "étrangères" (ni pergaméniennes ni attalides) découvertes à Pergame est fructueux : la présence de monnaies "étrangères", leur origine géographique et leur répartition chronologique illustrent l'histoire de cette cité qui est passée du statut de petite cité à la fin de l'époque classique à celui de capitale royale hellénistique et qui reste ensuite une des métropoles de la province d'Asie.

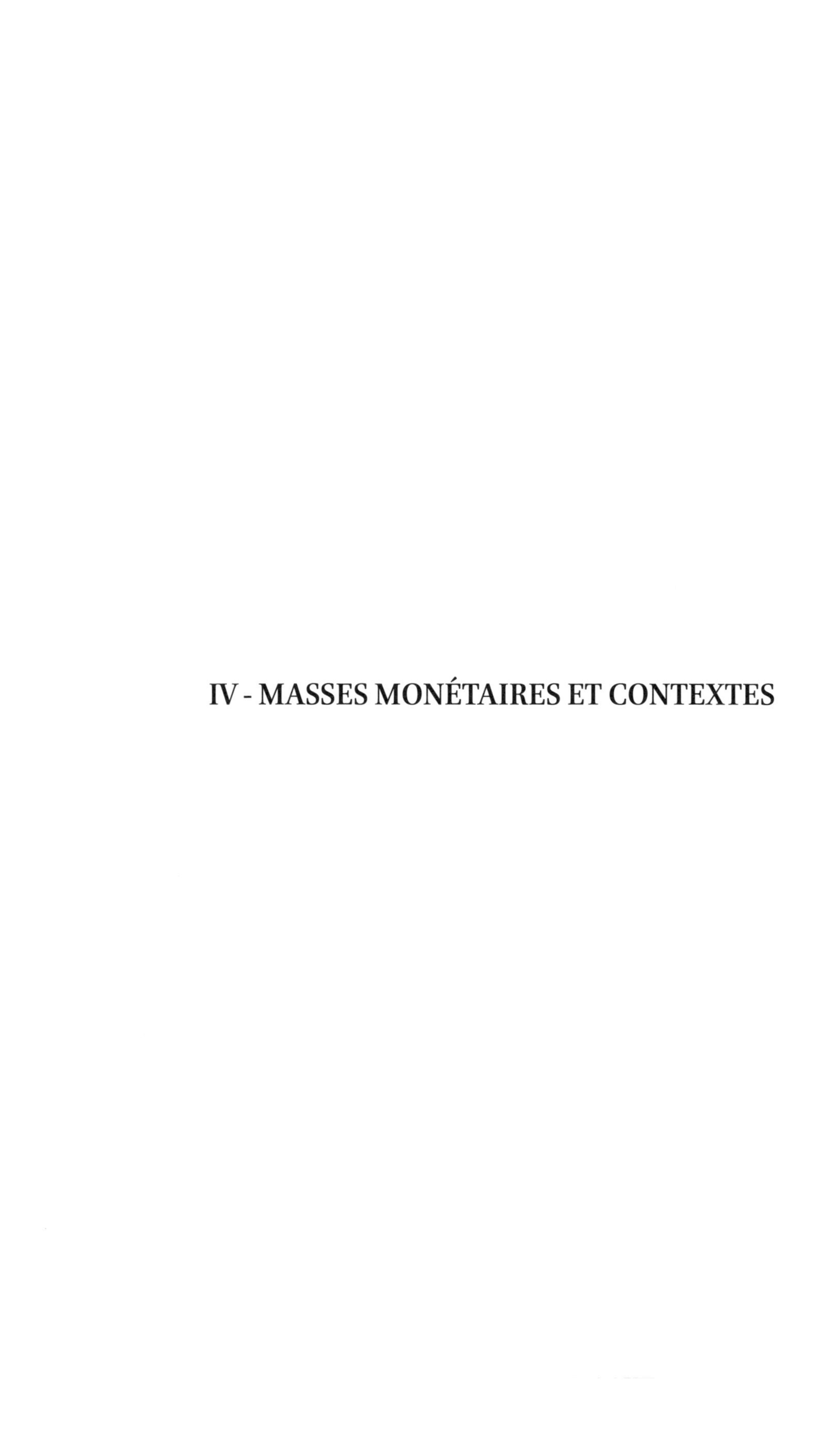

IV - MASSES MONÉTAIRES ET CONTEXTES

Coin Finds and the Monetary Economy: the Good, the Bad, and the Irrelevant

Kevin Butcher

What do coin finds tell us about the past? At a very elementary level, they can be appreciated for their contribution towards dating contexts. However, since we know very little about the longevity of coins in circulation, their utility in this respect is rather more restricted than non-specialists might imagine. Our monetary histories are still largely constructed via typologies rather than contextual dating. An alternative history, making use of contextual data to inform us when major changes to the circulating medium took place, is something that is sorely needed. While interest in this approach is gaining momentum, it will require far more contextual evidence than is currently available to us in order to construct an overview of coin use in antiquity[1]. If we knew more about the lifespan of coins we could be more sanguine about the precision of coins for dating contexts.

There are, of course, more interesting things to do with coin finds than using them to provide spot dates for archaeological features. Coins are social objects, and therefore have something to tell us about ancient social relations. They might have arrived at a site for a variety of reasons: as votive offerings, or as items of personal adornment, for example. In general, however, coin finds are considered to bear some relation to the ancient economy. This is, however, a very difficult topic, since it makes a grand claim for the material. The link between the ancient economy and the coins found on a site is far from obvious. Numismatists who work with site finds are well aware of the fact that they are dealing for the most part with low value denominations[2]. This sort of work has been characterised explicitly, if informally, as "small change studies". It concerns itself with the sort of money used in day-to-day transactions.

1 See the remarks by Collis 1988. This seems to me to be one of the imperatives for coin find studies, though I do not intend to deal with it here and mention it only in passing. For some attempts to phase coins using contextual data, see Butcher 2003 and Frey-Kupper 2013. The problem of deciding whether coins are residual or not can only really be tackled through analysis of the contexts: that is, by determining whether the relevant contexts otherwise contain non-residual material, or whether they contain material that has been re-deposited in such a way that the material's origin in an earlier deposit can be identified. Such studies require close cooperation between finds specialists and dirt archaeologists (especially those responsible for keeping contextual records). Given that categories of finds and the stratigraphy of a site are often studied independently of each other and timetables for publication do not always coincide, it is no easy task.

2 Casey 1980, 26-28.

K. Butcher, in : *Les monnaies de fouille du monde grec*, p. 225-237

While the sort of coins encountered on a site may well have been the sort used for day-to-day exchange, is there a strong correlation between the number of coins of a given period found, and the number of exchanges taking place? Does small change give us an accurate picture of economic circumstances in a given period? These are fundamental questions that impact on the significance and relevance of much that is done in archaeological numismatics.

It must be admitted that the humble nature of this material does not always endear it to historians of the ancient economy. They are quick to remind us that gold and silver coinage, being of much higher value, was of far greater economic significance than the small change that makes up the majority of site finds[3]. Furthermore, really large transactions might have been conducted through credit, at least in the Roman world[4]. If "small change studies" is an attempt to supply evidence for ancient economies, it is doing so in an environment in which most of the evidence is missing.

Despite these shortcomings, evidence of some sort is *present*, and it is of a kind that cannot be obtained from other sources. The archaeological record preserves two main sorts of evidence: coin hoards, usually (but not exclusively) composed of precious metal coins; and site finds. As we are all aware, these two sorts ought to be considered separately, even when they occur on the same site. That said, distinguishing dispersed hoards from single finds is not always easy. Unless the coins are found in a mass together, excavators may not recognise a group of coins as a hoard. Hoard material can end up dispersed over several contexts. My work on the coin finds from the Packard Humanities Institute's excavations at Zeugma revealed a number of likely hoards that had been dispersed through several different, and not even stratigraphically-related, contexts. The hoards were probably dispersed in this way not by human activity, but during the decay and collapse of buildings abandoned after the Sasanian sack of the city *c.* 252 AD. Some of the material appeared to have fallen from upper floors, resulting in coins from the same putative hoard being distributed over adjacent rooms of a building and even the street outside[5].

The only way to identify these dispersed hoards is by noting suspicious concentrations of the same issues or types of coins in a particular area of a site and checking the stratigraphic record to see how the coins were likely to have been deposited. Sometimes the record will yield a note by the excavator of a possible hoard among the coin finds. Often, however, the identification of hoard material is more problematic. Small hoards not recognised as such by the excavators can easily enter a finds processing system and become further disassociated from each other by being recorded alongside other coins from the same contexts. Some concentrations will always remain uncertain. For example, a context numbered 10,600 in the Beirut excavations yielded a variety of coins, including a slightly suspicious concentration of late 6th and early 7th c. Byzantine folles: 4 of Justin II (565-578 AD); 1 of Maurice (582-602 AD); and 3 of Phocas (602-610 AD)[6]. Are these a hoard? There were no other folles of Phocas from any other context excavated on the site, which is suggestive. Even so, it was not clear

3 Duncan-Jones 2003, 165; Lo Cascio 2008, 161-162.
4 Harris 2006; *id.*, éd. 2008; Hollander 2007.
5 Butcher 2013, 14-15.
6 *Id.* 2003, 269-274.

that all 8 coins went together. The same context 10,600 also yielded a small module follis and 20 nummi coin of Anastasius (491-518 AD), a 20 nummi coin of Justin I (518-527 AD), a 10 nummi coin of Justinian (527-565 AD) and a 20 nummi coin of Justin II[7]. Should they be considered as single finds, or part of the putative hoard? Other coins from the same context included an issue of Licinius I from the mint of Siscia, dated to 313-315 AD, a provincial issue of Berytus struck under Hadrian (117-138 AD), both of which are very unlikely to have formed part of an early 7th c. hoard[8]. In the end, there were too many uncertainties to warrant a listing of the suspected hoard coins in the section on hoards. Nevertheless an early 7th c. hoard from a major Near eastern city, even if composed of 8 coins, would be of some interest to specialists. In the Zeugma report, where there were many more examples of probable hoards, I attempted to discuss putative hoards, again without listing them separately[9]. Whether one decides to list them separately is to some extent a matter of taste; but such difficulties remind us how often the single finds from a site are potentially contaminated with unrecognised hoard material.

Of course, we are all aware of the fact that it can happen the other way around –that a hoard can be contaminated by alien material. There will always be grey areas, and these need to be reported, so that readers can make up their own minds.

Some specialists who work with site finds bemoan the scholarly focus on hoards; and it is true that historians of the ancient economy, when they consider archaeological evidence at all, tend to concentrate on hoards as evidence for the monetary economy. While there is something vaguely perverse about studying coin circulation through assemblages of coins that were unambiguously *not* in circulation, I feel that it is important to consider hoard evidence in parallel with site finds when interpreting the latter, precisely because they preserve complementary forms of evidence. Together they have preserved evidence of ancient perspectives on the nature of coined money. This is where I think the subject of small change becomes really exciting, and where the study of coin finds has a real contribution to make: not by using finds to chart the economic fortunes of a city over time, or to describe trade links between the site and other locations; but to draw comparisons, spatially, chronologically and between different categories of evidence. The archaeological record preserves evidence of tensions between the issuing authority and users, and about local or regional solutions to problems such as undersupply of coin. Without wishing to impose an agenda on "small change studies", it seems to me that an initial objective could be to explore and enrich our understanding of ancient monetary history rather than pursuing the broader but more elusive goal of shedding light on the ancient economy. Of course, monetary history is a part of economic history, but the subject of small change seems better suited to answering the needs of the former than the latter.

That said, the nature of money is itself a difficult topic, but this very difficulty could be a key to understanding what we see in the patterns of hoards and site finds. It is no secret that economists and monetary theorists are unable to agree on a precise definition of

7 *Ibid.*, 257, 259, 265, 268 et 270.

8 *Ibid.*, 149 et 180.

9 Butcher 2013, 14-17.

money, and perspectives have shifted back and forth over time, between money as a thing with intrinsic value, and money as a signifier of credit. There are some well-known ancient views on the subject, which merely serve to highlight the fact that people in antiquity faced similar difficulties in determining the nature of money. Aristotle puzzled over how money seemed to reconcile what to him was irreconcilable: the (proper) use value of a thing on the one hand, and its exchange value on the other[10]. In the Severan age, Paul the jurist declared money to be a price (*pretium*), not a commodity (*merx*), deriving its power not so much by its substance as by its quantity[11]. The fact that this needed elucidating suggests that not everyone saw it that way. His comments perplexed many medieval and Renaissance scholars and jurists, who tended to think of money as deriving its power from its intrinsic value as a commodity. Being unfamiliar with token base metal coins, some of these scholars proposed that scribal error was to blame: Paul had meant "quality", not "quantity"[12]. The Renaissance Italian jurist Girolamo Butigella disagreed, and took Paul at face value: all that mattered was the form, not the substance[13]. His opinions, and those of his contemporaries, paved the way for experiments with fiat money in base metal, among the first since ancient times.

This debate about the nature of money continued in the centuries that followed, and moved beyond the realm of theory to impact on the real world. England, having experimented with fiat money in the 17th c., famously reverted to the medieval commodity position in 1695, on the advice of the philosopher J. Locke: "Silver is the Instrument and Measure of Commerce in all the Civilized and Trading parts of the World. It is the Instrument of Commerce by its intrinsick value[14]". Yet his near contemporary J. Law saw money not as a thing, but as transferable credit: "Gold, Silver, Copper, Bills, Shells mark'd and strung are only representative Riches, or the Signs by which real Riches are Transmitted[15]". (Both views famously led to monetary catastrophe.) Here were two very different perspectives on money: either that it was material, and had value because of the commodity from which it was made; or that it was immaterial, transferable credit, which could be represented by any manner of substance.

What has any of this to do with coin finds? Apart from the fact that the two perspectives still compete, in various permutations, to this day, and so shape our own thinking about the nature of coinage, it is possible that they also competed in antiquity as well, leaving traces in the archaeological record. Some have seen Paul's declaration that money is a *pretium* and not a *merx* as a reflection of the age in which he was writing: after Septimius Severus debased the Roman silver denarius in 194 AD, the latter became a token coinage, whereas previously it had been a commodity currency[16]. However, it is equally possible that the legal position on coinage had always been that it represented value, rather than embodying it; in which case the precious metal was present as collateral, to convince all parties involved

10 Meikle 1995, 87-109.

11 *Dig.*, 18.1.1.

12 Sargent & Velde 2002, 110.

13 *Ibid.*, 108.

14 Locke 1695, 1.

15 Law 1720, 91.

16 Lo Cascio 1996, 274.

that the credit represented was good. However, given that the history of monetary theory is largely a history of a tension between the two positions, the coexistence in antiquity, at least unofficially, of a parallel opinion about money – that it embodied value by virtue of its substance – seems not unlikely, even if it was false from the jurists' perspective. It would certainly explain the choice of gold and silver for hoarding by private individuals, and why token base metal coinages often did not circulate widely compared with gold and silver. It also helps to explain the operation of Gresham's Law in antiquity: "better" coins were hoarded or exported[17]. Conversely, the presence of small change as single finds on sites could be explained not simply by their low value, but as a consequence of their value being regarded as representative rather than "intrinsic", and hence not suitable for hoarding.

In my original conference abstract, I promised to use a definition of money supplied by the Columbia economist R. Mundell, and here it is. Mundell is wary of token or fiat money, and sees it as the last stage in a succession of "bad" moneys that have driven out their "better" antecedents. He ended an essay on Gresham's Law with the following definition of money: "In the world of exchange, debts are settled in the cheapest medium possible[18]". This might seem like nothing more than an argument in favour of the efficiency of money as a medium of exchange, but it is not. Mundell argues that whatever becomes the primary medium of exchange effectively becomes the "bad" money that drives out other forms of money.

When we use the term "bad" money, we tend to mean that such moneys have less "intrinsic" value. The perjorative term, however, belies "bad" money's utility. It does not mean that people do not want "bad" money; on the contrary, it can even be more useful in exchanges than "good" money. Perhaps this is one way of thinking about site finds, as evidence for the medium considered most cost effective for exchanges. As long as there was a choice of denominations or coinages in different metals, one denomination or metal had a tendency to drive out other denominations from the realm of exchange, or at least from the realm of those types of exchanges that are likely to have left traces in the form of single finds.

In this paper I would like to look at three potential examples of this presumed tendency for the cheaper exchange medium to drive out others. All date to the third or very early 4th c. AD. In all cases the distinctions do not concern precious metal coins on the one hand and base metal on the other. The differences are more subtle than that. All the coins concerned are common issues of base metal or billon. We might readily expect them all to turn up regularly as single finds on sites, but some of the coinages do not. I suggest that the coexistence of these two ideas about the nature of money explains the patterns that we see.

All three case studies require revisiting some of the evidence from the Beirut excavations that I published in 2003. The first example concerns coinage in circulation from roughly the

17 Quite probably they were melted, too, but naturally this activity has left no unambiguous evidence. For hoarding of "better" Julio-Claudian and Republican denarii prior to Nero's reforms, see Butcher & Ponting 2014; for the export of Julio-Claudian denarii, some of which left the Roman empire after Nero's reforms, see Mac Dowall 1991; for the export of pre-Severan denarii to Barbaricum after the Severan debasement, see Lind 1993 and Reece 2008 (not all agree that the latter deposits date to after the Severan debasement, however: Berger 1996b; Bursche 2002).

18 Mundell 1998.

second half of the 3rd c., down to the end of the reign of Gallienus in 268 AD. The second spans the period of Aurelian's reforms of 274 AD down to Diocletian's reforms of *c.* 294 AD. The third concerns coins issued in the decade after Diocletian's reform. The conclusions are tentative, but can be viewed as invitations to further research on the topic.

Case study 1

In all three cases we need first to review the relevant monetary history as it currently stands. From about 260 to 274 AD there was effectively only one denomination produced in the Roman world: the debased radiate or antoninianus. Recent die studies suggest that production of gold coinage in this period was far from modest, but the paucity of surviving specimens suggests that gold did not survive long in circulation. Nor does it appear to have been regularly hoarded[19]. In contrast the ubiquity of radiates in hoards and as site finds implies that use of this denomination was widespread. In a fairly short space of time (230-270 AD) the coinage system had gone from one in which a suite of denominations was in regular production to what looks like a system involving the dominance of only one denomination. The picture may not be quite that simple, however, once we raise the question, briefly addressed at the beginning of this paper, of the longevity of coins in circulation. In the eastern empire cities had traditionally produced their own base metal denominations, but these too had all but ceased being produced after about 260 AD. How long the old denominations remained in circulation is less certain, and is one feature of monetary history that needs elucidating. At any rate, after about 260-268 (the sole reign of Gallienus) neither imperial mints nor many provincial cities in the east were investing in the production of small change. It is quite clear that the radiate went from a coin that is infrequently encountered as a single find on sites (and was therefore not treated like small change) and which instead was regularly hoarded, to one that is commonly encountered on sites as well as being commonly hoarded.

It looks as if the antoninianus had to do the work formerly undertaken by a suite of demoninations, serving as both a store of wealth and a medium of exchange. With gold very scarce, huge quantities of antoniniani were needed to perform the functions previously undertaken by high value denominations.

To illustrate the transition I refer to a chart originally employed for my report on the Beirut coins (fig. 1)[20]. It shows the proportions of three categories of radiates at nine different sites. At most sites it appears that the change comes in the sole reign of Gallienus (260-268 AD). Radiates of the period 244-253 AD, which were still silvery in appearance, are generally scarce to rare on sites (though they are common in hoards). Coins of the next period, the joint reign of Valerian and Gallienus (253-260 AD), witnessed a transition from a silvery-looking coinage to one that was more obviously billon. There is much more variation in the proportions of these coins at sites, and they are well-represented at Antioch (a major

19 Bland 2013. What happened to gold in the 3rd c. is uncertain. Perhaps it was exported and melted, or perhaps it was melted within the Roman world.

20 Butcher 2003, 78, fig. 33.

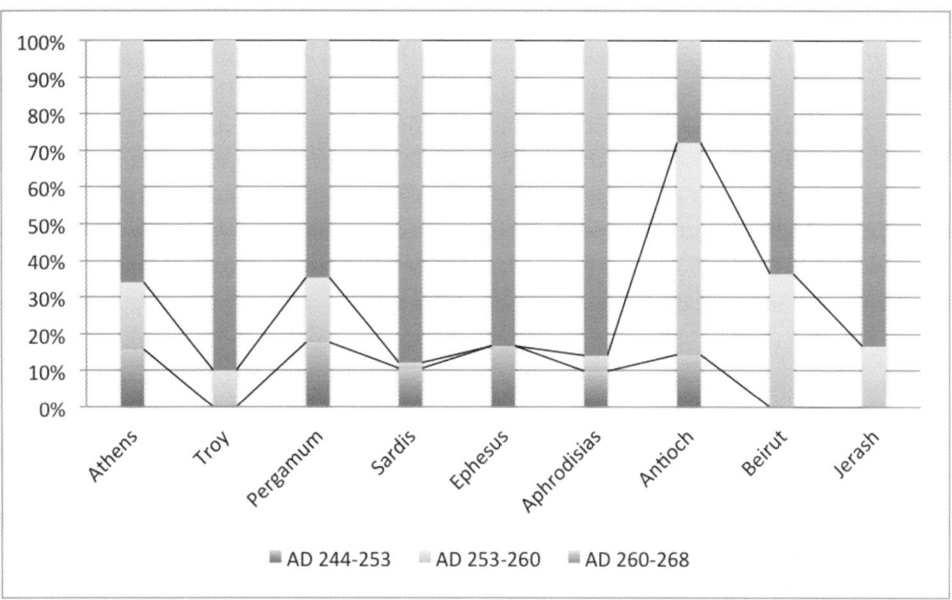

Fig. 1. Proportions of radiates of three successive periods at nine sites in the eastern Roman empire.

mint) and Beirut. Finally in the period of Gallienus' sole reign the antoninianus became a coin of base metal with only a minimal silver content. The proportions of this coinage dominate at all sites except Antioch.

One could take the scarcity or absence of coins of a period as evidence that they were not in circulation in any quantity, but often hoards from the vicinity or region of the sites furnish us with a corrective. The hoards suggest that the coins were there, but they were not being deposited as single finds. If we follow the reasoning above, antoniniani of 244-253 AD are absent or rare as site finds because they were not the cheapest means of settling debts. There were other forms of money available to do that. Antoniniani of the following period, 253-260 AD, became a cheap way of settling debts in some places, like Antioch, but in other places like Sardis they did not.

Naturally this raises the question as to what sort of money was the cheapest means of settling everyday debts if the radiates did not serve this function, and the pattern just described may hint at an answer. The strong showing for radiates of 253-260 AD at Antioch and Beirut may indicate that provincial base metal coinage had been demonetised, or was now harder to obtain, in Antioch and Beirut than elsewhere. Certainly there is no evidence for production of provincial coinage at Antioch later 253-254 AD, or at Berytus later than 254-255 AD, or the whole of the Near East later than 256-257 AD[21]. There are no coinages with portraits of Valerian II (Caesar 255/256-258 AD) or Saloninus (Caesar 258-260 AD) from any

21 Butcher 2004, 263-264.

Near Eastern city[22]. In contrast, cities in western Asia Minor continued to issue coins after 256-257, since there are coinages for both Valerian II and Saloninus and, indeed, a few for Claudius II (268-270 AD) and Aurelian (270-275 AD)[23]. It is possible, then, that a rise in the proportion of radiates as single finds at a site could be, at least in part, a symptom of radiates replacing provincial coinage as the cheapest medium of exchange there (either because the latter were no longer readily available, or because they were deemed of greater metallic value), but this needs further investigation to confirm or refute. If provincial coinages were "driven out" by "bad" radiates, this could explain why we have numerous hoards of provincial coins dating to the 250s-260s.[24].

There is another aspect to consider here: the relationship of the finds to the supply of coinage. In other periods the absence of gold and silver among the site finds would be a severe handicap to any such analysis, but in the 260s we are dealing with a currency predominantly composed of a single denomination. It is often argued that a vastly increased supply of debased radiates caused high inflation. Such arguments are often advanced following the observation that huge hoards of this material exist, but, as we have seen, huge hoards of radiates may be a symptom of a general absence of gold coinage for storing wealth. Furthermore, all that huge hoards tell us is that coinage was being removed from the monetary economy and left to languish in hoards, where potentially it was not put to work. It is hard to see how hoarded money can have contributed significantly to high inflation. On the other hand, there might be a relationship between the frequency of radiates as site finds and how hard that money was made to work. So an increase in the frequency of radiates as site finds could potentially be an indication that the quantity of money being used also increased, which might have resulted in rising prices. This is, however, conjecture, and the possibility that a high incidence of a coinage as site finds represents demonetisation could easily disrupt such an analysis (see below).

Case study 2

The second case study concerns the pattern that appears after Aurelian's reform in 274 AD. The precise character of Aurelian's reforms have long been debated. He introduced a new radiate coin of better quality than the ones issued in the decade immediately preceding the reform. The relationship of this new "aurelianus" or "aurelianianus" to the old radiate is far from clear. The late 4th c. historian Zosimus mentions that Aurelian gave out new silver in exchange for debased coin, but provides no further details[25]. Hoards seem to suggest that old radiates continued circulating in many places, although they may well have been successfully

22 Sawaya 2009, 262 has argued for a coinage in the name of Valerian II at Heliopolis dated to 255-256 AD, though the portrait is indeterminate and the titles are those of his grandfather Valerian I: IMP CAES P LIC VALERIANVS P F AVG.

23 The Pamphylian city of Perge even issued coins for Tacitus (275-276 AD).

24 Howgego 1985, 66.

25 Zosimus 1.61.3: ἤδη δὲ καὶ ἀργύριον νέον δημοσίᾳ διέδωκε, τὸ κίβδηλον ἀποδόσθαι τοὺς ἀπὸ τοῦ δήμου παρασκευάσας, τούτῳ τε τὰ συμβόλαια συγχύσεως ἀπαλλάξας.

demonetised in Italy and the Balkans[26]. Fortunately there are other ways of exploring the relationship between the "aurelianus" and other coinages that do not require full knowledge of their relative face values.

Fig. 2 shows the proportions of three categories of coin minted between 253 and 294 p.C. (the date of Diocletian's reforms) [27]. The three categories comprise: 253-274 p.C., the period of the debased radiate; "aureliani" of 274-294 p.C.; and "barbarous radiates" and coins of the Gallic empire. As is immediately apparent, while proportions of radiates of 253-274 p.C. are roughly similar at all nine sites, those that are rich in "barbarous and Gallic" are poor in "aureliani".

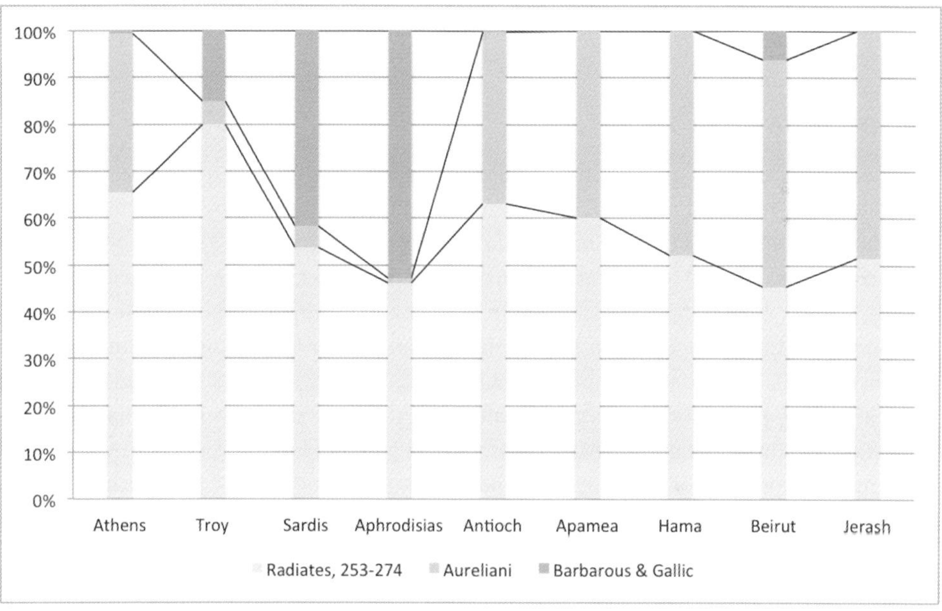

Fig. 2. Radiates and "aureliani" of the period 253-294 AC at nine sites in the eastern Roman empire.

To make full sense of this we need to consider the hoard evidence as well. While "aureliani" are rare as single finds at Troy, there was a major mint for these coins at nearby Cyzicus, and a hoard of these coins was found at the site (which was not included in the chart data)[28]. As was the case with the earlier radiates, the aureliani were probably present everywhere in the east, but are not commonly found as single finds at the three sites in western Asia Minor. The case of the barbarous and Gallic radiates is different. While hoards of these are known in the western Asia Minor, where they also commonly occur as single finds, there are no

26 Estiot 2012, 550.

27 Butcher 2003, 79, fig. 34. There is evidence that the reformed coinages of Diocletian were not introduced everywhere simultaneously, but for our purposes the differences in date do not matter.

28 Bellinger 1961, 201-211.

known hoards of these coins outside that region of the Roman east. They would appear to have been imported from the north western provinces of the empire to western Asia Minor at some point in the 270s or later, and somehow they were sustained in circulation there, and nowhere else did they have a significant role to play[29].

The presence of these barbarous and Gallic radiates seems to have given coin users in that region a choice that coin users at the other sites did not have: to use barbarous and Gallic coins (and perhaps old radiates) as the cheapest medium of exchange. Aureliani were driven into hoards, presumably because they were deemed to be more valuable as a store of wealth than a means of exchange. The pattern of single finds in western Asia Minor would appear to replicate that in the north western provinces of the empire, where barbarous and Gallic radiates predominate and aureliani are rare[30].

Case study 3

The final case also requires a little review of the background. The reforms of Diocletian are sometimes regarded as a further stage of the changes initiated by Aurelian[31]. The old aurelianus continued to circulate but was no longer produced; instead a radiate coin with no silver content was issued (mainly at eastern mints)[32]. The latter is hardly ever encountered in the west, either among the single finds or in hoards, and presumably it did not form a major component of the coinage circulating there. A larger, heavier billon coin, the nummus, was also introduced. The nummus is plentiful in hoards, but rare among single finds (fig. 3)[33]. In contrast, the post-reform radiate is abundant in the east. The finds imply that the post-reform radiate drove the nummus out of circulation and into hoards. As has been proposed, the nummus would appear to have been undervalued at some point, at least with respect to the post-reform radiate[34].

This pattern makes it hard to accept K. Harl's judgement that public confidence in the nummus rapidly waned and that its value declined because it was overvalued[35]. The hoarding of these coins seems to imply the opposite: that these coins were too highly valued to form the cheapest medium of exchange. Diocletian's currency edict of 301 AD mentions the doubling in value of a denomination, or some denominations, or perhaps all denominations. Opinions vary[36]. One position has it that only the value of the post-reform radiate was

29 Mac Donald 1974; Butcher 2003, 79.

30 In the north west, aureliani generally occur only in hoards (Burnett 1987, 126), but they are not common and it appears that they did not circulate in mass there (Estiot 2012, 551). In Britain the phenomenon of "legitimist" hoards, containing predominantly *aureliani* rather than those of the Gallic usurpers and central emperors prior to Aurelian's reform, is uncommon but well known (Bland 1992, 209-210).

31 Estiot 2012, 548.

32 Abdy 2012, 586.

33 Butcher 2003, 81. The same observation about the rarity of *nummi* among the single finds holds true in western provinces like Britain: Casey 1980, 42.

34 Estiot 2012, 548.

35 Harl 1996, 152-156.

36 Harl 1996, 153 (all denominations); Estiot 2012, 548-549 (some denominations); Abdy 2012, 585 (post-reform radiates only).

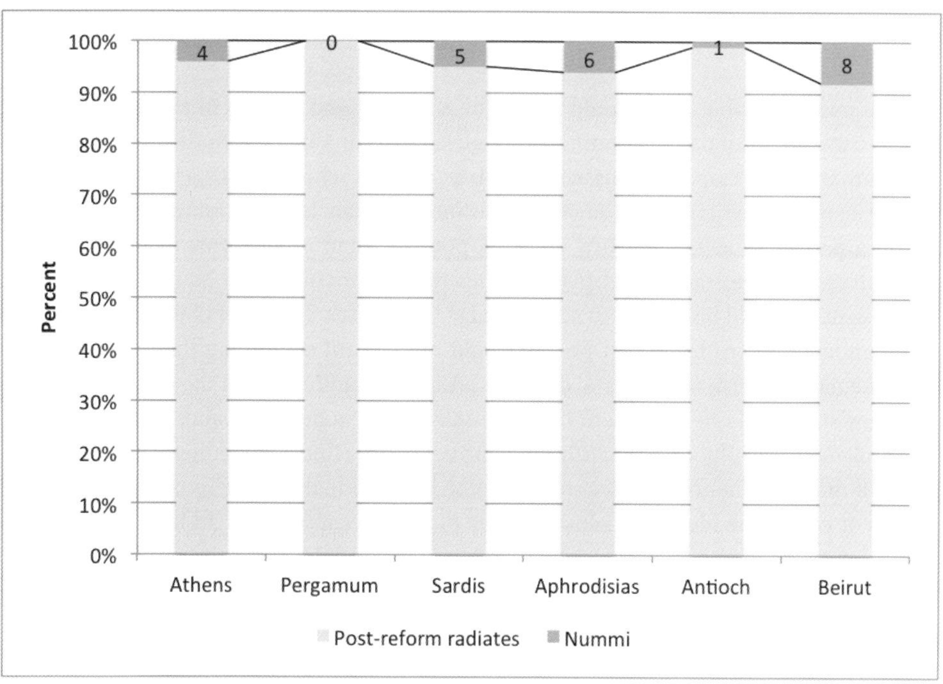

Fig. 3. Proportions of tetrarchic nummi and post-reform radiates, 294-305 AC, at six sites in the eastern Roman empire. The numbers in the columns denote the percentages for the two respective categories.

doubled. If this is so, it can only have exacerbated the situation; and perhaps the pattern that we see is the consequence of the revaluation. Whatever the case, if doubling of values in the currency edict was an attempt to deal with a reluctance to use nummi in everyday exchanges the rarity of nummi as single finds would seem to suggest that the problem was not resolved by the reform.

The bugbear of irrelevance: demonetisation and the archaeological record

So far we have been considering public treatment of "good" and "bad" coin, but there are also occasions on which certain coins can cease to function even as the cheapest medium of exchange[37]. Perhaps some of the coinages that predominate on sites, even some of those we have considered above, are common partly because there came a point when they ceased to have official backing from the state and became more difficult to use. There seems to be no easy way of distinguishing between presence due to frequent use and presence due to demonetisation of an issue. A horizon in which a certain coinage predominates could be an

37 Butcher 2003, 35; Reece 2002, 91-92.

indicator, but the contextual evidence is rarely so closely dated so as to permit one to draw such a conclusion.

The possibility that coins could simply be scrapped and end up in the archaeological record through redundancy is yet a further obstacle to linking coin finds with the ancient economy, which perhaps explains why there is a degree of scholarly resistance to it. However, even if demonetised coins are largely irrelevant to the ancient economy, demonetisation is still a part of monetary history, more so, perhaps, than other forms of non-economic numismatic evidence such as votive offerings of coin or coins used as items of personal adornment. It would be helpful to acknowledge likely cases. The chief objection to the idea of redundancy seems to be that people would not discard something that had value and could be melted down for its metal content[38]. A quick examination of the metal small finds from any site should be enough to convince that the objection is invalid. Scraps of bronze and broken bronze objects are hardly great rarities among finds on Mediterranean sites, and many of these fragments are more substantial than individual specimens of the commonest classes of coins. The idea that coins could be present because they had become irrelevant to economic exchanges does not mean that demonetised coins were always wilfully thrown away, but that is also possible, given that larger fragments of broken bronze objects were sometimes discarded. Such objects, like demonetised coins, no longer had use value, let alone exchange value.

Conclusions

Jurists like Paulus may have had a clear understanding of the symbolic nature of money, but the finds seem to me to speak of two conceptions: one, characterised by site finds, of money as largely symbolic of value; and a popular conception of money as a thing with intrinsic value, characterised by hoard coins that were removed from the realm of exchange, probably much to the chagrin of the issuing authorities. Symbolic money is most successfully sustained by strong institutions, and therefore the spatial and chronological patterning of site finds may have something to tell us about underlying institutional structures, providing a more finely-grained image than the evidence derived from hoards of “good” coins. Assuming that demonetised coins did not travel in large numbers after they had been rendered redundant, the “bugbear” of demonetisation would be no obstacle to the identification of these institutional structures.

Nothing in this paper should be read as an attempt to disparage the notion of a correlation between coin use and coin finds. If anything, it strengthens the links. The “bad” money predominates in the finds record because, perversely, it was “good” for exchange. One might even say it was desirable, and to that extent, it could have been worth importing, as in the case of barbarous and Gallic radiates in western Asia Minor. The finds record preserves public ideas about which coins were suitable for a particular purpose, suggesting to us

38 “Coins... are most emphatically not rubbish; they are a store of wealth, they represent security, food, shelter, diversion and all the other basics of existence. They are not usually deliberately thrown away...” (Casey 1988, 40).

the media in which exchanges were conducted; what it probably cannot do is help us to quantify the number of those exchanges over time. It perhaps hints more at the form of the monetary economy rather than its performance. Yet an ability to delineate with confidence the monetary economy of antiquity in any given period would be a significant advance.

De quoi les monnaies grecques trouvées en fouilles sont-elles le reflet ? Propos diachroniques de méthode

François de Callataÿ

À la mémoire de Mando Oeconomidès.
Son "étudiant belge" (1984-1985), en souvenir affectueux de tant d'heureux moments passés au *Musée numismatique*.

Un matériel monétaire immense a été dégagé tout autour de la Méditerranée et jusqu'à l'Indus depuis maintenant plus d'un siècle. Quoique, et de façon regrettable, une grande partie de ce matériel n'a pas été publié (et à vrai dire ne le sera jamais)[1], les publications de monnaies grecques trouvées en fouille constitue une riche bibliographie dont le rythme n'a cessé de s'accélérer. Pourtant, au-delà de ces entreprises spécifiques à un site, on a peu mené de réflexion concertée qui touche aux problèmes et aux méthodes. Vingt ans environ après le colloque organisé à Athènes en 1995 en l'honneur de M. Oeconomidès et son ensemble de contributions stimulantes[2], l'heure est venue d'un nouveau bilan en forme de réflexion panoramique[3].

La présente étude est résolument méthodologique. 1) Elle recadre d'abord les particularités des monnaies de fouilles par rapport aux trésors monétaires et aux monnaies isolées. 2) Elle s'en va ensuite faire un tour du côté des spécialistes de monnaies romaines, qui – bénéficiant

1 En partie parce qu'il est aujourd'hui désagrégé et réduit en poussière, notamment du fait de traitements inappropriés utilisés lors de leurs découvertes (Rotroff 1997, 9 évoque une solution d'hydroxyde de sodium et de zinc). En partie parce qu'il y a eu négligence (Grierson 1965, x-xi : sur l'attitude de Flinders Petrie à Naucratis ou le destin des monnaies des fouilles allemandes à Baalbek et Magnésie, dont un grand nombre furent reléguées avec les doubles par K. Regling voire même fondues). En partie parce que les vieux rapports de fouilles sont souvent inexploitables (Hackens 1975, 217 ; Grierson 1976, 179). En partie surtout – et c'est là un problème grandissant – parce que l'argent manque pour publier le produit des fouilles.

2 Sheedy & Papageorgiadou-Banis, éd. 1997 (voir en particulier : Picard 1997 ; Rotroff, 1997; Touratsoglou 1997 ; Walker 1997). Sur les monnaies de fouilles spécifiquement, voir aussi déjà Sorda, éd. 1989.

3 Les colloques sur la circulation monétaire en général, et traitant de trésors principalement, n'ont pas manqué : *Coin finds and coin uses in the Roman world* (Oxford, mars 1993 ; voir King & Wigg, éd. 1996) ; *Ritrovamenti monetali nel mondo antico: problemi e metodi* (Padoue, mars-avr. 2000 ; voir Asolati & Gorini, éd. 2002) ; *Coins in context. New perspectives for the interpretation of coin finds* (Francfort, oct. 2007; voir Kaenel & Kemmers, éd. 2009) ; *Nomisma. La circulation monétaire dans le monde grec antique* (Athènes, avr. 2010 ; voir Faucher *et al.* 2011).

F. de Callataÿ, in : *Les monnaies de fouille du monde grec*, p. 239-261 de conditions favorables – ont poussé plus tôt et plus loin la réflexion sur le sujet. 3) Elle esquisse ce que l'on peut attendre des études menées sur des monnayages contemporains. 4) Elle conclut enfin par quelques propos actualisés sur ce dont les monnaies de fouilles sont le reflet (ou pas).

Proportion et particularités des monnaies de fouilles par rapport aux trésors et aux monnaies isolées

Dans un de ses articles pionniers paru en 1965, P. Grierson écrivait : "My primary concern will be the light which coin finds can throw upon problems of coin distribution, both in space and time. For this single finds, whether coming to light by chance (stray finds) or as the result of systematic search (site finds) are more relevant than cumulative finds of hoards. Stray finds are our best guide to the area over which coins were used"[4]. On a beaucoup débattu depuis des mérites respectifs des différentes catégories de documents, en marge de débats plus vastes où pointent les lignes de fracture identifiées qui divisent les modernistes-économistes d'une part, les primitivistes-anthropologues de l'autre.

Proportion des monnaies de fouilles

Les fouilles officielles menées depuis plus d'un siècle à présent en Grèce et plus généralement sur les sites du monde grec antique ou en relation avec celui-ci, ont permis de mettre au jour un grand nombre de monnaies grecques. Ce nombre a très probablement aujourd'hui dépassé les cent mille. Parmi ce grand total, figurent les larges ensembles de l'agora d'Athènes (16 557 monnaies grecques identifiées)[5], des fouilles de Thasos[6] et de bien d'autres[7].

Il arrive cependant souvent qu'une partie du matériel soit illisible ou seulement vaguement identifiable en fonction d'un module propre à une époque. C'est particulièrement le cas en Égypte où la nature du sol mange le bronze (84 % de non identifiables pour la récente

4 Grierson 1965, ii ; voir aussi xiii : "One has to accept the fact that while the three categories of stray finds, site finds and hoards largely complement each other, there are certain things they cannot be asked to do. Site finds are more satisfactory than stray finds for the study of fluctuations in circulation density; stray finds are a more reliable guide than hoards to circulation areas and sometimes to the localization of mints".

5 Kroll 1993, 1 (mais le nombre de monnaies romaines est supérieur : voir Rotroff 1997, 9 qui évoque un grand total de 54 000 monnaies).

6 Picard 1997, 29 (plus de 20 000 monnaies).

7 Mais on notera aussi que près de 20 ans de fouilles n'ont amené la découverte que de *c.* 1 300 monnaies d'époque grecque à Monte Iato (Frey-Kupper 2013) et de 1 022 monnaies ptolémaïques sur dix chantiers différents à Alexandrie (Picard *et al.* 2012). À Némée, ce sont 985 monnaies grecques qui ont été trouvées en quelque 25 années de fouille (Knapp & Mac Isaac 2005). À Didymes, les fouilles allemandes menées de 1962 à 1998 n'ont permis la publication que de 490 monnaies d'époque grecque (Baldus 2006). À Cyrène, ce sont 736 monnaies grecques (Buttrey 1997, 2) qui ont été mises au jour en dix campagnes de fouille (1969-1978).

publication des fouilles du CEA à Alexandrie)[8]. Ailleurs, ce pourcentage peut dans les cas les plus favorables tomber sous les 10 %[9] mais on rappellera aussi que, pour les fouilles de l'agora d'Athènes, deux tiers des monnaies se sont révélées illisibles et la moitié non-identifiables[10].

Par rapport aux quelques millions de monnaies grecques aujourd'hui conservées dans les collections publiques et privées, cela représente un pourcentage qui, sans être dérisoire, est néanmoins très réduit, de l'ordre de quelques pourcents tout au plus[11].

De toute façon, n'attestant presque que le bronze, les monnaies de fouilles passent à côté de l'essentiel de la masse monétaire quand on sait que, dans la France du XVIIIe s., toutes les frappes de cuivre et de billon ne représentaient pas 2 % de la masse monnayée[12]. Ajoutons que, d'après la très imprudente estimation faite par le généralement très prudent R. Reece, ce qui est retrouvé à l'occasion d'une fouille extensive correspond à moins d'un 1/100 000e de tout ce qui a circulé[13].

Particularités des monnaies de fouilles par rapport aux trésors et aux monnaies isolées

Un des Graals du numismate est d'apercevoir, fut-elle partiellement déformée, l'image de la circulation monétaire propre à une aire géographique et une époque déterminées.

Ce qui suit vise à typer les qualités et les défauts propres aux trois grandes catégories de documentation factuelle généralement convoquée pour définir la circulation monétaire : 1) les monnaies de fouilles, 2) les trésors monétaires et 3) les monnaies isolées. Ces trois catégories ne sont pas étanches. En particulier, il est habituel que le matériel d'une fouille archéologique comprenne un ou plusieurs trésors et de nombreuses pièces isolées[14].

8 Picard *et al.* 2012 (3 529 identifiées sur *c.* 22 000 exhumées). Même valeur de *c.* 85 % pour Doura-Europos (2 177 monnaies sur 14 017 : Bellinger 1949 et Seyrig 1958, 171).

9 Voir Frey-Kupper 2013, pour Monte Iato : 6 % (86 [n° 1340-1425] sur 1425) ou Knapp & Mac Isaac 2005, 18 pour Némée (*c.* 5 % des monnaies d'époque classique : seulement *c.* 100 sur 2 000).

10 Rotroff 1997, 10. Voir aussi Walker 1997, 22.

11 5 % si on imagine qu'il se trouve 250 000 monnaies à provenir de fouilles (estimation généreuse) sur un total de 5 millions de monnaies conservées (estimation sans doute dépassée aujourd'hui ; voir Callataÿ 1997a, 21-94).

12 Voir Morrisson, 2002 qui cite Spooner : *c.* 1,5 % pour les années 1726-1785.

13 Reece 2003, 65. Le calcul pour y arriver mérite d'être résumé : comme celui de Richborough, le site de Cirencester (Corinium) est susceptible de livrer *c.* 60 000 monnaies (mais pas 200 000), soit l'équivalent de la recette d'une boutique prospère à Rome pendant *c.* 2-3 mois. Considérant l'existence d'une centaine de boutiques actives à Cirencester pendant *c.* 100 ans (41-138), on voit que ce qui pourrait être trouvé (*c.* 60 000 monnaies) "is probably not one hundred-thousandth part of the money in circulation in Corinium at any one time" (60 000 monnaies [lesquelles ?] x 100 boutiques x 100 ans = 6 000 000 000). Critiques de ce calcul dans Reece 1984 = *id.* 2003, 311.

14 La publication par G. Le Rider des trouvailles monétaires faites à Suse (Le Rider 1965) fait ainsi connaître 12 trésors, soit 1 847 monnaies d'argent (83 % ; 10 trésors) et 384 de bronze (2 trésors), pour 2 640 monnaies isolées, soit 2 527 en bronze (96 %) et 113 en argent (voir aussi Fischer 1968). Pour Doura-Europos, Bellinger publie 22 trésors (Bellinger 1949 et Seyrig 1958, 172). Sur les raisons qui poussent à enterrer un trésor dans un cadre urbain ou non avec référence à la littérature antique, voir MacDonald 1902-1903.

Monnaies de fouilles (excavations finds)

Les monnaies de fouilles privilégient de façon écrasante le petit numéraire (*nb* : on laisse ici entièrement de côté l'archéologie funéraire qui s'est de plus en plus constituée en champ autonome). Pour un ensemble de 38 sites, on a pu montrer que, dans quatre cas sur cinq, le pourcentage de monnaies de bronze s'élève à plus de 95 % du total des monnaies exhumées. Il est même supérieur à 99 % dans un cas sur trois[15].

Autrement dit, les chances de retrouver une pièce égarée sont inversement proportionnelles à la valeur de celle-ci[16]. C'est toute la différence qui existe entre un passage de Saint-Luc et un autre de Théophraste. À Saint-Luc, qui écrit : "Quelle est la femme qui, si elle a dix drachmes et vient à en perdre une, n'allume une lampe, ne balaie la maison et ne cherche avec soin, jusqu'à ce qu'elle l'ait trouvée ? Et quand elle l'a trouvée, elle assemble amies et voisines et leur dit : Réjouissez-vous avec moi, car je l'ai trouvée, la drachme que j'avais perdue[17]", Théophraste réplique en attribuant au seul mesquin le fait de rechercher une monnaie de bronze : "Sa femme a-t-elle laissé tomber un sou (*trichalkon*), il déplace tout, meubles, lits, coffres, et fouille le plancher[18]". Sachant que le pouvoir d'achat d'un statère ou d'un *aureus* dépassait de loin celui d'un billet de 500 euros de nos jours, on ne s'étonnera pas de leur absence en fouilles. En revanche, il est possible que les monnaies étrangères soient surreprésentées[19].

Les monnaies de fouilles sont donc, la plupart du temps, ce que l'on ne s'est pas mis en demeure de rechercher. Il en découle, a contrario, que l'absence de preuves ne peut être tenue pour la preuve de l'absence et que des monnayages plus précieux ont pu abondamment être utilisés sans laisser la moindre trace dans le matériel mis au jour.

En dépit des appels à collaborer[20] ou de la formulation de procédures à respecter[21], le dialogue entre archéologues et numismates est souvent demeuré très réduit en dépit de l'attente réciproque pour une amélioration de leurs chronologies respectives[22]. Le numismate se trouve frustré du peu de contextes utiles qui permettent d'affiner la datation de ses monnaies et l'archéologue dépité de ne pouvoir utiliser les dates de production, dans

15 de Callataÿ 2006, 180 (sur 38 sites, plus de 95 % dans 31 cas et plus de 99 % dans 13 cas).

16 Ce que R. Reece appelle le "risk factor" (Reece 1973 = *id.* 2003, 63). Cela vaut pour hier comme pour aujourd'hui.

17 Luc 15.8-9.

18 Thphr., *Char.*, 10.6. Voir aussi Petr. 43.4 : *ab asse crevit, et paratus fuit quadrantem de stercore mordicus tollere* [il n'avait pas un as à son début, et il eût ramassé avec ses dents un quadrans dans un tas de fumier] (à propos d'un certain Chrysanthe ("Fleur d'or" !), devenu riche). Si besoin, Furnham 1985, 571-575 a montré que la probabilité qu'une personne conserve une monnaie trouvée augmente de façon linéaire en fonction de la valeur de ladite monnaie.

19 Seyrig 1958, 174 ("Peut-être, à vrai dire, les monnaies d'une fouille donnent-elle un tableau plus disparate que ne l'était la réalité, et comprennent-elles un bon nombre de pièces rebutées, abandonnées çà et là et dénichées seulement par l'œil perçant du fouilleur").

20 Rotroff 1997.

21 Dolley 1974 ; Buttrey & Johnston 1981, XIV-XVII, Walker 1997 ; de Callataÿ 2006.

22 Voir entre autres Reece 1994 = *id.* 2003, 258 et Suchodolski 2002, 273-284.

le cas où elles auraient été fixées précisément (ce qui pour les monnayages grecs de bronze est loin d'être la règle)[23]. Les esprits ont évolué de part et d'autre.

On est loin de la situation d'il y a une ou deux générations qui voyait les numismates se plaindre de voir les archéologues, tout empressés qu'ils étaient à dater leurs couches, allègrement confondre date de production et date de perte. Il est très certain qu'un temps important, parfois plusieurs siècles, peut s'être écoulé entre la mise en circulation d'une monnaie et son abandon, et cette mise en garde a maintenant gagné les esprits sur tous les chantiers[24]. Sans surprise, les archéologues se sont donc tournés vers d'autres types de matériel, à commencer par la vaisselle céramique dont on peut présumer qu'elle ne résista pas dans l'ensemble à plus d'une génération d'usage. Mais il y a beaucoup mieux encore : en effet, quand elles contenaient de l'huile, les amphores n'étaient pas réutilisables, ce qui explique qu'on les ait détruites près de leur débarcadère comme l'illustre si bien le Mont Testaccio. Les archéologues des sites septentrionaux de la mer Noire ne jurent ainsi que par les amphores, sans attendre beaucoup des monnaies, pourtant découvertes en grand nombre. S. Rotroff a fourni des chiffres assez intéressants à propos des nombreux dépôts céramiques athéniens étudiés par elle. On peut les résumer ainsi[25] :

Nombre de dépôts céramiques	Utilité pour la chronologie
29 dépôts pour lesquels les monnaies sont les seuls objets datables	– 11 cas utiles – 18 cas où la céramique est largement postérieure aux monnaies
48 dépôts contenant des monnaies et des timbres amphoriques	– 5 cas où les monnaies et les timbres les plus récents sont contemporains – 26 cas où les timbres sont bien plus récents que les monnaies

On voit que les monnaies ne sont jamais plus utiles que les timbres pour dater les contextes archéologiques et qu'on aurait souvent tort de s'y fier. S'agissant de préciser la chronologie, S. Rotroff conclut donc avec modération : "in most cases, most excavation coins are not very useful in this pursuit[26]".

Les numismates ont eux aussi appris qu'une couche ne fait pas le printemps et que l'archéologie méditerranéenne, avec ses habitats continus sur plusieurs siècles et parfois

23 Grierson 1965, iii : "Archaeologists, who value numismatic evidence almost entirely for its use in dating other objects".

24 Le point est abordé dans presque chaque présentation de monnaies de fouille. Voir plus spécifiquement Collis 1988. Il est ainsi acquis, par exemple, qu'on a continué, en Méditerranée orientale, d'utiliser les bronzes du IVe s. au Ve et des IVe et Ve s. au VIe s. (voir Butcher 2003) et Guest 2012, 105-131 (avec référence à une littérature plus ample sur le sujet).

25 Rotroff 1997, 15.

26 *Ibid.*, 12.

millénaires, est prodigue en stratigraphies perturbées et en remblais tardifs[27]. On rappellera ici l'inquiétant bilan offert par les quatre seules monnaies d'or ou d'électrum trouvées à l'agora d'Athènes. Si le statère d'Alexandre provient bien d'une couche de remplissage sous une stoa hellénistique, le solidus d'Arcadius (377-408) a été retrouvé dans un contexte postérieur de deux siècles à son émission. Et la situation est pire encore pour le statère de Cyzique, recueilli sur un sol byzantin, et la darique perse d'Artaxerxès Ier exhumée dans un contexte romain[28].Que dire alors du groupe de bronzes romains du temps d'Hadrien retrouvé sous les fondations de la Stoa d'Attale ?[29]

Fondamental – mais c'est là une tâche très délicate – est de déterminer le degré d'usure des pièces due à la circulation, qui est donc à dissocier radicalement de l'état de conservation due aux facteurs de conservation (dont la corrosion). On le fait généralement de façon relative (en déterminant des degrés d'usure) et je ne crois pas qu'il soit raisonnable de travailler d'après les poids réels des pièces[30]. Dans les meilleurs cas, quand les contextes archéologiques sont datés de façon sûre ou que l'usure des pièces peut être déterminée avec précision, il est possible de faire comme S. Suchodolski et produire un double graphique qui donne les dates de production et d'abandon du matériel monétaire trouvé en fouille[31].

Quoique le plus opératoire, l'usure des pièces n'est pas le seul critère qui nous permette de statuer sur la longévité de circulation. Dans le cas d'un monnayage civique abondamment documenté comme c'est le cas de celui de Thasos, il est intéressant de se pencher, comme le fait O. Picard, sur le rapport du nombre moyen de monnaies par coin pour chaque émission tel qu'attesté par la fouille. On peut ainsi espérer définir des durées de circulation, mettre par exemple le doigt sur des retraits précoces (très faible nombre de monnaies par coin) ou des circulations particulièrement longues (très grand nombre de monnaies par coin)[32].

Il ne s'agit pas simplement d'aider l'archéologue à dater des contextes, mais plus fondamentalement d'observer la monnaie en mouvement. O. Picard fait ainsi remarquer que l'on trouve à Thasos des monnaies hellénistiques des IIe et Ier s. dans des niveaux romains et que ces monnaies hellénistiques se trouvent "dans un état d'extrême usure", ce qui montre "que des bronzes hellénistiques continuent à circuler sous l'Empire"[33].

La comparaison du matériel monétaire entre différents sites se doit de toujours prendre en compte le contexte général dudit site. On peut penser à différentes répartitions en catégories, dont, à tout le moins, 1) les cités de grande importance, 2) celles de taille moyenne ou modeste, 3) les sites ruraux, 4) les sites militaires et 5) les lieux sacrés[34]. De même, on ne

27 La plupart des monnaies grecques trouvées sur l'agora d'Athènes le furent dans des remblais tardifs inutilisables à des fins chronologiques (Kroll 1993, 2).

28 Rotroff 1997, 9.

29 Walker 1997, 25.

30 *Contra* Pilon 2011, dont la tentative d'évaluer la date estimative de perte (DEP) des sesterces d'après leur métrologie bute sur la réalité de la grande dispersion des poids à l'émission et de leur faible perte par circulation.

31 Suchodolski 2002, 281-283.

32 Picard 2002.

33 *Id.* 1997, 31.

34 Voir infra les travaux de R. Reece.

comparera pas de façon ingénue l'ensemble du matériel monétaire provenant de tel site A avec celui, restreint aux fouilles de tel temple, du site B. d'autant que, comme l'écrit T. Buttrey dans le cas du sanctuaire de Déméter à Cyrène, "the find coins may reflect intensity of worship rather than of monetary circulation[35]".

Le numismate attend de l'archéologue qu'il fournisse non seulement la localisation précise de chaque pièce mais encore sa position stratigraphique et son association éventuelle à d'autres types de matériel[36], ce qui se fait de plus en plus souvent. Encore faut-il pour cela que les monnaies ne soient pas des trouvailles isolées de surface et proviennent de couches archéologiques datables, ce qui élimine une bonne partie du matériel[37].

En revanche, très peu de rapports de fouille mentionnent la surface fouillée (ce qui peut encore se calculer à partir des plans fournis) et aucun pour ainsi dire le volume exprimé en mètres cube[38]. En dépit de tous les problèmes de comparaison que posent de tels chiffres bruts, ils seraient pourtant extrêmement utiles pour nourrir la réflexion. J'ai plaidé naguère pour un index qui donne le rapport entre la surface moyenne fouillée par monnaie retrouvée et j'avais été jusqu'à comparer les trouvailles de l'Îlot des Comédiens à Délos (507 monnaies pour *c.* 1 920 m^2 = 1 monnaie par *c.* 3,8 m^2) et la Maison de Dionysos à Paphos (596 monnaies pour *c.* 5 000 m^2 = 1 monnaie par *c.* 8,4 m^2)[39].

La comparaison se veut plus suggestive que démonstrative parce que, bien entendu, il s'agit de prendre en compte les durées respectives d'occupation (et de construction – voir infra pour le palais de Fishbourne). Tout de même, on ne peut qu'être frappé par les différences qui existent sous ce rapport entre les monnaies grecques de l'agora d'Athènes (avec un nombre de monnaies proche de celui de l'Îlot des Comédiens : 12 515 monnaies pour *c.* 60 000 m^2 [6 hectares] = 1 monnaie par *c.* 4,8 m^2), la richesse de ce qui a été trouvé à l'occasion du dégagement d'une petite structure à Risan (environ 1 monnaie par m^2)[40] et la très grande pauvreté des fouilles d'Aï Khanoum (181 monnaies grecques exhumées lors des campagnes menées de 1965 à 1978 sur une surface non spécifiée mais clairement de grande ampleur)[41]. On veut croire que ce type de considérations, encore dans les limbes

35 Buttrey 1997, 1.

36 L'indication "Zone X, couche Y" ne dira rien au numismate mais lui sera utile s'il lui est précisé que la monnaie a été retrouvée sur un sol de galets associée à de la céramique de la IIe moitié du IVe s. a.C. (adapté de Laing 1969, 85).

37 Pour Monte Iato (Frey-Kupper 2013), restent 227 monnaies, soit 16 % environ du matériel. La réduction est aussi très importante pour les sites de la région de Caltanissetta (13 monnaies sur les 117 trouvées à Gibil Gabib sont exploitables : *c.* 11 % [à côté des 78 isolées sans contexte et des 26 autres provenant d'un trésor]).

38 L'exception est ici constituée par les fouilles suédoises pour des habitats allant du XIIIe au XVIIe s. (Redin 1989, 12, fig. 3 et "The number of coins found at specific excavations must be considered in relation to the size of the excavated area and the volume of the layers investigated").

39 de Callataÿ 2006.

40 Ujes 2011, 117 : 133 monnaies trouvées en fouille à Risan pour une petite structure de 130 m^2 (il s'agit sans doute d'un trésor dispersé, peut-être caché dans le plafond).

41 Kroll 1993 et Bernard 1985. Pour le sanctuaire hors-les-murs de Déméter et Perséphone à Cyrène, on a retrouvé en dix années de fouilles 736 monnaies pour une surface fouillée de *c.* 40 x 65 m (Buttrey 1997, 2 et 70 [plan du site]), soit une moyenne élevée d'une monnaie par *c.* 3,5 m^2 comparable à celle de l'Îlot des Comédiens.

actuellement, est promis à des développements intéressants. Il vient d'ailleurs de recevoir un premier traitement global (et certainement très critiquable en l'état) portant sur 17 sites romains situés aux Pays-Bas et en Grande-Bretagne[42].

Trésors monétaires

La littérature sur les trésors monétaires est surabondante[43]. Nous y renvoyons pour l'essentiel en attirant l'attention au passage sur l'excellence théorique de l'ouvrage de D. Backendorf[44] ainsi que sur un point qui eût étonné nos devanciers : celui d'un récent et relatif *consensus* sur l'impraticabilité de la séparation entre "trésors de circulation" et "trésors de thésaurisation"[45].

Pour le présent propos, il importe seulement de bien marquer en quoi les trésors se différencient des monnaies de fouilles. La différence la plus importante tient dans la répartition par métaux[46]. J'ai ainsi calculé que, sur les 604 418 monnaies recensées tant par les 2 387 trésors de l'*Inventory of Greek Coin Hoards* que par les 1 257 supplémentaires repris dans les huit premiers *Coin Hoards*, on obtenait la répartition suivante : 73,7 % pour l'argent (445 772 monnaies), 21,5 % pour le bronze (129 873), 4,1 % pour l'or (24 528) et 0,7 % pour l'électrum (4245)[47]. Il faudrait du reste aller plus loin et, comme le fait D. Hollard pour le bronze romain, voir si les bronzes des trésors ne sont pas de plus gros modules que ceux des monnaies de site[48]. Avec Copernic et Gresham, il faut redire que, à l'inverse des monnaies de fouille qui font le contraire, les trésors privilégient la bonne monnaie.

Quoique trésors et monnaies de fouilles renvoient à des réalités différentes et que chacun puisse convenir que ces réalités sont complémentaires pour qui étudie la circulation monétaire, des voix se sont fait entendre pour préférer les secondes aux premiers[49], mais l'inverse a pu aussi s'écrire : "Hoards preserve the relative frequency of coins in the monetary pool in better detail than site finds[50]".

42 Buringh & Boskers 2014, 242, fig. 9.3. Total stray finds of Roman coins (in 1 000s of coins, y-axis) minted before 402 p.C. and settlement size in hectares (x-axis), et p. 243: "we also find a fair relationship between town sizes and the amount of coin in local circulation" (*NB* : ce qui est aller extrêmement vite en besogne).

43 Sur les significations du mot "trésor", on consultera les intéressantes observations d'Aubin 2007.

44 Backendorf 1998 et le compte-rendu dithyrambique de Buttrey 1999.

45 Backendorf 1998 repris par Buttrey 1999, 528-529.

46 Reece 2003, 322 : "Put very simply hoards are selected for their value and site finds are lost and not recovered because of their lack of value".

47 de Callataÿ 1997a, 64-65 (travail bénédictin dont Mme Martens prit en son temps sa part).

48 Hollard 1996, 215-216, tableau 3.

49 Voir Bruun 1978, 114 ; Butcher 1988, 28 : "The selectivity of hoards and the accident of their loss makes them of less use in studying circulation than coins dropped in the market place"; Reece 1991-1993, 61 : "The factors which bias hoards, and make them highly unsuitable as a source from which to write the monetary history of an area, are intrinsic value, and political and economic expediency, in addition to the regional problems which affect all coin finds... Hoards from a given period are therefore very bad indicators of the relative frequency of denominations in circulation or in production".

50 Casey & Reece, éd. 1988, 60.

Monnaies isolées (stray finds)

Naguère encore passées sous silence, les monnaies isolées (entendues comme trouvées hors de fouilles régulières) ont reçu une attention considérable ces dernières décennies. Certains n'hésitent pas de nos jours à leur trouver des vertus supérieures aux monnaies de fouilles (ce petit fretin tenu pour rien) et aux trésors (ces gros menteurs atypiques). Ce sont les chercheurs anglo-saxons qui ont le plus soutenu cette voie : P. Grierson en tête[51], suivi par M. Blackburn[52] et d'autres[53]. Il existe aujourd'hui de très puissantes bases de données consultables en ligne pour la Grande-Bretagne (Portable Antiquities Scheme) et les Pays-Bas (NUMIS)[54].

Les monnaies isolées ont pour elles d'offrir l'apparence d'une voie moyenne entre les témoignages irréconciliables des monnaies de fouille et des trésors. Bien plus que les monnaies de fouille et bien moins que les trésors, elles attestent l'existence d'une circulation des métaux précieux. Il n'en faut pas plus à l'imagination pour s'enflammer et croire tenir là les discrets vestiges de routes commerciales ou militaires. Ce doit être vrai dans quelques cas, mais il faut surtout redire avec force que cette différence de faciès tient d'abord aux facteurs modernes de transmission de l'information. En effet, alors que l'archéologue enregistre tout, tel n'est pas le cas ou est moins le cas du découvreur accidentel. C'est un échantillon non-aléatoire et tiré vers le haut qui est ici présenté, qui privilégie l'enregistrement de pièces remarquables à l'un ou l'autre titre et pénalise le petit bronze. De ceci découle notamment un surcroît d'attention aux monnaies étrangères, au détriment des numéraires locaux. Sauf raisons expresses, la découverte de monnaies grecques en Angleterre ou en Belgique, par exemple, ne doit pas conduire à imaginer *a priori* que ces monnaies ont circulé et été perdues dans ces régions durant l'Antiquité[55]. On ajoutera aussi, avec P. Grierson, que les monnaies isolées sont plus soumises que les monnaies de fouilles et même que les trésors à l'éventuelle malignité humaine[56].

S'agissant de l'étude d'un même monnayage (même métal, même dénomination), les différences entre trésors et monnaies isolées s'estompent quoique, en bonne logique, l'on puisse tenir le témoignage des trésors comme étant le produit d'une moindre dispersion que celui des monnaies isolées[57].

Pour le reste, les monnaies isolées présentent des risques de biais comparables à ceux mis en lumière pour les trésors. L'activité d'une personne, d'un cercle archéologique

51 Grierson 1965, ii (voir supra).

52 Blackburn 1986 ; *id.* 1989a ; *id.* 1989b.

53 Newton 2006.

54 Voir : http://finds.org.uk (plus de 300 000 monnaies) et http://numis.geldmuseum.nl/en/introduction (près de 50 000 monnaies).

55 Grierson 1965, vi-vii.

56 *Ibid.*, vi : "One has to remember that finders are often careless and not always truthful, that the planting of coins, whether for pecuniary gain or to prove an hypothesis, or even as a joke, is not unknown, that genuine mistakes may happen, and that ancient coins have sometimes been lost or discarded in modern times and not at those periods when they were in regular circulation".

57 Metcalf 1998, 90.

particulièrement actif ou l'existence d'un musée local risquent de fausser sensiblement les proportions relatives.

Pour les monnaies isolées, on s'est plus penché sur l'or que sur les autres métaux[58]. Pour l'or, Morrisson conclut en une meilleure représentativité des trouvailles isolées que des trésors, tandis que pour le bronze, cette représentativité serait à peu près égale[59].

Les monnaies de fouilles : l'apport des spécialistes des monnaies romaines

Par rapport au monde grec, le monde romain bénéficie de trois avantages structurels et de cas favorables particuliers. Dès lors, autant il est indiqué, s'agissant de monnaies antiques, de prendre connaissance des travaux méthodologiques réalisés par les spécialistes des monnaies grecques pour tout ce qui touche l'étude des coins et même plus généralement la production, autant il est fondamental de se frotter à la littérature romaine, surtout celle qui traite des séries impériales[60], pour tout ce qui concerne la circulation.

Avantages structurels

Primo, les spécialistes de numismatique romaine impériale bénéficient d'une base documentaire qui se situe à l'ordre supérieur de magnitude par rapport aux monnaies grecques. C'est vrai pour les trésors (*c.* 5 000 trésors pour le monde grec contre *c.* 30 000 pour le monde romain)[61]. C'est vrai aussi des monnaies de fouilles[62]. On dispose pour les monnaies romaines de davantage de sites et de monnaies publiées pour la seule Grande-Bretagne que de monnaies grecques pour l'ensemble du monde grec. En effet, les 140 sites retenus par R. Reece totalisent à eux-seuls 168 828 monnaies, contre 35 966 pour les trente-sept sites retenus dans mon *conspectus*[63].

58 Callu & Loriot 1990, *id.* 1992 et Loriot 2003 pour une interprétation du matériel.

59 Morrisson 2002, 236-239.

60 Pour un bon résumé de la question et les particularités du monnayage romain provincial, voir Butcher 2004, 143-149 (*3.1. Models for circulation and coin use*). *NB* : on s'accordera bien volontiers avec lui, et à la suite des travaux de C. Howgego, sur le fait que les émissions monétaires n'ont pas toutes été émises pour payer des troupes (le "coin-for-state-purposes-only" modèle) ; je ne suis pas sûr en revanche de le suivre quand il fait jouer, exagérément à mon sens, les règles fondamentales de l'économie *mainstream* contemporaine en imaginant que les cités, qui en tiraient un bénéfice au passage, se souciaient d'alimenter et de réguler la circulation monétaire.

61 Pour l'estimation du nombre de trésors de monnaies grecques, voir de Callataÿ 1997b.

62 Citons, pour s'en tenir à quelques données, les 56 000 monnaies de Richborough dans le Kent (Reece 1968), les 12 595 à Bath (Walker 1988, 281) ou les 7 800 monnaies de Coventina (Allason-Jones & McKay 1985). On rappellera que les fouilles romaines pratiquées dans le Tibre au début du XXe s. ont permis de récupérer plus de 30 000 monnaies de bronze, représentant quelque 274 kg, lesquels, en 1936 et sur ordre du ministère des Finances furent requis pour la fonte (qui toutefois n'eut pas lieu). On avait déjà trouvé à Rome auparavant, entre 1870 et 1902, quelque 75 000 monnaies (conservées au médaillier du Musée national romain, voir Kaenel 1984, 88-91 et Bertoldi 1997). Faute de contexte (les monnaies se trouvaient pêle-mêle dans cinq caisses en bois), ce matériel est presque inexploitable.

63 Reece 1991 (qui ne donne nulle part le total des monnaies mobilisées) et de Callataÿ 2006.

Or la capacité à pouvoir déterminer ce qui est normal de ce qui l'est moins suppose de pouvoir confronter le particulier au général et donc de disposer d'un cadre de référence. La robustesse des hypothèses émises dépend donc fortement de la solidité de ce cadre de référence. Pour les monnaies grecques de Sicile, on saluera ainsi le bel effort de S. Frey-Kupper qui, pour interpréter les 1 425 monnaies exhumées à Monte Iato (l'ancienne Ietas), s'est construit un grand cadre de près de 15 000 monnaies[64]. C'est encore l'abondance documentaire qui permet à D. Walker de se lancer, à partir du riche matériel retrouvé dans la source sacrée de Bath, dans des extrapolations sur la valeur totale de la monnaie de bronze circulant au IIe s. en Grande-Bretagne[65]. Mais, même en disposant d'une meilleure documentation, Reece rappelle que : "When we study site finds we are therefore working on a sample of 0,01 % of 4 % of the money which was about at the time (*NB* : littéralement 1/250 000e) ; this should explain my reluctance always to be positive and predictive and my preference for warning and scepticism[66]".

Secundo, le monde romain constitue un grand système fortement centralisé à la production et dont la circulation des monnaies assure un caractère plus ou moins homogène aux échantillons qui peuvent être prélevés sur celle-ci, en tout cas au niveau provincial. R. Duncan-Jones peut donc parler de "Empire-wide patterns in Roman coin hoards" (même si, en l'occurrence, c'est pour mieux en montrer les variances régionales)[67] et R. Reece déclarer que "all sites, excepting the most extreme, follow a general British pattern of coin loss[68]". Jamais, il ne sera possible de produire pour le monde grec un travail aussi fin que celui de D. Backendorf pour les trésors de monnaies romaines enfouis en Italie lors des deux derniers siècles a.C.[69]. Les seules exceptions potentielles sont les grands royaumes hellénistiques pour lesquels les bases de données rassemblées par P. Iossif pour les Séleucides (sa "Seleucid Excavation Database" comprend 8 334 monnaies [dont 8 273 bronzes = 99 %] pour 80 sites) et par T. Faucher pour l'Égypte Ptolémaïque (2 688 monnaies [dont 2 599 bronzes = 97 %] provenant de 36 localités) présentent une robustesse documentaire qui encourage l'analyse[70].

Tertio, les bronzes romains, à la différence des grecs, se laissent la plupart du temps dater précisément. Il en résulte qu'il est possible de déterminer des indices de fréquence par périodes, le fameux indice de Ravetz, dans sa version simple ou améliorée[71]. L'exercice de comparaison demeure toutefois extrêmement compliqué car il faut intégrer le temps de circulation moyen de chaque monnayage et ce que, publiant les monnaies de Carthage, T. V. Buttrey a appelé un "index of tolerable loss", à savoir les chances de perte calculées

64 Frey-Kupper 2013 (dont près de 10 000 il est vrai pour les seules fouilles de Serra Orlando [Morgantina]).

65 Walker 1988, 301-305 (dans un exercice dont la bravoure a été plus dénigrée qu'applaudie).

66 Reece 1973 = *id.* 2003, 314.

67 Duncan-Jones 1996 (appliqué aux deniers du IIe s.).

68 Reece 1996, 342.

69 Backendorf 1998.

70 Je suis reconnaissant envers P. Iossif d'avoir partagé le fruit de ses recherches en cours dans le cadre de son doctorat. Pour les monnaies ptolémaïques, voir Faucher 2011.

71 Ravetz 1963 ; *id.* 1964 ; Williams 1992. Pour la Gaule romaine, voir maintenant Gricourt *et al.* 2009.

d'après le diamètre et le poids des monnaies (et donc la moyenne de ces valeurs pour chaque règne)[72].

Cas favorables

En outre et mieux que le monde grec[73], le monde romain offre quelques opportunités de saisir un instantané de la circulation à la faveur d'une catastrophe soudaine : on pense bien sûr à l'éruption du Vésuve en août 79 mais aussi au désastre de la perte des légions de Varus en l'an 9 p.C., et – beaucoup moins spontanément – aux possibilités offertes par la fouille d'un camp militaire comme celui d'Oberraden.

Pompéi. Des fouilles menées à Pompéi de 1897 à 1971, on conserve 7 890 monnaies, dont 108 en or, 2 075 en argent et 5 707 en bronze[74]. Le projet de recherche portant sur les monnaies découvertes à Pompéi a identifié *c.* 24 000 monnaies, dont 550 en or, *c.* 7 000 en argent et *c.* 16 000 en bronze. Plus intéressant encore, il appert que *c.* 9 600 d'entre elles proviennent d'habitations, *c.* 6 300 d'implantations commerciales et seulement 1 300 d'édifices publics. On trouve aussi *c.* 5 900 pièces isolées et 508 trouvailles fortuites. Le faciès par métaux varie beaucoup en fonction du type de contexte. L'or se trouve de façon préférentielle à l'intérieur des édifices publics et des implantations commerciales alors que l'argent provient massivement des habitations[75]. Pour ce qui est du bronze qui forme, certes un peu moins qu'ailleurs, la presque totalité des trouvailles, le phénomène le plus remarquable et maintenant bien identifié est la présence massive de monnaies frappées à Ebusus (Ibiza) et amenées en bloc vers 130-120 a.C. avant d'être imitées localement Il est loisible de démontrer que ce phénomène n'est pas lié au commerce mais plus vraisemblablement à un butin de guerre pris par Quintus Caecilius Metellus en 123 a.C.[76].

Kalkriese. Identifié à Kalkriese, le site historique du massacre des légions de Varus, en l'an 9 p.C., dans la forêt de Teutobourg, a aussi livré un matériel pris sur le vif dont le faciès paraît intermédiaire entre le bronze des monnaies de fouilles et l'or et l'argent monnayés des trésors. Pour s'en tenir au matériel dispersé, on y dénombre 4 *aurei*, 125 monnaies d'argent (*c.* 20 %) et plus de 500 de bronze[77].

72 Buttrey & Hitchner 1978, 102 (Grierson 1985, 517).

73 Pour la Grèce, on pensera aux destructions à Olynthe en 348 a.C. (Robinson 1931 et Robinson & Clement 1938), à Koroni dans les années 260 (Vanderpool *et al.* 1964), à Morgantina lors de la seconde guerre punique (Buttrey *et al.* 1989) et à Corinthe en 146 (Price 1967).

74 Taliercio Mensitieri 2002, 80. Voir aussi Ranucci 2008, 151-175 ; *id.* 2014 (pour les fouilles menées par l'Université de Pérouse) ; Hobbs 2013.

75 Les quelque 1 500 monnaies découvertes dans l'*Insula* VI, 1, fouillée de façon extensive par une équipe anglo-américaine (Bradford University et British Museum) sont publiées par Richard Hobbs du British Museum, qui ne craint pas d'y voir un matériau de premier choix pour l'histoire économique de la cité (Hobbs 2013).

76 Stannard & Frey-Kupper 2008 et Stannard 2013.

77 Voir Berger 1999 et *id.* 2000. À quoi il faut ajouter 5 trésors totalisant 1 monnaie d'or et 304 d'argent (et aucun bronze).

Oberaden. D'une superficie de 56 hectares (840 x 680 m), le camp romain d'Oberaden est lié à l'offensive de Drusus contre les Germains[78]. Construit en 11 a.C. (datation sûre grâce à la dendrochronologie), le camp fut abandonné en 8/7 a.C. Dès lors que l'on peut se faire une idée de sa démographie (*c.* 10 000 ? : 2-3 légions plus des auxiliaires) et de la surface fouillée (*c.* 2 hectares [?]), il est possible – à titre bien entendu très exploratoire, plus ludique que démonstratif – d'avancer un taux de perte par occupant : en l'occurrence 1 monnaie par personne tous les *c.* 7 ans[79].

Divers. À ces cas favorables, on ajoutera la découverte de troncs d'offrandes ou *thesauri*, près de vingt au total dont celui de Sora (près de Frosinone) contenait encore scellé le fruit des dernières aumônes (50 monnaies)[80].

Ces circonstances favorables ont permis aux spécialistes des monnaies romaines de mener des réflexions qui ont toujours été méthodologiquement en avance sur leurs confrères spécialistes de monnaies grecques.

L'apport des numismates anglais

Plus spécifiquement, ce sont les numismates anglais spécialistes des monnaies romaines trouvées en Grande-Bretagne qui ont le plus contribué à enrichir nos connaissances et on reconnaîtra à R. Reece d'avoir tenu un rôle prééminent en la matière (mais voir avant lui P. Grierson et avec ou après lui R. Duncan-Jones, C. Howgego, N. Ryan, K. Butcher, A. S. Hobley, P. Guest ou P. Walton pour n'en citer que quelques-uns)[81].

Ce que professe R. Reece est résolument empirique et peut se résumer à des idées simples au maniement complexe[82]. Des monnaies elles-mêmes, nous pouvons espérer connaître

78 Ilisch 1991 (283 bronzes, dont 258 de Nîmes).

79 10 000 hommes pour 56 hectares = 435 hommes pour 2 hectares. Dès lors, 283 monnaies perdues par 485 hommes pendant 4 ans correspond au non recouvrement d'une monnaie par personne tous les *c.* 7 ans. On notera que le rapport monnaie/surface est d'une pièce par *c.* 70 m² (283 monnaies pour *c.* 2 hectares), soit un rapport bien moins élevé que celui hypothétiquement dégagé dans l'absolu (sans se prononcer sur la durée d'utilisation des sites) à Délos et à Paphos.

80 Catalli & Scheid 1994 (le *thesaurus* intact, encore recouvert de sa coiffe de bronze, a été retrouvé sous la cathédrale bâtie sur un temple romain). Les auteurs dressent la liste de 19 *thesauri* connus pour le monde romain, dont 3 ont livré des monnaies (voir à ce sujet Kaminski 1991).

81 Richard Reece qui, préfaçant, un florilège de ses articles, écrit: "The papers do not give the story of the application of a method to a body of material simply because there was, when I started, no method, and very little material" (Reece 2003, 3).

82 Typique de son approche est le propos suivant : "These coins are certainly not all the coins found in clearing the Chedworth buildings, and even if the list of coins could be made complete these would not be all the coins lost, in antiquity, on the site. Finally, we do not know the relationship of coins found to coins lost, coins lost to coins in circulation, or coins in circulation to coins minted. With all these barriers to any direct or absolute interpretation, it must be clear that any attempt to translate the presence of coins on a given site into a simple story of what happened in antiquity is pointless if the rules of formal logic are followed. If a story of the use of specific coins in a specific place is wanted, then it will be best to construct it from a general historical feel, common sense, and contemporary writings than to start from a coin list" (Reece 1988 = *id.* 2003, 99).

deux dates : celle de leur fabrication et celle de leur abandon. Au-delà de quoi presque toute l'affaire porte sur l'attention aux contextes et le danger des corrélations simples.

Chacun comprend qu'une région n'est pas une autre[83] et que les sites d'une même région peuvent différer par leur nature : milieu urbain, milieu rural (essentiellement alors les fouilles de villas)[84], forts militaires, temples, autres lieux cultuels (gués, fontaines) : l'archéologie de la Grèce ancienne a depuis longtemps déjà recouru aussi à de telles typologies, sans toutefois pouvoir ambitionner définir le profil type[85] de la distribution chronologique des monnaies propre à un fort, à un temple, etc. parce qu'elle n'a pas – et n'aura pas avant longtemps – l'équivalent d'un modèle aussi robuste que celui bâti par Reece pour la Grande-Bretagne, soit le produit des monnaies trouvées sur 140 sites dont les différences internes peuvent être tenues pour mineures par rapport aux faciès de n'importe quelle province continentale[86].

Mais les spécialistes de monnaies romaines nous invitent à aller bien plus loin en se montrant attentifs aux différences parfois étonnantes de faciès monétaires non seulement entre des "good towns" et des "bad towns", mais entre des zones archéologiques contiguës[87], apparemment dévolues à la même fonction, et bien entendu entre les pièces d'une même maison.

Un des thèmes très peu abordés par les spécialistes des monnaies grecques mais qui aura retenu l'attention de leurs confrères romains est de se demander si les monnaies exhumées par l'archéologie ont été perdues accidentellement (ce qui est l'explication retenue par l'*homo oeconomicus*) ou si elles n'ont pas été volontairement écartées, pour des raisons économiques (elles ne valaient plus rien) ou culturelles (bien faites pour susciter l'intérêt de l'anthropologue)[88].

De même, les spécialistes de monnaies romaines auront davantage exploré les multiples raisons qui font que les monnaies sont demeurées enfouies dans le sol jusqu'à ce qu'on les redécouvre récemment. À ma connaissance, aucune publication de monnaies de fouille en Grèce n'évoque de "robbing levels" (de niveaux où les monnaies ont été récupérées)[89]. Parmi ces raisons, la nature du sol joue un grand rôle. Chacun a entendu parler de l'"effet Fishbourne", popularisé par R. Reece[90], à savoir l'apparent paradoxe de recueillir bien plus de monnaies lors de la phase de construction du palais (122 monnaies en 30 ans) que durant la

83 Reece 1982 = *id.* 2003, 354 : "What can be said more factually is that the British system of coin use was not the Italian system, so that if the Italian system is the archaeological remnant of a market economy the British coin loss is not".

84 Reece 2003.

85 Comme Reece défend l'idée du "normal hoard" (Reece 1981).

86 Reece 1968 (les sites ont été divisés en cinq catégories : grandes villes, villas, temples, sites militaires et autres sites ruraux non précisés). Le modèle est tenu pour remarquablement prédictif : "Form the work of John Casey of myself, we can say roughly what coins will turn up on any site in Britain before it is excavated" (Reece 1987 = *id.* 2003, 137).

87 Pour un exemple dans le monde grec, voir à Délos la grande différence de faciès entre les trouvailles monétaires de l'Îlot des Comédiens (abandon lent) et celles de l'îlot voisin (abandon rapide) (Hackens 1970 et *id.* 1975, 217).

88 Sur cette question, voir Reece 1973 et *id.* 1996, 342-344.

89 Reece 2003, 33.

90 Reece 1971.

longue occupation du site une fois construit (31 monnaies en 125 ans), pour la simple raison qu'il est bien plus facile de perdre une monnaie dans un sol boueux que sur un pavement mosaïqué, surtout si le profil social des occupants est différent[91]. C'est aussi le social derrière l'archéologique que Reece recherche à partir des monnaies trouvées dans les villas romaines de Grande-Bretagne[92].

En espérant être conforme à la pensée de R. Reece, qui n'entend jamais fournir une méthode rigide mais procéder par réflexions empiriques, j'ai sélectionné quelques propos qui me paraissent utiles d'avoir à l'esprit au moment de publier le matériel monétaire dégagé en fouille :

· "It seems likely that most coins completed 90 per cent of their travelling, in terms of Roman miles, in the period, if not within five years, of their minting[93]".
· "but money which later came with individual detachments must pale into insignificance beside the periodic bulk movements of military pay, whatever they came from and whatever metals and denominations they comprised[94]".
· "This seems a very strange paradox; that economic prosperity and money should not be connected. Yet it seems to be the case if my model is correct. The position at the moment seems to be that in the Later Roman Empire coins are where the army are, and the greater part of the army is on the frontiers[95]".
· "A second barrier to a wide application of the theory of 'constant unit loss' is the absence of correlation, or more precisely, direct proportionality between the frequency of coin loss and the value of the coin. [...] Here is the main problem: a more valuable coin is being lost in preference to a less valuable coin. As the critical reader will see, such points depend on the assumption that all coins supplied during the reign of Hadrian were lost then; this is demonstrably untrue (Reece 1974). From coin loss we may comment on coin supply, but there is bound to be error when we transfer the evidence to the subject of coin use[96]".

Le constat général de ce qui a été écrit par R. Reece invite fortement à la prudence interprétative. Disposant pour les monnaies romaines trouvées en Grande-

91 Reece 2003, 34 : "Secondly, large numbers of coins lost, whether common or scarce, will only accumulate in what can best be described as middle or lower class conditions. [...] As this occurrence in building levels suggests, the coins of Vespasian are associated with an army of building labourers and craftsmen at work in the mud and dust of a building site. Coins of Domitian as Augustus, however, cannot have entered the site until it was a clean, well-kept place. Therefore, although the numbers of inhabitants was fairly constant, since the army of servants required to run the palace cannot have been much smaller than the army required to build it, the change in the number of coins found reflects not a difference in intensity of occupation, but a complete change in its quality".

92 Reece 1988 = *id.* 2003, 102-106.

93 Reece 1973 = *id.* 2003, 63.

94 Reece 1973 = *id.* 2003, 64. On a longtemps pensé différemment. À titre d'exemple, s'interrogeant sur la très étonnante masse de 1 200 *dupondii* frappés en 205/206 par cinq cités du Pont et retrouvés au loin à Doura-Europos, Bellinger s'interdisait d'y voir un déplacement de légion parce que, soutenait-il, on sait bien que la solde se réglait en argent (Bellinger 1949 et Seyrig 1958, 176).

95 Reece 1977 = *id.* 2003, 169.

96 Reece 1975 = *id.* 2003, 307.

Bretagne d'une documentation très nettement supérieure tant par la quantité que par la qualité par rapport à ce qui peut se concevoir pour le monde grec, il aura démontré combien il y a lieu de se défier de corrélations hâtives, et par exemple de celle qui lierait la fréquence des trouvailles à l'occupation du site, a fortiori à son dynamisme économique[97]. Il n'est pas le seul. Dans son grand livre sur l'économie monétaire byzantine, M. Hendy a d'emblée écrit combien il lui semblait : "pointless to analyse coin finds, and to derive 'monetary' or 'economic' conclusions from such analyses, either in total ignorance of the fundamental causative factors behind the production and circulation of a coinage, or on the basis of some superficial or faulty causative and behavioural framework[98]". On paraît s'accorder sur le fait que les bronzes impériaux sont injectés dans la circulation via la solde des troupes[99], mais les opinions divergent sur l'importance du commerce comme moteur du mouvement de ces monnaies ensuite[100].

En réalité, comme l'avait déjà observé P. Grierson, les pics de trouvailles sont souvent d'abord liés à l'histoire proprement monétaire et aux décris ("withdrawals" en anglais) à propos desquels en général nous ne savons rien et pour lesquels les monnaies de fouille sont précisément nos meilleurs guides[101]. C'est la même ligne de raisonnement qui a permis à O. Picard, en compagnie de T. Faucher et aidé de C. Lorber, de définir des périodes de circulation pour le bronze ptolémaïque à Alexandrie[102].

L'utilité des contrépreuves contemporaines ou modernes

En dépit de ses grands avantages par rapport à la numismatique grecque, la numismatique romaine permet rarement de contrôler le bien-fondé des hypothèses avancées[103]. Aussi y a-t-il profit à ne pas négliger des études portant sur des cas beaucoup plus récents pour lesquels

97 Reece 1973 = *id.* 2003, 169 ; Reece 1982 = *id.* 2003, 351-352. En cela, il s'oppose à Fulford 1978 (Reece 1982 = *id.* 2003, 352 : "Mike Fulford has suggested that much coinage moves around the Empire in course of trade; he has put forward his ideas well and carefully, and the whole scheme is very convincing except for one initial detail, and that is how the money first left the hands of the state and reached commerce. On my model I can find no place at all for distribution of coin by the state to merchants or traders, and until that point of entry for the coin can be found, Fulford's picture is invalid".

98 Hendy 1985, 1.

99 Casey 1986, 82 : "Military stations in the ancient world were places from which an injection of coinage into the regional economies took place".

100 C. Howgego, dans ce qui est alors une contre-attaque face aux excès de la raison militaire, aura argumenté finement sur le rôle non négligeable, voire important, du commerce (Howgego 1994 et 1995, 88-95 [mais 102 : "This suggests that the army was in terms of numbers the most significant mobile body of population within the Empire"]).

101 Grierson 1966, vi.

102 Picard *et al.* 2012. La publication des monnaies ptolémaïques des fouilles du CEA à Alexandrie est toute entière tournée vers l'identification des périodes de circulation, c'est-à-dire des moments de décri, sans chercher d'ailleurs à esquisser une pseudo-trame économique des échanges.

103 Grierson 1966, xiv : "Many of the principles on which we work were formulated in the sphere of ancient numismatics, where comparatively little counter-checking with other types of evidence is possible ; or else have come to be accepted merely because they seem to be 'obvious', which usually implies that no one has reflected upon them at all. We labour in consequence under a number of conceptions which reference to modern situations would almost certainly show to be false".

un tel contrôle est possible. Parmi la vaste littérature existante sur le sujet, je me limiterai à quelques exemples.

Cela fait longtemps qu'on a noté pour l'Angleterre une différence entre la circulation monétaire urbaine et rurale, la seconde étant composée de monnaies plus vieillies que la première[104].

Travaillant sur les constantes de diffusion (le temps mis par une pièce entre la frappe et l'utilisation pour les échanges) et de régression (le temps mis par une pièce entre sa mise en service et sa disparition), Goulpeau a développé un modèle qui, appliqué aux monnaies relevées à la faveur de quêtes paroissiales (en octobre et novembre 1978), d'une part, au contenu du trésor de Rance (début XVIIe s.), de l'autre, paraît indiquer que : "au XVIIe s. la vitesse de mise en circulation des doubles-tournois est donc la moitié de celle observée de nos jours pour les pièces d'un franc et leur durée de vie environ trois fois moindre[105]".

Dans *The random walk*, deux chercheurs australiens se sont astreints a étudier les 1 000 monnaies trouvées lors des 410 promenades autant pédestres qu'urbaines de 6-7 km faites par l'un d'entre eux à l'aube pendant 28 mois à Melbourne (déc. 2005-mars 2008)[106]. Il ressort que ces trouvailles isolées sont en remarquable adéquation avec les quantités produites de petites dénominations, qu'on y trouve 1,7 % de monnaies étrangères n'ayant pas cours en Australie, que les trouvailles ont été faites préférentiellement (44 %) à proximité des machines à sous (cabines téléphoniques et caisses de parking)[107], qu'il a été procédé à davantage de trouvailles en début de semaine, soit juste après le pic d'activités commerciales du week-end. En revanche, les mois d'été (janvier-février) ne correspondent pas à un pic, alors que la saison touristique bat son plein.

Dans leur article intitulé *La circulation des euros, reflet de la mobilité des hommes*, les auteurs de l'INED montrent comment les débuts de la diffusion de la nouvelle monnaie européenne traduisent le déplacement non pas des marchandises mais des personnes, essentiellement en fonction du tourisme avec des têtes de pont d'euros allemands sur la Côte d'Azur et d'euros espagnols à Paris[108]. Dix ans plus tard, on voit que le brassage a augmenté en fonction d'une logique de proximité géographique, sauf pour l'Italie[109].Une autre étude permet de montrer comment, en Belgique, les euros français ont davantage pénétré les

104 Glanville 1970 (voir aussi Kent 1974, 185 : "Even in 1967 it appeared that the currency of Great Britain was not uniform, there being a marked increase in the proportion of older coins in circulation outside London").

105 Goulpeau 1981, 298. Il ajoute : "La moins bonne tenue à l'usure du métal (cuivre contre nickel) et le volume limité des stocks disponibles de cuivre sont en grande partie responsables de ce recyclage rapide des flans".

106 Frazer & Touw 2010, qui cite une riche bibliographie sur la perte de monnaies telle qu'étudiée par les économistes aujourd'hui, en ce compris l'étude pionnière de Cole 1976.

107 Transposé au monde grec, on notera le bon sens de Knapp & Mac Isaac 2005, 29 lorsqu'ils observent: "As ancients' garb had no pockets, it was not as easy to lose coins as it is today. Coins had to be removed from a pouch [...] But the question remains why the coins would be taken out of a pouch during an athletic contest. Two reasons in particular come to mind, the purchase of snacks –available for a few chalkoi– and the incidence of gaming").

108 Grasland *et al.* 2002. Pour l'influence du tourisme voir aussi Grasland & Guérin-Pace 2004.

109 Grasland *et al.* 2012.

porte-monnaie (invariable) wallons que flamands[110]. Pour les euros allemands, le rythme auquel ils quittent l'Allemagne est de *c.* 5 % par an[111], etc.

Au-delà de la disparité des contextes et des époques, on voit l'intérêt pour l'historien de l'Antiquité de se pencher sur une littérature dont les modèles sont construits en fonction de paramètres bien mieux maîtrisés.

Retour aux monnaies grecques trouvées en fouilles : de quoi sont-elles le reflet ?

Passer de l'étude des monnaies de fouilles à celle de la circulation monétaire est donc un exercice particulièrement périlleux, tant les possibilités de distorsion sont grandes et les pièges interprétatifs nombreux. Pour rappel : ce qui est publié ne constitue qu'une partie de ce qui a été trouvé ; ce qui a été trouvé qu'une partie de ce qui a été perdu ; ce qui a été perdu qu'une partie de ce qui a circulé ; ce qui a circulé qu'une partie de ce qui a été émis et chacune de ces étapes est susceptible d'avoir été biaisée par des circonstances particulières, anciennes comme modernes[112].

Les seuls cas simples sont ceux qui dévient le plus par rapport à la normalité, à supposer qu'on puisse la définir de façon satisfaisante (le cadre de référence régional). Ainsi en va-t-il de Cabyle (Jambol) à l'époque hellénistique où l'essentiel des monnaies retrouvées dans les niveaux hellénistiques sont des bronzes au nom d'Antiochos II frappés à Sardes[113]. Non seulement, il ne fait pas de doute que ces bronzes ont été amenés lorsque la cité a accueilli une garnison séleucide mais il est encore patent qu'ils ont continué à former l'essentiel du numéraire disponible longtemps après le départ de ladite garnison. Ce schéma, qui répond bien au modèle plaidé par R. Duncan-Jones pour l'Empire romain (arrivée rapide d'un numéraire spécifique dans une province et immobilisation captive ensuite de ce numéraire)[114], est presque banal à l'époque hellénistique (garnisons macédoniennes sous Antigone Gonatas en Eubée et en Attique ; bronzes ptolémaïques dans le Péloponnèse) et prouve à l'évidence que les soldats pouvaient être payés en monnaies de bronze[115].

Dans la plupart des cas, toutefois, l'élément exogène se laisse moins facilement interpréter. La grande tentation de ceux qui ont publié les monnaies de fouilles des niveaux grecs aura été d'écrire à partir d'elles l'histoire économique de la cité. Cette ingénuité, dont les spécialistes de monnaies romaines sont revenus, doit hélas encore être dénoncée s'agissant de travaux parfois très récents et pour le reste des modèles de bonne méthodologie.

110 Berroir *et al.* 2005.
111 Stoyan 2002 et Stoyan & Döge 2012.
112 Grierson 1965, v. Voir le tableau donné dans Collis 1988, 174.
113 Draganov 1994.
114 Duncan-Jones 1990, 30-47.
115 Psoma 2009.

Monnaies locales : absence de lien entre la fréquence des trouvailles monétaires et la prospérité économique ?

“Que peuvent nous apprendre les monnaies de fouille sur l’histoire et sur l’économie d’une cité ?”[116]. À cette “question naïve” (dixit l’auteur), O. Picard apporte lui-même des éléments de réponse dans le cas de Thasos en indiquant ce dont les monnaies de fouille… ne sont pas le reflet. En particulier, il indique son fort scepticisme quant à lier une abondance de monnaies avec une prospérité économique[117]. Autant, cette démarche peut se révéler fructueuse pour des grands systèmes intégrés, fortement centralisés, où la monnaie se trouve brassée de manière à gommer l’incidence géographique des lieux de production (il évoque le haut Moyen Âge en Angleterre et même Thasos à l’époque byzantine)[118], autant cette liaison ne fonctionne pas pour des horizons monétaires aussi limités que celui des cités grecques[119].

Il est vrai que la liaison entre monnaies de fouilles et prospérité économique a souvent été posée ingénument comme allant de soi, alors que rien n’est moins sûr. Richard Reece va même plus loin en contestant le lien entre intensité des pertes monétaires et intensité de l’occupation d’un site[120]. C’est sans doute là faire l’avocat du diable (ce en quoi on sait qu’il excelle) mais il reste extrêmement difficile de cerner le rapport entre le monétaire et l’économique[121].

Il serait utile aussi – mais l’exercice est plus difficile à réaliser que pour l’époque romaine impériale – que les publications de monnaies grecques trouvées en fouille comparent non pas les nombres de monnaies trouvées à différentes périodes mais leurs pouvoirs d’achat[122].

116 Picard 1997, 29.

117 Sur le même sujet, voir Grierson 1966, xii-xv.

118 Voir Clarke & Schia, éd. 1989 et, pour Thasos, Saulnier 1993.

119 Picard 1997, 33 (“L’exemple de Thasos, où le volume du monnayage diminue à une époque de grande prospérité et d’intense activité commerciale, vient s’ajouter à celui d’Érétrie pour me convaincre que la production monétaire n’est fonction ni de la richesse ni des activités d’une cité”), avec renvoi à Picard 1994b et *id.* 1996, 190-192.

120 Reece 1980 = *id.* 2003, 117 : “Finally, and to me proving conclusively that the exercise is, at present, a waste of time, no one has attempted to prove any connection between intensity of coin loss, and intensity of occupation or use of a site. If, in Ostia, at a temple site, there is under Julian a rise in the number of dedications recorded, and a corresponding rise in the number of coins lost on the site, then I might begin to take the idea seriously at Uley (*NB*: un temple fouillé dans le Gloucestershire). This vital link has not been established, hence my reluctance to build historical sand-castles between material low and high tides”.

121 On notera que Peter Guest, formé par R. Reece, a récemment soutenu que la similarité de profils monétaires observée sur 15 sites permettait une exploitation économique de leurs résultats à l’échelle de la Méditerranée orientale entre le milieu du IVe et le milieu du VIIe s. (Guest 2012, 120 : “It has been possible to demonstrate a correlation between the coins lost at settlements and the production and supply of low-value coinage from the imperial mints. In turn, it is proposed that we can now begin to appreciate how the production of the late Roman and early Byzantine currency fluctuated between the end of the fourth and the seventh centuries, which to some extent must reflect imperial fiscal policy”). Pour une vision plus résolument économique encore des monnaies de fouille, voir Butcher 2004, 150.

122 Grierson 1966, v-vi ; Reece 1973 = *id.* 2003, 65 ; Hobbs 2007, 82-84 (qui mesure la valeur de tous les dépôts en les convertissant en grammes d’or (EGW = Equivalent Gold Weight)).

Monnaies étrangères : les cartes de distribution et leur interprétation

S'agissant des monnaies étrangères à la cité, "la première hypothèse qui vient à l'esprit, poursuit O. Picard, est qu'à défaut de nous permettre de retracer l'évolution du commerce de la cité, les monnaies de fouille feraient au moins connaître ses partenaires commerciaux. Il faut renoncer à cet espoir[123]". Et il démontre comment le commerce du vin, qui fut la grande affaire des Thasiens, n'a laissé aucune trace monétaire chez les partenaires commerciaux[124]. "La réalité qui se cache derrière la perte de ces menues monnaies, ce n'est pas le 'grand' commerce thasien, l'exportation de vin vers la mer Noire, mais l'activité sans doute beaucoup plus importante d'un cabotage qui faisait de Thasos une escale très vivante le long des côtes égéennes"[125].

C'est le même constat, *mutatis mutandis*, qui se déduit des cartes de répartition présentées dans leur important article par Z. Çizmeli-Öğun et M.-C. Marcellesi pour les monnaies étrangères retrouvées sur 14 sites d'Asie Mineure[126]. On signalera une innovation intéressante : comparer le faciès des monnaies de fouilles avec celui des inscriptions mentionnant la présence d'étrangers, ainsi qu'I. Savalli-Lestrade et J. Chameroy tentent l'exercice pour Pergame[127]. Là encore, ce sont les réseaux courts qui dominent nettement.

De telles cartes de distribution sont très suggestives et doivent être encouragées absolument dès lors que le matériel le justifie[128]. Je plaiderais pour adjoindre systématiquement aussi un graphique qui donne l'importance des monnaies étrangères par rapport aux monnaies de la cité, en établissant quelques catégories en fonction de la distance entre le lieu d'émission et celui de la découverte. Par exemple : 1) de 0 à 10 km, 2) de 10 à 50 km, 3) de 50 à 100 km et 4) plus de 100 km[129]. Cela fournirait un indice de proximité de circulation, très utile pour comparer les différents types de sites[130]. On ne peut d'ailleurs, à

123 Picard 1997, 36.

124 *Ibid.*, 36: "La contradiction est si flagrante entre les indications des amphores et celles des monnaies qu'il faut bien se résoudre à renoncer à voir dans le mouvement des monnaies de bronze un indicateur du mouvement des bateaux transportant le vin thasien".

125 *Ibid.*, 37.

126 Çizmeli-Öğun & Marcellesi 2011 (à quoi on ajoutera pour Pergame : Savalli-Lestrade & Chameroy à paraître).

127 Savalli-Lestrade & Chameroy à paraître.

128 Voir par exemple Picard 1984, 282 pour les nombreuses provenances des monnaies retrouvées dans l'Antre corycien.

129 Voir les cartes avec ronds concentriques données pour Némée et d'autres sites (Priène, Éphèse, Tralles, Smyrne, route sacrée entre Milet et Didymes : Knapp & Mac Isaac 2005, 20, 42-44 et 48).

130 Il est clair par exemple que Délos offre un faciès beaucoup plus international qu'Athènes, Corinthe ou Argos (Hackens 1975, 218). À Corinthe, pour les fouilles de 1896-1929, on trouve ainsi 63 % de monnaies corinthiennes (752 sur 1186), 9 % de monnaies de Sicyone (106) et 28 % pour le reste du monde grec (Edwards 1933 et Walker 1997, 23). Les monnaies de Priène constituent 68 % des pièces retrouvées en fouille (564 sur 833 ; Regling 1927, 187-193). S'agissant de provenances très lointaines, on citera à titre d'exemples les 2 bronzes de Mithridate Eupator trouvés dans le Tibre à Rome (Frey-Kupper 1995), ou, dans les fouilles de Carnuntum, la litra de Syracuse, datée de 475-450 a.C., ainsi que 3 bronzes d'Alexandre le Grand et 3 autres de Kymé (Dembski 1996, 123). Grierson cite aussi la présence d'une indo-grecque au Pays-de Galle (Grierson 1965, ii), Dolley de monnaies romaines dans les couches médiévales (Dolley 1974, 225), etc.

ce sujet, que formuler le vœu de voir se créer une base de données propres aux monnaies de fouilles du monde grec, à l'imitation du site *Nomisma.org* pour les trésors monétaires.

Au-delà d'attester un "réseau d'échanges" (pour rester prudent), il est difficile de qualifier ces monnaies étrangères : ont-elles été perdues accidentellement ou délibérément écartées parce que non acceptées dans le cadre de transactions locales ? Dans une perspective plus soucieuse d'envisager le document de façon anthropologique qu'économique, certains font valoir que – pour l'essentiel – ce qui est retrouvé par les archéologues de nos jours est, littéralement, "ce qui n'a pas circulé"[131]. Derrière ces critiques, on retrouve la tension naturelle entre deux conceptions : prédominance implicite de l'économique qui se laisse dès lors étudier comme tel, d'une part, économique enchâssé ("embedded") dans le social, de l'autre. Dénier a priori à ces monnaies étrangères d'avoir pu être acceptées paraît procéder d'un rigorisme économique dont on pressent l'anachronisme et qui est maintes fois démenti sur le terrain[132]. Il est bien plus probable que, comme le plaide notamment L. Lacroix (qui reprend un passage maintenant bien connu des souvenirs d'enfance de G. Schlumberger à Pau dans les années 1860)[133], le monde grec a fait preuve d'une souplesse sur ce point dont nous avons perdu l'idée[134].

On a souvent cité L. Robert, selon lequel la monnaie d'argent attesterait le voyage des marchandises et celle de bronze celui des hommes[135]. Il est difficile d'adhérer à cet adage[136]. Non pas que la monnaie de bronze ne soit pas indicative du déplacement des personnes (comme nous l'avons vu pour les euros qui leur servent d'équivalents aujourd'hui), mais parce qu'il est plus ruineux qu'approprié de lier la monnaie d'argent au commerce, selon une vision de la monnaie en général qui paraît très datée, aujourd'hui que la raison militaire a taillé d'importantes croupières au tout commercial d'hier.

131 Une position presque certainement fausse si l'on entend par là que les monnaies de bronze étrangères n'étaient jamais acceptées (voir Savalli-Lestrade & Chameroy à paraître).

132 Voir les nombreux exemples plus haut évoqués, dont Seuthopolis et Pompéi. Sur le transfert massif de bronzes de Kos en Italie centrale vers le milieu du IIe s., voir Frey-Kupper 1995 ; Stannard & Frey-Kupper 2008, 385-391 ; Stannard 2013, 138-139.

133 Lacroix 1969, 171-172 : "Aujourd'hui, où nous n'avons plus qu'une monnaie unique, on se ferait difficilement une idée de l'extraordinaire macédoine de pièces de cuivre de toutes sortes que pouvait contenir, vers le soir, un de ces grands tiroirs de magasin, alors que la foule de paysans des environs avait passé, dans la journée, à l'épicerie Malan ou à la mercerie Cazalis. À côté des sous flambant neufs de Napoléon III, des sous et liards déjà plus frustes des deux Républiques et de Louis XVI (les Bourbons des deux branches du XIXe siècle en ont relativement fait peu frapper), on y trouvait des pièces de cuivre de tous les rois d'Espagne, des papes, des rois de Portugal, de tous les princes d'Italie, Piémont, Lombardie, Naples, puis des jetons très nombreux, français et étrangers ; surtout une immense quantité de bronzes des empereurs romains, déterrés par la charrue des paysans, presque toujours très frustes, aussitôt remis en circulation. Tout était accepté. J'ai vu, dans ces extraordinaires tiroirs, jusqu'à quelques pièces grecques antiques et beaucoup de pièces celtibériennes, frappées par les populations d'Espagne avant et après l'occupation romaine… De même, les pièces d'argent qui circulaient appartenaient à toutes les nations de la terre. Aucune n'était refusée" (tiré de Schlumberger 1934, 38-39).

134 Pensons aux friandises et aux jetons de téléphone acceptés en Italie dans les années 1963-1964, alors qu'il était devenu plus intéressant de fondre les pièces officielles de 10 lires.

135 Robert 1951, 77, n. 8.

136 Picard 2007, 113.

Mais le militaire et le commercial[137] sont loin d'épuiser les motifs de voyage. Les concours panhelléniques et les grandes fêtes religieuses constituent une autre catégorie qui vient spontanément à l'esprit[138]. Les découvertes monétaires faites au stade de Némée ont même poussé les auteurs en charge de leur publication à imaginer des espaces réservés à différentes cités tout autour du stade, comme les tribunes d'un stade de football aujourd'hui où les supporters des équipes opposées sont placés dans des zones distinctes[139].

Micro-contextes et dimension anthropologique des monnaies de fouilles

Un aspect qui est destiné à recevoir de grands développements, parce que peu pris en compte jusqu'ici est l'étude du micro-contexte (pour lequel les avantages structurels des monnayages romains s'estompent).

Ce type d'étude a toujours d'abord concerné l'archéologie funéraire, pour laquelle il est fondamental de savoir où et comment était présenté le matériel monétaire : dans la bouche, dans la main, sur la poitrine ? Si sur la poitrine, quelle face de la monnaie était visible ? La monnaie est-elle percée ou montée en bijou ? La valeur de la monnaie (ou des monnaies) est-elle significative ? Le type iconographique choisi à dessein ? Se peut-il que l'on ait sélectionné deux monnaies dont les types se répondent ? A-t-on sélectionné un type féminin au moment de consacrer une pièce à une divinité féminine ? Peut-on, plus généralement, reconstruire des croyances à partir du matériel monétaire étudié dans son contexte fin ?

P. Grierson s'est certainement montré plus qu'un autre attentif à la dimension anthropologique des monnaies et il est toujours intéressant de se reporter à ses écrits sur le trésor de Sutton Hoo, le Wergeld et bien d'autres matières. J.-M. Doyen plaide aussi pour que les micro-contextes soient enfin pris en compte dans une perspective qui enchâsse résolument l'économique dans le culturel.

À un niveau plus global, ce sont les spécialistes du *Barbaricum* romain qui ont sans doute le plus développé une réflexion anthropologique dans le champ des monnayages antiques. Les collègues allemands, polonais et scandinaves ont depuis longtemps avancé des idées sur la nature des monnaies retrouvées très au-delà du *limes* et se sont interrogés sur la fonction de ce qui, de toute évidence, n'était plus du "*all-purpose money*[140]". Leurs réflexions s'inscrivent pleinement dans le courant dominant de l'histoire culturelle et tournent inévitablement autour des questions de statut social et d'identité, avec un retour aux travaux de M. Weber, de K. Polanyi[141] et de G. Dalton[142]. Il ne fait pas de doute que ce regard anthropologique soit

137 Pour un petit trésor de 46 monnaies de bronze trouvé dans les fouilles d'Ascalon et paraissant documenter les escales d'un navire marchand en Méditerranée orientale, voir Gitler & Kahanov 2002, spéc. fig. 19.2. Map of the eastern Mediterranean showing locations of seaports and mints).

138 Voir Baldus 1989 pour un lot très cosmopolite trouvé sur la voie sacrée entre Milet et Didymes.

139 Knapp & Mac Isaac 2005, 27 (fig. 9. Plan of the Stadium with coins plotted by minting city) et 28 ("The distribution of the mints also provides evidence for seating arrangements in the Stadium").

140 Voir les contributions parues dans Bursche *et al.* 2008 (notamment les contributions d'A. Bursche, de R. Ciolek, de J. van Heesch et d'A. Zapolska, et la large bibliographie donnée jusqu'à cette date). Voir aussi Ciolek 2007. Pour l'Allemagne, *e.g.* : Berger 1996 et Wolters 1999.

141 À un niveau théorique, on ne citera qu'un article qui en résume bien d'autres : Maucourant 2000.

142 Dalton 1965.

porteur d'un enrichissement potentiel considérable de nos connaissances et c'est là un secteur en grand développement.

Pour conclure en quelques mots ce qui n'est qu'un rapide survol d'une littérature de plus en plus riche, on plaidera fortement pour que ceux qui ont la charge de publier les monnaies grecques trouvées lors d'une fouille archéologique emploient une partie de leur temps à prendre connaissance des études de nature méthodologique réalisées à propos de périodes ultérieures pour lesquelles la qualité de l'information permet d'aller plus loin tant dans la modélisation des phénomènes de circulation que dans les réponses apportées aux questions que celle-ci suscite[143]. On devrait par là s'affranchir des ingénuités sur le commerce et la prospérité économique du lieu fouillé.

On plaide aussi pour une attention plus grande à tous les types de contextes situés en-dessous de l'unité régionale qui aura monopolisé l'attention, et en particulier aux micro-contextes fort négligés jusqu'ici et pour lesquels le regard anthropologique peut se révéler très stimulant.

143 Il est significatif que les deux publications récentes les plus remarquables sans doute s'agissant de monnaies grecques trouvées en fouille (Alexandrie et Monte Iato) ne fassent aucune référence aux travaux de R. Reece (Picard *et al.* 2012 et Frey-Kupper 2013). Et cette situation peut être étendue à l'ensemble de la littérature antérieure (*e.g.* Knapp & Mac Isaac 2005).

Using Site Finds as Basis for Statistical Analyses of the Seleucid Numismatic Production and Circulation. An Introduction to the Method

Panagiotis P. Iossif[1]

Many of the principles in which we work were formulated
in the sphere of ancient numismatics, where comparatively little
counter-checking with other types of evidence is possible;
or else have come to be accepted merely because they seem to be "obvious",
which usually implies that no one has reflected upon them all.
We labour in consequence under a number of conceptions which
reference to modern situations would almost certainly show to be false[2]

The posing of the problem[3]

Ten years ago, when K. Butcher published his *Coinage in Roman Syria*, the question of the kind of numismatic data to be used for determining the circulation patterns and the volume of production was crucial for his analysis[4]. Butcher was influenced in his approach and methodology by what had been done by other British numismatists working on Roman Britain, especially by R. Reece[5], J. Casey[6], or N. S. Ryan[7]. The "British" school was the first to ask crucial questions on the nature of coin finds during archaeological excavations interpreting them in their original archaeological context or, even more important for our purpose, how

1 I'm grateful to the following colleagues and friends for long discussions and remarks: François de Callataÿ, Warren Esty, Alain Bresson, Bas van Leeuwen, Makis Aperghis, Cathy Lorber, Kris Lockyear, John Ma, Andy Meadows, Jean-Marc Doyen, Petr Veselý, Jan Moens, and Christian Lauwers. Mary Lannin is to be thanked for improving the quality of my English text. All errors of fact or interpretation remain my sole responsibility.
Abbreviations : *SC* 1: Houghton & Lorber 2002 ; *SC* 2 : Houghton *et al.* 2008.

2 Grierson 1966, xiv.

3 The bibliography of this article doesn't contain any reference to the enormous number of publications recording excavation coins. The complete record appears in Iossif 2016.

4 Butcher 2004.

5 Reece 1991, 1993, 1995 and 2002, to cite his most important contributions.

6 Casey 1986, esp. 68-113.

7 Ryan 1988.

to interpret them as representative samples of the volume of coinage originally produced[8]. In his useful introduction, Casey determined five self-evident factors that govern coin losses which can be summarized as follows: 1. They are proportional to the volume of coinage originally issued[9]; 2. Coin losses are (inversely?) proportional to the intrinsic value of the coins issued (mostly related to the effort of recovery of coins based on their denomination and economic value)[10]; 3. These coin losses are proportional to political factors prevailing during the lifetime of coins; 4. They are proportional to economic factors prevailing during the lifetime of coins; 5. Coin losses are frequently proportional to the physical size of individual coins in the original coin population[11].

These self-evident points are regularly asked when studying Roman coinages, especially in the West[12], but are rarely considered in studying the Greek numismatic material from excavations, even if considerable progress has been made in the last two decades[13]. Even in the cases where excavation coins are used for the long term, the relevance of this material as a statistically reliable sample is virtually never considered. In this article, I will try to consider a statistical and quantitative approach based on the Seleucid numismatic material coming from 80 excavations/sites in Asia Minor, the Near and Middle East, the so-called "Seleucid Excavations Database" or SED. Since the focus of this analysis is methodological, in what follows, I will consider the possibilities offered by such an approach without providing too many answers[14]. In the following section, I will explain the formation of the SED, its nature, and characteristics. Section 3 will deal with the reliability of the database by comparing it with large numismatic collections. Section 4 will consider the questions of the influence of denomination (and module) in coin loss patterns and the coin production will be considered in time (by reign) and space. The final section will deal with one particular aspect of the potential offered by this analysis: the examination of the speed of circulation of Seleucid coins within the borders of the Empire; I will conclude with some additional thoughts and possibilities offered by this type of approach.

8 See also Butcher 2004, 136-142.

9 If we want to be more precise, we need to say that the coin losses were "proportional to the volume of coinage in circulation", since we ignore the part of coinage in the royal (or imperial) treasures.

10 Or simply related to the care taken to avoid loss.

11 Casey 1986, 69 sq. The term "proportional" is that used by Casey; in fact, in mathematics, the term has a specific meaning and use: it means that one quantity is a constant time the other. Therefore, in Casey's five factors, the term "proportional" is used in the sense of "related to". Only in factor 1 the use of the term can be considered as exact. I thank Warren Esty for drawing my attention to this specific point of vocabulary.

12 See the numerous contextual studies on Roman Britain, or those in Northern France and Belgium under the leadership of J.-M. Doyen. Butcher 2004 was a pioneer work for the application of these methods in an eastern context, even though Doyen 1987 was also the first to apply the contextual methods in eastern Hellenistic numismatics.

13 The cases of Athens (Kroll 1993), Thasos (Picard 1997) or Alexandria (Picard *et al.* 2012).

14 Iossif 2016.

Creating a database

When I started working on a project of Seleucid quantitative studies, the basic idea was to gather together all available numismatic material from published sources. This started with the creation of two databases. The first one focused on published hoards containing Seleucid material, the "SHD" or "Seleucid Hoard Database". 253 hoards containing at least one Seleucid coin were collected. The composition of this database is now: 10 230 tetradrachms, 826 drachms and smaller denominations of silver, and 1 559 bronzes[15]. The grand total is of 12 615 coins.

From the composition of the collected hoard material, it became obvious that bronze coinage was underrepresented and offered no reliable basis for any statistical analyses. Seleucid bronze should therefore be accessed via a different type of material than hoards. Published excavation reports were the obvious candidate. Thus far, since this is a work in progress, the Seleucid coins from 80 sites have been collected in "SED" or "Seleucid Excavations Database" currently totaling 8 334 coins. Confirming what F. de Callataÿ has already observed for the composition of the material from different sites, this material is 99,3% composed of bronze coins[16].

The most difficult task when creating a database is to decide its type and entries. These parameters are generally determined by the objectives of the research itself. Thus, 38 different attributes/entries were created, each of them reporting a different characteristic of the coin and the site (name of the site, region, mint, issuing authority, metal, denomination, identity of the site, the mint or the reign etc.). Since the focus of the research was quantification and coin-types, the coins from each site were divided by "*SC* type". This explains why two or more entries exist for the same site in the database. In order to facilitate the research, the database was digitized, *i.e.* a unique number was attributed to every entry. I included only coins that I could verify myself (or those personally examined by colleagues with whom I was in contact) and only coins identified with certainty (for this purpose, I coined a "certainty degree 0-6" where zero corresponded to a coin impossible to identify and 6 to a coin identified with 100% certainty – only coins with "certainty degree" 5 or 6 were included). This last remark explains some differences in the quantity between my data and that published in excavation reports and corpora. *E.g.* in D. B. Waage's list of excavation coins from Antioch, the major mint of the dynasty for the longest part of the Seleucid history, there are reported 844 coins (all bronzes); I was able to personally identify and attribute a *SC* number to 826 (and only those are included in my database)[17].

Limitations: Before further considering the evidence, it is necessary to point out some of the limitations of our sample. The first and most important limitation is the uneven geographical distribution of the sample. For obvious historical reasons, some areas are

15 Iossif 2016 and *id.* 2014. See also a methodological introduction to the SHD and method in *id.* 2011b.

16 de Callataÿ 2006, 180: 38 sites with 95% of the material found being bronzes (this reaches 99% when considering 31 sites). Coins identified as "hoards" from regular excavations are not included in this analysis, since it has been decided to be part of the SHD.

17 Butcher 2004, 138 uses the same method when considering the material from Antioch and Dura-Europos.

overrepresented in the sample, especially those in the Western part of the Empire. The material from a small territory like Israel for instance, covers about 46,6% of the total entries (3 859 bronzes from 40 different sites)[18]. This situation could introduce a serious bias in the database, because if one region is overrepresented in relative terms, all other regions are inevitably underrepresented in the database. Nevertheless, since the area of what is nowadays Israel was a crossroad of armies and commercial routes, we have no reason to suspect a typical "Israeli" profile considerably different from that of the surrounding areas (even if caution is imposed due to local patterns)[19]. Furthermore, the fact that we have a virtually complete record for the two most important Seleucid sites (and mints), *i.e.* Antioch and Seleucia on the Tigris, effectively counterbalances the geographic bias introduced by the overrepresentation of Israeli sites in the record (see below on how to determine data introducing statistical bias in the sample).

A second limitation concerns the unequal quality of excavation records. Older (and some more recent) excavation reports provide exact information for the archaeological context of every single find (cf. again, the Israeli reports or the Australian reports from Jebel Khalid)[20]. Other, among them Antioch and Seleucia on the Tigris, are simple lists of excavation coins with no contextual information provided at all. This problem makes the precise reconstruction of the original context and strata of a given find impossible, as well as discussions and analyses on circulation since we have no precise "burial" date for these coins. For example, at Apamea, only four Seleucid coins were found during the Belgian excavations, three of them (dating to the reigns of Antiochos I, Alexander I, and Demetrios II) were found in backfill from the 4th c. AD, while the fourth (a coin of Seleucos I) was found in a 2nd c. AD context in the Thermal building[21]. We soften the impact of this limitation by simply considering the data from the point of view of the issuing authority. In practice, when attempting macro-contextual analyses of the data, all bronzes are analyzed from the point of view of the king (filter: "Reign" in SED). My periods (shorter or longer, see below) represent the date the coins were struck and certainly not the date of their arrival at a given site (much less, the date of their deposition)[22]. If we want to propose micro-contextual analyses, then all coins without precise context of discovery must be eliminated[23]. Another way to reduce this methodological problem is to adopt broader periods in the numismatic history; by dividing the data in that way, dates of issue and of loss are more likely to fall within the same period. Thus, I introduced an eight-period division of the Seleucid history: Period 1: Seleucos I; Period 2: Antiochos I to Seleucos III; Period 3: Antiochos III (Achaios & Molon); Period 4: Seleucos IV to Antiochos V; Period 5: Demetrios I to Antiochos VI;

18 Different excavations conducted at different areas of Jerusalem are here considered as an individual site.

19 Voir Syon 2004 for the circulation around Gamla covering also a major part of southern modern Lebanese territory.

20 See *e.g.*, the numerous excavation reports by D. Ariel or Syon 2004; for Jebel Khalid, see Nixon 2002.

21 Lauwers 2013, 165-167.

22 Butcher 2003, 45-46 discusses the issue in detail.

23 For a comparable explanation and analysis of Roman British material, see Walton 2012. Here, the nature of the material (mostly stray finds) obliges the author to raise the methodological problem, be cautious, and yet continue to use the data getting extremely useful results.

Period 6: Diodotos Tryphon; Period 7. Demetrios II first reign to Demetrios II second reign; Period 8. Antiochos VIII to the end of the Seleucids[24]. With this analysis, we don't eliminate the problem but we get, at least, less-methodologically-fraught results since issue and burial dates are more likely to fall within the limits of a single period.

A last method can be used to overcome this difficulty and is inspired by the "Date Estimative de Perte" ("DEP") method used by Swiss archaeologists, as modified (and improved) by J.-M. Doyen under the form of "Date Minimale de Perte" (DMP)[25]. In a forthcoming article, Iossif and Lauwers argue that it is possible to establish a wear matrix for the Seleucid bronzes. The method is simple and straightforward: a wear-index ranging from 0 to 10 (where zero is impossible to identify and 10 is a mint condition coin) is assigned to bronzes. Then, the wear-index is related and compared to coins coming from dated contexts making possible to relate wear-index and burial date. As a last step, we subtract the burial date from the known issuing date making possible to relate wear-indexes with time period of circulation. In that case, these coins can be studied based not only on their issue dates but also on their exact burial dates making possible a precise and accurate analysis of the circulation patterns[26]. Since these data are not yet available, I will simply consider the material from the point of view of the "production" of the issuing authority, assuming equal periods of circulation for all coins[27].

Another limitation of this kind of database is the part of the "subjective" based on the personal element of the scholar. When Reece explained the way he recorded coins from

24 I would like to thank Arthur Houghton for his help with the division of the Seleucid numismatic history. See Lockyear 2000 for discussion on the use and utility of larger categories (with previous bibliography on the original period division proposed by Reece).

25 See Pilon 2011 for the "DEP" method; Doyen 2010, 339; *id.* 2013a, 142-145 for the improved "DEP" method based on a matrix created on the Garonne hoard for Roman *denarii*; *id.* 2013b, for a wear matrix Doyen applies for the material from the excavations at Nempont-Saint-Firmin (Pas-de-Calais, France). For the "DMP" method, see now Doyen, forthcoming: this method is also based on the wear of coins and the author arrives at tables with "DMP" data that he tests for the excavation data from the site of Remilly-les-Pothées (in the Ardennes area, France).

26 Iossif & Lauwers 2016. In fact, following this method, if a coin was produced in 200 and its wear-index is 4 (equal to *c.* 25 years of circulation), then the date assigned to the given coin is 200-25 = 175. Wear ("usure") must not be confused with the conditions of conservation of these coins due to their state of preservation (or restoration). A brilliant demonstration of the potential this method represents is given in Cardon & Lemaire 2015 where the numismatic material from the Napoleonian military camps from Étaples-sur-mer and Camiers (France) is treated using this method. The advantage of these study cases is that most of the dates involved in the archaeological analysis are known from other sources and the method can be tested against reliable data.

27 Some additional corrections can be considered by assuming an annual percentage of coin loss (2% estimated by Aperghis 2004, 229). This approach is more appropriate to be used for hoard data and was attempted in SHD (for an annual coin loss rate of 1,5%) with satisfactory results (even if I'm totally conscious that this percentage is quite high. What is important with this kind of approach is to assume a uniform rate and consider that this gives *maxima* for comparisons); see Iossif 2016 and *id.* 2014. Suchodolski 2002, 281-283 proposes an interesting alternative of double dating the finds (using double-axis histograms) when the archaeological context is well known: a first histogram based on the date(s) the coins were struck and a second one using the later burial period. Again, this method works better for hoard data, but can be attempted for site finds as well. This will offer considerable *termini post- and ante-quem* for the circulation patterns.

one of his 140 sites, he says: "Which coins in the Lincoln museum did I list? [...] If anyone attempted to check my work the result would be chaos because there were so many occasions on which I made a snap decision to include or exclude [...]. I have not looked up the day which I spent in the museum, so we could probably never get back to that point. It does not matter, because we SHOULD not get back to that point" (Reece's capitals in the text)[28]. It is not my opinion that results cannot (or should not) be checked and/or be repeated by others; the analysis is not only a matter of objectivity *vs.* subjectivity, it is also question of repeatability. For this reason, the SED presents not only a complete bibliographic record for each coin, but the granularity in the breakdown of the data (never attempted at such level in Greek numismatics) allows for others to test the data, add more evidence when available in the future, and verify hypotheses. Part of the subjectivity remains and cannot be totally eliminated; *e.g.*, longer periods discussed above are my own and others could analyze the period-division in different ways. The same is also true when sites are grouped based on the original status assigned to them by the Seleucids. Thus, Jebel Khalid is identified as "Military post" in SED but this is only partially true since the site evolved into a "Small city" at some point in its history[29]. Hesitation remains when it comes to these two criteria but the remaining 36 attributes/entries are objective and verifiable.

The last focus in creating and using the SED is the intrinsic, economic value of the coins. Not all bronze coins are of the same denomination, which vary from the very large ΔA issues produced in the East after Antiochos IV to the small "E" bronzes of 8-11 mm. of diameter weighing 0,6-1 gm[30]. For a proper comparison, it is necessary to convert all coins into a single "bronze-value", one I call the "C bronze value" following the terminology of the authors of *Seleucid Coins*[31] Lorber and more recently Charles Doyen convincingly argued that the *chalkous*, the unit of the Seleucid bronze denominational system, should be the *SC* "C" of 15-21 mm. diameter and 3,00-5,49 gm. weight[32]. Accepting "C" as the *chalkous*, it is easy to convert all coins in SED in "C bronze value" coins. Therefore, a column is added in the database where the actual number of single coins is converted into "C bronze value". By applying this conversion, we get a total of 9 859,5 bronzes.

As already mentioned, it is not generally accepted that the "C" denomination corresponds to the *chalkous*, the "unit" of Newell's terminology. Recent studies by O. Picard, S. Psoma and C. Grandjean argue that the *chalkous* should be identified with the smaller denomination of a system since any references to bronze fractions are (quasi) unattested from epigraphic and

28 Reece 1991, 8.

29 Clarke *et al.* 2002.

30 All types are not represented in SED. Their absence from the database is also informative of their relative sizes of production, period of emission, and areas of circulation. See below for an extended analysis.

31 *SC* 1.2, 1-4. The conversion of coins in "C-bronze value" (and "E bronze value") is part of a larger project, which aims to compare coin loss and contexts. This analysis also focusing on economic aspects of the coinage will be considered in a forthcoming work by the same author.

32 Doyen 2014, 261-299. The authors of *Seleucid Coins* (Houghton & Lorber 2002 and Houghton *et al.* 2008) offer a useful introduction to the question of which denomination might constitute the *chalkous* in the Seleucid bronze denominational system. They hesitate to adopt Newell's terminology.

papyrological sources[33]. Since the metrological studies for the Seleucid bronzes do not allow to proceeding to fine and detailed denominational analyses, the hesitation between "C" and "E" as the original Seleucid *chalkous* should remain. Thus, an additional column converting the bronze values into "E bronze value" is added.

The numerical data from SED (and SHD) are summarized in table 1:

Database	Hoards/ Sites	N° of parameters	Tetradrachms	Silver fractions	AEs	Total coins	"SHD tetra value"/ "SED C bronze value"	"SHD tetra value"/ "SED E bronze value"
SHD	253	41	10,203	826	1,559	12,615	10,437	10,437
SED	80	38	24	29	8,273	8,334	9,859.5	34,974

Table 1. Numerical data in SED and SHD (Iossif 2016).

Questions of reliability: SED and museum collections

It is well known that the quality of a quantitative/statistical analysis depends solely on the quality of the sample. In a 2011 article on how to "quantify" Seleucid religion based on the SHD, I argued that the best method for determining the relative frequency of royal coin types is the simple tabulation of as many specimens as possible known from published hoards[34]. We expect that this sample would have been representative of the coinage produced by royal mints and different issuing authorities. This method concerning the relative frequency of coin types based on tabulations has been used by I. Carradice and C. Norena for different Roman coinages[35]. Furthermore, in Kushan coins, R. Bracey showed a common pattern when considering relative frequencies of deities depicted on reverses on the issues of king Huviska in hoard and die records[36].

In order to test the representativeness of our SED, we should ideally have to dispose of a complete record of Seleucid dies for bronze coins, and then compare the set of dies identified in SED to this record. But since such a complete record does not and may never exist, the question is if there is any other type of data that could be used to test the representativeness of SED? The answer to this question turned out to be a crucial one and was unexpected: major museum collections. In a recent important article, A. Gândilă argued that instead of biases introduced in the collection because of the preferences of curators, large collections present

33 On the question of the bronze unit and the number of *chalkoi* in one obol, see Picard 1992; Psoma 1998; Grandjean 1998. These authors seem to agree that the chalkous should be identified with a very small coin – in the case of our discussion, the "E" denomination – and in the Attic system, there were 8 *chalkoi* to the obol; contra to the Aeginitan system with 12 *chalkoi* to the obol. The same interpretation is also adopted by C. C. Lorber (pers. comm. 10/9/2015).

34 Iossif 2011b, 217-222.

35 Carradice 1987; Noreña 2001 and 2011.

36 Iossif 2011b, 218-219; Bracey 2012.

common patterns when compared with site finds and hoards[37]. Therefore, and following the arguments by Gândilă, it would be logical to assume that if there is a correlation to be observed between major collections and SED, then the representativeness of SED should not be questioned[38]. If the patterns to be observed were common between SED and museum collections, this would have a reciprocal importance: not only SED would have been a representative sample for statistical analyses but museum collections would offer reliable samples as well.

Whether site finds can be considered random and therefore useful for statistical analyses has been debated for a long period. How justified are we in regarding site finds as evidence for original issues, relative volume, and circulation? M. Hendy simply rejects any relevance of site finds for monetary and economic conclusions due to the ignorance of causative factors in their structure and formation[39]. Butcher offers a general overview of the debate focusing on the "British" school's arguments before concluding in a rather cautious way that: "we should however be careful before accepting site finds as a random sample of what was in circulation [...] Given such problems, are site finds of any assistance for establishing patterns of circulation? The pattern of loss depends upon what was available for loss, even if there was a bias in favor of certain issues. The finds also allow us to make general comments about regional patterns, and allow us to perceive differences between site assemblages which might point to the existence of regional or highly localized patterns of circulation[40]". Therefore, the first step to test the representativeness of the SED was to group the bronze coins chronologically by reign and to analyze the observed pattern. Tables 2 and 3 record the data expressed in coins and "C bronze value" and "E bronze value" coins respectively (there are illustrated in fig. 1-2):

Reign	# SED	% SED
Seleucos I	164	2,04
Antiochos I	357	4,44
Antiochos II	328	4,08
Antiochos Hierax	0	0,00
Seleucos II	159	1,98
Seleucos III	201	2,50

37 Gândilă 2009; Butcher 2004, 137-142 used a similar method comparing the SC material he examined in Antakya museum with the SC coins from Antioch excavations. Katsari 2003, 52 also made a similar argument concerning the statistical reliability of museum collections focusing on Roman provincial bronzes found in Turkish museums.

38 It is important to point out that there is no overlap between the contents of my database and major collections; we should expect that some coins of the collections were originally parts of site excavations recorded in SED. In fact, as far as I can see from the records I studied in the major museum collections, there is no overlap to be observed.

39 Hendy 1985, 1.

40 Butcher 2004, 150-151. Butcher correctly rejects the usefulness of site finds as indicators of the relative proportions of silver *vs.* bronze produced, since virtually no silver coins are found in excavations.

Achaios	7	0,09
Molon	0	0,00
Antiochos III	4020	49,95
Seleucos IV	198	2,46
Antiochos IV	1140	14,17
Antiochos V	5	0,06
Timarchos	0	0,00
Demetrios I	368	4,57
Alexander I Balas	117	1,45
Demetrios II (1st-2nd reigns)	291	3,62
Antiochos VI	41	0,51
Antiochos VII	198	2,46
Tryphon	3	0,04
Alexander II Zabinas	85	1,06
Antiochos VIII	253	3,14
Antiochos IX	79	0,98
Seleucos VI	4	0,05
Antiochos X	2	0,02
Demetrios III	15	0,19
Antiochos XII	13	0,16
Antiochos XIII	0	0,00
Total	**8048**	**100**

Table 2. SED data grouped by issuing authority (Iossif 2016).

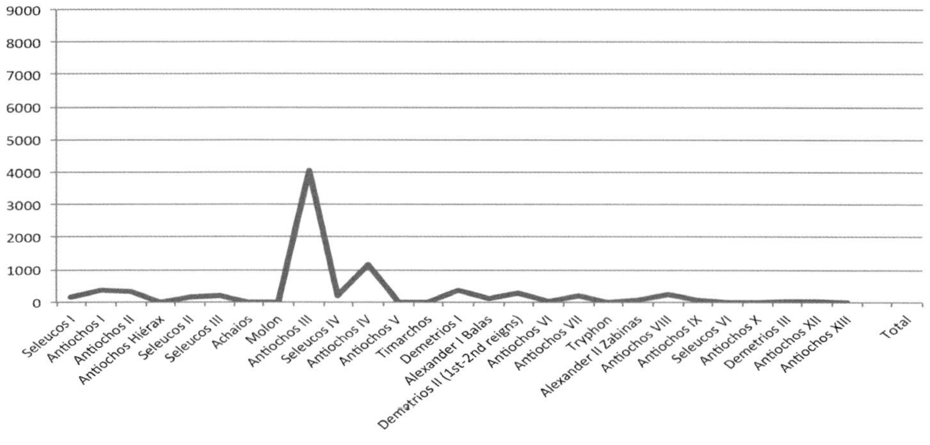

Fig. 1. Fluctuation of bronze coins in SED grouped by reign (Iossif 2016).

Reign	# SED 'C'	% SED C value	# SED 'E'	% SED E value
Seleucos I	231,5	2,35	740	2,12
Antiochos I	361,5	3,67	927	2,65
Antiochos II	583	5,91	2248	6,43
Antiochos Hierax	0	0,00	0	0,00
Seleucos II	249,75	2,53	807	2,31
Seleucos III	203	2,06	233	0,67
Achaios	8,25	0,08	21	0,06
Molon	0	0,00	0	0,00
Antiochos III	5302,5	53,78	19953	57,05
Seleucos IV	252	2,56	894	2,56
Antiochos IV	783,25	7,94	2797	8,00
Antiochos V	2,5	0,03	10	0,03
Timarchos	0	0,00	0	0,00
Demetrios I	335,5	3,40	787	2,25
Alexander I Balas	122	1,24	344	0,98
Demetrios II (1st-2nd reigns)	294	2,98	1119	3,20
Antiochos VI	48	0,49	99	0,28
Antiochos VII	268,75	2,73	916	2,62
Tryphon	6	0,06	24	0,07
Alexander II Zabinas	161	1,63	620	1,77
Antiochos VIII	452	4,58	1727	4,94
Antiochos IX	145	1,47	568	1,62
Seleucos VI	5	0,05	11	0,03
Antiochos X	4	0,04	16	0,05
Demetrios III	22	0,22	58	0,17
Antiochos XII	19	0,19	55	0,16
Antiochos XIII	0	0,00	0	0,00
Total	9859,5	100,00	34.974	100,00

Table 3. SED expressed in "C bronze value" and 'E bronze value' data grouped by issuing authority (Iossif 2016).

Having established the chronological pattern for SED, we can now compare it to the patterns based on major museum collections. Before doing so, it is necessary to add a few words on how numismatists deal with museum collections as statistically representative samples. It is a *topos* to read that these collections suffer from a series of flaws mostly in the

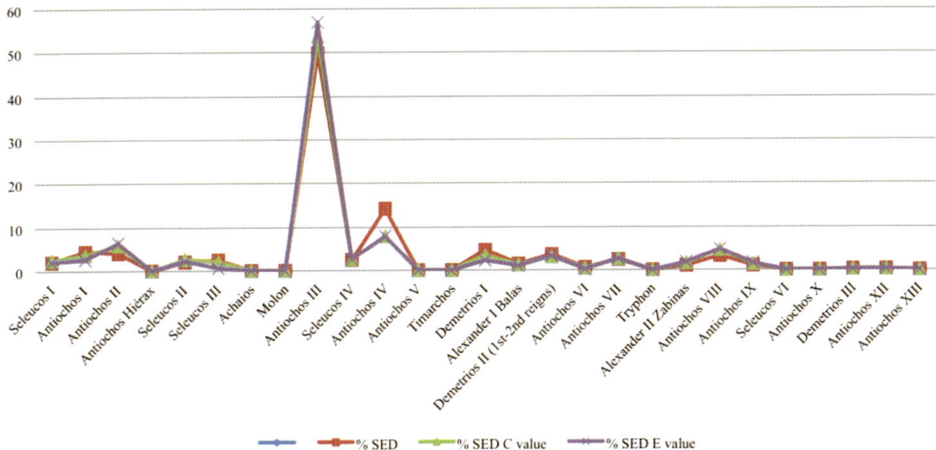

Fig. 2. SED. Fluctuation of bronze coins expressed in absolute coins and in "C bronze value" and "E bronze value" grouped by reign (Iossif 2016).

line of what I qualify as the "Grierson complex[41]"; Butcher considers collections as unreliable for estimating original output because they reflect the preferences of collectors[42]. This "collector behavior" might, indeed, affect choices biasing the collection as representative of the original volume of coins produced. Gândilă offers a series of arguments showing that "the fact that a collector's/curator's choice, although inherently present, does not have a dramatic effect on the type of material selected for this analysis[43]". Among these arguments, the fact that our study (and that of Gândilă) deals with petty coinage, *i.e.* bronze and copper respectively, softens the effect of selectivity which can indeed be expected when it comes to silver and more especially gold[44]. As can be observed in many large museum collections, bronzes of the exact same type (duplicates) are present in large numbers thus pointing to randomness in the way the collection was assembled. Furthermore, since most of the larger collections were created by accumulating partial donations, it is legitimate to assume that the original collectors applied different selection criteria thus globally limiting the possible effect of individual bias, and that the museum curator did not refuse to accept duplicates. Nevertheless, as will be shown below, very large issues will always be relatively under-

41 P. Grierson argued many times against the statistical representativity of large museum collections. Because of his influence in Ancient and Byzantine numismatics, his opinion seemed to dominate later generations of numismatists in disregarding the relevance of these collections for quantitative and statistical analyses.

42 Butcher 2004, 139. In fact, he applies the comparison using 533 SC coins from BnF, Berlin, and the ANS. The histograms from the collections are very different from the similar graphs he created from the excavations in Antioch and the Antakya museum.

43 Gândilă 2009, 158-160.

44 Nevertheless, the reliability of SHD was also tested against museum collections (and also against die data) and was confirmed. See Iossif 2014 and 2016.

represented in collections given that the number of duplicates of a given type seems to be capped after all (see below for the case of Antiochos III in SED).

Which collections? Considering these questions, it was necessary to find collections satisfying initial criteria of randomness and size. The choice was rather obvious: the "Big Four" [the American Numismatic Society (ANS), the Bibliothèque nationale de France (BnF), the British museum (BM), and Berlin] and in addition the large private collection created by the late Arnold Spaer in Jerusalem. Following the same methods as with the analysis of the SED, I personally examined and reviewed all evidence from the above mentioned collections (either during my visits or online) in order to attribute them a *SC* number and correct many mistakes of attribution.

- From the ANS: 2 754 bronzes;
- In BNF: 1 841 bronzes;
- In BM: 1 861 bronzes;
- In Berlin: 1 320 bronzes;
- Spaer: 1 757 bronzes;

In total, 9 533 bronzes were identified and introduced in their separate databases. Table 4 reports the data as gathered by reign for the major collections[45]:

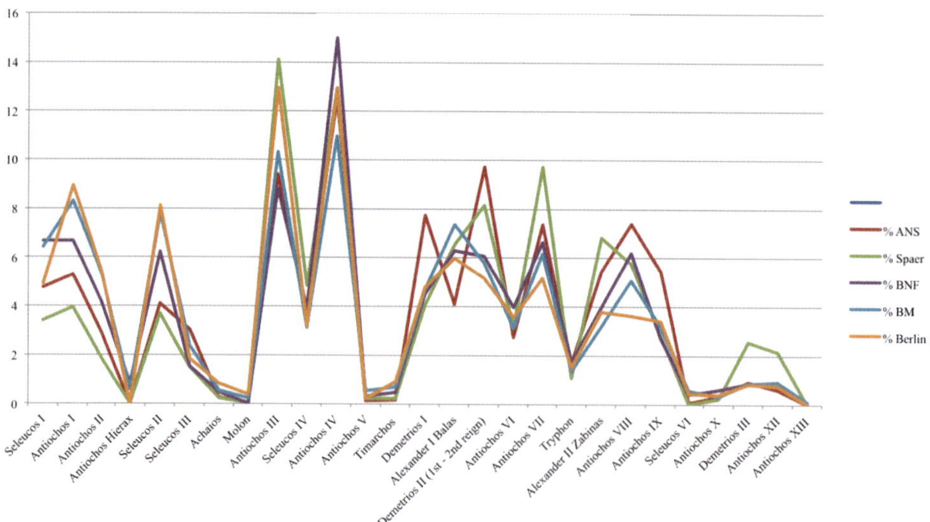

Fig. 3. Fluctuation of bronze coins in major collections grouped by reign (Iossif 2016).

45 Given the different sizes of these collections, it is necessary to compare relative percentages of coins for each king instead of absolute numbers. What interests us is the general relative fluctuation.

Reign	# ANS	% ANS	# Spaer	% Spaer	# BNF	% BNF	# BM	% BM	# Berlin	% Berlin
Seleucos I	131	4,76	164	3,41	123	6,7	119	6,43	65	4,92
Antiochos I	146	5,30	357	3,93	123	6,7	154	8,32	118	8,94
Antiochos II	79	2,87	328	1,82	76	4,1	119	5,29	71	5,38
Antiochos Hierax	0	0,00	0	0,00	15	0,8	0	0,59	0	0,00
Seleucos II	113	4,10	159	3,70	115	6,2	145	7,83	107	8,11
Seleucos III	83	3,01	201	1,48	28	1,5	44	2,38	24	1,82
Achaios	7	0,25	7	0,23	9	0,5	10	0,54	11	0,83
Molon	1	0,04	0	0,06	0	0,0	4	0,22	5	0,38
Antiochos III	259	9,40	4020	14,11	163	8,9	191	10,32	171	12,95
Seleucos IV	104	3,78	198	4,84	72	3,9	58	3,13	42	3,18
Antiochos IV	346	12,56	1140	12,92	276	15,0	203	10,97	171	12,95
Antiochos V	4	0,15	5	0,23	6	0,3	10	0,54	3	0,23
Timarchos	5	0,18	0	0,23	9	0,5	13	0,7	12	0,91
Demetrios I	213	7,73	368	4,04	83	4,5	87	4,7	63	4,77
Alexander I Balas	113	4,10	117	6,55	116	6,3	136	7,35	79	5,98
Demetrios II (1st-2nd reign)	268	9,73	291	8,14	112	6,1	107	5,78	68	5,15
Antiochos VI	76	2,76	41	3,13	73	4,0	58	3,13	47	3,56
Antiochos VII	203	7,37	198	9,73	122	6,6	114	6,16	68	5,15
Tryphon	46	1,67	3	1,08	32	1,7	25	1,35	20	1,52
Alexander II Zabinas	150	5,45	85	6,83	73	4,0	59	3,19	50	3,79
Antiochos VIII	204	7,41	253	5,75	114	6,2	94	5,08	48	3,64
Antiochos IX	150	5,45	79	2,85	50	2,7	59	3,19	45	3,41
Seleucos VI	2	0,07	4	0,00	8	0,4	11	0,59	6	0,45
Antiochos X	9	0,33	2	0,23	11	0,6	6	0,32	5	0,38
Demetrios III	25	0,91	15	2,56	16	0,9	16	0,86	11	0,83
Antiochos XII	17	0,62	13	2,16	14	0,8	17	0,92	10	0,76
Antiochos XIII	0	0,00	0	0,00	2	0,1	2	0,11	0	0,00
Total	**2754**	100,00	**8048**	100,00	**1841**	100,0	**1861**	100,00	**1320**	100,00

Table 4. Museum and private collections by absolute number of coins and as percentage of the total. Grouped by reign (Iossif 2016).

One cannot escape the striking resemblance between these five major collections in terms of structure. This visual impression is confirmed by the correlation coefficients r^2 between on the one hand, the composition of each individual collection (in terms of percentage of coins per reign), and on the other hand, the weighted average of the five collections: these correlation coefficients vary between 88% (for the Spear collection, probably not a surprise) and 94% (for the collection of the BnF), which shows that – if indeed there has been a bias in the way these collections were assembled – this must have been very similar, so probably close to inexistent. In other words, it seems reasonable to assume that these collections are indeed representative samples (*i.e.* chosen at random) of the total circulation.

Gândilă, who also studied five collections, convincingly interpreted this structural similarity in the formation of the museum collections as an expression of similarity in statistical terms as well[46]. Having established this randomness of the five reference collections, both individually (and hence also globally), we can now verify if the same or at least a very similar pattern can be observed using the data of SED. The results are represented in fig. 4, which shows an overall good similarity, except for the data point corresponding to the reign of Antiochos III, whose bronze coins represent nearly half of the total of SED, whereas the weighted average in the five reference collections is only about 11%. The value of r^2 between on the one hand, the weighted average of the five reference collections, and on the other hand, the SED data, is only about 40%, pointing to a poor correlation; but when we leave out the data for Antiochos III in both series[47], the value of r^2 increases to about 73%; although this is still smaller than the values we have observed for each of the reference collections, it shows that SED can be considered as sufficiently representative for all the reigns with the exception of Antiochos III, or perhaps are we closer to reality when stating that the five reference collections can be considered representative of the global coin circulation, with the exception of the reign of Antiochos III whose coins are underrepresented taking into account the size of his bronze emissions.

As it has been previously stated, when it comes to very large issues, it is obvious that collections tend to eliminate the extremely high number of duplicates. In that respect, the SED seems to better illustrate the very high production under this king.

There is also a geographical bias due to the overrepresentation of sites from Israel. In fact, one single site, Jerusalem, offers a huge number of coins from this reign; the single excavation from the Citadel (site n° 13 in SED) contained 1 936 bronzes of *SC* type 1089. Two interesting points are to be observed about this *SC* type: it is attributed to a military mint (Uncertain Mint 60) and bears clearly military types: Macedonian shield on the obverse and elephant on the reverse.

46 Gândilă 2009, 161, fig. 1. The late Arnold Spaer's collection presents the relatively strongest anomalies compared to the "Big Four"; this is an argument in favor of the randomness and reliability of these collections. Spaer's collection was heavily "region influenced" given Spaer's personal preferences as reported in his writings and also via private correspondence with A. Houghton.

47 Obviously, since the reign of Antiochos III is "overrepresented" and we are comparing compositions of the collections, all the other reigns are automatically under-represented (the total adding of course up to 100%); leaving out the overrepresented reign only partially eliminates this bias.

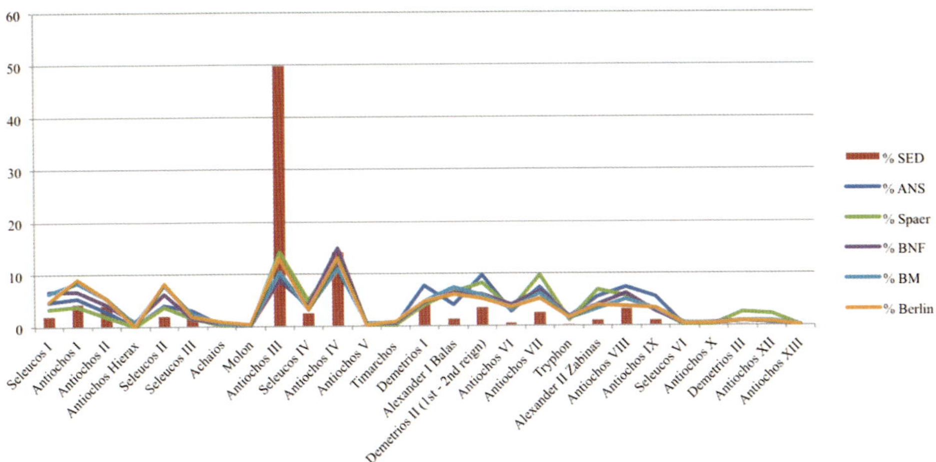

Fig. 4. Comparison of bronze fluctuation between SED and collections (Iossif 2016).

Fig. 5. UM 60, SC 1089. Macedonian shield with head of Medusa as episêmon*/Elephant walking r. Inscription: ΒΑΣΙΛΕΩΣ ΑΝΤΙΟΧΟΥ. Symbol: Anchor (in upper field). Monogram between elephant's legs.*

By excluding the Jerusalem data from the analysis, the percentage of Antiochos III bronze coins falls from about 50% to 34%. This shows clearly that this single find introduces a serious statistical bias in our sample, which can presumably be explained by the fact that the city of Jerusalem became a citadel and received a garrison under this king and was an important theater of military operations in the following years[48]. For this reason, the Jerusalem data were excluded from further statistical analyses[49].

48 Plb. 16.39; J., *AJ*, 12.131.

49 The data has also been tested with Jerusalem included but this will drive us far away from the purpose of this article meant to be methodological and introductory. For further analyses, voir Iossif 2016.

After running a "Correspondence Analysis" (CA) on the remaining data, it turned out that a series of different sites also introduced minor, but still significant, noise in the sample[50]. Therefore, those sites were also eliminated from the sample. The following table and map report the data and diagnosis of the CA.

In table 5 sites are classified based on their "quality[51]". Those sites for which I also provide their names in order to facilitate their identification by the reader are eliminated from the sample given the noise they introduce (and they also appear far removed from the general pattern on the factor map in fig. 6).

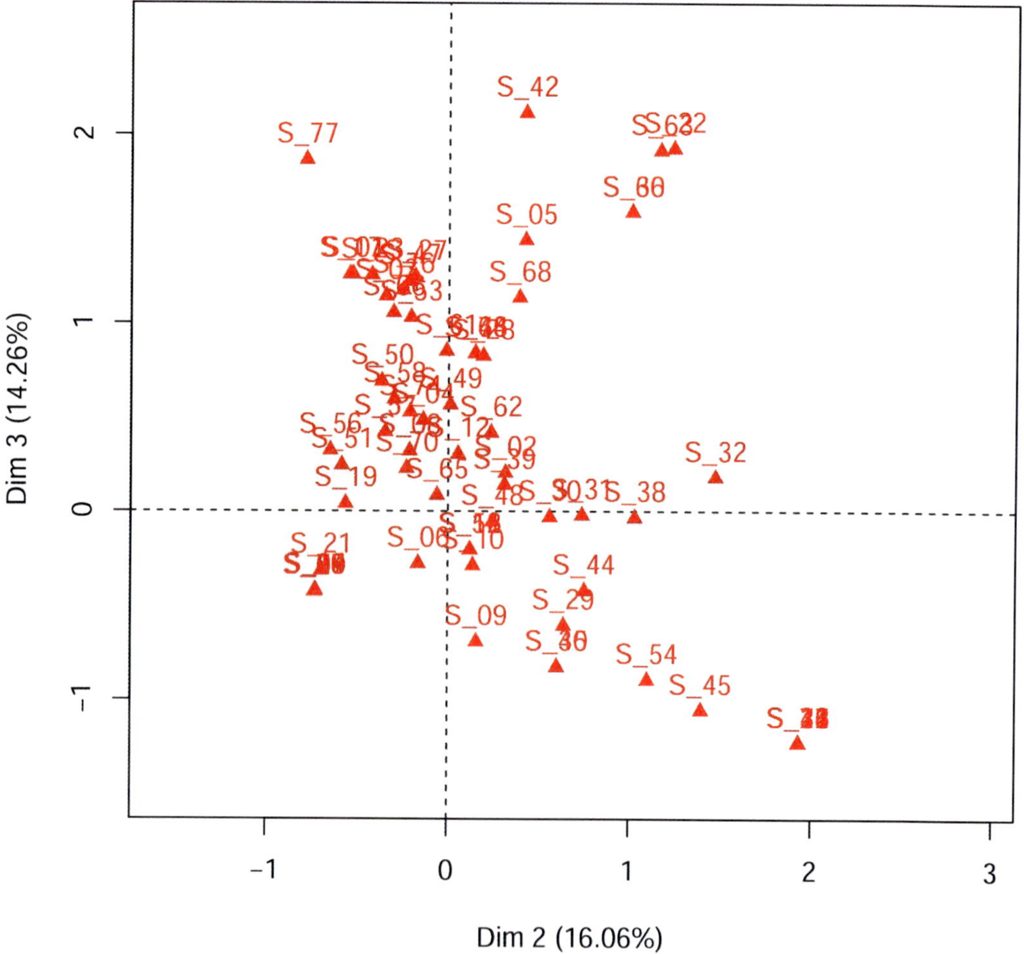

Fig. 6. Factor map after CA (Iossif 2016).

50 For the method, see Lockyear 2007 with extended previous bibliography. In general, this method is used quite extensively in archaeological excavations (most of Roman period) dealing with ceramics. To the best of my knowledge, Lockyear was the first to use it in the numismatic field, followed by Walton 2012. The method has never found its way into Greek numismatics.

51 On the term, its significance, and the way to read diagnostics in CA, voir Lockyear 2007, 57-59.

S_39	Jer Jews Quarter	59	49	1	-,08	-210	19	0	308	40	0	140	8	0	67
S_47	Nimrud	3	55	1	7,11	-167	1	0	-216	2	0	1223	53	3	56
S_42	Kelenderis	2	45	0	4,52	-184	0	0	421	2	0	2115	43	1	45
S_48	Orchoi	41	43	10	2,88	5	0	0	242	41	1	-54	2	0	43
S_43	Jer Khirbet	2	35	0	1,11	-121	1	0	146	1	0	839	34	0	36
S_46	Jer South Wall	2	35	0	-,53	-121	1	0	146	1	0	839	34	0	36
S_64	Shoham	2	35	0	-,53	-121	1	0	146	1	0	839	34	0	36
S_75	Jer 3rd Wall	2	35	0	-,53	-121	1	0	146	1	0	839	34	0	36
S_27	Istakhr	1	32	0	2	84	0	0	-184	1	0	1246	32	0	33
S_57	Samaria	14	26	0	1,54	-213	4	0	-346	10	0	422	15	0	29
S_50	Oumm-el-Mara	6	28	0	2,67	-20	0	0	-366	6	0	689	22	0	28
S_08	Beth Zur	10	21	3	6,27	-164	4	0	-212	7	0	322	15	1	26
S_53	Qalaat Bahrain	1	22	0	3,84	7	0	0	-207	1	0	1030	21	1	22
S_65	Susa	14	10	101	38,15	-109	11	2	-61	3	1	85	7	2	21
S_77	Xanthos	4	3	0	48.98	1892	3	1	-782	1	0	1866	3	1	7
S_12	Cankirikai	1	3	0	1,77	-146	1	0	53	0	0	305	2	0	3

Table 5. Diagnostics of SED CA (Iossif 2016).

The next step was to run correlation and dependence analysis, as well as a linear regression to the different datasets under consideration. The results show a strong statistical relationship between the different sets. Tables 6-8 summarize the evidence:

	ANS	SED	Spaer	*SC* types	BNF	BM	Berlin
ANS	100%	68%	90%	75%	90%	85%	84%
SED	68%	100%	79%	82%	69%	72%	81%
Spaer	90%	79%	100%	77%	88%	84%	84%
SC types	75%	82%	77%	100%	86%	94%	97%
BNF	90%	69%	88%	86%	100%	95%	93%
BM	85%	72%	84%	94%	95%	100%	97%
Berlin	84%	81%	84%	97%	93%	97%	100%

Table 6. Correlations observed among the seven datasets under consideration. Black marks the maximum and minimum correlations (Iossif 2016).

Statistic	ANS	Spaer	SC	BNF	BM	Berlin
Tolerance	0,127	0,154	0,042	0,056	0,035	0,020
VIF	7 843	6 493	23 667	17 927	28 685	50 030

Table 7. Multicolinearity statistics of the linear regression (Iossif 2016).

Observations	27 000
Sum of weights	27 000
DF	20 000
R^2	0,859
Adjusted R^2	0,817
MSE	0,001
RMSE	0,031
MAPE	289 733
DW	2 735
Cp	7 000
AIC	-182 288
SBC	-173 218
PC	0,240

Table 8. Regression of variable SED-Goodness of fit statistics (Iossif 2016).

From a statistical point of view, SED presents a very positive correlation with all other datasets varying from 68% (with the ANS) to 82% (with *SC* types), while the R^2 of the linear regression is high (to very high) positive (0,859). The average correlation between SED and the collections is estimated to 75,2%, a significantly high level of correlation proving that the excavation material, after removing local biases, is reliable for statistical analyses[52].

An additional reason that might have affected the sample and the overrepresentation of bronzes of Antiochos III could be the variable length of different reigns. It could be considered that the "longer the reign, the larger the sample". This postulates, above all, that the size and volume of coin productions is to be related to the years of production (an assertion often implied but never proved, also involving regular *annual* issues). In order to test this assertion and observe the possible biases inserted by the variable duration of individual reigns, I created an index reporting annual coin distribution. In fact, this index considers coins by reign (*e.g.* 164 bronzes under Seleucos I) divided by the years of the given reign (30 years for Seleucos I). As a next step, this index is given as a percentage of the total indices by reign. The results are reported on fig. 7:

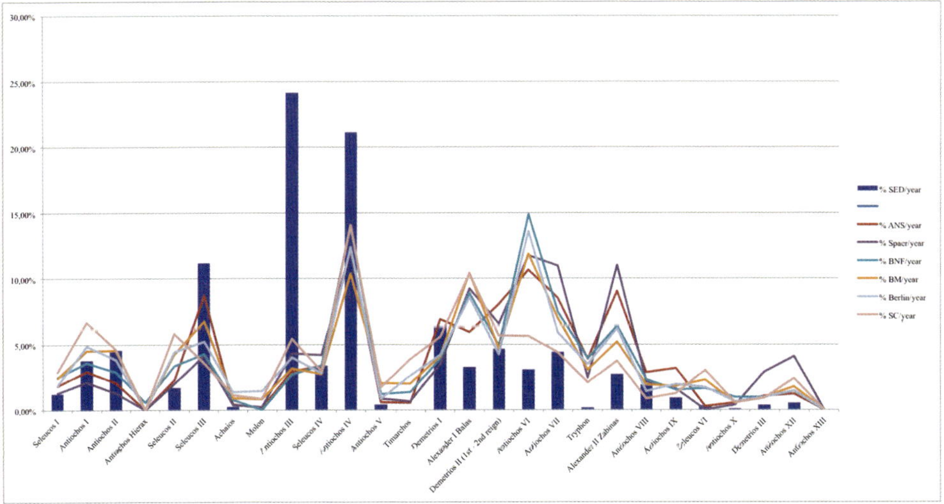

Fig. 7. Annual index of bronze fluctuation between SED and collections (Iossif 2016).

The annual index confirms that the very high representation of bronzes of Antiochos III in SED is independent of the length of the reign. It also confirms the general patterns observed in previous tables with some minor discrepancies between SED and collections on shorted reigns (Alexander I Balas and Antiochos VI).

52 It is not without interest to note that the correlation and linear regression analyses are also significantly high with Jerusalem included. We prefer though, for methodological reasons, to eliminate this site from the analysis until more results from other regions of the Seleucid realm diminish its statistical weight in the data.

The question of a possible bias introduced by the length of the reigns in quantity of coins in SED was also tested using a more sophisticated statistic method by measuring Cook's distance[53]. This method allows isolating peculiarities and outliers in the data. We suppose a linear model of the type "number of coins in SED = A*number of years per reign" [where A is a coefficient]. As can be seen on table 9 and fig. 8, the estimate for A is 33,7.

Reign	Years	# SED	Cook's distance	linear model	residuals	3 * mean Cook's distance
Seleucos I	30	164	0,335	1013,4	-849,4	0,820
Antiochos I	21	357	0,024	709,38	-352,38	0,820
Antiochos II	16	328	0,005	540,48	-212,48	0,820
Antiochos Hierax	16	0	0,031	540,48	-540,48	0,820
Seleucos II	21	159	0,058	709,38	-550,38	0,820
Seleucos III	4	201	0,000	135,12	65,88	0,820
Achaios	7	7	0,001	236,46	-229,46	0,820
Molon	3	0	0,000	101,34	-101,34	0,820
Antiochos III	37	4020	6,547	1249,86	2770,14	0,820
Seleucos IV	13	198	0,004	439,14	-241,14	0,820
Antiochos IV	12	1140	0,031	405,36	734,64	0,820
Antiochos V	3	5	0,000	101,34	-96,34	0,820
Timarchos	4	0	0,000	135,12	-135,12	0,820
Demetrios I	13	368	0,000	439,14	-71,14	0,820
Alexander I Balas	8	117	0,001	270,24	-153,24	0,820
Demetrios II (1st-2nd reign)	14	291	0,003	472,92	-181,92	0,820
Antiochos VI	3	41	0,000	101,34	-60,34	0,820
Antiochos VII	10	198	0,001	337,8	-139,8	0,820
Tryphon	5	3	0,000	168,9	-165,9	0,820
Alexander II Zabinas	7	85	0,000	236,46	-151,46	0,820
Antiochos VIII	30	253	0,269	1013,4	-760,4	0,820
Antiochos IX	20	79	0,061	675,6	-596,6	0,820
Seleucos VI	3	4	0,000	101,34	-97,34	0,820
Antiochos X	7	2	0,001	236,46	-234,46	0,820
Demetrios III	10	15	0,004	337,8	-322,8	0,820
Antiochos XII	6	13	0,001	202,68	-189,68	0,820
Antiochos XIII	0	0	0,000	0	0	0,820
Total	323	8048				
		mean Cook's distance:	0,273			
		3 * mean Cook's distance:	0,820			

Table 9. Calculation of Cook's distance ifor number of coins in SED per year (Iossif 2016).

53 Cook 1977. This part of the analysis was developed with the precious help of P. Veselý.

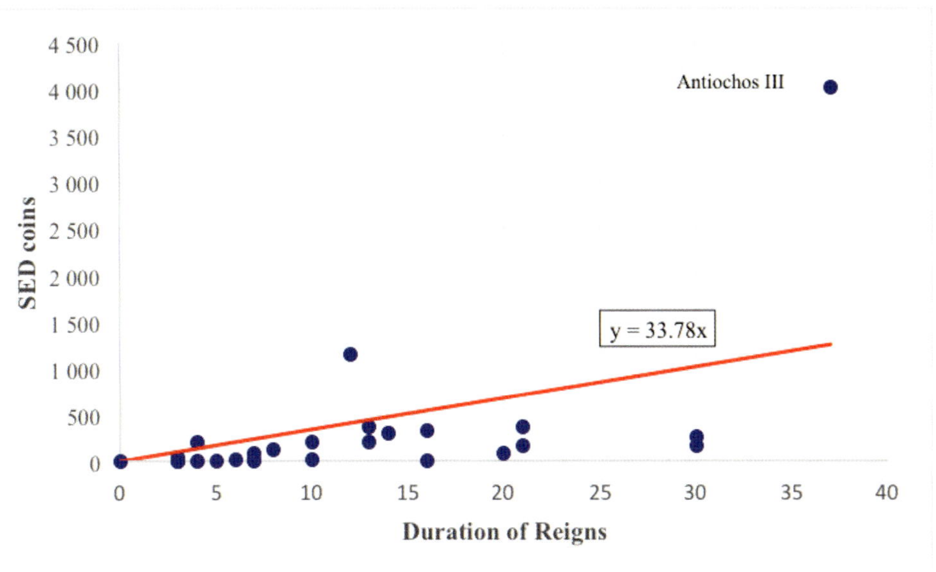

Fig. 8. Linear model for number of SED coins as related to duration of reigns (Iossif 2016).

As a second step, we measured Cook's distance for each observation. If that distance for some observations is greater than three times average of Cook's distance for all observations (which is the recommended conservative threshold value) then that observation should be an outlier. As can be observed on fig. 9, the number of coins of Antiochos III does not follow a linear model, *i.e.*, the number of Antiochos' III coins in SED cannot be expressed as a common coefficient times the length of the reign (note that all dots above the dashed line are outliers, *i.e.* the reign of Antiochos III being the only one falling under this category in our case).

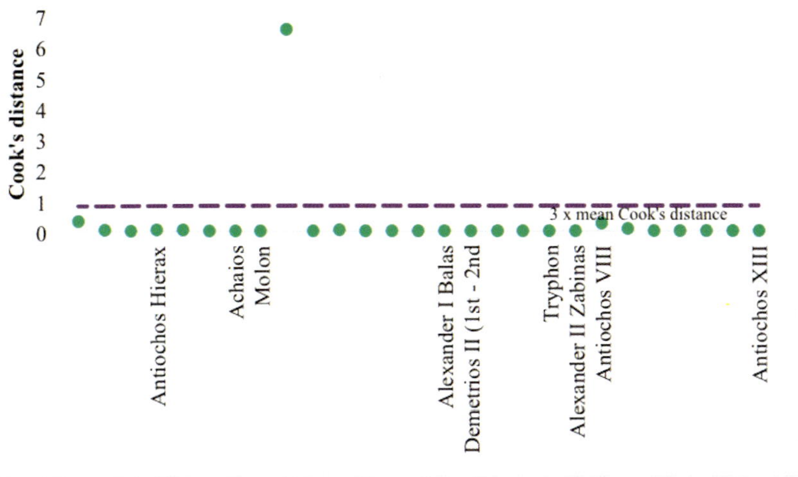

Fig. 9. Cook's distance per reign (Iossif 2016).

This type of analysis seems to strongly indicate that the duration of Antiochos' III cannot explain the high number of coins in SED (other exceptionally long terms fall under the dashed line in fig. 9). Therefore, it is legitimate to assume that the SED expresses a reliable image of the original production of bronze coins by reign and in that respect, the reign of Antiochos III was exceptionally prolific (see below for an explanation of the great volume related to a numismatic reform introduced by this king and his military activities, especially the installation of garrisons in newly conquered areas).

What questions to ask SED: bronze denominations and loss patterns

One *topos* in the analysis of site finds is the following: the smaller a coin, the easier to lose, and less effort would be given to find it[54]. In this section, I won't discuss the self-evident fact that precious metal coins are actually recovered; I will focus on bronze coins and the possible relation between denomination, and thus monetary value, and loss. Butcher, referring to Casey, writes: "site finds represent a random sample of what was in circulation, with a bias in favor of the smaller denominations which when dropped were harder to recover or not worth much effort recovering, is generally accepted by numismatists. The coins can therefore be used to put together a picture of economic activity, and clusters of coins are likely at places where they were exchanged or used for transactions[55]". Grierson also argued that the structure of site finds was biased by the overrepresentation of smaller denominations which were more easily lost[56]. Gândilă argued against this interpretation based on his sample and proves that such statements call for caution and must not be generalized[57].

Since SED offers such a reliable sample as well, it is necessary to test this hypothesis for the Seleucids and explore if smaller coins (denominations) were more easily lost than the larger (and more valuable) ones[58]. As has been explained in section 2, *SC* type identifications were given to every entry in SED; therefore, it was easy to explore relative percentages of bronze denominations. For the denominations, I'm using the conventional letters used by the authors of *SC*.

54 We must nevertheless remain cautious since in most of the cases, we are dealing with finds without precise contexts; therefore, it is not completely impossible that some of the finds are coming from specific areas where the deposition were originally intentional (a sanctuary) and these data might introduce some bias to the analysis. I would like to thank Jean-Marc Doyen for drawing my attention to this point.

55 Butcher 2004, 149-150 (discussing Casey 1986).

56 Grierson 1986, 42.

57 Gândilă 2009, esp. 156.

58 Another factor to be considered here is what has been demonstrated by a series of recent studies, that the smaller coins are those circulating less. This could also be a significant factor determining their loss but in the absence of further studies for the Seleucid East, it is impossible to go further in that direction. In any case, the approach I propose should be ideally combined with a large die study of the bronze material, one which is (and will probably remain) absent for the years to come.

SED-denomination	Quantity	% per denomination	Diameter (in mm)	Weight (in gr.)
D	3 297	39,89%	12-14	1.49-2.99
B	3 092	37,41%	17-22	5.49-8.49
C	1 767	21,38%	15-21	3.0-5.49
A	60	0,73%	22-28	11.0-16.99
E	48	0,58%	8-11	0.6-1.00
AA	1	0,01%	25-33	20.0-27.99
Total	**8265**	**100,0%**		

Table 10. SED. Bronze coins grouped by denomination (Iossif 2016).

Almost 40% of bronzes in SED belong to one of the two smallest modules issued by the Seleucids ("D") indicating that, at least, an initial pattern of coin loss based on the size of the coin can be observed. If we accept that "C" was the bronze unit, the *chalkous*, then it stands for about 22%. The "B" denomination rivals with "D" being represented by 37% of all finds in SED. In the case "E" was the *chalkous*, then it is represented by less than 1%.

The nature of SED allows us to go deeper into the detail and nuance of the above statement. There is no doubt that a pattern of coin loss based on the size of the coins is observed; but, does this pattern correspond to their real value? In SED, all bronzes are converted into their "C bronze value" and the grouping based on that criterion seriously modifies the pattern of the previous table:

SED 'C bronze value'	Quantity	% per denomination	Diameter (in mm)	Weight (in gr.)
B	6 184	62,72%	17-22	5.49-8.49
C	1 767	17,92%	15-21	3.0-5.49
D	1 648,50	16,72%	12-14	1.49-2.99
A	240	2,43%	22-28	11.0-16.99
E	12	0,12%	8-11	0.6-1.00
AA	8	0,08%	25-33	20.0-27.99
Total	**9859,5**	**100,00%**		

Table 11. SED. Bronze coins expressed in "C bronze value" grouped by denomination (Iossif 2016).

Contrary to what we observed in the previous table, the "B" denomination coins (double that of *chalkous*) were proportionally the most represented in Seleucid excavations data. The small denomination "D", the most represented in terms of absolute number of coins, stands for only *c.* 30%, while the *chalkous* represents 22% in terms of value. Therefore, nuances are to be introduced when discussing coin loss patterns. Even if smaller coins tend to be more easily lost due to their size, it is worth noting that coins worth of two *chalkoi* represent *c.* 44% of these coins expressed in terms of economic value.

SED 'E bronze value'	Quantity	% per denomination	Diameter (in mm)	Weight (in gr.)
B	24 736	70,73%	17-22	5.49-8.49
D	6 594	18,85%	12-14	1.49-2.99
C	2 590	7,41%	15-21	3.0-5.49
A	960	2,74%	22-28	11.0-16.99
E	62	0,18%	8-11	0.6-1.00
AA	32	0,09%	25-33	20.0-27.99
Total	**34 974**	**100,00%**		

Table 12. SED. Bronze coins expressed in "E bronze value" grouped by denomination (Iossif 2016).

The last table based on the "E" denomination as the *chalkous* doesn't change the relative value of denominations as observed in the previous "C bronze value" table (and this is not surprising). Nevertheless, it offers an interesting observation: the percentage of denomination "B", *i.e.* the "obol" of this system, is dominant touching *c.* 71% of the whole. Both the dominance of "B" and its very high percentage (*c.* 71%) are possible arguments in favor of a denominational system based on "E" as *chalkous* and dominated by the obol. This conclusion would be in accordance with the arguments proposed by Picard, Psoma and Grandjean for other bronze coinages in the Greek world[59].

In order to test if there is a proper pattern in the loss of excavations coins, I turned to my SHD. As already stated, 1 559 bronze coins were found in 22 hoards. From these, it was possible to assign *SC* denominations to 1 543[60].

SHD denomination	Quantity	% per denomination	Diameter (in mm)	Weight (in gr.)
B	677	43,9%	17-22	5.49-8.49
D	482	31,2%	12-14	1.49-2.99
C	367	23,8%	15-21	3.0-5.49
A	12	0,8%	22-28	11.0-16.99
E	4	0,3%	8-11	0.6-1.00
AA	1	0,1%	25-33	20.0-27.99
Total	1543	100,0%		

Table 13. SHD. Bronze coins grouped by denomination (Iossif 2016).

59 Picard 1992; Psoma 1998; Grandjean 1998.

60 For the remaining 16 bronzes, the hesitation is concerned about their classification to one or another denomination. For this reason, they were left outside the analysis.

SHD 'C bronze value'	Quantity	% per denomination	Diameter (in mm)	Weight (in gr.)
B	1354	67,1%	17-22	5.49-8.49
C	367	18,2%	15-21	3.0-5.49
D	241	11,9%	12-14	1.49-2.99
A	48	2,4%	22-28	11.0-16.99
E	1	0,0%	8-11	0.6-1.00
AA	8	0,4%	25-33	20.0-27.99
Total	2019	100,0%		

Table 14. SHD. Bronze coins expressed in "C bronze value" grouped by denomination (Iossif 2016).

SHD 'E bronze value'	Quantity	% per denomination	Diameter (in mm)	Weight (in gr.)
B	5392	67,57%	17-22	5.49-8.49
C	1404	17,59%	15-21	3.0-5.49
D	970	12,16%	12-14	1.49-2.99
A	160	2,01%	22-28	11.0-16.99
E	22	0,28%	8-11	0.6-1.00
AA	32	0,40%	25-33	20.0-27.99
Total	7980	100,0%		

Table 15. SHD. Bronze coins expressed in "E bronze value" grouped by denomination (Iossif 2016).

The hoarding process for bronze coins as it can be calculated from SHD is quite similar to the one observed for the "C bronze value" in SED but it is virtually the same as that observed for "E bronze value". Since coins were hoarded based on their economic value, this is not surprising even if, again, the largest denominations are virtually absent from hoards[61]. The small "D" denomination represents one out of three coins in SHD showing that its predominance in SED absolute numbers was not totally due to its small size. It is not without interest for our purpose to point out the importance of "B" denomination coins not only in terms of value, but also in terms of quantity. If we were to trust the database as a reliable sample for statistical analyses, this could mean that the Seleucid *bronze* economic system was based on the double *chalkous* (accepting the "C" denomination as the "unit") or the obol (following the "E" as the *chalkous*). Considering the (absolute and relative) importance of the "B" denomination in the above analyses, it seems quite possible that the Seleucid

61 This is to be considered against Hollard 1996, 215-216 who in his study of Roman bronzes concluded that hoards contained larger denominations compared to site finds. On the other hand, it cannot be excluded that the largest denominations were minted in smaller sizes, an answer only an extensive die study could offer.

bronze denominational system was indeed based on the Attic one, where the obol was the main denomination and was divided in eight *chalkoi*[62].

It is possible to further nuance the distribution and relative proportion of bronze coins by denomination offering a chronological and spatial analysis.

	A	AA	B	C	D	E	Total
Seleucos I	1		75	65	25		166
Antiochos I	2		57	179	111	20	369
Antiochos II			270	28	27	6	331
Antiochos Hierax							0
Seleucos II	5		80	66	6	3	160
Seleucos III			1	201			202
Achaios			2	4		1	7
Molon							0
Antiochos III	14		1979	500	1569	16	4078
Seleucos IV	14		14	151	34		213
Antiochos IV	5	1	40	165	1020	1	1232
Antiochos V					5		5
Timarchos							0
Demetrios I	6		20	188	167		381
Alexander I Balas			26	49	42		117
Demetrios II (1st-2nd reigns)	12		63	24	192		291
Antiochos VI			8	31	2		41
Antiochos VII	1		86	56	73	1	217
Tryphon			3				3
Alexander II Zabinas			76	9			85
Antiochos VIII			208	27	18		253
Antiochos IX			69	4	6		79
Seleucos VI			1	3			4
Antiochos X			2				2
Demetrios III			6	10			16
Antiochos XII			6	7			13
Antiochos XIII							0
Total	60	1	3092	1767	3297	48	8265

Table 16. SED. Bronze coins grouped by reign(Iossif 2016).

62 For other Greek coinages of this type, see Psoma 1998.

	A	AA	B	C	D	E	Total
Seleucos I	4		150	65	12,5	0	231,5
Antiochos I	8		114	179	55,5	5	361,5
Antiochos II	0	0	540	28	13,5	1,5	583
Antiochos Hierax	0		0		0	0	0
Seleucos II	20		160	66	3	0,75	249,75
Seleucos III	0		2	201	0	0	203
Achaios	0		4	4	0	0,25	8,25
Molon	0		0		0	0	0
Antiochos III	56		3958	500	784,5	4	5302,5
Seleucos IV	56		28	151	17	0	252
Antiochos IV	20	8	80	165	510	0,25	783,25
Antiochos V	0		0		2,5	0	2,5
Timarchos	0		0		0	0	0
Demetrios I	24		40	188	83,5	0	335,5
Alexander I Balas	0		52	49	21	0	122
Demetrios II (1st-2nd reigns)	48		126	24	96	0	294
Antiochos VI	0		16	31	1	0	48
Antiochos VII	4		172	56	36,5	0,25	268,75
Tryphon	0		6		0	0	6
Alexander II Zabinas	0		152	9	0	0	161
Antiochos VIII	0		416	27	9	0	452
Antiochos IX	0		138	4	3	0	145
Seleucos VI	0		2	3	0	0	5
Antiochos X	0		4		0	0	4
Demetrios III	0		12	10	0	0	22
Antiochos XII	0		12	7	0	0	19
Antiochos XIII	0		0		0	0	0
Total	240	8	6184	1767	1648,5	12	9859,5

Table 17. SED. Bronze coins expressed in "C bronze value" grouped by reign (Iossif 2016).

	A	AA	B	C	D	E	Total
Seleucos I	16		600	74	50	0	740
Antiochos I	32		456	197	222	20	927
Antiochos II	0		2160	28	54	6	2248
Antiochos Hierax	0		0		0	0	0
Seleucos II	80		640	72	12	3	807
Seleucos III	0		8	225	0	0	233
Achaios	0		16	4	0	1	21
Molon	0		0		0	0	0
Antiochos III	224		15832	743	3138	16	19953
Seleucos IV	224		112	490	68	0	894
Antiochos IV	80	32	320	317	2040	8	2797
Antiochos V	0		0		10	0	10
Timarchos	0		0		0	0	0
Demetrios I	96		160	190	334	7	787
Alexander I Balas	0		208	52	84	0	344
Demetrios II (1st-2nd reigns)	192		504	39	384	0	1119
Antiochos VI	0		64	31	4	0	99
Antiochos VII	16		688	65	146	1	916
Tryphon	0		24		0	0	24
Alexander II Zabinas	0		608	12	0	0	620
Antiochos VIII	0		1664	27	36	0	1725
Antiochos IX	0		552	4	12	0	568
Seleucos VI	0		8	3	0	0	11
Antiochos X	0		16		0	0	16
Demetrios III	0		48	10	0	0	58
Antiochos XII	0		48	7	0	0	55
Antiochos XIII	0		0		0	0	0
Total	960	32	24736	2590	6594	62	34974

Table 18. SED. Bronze coins expressed in "E bronze value" grouped by reign (Iossif 2016).

For practical reasons, these tables are illustrated as a demonstration of the potential represented by SED. Some initial remarks will focus on the "D" denomination: approximately 79% of all "D" coins in the database come from the reigns of Antiochos III and IV showing that a short-lived reformation took place under Antiochos III. They are not only the most voluminous in terms of absolute coins, but also in terms of value. Tables 19-22 show the mints producing these coinages, as well as their spatial distribution:

Antiochos III: Mints producing D bronzes	Quantity
Antioch	950
Ptolemaïs-Ake	402
ΔΕΛ	123
Tyre	36
Susa	28
Seleucia on the Tigris	20
Sardis	10
Total	1 569

Table 19. SED. "D" bronzes under Antiochos III grouped by mint (Iossif 2016).

Antiochos III: Sites with D bronzes	Quantity
Dura	606
Antioch	244
Marisa	232
Mt. Gerizim	120
Beirut	91
Jebel Khalid	50
Susa	42
Seleucia Pieria	26
Oumm el Amed	26
Ptolemaïs-Ake	18
Qalandiyah	18
Tel Kedesh	9
Gamla	8
Seleucia on the Tigris	8
Various Western Sites	71
Total	1 569

Table 20. SED. "D' bronzes under Antiochos III grouped by site (Iossif 2016).

Antiochos IV: Mints producing D bronzes	Quantity
Ptolemaïs-Ake	913
Seleucia on the Tigris	76
Tyre	21
Susa	8
Ecbatana	1
Uncertain Mint	1
Total	1 020

Table 21. SED. "D" bronzes under Antiochos IV grouped by mint (Iossif 2016).

Antiochos IV: Sites with D bronzes	Quantity
Mt. Gerizim	500
Marisa	281
Seleucia on the Tigris	52
Qalandiyah	42
Susa	27
Gamla	18
Beirut	17
Tell 'Ira	13
Ptolemaïs-Ake	10
Various Western Sites	60
Total	1 020

Table 22. SED. "D" bronzes under Antiochos IV grouped by site (Iossif 2016).

Under Antiochos III, *c.* 68% of "D" bronzes were produced at Antioch (or by the associated ΔΕΛ) mint, while Seleucia produced only 1,2% as the only Eastern mint to produce this denomination in some extent. As for the distribution of these coins under the Great King, only eight of the 1 569 coins were found at Seleucia (all local-0,5%) and eight more in Anatolian sites. The rest were found in Syrian and Palestinian sites. It is therefore difficult, not to say impossible, to dissociate these issues from the Fifth Syrian War (202-195 BC). A closer look at the identity and status of the sites shows that most of them were military bases or hosted a garrison (Dura, Marisa, site at Mt. Garizim, Jebel Khalid etc.). This quantitative data and analysis seem to closely corroborate what has been observed in other areas of the

Hellenistic world; it is even possible to associate, at least in the case of Antiochos III, small denominations with the payment of garrisons in particular sites[63].

The same picture seems to appear under Antiochos IV and it is also tempting to associate these issues with the Sixth Syrian War. These are some initial conclusions based on the quantification of SED which aim to show the potential of this type of analysis in testing historical hypotheses.

Using SED for calculating speed of circulation within the kingdom

Before concluding, it is tempting to test SED on a current question in modern economics: that of the speed of circulation. In a recent article, Iossif, van Leewen and Foldvari compared the Seleucid speed of coin circulation with that of EU coins[64]. Given all the limitations of SED already considered, I will examine the speed of circulation of bronzes within the Seleucid Empire.

Coin	Cases	Total	mean (per case)	st. dev.	min	max
Bronze (SED)	845	7 778	9,2	73,1	1	1936

Table 23. SED. Summary statistics (Iossif 2016).

SED gives 845 cases for bronze, 7 778 coins in total. The database offers the opportunity to identify whether a coin was buried in the same province where it was minted (called a "domestic" coin) or if it arrived from a different province (labeled "foreign" coin).

Seleucid coins are not generally dated, so the following assumption was to be made: the date of minting of a coinage was placed during the middle of the king's reign. In making this assumption, the share of "domestic" coins at the starting year will be below 100%. The reason

63 See the excellent overview in Psoma 2009 arguing that bronzes were used extensively to pay the troops. In a recent article, Aperghis argued that bronzes were produced and used in two ways during the campaigns of Antiochos III: in long-term campaigns, bronzes were produced in places where the army was. Then, if the intention of the army was to occupy the territories, these bronzes stayed in the area (as in Coele-Syria and Phoenicia); if, as during the *Anabasis*, the army didn't occupy the territories, the bronzes followed the movement of the army and were spread in different areas. Nevertheless, this approach defies long standing methodologies on how to define a mint and its production. Furthermore, the spread of bronzes in areas relatively close to their mint of production (as they are determined in *SC*) argues against Aperghis' interpretation (Aperghis 2010). It is not without interest for the purpose of this analysis to mention that Cardon & Lemaire 2005 arrived to the same conclusion in their analysis of the numismatic data from the military camp of the *Grande Armée* at Étaples-sur-Mer.

64 Iossif *et al.* 2014.

is simply that some coins will be minted (and hence circulated), before the middle of a given reign. Yet, since some coins are minted before the middle of the reign and others thereafter, the theoretical consideration would be that the share of domestic coins should be close to 100%. Therefore, the first assumption we need is that at (*time+c*) the share of domestic coins is 100%, where time is the available time difference between the minting and burial of coins and (c) is the average bias, which should be estimated.

The second assumption concerns the functional form of the relationship between the share of "domestic" coins. The theoretical expectation is that most of the diffusion should take place in the first years after the minting and gradually slowing down afterwards. Thus, we need a function that is monotonic, has a negative slope and is convex. One candidate is the ln(x+1) function, while the second is the power function, which has the additional advantage that its value is always positive. The two specifications employed are as follows:

(1)

and

(2)

where *i* denotes the observation number, *j* is the bronze coin type, *time* is the observed difference between the dates of burial and minting and *c* is the estimated mean bias in *time*. We also use the demeaned date of minting. Both (1) and (2) are designed so that when *time+c=0* the estimated share of "domestic" coins is 100% in accordance with our hypothesis.

For bronze coins the best fit is achieved with the power specifications. The bias caused by choosing the middle of a king's reign as the date of minting is estimated between 6-14 years (the first specification yields a statistically insignificant estimate of 31 years), which is within the expected interval, since the bias cannot be more than half of the expected ruling period of a Seleucid king and is strictly positive. We obtain positive coefficients for the year of the minting. The lack of statistical significance can be attributed to the measurement error which causes the coefficient to bias toward zero and the standard error is inflated as well. The positive coefficient means that in the latter period of the Seleucid Empire the diffusion of bronze coins slowed down and relatively fewer bronze coins left their region of origin, as can be seen on table 20:

	Unweighted		Weighted	
	1	2	1	2
logarithmic	-0,098	-	-0,072	-
	(-13.1)		(-40.2)	
power	-	-0,139	-	-0,084
		(-13.0)		(-34.2)
c	31,3	13,8	6,73	6,26
	-1,59	-1,68	-2,84	-2,7

mint date	0,001	0,001	0,0001	0,0002
	-3,3	-3,68	-0,38	-1,32
% correctly predicted	57,50%	63,20%	70,90%	70,90%
R^2	0,554	0,555	0,715	0,714
N	845	845	7778	7778

Table 24. "Domestic" dummy as function of time differential between minting and burial (Iossif 2016).

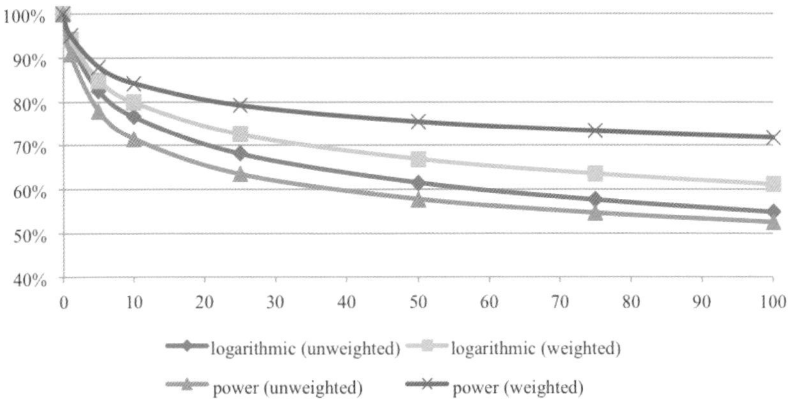

Fig. 10. Estimated percentage of "domestic" bronze coins in circulation (Iossif 2016).

In summary, after 100 years of circulation about 60-70% of the bronze coins were still in their province of minting[65]. At the same time, we observed that only 20-30% of silver coins remained in their province 100 years after their issue[66]. A quicker diffusion of the more valuable coins is not inexplicable, though. Obviously, there are two ways in which coins could have reached a different region quickly. The first way is by official payments, which even today is the standard way to release a new series of coins into the circulation: the government paid the wages of soldiers and officials, or other labourers working on state projects with the new coins. Such payments obviously were not limited to the same region where the coins were minted (but still limited to smaller areas around their original mint, as

65 See also in the same direction Meadows 2014c.
66 Iossif *et al.* 2014.

shown above)[67]. Another way is trade, when a stream of mints left the region with negative trade balance toward regions with positive trade balance. Carrying bronze coins must have been cumbersome both in terms of (high) volume and (low) value; hence silver coins were most likely the preferred coins for long-distance money transfers[68].

The speed of circulation can be further nuanced by region but this will drive us far away from the scope of the study. I will simply add a quick conclusion on Mesopotamia and Levant-Syria: these regions must have been the primary source of bronze coins, since in other regions such as Asia Minor and the rest of the Empire coins from these two regions are heavily represented. Yet, bronze coins may not have travelled too far, since they are found in nearby provinces. For example, Asia Minor had bronze coins originating mostly from the Levant region, while Babylon mostly received "domestic" coins[69].

Concluding thoughts and future perspectives

This article was intended to focus on the advantages of using quantification and statistics for the analysis of large numismatic samples. The goal was to introduce SED (and SHD) as a useful tool for accessing the numismatic production of the Seleucids. Much effort has been driven in proving the reliability of the sample for quantifications and statistical analyses, since this is the *sine qua non* condition for any further analyses. In the last part, I simply tried to show some limited aspects of the enormous potential this kind of databases offer to the numismatist. Other aspects, perhaps even more important, are not considered at all, as the determination of a numismatic profile for individual sites either by using cumulative percentages and determining a "Seleucid mean" of coin loss[70], or by applying the IF_R as calibrated by J.-M. Doyen for Roman sites[71]. The method presents thus far a great potential and further analysis will demonstrate the great possibilities in a more detailed and thorough study of excavation coins.

67 For coinage used as payment for the army, there is a very rich bibliography; see for the Hellenistic world, esp. the works by de Callataÿ 1997b; *id.* 2000; Psoma 1998 for bronze as mean of payments; for the Roman army, see among others: Casey 1986, 82; Reece 1991, 125-126; Duncan-Jones 1990, 30-47; Butcher 2004, 143 et 245-251.

68 This saying, it must be stressed that bronze coins could also be considered as commodities themselves. Evidence for this process is available for 4th c. AD Egypt and 5th c. AD Gaul. There, the transportation of tons of copper coins generated small percentage of gain (2 X 3,5%) for the moneychangers, which represented at the end a considerable profit. In that respect, the role of bankers/moneychangers was very important as was demonstrated in Reece 2003. See now Doyen 2013a, 139-143 for an analysis of the process of exchange between *solidi* and small change via the moneychangers. For the estimation of the moneychangers' percentage of profit, see Delmaire 2003.

69 Further analysis of average distance of travel of bronze coins is given in Iossif forthcoming.

70 In the line of Reece 1972, 273; *id.* 1991; *id.* 1995; Walton 2012, 36-37 for a "British mean".

71 Doyen 1987, 83-83; *id.* 2011, 21-24.

Some Recommendations for Publishing Coins from Excavations

Frédérique Duyrat

One of the major difficulties when starting a comparative study of coins from excavations is the absence of norms in the publications examined. There is no reference literature, no common guidelines, and each author chooses his own rules of publication. A significant number of authors of excavation reports are not numismatists but archaeologists who have a good knowledge of the coins they find, but fewer of the standards of the discipline. As a consequence, there is a very wide variety of form and content in publications of coins from excavations.

This symposium has offered a rather wide overview of the range of possible uses of coins from excavations, from their extraction from the earth to the reconstruction of historical episodes, from the excavation to a GIS.

Why standardize publications?

During the meeting, O. Picard underlined the limits of standardisation: it can lead to impoverishment. This is probably true if one considers the number of archaeological numismatic publications of any size and quality. However, standardisation makes data comparable and understandable by any reader. Therefore we must seek a standardisation with enough flexibility to avoid the impoverishment of catalogues. There are some good reasons to encourage the use of a norm:

1. Coins are a good chronological marker, especially if properly combined with other materials bearing chronological data, such as pottery[1].
2. In a regional perspective, standardisation of numismatic publications will make available the data on coin circulation from one or several excavations: nature, density, changes according to the period, proportion of local and foreign coins, relationships with neighbouring mints[2].
3. At a more general level, the capacity to compare numismatic data can highlight historically disruptive events, such as economic crisis, foreign armies, etc. Local and regional history is thereafter enhanced as showed by S. Psoma in this volume, with the long-lasting occupation of Olynthus after Philip II had destroyed the city, or by S. Kremydi and K. Kryssanthaki in this volume, who delineate episodes of the history of Aegae and

1 Butcher 2003; Doyen 2011.

2 See Grandjean in this volume.

F. Duyrat, in : *Les monnaies de fouille du monde grec*, p. 297-302

Amphipolis according to the contrasts they observe in the density of coinage found in excavations.
4. A standardized approach to coins from excavations can also shed light on the economy, especially concerning the monetisation of an area through a better knowledge of the use of bronze coins, of their value (are they valuable enough to be hoarded?) versus the use of silver, particularly silver fractions. Our knowledge of the output of bronze coins is tightly related to what excavations provide. The Thasian example is especially interesting: O. Picard finds very high die ratios for bronze coins from the excavations of the city, for obverse dies compared to the number of coins found as well as for obverse dies *vs* reverse dies[3]. Such results, quite unusual, would probably be commoner if such careful examination of the dies of coins from excavations were performed more frequently.
5. Finally, to standardise the publication of coins from excavations would allow mapping, quantification, and comparison on a broader and easier scale. Sharing data would be possible without the huge preparatory work needed today.

Current problems in the publication of coins from excavations

Numismatic studies are technical and often based on numerous and complex data: die studies, die ratio, survival index are concepts difficult to understand for a non-specialist. The content of the papers of this colloquium is not accessible to a neophyte. However, in this respect it is simply a reflection of the content of publications of coins from excavations, which are often similarly difficult to comprehend.

The size of publications can be very different, from short notes (less than one page in some articles of a periodical like *'Atiqot*) to volumes entirely dedicated to coins[4]. One of the major difficulties in these publications is that a large number of them only deal with one part of what was found. While selecting one part of these data, the authors often omit to provide information about the periods preceding the one they chose to publish: was the site already occupied or not? Is there an evolution in the period under consideration? To provide an overall framework, general figures are needed, such as the total number of coins found, and some general data about the activity of the site before and after the period studied.

From one publication to another, the criteria of classification can differ. Usually, Greek coins held in coin cabinets are classified according Strabonian geographical order, clockwise from Spain to North Africa. That makes the collections easily compared and used throughout the world. But this system is less obviously useful for coins from excavations. To begin with coins from Western Mints when excavating in Turkey would require the catalogue to start with rare foreign coins seldom found locally, when it might make more sense to begin with the most important coinages found on the site.

3 Picard 2015, 159-160.
4 Kroll 1993.

Formal choices can make a real difference in the clarity and use of a catalogue.

1. Numbering. The best solution is to choose a continuous numbering, from the first coin to the end of the catalogue. The practice of providing no numbering at all must be prohibited[5]. A wide range of complicated systems has been developed. For instance, in the publication of the excavations of Antioch and Seleucia Pieria, a catalogue number is given to the coin types, and the total numbers of items are given in two separate columns, one for each excavation, with totals by series and reigns[6]. The tables at the end of the volume give joint totals for the two sites. Thus, someone looking for the coins of one or the other site must go through the catalogue making their own calculations. Moreover, the use of *bis* numbers often leads to wrong results in tables.

2. Illustrations provided are often scarce, on the grounds that the items are to poorly preserved to justify a photograph. Therefore, the reader can almost never come to his own opinion, since he is deprived of the primary source. This raises the question of the choice of pictures: should it consist only of the best preserved items? Or of those essential for the dating of the stratigraphic layers? The whole corpus? Or even drawings?

3. Finally, the bibliography is often a problem. There is no complete overview of Greek coinage in the way that *Roman Imperial Coinage* or *Roman Provincial Coinage* are now universal references for Roman coinage. Therefore, Greek coins from excavations are often described according to very different books or articles, or according to the possibilities available to the person in charge of their identification.

Beyond this general context, one point must be made concerning hoards found in excavations. They are not so numerous and it is remarkable that, on many occasions, the publication places little or no value on the container in which it was found. It is often barely described, or not at all.

Publication criteria

A list of the criteria to standardize the publication of coins from excavations do not need to constitute a heavy document. They can be summarized as a series of items needed to allow a full use of data by numismatists or other researchers.

1. General information on the excavations:
– Context; possibly list of stratigraphic layers.
– Nature of the excavated site (street, agora, temple, house, harbour, etc.).
– Total number of coins found.
– Number of illegible coins after restoration.
– Number of coins destroyed by restoration.
– Surface area excavated.

5 As for the excavations of Hama for instance: Thomsen 1986.
6 Waage 1952.

2. Necessary fields:

– Mints.
– Description of the coin (obverse and reverse type, weight, dies, axis, metal, etc.). Legends must be noted in a Unicode font.
– Hoards: numismatic study and careful description of the container.
– Bibliographical references.
– Data specific to the site (stratigraphic layer in which coins were found, georeferencing of the precise location of the discovery, data about the context such as pottery in the same layer, etc.).

3. Photography

– Of the coin itself or of a plaster cast, often more legible when the coin is a corroded bronze.
– At actual size (1/1). If enlargements are provided, they should be in addition to actual size pictures.
– As many items as possible.

One difficult point remains the order of classification. Each archaeological site has its own characteristics and there may be no single method to suggest. But to make each solution reasonably manageable, some tools must be added to allow as full a use as possible of the data. There are two main types of classification.

1. Geographic, by mint, as in the publication of the excavations of Susa[7]. It is the usual system of classification for cabinet collections of Greek coins. This system was been adopted by J. Pellerin in his 1763 publication and then reused by J. Eckhel in 1792[8]. It follows the geography of the Roman provinces as described by Strabo, with an alphabetical classification of the mints into each province. It has been criticized but it remains the norm for general catalogues of Greek coins, such as the *Sylloge Nummorum Graecorum*. However, in an archaeological publication, the coins are mostly of local provenance, associated with other more scattered mints. The geographical order emphasizes that dispersion and requires mental gymnastics useless for a non-numismatic reader. E. Babelon insisted upon the interest of a geographical order centered on the region and emphasizing local specificities and influences[9]. L. Robert developed that idea, highlighting the interest of a purely regional classification of coins, with concentric circles[10]. The centre would be the local output, then the neighbouring mints, and the external circle the farthest coins. The main problem with such a classification, is to gather coins produced over very long periods of time under the name of the mint, and scatter coins of Archaic, Classical, Hellenistic and Roman periods through the whole catalogue. That means that any user wanting to have an overview

7 Le Rider 1965.
8 Pellerin 1763; Eckhel 1792.
9 Babelon 1914, vi.
10 Robert 1951, 89.

of one of these periods will need to extract all the data from the catalogue and rebuild it according to his needs. Thus, if this solution is preferred, an index of mints is necessary, with chronological tables, along with an introduction explaining which geography has been chosen, and according to which local frame.

1. Chronological, by periods – Archaic, Classical, Hellenistic, Roman, etc. – as for the excavations of Antioch[11]. This requires a classification by mint in each chronological section, with an index of mints making it possible to gather the output of those issuing through different periods. This classification has several advantages:

– It allows an easy historical use of the catalogue.
– It provides a differentiation of the periods, but takes into account the specificities of classification and dating of coins from excavations.
– It is enriched by an index by mint to reconstitute geographical links through periods if needed.

Whatever the choice, the basic principles to determine a type of catalogue should be:

– To make data usable for analysis of long periods.
– To make data ready for use without having to deconstruct the catalogue.
– To allow the archaeologist to find easily the dating elements he may need, and the historian to find points of comparison.
– Finally, commentaries and tools – maps, graphs, charts, indices – associated with the catalogue may help extracting historical informations by mint[12].
– *Indices* of mints, hoards, literary sources and inscriptions are basic, useful tools. A general conspectus as the one added to the masterful publication of the coins from the agora of Athens by J. Kroll is an excellent way to make sure that any reader can safely browse through the most complicated finds[13].

Conclusion

All of these suggestions apply to printed publications and do not solve the main problem. Many excavations are run on a yearly basis, outdating the publication of the preliminary report of the preceding year or postponing definitive publication to a final book. One possible answer to many of the difficulties noted through this article would be the digital publication through standardised databases communicating with each other through the semantic web. The interest of databases is obvious:

– Easy and free access from any place with a web access.
– No limit to the number of images available in colour.

11 Waage 1952.
12 de Callataÿ 2006, 187-190 highlighted the scarcity of chronological tables in publications devoted to coins from the Greek world when they are common for the Roman world. See particularly chart 7, p. 188.
13 Kroll 1993.

– Stable ids (URIs) giving a single digital identity to each item.
– Links with digital libraries and bibliographies.
– Links with other numismatic, archaeological, historical or economical databases.
– Sorting tools.
– Ongoing and timely publication.

This would lead to lighter printed publications, devoted to the discussion of the material and offering a selection of the most significant items discovered.

The École française d'Athènes has begun the discussion about creating an online database for coins from its excavations, and at the same time we are exploring the development of a general catalogue of Greek coins online (http://www.greekcoinage.org). The future of the discipline undoubtedly lies there.

Conclusions

John H. Kroll

Two perspectives

In the opening paper of this colloquium John Davies reviews a number of published accounts of coins from excavations in Greece and asks how much of this material has value for scholars whose areas of interest lay outside of the field of numismatics. His answer is that nearly all of it has potential value, so long as it is not treated as an end in itself but is recognized to be part of a larger whole and related to human activity in some identifiable way or another

This would seem to be not altogether different from the question asked in the title of F. de Callataÿ's essay, "De quoi les monnaies grecques trouvées en fouille sont-elles le reflet ?" But by this, F. de Callataÿ is referring more narrowly to specialist, *numismatic* concerns: How do excavation coins differ from coins recovered from hoards? What do they have to tell us about the history specifically *of money*? And even if his survey of the characteristics of excavation coins provides few surprises (their being almost entirely of bronze; their limitations in dating associated contextual material, etc.), the wealth of supporting bibliography and statistical data add unprecedented authority to his account.

Far from being antithetical, these two perspectives rather represent two complementary layers of analysis, the primary numismatic assessment and the subsequent and usually more selective analysis of discerning larger relevancies whether for economic history or political history or both. Good examples of such combined approaches at this colloquium are to be found in the paper on bronze coinage and the political history of Olynthos and Stageira by S. Psoma and C. Gatzolis and in the mass studies of coin finds in the Greek East by F. Duyrat and P. Iossif that have led to their identifying groups of coins that were originally deployed in the pay of military garrisons at Levantine and Seleucid sites.

Sites

For his pioneering earlier paper of 2006 comparing the coin profiles of excavated Greek sites, de Callataÿ assembled an inventory of thirty-seven sites[1]. I have not attempted to find out how much this number has increased since then, but it is growing at a good clip and

1 de Callataÿ 2006.

John H. Kroll, in : *Les monnaies de fouille du monde grec*, p. 303-305 now would include the appearance of three full-scale monographs, respectively on the coins excavated at Nemea, at Abdera, and at the two sites (one original, the other Hellenistic) of Maroneia[2]. Among the site-specific papers presented at the present conference seven are of sites that will soon be joining the inventory. In this connection, it is worth pointing out that since four of them – Pella, Aegae, Amphipolis, and Stageira – are sites that were, like Abdera and Maroneia, excavated by Greek archaeologists, they represent an especially welcome trend; for until very recently nearly all reported numismatic finds from excavations in Greece had come from excavations run by the foreign schools.

What do we learn from the site papers? That at Pella stratigraphical digging has been decisive in settling old problems of Macedonian numismatic chronologies. That at Thasos, one of the most unappreciated aspects of coins from long-term excavations, namely the sheer, vast harvest of specimens available for study, has enabled O. Picard to reconstruct an extraordinarily intricate system of dies and administrative details in a long bronze series. That at Argos we are confronted with an important Peloponnesian city whose own bronze coins were greatly outnumbered by coins minted elsewhere. That at Pergamon the accepted bronze chronologies are in need of fundamental revision. That even when available site records are limited to a mere list of identified coins, such lists almost always have something essential to tell or confirm, as, for example, in the replicated patterns of regal and then civic issues at the separate Macedonian centers of Aegae, Pella, and Amphipolis, or in the compelling historical narrative put together from the coin lists of Olynthus and Stageira. No new numismatic methodology here: only the batches of identified coins and a solid knowledge of the complex historical sources of the fourth-century Chalkidike to go with them.

To these terrestial sites the colloquium adds archaeological sites excavated underwater, both the entire submerged harbor-city of Herakleion-Thonis off the Nile Delta, and the more than two dozen micro-sites of sunken ships. While the coin harvest from Herakleion-Thonis is remarkable because of its rich historical data, A. Meadows reports that the problems it presents for numismatic analysis differ hardly at all from those of conventional excavations on land. And perhaps it not much different for groups of coins recovered from the shipwrecks reviewed by P. Tselekas. Apart from providing clues for the itineraries of the ships on which they were carried, they have in general close analogies with emergency burials of hoards on land.

Innovations

If the majority of the colloquium papers deal with *monnaies de fouilles* in familiar ways, the contributions of Duyrat and Iossif mark a dramatic departure by introducing a quantified regional approach that seeks to establish broad statistical conclusions from a massive compilation of coin data from a multiplicity of sites. Duyrat's compilation extends

2 Knapp & Mac Isaac 2005; Chryssanthaki-Nagle 2007; Psoma *et al.* 2008.

to fifty-eight excavated Levantine sites, Iossif's to the Seleucid material at eighty sites with a total of over eight thousand bronze coins that supplement his earlier database of over twelve thousand Seleucid silver and bronze coins from published hoards.

At the end of his essay, F. de Callataÿ notes another prospect that remains to be explored in the study of site coins by Greek numimatists, namely the highly sophisticated interrogations by specialists in finds of Roman Imperial coins, especially in the UK, regarding such issues as accidental loss vs. intentional discarding, longevity of use, and correlations (or not) of coin abundance with economic prosperity. The behavior of Roman coinage is so much better understood. And yet, as the paper of K. Butcher reminds us, when one reaches late 3rd c. AD, with its several debased coinages, inflationary prices, and repeated unsuccessful attempts at coinage reform, the complexity can be almost too daunting for expert Romanists.

Papers of a purely methodological nature also advance new possibilities in utilizing the full potential of mapping spatial representation of coin finds and assemblages, in applying the SIG digital system in site recording, and in encouraging standardization in the reporting of excavation coins. An account of the Israel Archaeological Authority's system of treating and storing for immediate retrieval all coins from excavations, hoards, and confiscations in Israel presents a standard of state numismatic stewardship that will probably never be surpassed.

Achievement

I doubt whether many of us at this colloquium had realized how much involvement with excavation coins has expanded since the international conference on numismatics and Greek archaeology in honor of M. Oeconomidou was held in Athens two decades ago. Admittedly, the focus of that conference was a good deal broader, but even so, the circumstance that only four of the papers dealt with *monnaies de fouilles*, and these from only three sites, gave the impression that this was an area of limited interest except for a very narrow circle of participants. As is obvious from the great range, variety, and quality of papers presented at this 2014 colloquium, there is no chance that anyone could entertain this impression any longer.

Bibliographie

IGCH = Thompson, M., O. Mørkholm et C. M. Kraay, éd. (1973) : *An Inventory of Greek Coin Hoards*, New York.

I.Smyrna = Petzl, G. (1982-1990) : *Die Inschriften von Smyrna*, 1-3, Inschriften griechischer Städte aus Kleinasien 23 et 24 (1-2), Bologne.

Abdy, R. (2012) : "Tetrarchy and the House of Constantine", in : Metcalf, éd. 2012, 584-600.

Abelli, L., M. Secci, P. G. I. Spanou (2014) : "The Roman Conquest of Pantelleria through Recent Underwater Archaeological Investigations: From Discovery to Public Outreach and Public Access to Maritime Cultural Heritage", *Underwater Archaeology Proceedings*, 345-355.

Adam-Veleni, P. (2000) : "Νομισματικοί θησαυροί από τις Πέτρες Φλώρινας", Οβολός, 4, 127-155.

Adam-Velenis, P. et K. Tzanavari, éd. (2012) : Δινήεσσα. Τιμητικός τόμος για την Κατερίνα Ρωμιοπούλου, Thessalonique.

AEMTH : Το Αρχαιολογικό Έργο στη Μακεδονία και στη Θράκη.

Akamatis, I. M. (1989) : "Πρόσθετα ανασκαφικά στοιχεία για τη χρονολόγηση της καταστροφής της αγοράς της Πέλλας", Εγνατία, 1, 173-193.

— (1993) : Πήλινες μήτρες αγγείων από την Πέλλα. Συμβολή στη μελέτη της ελληνιστικής κεραμικής, Athènes.

— (1995) : "Αγορά Πέλλας 1995", *AEMTH*, 9, 95-104.

— (2009) : "The Pella archaeological Site Development Project and the latest archaeological Findings", in : Einicke *et al.*, éd. 2009, 521-529.

— (2011) : "Pella", in : Lane Fox, éd. 2011, 393-408.

— (2012) : "L'agora de Pella", in : Chankowski & Karvonis, éd. 2012, 49-59.

Akamatis, N. (2008) : "Ερυθρόμορφη κεραμική από την Πέλλα", *ArchEphem*, 147, 1-78.

— (2013a) : "Τομείς δημόσιου λουτρού και εργαστηρίου κεραμικής της Πέλλας (1997-2013). Τα νομίσματα", *AEMTH*, 27, s.p.

— (2013b) : Ερυθρόμορφη κεραμική από την Πέλλα. Το τοπικό εργαστήριο, Thessalonique.

— (2014a) : "Ο θησαυρός Πέλλα/1998", Νομισματικά χρονικά, 32, 39-69.

— (2014b) : "Local Red-figure Potery from the Macedonian Kingdom: The Pella Workshop", in : Schierup & Sabetai, éd. 2014, 177-190.

— (à paraître) : "Τοπική παραγωγή της Πέλλας. Η μετάβαση από την κλασική στην ελληνιστική περίοδο", Θ′ *Ε*πιστημονική Συνάντηση για την Ελληνιστική Κεραμική.

Akamatis, N. et C. Aamodt (2015) : "Two late fifth century BC pits from the Public Bath of Pella", *AntK*, 58, 23-40.

Alfaro, C., C. Marcos et P. Otero, éd. (2005) : *Actas del XIII Congreso International de Numismática*, I, Madrid.

Alfen, P. van, éd. (2006) : *Agoranomia: Studies in Money and Exchange Presented to John H. Kroll*, New York.

Aliquot, J. (2014) : "Les cultes isiaques et le pouvoir dans la Tétrapole syrienne", in : Bricault & Versluys, éd. 2014, 135-146.

Allason-Jones, L. et B. McKay (1985) : *Coventina's Well. A shrine on Hadrian's Wall*, Hexham.

Amandry, P., éd. (1984) : *L'antre corycien*, BCH Suppl. 9, Athènes.

Andreau, J., G. G. Aperghis et P. L. Baker, éd. (2000) : *Économie antique. La guerre dans les économies antiques*, Entretiens d'archéologie et d'histoire 5, Saint-Bertrand-de-Comminges.

Andronikos, M. (1991) : *Vergina, The royal tombs*, Athènes.

Andronikos, M., G. Bakalakis, C. Makaronas et N. Moutsopoulos, éd. (1961) : Το ανάκτορο της Βεργίνας, Athènes.

Aperghis, G. G. (2004) : *The Seleukid Royal Economy: the finances and financial administration of the Seleukid Empire*, Cambridge.

— (2010) : "Recipients and End-Users on Seleukid Coins", *BICS*, 53 (2), 55-84.

Apostolou, E. (2004) : "Η κυκλοφορία των ψευδοροδιακών δραχμών στο θεσσαλικό χώρο κατά τους Μέσους Ελληνιστικούς χρόνους. Ερμηνεία του φαινομένου", Οβολός, 7, 259-276.

Archibald, Z. H., J. K. Davies et V. Gabrielsen, éd. (2005) : *Making, Moving and Managing. The New World of Ancient Economies, 323-31 B.C.*, Oxford.

— (2011) : *The Economies of Hellenistic Societies, Third to First Centuries BC*, Oxford.

Archibald, Z., J. Davies, V. Gabrielsen et G. J. Oliver, éd. (2001) : *Hellenistic Economies*, Londres-New York.

Arévalo Gonzalez, A., D. Bernal Cassola et D. Cottica, éd. (2013) : *Ebusus i Pompeya, ciudades maritimas. Testimonios monetales de una relación*, Cadix.

Ariel, D. T. (1998) : "Antiquities Law of the State of Israel", *Commission internationale de numismatique*, Compte rendu 45, 76-77.

Ariel, D. T. et Y. Shiloh (1990) : *Excavations at the City of David 1978-1985. 2. Imported Stamped Amphora, Handles, Coins, Worked Bone and Ivory, and Glass*, Qedem 30, Jérusalem.

Ariel, D. T. et H. Sokolov (2003) : "A Hoard of Silver Tetradrachms", *International Numismatic Newsletter*, 39, 16.

Arnaud, A. et P.-A. Davoine (2009) : "Approche cartographique et géovisualisation pour la représentation de l'incertitude", *SAGEO*, 1-20.

Asheri, D., A. B. Lloyd, A. Corcella, O. Murray, A. Moreno (2007) : *A commentary on Herodotus Books I-IV*, Oxford.

Ashton, R. et S. Hurter, éd. (1998) : *Studies in Greek Numismatics in Memory of Martin Jessop Price*, Londres.

Asolati, M. et G. Gorini, éd. (2002) : *Ritrovamenti monetali nel mondo antico: problemi e metodi*, Padoue.

— (2012) : *I ritrovamenti monetali e i processi storico-economici nel momdo antico*, Numismatica Patavina 12, Padoue.

Asskamp, R. et S. Berke., éd. (1991) : *Die römische Okkupation nördlich der Alpen zur Zeit des Augustus. Kolloquium Bergkamen 1989*, Boden Altertümer Westfalens 26, Münster.

Atik, N. et K. Rheidt (2004) : "Pergamenisches in Anatolien. Aizanoi und seine Beziehungen zur Hauptstadt der Attaliden", *MDAI (I)*, 54, 375-391.

Aubin, G. (2007) : "Les trésors (monétaires) antiques : le mot, les choses et les chercheurs", in : Baratte *et al.*, éd. 2007, 49-73.

Augé, C. (2000) : "Les monnaies de Ras Ibn Hani, près de Lattaquié et les guerres de Syrie", *Revue Numismatique*, 59-69.

Aylward, W., éd. (2013) : *Excavations at Zeugma*, Los Altos.

Babelon, E. (1914) : *Traité des monnaies grecques et romaines*, 2e partie : *Description historique*, III, Paris.

Backendorf, D. (1998) : *Römische Münzschätze des zweiten und ersten Jahrhunderts v.Chr. vom italienischen Festland*, SFMA 13, Berlin.

Baldus, H.-R. (1989) : "Das Münzdepot : ein späthellenistischer Geldbörsen-Inhalt(?)", *Archäologischer Anzeiger*, 204-206.

— (2006) : *Didyma*, III : *Ergebnisse der Ausgrabungen und Untersuchungen seit dem Jahre 1962*, 3 : *Fundmünzen aus den Jahren 1962-1998*, Darmstadt.

Barag, D. (1990-1991) : "Stella Ben-Dor, In Memoriam", *Israel Numismatic Journal*, 11, 1-2.

Baratte, F., M. Joly et J.-C. Beal, éd. (2007) : *Autour du trésor de Mâcon. Luxe et quotidien en Gaule romaine*, Mâcon.

Barbara, S. (2014) : "An Anepigraphic Bronze Close to the Pergamene Issue with Types Athena / Coiled Snake", in : Dörtlük *et al.*, éd. 2014, 49-58.

Barkay, R. (2003-2006) : "Undated Coins from Hellenistic Marisa", *Israel Numismatic Journal*, 15, 48-55.

Barron, J. P. (1966) : *The silver coins of Samos*, Londres.

Bass, G. F., éd. (2005) : *Beneath the Seven Seas. Adventures with the Institute of Nautical Archaeology*, Londres.

Bellinger, A. R. (1949) : *The excavations at Dura-Europos. Final report VI. The coins*, New York.

— (1961) : *Troy. Supplementary Monograph 2. The Coins*, Princeton.

— (1964) : "Philippi in Macedonia", *ANSMN*, 11, 29-52.

Berger, F. (1996a) : *Kalkriese 1. Die römischen Fundmünzen*, Francfort.

— (1996b) : "Roman coins beyond the northern frontiers: some recent considerations", in : King & Wigg, éd. 1996, 55-61.

— (1999) : "Kalkriese redécouvert par les monnaies. Le site du massacre des légions de Varus dans la forêt de Teutobourg (an 9 de notre ère)", *Dossiers d'Archéologie*, 248, 52-59.

— (2000) : "Die Münzen von Kalkriese. Neufunde und Ausblick", in : Wiegels, éd. 2000, 11-45.

Berges, D. (2010) : "Ein königlich-pergamenischer Beamter in Aizanoi?", in : Rheidt, éd. 2010, 38-43.

Bernard, P. (1985) : *Fouilles d'Aï Khanoum*, IV : *Les monnaies hors trésors ; questions d'histoire gréco-bactrienne*, Mémoires de la Délégation archéologique française en Afghanistan 28, Paris.

Bernholz, P. et R. Vaubel, éd. (2014) : *Explaining Monetary and Financial Innovation: a historical analysis*, Financial and Monetary Policy Studies 39, Cham.

Berroir, S., C. Grasland, F. Guérin-Pace et G. Hamez (2005) : "La diffusion spatiale des pièces euro étrangères en Belgique et en France", *Revue belge de géographie*, 4, 445-458.

Bertoldi, M. E. (1997) : *Antike Münzfunde aus der Stadt Rom (1870-1902). Il problema delle provenienze. Die Fundstellen*, SFMA 14, Berlin.

Bijovsky, G. (2012) : *Gold Coin and Small Change: Monetary Circulation in Fifth-Seventh Century Byzantine Palestine*, Polymnia Numismatica antica e medieval, Studi 2, Trieste.

Blackburn, M. (1986) : "Single finds of Anglo-Saxon and Norman coins", *British Numismatic Journal*, 56, 64-101.

— (1989a) : "What factors govern the number of coins found on an archaeological site?", in : Clarke & Schia, éd. 1989, 15-24.

— (1989b) : "Single-finds as a measure of monetary activity in the early Middle Ages", *Prace i materialy Muzeum archeologicznego i etnograficznego w Lodzi*, 9, 67-85.

Bland, R. (1992) : "Lacock, Wiltshire", in : Bland, éd. 1992, 208-216.

— (2013) : "What happened to gold coinage in the IIIrd c. AD?", *JRA*, 26, 263-280.

Bland, R., éd. (1992) : *The Chalfont Hoard and Other Roman Coin Hoards (Coin Hoards From Roman Britain IX)*, Londres.

Boehringer, C. (1972a) : *Zur Chronologie Mittelhellenistischer Münzserien 220-160 v. Chr.*, Berlin.

— (1972b) : *Pergamon, Ausstellung in Erinnerung an Erich Boehringer*, Ingelheim am Rhein.

— (1984) : "Münzen", in : Pinkwart & Stamnitz, éd. 1984, 163-164 et pl. 35.

Bomhard, A.-S. (2012) : *Decree of Sais: The Stelae of Thonis-Heracleion and Naukratis*, Oxford.

Bommelaer, J.-F., éd. (1992) : *Delphes. Centenaire de la "Grande Fouille", Actes du colloque Paul Perdrizet, Strasbourg, 6-9 novembre 1991*, Leyde-New York.

Bouyia, P. (2012) : "The era", in : Kaltas *et al.*, éd. 2012, 276-285.

Bowman, A. K. et A. Wilson, éd. (2009) : *Quantifying the Roman economy: methods and problems*, Oxford.

Bracey, R. (2012) : "Policy, Patronage, and the Shrinking Pantheon of the Kushans", in : Jayaswal, éd. 2012, 197-217.

Branigan, K. et D. Miles, éd. (1988) : *The economy of Romano-British villas*, Sheffield.

Bresson, A. (2005): "Coinage and money supply in the Hellenistic Age", in : Archibald *et al.*, éd. 2005, 44-72.

Bricault, L et M.-J. Versluys, éd. (2014) : *Power, Politics and the Cults of Isis, Proceedings of the Vth International Conference of Isis studies, Boulogne-sur-Mer, 13-15* octobre *2011*, Religions in the Graeco-Roman World 180, Leyde-Boston.

Bringmann, K. et H. von Steuben, éd. (1995) : *Schenkungen hellenistischer Herrscher an griechische Städte und Heiligtümer*, I : *Zeugnisse und Kommentare*, Berlin.

Bruneau, P., éd. (1970) : *L'ilot de la Maison des Comediens*, Exploration archéologique de Delos 27, Paris.

Bruneau, P. et J. Ducat, éd. (2005) : *Guide de Délos*, 4e éd., Paris-Athènes (1ère éd. 1965).

Bruun, P. (1978) : "Site finds and hoarding behavior", in : Carson, éd. 1978, 114-123.

Buringh, E. et M. Boskers (2014) : "Soldiers and booze. The rise and decline of a Roman market economy in north-western Europe", in : Spek *et al.*, éd. 2014, 236-266.

Burnett, A. et M. Crawford (1987) : *The Coinage of the Roman World in the late Republic*, BAR 326, Oxford.

Bursche, A. (2002) : "Roman coins in Scandinavia. Some remarks from the continental perspective", in : Pind, éd. 2002, 69-78.

Bursche, A., R. Ciolek et R. Wolters, éd. (2008) : *Roman Coins Outside the Empire. Ways and Phases, Contexts and Function, Proceedings of the ESF/SCH Exploratory Workshop, Nieborow, 3-6 septembre 2005*, Moneta 82, Wetteren.

Butcher, K. (1988) : *Roman Provincial Coins: An Introduction to the Greek Imperials*, Londres.

— (2003) : *Small Change in Ancient Beirut. The Coin Finds from BEY 006 and BEY 045 : Persian, Hellenistic, Roman, and Byzantine Periods*, Archaeology of the Beirut Souks 1, Berytus 45-46, Beyrouth.

— (2004) : *Coinage in Roman Syria, Northern Syria 64 BC-AD 253*, RNS Spec. Publ. 34, Londres.

— (2013) : "Coins and Hoards", in : Aylward, éd. 2013, 1-92.

Butcher, K. et M. Ponting (2014) : *The Metallurgy of Roman Silver Coinage. From the Reform of Nero to the Reform of Trajan*, Cambridge.

Buttrey, T. V. (1997) : "Part I: The Coins", *The Extramural Sanctuary of Demeter and Persephone at Cyrene, Lybia. Final Reports*, VI, 1-66 et pl. 1-12.

— (1999) : "The Content and Meaning of Coin Hoards", *JRA*, 12, 526-532.

Buttrey, T. V., K. T. Erim, T. D. Groves et R. R. Holloway (1989) : *The Coins*, Morgantina studies 2, Princeton.

Buttrey, T. V. et R. B. Hitchner (1978) : "The Coins", in : Humphrey, éd. 1978, 99-168.

Buttrey, T. V., A. Johnston, K. M. MacKenzie, M. L. Bates (1981) : *Greek, Roman and Islamic Coins from Sardis*, Archaeological Exploration of Sardis 7, Cambridge (Mass.).

Cahill, N. (2002) : *Household and City Organization at Olynthus*, New Haven (Conn.).

Cairncross, A. (1960) : *Introduction to Economics*, 3e éd., Londres (1ère éd. 1944).

Callu, J.-P. et X. Loriot (1990) : *L'or monnayé*, I : *La dispersion des aurei en Gaule romaine sous l'Empire*, Cahiers Ernest Babelon 1, Juan-les-Pins.

— (1992) : *L'or monnayé*, II : *Trouvailles de monnaies d'or dans l'Occident romain*, Cahiers Ernest Babelon 3, Juan-les-Pins.

Carcassonne, C. et T. Hackens, éd. (1981) : *Statistique et numismatique, Actes de la table ronde de l'EHES et de l'Université catholique de Louvain, Paris, 17-19 septembre 1979*, PACT 5, Strasbourg.

Cardon, T. et F. Lemaire (2015) : "Les sous des soldats de Napoléon au camp de Boulogne (1803-1805). Étude des monnaies issues des fouilles des camps napoléoniens d'Étaples-sur-Mer et Camiers (Pas-de-Calais, France)", *JAN*, 4, 67-176.

Carlier, P. éd. (1996) : *Le IVe siècle. Approches historiographiques*, Études anciennes 15, Nancy.

Carradice, I. (1987) : *Coinage and Finances in the Reign of Domitian, A.D. 81-96*, Bar Int. Ser. 178, Oxford.

Carson, R. A. G., éd. (1978) : *Scripta nummaria romana: Essays Presented to Humphrey Sutherland*, Londres.

Casey, P. J. (1980) : *Roman Coinage in Britain*, Aylesbury.

— (1986) : *Understanding Ancient Coins. An introduction for Archaeologists and Historians*, Norman.

— (1988) : "The Interpretation of Romano-British Site Finds", in : Casey & Reece, éd. 1988, 37-51.

Casey, P. J. et R. Reece, éd. (1974) : *Coins and the Archaeologist*, BAR 4, Oxford.

— (1988) : *Coins and the Archaeologist*, 2e éd., Londres.

Catalli, F. et J. Scheid (1994) : "Le thesaurus de Sora", *RN*, 6 (36), 55-65.

Chameroy, J. (2012) : "Chronologie und Verbreitung der hellenistischen Bronzeprägungen von Pergamon: der Beitrag der Fundmünzen", *Chiron*, 42, 131-181.

— (2013) : "Marie-Christine Marcellesi: Pergame de la fin du ve au début du ier siècle avant J.-C. Pratiques monétaires et histoire", *Gnomon*, 85 (8), 711-718.

Chankowski, V. (2011) : *Parasites du dieu. Pratiques financières et vie économique dans la Délos hellénistique*, mémoire d'HDR, EPHE.

Chankowski, V. et F. Duyrat, éd. (2004) : *Le roi et l'économie. Autonomies locales et structures royales dans l'économie de l'empire séleucide, Actes des rencontres de Lille (23 juin 2003) et d'Orléans (29-30 janvier 2004)*, Topoi Suppl. 6, Lyon.

Chankowski, V. et P. Karvonis (2012) : *Tout vendre, tout acheter, Actes du colloque d'Athènes, 16-19 juin 2009*, Scripta Antiqua 42, Bordeaux.

Chrysostomou, P. (1993) : Θησαυρός πρώιμων αργυρών μακεδονικών νομισμάτων από την Πέλλα, Αρχαία Μακεδονία V, Thessalonique, 621-644.

— (1996) : "Το ανάκτορο της Πέλλας", *AEMTH*, 10a, 105-142.

— (2008) : "Πέλλης βασίλειον", AEMTH, 22, 129-140.

Chrysostomou, P. A., éd. (2008) : Εθνική οδός Θεσσαλονίκης-Φλώρινας. Σωστικές ανασκαφές κατά το 2006-2008 στο τμήμα Νέας Χαλκηδόνας-Έδεσσας, Thessalonique.

Chryssanthaki-Nagle, K. (2007) : *L'histoire monétaire d'Abdère en Thrace (VIe s. avant J.-C.-IIe s. après J.-C)*, Meletemata 51, Athènes.

Ciolek, R. (2007) : *Die Fundmünzen der Römischen Zeit in Polen. Pommern*, Moneta 67, Wetteren.

Cipolla, C. (1956) : *Money, Prices and Civilization in the Mediterranean World*, Princeton.

Çizmeli-Ögün, Z. et M.-C. Marcellesi (2011) : "Réseaux d'échanges régionaux en Asie Mineure occidentale : l'apport des monnaies de fouilles", in : Faucher *et al.*, éd. 2011, 297-342.

Clarke, G. W., P. J. Connor, L. Crewe, B. Frohlich, H. Jackson, J. Littleton, C. E. V. Nixon, M. O'Hea et D. Steele, éd. (2002) : *Jebel Khalid on the Euphrates: Report on Excavations 1986-1996*, 1, Mediterranean Archaology Suppl. 5, Sydney.

Clarke, H. et E. Schia, éd. (1989) : *Coins and archaeology. Proceedings of the First Meeting at Isegran, Norway, 1988*, BAR Int. Ser. 556, Oxford.

Cohen, G. M. (1995) : *The Hellenistic Settlements in Europe, the Islands, and Asia Minor*, Hellenistic Culture and Society 17, Berkeley.

Cole, T. J. (1976) : "The Lifetime of Coins in Circulation", *NC*, 16, 201-218.

Collis, J. (1981) : "A Typology of Coin Distributions", *World Archaeology*, 13 (1), 122-128.

— (1988) : "Data for dating", in : Casey & Reece, éd. 1988, 189-199.

Conze, A., O. Berlet, A. Philippson, C. Shuchhardt et F. Gräber, éd. (1912) : *Stadt und Landschaft*, Altertümer von Pergamon I.1, Berlin.

— (1913) : *Stadt und Landschaft*, Altertümer von Pergamon I.2, Berlin.

Conze, A. et P. Schazmann, éd. (1911) : *Mamurt-Kaleh. Ein Tempel der Göttermutter unweit Pergamon, Jahrbuch des kaiserlich deutschen archäologischen Instituts*, Ergänzungsheft 9, Berlin.

Cook, B., éd. (2011) : *The British Museum and the Future of UK Numismatics*, Londres.

Cook, R. D. (1977) : "Detection of Influential Observations in Linear Regression", *Technometrics*, 19, 169-174.

Cosgrove, D. (2008) : "Cultural cartography: Maps and Mapping in Cultural Geography", *Annales de Géographie*, 660-661, 159-178.

Crawford, M. H. (1974) : *Roman Republican Coinage*, Londres-New York.

— (1985) : *Coinage and Money under the Roman Republic*, Berkeley.

Cunliffe, B., éd. (1968) : *Fifth Report on the Excavations of the Roman Fort of Richborough, Kent*, Oxford.

— (1971) : *Excavations at Fishbourne*, II, Society of Antiquairies Research Report 27, Londres.

— (1988) : *The Temple of Sulis Minerva at Bath*, II : *Finds from the Sacred Spring*, Oxford.

Dalton, G. (1965) : "Primitive, Archaic and Modern Economies: Karl Polanyi's Contribution to Economic Anthropology and Comparative Economy", in : Helm, éd. 1965, 1-24.

Darque, P., R. Étienne et A.-M. Guimier-Sorbets, éd. (2013) : Proasteion. *Recherches sur le périurbain dans le monde grec*, Travaux de la Maison René-Ginouvès 17, Paris.

Davesne, A. et G. Le Rider (1989) : *Gülnar II. Le trésor de Meydancıkkale (Cilicie Trachée 1980)*, Paris.

Davies, J. K. (2005) : "The economic consequences of Hellenistic Palaces", in : Arcibald *et al.*, éd. 2005, 117-135.

— (2013a) : "Ceramics and the Economic Historian: Mixed Messages and Unharmonised Agendas", in : Tsingarida & Viviers, éd. 2013, 11-17.

— (2013b) : "Corridors, Cleruchies, Commodities and Coins: the Pre-History of the Athenian Empire", in : Slawisch, éd. 2013, 43-66.

— (2016) : 'Towards a General Model of Long-Distance Trade: Aromatics as a Case-Study', in : Harris *et al.*, éd. 2016.

de Callataÿ, F. (1997a) : *L'histoire des guerres mithridatiques vue par les monnaies*, Publications d'histoire de l'art de d'archéologie de l'Université catholique de Louvain 98, Numismatica Lovaniensia 18, Louvain-la-Neuve.

— (1997b) : "Quelques estimations relatives au nombre de monnaies grecques : les collections publiques et privées, le commerce et les trésors", *Revue belge de numismatique*, 143, 21-94.

— (2000) : "Guerre et monnayage à l'époque hellénistique. Essai de mise en perspective suivi d'une annexe sur le monnayage de Mithridate VI Eupator", in : Andreau et *al.*, éd. 2000, 337-364.

— (2006) : "Greek Coins from Archaeological Excavations: a Conspectus and a Call for Chronological Tables", in : Alfen, éd. 2006, 177-201.

— (2011) : *Quantifying monetary supplies in Graeco-Roman times*, Bari.

— (2012a) : "Les statères de Pergame et les réquisitions d'Alexandre le Grand : l'apport d'un nouveau trésor ('Statères de Pergame 2004')", *RN*, 169, 179-196.

— (2012b) : "Control Marks on Hellenistic Royal Coinages: Use and Evolution toward Simplification ?", *RBN*, 58, 39-62.

— (2013a) : "Problèmes de terminologie en numismatique grecque : la classification des monnaies en périodes, séries, groupes, émissions, etc.", *RBN*, 159, 9-40.

— (2013b) : "The Coinages of the Attalids and their Neighbours: a Quantified Overview", in : Thonemann, éd. 2013, 207-244.

— (2014) : *Quantifying monetary supplies in Greco-Roman times*, Pragmateiai 19, Bari.

de Callataÿ, F. et D. Gerin (1992) : "Faut-il faire tomber les foudres", in : Westermark, éd. 1992, 103-109.

Debidour, M. (1986) : "En classant les timbres thasiens", *BCH*, Suppl 13, 311-334.

de Glanville, R. G. (1970) : *The Numbers of Coins in Circulation in the United Kingdom*, Studies in official statistics. Research Series 2, Londres.

Delmaire, R. (2003) : "Aspects normatifs de la politique monétaire du Bas-Empire : une nouvelle lecture de CTh IX, 23", *RN*, 159, 163-174.

Delrieux, F. (2011) : *Les monnaies du Fonds Louis Robert* (*Académie des Inscriptions et Belles-Lettres*), Mémoires de l'Académie 45, Paris.

de Luca, G. (1981) : *Das Asklepieion. Die Kultbauten aus römischer Zeit an der Ostseite des heiligen Bezirks*, Altertümer von Pergamon XI.3, Berlin.

— (1984) : *Das Asklepieion. Via Tecta und Hallenstrasse. Die Funde*, Altertümer von Pergamon XI.4, Berlin.

de Luca, G. et W. Radt (1999) : *Sondagen im Fundament des Grossen Altars*, Pergamenische Forschungen 12, Berlin.

Dembsli, G. (1996) : "Die Rolle von nichtreichs römischen Münzen im Geldumlauf Noricums und der Nachbarprovinzen", in : King & Wigg, éd. 1996, 121-127.

Dentzer, J.-M., P. Gauthier, T. Hackens, éd. (1975) : *Numismatique antique, Problèmes et méthodes, Actes du colloque organisé* à *Nancy du 27 septembre au 2 octobre 1971*, Études d'archéologie classique 4, Annales de l'Est Mémoire 44, Nancy-Louvain.

Descoeudres, J. P., éd. (1990) : *Eumousia: Ceramic and Iconographic Studies in Honour of Alexander Cambitoglou*, Mediterranean Archaeology Suppl. 1, Sydney.

Dittenberger, W. (1915-1924). *Sylloge inscriptionum graecarum*, I-IV, Leipzig.

Donas, A. (2008) : *Τα νομίσματα του ιερού της Εύκλειας. Η νομισματική μαρτυρία από την αγορά των Αιγών*, mémoire de master, Université de Thessalonique.

Dolley, M. (1974) : "Some thoughts on the manner of publication of coins found in the course of archaeological excavations", in : Casey & Reece, éd. 1974, 224-233.

Donceel, R. (2007) : "Canatha de la Décapole de Syrie. Contribution à l'établissement du catalogue des monnaies et à l'examen des types", in : Moucharte *et al*, éd. 2007, 229-266.

Dörtlük, K., O. Tekin, R. Boyraz Seyhan, éd. (2014) : *Proceedings of the I[st] international Congress of the Anatolian Monetary History and Numismatics, Antalya, 25-28 février 2013*, Istanbul.

Doyen, C. (2014) : "Le système monétaire et pondéral d'Antiochos IV", in : Feyel & Graslin-Thomé, éd. 2014, 261-299.

— (à paraître) : "Les monnaies gauloises et romaines du sanctuaire de Remilly-les-Pothées (Ardennes)", in : Souffi, éd. à paraître.

Doyen, J.-M. (1987) : *Les monnaies antiques du tell Abou Danné et d'Oumm el-Marra (campagnes 1976-1985). Aspects de la circulation monétaire en Syrie du Nord sous les Séleucides*, Bruxelles.

— (2010) : *Les monnaies du sanctuaire celtique et de l'agglomération romaine de Ville-sur-Lumes/Saint-Laurent (dép. des Ardennes, France)*, Bruxelles.

— (2011) : "Cliométrie et numismatique contextuelle : compter et quantifier le passé ? Petite histoire de la méthode (1960-2011)", *The Journal of Archaeological Numismatics*, 1, 9-46.

— (2013a) : "*Salus Reipublicae*: Modelling the Monetary Supply in the Middle Meuse Valley between 390 and 480 C.E.", in : Jacobs, éd. 2013, 127-144.

— (2013b) : "La circulation monétaire sous les Valentinies et les Théodosiens (364-vers 420 p.C.) dans le Nord-Ouest de la Gaule : l'apport des fouilles de la *rue du Warnier* à Nempont-Saint-Firmin (Pas-de-Calais, France)", *JAN*, 3, 1-105.

Draganov, D. (1994) : "Cabyle in the mid-third Century BC According to Numismatic Data", in : Draganov, éd. 1994, 277-282.

—, éd. (1994) : *Settlement Life in Ancient Thrace*, Acta Associationis Internationalis Terra Antiqua Balcanica 5, Sofia.

Dreyfus, R. et E. Schraudolph, éd. (1996) : *Pergamon. The Telephos Frieze from the Great Altar*, I, New York.

Drougou, S. (1989) : "Το αρχαίο θέατρο της Βεργίνας", *AEMTH*, 3, 13-23.

— (1997) : "Das antike Theater von Vergina. Bemerkungen zu Gestalt und Funktion des Theaters in der antiken Hauptstadt Makedoniens", *AM*, 112, 281-305.

— (2011) : "Vergina The Ancient City of Aegae", in : Lane Fox, éd. 2011, 243 256.

Drougou, S., D. Evgenidou, C. Kritzas, N. Kaltsas, V. Penna, E. Tsourti, M. Galani-krikou et E. Ralli, éd. (2009) : ΚΕΡΜΑΤΙΑ ΦΙΛΙΑΣ. Τιμητικός τόμος για τον Ιωάννη Τουράτσογλου, Athènes.

Drougou, S. et C. Saatsoglou-Paliadeli (2005) : *Βεργίνα. Ο τόπος και η ιστορία*, Athènes.

Drougou, S. et I. Touratsoglou (2012) : "Hellenistic Pottery from Macedonia. Twenty Years after", in : Tiverios *et al.*, éd. 2012, 263-271.

Duncan-Jones, R. (1990) : *Structure and Scale in the Roman Economy*, Cambridge-New York.

— (1996) : "Empire-Wide Patterns in Roman Coin Hoards", in : King & Wigg, éd. 1996, 139-152.

— (2003) : "Roman Coin Circulation and the Cities of Vesuvius", in : Lo Cascio, éd. 2003, 161-180.

Duyrat, F. (2002) : Compte rendu de G. Le Rider, *Antioche de Syrie sous les Séleucides. Corpus des monnaies d'or et d'argent. I. De Séleucos I à Antiochos V, c. 300-161*, Paris, 1999, *Revue Numismatique* 158, 408-417.

— (2004) : "La circulation monétaire dans l'Orient séleucide (Syrie, Phénicie, Mésopotamie, Iran)", in : Chankowski & Duyrat, éd. 2004, 381-424.

— (2005) : *Arados hellénistique. Étude historique et monétaire*, Bibliothèque archéologique et historique 173, Beyrouth.

— (2013) : "La frontière entre les possessions lagides et séleucides en Syrie", in : Gorre & Kossmann, éd. 2013, 1-25.

Duyrat, F. et O. Picard, éd. (2005) : *L'exception égyptienne ? Production et échanges monétaires en Égypte hellénistique et romaine, Actes du colloque d'Alexandrie, 13-15 avril 2002*, Études alexandrines 10, Le Caire.

École française d'Athènes (1968) : *Guide de Thasos*, Paris.

Eckhel, J. H. (1792) : *Doctrina numorum veterum conscripta*, Vienne.

Eder, W. (2016) : *s.v.* "Skytalismos", *Brill's New Pauly Online*, Leyde.

Edwards, K. M. (1933) : *Corinth. Results of Excavations Conducted by the American School of Classical Studies at Athens*, VI : *Coins 1896-1929*, Cambridge (Mass.).

Ehrhardt, C. (1973) : "The Coins of Cassander", *JNFA*, 2, 25-32.

Einicke, R., S. Lehmann, H. Lör, G. Mehnert, A. Mehnert et A. Slawisch, éd. (2009) : *Zurück zum Gegenstand. Festschrift für Andreas E. Furtwängler*, Langenweissbach.

Elayi, J. et A. G. Elayi (1993) : *Trésors de monnaies phéniciennes et circulation monétaire* (*v*[e]*-iv*[e] *siècles avant J.-C.*), Transeuphratène Suppl. 1, Paris.

— (2004) : *Le monnayage de la cité phénicienne de Sidon à l'*époque perse (*v*[e]*-iv*[e] *s. av. J.-C.*), Transeuphratène Suppl. 11, Paris.

— (2009) : *The Coinage of the Phoenician City of Tyre in the Persian Period* (*v*[th]*-iv*[th] *century BCE*), Louvain.

— (2014) : *Phoenician coinages*, I-II, Transeuphratène Suppl. 18, Paris.

— (2015) : *Arwad, cité phénicienne du Nord*, Paris.

Elkins, N. T. (2012) : "The Trade in Fresh Supplies of Ancient Coins: Scale, Organization, and Politics", in : Lazrus & Barker, éd. 2012, 91-107.

Emberling, G. (2010) : *Pioneers to the Past. American Archaeologists in the Middle East 1919-1920*, Oriental Institute Museum Publications 30, Chicago.

Errington, R. M. (1993) : *A History of Macedonia*, Berkeley.

Estiot, S. (2012) : "The Later Third Century", in : Metcalf, éd. 2012, 538-560.

Étienne, R. (1990) : *Ténos*, II : *Ténos et les Cyclades du milieu du iv*[e] *siècle av. J.-C. au milieu du iii*[e] *siècle ap. J.-C.*, BEFAR 263bis, Athènes-Paris.

Étienne, R. et J. P. Braun, collab. F. Queyrel (1986) : *Ténos I. Le sanctuaire de Poseidon et d'Amphitrite*, BEFAR 263, Athènes-Paris.

Faklaris, P. (1993) : "Βεργίνα. Ανασκαφή ακρόπολης", *AEMTH*, 7, 61-63.

— (1996) : "Βεργίνα. Ο οχυρωτικός περίβολος και η ακρόπολη", *AEMTH*, 10a, 69-78.

Faucher, T. (2011) : "La circulation monétaire en Égypte hellénistique", in : Faucher *et al.*, éd. 2011, 433-447.

— (2012) : "Coinage and Mapping", *Proceedings of the XVI*[th] *International Numismatic Congress, Glasgow*, 2012-2016.

Faucher, T., M.-C. Marcellesi et O. Picard, éd. (2011) : *Nomisma. La circulation monétaire dans le monde grec antique. Actes du colloque international, Athènes, 14-17 avril 2010*, BCH Suppl. 53, Athènes.

Fentress, E. (2013) : "Strangers in the City: Elite Communication in the Hellenistic Central Mediterranean", in : Prag & Quinn, éd. 2013, 157-178.

Feyel, C. et L. Graslin-Thomé, éd. (2014) : *Le projet politique d'Antiochos IV, Actes des journées d'études franco-allemandes, Nancy, 17-19 juin 2013*, Études lorraines d'histoire grecque 1, Nancy-Paris.

Fischer, T. (1968) : "Methodische Bemerkung zur historischen Auswerkung antiker Münzhortfunde an Hand der Silberfunde aus Susa: Depotfund und Münzversteck", *Schweizer Münzblätter*, 69, 9-13.

Fitz, J., éd. (1977) : *Akten des XI* Internationalen Limes*kongresses, Székesfehérvár, 30 août-6 septembre 1976*, Budapest.

Fontanille, J.-P. (2007) : "Two Unrecorded Hasmonean Coins", *Israel Numismatic Research*, 2, 89-92.

Fournier, J. et P. Hamon (2007) : "Les orphelins de guerre de Thasos : un nouveau fragment de la stèle des Braves (*ca* 360-350 av. J.-C.)", *BCH*, 131, 309-381.

France-Lanord, A. (1975) : "À propos de la conservation des monnaies de fouilles", in : Dentzer *et al.*, éd. 1975, 147-149.

Franke, P. R. (1957) : "Zur Finanzpolitik des makedonischen Königs Perseus während des Krieges mit Rom 171-168 v. Chr.", *JNG*, 8, 31-50.

Frazer, E. J. et J. van der Touw (2010) : "'The Random Walk'. A Study of Coins Lost and Found in an Urban Environment", *NC*, 170, 375-405.

Frey-Kupper, S. (1995) : "Monete dal Tevere: irinvenimenti 'greci'", *Bollettino di Numismatica*, 25, 33-73.

— (2013) : *Die antiken Fundmünzen vom Monte-Iato 1971-1990: Ein Beitrag zur geldgeschichte West siziliens*, Studia Ietina 10 (1-2), Lausanne.

Fritze, H. von (1906) : "Zur Chronologie der autonomen Prägung von Pergamon", in : Hill 1906, 47-62, pl. II.

— (1910) : *Die Münzen von Pergamon*, Berlin.

Fulford, M. J. (1978) : "Coin Circulation and Mint Activity in the Later Roman Empire", *Archaeological Journal*, 135, 67-114.

Furnham, A. (1985) : "The Perceived Value of Small Coins", *The Journal of Social Psychology*, 125 (5), 571-575.

Furtwängler, A. (1975) : "Münzen", in : Ziegenaus & de Luca, éd. 1975, 140-141.

— (1978) : "Katalog der Münzen", in : Nohlen & Radt, éd. 1978, 67-68.

— (2004) : "Beobachtungen zur Chronologie Antigonidischer Kupfermünzen im 3. Jh. v. Chr.", Οβολός, 7, 277-290.

Gaebler, H. (1930) : *Die Münzen von Stagira*, Berlin.

— (1935) : *Die antiken Münzen von Makedonia und Paionia*, Berlin.

Galili, E. et Y. Sharvit (1999) : "Haifa underwater surveys", *Hadashot Arkheologiyot – Excavations and Surveys in Israel*, 110, 15-20.

Game, J. (2009) : *Actes de vente dans le monde grec : témoignages épigraphiques des ventes immobilières*, Lyon-Paris.

Gândilă, A. (2009) : "Early Byzantine Coin Circulation in the Eastern Provinces: A Comparative Statistical Approach", *AJN*, 21, 151-226.

Garlan, Y. (1988) : *Vins et amphores de Thasos*, Sites et Monuments 5, Athènes.

Gatzolis, C. (2000) : "Δύο ελληνιστικοί θησαυροί από την Μακεδονία", Οβολός, 4, 103-126.

— (2010) : Η κυκλοφορία του χάλκινου νομίσματος στη Μακεδονία (5ος-1ος αι. π.Χ.), thèse de doctorat, Université de Thessalonique.

— (2011) : "Royal and Civic Bronze Coinage: Monetary Circulation between the Macedonian Kingdom and the Chalcidic Peninsula", in : Faucher *et al.*, éd. 2011, 185-198.

— (2012) : "A Reexamination of the Bronze Coinage of Alexander III and Cassander in the Light of the New Excavation and Hoard Evidence", in : Tiverios *et al.*, éd. 2012, 381-397.

— (2013) : "New Evidence on the Beginning of Bronze Coinage in Northern Greece", in : Grandjean & Moustaka, éd. 2013, 117-128.

— (à paraître) : "Alexanders in the Balkans until the Reign of Philip V (Macedonia and Greece)", in : *Les Alexandres après Alexandre : Histoire d'une monnaie commune*.

Gatzolis, C. et S. E. Psoma (2009) : "More on the Bottiaeans of Thrace", in : ΚΕΡΜΑΤΙΑ ΦΙΛΙΑΣ. Τιμητικός τόμος για τον Ι. Π. Τουράτσογλου, Athènes, 135-143.

— (2012) : "Αργυρή έκδοση με κεφαλή ίππου από την Σερμυλία. Παρατηρήσεις για την απόδοση μικρών υποδιαιρέσεων του αυτού τύπου στον Αλέξανδρο Α' της Μακεδονίας", in : Adam-Velenis & Tzanavari, éd. 2012, 617-20.

Giardino, C., éd. (2011) : *Archeometallurgia: dalla conoscenza alla fruizione, Atti del Workshop, Cavallino, 22-25 mai 2006*, Bari.

Gibbins, D. (2001) : "Shipwrecks and Hellenistic Trade", in : Archibald *et al.*, éd. 2001, 205-232.

Gibbs, M. (2006) : "Cultural Site Formation Processes in Maritime Archaeology: Disaster Response, Salvage and Muckelroy 30 Years on", *IJNA*, 35 (1), 4-19.

Gitler, H. et Y. Kahanov (2002) : "The Ascalon 1988 hoard (*CH* 9, 548). A periplus to Ascalon in the late Hellenistic Period?", in : Meadows & Wartenberg, éd. 2002, 259-268.

Gjongecaj, S. (2011) : "La circulation monétaire en Illyrie du Sud et en Epire", in : Faucher *et al.*, éd. 2011, 213-243.

Goddio, F. (2007) : *The Topography and Excavation of Heracleion-Thonis and East Canopus (1996-2006)*, Oxford.

Goddio, F. et D. Fabre (2006) : *Trésors engloutis d'Égypte*, catalogue de l'exposition présentée au Grand Palais à Paris du 9 décembre 2006 au 16 mars 2007, Milan-Paris.

Gorre, G. et P. Kossmann, éd. (2013) : *Espace et territoire de l'Egypte gréco-romaine, Actes des journées d'étude, 23 juin 2007 et 21 juin 2008*, Paris.

Goulpeau, L. (1981) : "Modélisation de la circulation monétaire à l'aide de deux constantes de temps", in : Carcassonne & Hackens, éd. 1981, 141-221.

Grandjean, C. (1998) : "La valeur des monnaies de bronze du Péloponnèse classique et hellénistique", *RN*, 153, 31-40.

— (2003) : *Les Messéniens de 370/369 au Ier siècle de notre ère Monnayages et histoire*, BCH Suppl. 44, Athènes.

— (2015) : "La monétarisation de l'astu et de la chôra des cités grecques (VIe s. av. n. è.-Ve s. de n. è.) en questions", *RBN*, 161, 3-15.

Grandjean, C. et A. Papadimitriou (à paraître) : "The 2005 Argos Hoard", à paraître.

Grandjean, C. et A. Moustaka, éd. (2013) : *Aux origines de la monnaie fiduciaire. Traditions métallurgiques et innovations numismatiques*, Scripta Antiqua 55, Bordeaux.

Grandjean, Y. (1988) : *Recherches sur l'habitat thasien à l'*époque grecque, I, Études thasiennes 12, Paris.

— (2010) : *Philathenaios. Studies in Honour of Michael J. Osborne*, Athènes.

Grandjean, Y. et F. Salviat, éd. (2000) : *Guide de Thasos*, 2e éd., Paris (1ère éd. 1967).

Grasland, C. et F. Guérin-Pace (2004) : "Mobilité européenne, tourisme et diffusion des pièces euros étrangères en France", *Revue d'économie régionale et urbaine*, 5, 793-822.

Grasland, C., F. Guérin-Pace, M. Le Texier et B. Garnier (2012) : "Dix ans de diffusion d'euros étrangers en France", *Population & Sociétés*, 488, 1-4.

Grasland, C., F. Guérin-Pace et A. Tostain (2002) : "La circulation des euros, reflet de la mobilité des hommes", *Population & Sociétés*, 384, 1-4.

Gricourt, D., J. Naumann et J. Schaud (2009) : *Le mobilier numismatique de l'agglomération secondaire de Bliesbruck (Moselle), fouilles 1978-1998*, Paris.

Grierson, P. (1965) : "The President's Address, delivered 16 June 1965, The Interpretation of Coin Finds (I)", *The Numismatic Chronicle and Journal of the Royal Numismatic Society*, 5, i-xii.

— (1966) : "The Interpretation of Coin Finds (2)", *NC*, 6, i-xxi.

— (1976) : *Monnaies et monnayage. Introduction à la numismatique*, Collection historique 17, Paris.

— (1985) : "Thirty Years of Numismatics", Acta Historica Bruxellensia, IV : *Histoire et méthode*, Bruxelles, 503-519.

— (1986) : "Circolazione monetaria e tesaurizzazione", in : Guillou, éd. 1986, 37-57.

Guarducci, M. (1946) : "Tripodi, lebeti, oboli", *RFIC*, 72-73, 171-180.

— (1974) : *Epigrafia greca*, III : *Epigrafi di carattere privato*, Rome.

Guest, P. (2012) : "The Production, Supply, and Use of late Roman and Early Byzantine Copper in the Eastern Empire", *NC*, 172, 105-131.

Guillou, A., éd. (1986) : *Les outils dans les Balkans*, Paris.

Guzzo, P. G. et M. P. Guidobaldi, éd. (2005) : *Nuove richerche archeologiche a Pompei ed Ercolano, Atti del convegno internazionale, Roma, 28-30 novembre 2002*, Studi della Soprintendenza archeologica di Pompei 10, Naples.

Haatvedt, R. A. et E. E. Peterson, éd. (1964) : *Coins from Karanis: The University of Michigan Excavations 1924-1935*, Ann Arbor.

Hackens, T. (1968) : "À propos de la circulation monétaire dans le Péloponnèse au IIIe s. av. J.-C.", in : Peremans, éd. 1968, 82-90.

— (1970) : "Les monnaies", in : Bruneau, éd. 1970, 387-419 et pl. 64-68.

— (1975) : "La circulation monétaire, questions de méthode", in : Dentzer *et al.*, éd. 1975, 213-222.

— (1976) : "À propos du monnayage d'Argos VIe-IIIe s. av J.-C.", *Actes du VIIIe congrès International de Numismatique, New York-Washington, 1973*, Paris, 83-85.

Hackens, T. et R. Weiller, éd. (1982) : *Proceedings of the IXth International Congress of Numismatics, Berne, septembre 1979*, Louvain.

Hadjidakis, P. I. (1997) : "Κτήριο νότια του "Ιερού του Προμαχώνος". Μια taverna vinaria στη Δήλο", in *Δ΄ Συνάντηση για την Ελληνιστική Κεραμική: Χρονολογικά Προβλήματα, Κλειστά Σύνολα, Εργαστήρια, Μυτιλήνη, Μάρτιος 1994*, Athènes, 291-307.

Hainzmann, M. (1997) : "Fundmuenzen aus Aigeira I: lokale praegungen", in : Sheedy & Papageorgiadou-Banis, éd. 1997, 40-46.

Hammond, N. (1970) : "The Archaeological Background of the Macedonian Kingdom", *Ἀρχαία Μακεδονία, I*, 53-67.

— (1972) : *A History of Macedonia*, I : *Historical geography and prehistory*, Oxford.

— (1992) : *The Macedonian State. The Origins, Institutions and History*, Oxford-New York.

Hammond, N. G. L. et G. T. Griffith (1979) : *A History of Macedonia*, II : *550-336 B.C.*, Oxford.

Hammond, N. G. L. et F.W. Walbank (1988) : *A History of Macedonia*, III : *336-167 B.C.*, Oxford.

Harl, K. (1996) : *Coinage in the Roman Economy, 300 BC to AD 700*, Baltimore.

Harris, E. M., D. Lewis et M. Woolmer (2016) : *Markets, Households and City States in the Ancient Greek Economy*, New York.

Harris, V. W. (2006) : "A Revisionist View of Roman Money", *JRS*, 96, 1-24.

Harris, V. W., éd. (2008) : *The Monetary Systems of the Greeks and Romans*, Oxford.

Hatzopoulos, M. B. (1991) : *Actes de vente d'Amphipolis*, Meletemata 14, Athènes.

— (1994) : "Apollonia Hellenis", in : Worthington, éd. 1994, 159-188.

— (1996a) : *Macedonian Institutions under the Kings*, I : *A Historical and Epigraphic Study*, et II : Epigraphic Appendix, Meletemata 22, Athènes.

— (1996b) : "Aigai. La localisation de la prémiere capitale macédonienne", *REG*, 109, 264-269.

Hatzopoulos, M. B. et L. Loukopoulou (1987) : *Two Studies in Ancient Macedonian Topography*, Meletemata 3, Athènes.

Hatzopoulos, M. B. et S. Psoma (1998-1999) : "Cités de Grèce septentrionale portant le nom de Dion", Τεκμήρια, 4, 1-12.

Head, B. V. (1886a) : "Coins Discovered on the Site of Naukratis", *Numismatic Chronicle*, 6, 1-18.

— (1886b) : "Chapter VIII. The coins", in : Petrie *et al.* 1886, 63-69.

Heckel, W. (2006) : *Who'Who in the Age of Alexander the Great. Prosopography of Alexander's Empire*, Malden (Mass.).

Heermann, V. (1980) : *Studien zu makedonischen Palästarchitektur*, Berlin.

Helm, J., éd. (1965) : *Essays in Economic Anthropology Dedicated to the Memory of Karl Polanyi*, Washinghton.

Hendy, M. F. (1985) : *Studies in the Byzantine Monetary Economy, c. 300-1450*, Cambridge-New York.

Heuzey, L. et H. Daumet (1876) : *Mission archéologique de Macédoine*, Paris.

Hill, G. F. (1906) : *Corolla Numismatica, Numismatics Essays in Honour of Barclay V. Head*, Londres-New York.

Hingley, R. et S. Willis, éd. (2007) : *Roman Finds. Contexts and theory. Proceedings of a Conference held at the university of Durham*, Oxford.

Hobbs, R. (2007) : "Mine's Bigger than Yours: Comparing Values of late Roman Hoards", in : Hingley & Willis, éd. 2007, 77-85.

— (2013) : "The Commercial Life of *Insula* VI, 1: the Coins from the Excavations of the Anglo-American Project in Pompeii", in : Arévalo Gonzalez *et al.*, éd. 2013, 167-180.

Hoepfner, W. (1996) : "Zum Typus der Basileia und der Königlichen Andrones", in : Hoepfner & Brands, éd. 1996, 1-43.

— (2002) : *Palast der makedonischen Könige in Aigai (heute Vergina)*, in : *Die griechische Klassik. Idee oder Wirklichkeit.*

Hoepfner, W. et G. Brands (1996) : *Basileia: Die Paläste der hellenistischen Könige, Internationales Symposion in Berlin, 16-20 décembre 1992*, Mayence.

Hoffmann, A. (2011) : *Das Asklepieion. Die Platzhallen und die zugehörigen Annexbauten in römischer Zeit*, Altertümer von Pergamon XI.5, Berlin, 2 vol.

Højte, J. M., éd. (2009) : *Mithridates VI and the Pontic Kingdom*, Black Sea Studies 9, Santa Barbara.

Hollander, D. B. (2007) : *Money in the Late Roman Republic*, Leyde.

Hollard, D. (1996) : "La circulation monétaire en Gaule au IIIe s. après J.-C.", in : King & Wigg, éd. 1996, 203-217.

Holleaux, M. (1952) : "Le papyrus de Gourob", in : *Études d'épigraphie et d'histoire grecque*, III, Paris.

Holmberg, E. J., éd. (1944) : *The Swedish excavations at Asea in Arcadia*, Leipzig.

Holmes, N., éd. (2011) : *Proceedings of the XIVth International Numismatic Congress, Glasgow, 2009*, Glasgow.

Hoover, O. D. (2006) : "A Reassessment of Nabatean Lead Coinage in Light of New Discoveries", *Numismatic Chronicle*, 166, 105-119.

Houghton, A. et C. C. Lorber (2000-2002) : "Antiochus III in Coele-Syria and Phoenicia", *Israel Numismatic Journal*, 14, 44-58.

— (2002) : *Seleucid Coins. A Comprehensive Catalogue*, Part I : *Seleucus I through Antiochus III*, New York-Lancaster.

Houghton, A., C. C. Lorber et O. D. Hoover (2008) : *Seleucid Coins. A Comprehensive Catalogue*, Part II : Seleucus IV through Antiochus XIII, New York-Lancaster.

Howgego, C. J. (1985) : *Greek Imperial Countermarks. Studies in the Provincial Coinage of the Roman Empire*, RNS Special Publications 17, Londres.

— (1994) : "Coin Circulation and the Integration of the Roman Economy", *JRA*, 7, 5-21.

— (1995) : *Ancient History from Coins*, Londres-New York.

— (2009) : "Some Numismatic Approaches to Quantifying the Roman Economy", in : Bowman & Wilson, éd. 2009, 287-295.

Humphrey, J. H., éd. (1978) : *Excavations at Carthage 1976. Conducted by the University of Michigan*, IV, Ann Arbor.

Huston, S.M. et C.C. Lorber (2001) : "A Hoard of Ptolemaic Bronze Coins in Commerce, October 1992 (*CH* 8, 413)", *Numismatic Chronicle*, 161, 11-40.

Ilisch, P. (1991) : "Die Münzen aus den Ausgrabungen im Lager Oberaden", in : Asskamp & Berke, éd. 1991, 141-147.

Imhoof-Blumer, F. (1884) : *Die Münzen der Dynastie von Pergamon*, Berlin.

Iossif, P. P. (2011a) : "Quantifying Greek Hoards", *Numismatic Chronicle*, 171, 435-455.

— (2011b) : "Seleucid Religion Through Coins: Is It Possible to Quantify 'Iconography' and 'Religion'?", in : de Callataÿ, éd. 2011, 213-249.

— (2014) : "Coin Diffusion Patterns in the Seleucid Empire. A Statistical Model", *Coins, Currency and Crisis from c. 2000 BC-c. AD 2000. On Silver, Paper and Trust in Historical Perspective*, international workshop tenu à l'université libre d'Amsterdam les 12 et 13 décembre 2014.

— (2016) : *"Favorites of the Gods". The Seleucid kings coping with the divine. A qualitative and quantitative approach of the numismatic evidence attesting the "discreet" divinization of the Seleucids*, Liège.

Iossif, P. P. et C. Lauwers (à paraître) : "Une matrice d'usure pour les monnaies de bronze séleucides. Une introduction méthodologique", *BCEN*.

Iossif, P. P., B. van Leewen et P. Foldvari (2014) : "The Speed of Coin Diffusion within the Seleucid Empire and the EU compared", *Coins, Currency and Crisis from c. 2000 BC-c. AD 2000. On Silver, Paper and Trust in Historical Perspective*, international workshop tenu à l'université libre d'Amsterdam les 12 et 13 décembre 2014.

Ivanov, S. (2011) : "Circulation of Bronze Coins of Amphipolis and their barbarian imitations from the 2nd Century BC to the 1st Century BC on the Territory of Southwest Bulgaria", *Archaeologia Bulgarica*, 15 (1), 35-51.

— (2012) : "Circulation of Bronze Coins of Thessalonica from the 2nd Century BC to the 1st Century BC on the Territory of Southwest Bulgaria", in : Paunov & Filipova, éd. 2012, 431-441.

Jacobs, I. éd. (2013) : *Production and Prosperity in the Theodosian Period*, Interdisciplinary studies in ancient culture and religion 14, Louvain.

Jayaswal, V., éd. (2012) : *Glory of the Kushans. Recent Discoveries and Interpretations*, New Delhi.

Jha, A K, éd. (1991) : *Coinage, Trade and Economy, 3rd International Colloquium, 8-11 January 1991*, Anjaneri.

Jursa, M. et J. Hackl (2010) : *Aspects of the Economic History of Babylonia in the First Millennium BC. Economic Geography, Economic Mentalities, Agriculture, the Use of Money and the Problem of Economic Growth*, Alter Orient und Altes Testament 377, Münster.

Kaltsas, N., E. Vlachogianni et P. Bouyia, éd. (2012) : *The Antikythera Shipwreck. The Ship, the Treasures, the Mechanism*, Athènes.

Kaminski, G. (1991) : "Thesauros. Untersuchungen zum antiken Öpferstock", *JDAI*, 106, 63-181.

Karvonis, P. et J.-J. Malmary (2012) : "Du quartier à l'agora : étude de cas dans le Quartier du Théâtre à Délos", in : Chankowski & Karvonis, éd. 2012, 263-275.

Katsari, C. (2003) : "The Statistical Analysis of Stray Coins in Museums: the Roman Provincial Coinage", *Nomismatika Chronika*, 22, 47-52.

Katzev, L. W. (1970) : "Kyrenia 1969", *Expedition*, 12 (4), 6-14.

Katzev, S. W. (2005) : "Resurrecting an Ancient Greek Ship: Kyrenia, Cyprus", in : Bass, éd. 2005, 72-79.

Kent, J. P. C. (1974) : "Interpreting Coin-Finds", in : Casey & Reece, éd. 1974, 184-200.

Kersel, M. M. (2010) : "The Changing Legal Landscape for Middle Eastern Archaeology in the Colonial Era, 1800-1930", in : Emberling 2010, 88-89.

King, C. et D. Wigg, éd. (1996) : *Coin Finds and Coin Use in the Roman World, The Thirteenth Oxford Symposium on Coinage and Monetary History, 25-27* mars *1993*, SFMA 10, Berlin.

Knapp, R. C. et J. D. Mac Isaac (2005) : *Excavations at Nemea*, III : *The Coins*, Berkeley-Londres.

Kool, R. (2000-2002) : "The Rediscovery of G.F. Hill's Original Plates of BMC Palestine and Phoenicia in Jerusalem", *Israel Numismatic Journal*, 14, 260.

Kosmidou, E. (2006) : "Greek Coins from the Eastern Cemetery of Amphipolis", *NC*, 166, 415-432.

Kottaridi, A. (2006) : "Έρευνα στις Αιγές, μια πόλη κατά κώμας Βεργίνα", *AEMTH*, 20, 767-780.

— (2009) : "The Palace of Aegae: The New Data", in : Kottaridi, éd. 2009, 12-59.

— (2011a) : "The Palace of Aegae", in : Lane-Fox, éd. 2011, 297-333.

— (2011b) : "The Chronology of the Hellenistic Coins of Thessaloniki, Pella and Amphipolis", in : Holmes, éd. 2011, 251-255 et pl. I-III.

Kottaridi, A., éd. (2009) : *The Palace of Aegae. 2007-2009. The Commencement of a Major Project*, Thessalonique.

Koukouli-Chrysanthaki, C. (2002) : "Excavating Classical Amphipolis", in : Stamatopoulou & Yeroulanou, éd. 2002, 57-73.

— (2011) : "Amphipolis", in : Lane Fox, éd. 2011, 409-436 et fig. 40-48.

Kourempanas, T. (2010) : "Απόδοση χάλκινων νομισμάτων στον Φίλιππο ΣΤ'", Νομισματικά Χρονικά, 28, 5-14.

— (2011a) : "Les monnayages de bronze en Macédoine après la fin de la monarchie", in : Faucher *et al.*, éd. 2011, 199-211.

— (2011b) : "The Chronology of the Hellenistic Coins of Thessaloniki, Pella and Amphipolis", in : Holmes, éd. 2011, 251-255.

— (2012) : Kourempanas, "Un atelier monétaire sur l'agora de Pella", in : Chankowski & Karvonis, éd. 2012, 333-339.

Kraay, C. M. (1969) : *Greek coins and history: some current problems*, Londres.

— (1976) : *Archaic and Classical Greek Coins*, Berkeley.

Kremydi-Sisilianou, S. (1999) : "Ένας νέος τύπος τετραδράχμου του Αλεξάνδρου Α'", Αρχαία Μακεδονία, VI, 643-654.

— (2007) : "ΜΑΚΕΔΟΝΩΝ ΠΡΩΤΗΣ ΜΕΡΙΔΟΣ. Evidence for a Coinage under the Antigonids", *RN*, 163, 91-100.

— (2009) : "The Tauropolos Tetradrachms of the First Macedonian *Meris*: Provenance, Iconography and Dating", in : Drougou, éd. 2009, 191-201.

Kritzas, H. (2006) : "Nouvelles inscriptions d'Argos ; les archives des comptes du trésor sacré (IVe s. av. J.-C.)", *CRAI*, 150 (1), 397-434.

— (2009) : "*Oboloi Argolikoi, Kermatia Philias*", Mélanges en l'*honneur de Ioannis Touratsoglou*, 9-23.

Kroll, J. H. (1979) : "Early Athenian Bronze Coinage", in : Mørkhlom & Waggoner, éd. 1979, 139-157.

— (1993) : *The Greek Coins*, The Athenian Agora 26, Princeton.

— (2011): "Athenian Tetradrachm Coinage of the First Half of the Fourth Century BC", *RBN*, 157, 3-26.

Krzyżanowska, A. et K. Myśliwiec (2009) : *Tell Atrib 1985-1995*, II : *Les Monnaies. Contexte archéologique*, Varsovie.

Kuhrt, A. (1995) : *The Ancient Near East, c.3000-330 BC*, I, Londres-New York.

Lacroix, L. (1969) : "La monnaie grecque et les problèmes de la circulation monétaire", *Bulletin de la Classe des lettres et des Sciences morales et politiques de l'Académie royale de Belgique*, 55, 169-180.

Lagos, C. (1996) : "A Hoard of the Chremonidian War", *NC*, 156, 272-277 et pl. 48.

Laidlaw, A. et M. S. Stella, éd. (2014) : *The House of Sallust in Pompei (VI. 2. 4)*, JRA Suppl. 98, Portsmouth.

Laing, R. K. (1969) : *Coins and Archaeology*, New York.

Lamboley, J.-L. et M. P. Castiglioni, éd. (2011) : *L'Illyrie méridionale et l'*Épire dans l'*Antiquité. V, Actes du Ve colloque international de Grenoble, 10-12 octobre 2008*, 1, Paris.

Lane Fox, R., éd. (2011) : *Brill's Companion to Ancient Macedon. Studies in the Archaeology and History of Ancient Macedon, 650 B.C.-300 A.D.*, Leyde-Boston.

Laurence, J. (1931) : *Money, Credit and Prices*, Londres.

Lauwers, C. (2013) : "Les monnaies des fouilles belges d'Apamée sur l'Oronte, Syrie (2005-2010)", *RBN*, 159, 151-186.

Lazaridis, D. (1972) : Αμφίπολις και Άργιλος, Αρχαίες Ελληνικές Πόλεις 13, Athènes.

— (1975) : "Ανασκαφαί και έρευναι Αμφιπόλεως", *PAE*, 131, 61-71.

— (1997) : *Amphipolis*, Athènes.

Law, J. (1720) : *The Present State of the French Revenues and Trade, and of the Controversy betwixt the Parliament of Paris and Mr. Law*, Londres.

Lazaridis, D., K. Romiopoulou et I. Touratsoglou (1992) : Ο τύμβος της Νικήσιανης, Athènes.

Lazrus, P. K. et A. W. Barker, éd. (2012) : *All the King's Horses: Essays on the Impact of Looting and the Illicit Antiquities Trade on Our Knowledge of the Past*, Washington D.C.

Lehmann, P.W., M. R Jones et K. Lehmann (1969) : *Samothrace 3, Text II: The Hieron*, Princeton.

Le Rider, G. (1956) : "Trésor de monnaies trouvé à Thasos", *BCH*, 80, 1-19 et pl. I-II.

— (1965) : *Suse sous les Séleucides et les Parthes. Les trouvailles monétaires et l'histoire de la ville*, Paris.

— (1973) : "Un tétradrachme d'Athéna Niképhoros", *RN*, 15, 66-79.

— (1977) : *Le monnayage d' argent et d' or de Philippe II frappé en Macédoine de 359 à 294*, Paris.

— (1986) : "L'atelier de Posideion et les monnaies de la fouille de Bassit", *BCH*, 110, 393-408.

— (1996) : *Monnayage et finances de Philippe II. Un état de la question*, Meletemata 23, Athènes.

— (1999) : *Antioche de Syrie sous les Séleucides. Corpus des monnaies d'or et d'argent I. De Séleucos I à Antiochos V (c. 301-161)*, Mémoires de l'Académie des Inscriptions et Belles-Lettres 19, Paris.

Le Rider, G., éd. (1989) : *Kraay-Mørkholm Essays. Numismatic Studies in Memory of C.M. Kraay and O. Mørkholm*, Louvain.

Liampi, K. (1998a) : "A Hoard of Bronze Coins of Alexander the Great", in : Ashton & Hurter, éd. 1998, 247-253.

— (1998b) : *Der Makedonische Schild*, Bonn.

— (2005) : *Argilos. A Historical and Numismatic Study*, Kerma 1, Athènes.

Liampi, K., éd. (2010) : Συμβολή στην οικονομική ιστορία του βασιλείου της αρχαίας Μακεδονίας: (6ος-3ος αι. π.Χ.), Athènes.

Lilimpaki-Akamati, M. (1993) : "Νέο εργαστήριο κεραμικής και κοροπλαστικής στην Πέλλα", *AEMTH*, 7, 171-182.

— (1996) : "Κτιριακά συγκροτήματα στην περιοχή του Καναλιού της Πέλλας", *AEMTH*, 10a, 93-104.

— (2000a) : "Νέες ανασκαφικές έρευνες στην Πέλλα", *AEMTH*, 14, 407-420.

— (2000b) : Θησαυρός από την περιοχή του καναλιού της Πέλλας", in : Pandermalis, éd. 2000, 377-391.

— (2000c) : Το ιερό της Μητέρας των Θεών και της Αφροδίτης στην Πέλλα, Thessalonique.

— (2003) : "Ανασκαφική έρευνα στην περιοχή του Φάκου της Πέλλας", *AEMTH*, 17, 465-483.

— (2005) : "Ανασκαφική έρευνα στην Πέλλα το 2005", *AEMTH*, 19, 391-406.

— (2008) : "Ανασκαφική έρευνα στην Πέλλα το 2006", in : Chrysostomou, éd. 2008, 35-47.

— (2011) : "Συντήρηση-Ανάδειξη Πέλλας. Το εργαστήριο κεραμικής (περιοχή νέας εισόδου αρχαιολογικού χώρου)", *AEMTH*, 25, s.p.

— (2013) : "Δημόσιο λουτρό Πέλλας. Εργασίες συντήρησης και νέα ανασκαφικά στοιχεία", *AEMTH*, 27, s.p.

— (2012) : "Pella from the Bronze to the Hellenistic Age", in : Tiverios *et al.*, éd. 2012, 5-25.

Lilimpaki-Akamati, M. et N. Akamatis (2007) : "Το δημόσιο λουτρό της Πέλλας. Ανασκαφική περίοδος 2007", *AEMTH*, 21, 99-108.

— (2008) : "Ένα νέο εργαστήριο κεραμικής στην Πέλλα", *AEMTH*, 22, 147-154.

— (2009) : "Ανιχνεύοντας την Πέλλα του πρώτου μισού του 4ου αιώνα π. Χ.", *AEMTH*, 23, 205-212.

—, éd. (2003) : Πέλλα και η περιοχή της, Thessalonique.

Lind, L. (1993) : "The Monetary Reform of Nero, Domitian and Septimius Severus and the Finds of Roman denarii in Eastern and Northern Europe", in : Moucharte & Hackens, éd. 1993, 289-295.

Lloyd, A. B. (1988) : *Herodotus: Book II. Commentary, 99-182*, Leyde-New York.

Lo Cascio, E. (1996) : "How did the Romans View their Coinage and its Function?", in : King & Wigg, éd. 1996, 273-287.

— (2008) : "The Function of Gold Coinage in the Monetary Economy of the Roman Empire", in : Harris, éd. 2008, 160-173.

Lo Cascio, E., éd. (2003) : *Credito e moneta nel mondo romano*, Bari.

Lochner, I. (2010) : "Der Siedlungshügel von Aizanoi in vorrömischer Zeit", in : Rheidt, éd. 2010, 22-37.

Locke, J. (1695) : *Further Considerations Concerning Raising the Value of Money, Wherein Mr. Lowndes's Arguments for it in his Late Report Concerning An Essay for the Amendment of the Silver Coins, are Particularly Examined*, Londres.

Lockyear, K. (2000) : "Site Finds in Roman Britain: A Comparison of Techniques", *Oxford Journal of Archaeology*, 19 (4), 397-423.

— (2007) : *Patterns and Process in Late Roman Republican Hoards, 157-2 B.C.*, BAR Int. Ser. 1733, Oxford.

Lombard, M. (1959) : "Un problème cartographié : le bois dans la Méditerranée musulmane (VIIe-XIe siècles)", *Annales. Histoire, Sciences Sociales*, 14 (2), 234-254.

Lolos, Y. A. (2008) : *Via Egnatia, Εγνατία Οδός*, Athènes.

Lönnquvist, K. (1997) : *Studies on the Hellenistic Coinage of Athens: The Impact of Macedonia on the Athenian Money Market in the 3rd Century B. C.*, Papers and Monographs of the Finnish Institute at Athens 6, Athènes.

Lorber, C. (1990) : *Amphipolis. The Civic Coinage in Silver and Gold*, Los Angeles.

— (2000) : "Large Ptolemaic Bronzes in Third-Century Egyptian Hoards", *American Journal of Numismatics*, 12, 67-92

— (2005) : "Development of Ptolemaic Bronze Coinage in Egypt", in : Duyrat & Picard, éd. 2005, 135-157.

— (à paraître) *: Coinage of the Ptolemaic Empire.*

Lorber, C. et T. Faucher (2010) : "Bronze Coinage of Ptolemaic Egypt in the Second Century BC", *American Journal of Numismatics*, 22, 35-80.

Loriot, X. (2003) : "Réflexions sur l'usage et les usagers de la monnaie d'or sous l'Empire romain", *RN*, 159, 57-74.

Lund, J. (1986) : *Sukas VIII. The Habitation Quarters*, Historisk-filosofiske skrifter 12, Copenhague.

Lykiardopoulou, M. et S. Psoma (2000) : "Η αργυρή βασιλική νομισματοκοπία των Τημενιδών της Μακεδονίας από τα τέλη της βασιλείας του Περδίκκα Β΄ έως το θάνατο του Περδίκκα Γ΄(413-360). Τεχνολογία κατασκευής, ανάλυση μετάλλου, ιστορική προσέγγιση", Οβολός, 4, 321-337.

Mac Alee, R. (2007) : *The Coins of Roman Antioch*, Lancaster.

Mac Donald, D. J. (1974) : "Aphrodisias and Currency in the East, AD 259-305", *American Journal of Archaeology*, 78, 279-286.

Mac Donald, G. (1902-1903) : "Coin Finds and How to Interpret Them", *Proceedings of the Royal Philosophical Society of Glasgow*, 34, 282-300.

Mac Dowall, D.W. (1991) : "Indian Imports of Roman Silver Coins", in : Jha, éd. 1991, 145-163.

Mackay, P. A. (1968) : "Bronze Coinage in Macedonia, 168-166 B.C.", *ANSMN*, 14, 5-13.

Mactoux, M. M. et E. Geny, éd. (1990) : *Mélanges Pierre Lévèque*, 5, *Antropologie et société*, Centre de recherche d'histoire ancienne 101, ALUB 429, Besançon.

Malkin, I, C. Constantakopoulou et K. Panagopoulou, éd. (2009) : *Greek and Roman Networks in the Mediterranean*, Londres.

Mamroth, A. (1928) : "Die Silbermünzen des Königs Perseus", *ZfN*, 38, 1-28.

— (1935) : "Die Bronzemünzen des Königs Philippos V von Makedonien", *ZfN*, 42, 219-251.

Maniatis, Y., I. Y. Fakorellis, D. Malamidou et C. Koukouli-Chrysanthaki (2010) : "Radio-carbon Sequential Dating Amphipolis Bridge", *Radiocarbon*, 52, 41-63.

Marcellesi, M.-C. (2012a) : "La question d'une subdivision du chalque : l'apport des sources épigraphiques et littéraires", *REG*, 125, 1-20.

— (2012b) : *Pergame de la fin du ve au début du Ier siècle avant J.-C. Pratiques monétaires et histoire*, Studi ellenistici 26, Pise.

— (2014) : "Monnaie, politique et économie à Cos de l'époque archaïque à l'époque d'Auguste", *RN*, 171, 747-758.

Marchetti, P. (1994) : "Recherches sur les mythes et la topographie d'Argos II-III", *BCH*, 118, 148-149.

— (1995) : "Recherches sur les mythes et la topographie d'Argos IV", *BCH*, 119, 437-477.

Maucourant, J. (2000) : "Échange, commerce et monnaies dans les économies non modernes – un réexamen de l'approche de Karl Polanyi", *Transeuphratène – Recherches pluridisciplinaires sur une province de l'Empire achéménide*, 20, 9-43.

Meadows, A. (2013) : "The Closed Currency System of the Attalid Kingdom", in : Thonemann, éd. 2013, 149-205.

— (2014a) : "Bronze Coins from Excavations in Alexandria", *Bulletin of the American Society of Papyrologists*, 51, 229-239.

— (2014b) : "Coin Circulation and Coin Production at Thonis-Heracleion and in the Delta Region in the Late Period", in : Robinson & Goddio, éd. 2014, 121-136.

— (2014c) : "The Spread of Coins in the Hellenistic World", in : Bernholz & Vaubel, éd. 2014, 188-191.

Meadows, A. et E. Gruber (2014) : "Coinage and Numismatic Methods. A Case Study of Linking a Discipline", ISAW Papers 7.15, [en ligne], http://dlib.nyu.edu/awdl/isaw/isaw-papers/7/meadows-gruber/.

Meadows, A. et U. Wartenberg, éd. (2002) : *Coin Hoards*, IX: *Greek Hoards*, Londres.

Meikle, S. (1995) : *Aristotle's Economic Thought*, Oxford.

Meshorer, Y. (1982) : *Ancient Jewish Coinage*, I : *Persian Period through Hasmonaeans*, Dix Hills.

— (2003-2006) : "The Coins from Qumran", *Israel Numismatic Journal*, 15, 19-23.

Metcalf, D. M. (1998) : *An Atlas of Anglo-Saxon and Norman Coin Finds, c. 973-1086*, RNS Spec. Publ. 32, Londres.

Metcalf, W. E., éd. (2012) : *The Oxford Handbook of Greek and Roman Coinage*, Oxford.

Migeotte, L. (1989): "Démocratie et entretien du peuple à Rhodes", *REG*, 102, 515-528.

— (2014) : *Les finances des cités* grecques *: aux périodes classique et hellénistique*, Epigraphica 8, Paris.

Miller, S. G. (1970) : *Hellenistic Macedonian Architecture: its Style and Painted Ornamentation*, thèse de doctorat, Bryn Mawr College.

Milne, J. G. (1925) : "J. T. Wood's Coins from Ephesos", *NC*, 5, 385-391.

Milojcic, V. et D. Theocharis, éd. (1976) : *Demetrias*, I, Bonn.

Moretti, J.-C. (dir.), L. Fadin, M. Fincker et V. Picard (2015): *Atlas. Exploration archéologique de Délos XLIII*, Athènes.

Mørkholm, O. (1991) : *Early Hellenistic Coinage. From the Accession of Alexander to the Peace of Apamea (336-188 B.C.)*, Cambridge-New York.

Mørkholm, O. et N. Wagonner, éd. (1979) : *Greek Numismactics and Archaeology. Essay in Honor of Margaret Thompson*, Wetteren.

Morrisson, C. (2002) : "Trouvailles isolées et trésors: réflets de la production monétaire à Byzance ?", in : Asolati & Gorini, éd. 2002, 235-245.

Moucharte, G. et T. Hackens, éd. (2013) : *Actes du XIe congrès international de Numismatique organisé à l'occasion du 150e anniversaire de la Société royale de Numismatique de Belgique, Bruxelles, 8-13 septembre 1991*, Louvain.

Moucharte, G *et al.* , éd. (2007) : *Liber Amicorum Tony Hackens*, Numismatica Lovaniensia 20, Louvain.

Moustaka, A. (1999) : "Die Fundmünzen der Südostgrabung", in : *Bericht über die Ausgrabungen in Olympia*, IX, Berlin-New York, 152-180 et pl. 42-45.

Muckelroy, K. (1978) : *Maritime Archaeology*, Cambrigde-New York.

Mundell, R. (1998) : "Uses and Abuses of Gresham's Law in the History of Money", *Zagreb Journal of Economics*, 2 (2), 3-38.

Newell, E. T. (1927) : *The Coinages of Demetrius Poliorcetes*, Londres.

Newton, D. P. (2006) : "Found Coins as Indicators of Coins in Circulation: Testing some Assumptions", *European Journal of Archaeology*, 9 (3), 221-227.

Nielsen, T. H. (1999) : *Hellenistic Palaces. Tradition and Renewal*, Studies in Hellenistic Civilization V, Aarhus.

— (2002) : *Arkadia and its Poleis in the Archaic and Classical periods*, Hypomnemata 140, Göttingen.

Nixon, C. E. V. (2002) : "The Coins", in : Clarke *et al.*, éd. 2002, 291-335.

Nohlen, K. et W. Radt, éd. (1978) : *Kapıkaya. Ein Felsheiligtum bei Pergamon,* Altertümer von Pergamon XII, Berlin.

Nollé, J. (2014) : " 'Panegyris coinages' – eine moderne Geisterprägung", *Chiron*, 44, 285-323.

Noreña, C. F. (2001) : "The Communication of the Emperor's Virtues", *JRS*, 91, 146-168.

— (2011) : *Imperial Ideals in the Roman West. Representation, Circulation, Power*, Cambridge-New York.

Oikonomidou, M. (1968), "Chronika", *Arch. Deltion*, 23, 12-15.

— (1989) : "Ένα νομισματοκοπείο στην αρχαία Πέλλα", Αρχαία Μακεδονία, V, 1143-1154.

Oikonomidou, M. et T. Kourempanas (2007) : "Ένα νομισματοκοπείο στην αρχαία Πέλλα. Μια δεύτερη προσέγγιση", *ArchEphem*, 146, 221-242.

Oikonomos, G. P. (1918) : "Νομίσματα του βασιλέως Κασσάνδρου", *ADelt*, 4, 1-29.

Paliadeli, C. (2007) : "Το ανάκτορο των Αιγών: προδημοσίευση", *AEMTH*, 21, 127-134.

Pandermalis, D. (1987) : "Η κεράμωση του ανακτόρου της Βεργίνας", Αμητός. Τιμητικός τόμος για τον καθηγητή Μανόλη Ανδρόνικο, 579-605.

Pandermalis, D., A. Despini, H. Koukouli-Chrysanthaki et P. Adam-Veleni (2000) : Μύρτος. Μελέτες στη μνήμη της Ιουλίας Βοκοτοπούλου, Thessalonique.

Papakonstantinou-Diamantourou, D. (1971) : Πέλλα Ι. Ιστορική επισκόπησις και μαρτυρίαι, Bibliothèque de la Société archéologique 70, Athènes.

Papanicolaou-Christensen, A., R. Thomsen, G. Ploug, éd. (1986) : *Hama, fouilles et recherches de la fondation Carlsberg, 1931-1938*, III.3 : *The Graeco-Roman Objects of Clay, the Coins and the Necropolis*, Nationalmuseets skrifter. Større beretninger, 10, Copenhague.

Papazoglou, F. (1988) : *Les villes de Macédoine à l'*époque romaine, BCH Suppl. XVI, Athènes.

Parker, A. J. (1992) : *Ancient Shipwrecks of the Mediterranean and the Roman Provinces*, BAR Int. Ser. 580, Oxford.

Paunov, E. et S. Filipova, éd. (2012) : ΗΡΑΚΛΕΟΥΣ ΣΩΤΗΡΟΣ ΘΑΣΙΩΝ. *Studia in honorem Iliae Prokopov sexagenario ab amicis et discipulis dedicata*, Veliko Turnovo.

Pavlovska, E. (2011) : "The Coinage of the Paeonian kings Leon and Dropion", in : Holmes, éd. 2011, 319-331.

Pellerin, J. (1763) : *Mélange de diverses médailles de peuples et de villes qui n'ont point encore été publiées ou qui sont peu connues*, Paris.

Peremans, W., éd. (1968) : *Antidorum W. Peremans sexagenario ab alumnis oblatum*, Studia Hellenistica 16, Louvain.

Perring, D. (1997-1998) : "Excavations in the Souks of Beirut: an Introduction to the Work of the Anglo-Lebanese Team and Summary Report", *Berytus*, 43, 9-34.

Petrie, W M.F, C.H. Smith, E.A. Gardner et B.V. Head (1886) : *Naukratis*, Part 1 : *1884-1885*, Londres.

Petsas, P. M, M. B. Hatzopoulos, L. Gounaropoulou et P. Paschidis (2000) : *Inscriptions du sanctuaire de la mère des dieux autochtone de Leukopetra (Macédoine)*, Meletemata 28, Athènes.

Picard, O. (1979) : *Chalcis et la Confédération eubéenne*, BEFAR 53, Athènes.

— (1982) : "L'organisation de l'atelier monétaire de Thasos", in : Hackens & Weiller, éd. 1982, 118-124 et pl. 21.

— (1984) : "Monnaies", in : Amandry, éd. 1984, 281-306.

— (1989) : "Le comblement d'un puits public à Thasos. I Les monnaies", *BCH*, 113, 473-476.

— (1990) : "Les oboles de Théogénès", in : Mactoux & Geny, éd. 1990, 315-323.

— (1992) : "Monnaies de bronze à Delphes", in : Bommelaer, éd. 1992, 349-354.

— (1994a) : "Deux émissions de bronzes d'Amphipolis", *BCH*, 118, 207-214.

— (1994b) : "Monnaies et commerce à Thasos", in : Andreau *et al.*, éd. 1994, 31-45.

— (1996) : "Chalcis revisité", in : Carlier, éd. 1996, 183-194.

— (1997) : "Monnaies de fouille et histoire grecque, l'exemple de Thasos", in : Sheedy & Papageorgiadou-Banis, éd. 1997, 29-39.

— (1998) : "La valeur des monnaies grecques en bronze", *RN*, 153, 1-12.

— (2001a) : "Monnaies", in : Grandjean & Salviat, éd. 2001, 303-314.

— (2001b) : "Le retour des émigrés et le monnayage de Thasos", *CRAI*, 144 (3), 1057-1084.

— (2002) : "Thasos : les fouilles de l'agora et les monnaies", in : Asolati & Gorini, éd. 2002, 52-57.

— (2007) : "Monnaie et circulation monétaire à l'époque classique", *Pallas*, 74, 113-128.

— (2010) : "Iconographie et mémoire monétaires : l'exemple de Thasos", Οβολός, 9, 45-57.

— (2011a) : "Un siècle de recherches archéologiques à Thasos", *CRAI*, 155, 1135-1159.

— (2011b) : "La circulation monétaire dans le monde grec : le cas de Thasos", in : Faucher *et al.*, éd. 2011, 79-109.

— (2012) : *Les monnaies des fouilles du Centre d'études alexandrines : les monnayages de bronze à Alexandrie de la conquête d'Alexandre à l'Égypte moderne*, Études alexandrines 25, Paris.

— (2013) : "La valeur du bronze : du métal à la monnaie", in : Grandjean & Moustaka, éd. 2013, 71-79.

— (2014) : "L'empreinte de la *Polis* sur la monnaie", in : *Hommage à Jacqueline de Romilly, L'empreinte de son œuvre*, Paris, 23-37.

— (2015) : "Corpus et classement des émissions : les bronzes hellénistiques de Thasos", in : Wartenberg & Amandry, éd. 2015, 153-165.

— (à paraître) : "Le type monétaire de la cité : pour une lecture institutionnelle", *Greek Coins and Their Images: noble issuers, humble users?*, *BCH Suppl.*

Picard, O. et T. Faucher (2012) : "Les monnaies lagides", in : Picard *et al.* 2012, 60-76.

Picard, O. et S. Gjongecaj (2000) : "Trésors de monnaies de bronze d'Apollonie", in : *Acten der XII Internationaler Numismatischer Kongress Berlin, 1997*, Berlin, 351-356.

Picard, O., C. Bresc, T. Faucher, G. Gorre, M.-C. Marcellesi et C. Morrisson (2012) : *Les monnaies des fouilles du Centre d'études alexandrines*, Études alexandrines 25, Paris.

Piérart, M. (1982) : "Argos, Cléonai et le *koinon* des Arcadiens", *BCH*, 106, 119-138.

Piérart, M. et G. Touchais (1996) : *Argos. Une ville grecque de 6 000 ans*, Paris.

Pilon, D. (2011) : "La 'Date Estimative de Perte' d'une monnaie: une aide à la datation des contextes archéologiques et de leurs mobiliers", in : Ossel, éd. 2011, 1-12.

Pind, J., éd. (2002) : *"Drik – og du vil leve skønt", Festskrift til Ula Lund Hansen, Årsdagen, 18 août 2002*, Studies in archaeology & history 7, Copenhague.

Pinkwart, D. et W. Stamnitz, éd. (1984) : *Peristylhäuser westlich der unteren Agora*, Altertümer von Pergamon XIV, Berlin.

Portolos, D. (1997) : "Some Early Issues of Philip II", in : *Μνήμη Martin J. Price*, Athènes, 111-118.

Poulios, B. D. (1982) : "Ταφικός θησαυρός χάλκινων νομισμάτων 4ου αι. π.Χ. από τον άγιο Χριστόφορο νομού Σερρών", *ADelt*, 37, 188-202.

— (2001) : "Συμβολή στη μελέτη της χάλκινης νομισματοκοπίας των Αντιγονιδών από τον Αντίγονο Γονατά έως τους πρώτους χρόνους του Φιλίππου Ε΄. Η περίπτωση πέντε 'θησαυρών' από την ανατολική Μακεδονία", *ADelt*, 56, 237-296.

Prag, J. R. W. et J. C. Quinn, éd. (2013) : *The Hellenistic West: Rethinking the Ancient Mediterranean*, Cambridge.

Price, M. J. (1967) : "Coins from some Deposits in the South Stoa at Corinth", *Hesperia*, 36, 348-388.

— (1979) : "The Coinage of Philip II", *NC*, 19, 230-241.

— (1991) : *The Coinage in the Name of Alexander the Great and Philip Arrhidaeus*, Zurich-Londres.

Psoma, S. (1996) : "Monnaies à la légende TPIH", in : *Μνήμη Martin J. Price*, Athènes, 97-110.

— (1998) : "Le nombre de chalques dans l'obole dans le monde grec", *RN*, 153, 19-29.

— (1999a) : "Monnaies de poids réduit d'Alexandre I et de Perdiccas II de Macédoine", *ZPE*, 128, 273-282.

— (1999b) : "Les Bottiéens aux Vᵉ et aux IVᵉ siècles av. J.C.", *RN*, 154, 41-55.

— (2000) : " Τάς παλαιάς πενταδραχμίας. Un stratagème de Polyen et le monnayage d'argent des rois de Macédoine de 413 à 360 av. J.-C.", *RN*, 155, 123-136.

— (2001) : *Olynthe et les Chalcidiens de Thrace : Études de numismatique et d'histoire*, Stuttgart.

— (2002) : "Le monnayage de Sparadocos des Odryses. Un État de la question", in : *Proceedings of the VIII International Congress of Thracology, Sofia, 25-29 septembre 2000*, Sofia, 513-521.

— (2003) : "Les "boucs" de la Grèce du Nord. Problèmes d'attribution", *RN*, 159, 227-242.

— (2006) : "The "Lete" coinage reconsidered", in : Alfen, éd. 2006, 61-85.

— (2008) : "Panygyris coinages", *AJN*, 20, 227-255.

— (2009) : "Τὰς σιταρχίας καὶ τοὺς μισθοὺς ([Arist.], *Oec.* 1351b). Bronze Currencies and cash allowances in Mainland Greece, Thrace and the Kingdom of Macedonia", *RBN*, 155, 3-38.

— (2011) : "The Kingdom of Macedonia and the Chalcidic League", in : Lane Fox, éd. 2011, 113-135.

— (2012) : "Royal bronze coinages versus civic bronze coinages. The tale of two stories for Greek history", in : Asolati & Gorini, éd. 2012, 49-64.

Psoma, S., C. Karadima et D. Terzopoulou (2008) : *The Coins from Maroneia and the Classical City at Molyvoti. A Contribution to the History of Aegean Thrace*, Meletemata 62, Athènes.

Raban, A. et E. Galili (1985) : "Recent Maritime Archaeological Research in Israel. A Preliminary Report", *IJNA*, 14 (4), 321-356.

Radt, S. (2006) : "Pergamon", in : Radt, éd. 2006, 279-288.

— (2009) : *Strabons Geographika: Bd. 8 Buch XIV-XVII*, Göttingen.

Radt, S., éd. (2006) : *Stadtgrabungen und Stadtforschung im westlichen Kleinasien. Geplantes und Erreichtes. Internationales Symposion, Bergama, 6-7* août 2004, Byzas 3, Istanbul.

Ranucci, S. (2008) : "Circolazione monetaria a Pompei. La documentazione numismática degli scavi dell'Università di Perugia", *AIIN*, 54, 151-175.

— (2014) : "The Coin Finds in their Archaeological Context", in : Laidlaw & Stella, éd. 2014, 241-254.

Ravetz, A. (1963) : *Roman Coinage of the Fourth Century in Britain*, thèse de doctorat, Université de Leeds.

— (1964) : "The Fourth-Century Inflation and Romano-British Coin Finds", *NC*, 7 (4), 201-231.

Raymond, D. (1953) : *Macedonian Regal Coinage to 413 b.C.*, ANSMusNotes 126, New York.

Redin, L. (1989) : "Medieval Coins in Recent Archaeological Excavations in Sweden", in : Clarke & Schia, éd. 1989, 9-14.

Reece, R. (1968) : "The Roman Coins Found in 1931-1938 and Summary of the Roman Coins from Richborough", in : Cunliffe, éd. 1968, 188-216.

— (1971) : "The coins", in : Cunliffe, éd. 1971, 97-100.

— (1972) : "Roman Coins Found on Fourteen Sites in Britain", *Britannia*, 3, 269-276.

— (1973) : "Roman Coinage in Britain and the Western Empire", *Britannia*, 4, 227-252.

— (1975) : "Roman Currency: New Thoughts and Problems", *World Archaeology*, 6 (3), 299-306.

— (1977) : "Coins and Frontiers. Or Supply and Demand", in : Fitz, éd. 1977, 643-646.

— (1980) : "Religion, Coins and Temples", in : Rodwell, éd. 1980, 115-128.

— (1981) : "The 'Normal' Hoard", in : Carcassonne & Hackens, éd. 1981, 299-308.

— (1982) : "Economic History from Site-Finds", in : Hackens & Weiller, éd. 1982, 495-502.

— (1984) : "The Use of Roman Coinage", *Oxford Journal of Archaeology*, 3 (2), 197-210.

— (1988) : "Coins and Villas", in : Branigan & Miles, éd. 1988, 34-41.

— (1991) : *Roman Coins from 140 Sites in Britain*, Cirencester.

— (1991-1993) : "Coins as Minted and Coins as Found", *Acta Numismàtica*, 21-23, 211-227.

— (1993) : "British Sites and their Roman Coins", *Antiquity*, 67, 863-869.

— (1994) : "The Regional Study of Coin Site-Finds", *JRA*, 7, 480-490.

— (1995) : "Site-finds in Roman Britain", *Britannia*, 26, 179-206.

— (1996) : "The Interprétation of Site Finds –a Review", in : King & Wigg, éd. 1996, 341-355.

— (2002) : *The Coinage of Roman Britain*, Londres.

— (2003) : *Roman Coins and Archaeology. Collected papers*, Moneta 32, Wetteren.

— (2008) : "Roman Silver Goes abroad", in : Bursche *et al.*, éd. 2008, 59-74.

— (2013) : "Roman Coins and Archaeology Collected Papers", *Moneta*, 32, 136-145.

Regling, K. (1913) : "Verzeichnis der bei den Ausgrabungen von Pergamon gesundenen Münzen", in : Conze *et al.*, éd. 1913, 355-363 (= 1914, "Münzfunde aus Pergamon", *Blätter für Münzfreunde*, 10-11, 5671-5685 et 5703-5718).

— (1927) : *Die Münzen von Priene*, Priene 3, Berlin.

Reinders, H. R. (2004) : "Coinage and coin circulation in New Halos", Οβολός 7. Το νόμισμα στο θεσσαλικό χώρο, Πρακτικά Γ' επιστημονικής συνάντησης, 185-206.

Rey-Coquais, J.-P. (1978) : "Inscription grecque découverte à Ras Ibn Hani : stèle de mercenaires lagides sur la côte syrienne", *Syria*, 55, 313-325.

Rheidt, K. (2001) : "Aizanoi. Die Ausgrabungen und Forschungen 1997 bis 2000", *Archäologischer Anzeiger*, 240-267.

Rheidt, K., éd. (2010) : *Aizanoi und Anatolien. Neue Entdeckungen zur Geschichte und Archaölogie im Hochland des westlichen Kleinasien*, Mayence.

Robert, L. (1951) : *Études de numismatique grecque*, Paris.

— (1966) : *Monnaies antiques en Troade,* Hautes études numismatiques 1, Genève-Paris.

Robinson, A. H., J. L. Morrison et P. C. Muehrcke (1977) : "Cartography 1950-2000", *Transactions of the Institute of British Geographers*, 2 (1), 3-18.

Robinson, D. M. (1931) : *Excavations at Olynthus*, III : *The Coins Found at Olynthus in 1928*, Baltimore.

— (1933) : *Excavations at Olynthus*, VI : *The Coins Found at Olynthus in 1931*, Baltimore.

— (1952) : *Excavations at Olynthus*, XIV: *Terracotas, Lamps and Coins Found in 1934 and 1938*, Baltimore.

Robinson, D. M. et P. A. Clement (1938) : *Excavations at Olynthus*, IX : *The Chalcidic Mint and The excavation Coins Found in 1928-1934*, Baltimore.

Robinson, D. M. et F. Goddio, éd. (2014) : *Thonis-Heracleion in Context*, Oxford.

Rodwell, W., éd. (1980) : *Temples, Churches and Religion in Roman Britain*, BAR 77, Oxford.

Rotroff, S. I. (1997) : "Coins and Stratigraphy", in : Sheedy & Papageorgiadou-Banis, éd. 1997, 8-16.

Rutter, N. K. (2001) : *Historia Numorum Italy*, Londres.

Ryan, N. S. (1988) : *Fourth Century Coin Finds from Roman Britain. A Computer Analysis*, BAR Brit. Ser. 183, Oxford.

Saatsoglou-Paliadeli, C. (2011) : "The Palace of Vergina-Aegae", in : Lane-Fox, éd. 2011, 271-295.

Safrai, Z. (1994) : *The Economy of Roman Palestine*, Londres-New York.

Salviat, F. (2013) : "La topographie d'Amphipolis au Ve s. av. J.-C. : en relisant Thucydide", in : Darque *et al.*, éd. 2013, 63-78.

Sargent, T. J. et F. R. Velde (2002) : *The Big Problem of Small Change*, Princeton.

Saulnier, J.-M. (1993) : *Thasos à l'époque paléochrétienne et byzantine. Étude de numismatique* et d'*histoire*, thèse de doctorat, Université Paris IV.

Savalli-Lestrade, I. et J. Chameroy (à paraître) : "Pergame, cité et capitale dynastique, au miroir de la prosopographie interne et des trouvailles monétaires", in : *Actes du colloque international* L'Éolide dans l'ombre de Pergame*, Paris, 23-24 novembre 2012*, Topoi 20, Lyon.

Sawaya, Z. (2009) : *Histoire de Bérytos et d'Héliopolis d'après leurs monnaies*, Bibliothèque archéologique et historique 185, Beyrouth.

Schazmann, P. et G. Darier (1912) : "Untersuchungen auf dem Kaleh Agili 1911", *MDAI(A)*, 37, 331-343.

Schierup, S. et V. Sabetai, éd. (2014) : *The Regional Production of Red-figure Pottery: Greece, Magna Graecia & Etruria*, Gösta Enbom Monographs 4, Aarhus.

Schlumberger, G. L. (1934) : *Mes souvenirs, 1844-1928*, I, Paris.

Schuchhardt, C. (1912) : "Historische Topographie der Landschaft", in : Conze *et al.*, éd. 1912, 61-143.

Schultz, H.-D. (1996) : "The Coinage of Pergamon until the End of the Attalid Dynasty (133 B.C.)", in : Dreyfus & Schraudolph, éd. 1996, 11-22.

Schwarzer, H. (2008) : *Die Stadtgrabung. Das Gebäude mit dem Podiensaal in der Stadtgrabung von Pergamon*, Altertümer von Pergamon XV.4, Berlin.

Seyrig, H. (1958) : "Monnaies grecques des fouilles de Doura et d'Antioche", *Revue numismatique*, 6 (1), 171-181.

Shachar, I. (2004) : "The Historical and Numismatic Significance of Alexander Jannaeus' Later Coinage as Found in Archaeological Excavations", *Palestine Exploration Quarterly*, 136, 5-33.

Shay, O. (2009) : "Collectors and Collections in Palestine at the Conclusion of the Ottoman Era", *Le Muséon*, 122, 3-4, 469.

Sheedy, K. et C. Papageorgiadou-Banis, éd. (1997) : *Archaeological Numismatics/Numismatics Archaeology*, Oxbow Monograph 75, Oxford.

Shiloh, Y. et D. T. Ariel (1990) : "Coins, Flans, and Moulds", in : Ariel & Shiloh, éd. 1990, 99-118.

Sismanidis, K. (1990) : "Έρευνες στην αρχαία Κασσάνδρεια και στα αρχαία Στάγειρα", *AEMTH*, 4, 371-383.

— (1991) : "Ανασκαφές στην αρχαία Σκιώνη και στα αρχαία Στάγειρα κατά το 1991", AEM*TH*, 5, 319-333.

— (1992) : "Ανασκαφή αρχαίων Σταγείρων 1992", *AEMTH*, 6, 451-465.

— (1993) : "Αρχαία Στάγειρα 1993", *AEMTH*, 7, 429-443.

— (1994) : "Αρχαία Στάγειρα 1994", *AEMTH*, 8, 275-287.

— (1995) : "Η συνέχεια της έρευνας στα αρχαία Στάγειρα κατά το 1995", *AEMTH*, 9, 383-393.

— (1996) : "Αρχαία Στάγειρα 1990-1996", *AEMTH*, 10, 279-295.

— (1997) : "Ανασκαφικά και αναστηλωτικά αρχαίων Σταγείρων 1997", *AEMTH*, 11, 469-479.

— (1998) : "Τα αποτελέσματα των πρόσφατων ανασκαφών στα αρχαία Στάγειρα" in : Άνδρος και Χαλκιδική. Πρακτικά Συμποσίου. Άνδρος, 23 *août 1997*, Ανδριακά Χρονικά 29, Athènes, 139-172.

— (2003) : Αρχαία Στάγειρα. Η πατρίδα του Αριστοτέλη, Athènes.

Slawisch, A., éd. (2013) : *Handels- und Finanzgebaren in der Ägäis im 5. Jh. V. Chr. – Trade and finance in the 5th c. BC Aegean world*, Byzas 18, Istanbul.

Smekalova, T. (2009) : "The Earliest Application of Brass and 'Pure' Copper in the Hellenistic Coinages of Asia Minor and Northern Black Sea Coast", in : Højte, éd. 2009, 233-248.

Sommerey, K. M. (2008) : "Die Chora von Pergamon. Studien zu Grenzen, Siedlungsstruktur und Wirtschaft", *MDAI(I)*, 58, 135-150.

Sorda, S. (1989) : *La moneta nei contesti archaeologici, Esempi dagli scavi di Roma, Atti dell'Incontro di Studio, Roma, 1986*, Rome.

Souffi, B., éd. (à paraître) : *8 000 ans d'occupations sur les bords de l'Audry: evolution d'un site en context de bas de versant, du Mésolithique à l'Antiquité*, Metz.

Stamatopoulou, M. (2009) : "Thessalians abroad, the Case of Pharsalos", in : Malkin *et al.*, éd. 2009, 204-229.

Stamatopoulou, M. et M. Yeroulanou, éd. (2002) : *Excavating Classical Culture. Recent Archaeological Discoveries in Greece. Studies in Classical Archaeology 1*, BAR Int. Ser. 1031, Oxford.

Stanley, J.-D, éd. (2007) : *Geoarchaeology. Underwater Archaeology in the Canopic Region in Egypt*, Oxford.

Stanley, J.-D., F. Goddio et G. Schnepp (2001) : "Nile Flooding Sank two Ancient Cities", *Nature*, 412, 293-294.

Stanley, J.-D., F. Goddio, G. Schnepp et T. F. Jorstad (2004) : "Submergence of Ancient Greek Cities Off Egypt's Nile Delta – A Cautionary Tale", *GSA Today*, 14 (1), 4-10.

Stannard, C. (2005) : "The Monetary Stock at Pompeii at the Turn of the Second and First Centuries B.C.: Pseudo-Ebusus and Pseudo-Massilia", in : Guzzo & Guidobaldi, éd. 2005, 120-143.

— (2013) : "Are Ebusan Coins at Pompeii, and the Pompeian Pseudo-Mint, a Sign of Intensive Contacts with the Island of Ebusus ?", in : Arévalo Gonzalez, éd. 2013, 125-155.

Stannard, C. et S. Frey-Kupper (2008) : "'Pseudomints' and Small Change in Italy and Sicily in the Late Republic", *AJN*, 20, 351-404.

Stefanaki, V. (2012) : Κως I, Νομίσματα – Νομισματική Αιγαίου, Athènes.

Stoyan, D. (2002) : "Statistical analyses of Euro coin mixing", *Mathematical Spectrum*, 35, 50-55.

Stoyan, D. et G. Döge (2012) : "Statistical Analyses and Modelling of the Mixing Process of Euro Coins in Germany and Europe", *Australian & New Zealand Journal of Statistics*, 46, 67-77.

Strauss, J. (2013) : *Shipwrecks Database*, [en ligne], <oxrep.classics.ox.ac.uk/databases/shipwrecks_database/>, page consultée le 30 avril 2015.

Stucky, R. A. (1983) : *Ras Shamra. Leukos Limen, die nach-ugaritische Besiedlung von Ras Shamra*, BAH 110, Paris.

Suchodolski, S. (2002) : "Les trouvailles monétaires et l'archéologie du haut Moye Âge. Quelques controverses entre les archéologues et les numismates au sujet de l'interprétation et de la datation", in : Asolati & Gorini, éd. 2002, 273-284.

Svoronos, J. N. (1899) : "Νομισματικὰ εὑρήματα (Μέρος Β')", *JIAN*, 2, 289-302.

— (1904-1908) : Τα νομίσματα του κράτους των Πτολεμαίων, 4 vol., Athènes.

— (1907) : "Εύρημα Σοφικού Επιδαυρίας", *JIAN*, 10, 35-46.

— (1919) : *L'Hellénisme primitif de la Macédoine prouvé par la numismatique et l'or de Pangée*, ΔΕΝΑ 19, Paris.

Syon, D. (2004) : *Tyre and Gamla. A Study in the Monetary Influence of Southern Phoenicia on Galilee and the Golan in the Hellenistic and Roman Periods*, these de doctorat, Université de Jerusalem.

Syon, D., C. Lorber et E. Galili (2013) : "Underwater Ptolemaic Coin Hoards from Megadim", *'Atiqot*, 74, 1-8.

Talbert, R. J. A et R. S. Bagnall (2000) : *Barrington Atlas of the Greek and Roman World*, Princeton.

Taliercio Mensitieri, M. (2002) : "Ritrovamenti monetali a Pompei: problemi di metodo e di ricerca", in : Asolati & Gorini, éd. 2002, 79-102.

Tekin, O. et A. Erol-Özdizbay (2012) : "Coins from Allianoi Excavations: Campaign of 1998", *Colloquium Anatolicum*, 11, 347-401.

Tiverios, M., P. Nigdelis et P. Adam-Veleni, éd. (2012) : *Threpteria. Studies on Ancient Macedonia*, Thessalonique.

Thomsen, R. (1986) : "The Graeco-Roman Coins", in : Papanicolaou-Christensen *et al.*, éd. 1986, 59-69.

Thompson, C. M. (2003) : "Sealed Silver in Iron Age Cisjordan and the 'Invention of Coinage'", *OJA*, 22, 67-107.

— (2011) : "Silver in the Age of Iron and the Orientalizing Economies of Archaic Greece: an Overview", in : Giardino, éd. 2011, 121-132.

Thompson, M. (1968) : *The Agrinion Hoard*, Numismatic notes & monographs 159, New York.

Tiverios, M., P. Nigdelis, P. Adam-Veleni, éd. (2012) : *Threpteria : Meletis gia tin Archaia Makedonia*, Thessalonique.

Thonemann, P. éd. (2013) : *Attalid Asia Minor. Money, International Relations and the State*, Oxford.

Tod, M. N. (1946) : "Epigraphical Notes on Greek Coinage II. *Chalkous*", *The Numismatic Chronicle*, 6, 47-62.

Tomlinson, R. A. (1972) : *Argos and the Argolid from the End of the Bronze Age to the Roman Occupation*, Ithaca.

Touratsoglou, I. (1987) : "Macedonia", in : Burnett & Crawford, éd. 1987, 53-72.

— (1993) : *The Coin Circulation in Ancient Macedonia* (ca. *200 B.C.-268-286 A. D.*). *The Hoard Evidence*, Bibliothèque de la société numismatique grecque 1, Athènes.

— (1997) : "Αρχαιολογική Νομισματική. Νομισματική Αρχαιολογία", in : Sheedy & Papageorgiadou-Banis, éd. 1997, 1-7.

— (2003) : "À la recherche du monnayage de bronze de Philippe II de Macédoine. Note préliminaire", *BSFN*, 58, 97-101

— (2010) : *Συμβολή στην οικονομική ιστορία του βασιλείου της αρχαίας Μακεδονίας* (*6ος-3ος αι. π. Χ.*), Athènes.

Touratsoglou, I. et S. Drougou (2000) : "Το ιερό της Μητέρας των Θεών στην Βεργίνα. Νομισματικές ενδείξεις και κεραμεική", Οβολός, 4, 307-319.

Trakosopoulou-Salakidou, E. (1993) : "Από τις ανασκαφές της Ανατολικής Χαλκιδικής", *AEMTH*, 7, 413-428.

Treister, M. Y. (1996) : *The role of metals in ancient Greek history*, Mnemosyne, bibliotheca classica Batava Supplementum 156, Leyde-New York.

Troxell, H. (1997) : *Studies in the Macedonian Coinage of Alexander the Great*, Numismatic Studies 21, New York.

Tselekas, P. (1996a) : "The Coinage of Pydna", *NC*, 156, 11-32.

— (1996b) : "Grave Hoards of Greek Coins from Greece", *NC*, 156, 249-259.

— (2012) : "The Coins", in : Kaltsas *et al.*, éd. 2012, 216-226.

Tsingarida, A. et D. Viviers, éd. (2013) : *Pottery Markets in the Ancient Greek World* (*VIIIth-I^st^ centuries B.C.*). *Proceedings of the International Symposium, Bruxelles, 19-21 juin 2008*, Études d'archéologie 5, Études d'archéologie classique de l'ULB 7, Bruxelles.

Tzamalis, A. P. (1999) : "Θράκο-Μακεδονικά Αβέβαια (Μέρος Γ΄)", *Nom.Chron.*, 18, 11-16.

Ujes, D. (1993) : "Nuovi ritrovamenti numismatici di Risan (Bocche di Cattaro, Montenegro, Jugoslavia)", in : Moucharte & Hackens, éd. 1993, 139-145.

— (2011) : "Ancient Greek Coin Finds from Risan", in : Lamboley & Castiglioni, éd. 2011, 115-132.

Ünal, E. (2009) : "Greek, Roman, Byzantine, Medieval and Islamic Coins from the Excavations at Kyme, Aiolis, 1951-1954", *NC*, 169, 407-423.

Valassiadis, C. (2005) : "A Contribution to Cassander's Bronze Coinage", in : Alfaro, éd. 2005, 405-413.

Vanderpool, E., J. R. McCredie et A. Steinberg (1964) : "Koroni. A Ptolemaic Camp on the East Coast of Attica", *Hesperia*, 31, 26-62.

van der Spek, R. J. (2011) : "The 'Silverization' of the Economy of the Achaemenid and Seleukid Empires and Early Modern China", in : Archibald *et al.*, éd. 2011, 421-440.

van der Spek, R. J., J. Luiten van Zanden et B. van Leeuwen, éd. (2014) : *A History of Market Performance: From Ancient Babylonia to the Modern World*, New York.

van Driesche, V. (2009) : *Des étalons pré-monétaires au monnayage de bronze*, Études de métrologie grecque I, Louvain.

Van Ossel, P., éd. (2011) : *Les céramiques de l'Antiquité tardive en Île-de-France et das le Bassin parisien. II. Synthèses / Contextes et contextualisation de trouvailles monétaires, Actes du 6e colloque international du groupe suisse pour* l'étude des trouvailles monétaires, *Genève, 5-7 mars 2010*, Diocesis Galliarum, Document de travail 9, Nanterre.

Varoucha-Christodoulopoulou, I. (1944) : "Hellenistic Asea, The Coins", in : Holmberg, éd. 1944, 167-171.

Voegtli, H. (1984) : "Münzen", in : de Luca, éd. 1984, 60-77.

— (1990) : "Zwei Münzfunde aus Pergamon", *SNR*, 69, 41-50 et pl. 8-13.

Voegtli, H., S. Bendall, L. Illisch et C. Morrisson (1993) : *Die Fundmünzen aus der Stadtgrabung von Pergamon*, Pergamenische Forschungen 8, Berlin.

von Kaenel, M. (1984) : "Roma. Monete dal Tevere. L'imperatore Claudio I. Roma. Museo Nazionale Romano", *BollNum*, 2-3, 85-325.

von Kaenel, M. et F. Kemmers, éd. (2009) : *Coins in Context. New Perspectives for the Interpretation of Coin Finds, Colloquium Frankfurt, 25-27 October 2007*, Mayence.

von Mosch, H. C. (2000) : "Das Kultbild des Zeus von Aizanoi", *SNR*, 79, 113-123 et pl. 8-10.

Waage, D. B. (1952) : *Antioch on the Orontes*, IV.2 : *Greek, Roman, Byzantine and Crusaders' Coins*, Princeton.

Walker, A. S. (1997) : "Excavations Coins: the Use and Misuse of Numismatic Evidence in Archaeology", in : Sheedy & Papageorgiadou-Banis, éd. 1997, 17-27.

Walker, D. R. (1988) : "Roman Coins from the Sacred Spring at Bath", in : Cunliffe, éd. 1988, 281-358.

Wallace-Hadrill, A. (2013) : "Hellenistic Pompeii: between Oscan, Greek, Roman, and Punic", in : Prag & Quinn, éd. 2013, 35-43.

Walton, P. (2012) : *Rethinking Roman Britain. Coinage and Archaeology*, Moneta 137, Wetteren.

Warren, J. A. (1985) : "The Autonomous Bronze Coinage of Sicyon. Part 3", *NC*, 145, 45-66.

— (2009) : "Sikyon: a Case-Study in the Adoption of Coinage by a Polis in the Fifth Century BC", *NC*, 169, 1-13.

Wartenberg, U. et M. Amandry (2015) : *ΚΑΙΡΟΣ: Contributions to Numismatics in Honor of Basil Demetriadi*, New York.

Weinstein-Evron, M. (2009) : *Archaeology in the Archives: Unveiling the Natufian Culture of Mount Carmel*, American School of Prehistoric Research Monograph Series 7, Leyde.

Weir, R. (2007) : "The Stymphalos Hoard of 1999 and the City's Defences", *AJN*, 19, 9-32.

Weisser, B. (2014) : "Die Fundmünzen aus dem Felsheiligtum Ost in Priene", in : Dörtlük *et al.*, éd. 2014, 653-668.

Westermark, U. (1979-1980) : "Notes on the Saida Hoard (*IGCH* 1508)", *NordNumArs*, 36-37, 22-35.

— (1987) : "Notes on Macedonian Bronze Coins", *Bolletino di Numismatica*, Suppl. 4, 179-181.

— (1988) : "The Coinage of the Chalcidic League Reconsidered", in : *Studies in Ancient History and Numismatics presented to Rudi Thomsen*, Aarhus, 91-103.

— (1989) : "Remarks on the Regal Macedonian Coinage *ca.* 413-359 B.C.", in : Le Rider, éd. 1989, 301-315.

— (1991) : "Bronze Coins of Pergamon", *NAC*, 20, 147-159.

— (1995) : "On the Pergamene Bronze Coins in the Name of Athena Nikephoros", *StCercNum*, 11, 29-35.

Westermark, U., éd. (1992) : *Florilegium Numismaticum, Studia in honorem U. Westermark edita*, Numismatiska meddelanden 38, Stockholm.

Wiegels, R. éd. (2000) : *Die Fundmünzen von Kalkriese und die frühkaiserzeitliche Münzprägung. Akten des wissenschaftlichen Symposions, Kalkriese, 15-16 avril 1999*, Osnabrücker Forschungen zu Altertum und Antike-Rezeption 3, Möhnesee.

Williams, G. (2011) : "Building the Collection – Past, Present and Future", in : Cook 2011, 34-41.

Williams, H. (1992) : "Coin Supply in Britain in the Late Third Century as Evidenced by a Mathematical Interpretation of Site Finds", *NC*, 152, 49-56.

Wilson, A. (2013) : "Trading across the Syrtes: Euesperides and the Punic world", in : Prag & Quinn, éd. 2013, 120-156.

Winter, E. (1999) : "Τα ίχνη των πόλεων της ανατολικής Χαλκιδικής", *AEMTH*, 13, 282-294.

Wojan, F. (2016) : "Le monnayage de 'bronze' des Éléens à l'époque hellénistique", *BSFN*, sous presse.

Wolf, D. (2013) : "A Metrological Survey of Ptolemaic Bronze Coinage", *American Journal of Numismatics*, 25, 49-118.

Wolters, R. (1999) : Nummis signati. *Untersuchungen zur römischen Münzprägung und Geldwirtschaft*, Vestigia 49, Munich.

Worthington, I., éd. (1994) : *Ventures into Greek History*, Oxford.

Yalouris, N. (1990) : "The Shipwreck of Antikythera: New Evidence of its Date after Supplementary Investigation", in : Descoeudres, éd. 1990, 135-136.

Yaraş, A. et D. S. Lenger (2009) : "Coins from the Necropolis of Maymum Sekisi Tepesi near Pergamon", *NC*, 169, 401-403.

Yoyotte, J. (1958) : "Notes de toponymie égyptienne", *MDAI(K)*, 16, 414-430.

Zahrnt, M. (1971) : *Olynth und die Chalkidier. Untersuchungen zur Staatenbildung auf der Chalkidischen Halbinsel im 5. und 4. Jahrhundert v. Chr.*, Vestigia 14, Munich.

Zias, J. et A. Kloner (2013) : "Levi-Yitzhak Rahmani (obituary)", *Israel Exploration Journal*, 63, 233-234.

Ziegenaus, O. et G. de Luca, éd. (1968) : *Das Asklepieion. Der südliche Temenosbezirk in hellenistischer und frührömischer Zeit*, Altertümer von Pergamon XI.1, Berlin.

— (1975) : *Das Asklepieion. Der nördliche Temenosbezirk und angrenzende Anlagen in hellenistischer und frührömischer Zeit*, Altertümer von Pergamon XI.2, Berlin.

—, éd. (1981) : *Das Asklepieion. Die Kultbauten aus römischer Zeit an der Ostseite des heiligen Bezirks*, Altertümer von Pergamon XI.3, Berlin.

Ziesmann, S. (2016) : "Vier unedierte Bronzemünzen aus Pergamon", sous presse.

Index général

Nous distinguons les noms géographiques par l'usage des petites capitales et les entrées numismatiques par l'italique.

O

P

Q

R

S

Index des personnages historiques

Index des personnages historiques, p. 339-341

Index des trésors

Index des sites archéologiques

Index des sources écrites

Sources issues de la transmission manuscrite

Inscriptions

Résumés

John K. Davies, *An economic historian's agenda*, p. 19-34

Les monnaies de fouille peuvent-elles apporter des informations sur l'histoire économique ? En dépit des réserves exposées ci-dessous, il paraît possible de répondre affirmativement à cette question dès lors que l'interprétation de données obtenues de manière fiable est correctement menée. Le traitement des monnaies et leur catalogage ne constituent en effet que la première étape du travail sur les monnaies de fouille. Il faut ensuite prendre en compte pour l'interprétation historique des données toutes les données sur la vie économique (objets produits et échangés, services, transactions, mouvements de population et de marchandises, etc) du site ou de la région étudiée.

Underlying this entire paper has been the core question "Can *monnaies de fouille* be made to yield substantive economic information?" In spite of the four warning flags which I raise, it is possible, in the light of two extended examples, to offer the more positive answer "Yes, with the right interpretative approaches and practical procedures". That is to say, though the practical procedures involved in cataloguing are obviously essential and primary, they are only the start, for what ultimately matter are the movements of people into, through, and beyond this or that specific site or region: and the absolutely basic drivers of those movements are commodities in the widest possible sense (intangible services as much as tangible objects) and the consequential exchange transactions, private or public.

F. Duyrat, *Les monnaies de fouille au Levant. Une approche régionale*, p. 35-50

Les monnaies trouvées isolées dans les fouilles sont d'abord un matériel archéologique étudié en stratigraphie et incorporé dans des rapports intermédiaires et, en principe, dans le rapport final d'un site. Leur utilisation comme source d'histoire à l'échelle régionale reste exceptionnelle dans le monde grec. L'examen du produit de 58 sites archéologiques en Syrie, dans la région d'Antakya en Turquie, au Liban, en Jordanie et en Israël est l'occasion de proposer quelques réflexions méthodologiques et d'évaluer la qualité de ce matériel comme source d'histoire. En effet, l'absence de normes de publication, la grande variété des informations données, l'obsolescence des identifications qu'il n'est pas toujours possible de mettre à jour rendent difficile l'exploitation statistique du corpus créé. Cependant, les monnaies de fouilles étudiées à l'échelle régionale donnent un visage de la circulation monétaire différent de celui, mieux connu, tiré des trésors. Mettre ces deux types de données en regard représente un enrichissement notable de notre compréhension des usages de la monnaie au Levant.

Coins found individually in excavations are first of all archaeological objects studied in the context of stratigraphy and incorporated in provisional reports and, in principal, in the final report of the excavation of a site. Their use as a historical source on a regional basis remains unusual for the Greek world. A study of the finds from 58 sites in Syria, form the regions of Antakya in Turkey, Lebanon, Jordan and Israel provides the opportunity to offer a number of methodological observations and to evaluate the quality of this material as a historical source. In fact, the absence of publication standards, the great variety of information provided, the obsolescence of identifications that cannot always be updated, make statistical exploitation of the corpus of material difficult. However, excavation coins studied on a regional basis present a different pattern of monetary circulation from that, better known, provided by the hoards. To compare these two types of find offers a significant enrichment of our understanding of monetary use in the Levant.

C. Grandjean, *Les monnaies grecques des fouilles de l'École française d'Athènes à Argos*, p. 51-64

Les fouilles de l'EfA à Argos ont livré un millier de monnaies grecques identifiées antérieures à Auguste. Il est illusoire de prétendre reconstituer la circulation monétaire à partir de cet échantillon. Près de 60 % du matériel sont des monnaies étrangères en bronze provenant surtout d'ateliers proches, principalement Corinthe, Phlionte et Sicyone. Ces pièces de faible valeur, associées aux argiennes dans la quasi-totalité des sites fouillés, datent surtout de la période antérieure à 229, qui vit l'adhésion d'Argos au *koinon* achaien. Rien ne laisse croire qu'il s'agisse de monnaies mises au rebut et leur présence massive pose question.

Almost 1 000 Greek coins have been excavated by the EfA at Argos. "The coins that have been found are only a sample of those which were lost. These in turn were only a sample of those that had originally been in circulation" (Grierson 1965, n. 25). Almost 60% are foreign coin, mostly from Corinth, Phlious and Sicyon. Most of these foreign coins are dated to the IVth-IIIrd c. a.C., before 229 a.C., when Argos joined the Achaian *koinon*. That paper is focused on the question of "small change" and on the fact that the policy regarding foreign coinage may have been different concerning silver and bronze coins.

O. Picard, *Les monnaies de fouilles du monde grec : l'apport de Thasos*, p. 65-82

Les fouilles de l'EfA à Thasos ont mis au jour plus de 6 800 monnaies de la cité, presque exclusivement en bronze. Cette masse permet de reconstituer toutes les formes institutionnelles qu'a prises la monnaie : les types et valeurs qui sont émis, les systèmes de contrôle des émissions. Sauf les petits modules, trop souvent abîmés, tous les coins utilisés ont été identifiés, fournissant une image complète de la production des bronzes. Le deuxième apport provient des contextes archéologiques, qui apportent quantités d'informations chronologiques, que j'utiliserai ici sans les détailler. Il est ainsi possible de reconstituer la politique monétaire de la cité à partir de la succession des monnayages en distinguant les séries et les monnayages hétérogènes, d'analyser le choix des valeurs émises, d'estimer la part du métal réutilisé. On s'interrogera sur le rôle économique de la monnaie.

The excavations of the French archaeological School at Thasos have given more than 6 800 coins from the city, for the most part in bronze. It has been possible to reconstitute all the institutional elements of the Thasos' monetary policy: the types, the coins values, the supervision system of the coinage. Except the small pieces, which are too damaged, all the dies have been identified, giving a complete chart of the bronze emission. The second information concerns the archaeological contexts, very useful for the chronology. We are studying the development of the monetary policy, with the successive series, and the extraordinary coinages, the module choice, the metal reuse. We are examining the economical function of the coinage.

C. A. Gatzolis, S. E. Psoma, *Olynthos and Stageira: Bronze Coinage and Political History*, p. 83-96

L'objet de cette contribution est l'étude des monnaies de fouille en bronze exhumées lors des fouilles d'Olynthe et de Stagire. Situées en Chalcidique et membres de la Ligue chalcidienne, ces deux cités furent détruites à la fin de l'été de 348 par Philippe II. Olynthe était la capitale de l'État fédéral tandis que Stagire était un membre de ce dernier. Olynthe était la principale cité de Thrace tandis que Stagire était une modeste cité. Olynthe ne fut jamais refondée, à la différence de Stagire. Les monnaies de fouille révèlent l'histoire politique de ces deux cités.

The aim of this paper is to examine the bronze coins excavated at two cities, Olynthos and Stageira. Both cities were situated in the Chalcidic peninsula, were members of the Chalcidian League and were destroyed in late summer of 348 a.C. by Philip II. Olynthos was the capital of the federal state while Stageira was a member of this state. Olynthos was considered as the largest city in Thrace while Stageira was less significant by far. Olynthos was never re-founded while Stageira was. Excavation coins reveal the political history of the two cities.

D. T. Ariel, *Coins from a small country: How excavated coins are managed in Israel, from the dig to the bookshelf*, p. 99-112

La collection nationale israélienne possède probablement la plus grande collection au monde, conservée dans un lieu unique, de monnaies dont la provenance est connue (87 %). 150 000 sont méticuleusement enregistrées sur un total actuel d'un demi-million – et plus de 30 000 complètement publiées. La plupart des monnaies avec provenance proviennent de fouilles archéologiques contrôlées, les enrichissant d'une valeur scientifique supplémentaire.

Les métadonnées de la collection sont significatives. Par exemple, elles expliquent l'impact de la guerre et de l'inflation sur le numéraire du Levant Sud, et limitent la portée de certaines séries juives, quand nombre d'entre elles proviennent des niveaux de destruction de sites comme Jérusalem, Gamala et Masada.

L'équipe de trois personnes enregistre et identifie 8 000 monnaies chaque année, provenant de plus de 100 fouilles différentes, tout en publiant des rapports numismatiques de grande qualité et en poursuivant la saisie numérique des pièces. Par ailleurs, leur action, et non la moindre, vise aussi à étudier équitablement les monnaies de toute période, dont les ensembles remarquablement riches de monnaies musulmanes.

The Israel national collection has probably the largest predominantly provenanced (87%) coin collection concentrated in one place in the world. 150 000 of an actual total of over a half-million coins are meticulously registered – and over 30 000 are fully published. Most of the provenanced coins derive from controlled archaeological excavations, endowing them with added research value.

The collection's metadata are significant. For example, they elucidate the impact of war and inflation on the coin currency of the southern Levant, and downgrade the import of certain Jewish coin series, when so many are seen to derive from destruction layers at sites such as Jerusalem, Gamla and Masada.

The collection's three-man staff accesses and identifies 8 000 new coins annually, from over 100 separate excavations, all the while publishing high quality numismatic reports and advancing the coins' computerization. Another hallmark is their efforts in equitably studying coins of all periods, not the least being the remarkably rich, Islamic assemblages.

T. Faucher, *Cartographie des monnaies de fouilles (1950-2050)*, p. 113-122

La cartographie a fait d'immenses progrès ces dernières années. Il est difficile d'établir des normes de cartographie des trouvailles archéologiques pour des cas aussi nombreux que particuliers mais certaines règles peuvent être suivies. La carte doit être lisible et pour cela ne doit pas compter un trop grand nombre d'informations. Il s'agit pour l'auteur d'illustrer son propos et pour le lecteur de disposer d'une information claire et mémorisable facilement. *À côté de la cartographie traditionnelle, le développement des outils numériques propose maintenant de nouvelles perspectives à la cartographie des monnaies de fouilles. La participation aux bases de données conn*ectées peut permettre, d'un côté, aux archéologues d'avoir la possibilité d'offrir au plus grand nombre le matériel numismatique issu de leurs fouilles et, de l'autre, aux chercheurs de disposer d'outils puissants de cartographie.

The field of cartography has seen immense improvements in the past few years. It is difficult to establish standards for mapping archaeological finds because circumstances are numerous and different, but a number of rules can apply. The map should be legible and, in that respect, should not include too large a number of items. The aim for the author is to illustrate his text and for the reader to have access to a clear and easily memorisable information. Alongside traditional cartography, the development of digital tools now offers new perspectives to the cartography of excavation coins. The inclusion of coins in databases can provide, on the one hand, the possibility to archaeologists of making their excavation material available to a broader audience and, on the other hand, access for researchers to powerful cartographic tools.

L. Fadin, V. Chankowski, *Monnaies de fouille et SIG : l'exemple de Délos*, p. 123-130

L'intégration d'une partie des données issues des trouvailles monétaires de Délos dans le SIG de l'île permet de faire apparaître, grâce à cet outil de visualisation, plusieurs caractéristiques de la circulation monétaire délienne. Les modalités d'intégration des données numismatiques ainsi que le fonctionnement de l'interface construite dans le SIG de Délos sont présentées ici. Est abordé en particulier le problème du traitement de localisations qui, dans l'état de la documentation (archives de fouilles anciennes, données de fouilles récentes, publications diversement renseignées), présente un caractère très disparate.

The integration of one part of the data concerning coin finds from Delos into the SIG of the island makes it possible to show, thanks to this visualization tool, a number of characteristics of Delian monetary circulation. The means of integration of numismatic data as well as the functioning of the Delian SIG interface are presented here. A particular focus is the problem of the treatment of find-spots, which, according to their documentation (old excavation archives, data from recent excavations, publications resulting from various research projects), is particularly disparate.

A. Meadows, *Coins from Underwater Excavations. The Case of Thonis-Herakleion*, p. 133-146

Les épaves provenant de Méditerranée, de l'Égée et de la mer Noire ont livré parmi les plus remarquables trouvailles archéologiques antiques. Elles sont riches d'informations sur l'histoire des techniques navales, sur les itinéraires maritimes, sur les passagers et le fret transportés. Cette contribution porte sur les quelques épaves s'échelonnant entre le IVe s. et le Ier s. a.C. qui ont livré des monnaies. Ces dernières étaient tantôt destinées aux dépenses personnelles de l'équipage et des passagers, tantôt destinées à des dépenses militaires et commerciales. Elles apportent, en relation avec la céramique et d'autres objets présents à bord, des informations pour dater les naufrages et des indications sur les itinéraires empruntés par les navires.

In this paper I describe some of the difficulties presented and opportunities offered by coins recovered in underwater excavation of the city of Thonis-Herakleion, off the north coast of Egypt. While noting some obvious problems in working with heavily corroded coins from a site that cannot be seen or visited, I point out that the methods adopted for the excavation of such a site in fact present us with much better information about the coin finds than is often the case in terrestrial excavations. This fact, combined with the peculiar nature of Egyptian finds, including the dominance of Ptolemaic royal coinage, allow for interesting forms of analysis, both across the site itself, and by comparison with other sites.

P. Tselekas, *Treasures from the Deep: Coins from Hellenistic and Roman Republican Shipwrecks*, p. 147-156

Les épaves provenant de Méditerranée, de l'Égée et de la mer Noire ont livré parmi les plus remarquables trouvailles archéologiques antiques. Elles sont riches d'informations sur l'histoire des techniques navales, sur les itinéraires maritimes, sur les passagers et le fret transportés. Cette contribution porte sur les quelques épaves s'échelonnant entre le IVe s. et le Ier s. a.C. qui ont livré des monnaies. Ces dernières étaient tantôt destinées aux dépenses personnelles de l'équipage et des passagers, tantôt destinées à des dépenses militaires et commerciales. Elles apportent, en relation avec la céramique et d'autres objets présents à bord, des informations pour dater les naufrages et des indications sur les itinéraires empruntés par les navires.

Shipwrecks in the waters of the Mediterranean, the Aegean and the Black Sea comprise some of the most exciting and revealing finds of antiquity. These destructive sites offer valuable information on the study of ancient marine technology, maritime trade routes, transportation of people and goods.

The paper surveys the few shipwrecks dating from the IVth to the Ist c. a.C. that have yielded coins. Although their number is rather modest, the existing data indicate that coinage was carried aboard as personal cash of the crew and passengers as well as for military and trading purposes. The coins – whether isolate specimens or hoards – recovered from wreck sites constitute an important piece of evidence for the maritime record of the Hellenistic and Roman Republican era. They can offer alongside pottery and other datable artefacts valuable information on the dating of wrecks as well as indications for the possible ship traveling routes.

S. Kremydi, K. Chryssanthaki-Nagle, *Aigeai and Amphipolis: Numismatic circulation in two major Macedonian cities*, p. 157-176

Le propos de cette contribution est de présenter de façon liminaire les trouvailles monétaires d'Aigeai et d'Amphipolis et d'offrir une vue générale de la circulation monétaire dans ces deux cités, basée sur du matériel inédit. Notre ambition est de montrer les similarités et les différences de situation entre deux cités importantes du royaume macédonien et dotées de statuts différents. Pour ce faire, nous abordons des thèmes tels que le rôle de la monnaie locale de chacune de ces cités ou la distribution géographique des monnaies étrangères qui circulaient sur leurs territoires. De plus, nous discutons de l'apport du monnayage à la datation et à l'histoire de monuments importants spécifiques à chaque cité, en combinant les données archéologiques et numismatiques.

This paper aims at a preliminary presentation of coin finds from Aigeai and Amphipolis, by drawing a general outline of numismatic circulation in these two cities, based on so-far unpublished material. Our intention is to trace similarities and differences between two important cities with a different status within the Macedonian kingdom. In order to achieve this, we shall discuss topics such as the role of local currency and the geographical range of foreign coins that circulated within them. Furthermore, we shall discuss the contribution of coins to the dating and history of specific important monuments in each city, combining numismatic and archaeological evidence.

N. Akamatis, *Numismatic Circulation in the Macedonian Kingdom. The Case of Pella*, p. 177-202

Cette contribution présente environ 2 400 monnaies trouvées lors des fouilles du sud de Pella, au sud du rempart septentrional classique. Ces monnaies proviennent principalement de trois zones de fouille : la nouvelle entrée du site, où un établissement de bain, des ateliers de potiers et de métallurgistes ont été exhumés ; la zone des sanctuaires, avec notamment le sanctuaire du héros local Darron et d'autres édifices cultuels ; Phakos, l'île fortifiée du lac Loudias, où se trouvaient le port et le trésor de Pella. Des monnaies provenant de fouilles de sauvetage de maisons et sept trésors seront aussi évoqués.

In this paper, numismatic material from the southern part of Pella, south of the city's north wall of the Classical period is presented. This material is very representative, because it derives from the city of both Classical and Hellenistic eras. Around 2400 coins have been studied from three major excavation areas: 1) The new entrance of the archaeological site where three town blocks came to light, in which public buildings, such as a bath, and also pottery and metal workshops have come to light. 2) The area of the sanctuaries, where the sanctuary of Darron, a local healing god has been unearthed, as well as a circular building that is probably related to a hero cult and other buildings related to cult needs. 3) Phakos, the fortified island inside lake Loudias, where Pella's harbor and treasury was located. Furthermore, coins from rescue excavations of the surrounding plots have also been included. These come from various buildings, mostly houses. Apart from single coins, seven coin hoards from the above mentioned areas are also presented. Numismatic material from Pella can be placed in three categories according to issuing authority: a) regal coins b) issues of the Macedonian cities and the "Macedonians" c) coins from areas outside Macedonia. These coins offer valuable information regarding the economy and the numismatic circulation during the Classical and Hellenistic period as well as the chronology of the buildings under study.

M.-C. Marcellesi, *Territoire, institutions et rayonnement de Pergame : l'apport des monnaies de fouille*, p. 203-222

Les publications de monnaies trouvées dans les fouilles de Pergame, de l'Asclépieion et de sanctuaires ou nécropoles des environs offrent un ensemble de 1 228 monnaies antérieures à Auguste, parmi lesquelles on identifie 839 bronzes frappés à Pergame, par la cité ou les Attalides, et 294 monnaies "étrangères". Les fouilles n'offrent que peu d'éléments pour préciser la chronologie des séries pergaméniennes ; la répartition des monnaies reflète plutôt l'histoire des sites ou les choix scientifiques. La part des monnaies "étrangères" est peu importante à Pergame même ; le sanctuaire de la Mère des Dieux à Mamurt Kale, aux confins du territoire de plusieurs cités, présente un faciès différent. L'origine des monnaies "étrangères" dans la ville et ses abords proches illustre les réseaux d'échange privilégiés de Pergame et l'évolution de son rayonnement.

The publications of the coins found in the excavations of Pergamon, of the Asclepieion and of the sanctuaries or *necropoleis* of the surrounding area, offer us a total of 1 228 coins struck before Augustus, among which we can identify 839 bronze coins struck in Pergamon, by the city itself or by the Attalids, and 294 "foreign" coins. The excavations offer only a few opportunities to refine the chronology of the Pergamene series, while the distribution of the coins mostly reflects the history of each site or scientific preferences. The share of "foreign" coins is not very important in Pergamon itself; the sanctuary of the Mother of Gods at Mamurt Kale, at the borders of the territories of several cities, presents a different picture. The origins of "foreign" coins in the town and its surrounding area demonstrate the exchange networks of Pergamon and the evolution of its influence.

K. Butcher, *Coin Finds and the Monetary Economy: the Good, the Bad, and the Irrelevant*, p. 225-238

Les numismates supposent généralement qu'il y a un lien direct entre l'usage de la monnaie et les exemplaires trouvés sur un site. On constate une réticence générale à considérer les trouvailles monétaires comme des témoignages de démonétisation ou de décri. En conséquence, les trouvailles monétaires sont prises comme des témoignages du comportement de la monnaies ancienne. La compréhension des fonctions élémentaires de la monnaie peut-elle nous aider à mieux apprécier les trouvailles monétaires ? Cet article étudie la définition simple de la monnaie employée par l'économiste Robert Mundell, et comment elle pourrait être utilise pour comprendre les schémas des dépôts monétaires.

Numismatists generally assume that there is a direct link between coin use and the coins found on a site. There is a general reluctance to consider coin finds as evidence of demonetisation or redundancy. Consequently coin finds are taken to be evidence of the behaviour of ancient money; but can an understanding of the basic function of money help us to better appreciate coin finds? This paper will consider a simple definition of money, employed by the economist Robert Mundell, and how it might be used to help understand patterns of coin deposition.

F. de Callataÿ, *De quoi les monnaies grecques trouvées en fouilles sont-elles le reflet ? Propos diachroniques de méthode*, p. 239-262

La présente étude entend 1) brièvement rappeler ce que l'on peut attendre des monnaies de fouille par rapport aux trésors et aux monnaies isolées ; 2) résumer ce que les numismates grecs ont à apprendre des spécialistes des monnaies romaines qui – bénéficiant de conditions favorables – ont toujours poussé plus loin la réflexion à ce sujet ; 3) donner quelques pistes sur l'intérêt de comparer avec des situations contemporaines ; 4) enfin, procurer une série de propos actualisés sur ce dont les monnaies de fouilles sont le reflet (ou pas), en incluant l'approche anthropologique assez négligée jusqu'à présent.

The present paper aims 1) briefly to survey what we can expect from excavation coins with respect to hoards and isolated finds; 2) to sum up what Greek numismatists have to learn from the specialists of Roman coinage who – with the benefit of favourable circumstances – have always advanced further consideration of this topic; 3) to offer views on the potential benefit of comparing modern cases; 4) lastly, to provide a set of updated comments about what it is that excavation coins reflect, including the hitherto much neglected anthropological perspective.

P. P. Iossif, *Using site finds as basis for statistical analyses of the Seleucid numismatic production and circulation. An introduction to the method*, p. 263-296

Cette étude est consacrée à l'analyse des monnaies de fouilles séleucides et sert d'introduction aux méthodes de "numismatique appliquée" dans le monde hellénistique. Une grande base de données est ainsi constituée, qui proviennent de *c.* 70 différents sites archéologiques du Proche et Moyen Orient. Différentes méthodes statistiques sont appliquées afin de montrer que cet échantillon ("SED") constitue une base représentative pour tirer de conclusions valables pour l'ensemble du territoire séleucide et pour toute l'histoire de la dynastie. Une fois sa fiabilité démontrée, des conclusions sont tirées : la forte prédominance du petit module "D", dont la plus grande quantité provient des règnes d'Antiochos III et IV, est interprétée comme la preuve d'une brève réforme introduite sous le premier. Leur provenance des sites de la Coelé-Syrie est associée aux cinquième et sixième guerres de Syrie. Enfin, des questions de vélocité de circulation des monnaies de bronze à l'intérieur de l'empire sont examinées.

This paper analyzes Seleucid coins from excavations and is meant to be an introduction to the methods of "applied numismatics" in the Hellenistic world. A large database is created coming from *c.* 70 different sites in the Near and Middle East. Different statistical methods are used to show the reliability of the SED for conclusions concerning the whole Seleucid history and territory. Once the reliability of SED established, some initial conclusions are considered: the pattern of coin loss of the small "D" module mostly associated with the reigns of Antiochos III and IV is interpreted as an indication of a short-lived reform introduced by the former. The provenance of these coins from sites in Coele-Syria is connected to the fifth and sixth Syrian wars. In the last part, questions of speed of circulation of bronze coins within the Empire are also considered.